GOOD READ But way too
much RepeTITION.

Praise for
Pickett's Charge

"Contains much to interest and provoke Civil War enthusiasts."

—*Kirkus Review*

"In his almost minute-by-minute account of the most famous infantry charge in history, Phillip Thomas Tucker provides a thoughtful and challenging new look at the great assault at Gettysburg, from planning to aftermath. Not afraid to lay blame where he thinks it belongs, Tucker is fresh and bold in his analysis and use of sources. Even though any reader knows in advance the outcome, still Pickett's Charge maintains suspense to the sound of the last gun."

—William C. Davis, author of *Crucible of Command:*
Ulysses S. Grant and Robert E. Lee—
The War they Fought, the Peace they Forged

"No action in the Civil War is more iconic than the misnamed 'Pickett's Charge,' and yet few episodes of this most-studied of wars is in need of more enlightened and enlightening reexamination. Phillip Thomas Tucker's magisterial *Pickett's Charge: A New Look at Gettysburg's Final Attack* replaces 150-plus years of uninterrogated mythology with meticulously researched history to give us a new and long-overdue understanding of what tradition dismisses as Robert E. Lee's most tragic error in pursuit of a 'Lost Cause.' Tucker persuasively argues that Pickett's Charge, though failed in its execution, actually reveals Lee at his most masterful. This book is one of a handful essential to gaining a full strategic and tactical appreciation of both Gettysburg and the war in which it was the turning point."

—Alan Axelrod, author of *The Horrid Pit: The Battle of the Crater, the Civil War's Cruelest Mission* and *The 20 Most Significant Events of the Civil War*

"Phillip Thomas Tucker cuts through the myths and misconceptions that surround Pickett's charge to offer a fresh defense of Robert E. Lee and a probing examination of what happened that fateful afternoon. The result is a thought-provoking and eye-opening study of this pivotal moment in American history."

—Louis P. Masur, Rutgers University History professor,
and author of *The Civil War: A Concise History*

"In nearly all recent surveys, Americans list the Battle of Gettysburg as the most recognizable and most important of all battles in our history. And, when asked what they know about Gettysburg, to top of that list is Pickett's Charge. When pressed a little harder, if they know anything about the charge, most will say it was a disaster, that General Lee didn't know what he was doing, that there was no way it could have succeeded, and so forth. Relying heavily on the combatants's first-hand accounts, Phillip Thomas Tucker cuts away the myths and offers a fresh new interpretation that challenges long held views of the story. Rather than seeing Pickett's Charge as foolhardy, Tucker considers Lee's plan as a stroke of genius, and that, had a few things gone differently, could well have ended the war in favor of the Confederacy.

—Robert K. Sutton, former Chief Historian, National Park Service

Introduction

Pickett's Charge was the greatest assault of the greatest battle of America's greatest war. Even more, this iconic attack was truly one of the most dramatic episodes and defining moments in American history. Consequently, Pickett's Charge has earned a revered and lofty place in the American memory and popular imagination.

No chapter in the Civil War saga has become more romanticized than Gettysburg, the largest battle ever fought on North America. Likewise, no chapter of Gettysburg's dramatic story has been more excessively glorified than the massive assault on the last day, July 3, 1863, of the three-day battle, however. Myths and stereotypes abound. Even the famous name, Pickett's Charge, is a misnomer, because Major General Edward Pickett only commanded a single division, or barely one-third of the troops in the assault. But the most persistent myth about Pickett's Charge has been that it was a doomed assault from the beginning.

Consequently, it is time for a more comprehensive look at the most famous charge in American history, because the unvarnished story of Pickett's Charge and its hidden history are actually far more fascinating than the romantic legends and myths.

The North Carolina troops on Pickett's left flank were long blamed for having failed the Virginians, sabotaging their best efforts: another myth, because the North Carolina, Tennessee, Alabama, Florida, and Mississippi soldiers fought just as well as Pickett's Virginians. In fact, General James Johnston Pettigrew's division lost more men than Pickett's division during the assault, testifying to their resolve and courage.

Pickett's Charge also revealed an inordinate share of cowardice among many soldiers, however. Thousands of Confederate soldiers refused to go all the way in the assault, helping to thwart General Robert Edward Lee's best-laid tactical plans. An entire brigade of Virginians (not of Pickett's division) broke early, creating a crisis on the assault's left flank. Clearly, Pickett's Charge witnessed an unparalleled degree of bravery, cowardice, and tragedy.

Other commonly held perceptions about Pickett's Charge need to be reevaluated and looked at anew, especially without the usual regional bias, stereotypes, and Lost Cause mythology. Lee fully realized that if only his foremost attackers had been provided the support as planned, decisive victory would have been won. Twentieth-century historians have erroneously portrayed Pickett's Charge like the doomed British and French infantry assaults on German defenses in the 1916 Battle of the Somme, in France, which caused unprecedented casualties. Contrary to today's popular consensus, Pickett's Charge was not doomed from the beginning. Here, the technological advances of modern weaponry (machine gun and heavy artillery) truly guaranteed that frontal infantry assaults over open ground were doomed. Viewed too often within the context of the advanced technology of modern warfare, twentieth-century historians, influenced by pervasive Lost Cause romance, have been long thoroughly convinced that Pickett's Charge was likewise doomed from the start. However, this traditional fatalistic scenario was simply not the case.

One must fully understand today the relevancy of Lee's greatest assault, because no single episode has been more poignantly represented as the Civil War's climactic and defining moment than Pickett's Charge, symbolizing the central tragedy of America's Iliad of 1861–65. On the final day of the largest and deadliest battle in American history (more than 51,000 casualties), more Americans died that day (more than 7,860) than the total American casualties during the Normandy invasion of early June 1944.

Most importantly, Pickett's Charge also effectively sealed slavery's fate. If Pickett's Charge had succeeded, two sister republics might well exist to this day. Paradoxes dominate the story of Pickett's Charge. At the assault's most climactic moment, the much-celebrated leader of the attack (Pickett) was not leading his troops at the front, when inspired leadership was most needed—a mockery of the misnomer of Pickett's Charge. However, the name of "Pettigrew's Charge" (Pettigrew's division, four brigades, on the assault's left wing complemented Pickett's three brigades of his Virginia division, the attack's right wing) is equally unsuitable. The great assault was actually "Longstreet's Charge, " as survivors called it before the influential Richmond press (five leading newspapers) conjured up the catchy name of Pickett's Charge, as if Hollywood scripted. Not only have the vital contributions of non-Virginians been minimized by historians, but also prominent Virginians (soldiers, civilians, and the powerful Virginia press) early placed blame for the attack's repulse on them. The early, common misconception of the all-Virginia charge (hence, the popular sobriquet Pickett's Charge) obscured the significant fact that Pickett's attackers were a minority. Therefore, Pickett's Charge can be more accurately called the "Pettigrew–[Isaac] Trimble–Pickett Charge."

Likewise shattering the self-serving myths of the influential postwar Virginia School of Civil War historiography and subsequent Virginia-first Lost Cause romanticism, it was an all-Virginia brigade—of Ambrose Powell Hill's corps—on the far left (or north) that first broke during the assault. This early tactical setback started a disastrous chain of events (the left flank's collapse) that helped to ensure the attack's repulse. The truth of Lee's greatest assault was actually the antithesis of the carefully orchestrated myth that the failures of non-Virginia attackers doomed Pickett's Charge.

Endlessly derided by historians, Lee's decision to unleash his last attack at Gettysburg was his only realistic one because this was the Confederacy's *last* chance to win the war in one decisive stroke. Contrary to today's traditional view that Lee's decision to attack the Union right-center (an area weakened by General George Gordon Meade, the Army of the Potomac's new commander, after he had shifted troops from his center to bolster his hard-pressed flanks on the previous day) was the height of folly, the truth of Pickett's Charge was altogether different. Quite simply, the attack was Lee's best opportunity to reap a decisive success after July 2's tactical opportunities had passed. Based on careful calculation (instead of the stereotypical view of a gambler's recklessness), Lee correctly targeted the weakest point in Meade's line, a weak spot distinguished by a copse of trees located at a high point along the open Cemetery Ridge. Lee correctly calculated in striking at exactly the right place and the right time, while utilizing a bold battle plan that was as brilliant as it was innovative.

Gettysburg's most dominant romantic myth has been that Pickett's Charge was automatically fated for failure, the traditional explanation that has been based upon the Lost Cause romanticism of an underdog South succumbing to impossible odds. Pickett's Charge, therefore, became the most symbolic representation of the vanquishing of a Southern Anglo-Saxon nation (still another myth) by overpowering might. In consequence, this crucifixion-like final demise of the greatest offensive effort ever launched by the South's most primary army on July 3 became the most dominant symbol of a tragic martyrdom that served as the principal foundation of Lost Cause mythology of a defeated nation. Dismayed by postwar mythology, Colonel Armistead Lindsay

Long, a talented West Pointer (Class of 1850) and Lee's military secretary, concluded that Pickett's Charge erroneously compared to the famous charge of the Light Brigade during the Crimean War: the traditional myth that has persisted to this day.

Lee's tactical plan to pierce the Union right-center along Cemetery Ridge with 12,500 veteran troops of eleven brigades (and even more units if Longstreet had properly supported the assault and exploited the break-through) was masterful, especially with regard to its most overlooked com-ponent: the simultaneous attack of more than 6,000 Confederate cavalry, under Lee's top cavalry commander, James Ewell Brown (Jeb) Stuart, from the east and into the rear of the Union at the clump of trees, while masses of infantry struck from the west. Significantly, these more-than-6,000 Southern cavalrymen represented a larger number than the bluecoat defenders, who manned the vulnerable right-center: the ideal tactical situation that presented Lee with his best tactical opportunity on July 3. The son of one of General George Washington's finest cavalry commanders, "Light-Horse Harry" Lee, Robert E. Lee fully appreciated the importance of utilizing his cavalry arm to the fullest.

Unfortunately, the vast majority of today's historians, who have loyally fol-lowed the traditional Gettysburg faithful that have kept romantic myths alive, have either minimized or ignored Stuart's vital role. They have dismissed out of hand the importance of the Southern cavalry role partly to ensure credibility for their own past works in adhering to traditional Gettysburg gospel. However, Union leaders knew the truth. General Meade wrote that the repulse of Stuart's bid to strike the Union rear with the bulk of the Army of Northern Virginia's cavalry, including horse artillery, was of extreme importance. However, the excessive focus placed on Pickett's Virginians has resulted in a myopic view that has automatically minimized Stuart's important role.

Lee's plan was based upon an unprecedented tactical complexity that required precise timing and close coordination of all three arms: infantry, artil-lery, and cavalry. Clearly, Pickett's Charge was far from a simplistic frontal assault as long represented. This was a brilliant tactical plan that actually came surprisingly close to achieving decisive success with infantry alone, and even *after* the failure of two of the three central elements of his battle plan. (Stuart's cavalry was thwarted from striking Meade's rear, and the Confederate artillery failed to deliver a knockout blow with a massive cannonade and then to advance as "flying artillery" to protect the attacker's flanks.)

Indeed, even after these tactics failed, Pickett's Charge succeeded in breaking through Meade's right-center. But early heavy pressure of Union flanking forces on the attack's left flank on the north and on the right flank to the south played a key role in undoing the tactical success in breaking through on the right-center. The wisdom of attacking the weak right-center, in contrast to Meade's impregnable flanks (Little Round Top on the south and Cemetery Hill and Culp's Hill on the north), also becomes evident in regard to an appreciation of the most forgotten part of Lee's plan.

Lee's decision to launch his massive attack was based upon a complex tactical plan that was not only classically Napoleonic, but also a tactical notch above the French general, because of the novel tactical concept of simultaneously striking the same weak defensive point from two directions to negate Union advantages of weaponry (the rifled musket) and high-ground defensive positions. In fact, Napoleon failed to develop a comparably complex tactical plan that called for a massive infantry assault coinciding with a cavalry charge in the rear.

After having narrowly failed to reap a decisive success on July 2, Lee's decision to launch an all-out assault the next day was especially wise because of the overall political and strategic situation. The manpower-short South was caught in an unwinnable war of attrition, and Lee lacked the logistical support to remain north of the Potomac any longer: a classic case of now or never for the Confederacy. In truth, no other realistic tactical option existed for Lee, because his army and nation were literally racing the clock when precious time was running out.

Consequently, Lee exploited the best tactical opportunity in the hope of scoring a psychological, strategic, and political knockout blow to reverse the inevitable fate of the slowly dying Confederacy and win the war. Pickett's Charge was the South's final bid to truly "conquer a peace" (the winning strategy of General Winfield Scott in capturing Mexico City during the Mexican–American War campaign, in which a young Lee had served)—to exploit the increasing vulnerabilities of a war-weary northern populace and encourage the northern peace party to negotiate a settlement.

By targeting the weak Union right-center (Cemetery Ridge's most vulnerable sector) and enjoying a significant manpower advantage at this vulnerable point after an unprecedented bombardment had wreaked havoc among the batteries protecting the right-center, Lee was presented with his greatest tactical opportunity. To stack the odds in his favor as much as possible, Lee masterfully employed all three arms (a secret formula of Napoleon's remarkable successes) to act in concert in going for broke in a highly favorable tactical situation.

Nevertheless, the central romantic myth that Pickett's Charge was doomed before it was even launched has become Gettysburg's most enduring romantic stereotype. This myth has partly resulted because of a lack of appreciation of the complexities of Lee's battle plan that called for carefully orchestrating all three arms of his army (infantry, cavalry, and artillery): first the artillery bombardment and then for the guns to advance to closely support the infantry attackers, while thousands of Stuart's cavalrymen struck from the rear.

Besides serving as a core foundation of Lost Cause mythology, the common assumption that the assault's failure was inevitable from the beginning also supported the winner's conviction that victory at Gettysburg was a great moral victory preordained by God. For a variety of reasons, no single defining moment in American history has more thoroughly captured the popular imagination, both North and South. However, fundamental truths have been hidden behind the enshrinement of the enduring romance of Pickett's Charge. The vanquished people of the postwar South needed saintly heroes to restore lost pride. Therefore, Pickett's Virginians, as constructed by Virginia writers, were transformed into virtuous Anglo-Saxons (a stereotype) who represented an inordinate amount of chivalry and courage. White Virginian virtues—as glorified in the heroics of Pickett's Charge—were portrayed romantically to represent an allegedly superior Anglo-Saxon society, culture, and people. Clearly, the romantic glorification of Pickett's Charge fulfilled a host of much-needed political, moral, racial, and psychological requirements for generations of white Southerners. The fabrication of the romantic Lost Cause mythology found its greatest fulfillment in the heroic image of Pickett's Charge (the doomed attackers in the romantic tradition of "The Charge of the Light Brigade") to demonstrate the superiority of Virginia virtues.

Pickett's Charge also represented the greatest what-if of American history. Only adding to the seemingly endless mythical qualities of Pickett's Charge, Michael Shaara, in his novel *The Killer Angels* (1974), gave long-existing stereotypes new life, solidifying the most romantic Lost Cause legends. Then, the film *Gettysburg* (1994), which was based upon the popular novel, continued the glorification of Pickett's Charge to a new generation.

As part of the Lost Cause romance that endlessly glorified sacrifice and decisive defeat, so the most romantic of Gettysburg myths was created to explain the attack's failure: the war's most glorious charge that allegedly never stood a chance of succeeding against superior numbers, logistics, and economic might (rather than Union courage and fighting spirit). Portrayed in the Lost Cause romance as the moral equivalent to ancient Anglo-Saxon knights, these Southern fighting men fell in a doomed assault like martyrs, valiantly sacrificing themselves in a Christ-like crucifixion: the fundamental basis of the doomed assault stereotype that was more culturally based than historically based.

However, Pickett's Charge can be seen very differently without the blinding haze (more disorienting than the fog of war) of regional pride, glorification, and romance. Lee was so close to winning his most important victory that Longstreet was even congratulated for the success of the assault. Lee's faithful staff officer Colonel Walter Herron Taylor emphasized in a December 1863 letter how close Pickett's Charge came to succeeding. Indeed, much of the real truth of Pickett's Charge can be best understood from the words of soldiers' letters, especially leading officers, written at the time, before the emergence of politically and self-serving postwar Lost Cause romance became holy writ.

Ironically, in still another glaring omission, the historical and tactical antecedents of Pickett's Charge have not been adequately explored by historians—another gap filled by this work. Most importantly, the overall purpose of this book will *not* be to present another outdated, traditional narrative of Pickett's Charge. Instead the primary purpose has been to focus on the hidden history and forgotten or overlooked truths of the most famous attack in American history. The overall goal has been to present as many new aspects of America's most famous attack as possible to go well beyond the pervasive myths, stereotypes, and romantic legends to reveal the truths about Pickett's Charge. This approach has revealed some ugly truths, including widespread cowardice in the face of the enemy even before the assault's beginning: the human side of the story of Pickett's Charge. Consequently, all aspects (including the blemishes) of Pickett's Charge will be presented in this work to tell the full story of this pivotal moment in America's story.

Appreciating exactly how close the attackers actually came to splitting the Army of the Potomac in two, one Union general emphasized how the Confederacy nearly won its independence to a captive Virginia major not long after the assault was repulsed. The 9th Virginia Infantry's adjutant placed the attack's repulse in the proper historical perspective by writing how Pickett's

Charge was the Confederacy's Waterloo. Like Napoleon's decisive defeat at Waterloo, the repulse of Pickett's Charge altered the course of history on both sides of the Atlantic. Pickett emphasized how if the great attack had been supported, then Lee's army would have shortly marched into Washington, DC: no exaggeration as long assumed.

In contrast to the popularity of Lost Cause mythology, there was nothing romantic to its participants about Lee's greatest attack. Nevertheless, even today's most recent books about Pickett's Charge have emphasized the word "glory" in the title or subtitle. But only hell on earth was experienced by more than 6,500 Southerners, who were killed, wounded, or permanently crippled on July 3, causing endless suffering to grieving families, widows, and orphans across the South. Quite simply, there was no glory to the victims of Pickett's Charge.

Confederate Colonel William Allen emphasized how there was absolutely nothing rash or foolhardy about Lee's attack, which would have succeeded if properly executed as planned. Contrary to the popular doomed assault scenario against the alleged impossible odds and impregnable position, Lee's attackers significantly outnumbered the defenders (at least eight to one), but these would have been greater if Stuart's thousands of cavalry had struck from the rear at the targeted copse of trees as planned.

Because so much of the story of Lee's assault has been distorted and romanticized, this book has relied heavily upon wartime letters of the common soldiers. These letters were written before the agenda-driven writings dominated the postwar period to overshadow the facts. Consequently, this book will emphasize the human-interest side of Pickett's Charge to present a highly personalized history. The author's overall goal has been to de-romanticize and de-glorify the assault to provide a more realistic view. This book also has been written not only to present new tactical analysis, but also to finally end a long-existing debate: Did Lee commit his greatest folly by launching Pickett's Charge?

After more than 150 years, the full story of Pickett's Charge has been revealed in all of its many complexities and contradictions by presenting as much of its hidden history as possible: the first true *comprehensive* view of Pickett's Charge by revealing Lee's plan of Stuart's cavalry attacking into the defender's rear; the forgotten mini–civil war between the Irish (and Germans to a lesser extent) in blue and gray; the Virginia Military Institution's significant influence; how the common soldiers—not always generals—on both sides rose to the fore in splendid fashion; the assault's tactical antecedents; etc. These are just some representative examples of fresh perspectives that have filled long-existing gaps in the historical record. Because the story of this pivotal moment in American history has been shrouded in myth to this day, it is time for a new look at the most iconic charge in the annals of American history.

Phillip Thomas Tucker, PhD
Washington, DC
January 1, 2016

This book reproduces original correspondence of many Civil War–era soldiers and civilians. We apologize for the inconsistencies in spelling and capitalization, when set in modern context. In addition, the timing of some events varies from source to source, sometimes depending on what side the soldiers were on or how their watches were set.

Chapter I

Genesis of Pickett's Charge:
Evolution of a Brilliant Tactical Plan

When the summer sun broke over South Mountain at 4:50 a.m. on July 3, 1863, it illuminated the carnage of the killing fields around Gettysburg, Pennsylvania.

By the third summer of America's most murderous war, it was abundantly clear that the Confederacy was slowly dying. Consequently, after the first two days of combat at Gettysburg, General Robert Edward Lee's battle plan for the afternoon of July 3 was based upon a host of urgent political, military, and economic requirements. Because the manpower-short South was trapped in a fatal war of attrition that guaranteed decisive defeat, Lee was determined to rearrange this cruel equation to end the Confederacy's death spiral by delivering a decisive knockout blow upon the Army of the Potomac in Adams County, Pennsylvania.[1] Lee felt confident of victory because his troops had reaped "partial successes" during their attacks on July 2 that he was determined to fully exploit on the third day.[2]

With everything now at stake, Lee needed a winning tactical plan that maximized his limited available resources to deliver a powerful blow. The tantalizing concept of achieving the perfect victory was the long-sought, but rarely achieved, ambition of military commanders from time immemorial. As long taught in military schools, only one battle was defined as tactically perfect: the Battle of Cannae on the Italian Peninsula on August 2, 216 BC, that resulted in Carthage's greatest victory over Rome. Since that time, no commander had matched Hannibal's tactical brilliance in vanquishing sixteen Roman legions during the greatest battle of ancient times. Hannibal's innovative tactic of a double envelopment with his experienced multiethnic army was a masterpiece.

A careful student of history, Lee knew that Hannibal had utilized all of his troops in an innovative way at Cannae. With the Romans pressured in front by Carthaginian (or Punic) infantry of north Africa in the center and cavalry attacking both flanks, the turning point of this decisive battle resulted when Hannibal's Numidian (north Africa) cavalry, as well as Spanish and Gallic horsemen, rode around the Roman flank and attacked in the center of their rear. Hannibal delivered his masterstroke to inflict the greatest defeat ever suffered by the Roman Republic, annihilating an army of about 75,000 men. Lee hoped to achieve his own Cannae at Gettysburg on July 3 to win it all.[3]

Of course, few of the Army of Northern Virginia's common soldiers knew anything about the victory at Cannae, Italy, so long ago. Young Lieutenant George Williamson Finley, Company K, 56th Virginia Infantry, Major General George Edward Pickett's division, Lieutenant General James Longstreet's 1st Corps, described the situation on Gettysburg's third day in fundamental tactical terms: "[W]ith food running low and ammunition running low, General Lee [now] decided to risk it all on one throw of the dice. He had tried the Union right, and he hadn't broken it. He had tried the Union left, and he hadn't broken it, so he reasoned that the only place left to strike was the Union [right] center."[4]

Thanks to the benefit of hindsight, generations of armchair historians have widely denounced Lee's final decision to launch a massive assault against General George Gordon Meade's right-center on Cemetery Ridge. However, for the most part, these modern historians had merely projected the folly of the Army of the Potomac's assault on Fredericksburg's Marye's Heights and Lee's attacks on Malvern Hill onto Pickett's Charge with a generalized, broad brushstroke. These two 1862 attacks were doomed because of tactical breakdowns, especially the lack of coordination, rather than the assumed inherent folly of the tactical offensive. Nevertheless, an enduring myth has been created by historians: the unchallenged axiom that the tactical defensive always decisively prevailed regardless of the tactical situation. This exaggeration of the superiority of the tactical defensive has fostered the myth of the alleged folly of Pickett's Charge.

But in fact, the true situation as presented to Lee on July 3 was the very antithesis of this alleged folly. Contrary to conventional wisdom, Lee's planned assault was in fact the best tactical recipe for achieving a decisive success calculated to reverse the war's course with one blow. An officer who served under Napoleon Bonaparte described the Corsican's secret of success: "The emperor's favourite tactic of attacking the enemy in the centre, splitting it in two and paralysing both flanks."[5]

Lee knew that a "proper concert of action" had denied him success on bloody Thursday, July 2.[6] From his vantage point of Seminary Ridge's crest and with the trained eye of a West Point–trained engineer whose tactical brilliance and reconnaissance skills were legendary in two wars, Lee searched for an Achilles' heel in Meade's Cemetery Ridge line with a trained eye. He was convinced that a weak point, even along the high-ground, could be taken by storm if a larger and more coordinated offensive effort was launched. Lee had originally planned to exploit previous tactical gains by hitting both Union flanks simultaneously. Lee and Lieutenant General Richard Stoddert Ewell, commanding the 2nd Corps, had decided that Culp's Hill, just southeast of Gettysburg and the anchor of the northeastern corner of Meade's line, and its stubborn defenders, could be overwhelmed on the morning of July 3. Likewise, with his units already in frontline positions on the right, Longstreet was ordered to continue his assault on Meade's left (with John Bell Hood's division) and left-center (with General Lafayette McLaws's division) as on July 2, while Pickett's division played only a supporting role. Therefore, the initial battle plan for July 3 was unchanged, with Ewell and Longstreet ordered to attack simultaneously on the early morning of the third day.

However, Lee's original plan on the north was spoiled early on July 3, when Union troops launched an early morning counterattack along Ewell's front at Culp's Hill. Ewell was now tactically thwarted. But the escalating gunfire echoing over heavily timbered Culp's Hill correctly convinced the tactically flexible Lee that Meade's right flank, and certainly his left flank as well, was now certainly stronger than he originally thought. The astute Lee was convinced that Meade had considerably strengthened his flanks at his center's expense. Indeed, Meade had rushed thousands of troops to face Longstreet's hard-hitting echelon assaults and strengthened his battered position on the far south on July 2, including with the 6th Corps now occupying a reserve position on his left. Meade's right and left flanks, situated on high ground and reinforced, were now impregnable.

Therefore, Lee was now forced to compensate because his original plan of attack on Meade's right flank at Culp's Hill had been spoiled early and Pickett's division was still not up to playing a support role for Longstreet's morning attack. Longstreet was not able to unleash an attack on that morning as ordered, because of Pickett's absence. Lee, therefore, had been forced to create a new battle plan. Hoping to overcome the twin setbacks of Ewell's failure to achieve gains and Pickett's belatedness, Lee became more tactically innovative out of urgent necessity. After carefully surveying Cemetery Ridge's lengthy expanse, he finally discovered a glaring tactical weakness in Meade's position. He was now determined to break Meade's right-center with a concentrated blow at a weak point along an overextended line. Indeed, Meade's right-center was now even more vulnerable than ever before with reinforcements having bolstered the Union line's northern and southern ends. If his attacking units would only act in "proper concert of action"—as at Chancellorsville in May 1863 and unlike on July 2, when dramatic Confederate breakthroughs were not supported by reinforcements—then Lee was convinced that decisive victory could be won.[7]

As emphasized by Lee, if Pickett's division was fully available early on July 3, "I will strike them between the eyes [as] I have tonight [July 2] been reinforced by Pickett's division, the flower of my army [and the only division yet to see combat at Gettysburg], and by [Jeb] Stuart's cavalry."[8] Indeed, Pickett's three brigades of Virginia troops were "the freshest, strongest, and most eager" troops available.[9] Even more, the three brigade commanders of Pickett's division (consisting of around 5,830 infantrymen and more than 400 Virginia artillerymen of the attached "long arm" battalion) were experienced and capable.[10]

More confident with Pickett's and James Ewell Brown (Jeb) Stuart's dual availability for the first time at Gettysburg, Lee now possessed his best tactical opportunity to achieve a decisive result. Lee was encouraged by the previous day's success of General Ambrose Ransom Wright's Georgia brigade, although unsupported, in attacking so near Cemetery Ridge's crest on the right-center. Therefore, a decisive success seemed most probable at this same point if a far larger number of troops struck this weak spot on the battered right-center. The tactical opinion of General Wright, whose Georgians had allegedly penetrated Meade's right-center (which Lee had watched through his binoculars), now coincided with Lee's newly formed tactical view: "It is not as hard to get there as it looks."[11]

Enduring Myths

Certainly the greatest myth about Gettysburg was that what Lee launched was nothing more than a doomed offensive effort. In hindsight, the basis of this myth has been founded on the concept that Cemetery Ridge and the defenders were simply too strong (by nature and numbers of infantry defenders and artillery) to be overwhelmed. In later years, to explain their dismal failure, Confederate veterans described Meade's right-center as far more formidable than was actually the case. In contrast to the myth of impregnability, Meade's stretched-thin right-center was much weaker and more vulnerable than has been generally recognized by historians.

However, the invincibility (a postwar creation that transformed Cemetery Ridge in the popular imagination into another impregnable Marye's Heights) of Meade's right-center has become a common assumption. But ample evidence of nineteenth-century warfare on both sides of the Atlantic revealed how massive frontal assaults were often successful against high-ground positions defended by veterans with modern weaponry. As Lee fully understood, decisive victory could only be won by offensive tactics because any "collapse at all was likely to be total and disastrous."[12]

Smashing through Meade's right-center meant that "*Uncl. Sam* would recognize his nephew and give us peace."[13] One of Longstreet's men penned to his wife that "I think we will end the war [with] this campaign [and] I hope I will be able to write to my dear from Baltimore or Philadelphia [and] I would pray to God that this war would end soon [or] both nations [will be] ruined forever."[14] In the words of a 71st Pennsylvania Volunteer Infantry, now defending Cemetery Ridge: "A sort of fatality had [descended and we] must depend Only on [our]selves for fighting out an honorable peace."[15] Quite simply, the South's peace could only come with decisive victory on July 3.

Most of all, Lee knew that time was not on his side. President Abraham Lincoln was gearing up for total war on a scale never before, in American history, to totally eliminate the Confederacy. On June 15, 1863, Lincoln issued a call for another 100,000 troops. As he fully realized, Lee now needed to secure a decisive victory on July 3 before another 50,000 men for federal service from Pennsylvania, 30,000 troops from Ohio, 10,000 soldiers from Maryland, and another 10,000 men from West Virginia (which broke away from Virginia in 1862) joined the great crusade. Additionally to meet Lee's invasion, state governors were directed by Secretary of War Edwin M. Stanton to raise nearly fifty state militia regiments from New York and Pennsylvania, for the defense of the Pennsylvania capital of Harrisburg and other major northeastern cities.[16]

Gettysburg's third day was the final showdown that had been long and eagerly awaited. General William Dorsey Pender, who fell mortally wounded at Gettysburg, had recently penned in a letter, "I wish we could meet [the Army of the Potomac in a final showdown] and have the matter settled at once."[17] But securing the North's recognition as an independent nation now called for the Army of the Potomac's destruction on Pennsylvania soil. Only vanquishing Meade's army by an overpowering blow on July 3 and then marching on major northern cities, such as Philadelphia and especially Washington, DC, could now transform the great dream of conquering a peace into a reality.[18] With this goal in mind, Lee was presented with a "unique opportunity" on July 3 to defeat the only slightly larger Army of the Potomac that had suffered devastating losses on the first two days: a long-sought favorable equation.[19]

Lee had emphasized his central objective to General Isaac Ridgeway Trimble while on the road to Gettysburg: "destroy the army" now mostly aligned on Cemetery Ridge.[20] However, innovative tactics were now needed for decisive success, because of Meade's high-ground advantage. Lee now thought much like Lincoln, who had recently ordered General Joseph Hooker (the army commander before being recently replaced by Meade): "Fight him [Lee] when opportunity offers."[21] Lee's tactical objective was revealed in full when he pointed to Cemetery Ridge: "The enemy is there, I am going to strike him."[22] Ascertaining a shortcut to decisive victory, Lee planned to strike Meade with a powerful blow right "between the eyes."[23]

However, Lee's offensive-mindedness on July 3 has been viewed by modern historians as emotion driven and entirely reckless without careful tactical calculation—the epitome of tactical folly, if not stupidity, which had become one of the great myths of the Civil War. But Lee's men knew better, because their commander's tactical astuteness and aggressiveness had led to so many past victories. One of General John Bell Hood's soldiers concluded that Lee "was in temperament a gamecock [known for] his pugnacity."[24] John Singleton Mosby concluded that Lee was "the most aggressive man I met" during the war years.[25] But it would take more than aggressiveness alone to achieve decisive victory on July 3. South Carolinian Mary Chesnut, who was part of President Davis's inner circle in Richmond, made a significant point, noting another quality (verified fully at Gettysburg on July 3) in her diary, "Gen. Robert Lee . . . is not a *lucky* man."[26]

Lee's Greatest Personal Challenge

Clearly, the stakes could not have been higher than on this Friday when two mighty armies faced each other on parallel ridges (Seminary and Cemetery, from west to east) in an idyllic agricultural setting. As the son of "Light-Horse Harry" Lee, who had earned fame as the hard-hitting commander of "Lee's legion" in the southern theater of operations during the American Revolution, Lee seemed to have been born for exactly this climactic moment. If Lee now reaped a decisive victory on July 3, then he would become the revered George Washington of a new republic.

But a streak of bad luck had long followed the Lee family like a dark cloud. After winning fame as Washington's finest cavalryman, the life of "Light-Horse Harry" had then abruptly taken a drastic turn for the worst. He became a debtor in the Spotsylvania County House (Virginia) Jail, and eventually went into a self-imposed West Indies exile. However, Lee possessed all the sterling qualities, including a brilliant mind, of his father, who had "come out of his mother's womb a soldier." The son had been molded by his father's wartime legacy and tragic fate. Even Lee's limitations as a strategist (unlike as a tactician), with his obsession on Virginia-first strategic priorities that ensured a stubborn inability (for provincial, cultural, and psychological reasons) to see beyond Virginia's requirements, had been now transformed into a laser-like focus to pierce Meade's right-center to save Virginia from conquest.[27] South Carolina soldiers of General Joseph Brevard Kershaw's brigade correctly reasoned "that Lee would not yield to a drawn battle without, at least, another attempt to break Meade's front" in a final attempt to reverse the course of the war.[28]

After two days of intense fighting across the picturesque hills and wheat, corn, and oat fields of Adams County, Lee embraced his long-awaited tactical opportunity to win it all. From Seminary Ridge, Lee ascertained the sight that convinced him that he could deliver a decisive blow to smash through Meade's vulnerable right-center held by only 5,300 2nd Corps infantrymen. Since taking command of the army just outside Richmond during the 1862 Peninsular Campaign, the cerebral Virginian had long waited for this moment. All the Confederate lost lives and heroics during the past two summers had been made to now present Lee with this opportunity to deliver a masterstroke to cut Meade's army in two. If he drove a wedge into Meade's vulnerable right-center and then turned on each side to roll up the enfiladed flanks, then Lee would be presented with an open road all the way to Washington, DC, less than 100 miles to the southeast: the long-sought magical formula for conquering a peace.

Here was a rare tactical opportunity to "end the war," as Lee had long hoped and prayed. Trapped in an unwinnable war of attrition against a vastly superior opponent and handicapped by outdated cultural and romantic concepts about waging war (versus irregular or asymmetric warfare) in the "European tradition of regular combat," the South desperately needed a bold masterstroke. By this time, the chances for the Confederacy's recognition from France and England had all but evaporated, after the Battle of Antietam, Maryland, on September 17, 1862, had opened the door for Lincoln's Emancipation Proclamation. Lee, consequently, was now determined to erase the war's brutal "arithmetic" of a vast northern war machine systematically grinding down his army to oblivion.

Therefore, Lee's upcoming tactical offensive was neither a mindless or reckless gamble, as long assumed, but a well-calculated bid to win it all, because the odds were actually now stacked in his favor. After attacking the Union flanks that had been reinforced on July 2, Lee calculated correctly in having pinpointed the weakest spot in Meade's position: the vulnerable right-center, which was now the Achilles' heel of the sprawling defensive line that was stretched exceptionally thin, except on the flanks, for three miles. Even Ewell's failed assaults on Cemetery Hill and Culp's Hill now paid tactical dividends to Lee, because these furious attacks kept the Union defenders on the north firmly in place and away from reinforcing Meade's weak right-center.

Lee, consequently, planned to deliver a mighty blow to this thinly defended soft spot, after unleashing the most massive artillery bombardment of the war. This targeted area was distinguished by a tiny (but especially conspicuous because of its distinctive umbrella shape on the sun-hazed eastern horizon atop the otherwise-open Cemetery Ridge) grove of chestnut oak trees—the famous copse of trees. Part of the white oak family, this clump of chestnut oaks, growing on property owned by farmer Peter Frey, consisted of ridgetop trees that grew so well on thin, rocky soil that they earned the nickname of "rock oak."

Most importantly when Lee struck his winner-take-all blow, he would enjoy an eight-to-one advantage at the most decisive moment, after his right wing (Pickett's division) and left wing (General James Johnston Pettigrew's division) converged and descended upon the copse of trees in a compact strike force. Significantly, Meade's right-center was unfortified. Even the open terrain before Cemetery Ridge enhanced Lee's chances for a more rapid and orderly advance. The approach to Meade's right-center was entirely open and free of obstacles, except an occasional flimsy rail fence: a tactical situation that guaranteed a relatively swift advance to minimize losses and maximize momentum. Contrary to the traditional opinion of historians and for a host of valid reasons, Lee was certainly not "no longer in possession of his full faculties as a military commander."[29] As he emphasized, Lee hoped to now deliver the devastating blow to "end the war if Providence favours us."[30]

Although he was now guilty of sharing Napoleon's overconfidence, the 56-year-old Lee had not deteriorated in deftness and flexibility of mind like the famed French emperor, who was only in his early forties by the time of the 1812 Russian Campaign. Lee still basked in his most remarkable tactical success (the envelopment of the Union army's right flank) at Chancellorsville, which was his "Boldest and Most Daring Strategy" to date.[31] Lee's tactical analysis was now correct because Meade's right-center was so weak that gifted West Pointer General Winfield Scott Hancock, who commanded the thin blue line of 2nd Corps's troops around the copse of trees, lamented that because his "corps had been so weakened by its [July 2] losses it required every available man in line of battle to cover the ground held the previous day."[32]

Lieutenant Colonel Rawley White Martin, 53rd Virginia, Pickett's division, was confident they could plant "their tattered banners upon the crest of Cemetery Ridge."[33] After all, Lee's veterans "had almost always defeated their more numerous opponents [and Lee's army now] constituted as fine a unit as ever marched to battle on this continent."[34] As revealed in a May 21, 1863, letter, Lee's faith in his battle-hardened veterans was boundless: "There never were such men in any Army before & there never can be better in any army again [and they will] never falter at the work before them."[35]

In the words of Lieutenant John Henry Lewis, Jr., 9th Virginia, Pickett's division, Lee had made up his mind "that he must cripple his adversary [and] carry Meade's lines by assault."[36] Lee's army now represented the last "great hope of the South," in the words of Major Edgeworth Bird, 3rd Georgia Infantry, in a letter to his wife.[37]

Destiny itself seemingly called Lee to this situation that presented a golden tactical opportunity on July 3. Former attorney Colonel Eppa Hunton, 8th Virginia, Pickett's division, had just learned that Lee believed that he could "end the war" once and for all.[38] Lieutenant John Henry Lewis, Jr., 9th Virginia, Pickett's division, emphasized how this was now the long-awaited chance to finally say a last "goodbye to Meade's army" forever.[39] Colonel David Wyatt Aiken, the commander of the 7th South Carolina, Kershaw's brigade, revealed the extent of the opportunity in a letter to his wife: "Genl. Lee ordered Genl. Pickett . . . to attack the most vulnerable portion of the enemy's line": the weak right-center.[40]

Allan Guelzo correctly concluded, "In retrospect, the kind of head-down, full-in-front attack which became Pickett's Charge wears all the appearance of folly that over-the-top assaults acquired on the Western Front half a century later. But 1863 was closer on the clock of war technology to Waterloo than the Somme. . . ."[41] Nevertheless, and as mentioned, the alleged folly of Pickett's Charge has become Gettysburg's most enduring stereotype and myth. Faithfully perpetuating the myth, common headlines of 150th-anniversary newspaper articles in America emphasized: "Pickett's Charge: a deadly mistake by Gen. Lee."[42]

The Golden Tactical Opportunity

But this alleged most egregious of Lee's tactical mistakes was in fact the best tactic for reaping decisive victory. If the assault succeeded, then the Army of the Potomac, in the words of Captain Joseph Graham, 1st North Carolina Artillery, from a July 1863 letter to his father, "would have been ruined [and] They would have been scattered over the whole country."[43]

Overlooked by those who have deemed Lee's last offensive at Gettysburg the ultimate folly, unleashing the infantry of Pickett's Charge was only one phase of the planned offensive effort, however. In a masterful employment of available resources, Lee planned to utilize all three arms (infantry, artillery, and cavalry) to the fullest in a well-coordinated fashion: the longtime true secret to battle-field success. Lee's tactical formula emulated those of Napoleon, whose "passion for the strategy of annihilation and the climactic, decisive battle" transformed him into Europe's conqueror.[44] Indeed, throughout the Napoleonic period, what most often brought decisive success was "the correct tactical formula—a coordinated attack by all arms."[45]

Lee, therefore, placed great faith in his long arm, like Napoleon. He planned to unleash the war's largest artillery bombardment along the entire line to prepare the way for his massive assault. This unprecedented cannonade was calculated to knock out Union guns and to support infantry situated on the open, unfortified right-center. Lee's initial tactical plan had been first formu-lated late on July 2 at Lee's headquarters at Mary Thompson's one-and-a-half-story stone house, located just north of the Chambersburg Pike on Seminary Ridge. Boding ill for future developments, Longstreet was not present at Lee's headquarters that night. Deviating from the norm, Longstreet only submitted a report of the second day's activities of his 1st Corps. Nevertheless, Longstreet, the burly Georgian with an outsized ego, was assigned by Lee to make the final dispositions for the charge on July 3.

Despite Longstreet's previous "bad" management and repeated disincli-nations to take the tactical offensive, this upcoming offensive effort was the Georgian's charge, and not Pickett's charge. At Lee's Gettysburg–Chambersburg Pike headquarters at the Widow Thompson House (the modest home of a homespun woman born in 1793 located on Seminary Ridge's crest), Lee ordered that "the assault was to have been made with a column of not less than two divisions, and the remaining divisions were to have moved forward in support of those in advance," in the words of Colonel Walter Herron Taylor of Lee's staff.[46] After the modification of the original offensive plan, Lee actually gave himself a better chance for success by correctly targeting Meade's unfortified right-center, which was "the weakest part" defended by only around 5,300 infantrymen.[47]

Lee now possessed 37 brigades in total. Despite the fact that the majority of these veteran brigades had been bloodied on July 1–2, Lee's offensive plan was based on utilizing the army's freshest troops: Pickett's division of three brigades.[48] However, the two primary divisions to spearhead the great assault on Meade's right-center were designated more out of circumstances than design. Because Pickett's command "was [now] fresh," and Major General Henry "Harry" Heth's division (now led by erudite James Johnston Pettigrew) was already available because of its position in the line (on the left) next to Pickett's division once up, they had been selected. The seemingly ill-fated Heth, who had been with Lee's army for only three months, had been knocked unconscious when a bullet grazed his head on July 1.[49]

Other veteran divisions, especially those of Hill's 3rd Corps, were ordered to provide support. The 3rd Corps possessed fresh brigades, including General William "Billy" Mahone's Virginia brigade and General Carnot Posey's Mississippi brigade. These commands were to advance on the flanks of Pickett's and Pettigrew's divisions close enough to exploit the initial breakthrough in Meade's right-center by the first wave attackers. To protect Pettigrew's left, two 3rd Corps brigades of Pender's division were to advance on the north. Significantly, after suffering only light losses on the first two days, Pender's brigades were in good combat shape.

Likewise, the four brigades of General Richard H. Anderson's division, of Hill's 3rd Corps, were envisioned by Lee to support the flanks. Two brigades (under Generals Cadmus M. Wilcox and David Lang) of this large division were chosen to protect the right of Pickett's division on the south—a vital guardian role. Therefore, Lee expected not only "all of Anderson's troops [but also] perhaps [General] Robert Rodes's remaining [Ewell's 2nd Corps] units to move in support of the main attack." Lee naturally expected Longstreet and Hill to "act in concert" in closely supporting the assault, a risky assumption because of their fractured relationship. But Anderson's division had already faltered in adequately supporting Longstreet's assault on July 2, because of the lack of coordination between Hill and Longstreet—an inept leadership team, which was an ominous development for July 3.[50]

More importantly, with two high tactical hands to play that were not readily available to him on July 1–2, Lee planned to utilize not only Pickett's fresh division, but also more than 6,000 veteran cavalrymen, including horse artillery, under Stuart. In Lee's tactical reasoning on July 2, which set the stage for the final day: "I have been reinforced by Pickett's division and Stuart's Cavalry [and] Tomorrow I will mass Pickett's division . . . in front of Meade's [center], well supported to the right and to the left [and] I will dispatch Stuart around Meade's right flank to make an attack in conjunction with Pickett's front attack; then let every battery and every gun along our line open and concentrate their fire upon that point in Meade's line, the center of which is designated by that umbrella-shaped clump of trees that shall be Pickett's objective point, and when the bombardment shall cease, then shall Stuart and Pickett charge, and I will cut Meade's army in two and destroy it in detail."[51] James M. McPherson described the brilliance of Lee's innovative battle plan, especially with regard to Stuart's planned strike from the rear: Lee "still hoped and planned for a Cannae victory [based upon] not only the attack we now call Pickett's Charge . . . but also an attack on Culp's Hill and a coup-de-grace strike by Stuart's six thousand cavalry swooping down on the Union rear. . . ."[52]

Lee's bold tactical concept of striking Meade's rear with cavalry was in keeping with an ancient axiom of war that emphasized: "Do not mass all your troops in front, and even if the enemy is superior in numbers, direct your operations against his rear. . . ."[53]

Stuart's cavalry would strike the right-center's rear, after the war's most extensive Confederate cannonade swept the Cemetery Ridge. Lee had wisely concentrated the army's cavalry (the South's finest horse-soldiers) under Stuart, who now headed three veteran horse brigades, to smash into the Union army's rear precisely where the defenders were most vulnerable, while thousands of infantrymen struck from the opposite direction.

Likewise, because of Longstreet's failed performance in providing adequate artillery support and properly coordinating an assault on Malvern Hill that turned into a costly disaster on July 1, 1862, Lee had wisely not completely placed his faith entirely on Longstreet. Therefore, Stuart's strike into Meade's rear would compensate for any repeat of Longstreet's Malvern Hill–like failures. Lee had masterfully planned to maximize the best of his artillery, cavalry, and infantry in a coordinated effort. Clearly, success was now based upon a "proper concert of action" (the vital ingredient missing on July 2) to win it all in one masterstroke.[54]

Lee planned for his eleven infantry brigades to advance across a broad front and then to converge in a concentrated wedge-like formation to strike at a single point at the weak right-center to eventually achieve an eight-to-one numerical advantage (even without tabulating Stuart's strike from the rear). Achieving this strategic objective was made easier because of Lee's decision to funnel the attackers to strike at a highly visible point of a clump of trees. The combination of this copse of oak trees at a dominant high point along the lengthy ridge was significant for another reason as well: Not only was the copse to serve as an elevated beacon for the infantry attackers from the west, but also for thousands of Stuart's cavalry from the east. If everything went as planned, especially Hill's divisions supporting Pickett and Pettigrew and closely following up on these frontline attackers and also to protect the northern and southern flanks, then thousands of attackers would converge in a compact wedge like a giant battering ram at the copse of trees, while Stuart's three experienced brigades of more than 6,000 cavalrymen (bestowing Lee with more than a 10-to-one manpower advantage) simultaneously struck from behind at the same point, then "Lee would find an open road before him—one he might take, surrender demand in hand, to Washington, DC."[55]

Recently, some historians have postulated the thesis that the real target of Pickett's Charge was in fact Ziegler's Grove, located just southwest of Cemetery Hill and north of the copse of trees. However, this latest revisionism has been nothing more than idle speculation. These recent assumptions have been based upon faulty conclusions without realizing that the copse of trees was larger in overall size (more in terms of width than height) in July 1863 than today. The trees did not have to tower high to provide a visual guide because of their high visibility on the crest of the ridge. The height of the clump of trees was stunted because these ridgetop-growing trees (scrub oaks) never reached great heights (like other local trees planted on infertile soil), especially on the thin, rocky soil atop Cemetery Ridge.[56]

Confederate survivors almost exclusively and early on designated the copse of chestnut oak trees as Lee's ultimate target. Major Walter Harrison, the inspector general of Pickett's division and a staff officer (Pickett's acting adjutant at Gettysburg who was privy to the assault's intimate details), knew the truth. He emphasized that the objective of the attack was the "clump of trees." In an early publication (1870) before the Lost Cause glorification of Pickett's Charge, he wrote how a "small clump of trees made the enemy's centre a prominent point of direction."[57] Harrison also penned: "[W]hat an important feature that copse of trees was at the time of the battle; and how it had been a landmark towards which Longstreet's [correctly named] assault . . . was directed."[58]

Most of all, Lee needed a good, visible high-ground point to guide his assault for multiple directions so that thousands of attackers could converge at a single vantage point. Therefore, when he surveyed Cemetery Ridge's length, he had overlooked lower points along the ridge south of the clump of trees. Clearly, a highly visible point was crucial for guiding the attackers from opposite directions toward a central focal point. However, some critics of the copse of trees as Lee's targeted point have maintained that these trees stood only about 10 feet tall in 1863. However, these revisionists have overlooked the fact that it was the combination of this elevated position along the ridge and the unique shape of the clump of trees that made this targeted point more highly visible (to both infantry and cavalry attackers) and ideal for guiding the attackers than simply the tree's height.

Likewise, because the highly visible Nicholas J. Codori House and large red barn were located on the lower ground (west of Cemetery Ridge) along the Emmitsburg Road almost directly (west) before the clump of trees, the Codori House and barn also served as an initial guide for the attackers. But the chestnut oaks of the clump of trees that dominated the ridge's skyline and were more visible on higher ground just east of the Codori House were the most crucial point, especially after the attackers passed the house. Therefore, this elevated perch upon which the copse of trees stood was a distinctive, easily seen high point. Almost a knoll atop an open, commanding plateau of the lengthy ridge that dominated the eastern horizon, this right-center point in terms of an elevation was as prominent as the tree-covered spot along an otherwise-open ridge. Therefore, in relative terms, the height of the copse's trees was not as important as the ridge's overall height at this strategic location in serving as the assault's guiding point. The clump of trees (south of Zeigler's Woods located higher up this north–south ridge) served as an ideal highly visible general guide for the two assault wings (Pettigrew and Pickett) from the west (not to mention Stuart from the east) that were to converge at this strategic point.[59]

The copse of trees was also described as a "clump of dwarfed trees" by an observer who was more familiar with tall timber growth on fertile, less rocky ground with ample topsoil. But as mentioned, the timber's height was actually much less important than location at a high point along the ridge in serving as a highly visible guide for attackers.[60]

Lee had chosen this point because Meade's right-center was almost entirely free of trees and underbrush (hence, the prominence of the copse of trees—thanks to its high-ground perch—that dominated the skyline to the attacker's view), because of thin topsoil and rocky ground. The clump of trees, struggling for life without sufficient topsoil, was centered on a rocky outcropping long avoided out of necessity by farmers' plows. However, elsewhere on the ridge in the 2nd Corps's sector on the right-center, this lack of natural cover guaranteed no protection for either Union artillerymen or infantrymen exposed on the open slope. Boding well for Lee's plan, these bluecoat foot soldiers were without fortifications, trenches, or even rifle pits. Only the north–south running stone wall, except at the Angle (where the light-colored wall of rocks just north of the copse turned a short distance east before continuing on its north–south direction, just below the crest) offered protection for the 2nd Corps's infantrymen. But even this stone wall was low and anything but formidable. Without earthen emplacements for protection, Federal artillery poised along the open ridge around the copse of trees was vulnerable. As planned by Lee, consequently, these exposed guns could be knocked out by a massive artillery bombardment.[61]

Contrary to conventional wisdom, therefore, Lee deliberately targeted one of the ridge's highest and "most prominent" points for attack: an ideal target not only for the infantry attackers of nine brigades, immediately supported by two brigades (and additional brigades to be hurled forward in support by Longstreet) in front, but also for Stuart's cavalry of three veteran brigades. Lee's tactical decision has long seemed incomprehensible to modern historians, especially those imbued with the lessons (the folly of frontal assaults) of western-front warfare during World War One and with the disastrous assaults on Malvern Hill and Fredericksburg. Therefore, without grasping the full complexity of Lee's plan, armchair historians have long emphasized that assaulting Cemetery Ridge was suicidal, especially without taking into account Stuart's key role in charging into Meade's rear. While the popular "attack and die" thesis has applied to the folly of frontally attacking a fortified, high-ground defensive position because technical advances in weaponry (rifled musket) had outpaced tactics, the targeting of an unfortified high-ground defensive position (simultaneously from front and rear) was another tactical matter altogether, as Lee fully realized, especially one that was stretched thin and short on men.

Consequently, Lee concluded that this unfortified position could not be defended by adequate numbers of defenders because of not only the threats of Confederate pressure (Ewell on the north and Longstreet on the south) on the flanks, but also because Lee knew that Meade believed that this was the least likely of places to be attacked. Interestingly, this was the same tactical reasoning that had caused Mexican General Antonio Lopez de Santa Anna to incorrectly believe that General Winfield Scott's September 1847 threat before the 200-foot-high hill was only a feint. Santa Anna had made the key tactical mistake of only lightly defending Chapultepec's heights, believing that its imposing natural strength would deter an attack, an erroneous assumption that led to the hill's capture and Mexico City's capture. For this reason, along with the fact that Meade had obviously strengthened his line's northern (Cemetery Hill) and southern ends (Little Round Top) that had nearly been overwhelmed on July 2, Lee concluded that Meade's right-center was weak not only with regard to numbers, but also thanks to commonsense assumptions of Union leadership that Lee dare not attack over such a wide stretch (three-quarters of a mile) of open ground.[62]

Internal Obstacles

Ironically, Lee's first obstacle was his own top lieutenant, Longstreet, who still advocated the impractical turning movement around Meade's left early on July 3. As mentioned, Lee had originally desired to unleash a simultaneous "pincer move" that included Ewell striking Meade's right and Longstreet's entire 1st Corps attacking the other flank, but "Old Peter" would have none of it. Lee, therefore, was forced to literally work around a reluctant Longstreet. After having launched bloody assaults against General Dan Sickles's left (3rd Corps) at Houck's Ridge and the jumble of giant boulders (Devil's Den) at Houck's Ridge's southern base, and then later at Little Round Top on July 2nd, Longstreet had early declared that his commands were too weak to take the offensive on July 3: the intransigence that forced Lee to hastily create his second battle plan.

After the morning of July 3 conference, the final formulation of Lee's complex plan revealed that he had accepted Longstreet's arguments: unleashing an assault on the right-center (where Wright had struck on July 2) and not the left-center (where General William Barksdale's Mississippi brigade attacked on the previous day) and left (where Hood struck on the second day).

Consequently, this last-minute shift of focus of the assault farther north now meant that General Joseph Robert Davis's inexperienced Mississippi and North Carolina brigade and Colonel John Mercer Brockenbrough's Virginia brigade— the two least reliable brigades now understrength—were now assigned to the assault force (instead of McLaws's and Hood's superior combat troops to the south). Worst of all, these two weak brigades were assigned to the vital mission of advancing on the assault's extreme left flank, a certain tactical arrangement for a collapse. The inexperienced Mississippi and North Carolina brigade (new to Lee's army) had been cut to pieces on July 1. Additionally, this brigade was led by President Jefferson Davis's nephew of unproven leadership ability. Davis's and Brockenbrough's brigades were the worst possible choices for this crucial assignment.

But Lee had been convinced by Longstreet that these vastly inferior troops were preferable to McLaws's and Hood's divisions. In consequence for the upcoming attack, Pickett's division alone represented Longstreet's corps, and Pettigrew's division (Heth's command before he fell wounded on July 1) had been substituted for McLaws's division. And Pender's division, of two brigades, took the place of young Evander M. Law's division (formerly commanded by Hood until he fell wounded from a bursting shell at the assault's beginning on July 2). Because Pender's troops now lacked experienced leaders, Lee had placed General Trimble (West Point Class of 1822) in command, despite being the oldest division commander (age 61) in the assault.

Because of Longstreet's insistence, Hood's and McLaws's divisions, from south to north, now remained in stationary positions. Sudden substitutes to go in with Pickett's division, six brigades (or one and a half divisions) of Hill's corps now replaced Hood's and McLaws's crack troops for the assault. Pettigrew's division (the assault's left wing) of four brigades was designated to advance alongside Pickett's division (the attack's right wing) in the first assault wave. But more than 40 percent of Pettigrew's division had been killed, wounded, captured on, or was missing on July 1. At Gettysburg, one-fourth of Lee's total losses were North Carolina soldiers, mocking the ill-named Pickett's Charge, the excessive focus on the Virginians' minority role, and the alleged inferior performance of these "Old North State" troops. However, Trimble's ten North Carolina regiments were in overall bad shape compared to Pickett's fresh regiments. Nevertheless, the army's elite units of Longstreet's corps (Hood's and McLaws's divisions) would now sit out the massive attack.

Nine veteran brigades of about 12,500 men (about one-third of Lee's army) from three divisions would be hurled toward Meade's right-center, while two other brigades served as flank support—a total of eleven brigades. However, the 46 regiments designated for the upcoming assault were depleted from the prior two days. Most importantly, Lee envisioned unleashing the bulk of the army's units in support of the frontline attackers. Pickett's fifteen regiments (three brigades) were in the best shape of any troops. Lee additionally hoped that Longstreet would still send forth Hood's and McLaws's divisions (another eight brigades) to exploit initial gains reaped by the frontline attackers of Pickett's and Pettigrew's divisions. Therefore, Longstreet possessed the authority to utilize more than nineteen brigades in the upcoming offensive effort.[63]

Colonel Walter Herron Taylor described the last-minute adjustments made more complex by the utilization of eleven brigades from four divisions (Pickett, Pettigrew, Anderson, and Pender) of two different corps, 1st and 3rd: "[I]t was only, after because of the apprehensions of General Longstreet that his corps was not strong enough for the [attack], that General Hill was called on to reinforce him [therefore] Orders were sent to General Hill to place Heth's division and two brigades of Pender's at General Longstreet's disposal. . . . "[64] To protect the assault's right flank and to fully exploit gains made by the frontline troops, Lee also wanted two reserve brigades of General Richard H. Anderson's division, and the division's other three brigades to support the attack's left flank, and "perhaps Robert Rodes remaining units to move in support of the main attack."[65]

However, not only Pettigrew's brigades, but Hill's 3rd Corps brigades (except for General William "Billy" Mahone's Virginia and Carnot Posey's Mississippi brigades, which were not involved in the previous day's attacks) were also in worse shape than Hood's and McLaws's divisions, after having been hard hit on July 1: a nullification of Longstreet's arguments not to utilize the crack troops of McLaws's and Hood's divisions.[66]

Consequently, the main support for Pickett's and Pettigrew's divisions fell on the units of Hill's corps. However, General Ambrose Powell Hill was physically exhausted and ailing. Besides being mentally war-weary, Hill was also obsessed about the welfare of his pregnant wife, Kitty Morgan Hill, or "Dolly," who gave the general much anxiety. Hill was also a changed man, much like Ewell (due to a recent marriage and an amputated leg), and no longer the relentless fighter. Therefore, all three of Lee's three corps commanders were far below their prime, ensuring subpar performances on July 3. Hill's contributions to enhance the assault's success were practically nonexistent. Hill had already failed to work closely with Longstreet in coordinating assaults of the two corps on the second day. The personal relationship between Longstreet and Hill was nearly as dysfunctional as that of Lee and Longstreet.

Hill had recently reorganized his corps. Hastily cobbled together and lacking overall cohesion, Hill's 3rd Corps consisted of thirteen brigades representing eight different states. Hill's corps had never fought together before. Likewise, half of the army's corps had never operated on the battlefield together with the other half just before their greatest challenge to date. No corps was more ill-prepared than Hill's ad hoc corps of divergent units, which were less capable because of relatively little experience and dysfunctional leadership at high levels, including jealousy in regard to Hill's political-based promotion of corps command.[67]

Consequently, Hill's assault force was inherently weaker and actually much smaller than envisioned by Lee. Lee's original assault plan, which called for a larger strike force that had been initially agreed upon by the commander and his top lieutenants at the July 2 conference, had evolved and now included a weaker attack force. Despite Longstreet's strong stance against offensive operations on successive days, Lee still hoped for the best. Longstreet was now in charge of orchestrating the assault directed against fellow West Point classmate (1839) Winfield Scott Hancock's sector, when an energetic hand was needed.[68]

Lee was relying too much upon his top lieutenants partly because he was a sick man. He was hampered by heart disease, which resulted in his death barely five years after the war's end. Lee was stricken not only from a debilitating case of diarrhea, but also from long-term coronary problems. He even suffered a mild heart attack the previous April.[69]

Nevertheless, Lee overcame failing health and uncooperative top lieutenants to perform his old tactical magic to increase the chances for the assault's success. Lee now "had thirty-seven brigades of infantry [and] eight of these were pinned down on the right, and ten on the left. But this means that Lee had been able to concentrate nineteen brigades, more than half of his army, in his center, where they could be used to launch or to support the climactic attack [and] at this time thirty of the brigades were more or less worn down by hard fighting and seven were fresh or comparatively so. All of these seven were among the nineteen brigades massed in the center. Obviously Lee had been able to effect this concentration only because he was playing Meade for what he was, that is, a not-very-aggressive fighter, doubly hesitant at Gettysburg because he had been in command of his army for only a few days. Thus, for the launching of the great attack, Lee had effected a magnificent concentration, especially of fresh troops, especially Pickett's division.[70]

To cut Meade's line in two, Lee not only expected Longstreet to throw eight brigades of McLaws's and Hood's divisions into the breach once ripped in

Meade's right-center, but also for Hill on the north to do the same. Therefore, if Longstreet's and Hill's readily available troops were hurled forward to exploit the gains of the frontline attackers, then Lee would have about another 10,000 troops added to the assault.[71] In total, Lee possessed "some 25,000, and perhaps closer to 30,000," ready to strike, including the initial spearhead of around 12,500 men.[72]

Without a doubt, his was a "magnificent concentration" of assault troops to exploit a magnificent tactical opportunity to overwhelm an unfortified, weak position.[73] Lee also possessed a novel tactical solution of advancing so many troops across open ground so that they would then simultaneously converge at a single point on Meade's right-center: when relatively near the strategic objective, the assault's left wing (Pettigrew) was to advance east, turn and march south, and then turn east again to strike at the copse of trees; while the right wing (Pickett) was to initially march east, turn and march north, and then turn east at hit the clump of trees sector in a convergence of attackers to then form the wedge-like spearhead of a battering ram to punch through Meade's weak right-center. This "indirect approach" over a wide stretch of open ground was guaranteed to confound the opponent, disguising Lee's targeted point (clump of trees) so that Union reinforcements would not be rushed forth in time to bolster the right-center: a clever means of stacking additional odds in Lee's favor of about eight to one at the copse of trees at the most critical moment. Even more, Lee counted on a more than massive concentration for a frontal assault, but also a lengthy flank march (or ride in this case) early on July 3 around Meade's right by Stuart's cavalry to ease into position behind the right-center's defenders in preparation for catching the Yankees by surprise from the rear, while the infantry struck from the front.[74]

Colonel Taylor, Lee's darkly handsome adjutant, described the fundamental basis of Lee's final decision to attack on Meade's vulnerable right-center in a July 17, 1863 letter: "Their two flanks were protected by two insurmountable, impracticable rocky mountains," and therefore, the soft right-center was the best point of attack.[75] Partly forested Little Round Top (a barren western face) and heavily timbered Big Round Top, from north to south, anchored Meade's left before Hood's division, and Culp's Hill and Cemetery Hill solidly anchored the Union line's right. Compared to these mostly timbered heights (the defensive line's highest points) at the opposite ends of Meade's line, the right-center was open, weakly defended, and comparatively a lower point than north higher up Cemetery Ridge and lower than the high-ground on the northern and southern flanks—realities conveniently ignored by historians who had long decried Lee's July 3 folly because of the central paradox that Cemetery Ridge was in fact an overall easier target also in regard to elevation.

Verifying Lee's tactical wisdom, Taylor wrote: "It was out of the question to turn them [the high-ground at both ends of Meade's line and] Besides the natural advantages of the place the enemy had strengthened themselves very much by artificial works [and] There was no opportunity whatever for a successful flank movement . . . on the third day." Consequently, at the right place and with the right tactical plan, Lee correctly planned to smash through Meade's vulnerable right-center, where barely 5,000 Yankee infantry held the thin, overly stretched line exactly where the attackers were to converge in overwhelming numbers.[76]

Presented with the best available tactical opportunity that he planned to exploit to the fullest, Lee was now in fact at his very best (not his worst, as long assumed) in deciding to launch a frontal assault at a weak, unfortified point. The ever-cautious Meade, who possessed no prior experience in handling an entire army, had allowed Lee a free tactical hand. Because of such reasons, the Virginian planned to unleash two masterful surprises from the west that were guaranteed to deliver a powerful one-two punch to split Meade's army in two: 1) the war's most massive artillery bombardment from a lengthy row of guns positioned along the advantageous high-ground of the Joseph Sherfy Peach Orchard and the Emmitsburg Road ridge, in softening up the defenders, and 2) thousands of veteran troops massed in the thick woodlands on Seminary Ridge's reverse slope to hide them from prying Yankee eyes, before they emerged from hiding to advance over the open fields without natural obstructions to guarantee a relatively swift advance.

Last but not least, Lee was inspired by the memory of the remarkable tactical offensive achievements of the superb American fighting men during the Mexican–American War, especially in overrunning Chapultepec, which was far more naturally formidable than Cemetery Ridge at the right-center. The high-ground of Chapultepec was a seemingly impregnable bastion on September 13, 1847, until overwhelmed by a frontal assault that led to Mexico City's fall and the war's end. If the seemingly impregnable heights of Chapultepec could be carried by a headlong bayonet attack, then surging up the gentle, open western slope of Cemetery Ridge—especially when compared to the more daunting rocky heights at both ends of the defensive line (Cemetery Hill on the north and the Round Tops on the south)—and then smashing through Meade's right-center would be much less challenging.

Most symbolic, America's greatest hero of Chapultepec's storming just happened to be the officer chosen to lead his division in spearheading Lee's greatest assault, George Edward Pickett. Lee envisioned that if Pickett (then a young West Pointer, Class of 1846) could lead the way in overrunning formidable Chapultepec, then almost certainly the long-haired Virginian (now a major general) could now accomplish a comparable tactical feat with thousands of expert fighting men. The capture of Cemetery Ridge was now seen by Lee as easier to overrun than Chapultepec. Upholding the valor of his French ancestors (later Huguenots, or French Protestants) in battling English invaders, Pickett had been "the first American to scale the ramparts of Chapultepec, a daring exploit noted in official reports as well as in the newspapers."[77]

Pickett would not have placed the United States flag upon Chapultepec's ramparts if not for his friend "Pete" Longstreet (a fellow West Pointer, Class of 1842). Longstreet had been leading his Company H, 8th United States Infantry, which advanced before Pickett's Company A, when he had been cut down with a serious thigh wound while carrying the United States banner, recently grabbed from a fallen regimental color-bearer. When Longstreet fell atop the first parapet, Lieutenant Pickett was then handed the colors by his friend "Pete." Pickett then reached the site of the palace of the ancient Aztecs. After hauling down the Mexican colors, Pickett raised the "Stars and Stripes."[78] Pickett's colors flew proudly over Chapultepec, while American victory cheers rang across the heights once conquered by Cortez and his Spanish conquistadors.[79]

And now at Gettysburg on a day as equally hot as that day central Mexico in September 1847, Pickett possessed still another opportunity to accomplish great things. Once again, a strange destiny had placed Pickett in a key situation with a chance to again become famous as during his youth. Then, Lee, Longstreet, Pickett, and other former West Pointers would again shortly march triumphantly in still another fallen enemy capital (Washington, DC) like they had done at Mexico City.[80] Partly because of the Mexican–American War's tactical lessons that had been taught at West Point, Lee now fully embraced the wisdom of offensive-minded tactics as the ultimate solution to the South's ultimate dilemma.[81]

Enduring European Military Legacies

The timeless lessons of Napoleon's battlefield successes based upon his reliance on the tactical offensive also loomed large in Lee's mind. The Civil War generation of leadership had learned that "Napoleon never failed in carrying any lines which he attacked."[82] When Lee became West Point's superintendent, he supported the Napoleon Club, where faculty, especially its influential president Dennis Hart Mahan, espoused the wisdom of Napoleonic tactics, especially the tactical offensive. Here, young cadets had hotly debated and written essays about the merits of Napoleon's tactics.[83]

Austerlitz was Napoleon's tactical masterpiece. It was there, on December 2, 1805, that Napoleon's troops overran the Pratzen Heights to smash through the enemy's center. Even Lee's grand strategy of capturing Washington, DC, to force a peace was taken out of Napoleon's most relied-upon chapter in the art of waging war. The brilliant Corsican had conquered one European capital after another, marching into Berlin and Vienna to fulfill his insatiable imperial ambitions.[84] Historian Paul Johnson emphasized the simple secret of Napoleon's amazing winning streak across Europe: "Once his army was deployed on ground of his choosing, he simply attacked."[85]

Lee's decision to launch a massive attack to pierce Meade's right-center was entirely in keeping with the day's most advanced military thought as taught at leading military schools on both sides of the Atlantic. Baron Antoine Henri Jomini, who had served on Napoleon's staff as official historian, emerged as a leading war theorist. Based upon Napoleon's art of war, Jomini's concepts were embraced by generations of West Point cadets, including a young Lee (Class of 1829). In consequence, Civil War generals carried Jomini's concepts into battle, even his 1838 *Summary of the Art of War,* at Gettysburg.

America's top military theorist during the antebellum period, Professor Dennis Hart Mahan, had popularized Jomini's strategic and tactical ideas, including at West Point, with his own 1848 book about the art of war. Lee's Chancellorsville's victory was a product of a masterful utilization of a "classic Jomini-style" tactic of the "strategic envelopment." In regard to Lee's tactical reasoning on Gettysburg's third day, Jomini, who learned of Napoleon's winning ways firsthand, emphasized that the enemy's weakest spot was the most decisive point to strike with a concentrated mass of infantry. Lee now planned to do what Mahan had long emphasized: the strategic wisdom of invading enemy territory and then delivering a decisive knock-out blow to reveal "true genius."[86]

Indeed, Lee was the Confederacy's "greatest Jominian."[87] He concurred with Jomini's axiom based upon what the military theorist had learned, while serving by Napoleon's side: "A general who waits the enemy like an automaton without taking any other part than that of fighting valiantly, will always succumb when he shall be well attacked."[88] David D. Chandler summarized how the fundamental basis of Napoleon's success was deceptively simple: "For it is by upsetting the enemy's 'balance' that the victory is won; the concentration of fire and the opening of a breach are the only means to the true end—which is the psychological destruction of the enemy's will to continue resistance."[89]

The moral factor also now fueled Lee's desire to unleash the tactical offensive. Lee passionately denounced the "evil designs of the North" against the "most puritan of all American regions [the South]." Lee was also determined to attack because he admitted that "in view of the disparity of resources, it would have taken a miracle, a direct intervention of the Lord on the other side, to enable the South to win."[90] Like Lee, Napoleon fully understood that the key to success, especially in regard to the tactical offensive, involved the moral factor: "[M]oral considerations in war were three-quarters of the equation" for decisive success.[91]

Lee might have reflected back on the statement made by one dismayed Mexican officer, who remarked to Santa Anna when the tricolor Mexican flag was lowered from atop Chapultepec just before young Lieutenant Pickett raised the United States flag, "God is a Yankee."[92] In moral terms, Lee was betting—although he was doing so with careful calculation to stack the odds in his favor as much as possible, especially in regard to Stuart's attack into Meade's rear—that God was definitely not a Yankee on July 3.

But now Lee was not as much relying upon God as he was depending upon the combat prowess of the average fighting man, infantry, cavalry, and artillery. Especially among Lee's July 3 critics, the much-touted theory of the alleged vast superiority of the tactical defensive has overlooked the most crucial factors for a successful tactical offensive: a righteous cause, experienced officers commanding veterans, fighting spirit, esprit de corps, and élan. In a July 1, 1863, letter that described what Lee also counted upon to win it all, a confident Lieutenant Benjamin Lyons Farinholt, 53rd Virginia, Pickett's division, wrote to his wife: "Our Army is in excellent health, and if we keep up our present state of organization there is nothing to fear from any force that can be brought against us [and] Our Army is in fine spirits and [is] confidently expecting success under the able leadership of Genl. Lee."[93] Confederate Alexander McNeill explained in a letter that "We came here [Pennsylvania] with the best army the Confederacy ever carried into the field. . . ."[94]

For a host of pressing political, military, and diplomatic factors, Lee was now obsessed with delivering a massive blow for all the right reasons. Ironically, this bold decision based upon a keen tactical calculus has been interpreted by modern historians as a classic case of faulty decision-making of the lowest order: an inexplicable aberration for the most successful commander in American history on a single early July afternoon when he was simply not himself, as generally believed.

Ironically, while Chapultepec had presented the formidable objective of its imposing heights that overlooked Mexico City like an Aztec Mount Olympus, Cemetery Ridge was a different kind of elevation altogether. From Seminary Ridge, Cemetery Ridge hardly looked worthy of its designation as even a ridge because of its gently ascending open slope. A lush patchwork of green pastures, crops of oats and rye, and yellow fields of wheat filled the gently rolling terrain before Cemetery Ridge. However, this pristine agricultural landscape was deceiving, appearing almost flat from a distance on Seminary Ridge. A lengthy, narrow ridge, the Emmitsburg Road ridge, lay between the two main parallel ridges (Seminary and Cemetery), running northeastward to Gettysburg's southern end. Especially with regard to its open western slope, Cemetery Ridge was anything but a commanding height like Chapultepec that rose sharply from an open plain filled with cornfields.

At first glance, in retrospect, therefore, Lee's decision to launch his attack across the open, relatively level ground of about three-quarters of a mile has been long viewed as suicidal according to popular lore. But this broad expanse of open, gently ascending terrain has caused historians to emphasize Lee's alleged tactical folly without considering that it offered an easy avenue for a relatively swift advance for thousands of troops to more quickly gain their strategic objective when time was of the essence—additional proof of the tactical opportunity, because the lay of the land would not impede the sweeping Confederate advance all the way to Cemetery Ridge, ensuring a relatively rapid advance across open fields.

Compared to Virginia's battlefields (distinguished mostly by rough, wooded terrain), nature herself seemed to have created this relatively smooth avenue for thousands of attackers to more quickly reach Cemetery Ridge. Because nineteenth-century armies had long fought by the axiom that "armies did not attack in dense forests" (the daunting reality had Lee approved Longstreet's impractical proposed turning of Meade's left at the heavily-timbered Round Tops and one explanation of Ewell's failure to overwhelm densely wooded Culp's Hill), the broad, open fields lying before Cemetery Ridge and its gentle slope were actually promising for the fulfillment of Lee's tactical plan. Revealing as much, General Wright, whose Georgia brigade (three regiments and a battalion) had pushed across this same open ground and struck Meade's right-center on July 2, emphasized: "It is not as hard to get there as it looks." Indeed, the ground was actually highly favorable for a massive assault, especially when compared to the rugged, rocky terrain and heavy woodlands on the Round Tops and Culp's Hill. Embittered survivors described Little Round Top as a "Gibraltar" that was truly "impregnable," unlike Meade's right-center that paled in comparison as an imposing elevation.

While the relatively gentle terrain over which Pickett's Charge would be launched presented the deceptive initial appearance (the ground was more rolling than level), what was now presented before Lee was actually the easiest and best natural avenue (as General Wright verified) leading toward decisive victory. Again at first glance, Lee's prospects of overrunning the high-ground might seem improbable, but such was simply not the case. But in relative terms rather than Lee's attack demonstrating the height of folly, the inevitable losses were alone justified to exploit the long-awaited opportunity to fulfill the South's greatest ambition of "conquering [a] Peace."[95] Therefore, in the words of Sergeant James Walker, 9th Virginia of General Lewis Addison Armistead's brigade, Pickett's division, "the men did not seem to dread this battle as many others" in the past, because a possible decisive success now could be won instead of just another wasted effort and pyrrhic victory as so often in Virginia.[96]

Despite initial objections to a northern invasion and leaving his own home state (Mississippi) to its uncertain fate, President Davis now wanted Lee to exploit "some opportunity [that] should be offered so as to enable us to defeat the army on which our foe most relied, [then] the measure of our success would be full."[97]

And now that great opportunity was now presented by the thin, weak, and unfortified Union line on Meade's right-center that was ripe for delivering a devastating blow. Lee felt that this greatest of all prizes of finally vanquishing the Army of the Potomac was now well within his grasp. Therefore, Lee's determination to pierce this weak defensive point was not a product of delusion or because he was "no longer in possession" of his mental faculties as long assumed.[98] Colonel Walter Herron Taylor, Lee's adjutant, felt that all was well because of "our wise Chief" and his decision making.[99] Lee knew that his veterans could advance rapidly across (in timely and organized fashion) the wide stretch of open ground—precisely because it was so open and obstacle-free—with relatively few casualties.[100] From what he learned from General

Wright, Lee reasoned that the attackers could gain Cemetery Ridge in only about twenty minutes, a correct estimation.[101]

Lee's tactical calculations and deductions were right on target. Contrary to today's prevailing stereotypes and myths, the planned assault was not a case of "not war [but] murder" as at Malvern Hill and Fredericksburg.[102] To Lee's trained eye, Meade's right-center did not even appear as formidable as the Union-fortified defensive position at Gaines's Mill, which had been pierced by a frontal assault.[103] To fulfill this delicate timetable (precious minutes meant lives) of gaining Cemetery Ridge in less than a half hour thanks to the open, rolling terrain, Pickett informed General Garnett to "Get across the field as soon as you can. . . ."[104]

The motivations of Lee's veterans could not have been higher, because they were consumed with the vision of "our banners [soon] wav[ing] in the streets of Washington" and atop the Capitol dome and the statue of Freedom, Columbia. Catching the army's prevailing ethos, "Old Pete" Longstreet had earlier declared with regard to his country's enemies, "I will kill them all."[105] Teenage Corporal George M. Setzer, a former carpenter of Company F (Farmville Guards), 18th Virginia, Pickett's division, and fated to be killed during Pickett's Charge, wrote with jubilation in a letter to his parents, after the slaughter at Fredericksburg, "We just slayed them" with businesslike efficiency.[106]

Best of all, after Lee's "magnificent concentration" of assault units, the attackers were destined to have an eight-to-one advantage against only 3,000 defenders upon reaching Meade's right-center—the long-sought tactical formula that provided the best opportunity ever presented to Lee to finally deliver a mortal blow to the Army of the Potomac. Perhaps learning from prisoners of the exact location of Meade's headquarters, on the west side of Taneytown Road and just southeast of the copse of trees, Lee might have known that a breakthrough at this point would also knock out his opponent's command and control center.

Meade's right-center was not dominated by overwhelming numbers of defenders, heavy reserves, and rows of cannon that automatically doomed an assault. Only the hindsight of academic historians has created the myth of the impregnability to Meade's right-center. After correctly ascertaining Meade's strengthening of his flanks instead of his inadequately defended center, Lee now planned to smash through this weak sector defended by only a single brigade (General Alexander S. Webb's 2nd Brigade, 2nd Division, 2nd Corps) without the advantage of defenses, except for the north–south running stone wall (low and hardly formidable), which turned a short distance east–west to form the Angle.[107]

Of course, the other key to a successful assault was adequate support, both infantry and artillery (especially on the flanks), for the attack: Longstreet's responsibility. Barksdale's and Wright's deep penetrations (left-center and right-center, respectively) and other determined Rebel assaults, including those on Little Round Top, on July 2 were thwarted because of the breakdown of the execution of Lee's echelon attack, thanks to either nonexistent or entirely inadequate support. Longstreet and his division commanders failed to closely coordinate the assaults of their units on the previous day. Therefore, not taking any chances of coordination again breaking down on July 3 (Longstreet had failed at Malvern Hill for these same reasons), Lee thought he had diminished this fatal flaw by planning for his eleven brigades—and then other close support brigades that Longstreet was to advance—to simultaneously converge at a single point, the copse of trees.[108]

Colonel Edward Porter Alexander wrote of the ultimate target chosen by Lee and upon which the assault formations were to converge: "A clump of trees in the enemy's line was pointed out to me as the proposed point of our attack. . . ."[109] Although situated on a high part of Cemetery Ridge and lower than the ridge's northward continuation, which gently ascended toward the tall oak trees of Ziegler's Grove, the defensive line at the little clump of oaks was paradoxically a rare high-ground weak point. The "angle of the stone fence was lightly held [as] comparatively few Federals who were there. . . ."[110] In a letter to his wife, 36-year-old Colonel David Wyatt Aiken, who commanded the 7th South Carolina, General Joseph Brevard Kershaw's South Carolina brigade, wrote how Lee had orchestrated a formidable "magnificent concentration" of veteran troops "to attack the most vulnerable portion of the enemy's line."[111]

As revealed in a letter to his father, whose five sons served as Confederate officers, an experienced Captain Joseph Graham was correct in his analysis. He was a North Carolina medical man who had graduated from the University of North Carolina with two degrees. Graham now commanded the high-spirited Tar Heels of the 1st North Carolina Battery, Hill's corps, and rode a "magnificent dark bay stallion." Graham summarized an undeniable truth in regard to Pickett's Charge: "Gen'l Lee's plan was excellent."[112]

Meade's vulnerable right-center was the fragile, vulnerable "hinge" of the Union army's two reinforced wings that now thinly held together the two impregnable high-ground defensive bastions at the opposite ends of Meade's line: a weak link. If the right-center was pierced, then Meade's greatest strengths and concentrations of firepower, especially artillery, would be negated by a single blow without expending a good many Confederate lives in attempting to overwhelm high-ground bastions anchoring impregnable flanks.[113]

After he unleashed an "unprecedented artillery bombardment" from the largest concentrated array of artillery ever seen on the North American continent because Lee realized that the "grandest results are obtained by the reserve artillery in great and decisive battles," eleven Confederate brigades would then emerge from their hidden positions on Seminary Ridge's reverse slope and then storm forward. An ample number of other veteran brigades, including fresh units, were in position to immediately reinforce these spearhead attackers, because "the intact reserves of infantry [were to] advance [and then] victory is won" by this tactical formula. Besides Pickett's division spearheading the assault on the right and serving as "the guide for the attack" according to his master plan, Lee placed his faith upon what only recently [before bloody July 1] had been his "largest, best equipped, finest looking brigade [Pettigrew, who would advance to Pickett's left] of the whole army," in the words of one of Lee's finest artillery officers, Major William Thomas Poague, a talented graduate of Washington College, discussing Hill's 3rd Corps.[114]

Perfecting the Offensive Plan

As importantly, two brigades of Hill's corps were to advance and provide timely support to exploit any breakthrough by the lead attackers to drive a deeper wedge, after the breakthrough on the right-center of Meade's overextended line on both sides of the clump of trees. Realizing the wisdom of Lee's plan, Hill initially wanted to employ his entire 3rd Corps of six brigades in the assault. Lee ultimately decided to add four additional veteran brigades of Hill's corps "just to make certainty certain."[115] Again, the key to success was a thorough utilization of all support troops (including 2nd Corps units) in a timely manner to exploit gains achieved by the spearhead troops (of around 12,500 men primarily Pickett's and Pettigrew's divisions), then "some 25,000, and perhaps closer to 30,000 men, would be available to press the Federal lines."[116]

Interestingly, one of Hill's men was a young soldier of Edward A. Perry's Florida brigade, handsome Lewis Thornton Powell, Company I, 2nd Florida Infantry. The Florida brigade had made significant gains on July 2, after striking the Emmitsburg Road sector, north of the Peach Orchard, before lack of support doomed their best efforts. Ironically, Powell eventually reached Washington,

DC, and resided there, where Lee's men hoped on July 3 that Confederate flags would fly in glorious triumph, but to no avail. After having survived Pickett's Charge with a wound and his subsequent capture, the dark-haired Powell (alias Lewis Payne) was hung in Washington, DC, as a Lincoln assassination conspirator on July 7, 1865, two years and four days after Lee's greatest attack.[117]

With Pickett's fresh command guiding and spearheading the way, Lee's plan was not only "logical [but also entirely] achievable."[118] Again, the most overlooked tactical ingredient of the attack, Meade's stretched-thin line, was even more likely to be broken in two by Stuart's projected cavalry attack from the rear.[119] Indeed, even if Lee's infantry was repulsed, Lee still possessed an ace in the hole with the South's greatest cavalry. If the charging Southern infantry failed to simultaneously strike with the cavalry, then the three hard-hitting brigades of Stuart's cavalry (more than 6,000 attackers) could very likely still reap a decisive success: Lee's forgotten insurance policy. Clearly, even "had Pickett failed as he did, Stuart still had the chance to . . . rescue the day for the Confederacy."[120] If mutually successful as Lee planned, then "Pickett and Stuart would have shaken hands on Cemetery Ridge and prepared to destroy portions of Meade's army at their leisure."[121]

At this time, Lee's lines (exterior lines that left him at a disadvantage) extended for nearly half a dozen miles and beyond Cemetery Ridge, and his lengthy line of artillery batteries had Meade's army "bracketed between convergent fire." Therefore, Lee now "readily assume[d] he had fire superiority over the Federal guns north and south of the copse of trees" on Meade's right-center.[122]

As Lee firmly believed, this was now the golden opportunity to bring "the end of the war," in the words of Colonel Eppa Hunton, who now led the 8th Virginia.[123] General Pickett was also confident for success. One officer never forgot how Pickett, like Lee, was "entirely sanguine of success in the charge, and was congratulating himself on the opportunity."[124]

In massing about 12,500 veteran troops of eleven brigades to strike Meade's weak right-center, held by 5,300 infantrymen of depleted units along an unfortified front stretched to the limit, Lee had "in fact found just about the best spot to attack anywhere along the Federal line [and now enjoyed] a very rare advantage for the Southerners of [not] 2.2. [to] 1," but nearly two-and-a-half to one.[125] But most importantly, these odds would be far greater if Longstreet utilized all of the troops, including McLaws's and Hood's divisions, that Lee expected to be hurled forward to support the assault: the majority of Lee's army.[126] And if thousands of Stuart's cavalrymen joined in the attack at the clump of trees when the odds were even more favorable (eight to one) when the attack struck home, then the odds would be more than 10 to one in Lee's favor.[127] Most significant in regard to Mexican–American War lessons (not to mention Napoleonic) and the favorable odds that promised a dramatic breakthrough at a weak point, Lee also felt sanguine for success also because "[s]ome of our divisions exceed the army Genl. Scott entered the city of Mexico" in triumph.[128] But at the most decisive moment of striking the clump of trees and Angle sector, Lee would possess an eight-to-one advantage, which verified that his battle plan was a tactically astute one.[129]

Lee also saw how the ground gently ascended from east of the Emmitsburg Road, ensuring that even veteran Yankees on higher ground would commit the usual sin of overshooting (especially in the excitement of battle) their targets on lower ground. The previous gains emphasized the wisdom of Lee's plan: This relative high point on Cemetery Ridge—the clump of trees on the high-ground beyond the Codori House and large barn—had been allegedly reached by Wright's single brigade (about 1,400 Georgians) the previous day. And just to Wright's south, Barksdale's Mississippi brigade had made an even deeper penetration of Meade's left-center on July 2, sweeping everything (including most of the 3rd Corps) before it until the fatal mixture of high casualties, low ammunition, and arriving Union reinforcements negated the second day's most dramatic gains. Dual deep penetrations on Meade's left-center (Barksdale) and right-center (Wright) convinced Lee that Meade's right-center now could be relatively easily pierced by a far larger number of attackers. In consequence, Lee "would return [on July 3 where Wright had struck], but this time with almost ten times that number."[130]

In analyzing Lee's chances for success, almost all historians have failed to tabulate Stuart's 6,000 cavalrymen striking from the rear. But even more overlooked has been the fact that if all of the available support troops were utilized, then Lee would have at least 25,000 troops in total in the offensive effort. Revealing the extent of Lee's unprecedented tactical opportunity, Captain Franklin Aretas Haskell deplored the right-center's vulnerabilities. Serving as the aide-de-camp of grizzled West Pointer (Class of 1847) General John Gibbon, Haskell described how with regard to the targeted right-center, now held by the 2nd and 3rd Divisions (from south to north) of the 2nd Corps, "the losses were quite heavy yesterday [July 2], some regiments were detached to other parts of the field—so all told there are less than six thousand men now in the two Divisions, who occupy a line of about a thousand yards."[131] And most importantly to verify the fact that Lee had indeed chosen exactly the right point to attack after a masterful concentration of troops, Haskell lamented how the thin line of blue along the right-center was now "without reserves," just before Lee unleashed his greatest offensive effort.[132]

Without the biased accounts and Lost Cause mythology, the realities of Pickett's Charge have demonstrated the entirely erroneous nature of Longstreet's prejudicial and endlessly quoted declaration (his postwar defense): "It is my opinion that no fifteen thousand men ever arrayed for battle can take that position."[133] Such self-serving statements laid the foundation early of the popular concept of the assault's folly.

Vulnerable Targeted Sector

As Lee saw during his observations, the fact that no Union defenses had been dug into the thin, rocky soil along Cemetery Ridge (the very antithesis of Chapultepec) also pointed to the tactical plan's wisdom. As mentioned, the ridge's topsoil was too thin—underneath was loose, hard shale—to dig trenches or even rifle pits. And even the stone wall that ran just below the ridge's crest on the western slope was only two to three feet high. The wall was not the sturdy defensive structure that ordained impregnability, as later imagined by historians. But in truth, Lee marveled at the magnificent tactical opportunity through his binoculars, because the lack of entrenchments and numbers partly negated the high-ground advantage. Not even the Union army's artillery along the crest on the right-center benefitted from earthen emplacements (as on Cemetery Hill) for protection against the dual threats of shell-fire and infantry attack. For the defenders, even the low stone wall offered no protection to Confederate shells exploding overhead or immediately to the rear.

Because of the rapid march north from the Rappahannock River country to catch up with Lee's army, the Federals were unable to bring entrenching tools. Ironically, although ample time had permitted, the vast majority of Yankees had not systematically scoured the woodlands in an organized effort to gather logs or secure fence rails to bolster the low stone wall. As "far as Lee could see, the Federals had not entrenched themselves along the ridge—all that was visible in the way of works was a low stone wall."[134] (Lee, of course, did not know that this lengthy stone wall—rare in the South—running along the high-ground had been partly erected by slaves, including by the town's founder, James Gettys, and continued to be improved by free blacks over the years.[135]) Anything but truly formidable in any sense or stretch of the imagination, the stone wall—more of a property boundary marker than a wall proper—was not even high enough to keep hogs or cattle inside.[136]

In the 2nd Corps sector that included the clump of trees area, Captain Haskell described the stone wall's glaring weaknesses: "Most of the way along this line upon the crest was a stone fence, constructed of small, rough stones, a good deal of the way badly pulled down, but the men had improved it [but overall the] works are so low as to compel the men to kneel or lie down generally to obtain cover."[137]

For good reason, Captain Haskell and other 2nd Corps officers were worried about the distinct possibility that Hancock's weak right-center would not be able to hold firm under any attack, much less an all-out offensive effort: "I could not help wishing all the morning that this line of the two divisions [under Alexander Hays's 3rd Division—north of the Angle—and John Gibbon's 2nd Division—south of the Angle—that was separated by the Angle in the stone fence] of the 2nd Corps was stronger; it was, so far as numbers constitute strength, the weaker part of our whole line of battle. What if, I thought, the enemy should make an assault here to-day, with two or three heavy lines—a great overwhelming mass; would he not sweep through" the defenders.[138]

Near the virgin stand of chestnut oak trees of Ziegler's Grove (as known to locals) on Cemetery Ridge just northeast of the copse of trees, Lieutenant Tully McCrea, of Scotch-Irish descent and a member of Battery I, 1st United States Artillery, caught the representative mood among the inadequate number of defenders to verify Lee's tactical wisdom: "[K]nowing that we had but one thin line of Infantry to oppose them, I thought that our chances for Kingdom Come or Libby Prison [in Richmond, Virginia] were very good."[139]

Contradicting the popular stereotype that Lee's massive assault was the war's greatest possible tactical miscalculation, such representative views of veteran Union officers were correct. After all, these were not the words of experienced fighting men, who believed in the popular postwar myth that the right-center was impregnable or that Lee's assault was doomed even before it was launched. As Haskell explained the crisis situation on the right-center, as "few as were our numbers we could not be supported or reinforced" until it was too late.[140] Clearly, Lee was now presented with his long-awaited opportunity to deliver a knockout blow, as the boys in blue, especially officers, realized at the time.[141]

Furthermore, on July 3, General Meade, wrote Haskell in his letter, "was not of the opinion that the enemy would attack the center [and that] this was not the favorite point of attack." Of course, Meade's incorrect assumption and tactical miscalculation threw an even greater percentage of the odds in Lee's favor.[142] The young captain also described how "General Meade still thought the enemy would attack his left again. . . ."[143] Ironically, targeting Meade's left with a flank movement was exactly the plan that Longstreet had strongly advocated to Lee since July 2.[144] However, as Lee realized, Longstreet's turning, or flanking, plan was "impractical," because of rough, wooded terrain and the position of Meade's powerful reserve, the 6th Corps, on the left.[145]

As mentioned, Lee planned an indirect assault in order to increase his chances for success, with the planned convergence of attackers at the copse of trees. However, by attacking via a frontal assault—and refuting the popular "attack and die" thesis that has emerged from hindsight, that deemed every frontal assault was folly—Lee determined "the most vulnerable position" at the weak right-center was the best chance to achieve a decisive success. Longstreet's proposed flank movement only promised, even if successful, to extend the campaign by forcing Meade to evacuate the high-ground.[146] With soaring optimism and unrealized by the unsuspecting Federals, Lee envisioned his brigades moving across a broad front relatively quickly and then redirecting their movements to concentrate toward the clump of trees to create a pointed and compact wedge formation of maximum strength (like the point of a sword) to deliver a mighty punch to tear a hole through Meade's right-center.[147]

Time-Proven Tactical Concept of the "Blitzkrieg Attack"

In this tactical sense, Lee faithfully followed the time-proven Napoleonic formula that was actually twentieth century–like: the "blitzkrieg attack." Napoleon revealed the secret to his successes that exploited the passivity of Europe's upper-class generals: "I see only one thing, namely the enemy's main body [and] I try to crush it"—Lee's precise tactical thinking on July 3.[148] Indeed, "the central theme, of Napoleon's concept of warfare [was] the blitzkrieg attack aimed at the main repository of the enemy's military power—his army."[149]

In overall tactical terms, Lee was now basically in the process of following Napoleon's tactical model of Austerlitz. Setting the stage, Napoleon deliberately allowed his opponent to take possession of the area's most dominant high-ground (Lee did not, of course, allow this), Pratzen Heights, despite being outnumbered more than two to one by a powerful Austrian–Russian army. However, this tactical cleverness, including exhibiting a tentative fear before a strong opponent, was all part of Napoleon's deceptive plan of feigning weakness to engender a fatal overconfidence to ensure that his opponent made a grievous tactical error.

When his adversary was convinced that the day was won, Napoleon had then hurled some of his best light troops toward the Pratzen Heights to smash through the weakened Allied center, after his opponent had taken the bait and massed troops to strike the French right to leave his center vulnerable, to gain the Russo-Austrian army's rear. Doing exactly what his enemy least expected, Napoleon then hurled his veteran grenadiers forward in a 20-minute advance (almost exactly the same time that it would take Pickett's Charge to reach Cemetery Ridge) over a wide stretch of open ground between two ridges (like Pickett's Charge) and then up the long slope of Pratzen Heights (much higher and steeper than Cemetery Ridge). Napoleon smashed through the Allied army's center, achieving his greatest victory at Austerlitz on December 2, 1805.[150]

For the most part, Lee had basically now taken the tactical core of Napoleon's Austerlitz battle plan—an infantry assault on the enemy's vulnerable center on high-ground—by including an entirely novel tactical dimension. He added more complexity to his innovative battle plan to considerably ensure his overall chances for success, by taking it higher to a more intricate, tactical level of sophistication. While Napoleon's brilliant success at Austerlitz resulted from a frontal assault up the open slope of the Pratzen Heights to rip a gaping hole in the Allied army's center, Lee developed a highly complex plan that was based upon a masterful two-pronged attack to strike not only the front, but also the rear of Meade's weak point at the same time. As mentioned, while more than 12,000 attackers hit the Union right-center, defended by 5,300 infantrymen (that would be reduced by this time), from the west, more than 6,000 of Stuart's elite cavalrymen would ride around Meade's right to gain the Army of the Potomac's rear, before turning west to smash into the copse of trees sector from the rear and thousands of more troops were to follow. Stuart's surprise attack called for his troopers to charge into the rear of the 2nd Corps, while its thin line of infantrymen hoped to hold a weak position at the small clump of trees sector against the full onslaught of thousands of veteran infantrymen: a powerful one–two punch guaranteed to deliver the coup de grace to the Union army.

Past Tactical Lessons

As mentioned, the key to smashing through Meade's right-center was maximizing all three arms. Lee planned to utilize his cavalry arm more masterfully than at any other time in the past. After all, no tactical force in Lee's army provided greater shock power than his veteran cavalry: the "historical equivalent of the shock of a modern tank." And this previously untapped power would now be employed by Lee in its most lethal form in a hard-hitting surprise attack from the rear. Again, Lee relied upon time-proven tactical lessons, because Napoleon had been the undisputed "master" of utilizing his cavalry "for shock action" to smash through enemy resistance.

But the greatest challenge of fulfilling Lee's master plan was precise timing and proper coordination. The Army of Northern Virginia now had to achieve what it had failed to accomplish on July 2: a "proper concert of action," in Lee's words, which was now the true key to decisive victory. Of course, thousands of Stuart's cavalrymen slashing into Meade's rear was the greatest tactical gamble, because this stealthy attack had to be perfectly timed to meet the attacking infantry at a single point (Meade's right-center), because Lee had to leave his flanks unprotected by adequate numbers of horse-soldiers.[151]

Lee placed great emphasis on the largest concentration of artillery on high-ground (the peach orchard and the Emmitsburg Road ridge) ever assembled on the North American continent to prepare the way for the attackers from *both* front and rear. In Napoleon's words: "The artillery, like the other arms, must be collected in mass if one wishes to attain a decisive result."[152] The Corsican emphasized that "[g]reat battles are won by artillery." Lee now faithfully followed this timeless axiom in preparing the way with a massive cannonade for not only Pickett's Charge, but also Stuart's charge from the rear.[153]

Even more, Meade and leading officers, like 40-year-old General John Newton (a trained engineer, Virginia-born West Pointer, and now commander of the 1st Corps), were not expecting any attack, much less two from opposite directions. Newton was convinced that Lee was simply not "fool enough to launch a massive assault," especially after two days of hard fighting.[154] Therefore, as intended, Lee possessed the vital element of surprise in attacking from not only one, but from two directions: front and rear.

What Lee had developed was the magical formula for decisive battlefield success as long employed by Napoleon but with his own innovative twists. Napoleon knew that "the true secret of success in the field lay in the careful coordination of cavalry, infantry and guns into one continuous process of attack, each arm supplementing the activities of the other two [therefore] [t]hrough inter-arm cooperation lay the road to victory."[155] And in almost exactly the same way, Lee was now relying on all three arms—an unprecedented massive artillery bombardment, infantry assault from the west, and a "shock" cavalry attack from the east—of a well-designed battle plan to cut Meade's army in two.[156]

Therefore, Lee envisioned an overpowering infantry attack, especially if there were timely reinforcements by a good many supporting brigades, which was only one part of an intricate three-part plan to smash through Meade's right-center. With his ample tactical gifts, experience in reaping victory, and ongoing winning streak, Lee was not about to just hurl more than 12,000 men (the spearhead attackers) against a high-ground position without a large number of supports and doing everything possible to enhance their chances for success. He was not about to allow most of his army to sit idly by when the nation's life was at stake during the war's turning point.[157]

This complex battle plan was based on exactly the right timing (especially hurling forward support troops) and the "proper concert of action," in Lee's words. Proper timing and coordination were absolutely necessary (especially with regard to infantry and cavalry striking the same point simultaneously from opposite directions) to reap a decisive success.[158]

Civil War historians have long overlooked the fact that Lee's decision to attack Meade's weak right-center was entirely in keeping with the central axiom of Napoleon's successful means of waging war.[159] Napoleon emphasized the secret to success: "Make war offensively; it is the sole means to become a great captain and to fathom the secrets of the art" of war.[160] Lee not only embraced the very core tactical foundation of the most successful Napoleonic formula for delivering the most decisive blow to end a war, but had also elevated it to a more sophisticated tactical level, especially with regard to an unprecedented cavalry role.[161] No doubt Lee's brilliant cavalryman father, "Light-Horse Harry" Lee, who studied the ancient military classics, would have been impressed by his son's mastery of what he called "the study of Mars" in a masterful utilization of all three arms, especially with regard to Stuart's role.[162]

Describing the tactical evolution that Lee had now brought to its zenith, Chandler explained Napoleon's secret to success, which was "the concept of the offensive battle—based on the all-out attack—which aims to end the war at one blow."[163] The key to Napoleon's success had most of all rested on a single central foundation, the "correct tactical formula, of a coordinated attack by all arms."[164] Certainly not lost to Lee, another appropriate tactical lesson lay in regard to Napoleon's remarkable victory at Marengo on June 14, 1800. When it appeared that the battle was lost to attacking Austrians, the Corsican prepared to lead a desperate headlong attack into the Austrian center, "staking everything on one last charge." After ascertaining a weakness in the Austrian center, Napoleon assaulted the heart of the Austrian line, snatching victory from the jaws of defeat.[165]

But even more than Marengo, the Battle of Wagram on July 6, 1809, provided the best Napoleonic tactical lesson to Lee. After the attacks were repulsed on the first day and his tactical plan was in disarray, Napoleon demonstrated tactical flexibility (another secret to Lee's success) by unleashing a mass assault on the overextended Austrian center (weak, like Meade's right-center) that resulted in decisive victory. Napoleon's flying artillery had played a key role, advancing before the infantry and moving sufficiently close to the enemy to knock out Austrian guns.[166]

Destiny Beckons

Lee's plan was, in fact, the very antithesis of Longstreet's glum assessment that justified his own biases and actions. Significantly, this audacious plan revealed the evolution and full maturation of Lee's tactical thought, which reached its highest level on the third day. Although Longstreet's and Ewell's offensive efforts never materialized, as expected by Lee, the most important parts of Lee's battle plan—Pickett's Charge from the west and Stuart's charge from the east—possessed sufficient tactical merit to achieve decisive victory. Quite simply, nothing could stop a powerful wedge formation of more than 12,000 veteran infantrymen striking the clump of trees along a concentrated front, while Stuart's cavalrymen slashed into Meade's rear at the copse of trees.[167]

Ironically, Lee's intricate plan (especially Stuart's attack in the rear) never appeared in the general's writings or in the volumes of the *Official Record of the War of the Rebellion*, a postwar creation that has long obscured the overall plan, partly because Lee (whose death after the war also guaranteed silence) did not want to place blame to damage the Southern people's and army's morale at a critical time (the same reason that he eventually rejected Pickett's post-battle report that pointed out failures and culprits in high places, especially Stuart).

Especially when compared to Longstreet's unrealistic plan, Lee could not have chosen a more opportune or better target at the clump of trees, because of its visibility on a commanding high-ground perch that dominated the eastern horizon just east of the Codori House and huge, red-painted barn: a two-tier set of highly visible beacons at different elevations for the attackers' line of vision to ensure proper coordination, especially when under fire. During their respective advances from opposite directions, Confederate infantrymen, from the west, and cavalrymen, from the east, could see (an extremely important factor on a smoke-covered field and when under fire) their elevated high-ground target, thanks to the clump of trees near the open crest—enhanced visibility in the midst of battle to greatly assist in the proper coordination of offensive efforts of so many diverse units for not only striking from two directions but also at the same time.

Without completely understanding Lee's plans of striking Meade's rear with Stuart's cavalry at the copse of oak trees—the tactical decision of assaulting Cemetery Ridge from the west—has also mistakenly convinced modern historians that Lee's offensive effort was the height of folly. And without understanding exactly why Lee decided to strike at this highly visible elevated point not only where Pickett's and Pettigrew's divisions were to converge, but also where Stuart's cavalry to the east could clearly see this elevated target (distinguished by this elevated, umbrella-shaped copse of oak trees), then it does seemingly appear that Lee inexplicably committed his greatest tactical blunder at Gettysburg. For Lee's tactical, masterful plan to work as envisioned from both directions, then the targeted high-ground (an actual asset instead of a liability in this case, which was a rarity in this war) actually offered a greater advantage for the prospect of ripping through Meade's right-center.[168]

As realized by Napoleon and Lee, who were kindred spirits, "the true secret of success in the field lay in the careful coordination of cavalry, infantry, and guns into one continuous attack, each arm supplementing the activities of the other two [and] [t]hrough inter-arm coordination lay the road to victory."[169]

Relying on Hardened Veterans

Lee now possessed the best fighting troops—battle-hardened infantrymen, troopers, and artillerymen (the correct three-part Napoleonic formula for success) who would work closely together as one—to fulfill his lofty tactical goal. These young men and boys (who now looked older and hardly like elite soldiers because of unkempt beards and dirty features) were determined to succeed at any cost. At a time when esprit de corps and élan were high (always the keys to success), the prevailing attitude was best summarized by one Confederate who boasted, "We will fight them until Hell freezes over, and then fight them on the ice."[170]

South Carolinian Tally Simpson, Longstreet's corps, penned in a July 1863 letter how, at this time, "Genl. Lee had the finest Army that ever was raised in ancient or modern times—and commanded by as patriotic and heroic officers as ever drew a sword in defence of liberty."[171] One of Lee's Georgia boys and a future minister, pious William Ross Stilwell, who had informed his wife to name his unborn son "Bull Run" in honor of past Confederate successes, made the appropriate biblical analogy in a letter: "We in our army always keep our armor bright and our powder dry and when they come we let fly and sure to be a Yankee die."[172] Equally confident, a soldier of the 2nd Florida Infantry, Florida Brigade, Hill's corps, Sergeant John B. Bird summarized, "We have a mighty foe to contend with [but] they are not our equals in battle, if Genl. Lee can meet them with one to their three [then] you need have no fear."[173] One of the finest regimental commanders of General Lewis Addison Armistead's brigade, former physician Lieutenant Colonel Rawley White Martin, leading the 53rd Virginia, recalled how the "esprit du corps could not have been better; the men were in good physical condition, self-reliant, and determined [and now] they were serious resolute, but not dishearten[ed]" by the formidable challenge.[174]

Not realizing that his analogy was far more appropriate than he imagined, 21-year-old Colonel Henry King Burgwyn, Pettigrew's division, placed the overall quality of Lee's fighting men in a proper historical perspective. He possessed an early interest in classical history (he had memorized Virgil's *Aeneid* before his teenage years) and graduated near the top of the Virginia Military Institute (Class of 1860). Burgwyn had fallen mortally wounded on July 1 in leading the 26th North Carolina Infantry, which lost 588 men for a staggering 73 percent loss. The handsome colonel penned in a May 1863 letter to his father of the superiority of Lee's troops: "I believe they will compare favorably with those of the Roman [Legions] or of Napoleon's Old Guard [and] The army that he has now can not be whipped by anything in Yankeedom."[175]

Known as the "Boy Colonel," he hailed from the low-lying Tidewater (the Atlantic coastal plain) of Northampton County, northeastern North Carolina. Burgwyn had only recently exacted a promise from a fellow 26th North Carolina officer to recover his body if killed (achieved by Iron Brigade troops on July 1). He had written in a prophetic letter how he expected Lee to "strike a tremendous & a successful blow."[176]

However, Lee was handicapped by liabilities that had fully manifested themselves on the previous two days. He possessed a staff that was entirely too small for the upcoming challenge—the antithesis of Napoleon's expansive imperial staff. Lee also continued to avoid direct personal confrontations of a contentious nature with his independent-minded top lieutenants and strong-minded generals—the direct opposite of Napoleon's in-your-face leadership style that got the best results from his badgered top lieutenants, thanks to well-calculated manipulation and intimidation (physical and mental).[177] Combined with the death of his top lieutenant (Stonewall Jackson) and the loss of many other veteran officers in past battles, Lee's disadvantages had been maximized by President Davis's ill-fated policy of scattering manpower widely—instead of concentrating nearly 200,000 available troops east of the Mississippi—to protect the Confederacy's immense territory (an impossibility). All of this virtually guaranteed a chronic manpower shortage at Gettysburg on July 3.

Although unrealized at the time, Lee was also hampered by the sheer determination (thanks to defending home soil) of not only the boys in blue who outnumbered him by about 15,000 men at Gettysburg, but also by their new commander. The homespun-looking Meade was an experienced West Pointer of outstanding ability. Lee now faced his most capable opponent. Born in Spain of American parents, Meade was also noted for his hot temper, exacting standards, and overall excellence as a frontline commander. Meade's laser-like focus on thwarting Lee was so intense that he was "indifferent to everybody when he was occupied" on the decisive day of July 3.[178]

As mentioned, historians who have long condemned Lee's attack have minimized the supreme importance of high levels of experience, highly qualified officers, superior morale, and esprit de corps that were the key ingredients necessary for successful assaults, including the overrunning of high-ground defensive positions held by infantrymen with modern weaponry: key advantages now possessed by Lee and his men in abundance.[179]

Final Preparations to Attack

Before the belated arrival of Pickett's division on the field, which resulted in Lee's disappointment at the upsetting of his early-morning assault plan, the other first phase of Lee's July 3 battle plan was functioning like clockwork. Before sunrise, Stuart and his troopers of four brigades had saddled up near Rock Creek, which flowed north–south just east of Gettysburg and just north of Benner's Hill. The South's legendary cavalrymen had then galloped down the York Pike and northeast from Gettysburg. These veteran cavalrymen had ridden through the relative cool of the predawn blackness in preparation for riding around Meade's right flank to maneuver into position to strike Meade's rear at the copse of trees. Stuart now commanded a larger number of cavalrymen than at any time during this campaign: more than 6,000 troopers. The slight early-morning chill and lingering ground fog soon faded away with the rising heat of another hot summer day, while Stuart eased into an advanced position amid the open fields between Hanover Road and Baltimore Pike.[180]

Because of Longstreet's obsession with his "impractical" flank march around Meade's left, he had been unready to launch an attack that morning. But Longstreet's inactivity also resulted because Pickett's division's belated arrival eliminated the possibility of an early morning attack. Therefore, a good many of Lee's men would have to be sacrificed for Longstreet's intransigence and Pickett's late arrival much later on July 3 than planned. The heat had slowed Pickett's arrival. Thirty-one-year-old Colonel John Amenas Fite, an attorney from Carthage, Tennessee, located just northeast of Nashville in command of the 7th Tennessee, Pettigrew's division, swore that this was the "hottest day I think I ever saw."[181]

As a result of straggling, Pickett's Virginia division of 5,830 men was only belatedly ready for action. In the Confederate center behind (west of) Seminary Ridge's crest, Pickett had placed the brigades of James Lawson Kemper on the right, Richard Brooke Garnett in the center (from south to north), and Louis Addison Armistead in the rear. Each brigade, from right to left, was extended slightly more advanced than the other. These positions behind the timbered crest on the reverse—or western—slope (both open and wooded ground) on Seminary Ridge provided concealment from prying Yankee eyes. Here, southwest of Gettysburg and mostly on the eastern edge of the Henry Spangler Woods, Pickett's three brigades (15 Virginia regiments) waited for Longstreet's order to advance.

Pickett's Virginians had been positioned in a broad "hollow," or swale (also described as a shallow "valley") behind the Henry Spangler farm and sheltering nearby wood-lots, especially Spangler Woods. Here, at the Spangler Woods, Samuel Pitzer's Lane (by which Pickett's division had belatedly trudged east to gain the ridge's western slope) entered this cool patch of full-leafed timber. The division's stealthy placement was judicious to disguise the heavy concentration of troops. A belt of virgin hardwood timber lining the crest of Seminary Ridge (named after the three-story and brick Lutheran Theological Seminary to the north) hid the massed formations and disguised the impending assault.

In the ranks of the 1st Virginia, under Colonel Lewis Burwell Williams, Jr., Kemper's brigade, Lieutenant John Edward Dooley, Jr., described how he and his comrades were sheltered in a "temporary position in the hollow of a field [and] Before us is a rising slope [of Seminary Ridge] which hides the Yankee position from view."[182] Here, in a broad field of green rye, Kemper's veterans were aligned under the blazing sun. Inspector general and acting adjutant of Pickett's division, Major Walter Harrison described how in the shallow valley before Seminary Ridge, "the usual inspection of arms and loading for action [was] perfected."[183] After inspecting and the like on Cemetery Ridge that revealed a glittering array that extended for miles under the bright sunshine, arms were stacked in neat rows as if this Friday was just another ordinary day.[184]

Ironically, from a high-placed source privy to developments at Lee's head-quarters that revealed his first plan before tactical modifications, many of Pickett's men earlier had been led to believe that their mission today would be only "to mop up an already broken Federal army."[185] Consequently, the mood was sufficiently light-hearted among Garnett's troops that some rambunctious men climbed apple trees near the edge of Spangler Woods. After having early consumed their three day's rations that had been cooked on the night of July 1, agile soldiers "shinnied up the apple trees and shook those apples down [and then] The boys began to stuff themselves with green apples [but] they didn't get sick [which] might even have saved their lives," wrote an amused Lieutenant George Williamson Finley.[186]

After eating their fill, the young soldiers then began hurling apple cores at each other. The frolicking continued until abruptly stopped by the 56th Virginia's stern commander, Colonel William Dabney Stuart, Virginia Military Institute graduate (Class of 1850). The 32-year-old Stuart "lost his temper." He admonished: "You boys stop throwing those apples," and "not another apple was thrown."[187]

Lieutenant John Edward Dooley, Jr., knew that something significant was taking place. In his 1st Virginia (situated in the center of Kemper's brigade on Pickett's right), the young man from Richmond described how "Genls. Lee, Longstreet, and Pickett are advising together and the work of the day is arranged [and] Soon we are ordered to ascend the rising slope and pull down a fence in our front" on the western edge of Spangler Woods.[188]

And on the Virginian's left and north of Pickett's division, the veterans of the Tennessee and Alabama brigade, Heth's division (now under Pettigrew), Hill's corps, also warily eyed the army's top commanders in their front. These good fighting men had been recently served under a scholarly bachelor General James Jay Archer, whose good looks had earned the Marylander the nickname of "Sally" as a college student. He had become a sullen prisoner—the first general captured at Gettysburg—on bloody July 1. These veterans intently watched

Lee, Longstreet, and Pickett and their thoughtful discussion. The three officers were sitting on a log near the left of Pickett's division.[189] The wide tactical disconnect between Lee and Longstreet, both veterans of Scott's march on Mexico City, had been smoothed by this time, after the Georgian's turning movement had been correctly dismissed out of hand.[190]

During this ad hoc commander's conference along Seminary Ridge's crest, Lee and his top lieutenants hammered out the final details of Longstreet's assault. In his diary, Sergeant Levin Christopher Gayle, Company G, 9th Virginia, penned how Lee, Hill, and Pickett "are pasing up and down our line and we hav been tolde what to do that is to Charge that Hill and take those cannon."[191] Lieutenant John Edward Dooley, Jr., described the moment when "orders come for us to lie down in line of battle [and we learned] *that all the cannon* on our side will open at a given signal . . . and upon their ceasing we are to charge straight ahead over the open field and *sweep from our path* anything in the shape of a Yankee that attempts to oppose our progress. This order is transmitted from Regt. To Regt., from Brigade to Brigade" under the scorching sun.[192] Ominously, Lee's orders also released all soldiers, especially officers, who were under arrest. Clearly, every soldier was now needed for the army's greatest undertaking.[193] Then, the word quickly passed down the ranks that Pickett's division had been chosen by Lee to occupy "the post of honor" in the assault.[194]

General Louis Addison Armistead was one of Pickett's brigade commanders (who had joined Pickett's division on November 6, 1862) and who had yet to reach his potential in this war. Of mixed English and German heritage, the Tidewater Virginian was a veteran of nearly a quarter century of faithful service to the United States. Lee and Armistead were united by the brotherhood of prewar service under the "Stars and Stripes." While serving at the newly established post of Fort Dodge, Iowa, on the muddy Des Moines River, and when his spouse was housed at the officer's quarters of Fort Snelling, Minnesota Territory, Armistead had lost his first wife, young Cecilia Lee Love, to a cholera epidemic. His six-year-old son, Walker Keith Armistead, was left without a mother. With sadness over Armistead's personal loss, Lee described in a November 1855 letter to his wife, Mary Custis Lee, "A soldier has a hard life and but little consideration."[195]

Armistead still recalled the triumphant assault on Churubusco and Chapultepec, when he was a young 6th United States Infantry officer. His regiment had charged the mission-fortress of Churubusco just to the left of the onrushing 8th United States Infantry in which Longstreet and Pickett served.

Armistead was part of the bayonet attack on the strong fortified position (known as the tete de point, part of the Churubusco defensive complex) guarding the bridge across the Churubusco River just northeast of the San Mateo Convent. Armistead still recalled how Pickett and Longstreet were among the first Americans to charge into the fortified point just outside Mexico City.[196]

Generals Longstreet, troubled by the relatively recent tragic loss of three children, Armistead, who was likewise a victim of life's cruel twists of fate, and Pickett, lovesick over a pretty teenager, were all together once again. Armistead was aware of the twisting contours of not only life but also history. Armistead's uncle, Major George Armistead, had commanded the small garrison at Fort McHenry, Baltimore, Maryland, during the British bombardment of mid-September 1814. He had commissioned the sewing of an outsized United States flag so that the enemy could see it from a distance. At Fort McHenry, the American republic gained its national anthem as penned by Georgetown lawyer Francis Scott Key. And now a good many "Star Spangled" banners (now with more stars) flew from Cemetery Ridge. Hancock's 2nd Corps's defenders were about to make their spirited defensive stand like Fort McHenry's United States regulars, including one African-American soldier. General Armistead now hoped to capture those United States flags under which so many of Armistead family members (including Lewis) had served under with distinction.[197] With history coming full circle in Adams County, Pennsylvania, one free black resident of Gettysburg (Clem Johnson) had been emancipated by Francis Scott Key in 1831.[198]

Ironically, General Dan Sickles, the man who had killed the son of Francis Scott Key, Philip Barton Key, was now Meade's 3rd Corps's brash commander. The outspoken New York general had nearly lost his own life on July 2 when an artillery shell exploded near the red-painted Abraham Trostle barn that stood near Plum Run on Meade's left-center. Here, northwest of Little Round Top, Sickles lost his right leg. When a New York Congressman, Sickles had shot the handsome Key down in the streets just across from the White House, because he had caught the young man seducing his wife, Teresa Bagioli-Sickles.[199]

Like his brigade commander descendant-general in gray, Major George Armistead, the celebrated "Hero of Fort McHenry," had been similarly ill-fated. One of the major's brothers had been killed in the War of 1812. In his first letter after Fort McHenry's defense, the major wrote proudly to his wife how "your husband has got a name for himself and standing that nothing but divine providence" bestowed.[200] While Major Armistead emphasized to his wife that "I pray to my Heavenly Farther that we may long live to enjoy" a good life, he died less than four years later from "heart disease . . . aggravated by the strain of the siege Fort McHenry."[201]

Young Lieutenant Armistead had faced a greater challenge than now posed by Cemetery Ridge when he had been part of the "forlorn hope" at the head of the two assault columns that targeted Chapultepec. He was the first blue-coat soldier to reach the deep ditch that protected Chapultepec Castle. Despite his wound (more serious than his September 18, 1862 wound), Armistead led the way into the stately castle itself, as he now planned to lead his troops to Cemetery Ridge's strategic crest.[202]

Even more surreal of all in terms of history repeating itself, Major Armistead had sent his pregnant wife, Louisa, safely out of harm's way (away from Baltimore) just before the September 1814 showdown at Fort McHenry. Of all places, she had journeyed to the peaceful town of Gettysburg, where she gave birth to their second child, a girl. Clearly, the fate of the Armistead family was strangely intertwined with Gettysburg. And now if Lee emerged victorious on July 3, then the Army of Northern Virginia might well be soon marching southeast upon Baltimore and Fort McHenry along the Baltimore Pike (located just east of town) in triumph.[203]

The defensive position occupied by his 2nd Brigade, under General Alexander Webb, of General John Gibbon's 2nd Division, 2nd Corps, that held Cemetery Ridge just south of the Angle and just north of the copse of trees, was about to become the eye of the storm. Of Scotch-Irish descent, teenage Private Anthony McDermott, 69th Volunteer Infantry, General Alexander S. Webb's brigade, 2nd Corps, described how when the sun was high in the sky, "a death like stillness prevailed [and] The sun was shining in all its glory, giving forth a heat almost stifling and not a breath of air came to cause the slight quaver" of a "blade of grass."[204]

Meanwhile, Chaplain John C. Granberry, 11th Virginia, Kemper's brigade, bolstered religious faith among the common soldiers, now "thoughtful as Quakers." Granberry busily attended to the spiritual needs of the men. The Methodist preacher knew that many soldiers would meet their Maker on this beautiful day that mocked man's folly. Chaplain Granberry would never be the same after what he saw that day, retiring in only twenty days.[205] One of Lee's men expressed the view of so many soldiers that now fueled resolve, emphasizing in a letter that "if God don't help us we are gone sure and certain."[206]

The midday interlude was so quiet and calm. An immense flock of passenger pigeons (now extinct from overhunting) flew past the lengthy lines of boys in blue and gray.[207] Some soldiers might have looked up and wished that they were now hunting pigeons back home instead of fighting for abstract ideas so artfully articulated by ambitious, smooth-talking politicians (now not serving at the front) on courthouse squares on both sides of the Mason–Dixon Line.

Disillusioned by this "unholy war," one of Longstreet's men, William Ross Stilwell, who now wore a straw hat acquired from a Pennsylvanian, perhaps best summarized the mood of Lee's soldiers in a letter to his wife: "Molly, this war will close sometime and God grant how soon it may be and let us get home to our family. They may talk of liberty and they may talk of me dying in war but I want to live with my family and live in peace."[208] As these men now realized, the only way to end the greatest horror that they had ever known was to smash through Meade's right-center and secure the decisive victory that might well bring peace to a blood-soaked land.

Chapter II

The War's Greatest Artillery Bombardment

To ensure that as many troops as possible crossed the roughly three-quarters of a mile of open ground in relatively good shape in order to converge on the copse of trees sector, Lee relied heavily on his artillery arm to inflict maximum damage. Lee planned to utilize every available gun to unleash "a cannonade unparalleled in the annals of warfare" to inflict high casualties and cause widespread demoralization. Equally important, Lee also planned for the artillery to move forward to protect the attackers' exposed flanks. As Colonel Porter Edward Alexander, Longstreet's top artillery officer, explained his key mission: "I was to advance such artillery as [I] can . . . in aiding the attack."[1]

Meanwhile, like the southern Pennsylvania heat, a haunting quiet hovered over the field, except for the occasional distant bark of a sniper's rifle or skirmishers firing in the shallow valley of green and yellow before Seminary Ridge. Lasting from 11:00 a.m. to 1:00 p.m., this strange quiet was confounding. Major Walter Harrison, the capable inspector general and acting adjutant of Pickett's division, called it a most "inauspicious calm" that had settled over the sprawling fields that seemed without end.[2]

This strange stillness told Lee's cynics and veterans to be wary of what was inevitably to come, the proverbial calm before the storm. More naive soldiers assumed that the two armies would disengage after two days of brutal fighting. During the soothing lull of another beautiful, early-summer day, young men thought about their families, farms, homes, and river valleys back home that they would never see again. This sweltering day was passing lazily under the bright midday sunshine that seemed as sultry as along the gulf coast.

In the 2nd Corps's sector (right-center) along Cemetery Ridge, Captain Haskell "dozed in the heat [while] A great lull rests upon all the field. . . . It was five minutes before one o'clock [and] I thought possibly that I might go to sleep, and stretched myself upon the ground accordingly [and] My attitude and purpose were of the General and the rest of the staff."[3] Meanwhile, in

Company G, Portsmouth Rifles from Portsmouth, 9th Virginia, Armistead's brigade, Sergeant Levin Christopher Gayle scribbled in his diary, "[T]here is a great deal of Artillery here with us and it dose look Beautiful [and] all in an open Field and A clear day and sun shines Beautiful."[4] However, fearing the worst, Chaplain Granberry, 11th Virginia, Kemper's brigade, described how the "quiet hours of just waiting were very trying."[5]

Equally suspicious of the haunting silence, some Yankees sensed something ominous in the air. Lee had only recently eliminated the army's general artillery reserve, unlike the Army of the Potomac. Since February 1863, Lee's artillery reserve had farmed out its guns to each of the three corps to strengthen their firepower. Therefore, Confederate batteries were no longer assigned to brigades after having been formed into battalions (mostly containing four batteries) for each division, allowing experienced battalion commanders greater tactical flexibility. However this realignment took away a single head of artillery—a fundamental mistake, because the army now needed an expert like General Henry Jackson Hunt, artillery chief (Meade's master artilleryman), to closely coordinate the army's artillery arm. This significant long arm reorganization also had resulted from service amid Virginia's rough terrain, mostly tangled woodlands with only an occasional field hacked out of dense forests. However, the open fields of the fertile farmlands south of Gettysburg far more resembled the open plains of central Europe, where Napoleon had reaped his great victories in part by replying upon the superior mobility over open terrain and massive firepower from a highly effective general artillery reserve. Seemingly forgetting the key role played by reserve artillery in smashing Union assaults on Fredericksburg's open plain in contrast to Chancellorsville woodlands, Lee would have benefitted immensely from the time-tested Napoleonic formula of a general artillery reserve. The army's lack of the Napoleonic reserve concept, especially when combined with the overall loose organization of the artillery arm, was about to come back to haunt Lee's efforts.[6]

Lee also should have replaced his incompetent chief of artillery, General William Nelson Pendleton. Instead, the too-kindly Lee merely circumvented Pendleton by organizing the artillery battalions for each division, giving battalion commanders greater authority. Pendleton was a Virginian (more detrimental cronyism that Longstreet deplored) in the Old Dominion–dominated army who had been promoted far beyond his limited abilities. Pendleton possessed strong political connections, including with President Davis. He was a respected Episcopalian rector from Lexington, Virginia. Pendleton was the very antithesis of his counterpart, General Hunt, Meade's brilliant chief of artillery, who was a master in the art of orchestrating his guns to the best advantage.[7] Known as "Old Penn," Pendleton was sufficiently religion-minded that he neglected his military duties. The dapper little holy warrior had bestowed his first guns of Virginia's Rockbridge Artillery with biblical names of Matthew, Mark, Luke, and John. Pendleton's too-thorough "mixing of the two professions [killing and saving men]" even brought disapproval from devout Confederate officers.[8] He was also known for having declared: "Lord preserve the soul while I destroy the body" upon sighting his guns on Yankees.[9]

One astute Union soldier, Robert K. Beecham, emphasized how "Meade had the advantage in reserves with which to replace his crippled and exhausted batteries. . . ."[10] Nevertheless, Lee benefitted from Napoleon's wisdom of massing artillery for a concentrated fire against a weak defensive position. At the Battle of Marengo, Napoleon emphasized that the key to his successful counterattack against the Austrian center to save the day was absolutely dependent upon what his artillery accomplished against infantry. As the Corsican informed one officer, "We must have a rapid artillery fire imposed on the enemy before we attempt a new charge; without which we shall fail [because] That General, is how one loses a battle."[11] To that general at Marengo, Napoleon had stressed the wisdom which was now embraced by Lee: "If there isn't an artillery bombardment made which lasts [a] quarter of an hour, we will lose" the battle.[12] Therefore, Lee believed that he could tip the scales in his favor by unleashing "the fiercest cannonading known to warfare," in the words of Captain Jacob B. Turney, 1st Tennessee, Pettigrew's division.[13]

Confederate Artillery Preparations

In the darkness long before daylight, on July 3, the army's artillery had been eased into the best firing positions that stretched northeastward from the body-strewn Peach Orchard (at a commanding point on the Emmitsburg Road ridge) of farmer Joseph Sherfy. Some Rebel artillerymen accidently rolled their field pieces over wounded Yankees, who cried out in the eerie blackness. Each artillery battalion commander aligned his batteries in conjunction with advice from corps artillery commanders. Colonel Alexander orchestrated the alignment of Longstreet's guns with his usual skill. He was a gifted West Pointer (Class of 1857) and former instructor at the military academy. At age 28, Alexander was now considered the army's finest artillery officer. Part of Longstreet's "inner circle," Alexander headed the Reserve Artillery, Longstreet's

1st Corps. Businesslike and highly efficient, he was not one to name artillery pieces after his favorite Bible chapters like the dour "Parson" Pendleton, who was well past his prime.

Alexander now commanded all of Longstreet's guns and 75 field pieces from 17 batteries. In total, Lee possessed 22 batteries of five artillery battalions. Appropriately, because of Pickett's upcoming spearhead role and advantageous high-ground, especially at the Peach Orchard, more guns were aligned on Pickett's front than Pettigrew's sector. Alexander had earned a lofty reputation for his splendid artillery performances at Fredericksburg and Chancellorsville. Laboring half the night to make sure that his 75 guns were carefully positioned, Colonel Alexander performed the responsibilities of Longstreet's appointed chief of artillery Major James B. Walton (older and less competent). By noon, Alexander had placed all 75 guns of Longstreet's 1st Corps in good firing positions along a 4,000-foot front of open, high ground that stretched from the commanding elevation of the Sherfy Peach Orchard to the northeastern edge of the Spangler Woods. Ironically, the boys in blue paid relatively little attention to the massive artillery buildup across the low valley draped aglow in nature's splendor. Born in Washington, Georgia, and riding a horse named Dixie, Alexander was a rising star. The heavy price (more than 50 percent casualties on July 2) paid by Barksdale's Mississippi brigade in overrunning the Peach Orchard and the Emmitsburg Road ridge, which spanned northeast toward Gettysburg, now allowed Alexander to utilize this strategic high-ground perch once held by Sickles's 3rd Corps.

Covered in the colorful patchwork of farmer's rich fields and fruit orchards, this open northeast-running ridgetop (upon which the slightly sunken dirt road ran from the Peach Orchard to the high-ground at the Daniel Klingel House—southwest of the Codori House—on the Emmitsburg Road ridge and beyond toward Gettysburg) provided an excellent elevated firing platform. From these vantage points, Southern artillery could pound Cemetery Ridge's defenders, especially on the right-center, perhaps into submission. Nearly 140 Confederate cannon, with 150–170 rounds in each wooden ammunition limber, were aligned in the open fields west of the road.

Representing Lee's largest concentration of Confederate guns, these field pieces extended northeast from the Peach Orchard and all the way to Oak Hill. At opposite ends of this lengthy artillery line, the open ground of Oak Hill (the line's northern anchor) and the Peach Orchard (the southern anchor) offered ideal elevated vantage points and wide-open fields of fire: a vast array of artillery pieces that spanned a two-mile arc. Stretching south from Lee's command post on the field and to the Emmitsburg Road ridge and the Sherfy Orchard, the iron and bronze barrels of the field pieces extended as far as the eye could see. After having just sipped an invigorating cup of sweet-potato coffee (brewed from peeled sweet potatoes cut into thin pieces, dried slowly, and then ground like coffee beans), a confident Alexander was consumed by a can-do spirit.

The ambitious Georgian hoped to add to his Fredericksburg success in decimating the surging blue ranks. Awaiting the order to open fire, Colonel Alexander, simply known as "Porter" to his friends, continued to refresh himself on the popular drink (which had replaced coffee, now denied to the South by the Union naval blockade). Instead, he should have checked to make sure that a proper amount of ammunition was available for the bombardment (especially after the previous day's vast expenditure of rounds), upon which so much depended.[14]

Alexander was especially confident because he had arrayed his guns without drawing significant Union counter-battery fire that usually impeded such massive artillery buildups.[15] Targeting Meade's right-center, Alexander's vital mission was now to "cripple him—to tear him limbless, as it were, if possible," in the Georgian's words, paving the way for Lee's massive assault.[16] In a letter to his wife, Emily, General Lafayette McLaws, who was disgruntled by service (like Longstreet) in an army dominated by Virginians, wrote, "On the 3d inst, all our available arty was put in position along our lines" for a great undertaking.[17]

However, an increasingly anxious Alexander experienced increasing frustration, because of the delay—thanks to infantry belatedly moving into their assigned positions—while awaiting Longstreet's directive to commence firing. Not long after noon, Longstreet dispatched a courier to Colonel James B. Walton, who officially commanded the 1st Corps's artillery although Alexander, officially only second in command, possessed immediate charge of the guns. Walton carried the long-awaited order to "[l]et the batteries open [and take] great care and precision in firing."[18]

Commanding the 1st North Carolina Artillery (known as Graham's Battery) of Hill's corps, Captain Joseph Graham, a University of North Carolina graduate (Class of 1859) who had his own faithful Irish orderly, now checked the time "by watch." The artillery bombardment's beginning was to be the prearranged signal of the firing of two Washington Artillery cannon under Major Benjamin Franklin Eshleman. Of Swiss heritage and from New Orleans, although he was born in nearby Lancaster County, Pennsylvania in 1830, Eshleman commanded the four companies of the Washington Artillery from New Orleans. Known to often sing a popular "little French song" called "Upi-De," many Washington Artillery gunners were of French heritage (Creoles) and from the Crescent City's leading families. Walton recorded how the two New Orleans guns in the line's center unleashed their eagerly awaited signal at exactly "12 ½ P.M."[19] The actual time of the cannonade's opening was seven minutes after 1:00 p.m.[20]

The Eruption That Shook Adams County

In a July 1863 letter to his father, Graham described the massive cannonade's opening: "[W]e began shelling their position [in what was] the heaviest Artillery duel of the war. . . ."[21] In less dignified words not heard by his mother, one of Pettigrew's soldiers described how "hell itself had broken loose."[22] In a letter to his wife, another Southerner wrote: "If the crash of worlds and all things combustible had been coming in collision with each other, it could not have surpassed it."[23]

Confederate spirits rose upon hearing the thunder exploding from rows of Southern cannon. Although now dying, a spunky Rebel in the makeshift hospital at the Christ Lutheran Church, on east–west-running Chambersburg Street in Gettysburg, suddenly came to life and shouted, "Give 'em hell!"[24] And in his July 7, 1863, letter to his wife, the full-bearded General McLaws described how what "commenced [was] the most tremendous artillery fire I ever heard on our continent."[25] Commanding the 7th Tennessee, Colonel John Amenas Fite, a Columbia University, New York City, graduate, wrote of "the grandest cannonading of the world."[26]

In the 1st Virginia's ranks, Lieutenant John Edward Dooley, Jr., described, "The earth seems unsteady beneath this furious cannonading" that was unprecedented.[27] Beside his 56th Virginia comrades of Company K (Harrison's Guards), pious Lieutenant George Williamson Finley described the bombardment in biblical terms, because Armageddon seemed to have arrived: "It was like the final day of judgment when the great scroll of life in the heavens is rolled shut with an overpowering clap of thunder!"[28] In Company G (Portsmouth Rifles), 9th Virginia, Armistead's brigade, Lieutenant John Henry Lewis, Jr., penned how the bombardment was like "a gigantic thunder-storm" that broke with a fury upon the land.[29]

And the correspondent of the *Richmond Enquirer*, of Richmond, Virginia, wrote with astonishment: "I have never yet heard such tremendous artillery firing [because] The very earth shook beneath my feet [and] made a picture terribly grand and sublime."[30] Perhaps reminded of the British bombardment of Fort McHenry fame (almost certainly in General Armistead's case), Captain Robert A. Bright, one of Pickett's staff officers, concluded, "Had this [bombardment] occurred at night, it would have delighted the eye more than any fire works ever seen."[31] With South Carolina roots, Rufus K. Felder, Hood's division, scribbled in a letter how "the canonading was terrific in the extreme, surpassing anything perhaps in the annals of warfare."[32]

A member of Gibbon's staff, Captain Haskell described the shock of the thunderous bombardment, when "the report of gun after gun in rapid succession smote our ears. . . ."[33] The "enemy's fire is chiefly concentrated upon the position of the 2nd Corps," in the clump of trees sector, wrote an alarmed Haskell, who feared the worst.[34]

Shells fell around Meade's headquarters from overshooting. In one of the battle's ironies, Meade's black servant was killed at the cannonade's beginning, when a projectile exploded in the yard of the small, two-room Lydia Leister House. Hired by Meade, he was the only African American killed in the war's largest battle. This one-story, wooden house served as a good central location for Meade to manage the battle. The Leister House was situated on level ground beside (just west of) the Taneytown Road and just northeast of the clump of trees. Symbolically, in a battle about to decide the fate of slavery, this free black man was very likely the first person killed in relation to Pickett's Charge.[35]

Located just south of Captain William A. Arnold's battery, Company A, 1st Rhode Island Light Artillery, which was positioned on the ridge's crest just northeast of the copse of trees, England-born Sergeant Benjamin Hirst, Company D (the "Rockville boys"), 14th Connecticut Infantry, described in a letter: "About noon commenced the Fiercest Canonading I ever heard [and] it seemed as if all the Demons in Hell were let loose [and] Principally upon the old 2nd Corps whom they desired to attack [and] we did [h]ug the ground expecting every moment was to be our last."[36]

Reliance on the Napoleonic Tradition

In unleashing this massive artillery storm, Lee relied on Napoleon's successful formula of "blitzkrieg" warfare.[37] After all, a large concentration of "big batteries was the true secret of victory" during the nineteenth century.[38] Ironically, Napoleon's axioms of employing massed artillery had been "entirely forgotten" at the Civil War's beginning. But now like a phoenix rising, these invaluable lessons were resurrected in their purest form by Lee on July 3.[39]

Napoleon's winning tactical formula for decisive victory was relying on an army "trained and organized for attack [preceded by] an intense artillery barrage [and] Bonaparte had good guns, plenty of them, and good gunners."[40] As Napoleon emphasized, the axiom held true on Gettysburg's third day: "Great battles are won by artillery."[41] As Lee now demonstrated in regard to his greatest attack, Napoleon "could never have enough guns," especially in preparing the way for a great infantry assault.[42]

Napoleon had long demonstrated how a massive artillery bombardment wrecked an opponent's morale and capability to resist an infantry onslaught. Indeed, as Lee now envisioned, a great cannonade always served "as the precursor to the main attack against the selected weak point of the enemy's line . . . in order to batter a breach into which the mass de decision could plunge" to achieve a decisive breakthrough.[43]

Clearly, in "a general rule [to reap decisive success], Napoleon placed heavy reliance on massed batteries of 100 or more guns to batter his foes into submission."[44] Napoleon explained a secret (well understood by Lee) of his remarkable successes: "The artillery, like the other arms, must be collected in mass if one wishes to attain decisive results."[45] The sage-like Jomini emphasized the wisdom of concentrating "a very strong artillery mass upon a point where we should wish to direct a decisive effort, to the end of making a breach in the hostile line, which would facilitate the grand attack upon which might depend the success of the battle."[46]

Therefore, Lee had concentrated more than 130 guns for a converging concentration of fire, especially on Meade's right-center. Like Lee, Napoleon knew "that big batteries are the true secret of victory. . . ."[47] After analyzing the opponent's positions and topography with care, Lee also realized that Meade could "bring fewer guns to bear" compared to his own, more concentrated artillery arm.[48] In the14th Tennessee, Fry's brigade, Pettigrew's division, to the left, or north, of Garnett's brigade, Sergeant Junius Kimble (affectionately nicknamed "June," without feminine connotations) described the cannonade: "the equal of which was never fought on this earth [and] The very earth shook as from a mighty quake."[49]

But Alexander was wisely not concentrating all his fire on Meade's right-center at the copse of trees so as not to betray the infantry's ultimate target. However, Alexander and battery commanders made the fundamental error of assuming that Meade's infantry was deployed on the ridge's reverse (eastern) slope for protection against artillery fire, like Lee's infantry on Seminary Ridge's west side. No Confederate officer (not Lee, Longstreet, Pickett, or Alexander) ascertained the most critical piece of intelligence: that the two veteran divisions of 2nd Corps's infantry defending the right-center, including the copse of trees area, were *not* positioned on the ridge's reverse slope, but on the opposite, or forward, western slope. Here, behind the low stone wall, "built of Blue Limestone," wrote one Rebel, "that will last for ages," which ran mostly north–south (except at the east–west-running Angle toward the crest) along Cemetery Ridge just below the crest, hundreds of Yankees waited quietly on the ridge's western slope. In consequence, these boys in blue were relatively unaffected by the greatest bombardment ever unleashed by Lee's army. Thinking that they were driving Union infantrymen away from Cemetery Ridge by their intense fire, Southern artillerymen continued to pound the reverse slope, where no blue lines of infantry were aligned.[50]

Meanwhile, the Union guns along Cemetery Ridge responded belatedly (15–20 minutes later) with their own cannonade, after General Henry Jackson Hunt issued wise orders to conserve ammunition by firing more slowly. He had about 175 artillery pieces (more than Lee) available to him, and 132 of these guns, aligned between Little Round Top to the south and Cemetery Hill to the north, fired from high-ground positions that provided a wide, panoramic view to the west. Major Walter Harrison described how "the enemy replied with interest to our artillery salute [and] Such a tornado of projectiles [were seldom seen while] The sun in his noontide ray was obscured by clouds of sulfurous mist, eclipsing his light, and shadowing the earth as with a funeral pall."[51] This massive artillery bombardment made Lee believe that the relentless pounding was wreaking havoc and that the already-thin defensive sector around the copse of trees was steadily getting weaker by the minute.

However, what was essentially "a fluke" was insidiously sabotaging chances for Confederate success.[52] A key tactical change had subtly occurred in the role of artillery since the Mexican–American War. General Zachary Taylor's early successes, especially on the wide, arid coastal plain of Palo Alto just north of the Rio Grande River, had been won by the aggressive use of flying artillery. These highly mobile guns had been aggressively employed by young artillery commanders from West Point. Thomas Jonathan "Stonewall" Jackson, when he had been motivated to distinguish himself, as he penned in a letter, had skillfully employed his guns as flying artillery at Chapultepec, when he launched his own "audacious charge" with his field pieces. Such tactical lessons of flying artillery were an enduring legacy of the Napoleonic Wars. Napoleon was an old artilleryman who first won recognition for his aggressive use of the long arm. He had thoroughly mastered the art of flying artillery: the employment of highly mobile light guns quickly and with swiftness (thanks to fast, well-trained horses) to unleash hard-hitting firepower, especially with grape and canister, to smash enemy formations at close range. Because opposing ranks were tightly massed in linear formations to maximize musketry firepower, the flying artillery fired at triple the usual rate of fire. Then, these light guns were quickly taken out of harm's way if the enemy counterattacked, even with cavalry. But now a "fluke in technological development" minimized flying artillery capabilities.[53]

The rifled musket (which was more deadly at long range compared to the smoothbore musket because of the barrel's rifling, which enhanced velocity and hence accuracy) reduced the effectiveness of the traditional role of flying artillery. Now the longer range and greater accuracy of common soldiers' weaponry meant that deadly grape and canister could not be utilized so easily at close range against infantry as during the Napoleonic Wars and the Mexican–American War, because advanced artillery now had to stay further rearward in supporting infantry assaults.[54]

However, the urgent requirements of July 3 now superseded theory, recent tactical evolutions, and conventional wisdom. Lee understood that he needed to rely upon every possible trick in the book, especially with regard to incorporating the most applicable Napoleonic and Mexican–American War lessons. Therefore, Lee planned to utilize his guns as flying artillery, because the vulnerable flanks of the assault formations in a linear formation needed protection. This was now especially the case because wide stretches of open ground lay on either side (north and south) of the assault. However, folds and swales (on both sides of the Emmitsburg Road) in the rolling terrain and battle smoke would allow Southern guns to fulfill a traditional flying artillery role, negating the rifled musket's lethality in such protective depressions from which field pieces could fire at relatively close range. Likewise, the marked tendency of Union infantrymen on higher ground to overshoot targets on lower ground also promised to make the flying artillery effective that afternoon. Also many defenders on the right-center (at the clump of trees and both north and south of the Angle) possessed smoothbores (only effective at short range) and not rifled muskets.

During his final assault on the British center at Waterloo, Napoleon had hurled the Imperial Guard forward with two batteries of horse, or flying, artillery to play its customary role. Jomini emphasized the supreme importance of utilizing artillery in a tactical offensive role. Mahan stressed that guns should be advanced with infantry to protect the ever-vulnerable flanks. Therefore, once the cannonade ended, Lee's artillery was ordered to advance and closely support the infantry to prevent the Union from launching spoiling attacks that might be launched on the assault's vulnerable northern and southern flanks. However, young Colonel Alexander lacked the necessary experience to fulfill Lee's vision of flying artillery on such an unprecedented scale.

General Pendleton's only sound decision to bolster Alexander's extensive efforts was to create a "mobile battery" (a special reserve) for supporting the attack as flying artillery, taken from Hill's 3rd Corps because their short range negated their effectiveness in the general cannonade. Gathered from various units, these nine howitzers (highly maneuverable and effective at close range) were to advance with the infantry to protect the attack's flanks that would be vulnerable on the open fields, especially on the south. These flying artillery guns were placed by Alexander in a concealed position, a shallow hollow behind the Henry Sprangler Woods, in preparation for advancing and providing close support to the attackers. Thanks to Pendleton's meddling, Alexander's plan for the employment of the nine howitzers, so vital in the highly anticipated flying artillery role, was shortly sabotaged by an order without the Georgian's knowledge, however. These nine howitzers were under the command of Major Charles Richardson of Lieutenant Colonel John J. Garnett's 3rd Corps Artillery Battalion.

Kept in what he thought was a safe reserve position—near the Emanuel Pitzer House—by Alexander and sufficiently close to support the assault when the time came, the nine howitzers, ineffective at long range, were not engaged in the bombardment. As planned by Alexander, consequently, these guns, with fresh ammunition reserves, men, and horses, would be in an ideal position to play a key role to protect the assault's flank. With Major William Thomas Poague's Virginia Artillery Battalion, Pender's division, directed to cover the northern, or left, flank and Major James Dearing's Artillery Battalion, four Virginia batteries (18 guns) that were part of Pickett's division, Longstreet's corps, covering the southern, or right, flank by advancing as flying artillery, Lee believed that the assault's flanks would be sufficiently safeguarded.[55]

As Lee envisioned, Alexander planned for all of his guns to advance "to follow any success, as promptly as possible." But young Poague's understanding of his mission revealed two central flaws: First and foremost—and seemingly forgotten by Confederate artillery commanders—the cannonade could not last too long so that insufficient ammunition remained to support the infantry assault. Additionally, the timing of the advancing artillery had to be exact to provide maximum fire support and timely flank protection. This vital requirement meant moving the guns forward long before the attackers actually struck the right-center. However, oral communications had broken down with regard to this key mission. Therefore, positioned before Pettigrew's division and like other guns, Major Poague's guns rapidly expended 657 rounds far too quickly. He explained his mission: "that as soon as our infantry . . . reached the crest [he was only then] to proceed as rapidly as possible to the summit with all my guns [but] [n]ot a word was said about following the infantry as they advanced to the attack."[56]

Faulty Confederate Artillery Fuses

As if this situation (especially the shortage of artillery ammunition) was not enough to diminish chances for success, other mishaps and general confusion also began to sabotage Lee's well-laid artillery plans. A serious problem with artillery-shell fuses now came back to haunt the gunners' best efforts. Alexander had been early concerned about the overall quality of the Bormann fuses, because of their "very high" rate of failure, resulting in an ineffective fire. Captain Haskell described the situation: "We went along the lines of the infantry [along Cemetery Ridge] as they lay there flat upon the earth, a little to the front of the batteries [on the crest and] [t]hey were suffering very little . . . . How glad we were that the enemy were no better gunners, and that they cut the shell fuses too long."[57]

But this disastrous situation for Southern fortunes was not completely the gunners' fault. As veterans who were experts at setting time fuses (the most commonly used fuses) to explode in a predetermined number of seconds, they knew better than to cut fuses too short. The true source of the problem lay in the recent explosion in the main Richmond factory—perhaps sabotaged by slave workers or the secret Unionists of an active spy network in Richmond. This mishap meant that a new fuse supplier in Charleston, South Carolina, now provided fuses.[58]

So many Rebel shells had prematurely exploded during the battle of Chancellorsville in early May 1863 that the Confederate Ordnance Department had launched an official investigation about what was responsible for negating the artillery's effectiveness. Rebel artillerists cut the length of fuses so that shells exploded at the estimated measured distance to hit a target, but there no longer existed the previous uniformity in fuse quality, which affected the time that the fuse burned and the shell exploded. The fuses long made in the Confederacy's principal war munitions manufacturing Richmond had been of the highest quality. Therefore, veteran gunners unwittingly continued to base their timing and targeting calculations on fuses produced at the nation's capital on the James, although they weren't.

However, the new supplies of new fuses manufactured in Charleston, in Atlanta, Georgia, and in Augusta, Georgia, were of inferior quality: more inconsistent and slower burning than the more dependable Richmond fuses. Artillerymen made time estimations with Richmond fuses in mind: a guarantee that shells were passing their targets on Cemetery Ridge, because these fuses burned too long and slower than Richmond fuses.[59]

Compounding the problem in believing that the target was much farther than was actually the case, some Confederate artillerymen cut fuses for the wrong distance. General Pettigrew's top staff officer, Captain Louis Gourdin Young, wrote in a letter how "the fuses for the shell used by the artillery, stationed immediately in our front, were cut for 1 1/4 miles," when Cemetery Ridge was three-quarters of a mile away.[60] Therefore, cutting fuses for a distance of a mile and a quarter was, in fact, more than a quarter mile too much.[61] The problem also lay with the absence of expert artillerymen (thanks partly to attrition), who lacked proper practice because of black powder shortages. Therefore, "[f]ortunately for most Federals on Cemetery Ridge, their aim was terrible."[62] As mentioned, it was not exclusively a question of problems with aim and fuses, because the Rebel gunners also believed that Cemetery Ridge's defending infantry had aligned along the reverse slope for protection.

Captain Haskell correctly reasoned how Lee "probably supposed our infantry was massed behind the crest [on the reverse slope] and the batteries; and hence his fire was so high, and his fuses to the shells were cut so long, too long."[63] With smoke covering the field, Rebel gunners were unable to ascertain exactly where their shells fell, eliminating much-needed adjustments in aim. Consequently, iron and brass cannon barrels were not sufficiently lowered with elevation screws to make necessary adjustments. Some shells even exploded on Taneytown Road's east side. Other Confederate shells failed to explode, revealing the usual manufacturing defects, because of the South's preindustrial limitations. In consequence, the Yankee infantry defenders, except on the ridge's crest at the targeted right-center, were relatively safe from this ineffective cannonade.[64]

Other Weaknesses of the Southern Cannonade

Some basic Napoleonic lessons, especially when Arthur Wellesley, Duke of Wellington, had wisely protected his infantry at Waterloo by positioning his redcoats on a ridge's reverse slope before a wide plain, began to early back-fire on Lee. Yankee infantrymen along Cemetery Ridge were far safer on the western slope rather than on the reverse slope: an atypical battlefield situation.[65] However, numbers of Union infantrymen were hit in the cannonade. North of the copse of trees and just below the Abraham Brien barn, the low stone wall could not save some 111th New York boys. About to be wounded from an exploding shell, Corporal Manley Stacey, who was fated to die the day after Christmas 1863, wrote in a letter: "Three men were killed and thrown across me [by one shell explosion], covering men with blood."[66]

Because of the rapid and excessive expenditure of ammunition (the nearest reserve supplies of artillery ammunition was located about 150 miles away in the Shenandoah Valley) during an increasingly lengthy duel, flying artil-lery capabilities were steadily eroded.[67] The combined effect of dysfunctional Confederate artillery leadership, casualties among gunners and battery horses, low ammunition, and a too-lengthy bombardment ensured that flying artillery would be unable to adequately support the assault.[68]

Lee's artillery arm (unlike Hunt's guns) possessed relatively few rifled cannon for accurate long-range firing. Confederate "smoothbore artillery [not effective at long range], when firing cannon balls, had relatively little effect on infantry in defensive positions."[69] Southern artillery fire now left Union officers contemptuous: "The Rebels had about as much artillery as we did [and] They have courage enough, but not the skill to handle it well. They generally fire far too high, and the ammunition is usually of a very inferior quality."[70]

Emphasizing the importance of flying artillery this afternoon, Rebel smoothbore artillery possessed greater potential at close range compared to rifled field pieces, thanks to the devastating effect of grape and canister on infantry.[71] Dismayed by the confusing variety of long arm weaponry that cre-ated a logistical and supply nightmare, Colonel Arthur J. L. Fremantle, official British observer attached to Lee's army, explained how the Southern "artillery is of all kinds—Parrots, Napoleons [named after Napoleon III, not Napoleon I], smoothbores, all shapes and sizes."[72]

Punishing Return Fire

Meanwhile, Union artillery from Cemetery Hill, Cemetery Ridge, and Little Round Top (from north to south) continued to respond with spirit. As mentioned, General Hunt, the long-arm genius, had ordered his guns to slow their fire to conserve ammunition for the expected infantry assault. However, Hancock, now leading the 2nd Corps with his usual skill, thought otherwise. He believed that roaring Union guns bolstered the infantry's morale.[73] In one of the battle's ironies, some Southern artillery officers had been trained by Hunt in artillery tactics at West Point. Because of ineffectiveness of Confederate long-arm fire, Hunt's sense of humor rose to the fore. He wondered with amusement, "Was I that bad of an instructor" at West Point?[74]

Despite the fact that Lee possessed capable artillerists who had been educated at not only the Virginia Military Institute (the majority) but also at West Point, the overall Confederate bombardment was entirely ineffective against the concealed infantrymen for a variety of reasons. Yankees crouched low and unseen behind the lengthy stone wall that ran just below the open spine of the ridge. However, Confederate shell-fire caused destruction on the right-center, knocking out field pieces, cannoneers, and artillery caissons around the clump of oak trees. Lee's chances for success gradually increased "because of the decimation of the Federal guns" on the battered right-center.[75]

Conversely, the heavy Union cannonade inflicted a good deal of physical and psychological damage among the Confederate infantry. From the guns of Lieutenant George A. Woodruff's battery I, 1st United States Artillery before Ziegler's Grove on the north to Little Round Top to the south, nearly 90 cannon roared. Garnett's and Kemper's brigades, positioned on Seminary Ridge's reverse slope before Armistead's brigade, whose left (the 38th and 57th Virginia, from left to right, or north to south) lay in the northeastern half of the Spangler Woods, were unmercifully swept by shell-fire. Virginia soldiers were aligned close together in grassy swales that provided no protection from the rain of projectiles. Consequently, these grassy swales were soon transformed into bloody bowling alleys from the rifled artillery firing from Little Round Top's summit, enfilading the swales from the southeast. Ironically, the Virginians now suffered heavy casualties quite by accident because Union gunners had only targeted Confederate artillery aligned before the infantry.

Therefore, like Pickett's other brigade commanders, Kemper ordered his hard-hit troops to the ground in the hope of saving lives, but this measure was not enough. Located closer to Seminary Ridge's crest than its sister brigade to the north, and with the Washington Artillery positioned before it drawing shell-fire, Kemper's brigade took a severe beating in the open fields southeast of the Spangler House: an attrition usually suffered only during offensive operations. Unlike Armistead's brigade farther in the rear, and whose left on the north was partly protected by the Spangler Woods, Kemper's brigade suffered heavier than any of Pickett's brigades. Positioned on the far south of Pickett's division, Kemper's troops were swept by Lieutenant Benjamin F. Rittenhouse's rifled Parrotts of Battery D, 5th United States Artillery, blasting away from Little Round Top's crest. Rittenhouse's enfilade fire from half a dozen long-range guns was so effective that some Confederate field pieces were shifted to fire on "the battery on the mountain." This new focus took some pressure off the battered 2nd Corps batteries on the targeted right-center.[76]

Meanwhile, Pickett's losses continued to spiral. In a letter to his brother, Captain John A. Herndon, who commanded Company D (Whitmell Guards) of the 38th Virginia and on the far right of Armistead's brigade, lamented, "Under this Shelling, I had one man killed (Tap Eanes) and two (Privates James F. Gregory and John S. Robertson) severely wounded."[77] Company D was lucky, with Private William T. Eanes (Tap) the company's lone fatality.[78]

With Dearing's four Virginia batteries, located west of and roughly parallel to the Emmitsburg Road on the crest of Seminary Ridge, positioned primarily before Garnett's brigade (but also Kemper's brigade to a lesser degree), the overshooting by Union cannon in attempting to knock out these Old Dominion guns was fatal to an escalating number of Virginia infantrymen.[79]

In the broad fields on the south below Garnett's brigade, General Kemper was horrified by his mounting losses. He watched as "the enemy's hail of shot pelted them and ploughed through them, and sometimes the fragments of a dozen mangled men were thrown in and about" the horrified survivors.[80] One of Garnett's officers, Lieutenant George Williamson Finley, described the "incoming storm of shot and shell killed and wounded many a man lying face down in the tall grass" on the reverse slope.[81] One 7th Virginia soldier, from Kemper's brigade, described the living nightmare: "In any direction might be seen guns, swords, haversacks, heads, limbs, flesh and bones in confusion or dangling in the air or bounding on the earth."[82]

Lieutenant John Edward Dooley, Jr., was sickened by the sad plight of Kemper's brigade: "We were immediately in rear of Genl. [Major James] Dearing's [Virginia] batteries and receive nearly all the missiles intended for his gallant troops. In one of our Regts. alone the killed and wounded, even before going into the charge, amounted to 88 men; and men lay bleeding and gasping in the agonies of death all around, and we were unable to help them in the least. Ever and anon some companion would raise his head disfigured and unrecognizable, streaming with blood, or would stretch his full length, his limbs quivering in the pangs of death. Orders were to lie as closely as possible to the ground, and *I like a good soldier* never got closer to the earth than" before.[83]

Commanding the 3rd Virginia on Kemper's right flank, Colonel Robert Mayo watched in stunned silence as his Company F (Nansemond Rangers) took a severe beating. Two brothers were killed: Second Lieutenant Patrick H. Arthur, a 21-year-old farmer, and Lieutenant John C. Arthur, an agriculturalist of age 23, mortally wounded in one shell's fiery explosion.[84] A former mechanic in his midtwenties from Portsmouth, color-bearer Joshua Murden was killed in one fiery explosion. Because of his firm death grip in still fulfilling his promise to protect the 3rd Virginia's flag, Murden's bloody right hand was pried from the wooden staff of the new battle flag.[85] Kemper was incensed at taking high losses for no gain. Confronting Longstreet, Kemper angrily denounced such "a terrible place," hoping to gain permission to move his brigade. But Longstreet only responded for Kemper to remain "a while longer [since] we are hurting the enemy badly" with the cannonade. One of Kemper's disgusted soldiers concluded how it was "as if we were placed where we were for target practice for the Union batteries."[86]

Lieutenant Colonel Alexander D. Callcote, of French heritage, born in the Isle of Wright County, Virginia, and a VMI graduate (Class of 1851) who would not survive the upcoming assault, and Colonel Joseph Mayo, Jr., 3rd Virginia and another VMI graduate (Class of 1852), watched the cruel culling of the ranks. With bitter resignation, Mayo described how "Company F suffered terribly, First Lieutenant A[zra] P. Gomer [a former clerk in his mid twenties], legs [the left leg was amputated] shattered below the knee; of the Arthur brothers, second and third lieutenants, one killed [and] the other badly hit."[87] A former attorney in his late twenties, Colonel Mayo wondered if he would ever again see his home and loving wife, Mary Armistead Tyler-Mayo.[88]

Heavy damage was inflicted upon hapless Company G (Lynchburg Home Guards), 11th Virginia, on Kemper's right-center. Here, in the open fields, 22-year-old Captain John Holmes Smith watched as a full third of his men were killed or wounded. Nineteen-year-old Sergeant DeWitt C. Guy, a former merchant, fell wounded.[89] And in the 8th Virginia on the far right of Garnett's brigade, the head of Private Albert J. Morris, Company D (Champe Rifles), was torn off by a screaming shell. Morris's brains were splattered over his comrades, including over Major Edmund Berkeley's hat. Thankful for having survived another close call, the major was also relieved that his brothers, Lieutenant Colonel Norborne Berkeley, Captain William Noland Berkeley, and Lieutenant Charles Fenton Berkeley, were spared in this artillery hell.[90]

Mayo described the "fearful havoc was made in our lines, the 3d and 7th Regts suffering with particular severity."[91]Amid the bombardment, mounted officers, including Longstreet, who ignored the danger, rode along the front to steady the troops to withstand the punishment.[92] Meanwhile, Chaplain John C. Granberry, 11th Virginia of Kemper's brigade, provided spiritual comfort amid the whizzing shell fragments. In the words of Lieutenant Colonel James Risque Hutter, commanding the 11th Virginia on the brigade's right-center: "Our chaplain the Reverend John C. Granberry … . whenever he saw a man badly wounded would go and kneel by him and pray for and with him."[93]

Suffering on the opposite flank (north) even more than Kemper's brigade, Colonel John Mercer Brockenbrough's brigade was enfiladed by the massive array of guns atop Cemetery Hill to the northeast. These northernmost Virginians were positioned to the extreme left of Pettigrew's division. Along with the brigade's other units, the undersized 22nd Virginia Infantry Battalion—including six companies of soldiers originally organized as members of the 2nd Virginia Light Artillery and now consisting of only 237 men (the smallest unit in the assault)— showed signs early of uneasiness under the severe pounding.[94] The awful "roar of artillery drowned all [and was worse than] I have seen in all the heavy battles in Virginia and Maryland [and] I never heard such artillery firing before," wrote one incredulous Tar Heel cannoneer in a letter.[95] Knowing that Lee had a tactical trick up his sleeve, one veteran Union officer expected the worst, because the Southern artillery had never before expended "so lavish [an amount] of ammunition."[96]

In just his early twenties and commanding his battalion's 18 guns of Pickett's division, Major James Dearing should have ensured that his gunners possessed plenty of ammunition for the crucial flying artillery role to follow on the infantrymen's heels once the advance began. A ladies' man who would be married in January 1864, Dearing was the son of an old, aristocratic family, whose plantation was known as "Otterburne" in Campbell County, Virginia. Dearing had received a fine education at the Hanover Academy, Virginia, and also at West Point, where he racked up many demerits for his high-spirited antics. Dearing hailed from Lynchburg, Virginia, and began the war with the famed Washington Artillery. Dearing was fated to be mortally wounded in hand to hand combat only three days before Lee's surrender at Appomattox Court House: the last Confederate general to die of combat wounds.[97]

Meanwhile, under the rain of shells, large numbers of Pickett's soldiers were now "being slaughtered like cattle in a pen."[98] The most exposed of Pickett's brigades, Kemper's brigade, aligned on the open ground on the south and without the protective cover of the Spangler Woods (like Armistead's left), continued to suffer the worst punishment. On the left flank of Kemper's brigade, 3rd Virginia soldiers witnessed the sickening sight of the death of Color Sergeant Joshua Murden, a 25-year-old former mechanic from Portsmouth, Virginia.[99] But the 11th Virginia, on the brigade's right-center, took even greater losses. Captain John Holmes Smith, a 22-year-old former merchant, watched as his company (G, the Lynchburg Home Guard) lost 20 out of 29 men, while the adjacent company lost even more members. Company G's most tragic loss was two brothers: Privates Thomas and William Jennings, who were killed by one shell explosion. Another pair of brothers, Privates Edward W., a teenager, and Joseph A. Valentine, an ex-merchant of age 27, were relatively more fortunate, with only the youngest of the two siblings fatally hit.[100]

Perhaps as high as 20 percent of Kemper's brigade were killed or wounded by the shell-fire. Kemper's high losses were excessive because the brigade had been assigned to anchor the assault's right flank (a hard-hit counterpart to Brockenbrough's Virginia brigade on the opposite flank).[101] Likewise, Armistead's right, especially the 14th Virginia on the far right (or south), was swept by the enfilade fire of Little Round Top's long-range cannon. Armistead's units on the right were vulnerable in the open below the Spangler Woods that protected at least two regiments on Armistead's left, the 57th Virginia and the 38th Virginia (on the extreme left flank), from south to north. In total, more than 500 men of Pickett's division were hit during the bombardment at a time when every soldier was needed for the assault.[102] A shocked Kemper saw one of his boys lifted several feet high from a shell explosion, which killed him.[103]

Significantly, Pickett lost valuable officers either killed or wounded, including some of the highest-ranking officers. The popular commander of the 53rd Virginia, positioned in the center of Armistead's brigade (which suffered relatively few losses compared to Kemper's regiments, and thanks to partial concealment in the Spangler Woods), was hit. Promoted to regimental command on March 1863, Colonel William Roane Aylett was seriously wounded. The grandson of Virginia lawyer–patriot Patrick Henry of "Give Me Liberty or Give Me Death" fame and University of Virginia graduate (Class of 1853) was carried rearward by stretcher bearers. Splattered in blood, dark-haired Colonel Aylett, only age 32, hailed from King William County (the Richmond area). In 1830, he had been born at the family mansion of "Montville." Meanwhile, wife Alice Brockenbrough Aylett prayed for her husband's safe return. Assuming regimental command, Lieutenant Colonel Rawley White Martin was a former physician who was now dedicated to taking lives instead of saving them.[104]

Also named after America's revolutionary hero and Virginia governor from 1776 to 1779, Patrick Henry Fontaine, who was later appointed regimental chaplain, was not now available to provide spiritual comfort when needed. Lieutenant Colonel Rawley White Martin had been educated at the University of Virginia (like Colonel Aylett) and the University of New York, from which he obtained a medical degree in 1858. He realized his men "felt the gravity of the situation [and] they were serious and resolute, but not disheartened. None of the usual jokes, common on the eve of battle, were indulged in" to lighten the mood.[105]

General Armistead had a close call under the relentless bombardment. Pickett's division nearly lost one of its finest brigade commanders when a shell smashed into a small hickory near where General Armistead stood before his troops. The shell explosion wounded a few unlucky men, while "almost cutting the tree off" and nearly abruptly ending Armistead's career.[106]

Virginia Military Institute's Distinguished Legacy

One of the best leaders of Garnett's brigade suffered a tragic fate. Lieutenant Colonel John Thomas Ellis, 19th Virginia, Garnett's brigade, found himself under the vicious enfilade fire from Little Round Top that punished Kemper's and Garnett's brigades. On Little Round Top's crest, a half-dozen 10-pounder Parrotts of Lieutenant Charles E. Hazelett's Battery D, 5th United States Artillery, roared incessantly. Born in Amherst County, among the Piedmont's rolling hills in west-central Virginia, Ellis first learned about the axioms of nineteenth-century warfare at the Virginia Military Institute (VMI) at Lexington, Virginia, in the picturesque Upper Shenandoah Valley. On the manicured parade ground, smartly uniformed cadets had long drilled before George Washington's statue, before marching off to war when none had imagined that defeat was possible.

From the southeast, Little Round Top's guns continued to hurl an enfilading fire down the ranks. One projectile ricocheted along the ground and
toward the 19th Virginia's right flank, where the troops lay amid the grassy
"hollow." A private raised the cry, "Look out!" Ellis raised his head up from a
"small wash." Lieutenant William N. Wood described the lieutenant colonel
as a "good man as well as a polished gentleman" cited for valor. The round shot
bounded up, striking Ellis square in the face. The blood-stained regimental
commander was carried by his grieving men to Pickett's divisional field hospital at the John F. Currins farm. Ellis died shortly after and was buried under
the shade of a little apple tree.[107] Colonel Alexander declared in horror, "I
never saw so much blood fly."[108]

However, the much-lamented Lieutenant Colonel Ellis was only one of
many fine VMI–educated officers cut down in Pickett's division. Dark-haired
and bearded Colonel Lewis B. Williams, Jr., now commanding the "Old First"
Virginia (Pickett's smallest regiment, with about 220 men in the ranks) was
another VMI graduate in danger. Colonel Williams relied upon high-quality
VMI–trained officers, such as Adjutant John Stockton. A total of 11 of Pickett's
15 regiments were commanded by VMI men of considerable ability. All of these
seasoned leaders were fated to be killed or wounded on that bloody afternoon.
On the left (or northern) flank of Armistead's brigade was Colonel Edward
Claxton Edmonds (VMI Class of 1858), who was born in Paris, located near
the Appalachians at Virginia's northern tip in January 1835. He was about to
be killed in the upcoming attack, while leading the 38th Virginia of around 480
soldiers. One of Pickett's brigade commanders possessed extensive VMI connections. Now commanding his brigade of around 1,800 men, General James
Lawson Kemper had served as the president of the Board of Visitors of VMI,
which had been modeled after West Point.

The promising VMI Class of 1855 was especially ill-fated. All Class of 1855
graduates serving as regimental commanders of Pickett's division—Colonels
Lewis Burwell Williams, Jr. (a bachelor); Waller Tazewell Patton (an ancestor
of General George Patton of Second World War fame and who was affectionately known as "Taz" to his fellow officers), commanding the 7th Virginia, on
Kemper's left-center; and Robert C. Allen, who led the 28th Virginia—were
destined for death in Pickett's Charge. All three leaders—Williams, Allen, and
Patton—had been gray-uniformed roommates in Room No. 13 (today's Room
201) in VMI's three-story brick barracks. They had been lawyers before the
war.

Additionally, Colonel John Bowie Magruder, in his midtwenties and a former teacher from the Piedmont town of Culpeper, Virginia, located just more than 200 miles northeast of VMI, led the 57th Virginia. Magruder was ably assisted by staff members Adjutant John Davis Watson, age 22, and Captain William S. Smith, VMI Class of 1861. Colonel Magruder was about to fall mortally wounded "within 20 steps" of the artillery on Meade's right-center.[109]

While the contributions of America's military academy at West Point in the molding of Civil War leaders have been widely recognized in a war that was "pre-eminently a West Pointers' fight," the role of small Southern military academies in creating an equally capable, if not superior, leadership corps—a sturdy foundation for Lee's army—has been relatively forgotten.[110] Ironically, VMI has been overlooked by historians, although it was one of the Confederacy's leading military colleges. Based "closely" upon the West Point model, VMI was a prestigious state-supported military college founded in 1839.

The Institute's first president had been a lucky survivor of Napoleon's 1812 invasion of Russia: Colonel Claude Crozet. A graduate of the Ecole Politechnique in Paris, France (like many of Napoleon's top officers), Crozet and VMI produced some of America's finest soldiers. With its high academic standards, VMI allowed the entry of Jewish students (such as Moses Jacob Ezekiel), mostly from Richmond, where a large Hebrew community thrived at the Confederacy's capital. Jewish Rebels were sprinkled throughout Pickett's division, especially the 1st Virginia, whose members hailed primarily from Richmond. On this day, these forgotten Jewish Confederates continued the ancient traditions of fiery Hebrew warriors of the Old Testament and the Torah. The exacting standards of VMI's three-year program were exceptionally high for the teenagers, whose neat gray uniforms were lined with three vertical rows of brass buttons. The bulk of the nearly 2,000 VMI alumni formed a sturdy foundation to the officer corps of not only Pickett's division, but also of the Army of Northern Virginia. VMI was "the West Point of the Confederacy."[111]

"What little drill and discipline the Southern armies had, they owed largely to VMI men," especially in the war's beginning.[112] With some undisguised malice, President Lincoln himself theorized that he had been unable to early crush the Southern rebellion primarily because of "a certain military school in Virginia which made it impossible."[113]

But no single chapter of the war was more disproportionately influenced and shaped by VMI than Pickett's Charge.[114] Indeed, "nearly every field officer who participated in Pickett's charge was [a product of] the Virginia Military

Institute."[115] On VMI's parade ground, the afternoon parade of lines of cadets had been long led by two free black musicians, Michael Lyle and Reuben Howard, with fife and drum. The army's large number of VMI graduates, including Lee's handsome Adjutant Colonel Walter Herron Taylor (Class of 1857) and especially men in Pickett's division, were motivated to now uphold the institute's high standards that afternoon.[116]

VMI's influence even reached down to the lower grade officers, lieutenants and captains, and even noncommissioned officers of Pickett's division. In the 11th Virginia, Kemper's brigade, VMI–educated company commanders included Captain John C. Ward (Class of 1853), a former teacher, age 29, who led Company E (Lynchburg Rifles) and Captain James Risque Hutter, age 19 and graduate of VMI Class of 1860. Hutter was a rising star. Only hours before, he had been relieved of regimental command by Major Kirkwood Otey (VMI Class of 1849), who had been just released from arrest to lead the 11th Virginia in the attack. Likewise, Captain William W. Bentley, who led Company E (organized at Newbern, Pulaski County, Virginia), 24th Virginia, was a VMI graduate (Class of 1860), while VMI's Lieutenant Benjamin P. Grigsby fulfilled the same role in Company G (organized in today's West Virginia), 24th Virginia. And in Company B (Danville Greys), 18th Virginia, Garnett's brigade, Captain Robert McCulloch, a Scotch-Irishman known for his Celtic fighting spirit, was part of VMI's Class of 1864. Lieutenant John Wesley Hill, age 27 and VMI Class of 1859, served in Company A (Monticello Guard), 19th Virginia. Leading Company H (Southern Rights Guard), 19th Virginia, Captain Benjamin Brown, Jr., a 19-year-old ex-farmer, was a member of VMI's Class of 1864.

Besides its VMI commander Colonel Lewis Burwell Williams, Jr., other VMI leaders of the 1st Virginia included Captain George F. Stockton (Class of 1860), who led Company D (Old Dominion Guards). The top 3rd Virginia leadership were educated at VMI: Colonel Joseph Mayo (Class of1852) and a former attorney; Lieutenant Colonel Alexander Daniel Callcote (Class of 1851); and Major William Hamlin Pryor (Class of 1848). And VMI's Colonel Waller Tazewell Patton, born in Fredericksburg and former attorney who led the 7th Virginia, was ably assisted by 20-year-old Lieutenant Colonel Charles Conway Flowerree, born in Fauquier County, Virginia, who was also a VMI man. In Kemper's brigade, the 24th Virginia was likewise dominated by outstanding VMI–trained leadership of superior quality: Colonel William Richard Terry (Class of 1850), a former merchant who eventually earned a brigadier general's rank, and his top lieutenants, 30-year-old Major Joseph Adam Hambrick (Class of 1857) and Adjutant William T. Taliaferro (Class of 1845). Hambrick, a former lawyer, and Taliaferro, of Italian (name meant "ironcutter") heritage and with a lieutenant's rank, were about to be cut down in the upcoming assault.

Likewise in Garnett's brigade, VMI was well represented by the top leadership of the 8th Virginia: Colonel Eppa Hunton, Lieutenant Colonel Norborne Berkeley, and Major Edmund Berkeley. Garnett's brigade's combat capabilities were also enhanced by 32-year-old Colonel William Dabney Stuart (VMI Class of 1850). Stuart reminded one of his lampooning lieutenants of his mother, because of his sheer willpower and determination to achieve an objective. A stern disciplinarian who maintained lofty VMI standards and who was taller than most of his men, Stuart commanded the 56th Virginia. He made an exceptional leadership team with Adjutant Richard Wharton (VMI Class of 1862). Also in the 56th Virginia, Captain John W. Jones, who could be counted upon in a crisis situation, was a distinguished a VMI graduate (Class of 1842).

In the same brigade and now leading the 18th Virginia, 30-year-old Lieutenant Colonel Henry Alexander Carrington, married since 1856 to Charlotte E. Cullen, was also VMI graduate (Class of 1851). Also in the 18th Virginia, Garnett's brigade, Lieutenant James C. Walthall, an ex-agriculturalist of age 22 who now led Company D (Prospect Rifle Grays), was part of VMI's Class of 1864. And the 19th Virginia, Garnett's brigade, was led by Colonel Henry Gantt (VMI Class of 1851), a farmer from Scottsville, Virginia, and his top lieutenant, John Thomas Ellis (VMI Class of 1848). In the same veteran brigade, the 28th Virginia was commanded by Colonel Robert Clotworthy Allen (VMI Class of 1855), a former lawyer from Salem, Virginia. He had been born in the idyllic Shenandoah County, Virginia on June 22, 1834. Allen was now assisted by his top lieutenant, Major Nathaniel Claiborne Wilson, who was trained in the art of war at VMI.

General Armistead was well served not only by his aide-de-camp, Alabama-born Lieutenant Walker Keith Armistead (his teenage son just assigned to the general's staff on April 30), but also by his acting Adjutant General Captain James D. Darden, in his midthirties and planning to eventually graduate from VMI's hallowed halls. VMI's Lieutenant Thomas Flournoy Barksdale and young Captain William Harvie Bray, VMI graduate (Class of 1861), who led Company B (Barhamsville Grays), served in the 53rd Virginia, Armistead's brigade. Sergeant Thomas Booker Tredway, who was fated to fall mortally wounded in the upcoming attack, also attended VMI. Even a lowly private,

Thomas Jefferson Green, who was early detailed as a clerk in the Confederate commissary department, was a VMI graduate (Class of 1848).

Also of Armistead's brigade, Lieutenant Thomas A. Hatcher, a 23-year-old planter of Company A (Paineville Rifles), 14th Virginia, was a graduate of VMI Class of 1858, along with 31-year-old Captain Richard Logan, Jr., who led Company H (Meadville Greys) of the same regiment. Colonel Edward Claxton Edmonds (VMI Class of 1858) headed the 38th Virginia, Armistead's brigade. And Captain George K. Griggs, who commanded Company K (Cascade Rifles), 38th Virginia, Armistead's brigade, was part of VMI Class of 1862. Leading Company E (Pamunkey Rifles), 53rd Virginia, Captain Benjamin L. Farinholt counted on his top lieutenant, William Harvie Bray (VMI Class of 1861).

These tactically astute VMI graduates of the 53rd Virginia were only some of the most notable representative examples of the VMI's significant influence in Pickett's other regiments. Such reliable VMI men, including Captain Bray, who was destined to charge *beyond* the stone wall and lose his life, at the lower officer ranks in Pickett's division were a long-overlooked secret that explained the near success of Pickett's Charge.[117]

The young Tidewater men and boys, including boatmen, sailors, and fishermen, of the 9th Virginia, Armistead's brigade, had been molded by lofty VMI standards, based on West Point's rigid guidelines. Consequently, this veteran Tidewater regiment could "boast of the finest officers in the South."[118] John Thomas Lewis Preston, the regiment's first lieutenant colonel, was one of VMI's respected founders. The regiment's first commander, Colonel Francis Henney Smith, born in 1812 and a West Point graduate (Class of 1833), was also VMI's first superintendent, beginning in 1839. Making significant contributions in creating a splendid regiment, the first major of the 9th Virginia, Stapleton Crutchfield, graduated from VMI with honors. And other leading regimental officers likewise possessed VMI training.[119]

Major Walter Harrison, the inspector general of Pickett's division, was also a product of VMI, which he entered at age 16. Harrison racked up many demerits, including one following a wild ride through the VMI barracks on horseback (evidently fueled by liquor consumption)—an outrageous escapade that ensured he never graduated. Harrison had prospered in New York City before the war. But with the call to arms, he immediately returned to his home state, and then volunteered to serve without an officer's commission on Pickett's staff.[120]

A close look at only a single regiment of Pickett's division has revealed VMI's supreme importance, which has been long overlooked, partly because on an overemphasis on the importance of West Point. In the 11th Virginia's ranks, VMI was represented at every level. Lynchburg, Virginia–born Major Otey Kirkwood (known as "Kirk"), in his midthirties, graduated from VMI (Class of 1849). Destined to lead Company D (Fincastle Rifles), 11th Virginia, in the upcoming assault, Lieutenant John Thomas James, who had seen his teenage brother, Private Edward W. James, killed by his side during combat in 1862, had first learned the ways of war as an 18-year-old cadet at VMI in 1859. Meanwhile, Captain John C. Ward led Company E (Lynchburg Rifles), 11th Virginia, represented VMI Class of 1853. Captain Ward was about to fall wounded, along with so many other fine leaders from the prestigious Lexington, Virginia, institution. Commanding Company H, the Jeff Davis Guard (also known as the Jefferson Davis Riflemen), 19-year-old Captain James Risque Hutter (VMI Class of 1860) shortly led his 11th Virginia (as the acting lieutenant colonel) all the way to the stone wall.[121]

Most importantly, VMI graduates had instilled an esprit de corps and fighting spirit among Pickett's men at every level. Although this detail had been forgotten, Pickett's Charge became famous because of its parade-ground-like precision born on VMI's parade ground that lay before the Gothic-style brick barracks. Eleven of 15 regimental commanders of Pickett's division (among the South's best and brightest) played key roles that July afternoon.[122]

However, West Point's less significant influences were also fully represented in Pickett's division (and Pettigrew's division), not only with regard to General Armistead, but also to junior officers in the ranks. In the 53rd Virginia, Armistead's brigade, Major John Corbett Timberlake was a West Pointer, who now served beside "our [former] drill master at West Point," Lieutenant William Harvie Bray, of Company E (Pamunkey Rifles).[123]

Meanwhile, under the cannonade, young Lieutenant John Thomas James, the former VMI cadet, watched as two mounted officers carefully surveyed Cemetery Ridge before Kemper's brigade. As the officers drew closer, Lieutenant James recognized Lee and Longstreet. Proud of his solid VMI training, the Fincastle, Botelourt County, Virginia, native knew exactly what this field conference meant. As he penned in a letter, "As soon as we saw this we knew a fight and a big fight at that was brewing, and it was hardly necessary for General Kemper to come around, as he did, and tell us that our division was assigned the task of storming the heights."[124]

Despite VMI's pervasive influence at every level of Pickett's division, success today also depended upon the young, but experienced, officers who may have lacked the best military educations available in America. After the terrible culling of the ranks, Company B (the Albemarle Rifles), 19th Virginia, Garnett's brigade, was now led by teenage officers, like Lieutenants Pulaski P. Porter, Richard B. Wood (soon to be killed), and William P. Hamner (shortly would be wounded); and noncommissioned officers, such as Sergeants Rufus W. Robinson, Eugene G. Taylor (about to fall wounded), and Leonidas R. Bowyer (fated to be shortly killed). Lee now relied upon such determined young men, from Albemarle County in the Virginia Piedmont, to achieve decisive victory.[125]

Furious Cannonade Continues

Unable to ascertain the elimination of opposing batteries on the right-center, Colonel Alexander originally believed that the assault should begin 20–30 minutes after the cannonade's beginning, but that time had long passed while Pickett's losses steadily spiraled higher. One of Kemper's brigade officers educated at Georgetown College, Lieutenant John Edward Dooley, Jr., described how "the air is shaking from earth to sky with every missile of death fire from the cannon's mouth [while] we are obliged to lie quietly tho' frightened out of our wits and unable to do anything in our own defence or any injury to our enemies."[126] Two Company H (Potomac Greys), 8th Virginia, soldiers were "literally [cut] in two" by a shell.[127]

However, with the cannonade lasting far longer than planned by Alexander, Dearing's guns had already expended far too much ammunition. In consequence and like other Southern cannon, Dearing's four Virginia batteries fired too fast, expending so much ammunition that an adequate supply to fulfill Lee's flying artillery support mission was rapidly slipping away.[128] In Dearing's words describing this disturbing situation, which threatened Lee's plan of providing close artillery support: "About this time my ammunition became completely exhausted, excepting a few rounds in my rifled guns [and] I had sent back my caissons an hour and a half before for a fresh supply, but they could not get it."[129]

Knowing that artillery officers needed to be all business, and especially when Major Dearing was drawing artillery fire that was cutting down even more of Pickett's men to the rear, Lee became irritated by Dearing's showboating. Lee correctly sensed that the battalion commander's display indicated an inattention to details. Therefore, when the "handsomely equipped" Dearing galloped near, Lee unleashed a stinging rebuke as if he were still West Point's superintendent: "Ah! Major, excuse me; I thought you might be some countryman who had missed his way. Let me say to you and to these young officers, that I am an old reconnoitering officer [the United States Army's most capable topographical engineer in Scott's Army on the march to Mexico City] and have always found it best to go afoot, *and not expose oneself needlessly.*"[130] Dearing's bravado abruptly ended, when the embarrassed artillery battalion commander quietly retired.[131]

Meanwhile, the army's greatest artillery bombardment continued to boom far longer than planned by either Lee or Alexander. In a letter to his wife, one Confederate described the inferno swirling around him as "the crash of worlds. . . ."[132] Lee and Alexander had no way of knowing that more than 170 guns, blasting away from a distance of 1,000–1,400 yards, had failed to drive the Union infantrymen from the right-center. Along Cemetery Ridge, the bluecoat infantrymen were still protected, while hidden behind the stone wall just below the crest.

As Napoleon had emphasized and Lee now hoped, "A good infantry is without doubt the backbone of the army, but if it had to fight long against superior artillery it would be discouraged and disorganized." Like Lee, Pickett believed that the massive cannonade was certain to "demoralize" the 2nd Corps defenders around the clump of trees. Colonel David Wyatt Aiken, commander of the 7th South Carolina, was emboldened by the spirited artillery performance. The South Carolina colonel wrote to his wife: "175 cannons [all fired] at one time, and the enemy replied with perhaps half as many [and] I know [our cannonade] killed and wounded hundreds, if not thousands, of the enemy."[133]

Major Benjamin Franklin Eshleman, a West Pointer born in nearby Lancaster, Pennsylvania, and a New Orleans resident at the war's beginning, also believed that the lengthy row of Confederate guns had "caused immense slaughter to the enemy."[134] Such lofty estimates of the Southern artillery's effectiveness were a gross exaggeration, but only with regard to the Union infantry.

Meanwhile, additional Federal cannon aligned along the dominate perch of the distant crest grew silent. Southern cannon either knocked out or disabled an increasing number of field pieces in the targeted 2nd Corps sector around the clump of trees. Captain Graham was elated by the direct hits inflicted by his 1st North Carolina Artillery, which had been organized in April 1861 in Raleigh, the capital of North Carolina, during "the heaviest Artillery duel of the war. . . ."[135] The captain, who left behind a lucrative medical practice to join the Charlotte Artillery (the nucleus of the 1st North Carolina Artillery), marveled how "we whipped them fairly in the Artillery."[136] Paradoxically, the cost of "winning" the artillery duel came at a high cost, because Confederate guns all along the line had fired too fast and too long, leaving an insufficient amount of long-range ammunition to support the assault by firing over the advancing infantrymen's heads.[137]

Lee had achieved his goals of mauling the frontline Union batteries of the 2nd Corps, disabling a good many guns around the clump of chestnut oak trees. Lieutenant Alonzo Hersford Cushing's battery A, 4th United States Artillery, was especially hard hit (leaving only two guns operational). But Lieutenant T. Fred Brown's Company B, 1st Rhode Island Light Battery, just south of the clump of trees, suffered an even greater pounding. Besides having one of his guns disabled, Captain James McKay Rorty, the dashing Irish commander of Company B, 1st New York Artillery, which was positioned below, or south, of the clump of trees and east of the north–south stone wall, was mortally wounded when an ammunition limber exploded from a direct hit. Two of Rorty's four guns were disabled by exploding shells.

Therefore, Union leadership now worried about the ultimate fate of the thin defensive line along Cemetery Ridge. However, the damage inflicted on Cushing's and Brown's hard-hit batteries indicated to more defenders that Lee had deliberately targeted the 2nd Corps and the Angle, the right-angle section of the stone wall about 250 feet north of the clump of trees, and the area around the clump of trees.[138] Haskell was astounded by the bombardment's fury: "[A] shell exploded over an open limber in Cushing's battery, and at that same instant, another shell over a neighboring box [and] the ammunition blew up with an explosion that shook the ground, throwing fire and splinters and shells far into the air and all around, and destroying several men."[139] Meanwhile, the 2nd Corps's infantrymen, crouched low behind the stone wall on the western slope, continued to suffer relatively little damage, with the vast majority of shells continuing to roar overhead.[140]

The Confederate cannonade continued to roar far longer than the anticipated 20–30 minutes originally envisioned by Alexander. Haskell was astonished: "Half-past two o'clock, an hour and a half since the commencement, and still the cannonade did not in the least abate."[141] Most importantly, Lee's ambition was fulfilled by the growing silence among the Federal guns, because a total of 34 Union artillery pieces were withdrawn, disabled, or knocked out.

Federal guns along the 2nd Corps's battered front had also used up most long-range ammunition during the lengthy artillery duel, which partly explained the increasing silence. Indeed "most of the 2nd Corps batteries had exhausted their long-range ammunition . . . and had to wait until the Confederates came into canister range—roughly, 250 yards—before they could effectively get into action."[142] Captain Graham was delighted by what his North Carolina guns had helped to accomplish, writing in his letter with triumph of how "we silenced all their guns."[143]

However, Hunt's artillery on either side of the mauled batteries of the 2nd Corps remained securely in positions to provide support with enfilade fire when the assault began. In total, 132 guns were arrayed between Cemetery Hill and Little Round Top.[144] But much damage was inflicted on Union artillery. In a letter, Sergeant Hirst, 14th Connecticut (just northeast of the copse of trees) described: "I saw one of Caissons [of Arnold's battery] blown up. . . . But all this could not last much longer, our fire began to lose its vigour for want of Ammunition, and as the Smoke lifted from the Crest we saw our Guns leaving one after the other. : . ."[145]

Peering anxiously through his field glasses and unfairly burdened with inappropriate orders from Longstreet (a clever deflection of responsibility) to inform Pickett of the best time to attack based upon his cannonade's effectiveness, Alexander saw Union artillery pieces leaving from the Angle sector: the long-awaited sight that suddenly appeared through the drifting clouds of smoke. Therefore, he dispatched his "fateful summons" to Pickett at 1:40 p.m.: "The eighteen guns [an overestimation] have been drawn off. For God's sake come on quick or we cannot support you" in the assault.[146] As planned, the cannonade had succeeded in its central mission of knocking out or forcing the withdrawal of guns from the targeted right-center.[147]

Unknown to Alexander, the sudden lack of fire from the Union guns also stemmed from the day's wisest artillery order from the savvy Hunt and also Major Thomas Ward Osborn on Cemetery Hill. Knowing that an attack was about to be launched, Hunt had made sure that his batteries conserved their ammunition (unlike Southern artillery officers). Of course, Alexander failed to realize that this silencing was also a deliberate ambush to provoke the Southern infantry into advancing out into the open: prematurely forcing Lee's hand before all assault preparations were ready. Never before had so many Union gunners disengaged from a raging artillery duel for the express purpose of preserving rounds to greet the attackers.[148]

The Finest Day for Union Artillery Commanders

Hunt had created a clever "blue ruse." As explained Colonel James C. Biddle, who served on Meade's staff, although he got the order's original author (Hunt) wrong, "General Meade [had early and] well understood that the object of the enemy in [the cannonade] was to demoralize our men, preparatory to making a grand assault. He, therefore, directed our artillery to slacken their fire, and, finally, to cease altogether, with the view of making the enemy believe that they had silenced our guns, and thus bring on their assault the sooner."[149]

However, the devastation of 2nd Corps's batteries was also the price paid for Hancock's insistence—against Hunt's orders—that his corps's guns should continue firing to fortify the infantrymens' morale. The key advantage of Meade's sizeable artillery reserve now paid immense dividends, verifying the axiom that the "grandest results are obtained by the reserve artillery in great and decisive battles." Withdrawing Union batteries were in the process of being replaced by fresh batteries from McGilvery's reserve artillery, including Captain Andrew Cowan's 1st New York Battery. But this substitution across a broad front would take time. Therefore, Lee now possessed an excellent, but narrowing, window of opportunity to strike a devastating blow on the right-center before the replacement guns arrived.[150]

Most importantly, the lack of return artillery fire testified to the effectiveness of Confederate artillery that scored a good many direct hits in 2nd Corps's battered sector. Not long after two o'clock, Captain Haskell felt greater unease over a true crisis situation when one mauled battery departed "from the line, too feeble for further battle [as] Its commander was wounded, and many of its men were so, or worse; some of its guns had been disabled, many of its horses killed; its ammunition was nearly suspended [and] Other batteries in similar case, had been withdrawn" after taking a beating.[151] Bestowing Lee with his best tactical opportunity as planned, 34 artillery pieces, around the Angle and clump of trees, were either disabled or withdrawn. Inside the Angle, Cushing's battery had four guns knocked out.[152]

Captain Haskell surveyed the increasingly desperate situation on the right-center: "The batteries had been handled much more severely [than the infantry.] A great number of horses had been killed, in some batteries more than half of all. Guns had been dismounted. A great many caissons, limbers, and carriages had been destroyed, and usually from ten to twenty-five men to each battery had been struck, at least along our part of the crest" of Cemetery Ridge.[153] On Meade's hard-hit right-center, "the fire of the enemy had injured us [the artillery arm] much [and] exhausting our ammunition and fouling our guns, so as to render our batteries unfit for further immediate use."[154]

Lee's massive bombardment succeeded in mauling the frontline Union artillery on the right-center. However, McGilvery's reserve batteries and the guns of Little Round Top and Cemetery Hill remained in good shape.[155] Then, with Union artillery having gone silent, the Confederate bombardment finally ceased to roar after its mightiest effort. The planned Southern bombardment of 20–30 minutes had continued for more than two hours, expending most long-range ammunition. Near the clump of oak trees, Captain Haskell concluded how "the cannonade was over [and it was clear that] [t]he purpose of General Lee in all this fire of his guns . . . was to disable our artillery and break up our infantry upon the position of the 2nd Corps" around the clump of trees.[156]

However, although knocking out or forcing the withdrawal of more than 30 Yankee cannon, the intensity of the bombardment was wasted on the veteran Union infantrymen. Napoleon's axiom that such a heavy cannonade was guaranteed to break the defender's morale was unrealized on Cemetery Ridge.[157] One Confederate sullenly concluded: "There was sure noise enough, from the roar of the guns and bursting of shells, to have moved the Yanks . . . but they [now] had a good thing [defending home soil] and knew it," remaining firmly in place.[158]

To inspire his defenders, Meade had already ordered his officers to inform their troops that the "whole country now looks anxiously to this army to deliver it from the presence of the foe."[159] One of Lee's confident men bragged in a recent letter: "We are the boys to make Yanks get up and dust, cowardly pups."[160] In striking contrast to such optimism, one Confederate officer offered General Pickett, who did not ride down the lines to encourage his men under the bombardment, a flask of whiskey and remarked, "Take a drink with me; in an hour you'll be in hell or glory."[161]

Meade's Businesslike Efficiency

A good stiff drink (more stimulating than Alexander's sweet-potato coffee) was indeed appropriate, because the 2nd Corps's infantry remained in position. Pickett took a drink, which was becoming increasingly his custom. Even his own Virginia comrades later criticized Pickett for nipping too much at the bottle on July 3. But in fact, perhaps Pickett would have needed more to drink had he known that Meade's solid performance in thwarting Lee's hardest hitting blows on July 2 had infused new confidence among his troops.

This commonsense Pennsylvanian was no prima donna like General George B. McClellan or the bombastic Joe Hooker. The businesslike Meade was now vindicating Lincoln's faith in the "tall, spare" Pennsylvanian. This West Pointer (Class of 1835) was proving to be as solid as a rock, while displaying an "impregnable imperturbability" that inspired his men. Maintaining his trademark "careless appearance," Meade had recently implored his troops to eliminate the "disgrace of a hostile invasion" on northern soil.[162] Tipped off by the artillery bombardment and not taking any chances, Meade prudently ordered up some reserve units (including a division from Cemetery Hill's rear to the north, to reinforce the weak right flank of General Alexander Hays's 3rd Division, 2nd Corps before Pettigrew's division). And from the south, two 6th Corps brigades were hurried into a reserve position behind the 2nd Corps, including near Meade's headquarters, for judicious deployment. Other troops were also shifted by Meade into supporting positions. However, these reinforcements were still far too insufficient and not enough to thwart Lee's plan, if everything worked as envisioned.[163]

Colonel James C. Biddle, age 32, from the Holmesburg section of Philadelphia, and one of Meade's aide-de-camps, explained, "Fredericksburg and Chancellorsville had demonstrated how little the valor of the troops could accomplish when incompetently led; [but now] at Gettysburg" this equation was now reversed.[164]

The extremely capable Hancock now had his veteran 2nd Corps ready for its greatest challenge. General John Gibbon had temporarily commanded the corps during the first two days of combat, when Hancock led the "left wing" units to Gettysburg, after General John Fulton Reynolds was killed on July 1. Gibbon, a hard-fighting Mexican–American War veteran and now a division commander of the 2nd Corps, had been convinced that the Confederate bombardment was nothing more than a clever screen. Revealing the wisdom of Lee's hiding of his assault troops along Seminary Ridge's reverse slope, Captain Haskell described how Gibbon believed "that the enemy was falling back, and that the cannonade was only one of his noisy modes of covering the movement."[165]

Other nervous Federals expected a stealthy Rebel flank attack to the south like at Chancellorsville. As mentioned, Longstreet had been imploring Lee in a "constant refrain" not to attack Meade's center, but to allow him to conduct flank movement around Meade's left, anchored on Little and Big Round Tops. Although "Longstreet's plan sounds like a good idea at first hearing [the] very real logistical problems made Longstreet's proposal impossible [and perhaps only leading] disaster" at Gettysburg.[166] However, despite what historians, thanks to hindsight, have long maintained, Lee now possessed a far more masterful battle plan that promised decisive results.[167]

Already on July 3, Lee had demonstrated considerable tactical flexibility by so quickly adapting to exploit a newly developed tactical opportunity—a central feature of Napoleon's winning formula. Meanwhile, Ewell's threatening presence on the north continued to work in Lee's overall tactical advantage, because he had "prevented Meade from shifting [additional] troops to meet" the upcoming assault.[168]

However, severe shortages of artillery ammunition were in the process of negating Lee's advantages. In the words of Georgia's General Ambrose R. Wright, a 36-year-old former attorney known affectionately as "Rans" (short for Ransom), from a July 7, 1863, letter to his wife, Mary Savage-Wright: "Our artillery now ceased firing, and upon inquiry, I learned they had exhausted their ammunition! And at such a time!"[169] And a shocked North Carolina artilleryman of Longstreet's corps described how "our Ordnance trains were pretty well exhausted—nearly all the Artillery ammunition was expended [and] every shot was out of the trains."[170] Worst of all, what little remained of the artillery ammunition was beyond immediate reach, because the 1st Corps's ordnance train had been removed farther rearward to escape the cannonade.[171]

Ironically, while young Rebel soldiers believed that God was on their side, they should have been praying for more competent Confederate leadership, especially in the artillery arm. Major Nathaniel Claiborne Wilson, who was acting lieutenant colonel of the 28th Virginia positioned on Garnett's left-center, realized that orders to advance were drawing near. The twenty-three-year-old, a University of Virginia graduate who had also attended VMI, placed his faith in God. The former attorney hastily penned his last diary entry: "In line of battle, expecting to move forward every minute. With our trust in God, we fear not an earthly enemy. God be with us!" Major Wilson was about to find a final resting place in a lush meadow on Pennsylvania soil under the shade of a walnut tree.[172]

Meanwhile, the veteran troopers of Stuart's cavalry made their final preparations to strike in conjunction with Pickett's Charge. In one historian's words: "For two hours that fateful afternoon [the cavalrymen in gray] all heard the thunder of artillery as Porter Alexander's guns, some four miles to the west, prepared the way for [Pickett's] charge [and therefore] Stuart attempted to move his troopers, shielded by woods, into a position where they might hit the enemy's rear."[173]

Lee's chances of pushing the Yankees off the targeted position greatly increased because of the extensive damage inflicted upon the batteries of Captain William A. Arnold, Lieutenant Alonzo Hersford Cushing, Lieutenant T. Fred Brown, and Captain James Rorty, before the arrival of replacement batteries. Quite a few guns defending the right-center were eliminated, and "the great prize [of vanquishing the Army of the Potomac was] well within [Lee's] grasp."[174] Lee had done everything possible to insure that he would not again be denied a decisive victory, because of a strange "perversity of Fate" as on July 2.[175]

Meanwhile, an equally strange fate had seemingly placed Pickett's command in a leading role. Back in May 1863, when Lee first learned that the Davis government had planned to send Pickett's division west to assist in Vicksburg's defense, he embarked on the diplomatic offensive. Upset at the possibility of losing a full division, he emphasized to the Secretary of War how he felt great "doubt [about] the policy of sending" Pickett's division far from the army. Because he had emphasized how the division's "removal from this army will be sensibly felt," Lee now relied heavily on Pickett's three brigades, after having successfully checkmated the highest-ranking officials in the Confederate government.[176] Lee hoped to deliver the decisive blow to fulfill the prayers of people across the South, including William Ross Stilwell, who had written in a recent letter: "I hope that the war will close before another winter."[177]

Chapter III

Orchestrating the War's Most Magnificent Charge

Lee calculated that his massive offensive effort would bestow a great gift, anticipating that he shortly "would find an open road before him, one he might take, surrender demand in hand, to Washington, DC".[1] He had correctly targeted the Union army's "really weak point [which] was the salient at the angle near the Clump of Trees," and had inflicted severe damage on the 2nd Corps batteries that protected this increasingly vulnerable point.[2] Once they emerged from their hidden positions, moved up Seminary Ridge's western slope, and aligned in the open fields on the eastern side of the ridge for a length of about two miles, Lee's massed infantry would then push around 1,200–1,400 yards across open ground, an advance calculated to take about 20 minutes, or about 70 yards per minute.[3]

Lee's tactical objective of disguising his target point of Meade's right-center—including by not concentrating all artillery fire on the copse of trees sector and especially by hiding his massed infantry behind Seminary Ridge—had succeeded. Meade had expected Lee to continue his previous day's main offensive effort to turn the Union army's left flank. Still haunted by Lee's hard-hitting flank attack that had suddenly exploded out of Chancellorsville's woodlands, Meade kept his mighty reserve of his veteran VI Corps massed far to the south not far from Big and Little Round Top. Meade had only lightly strengthened his center: an insufficient bolstering of the thin line.[4]

Major Walter Harrison, on Pickett's staff, realized that the "great question of [the Pennsylvania] campaign, perhaps of the whole war, was [now] hanging on the next few hours."[5] Lieutenant George Williamson Finley, 56th Virginia, lusted at the most tantalizing prospect: "if we could punch through" Meade's damaged and vulnerable right-center.[6] Captain Charles Minor Blackford, now attached to Longstreet's staff, concluded: "If success crowns our efforts . . . here it will be the beginning of the end" of the war.[7] Therefore, Lieutenant William Nathaniel Wood, Company A (Monticello Guard), 19th Virginia, was resolute, because "[t]hat hill must fall" at all costs. But instead, it was Lieutenant Wood who was about to fall near the stone wall.[8]

As another Confederate soldier penned from the promised land of Pennsylvania: "Our men feel there is no back-out [because] A defeat here would be ruinous [therefore we must] come out of this country triumphant and victorious, having established a peace" for the Southern people.[9] One of Longstreet's optimistic soldiers penned in a letter that "we will end the war [with] this campaign."[10] In a letter to his Presbyterian minister father, Abraham D. Pollock, who ironically had been born in Pennsylvania, Captain Thomas Gordon Pollock, the Adjutant and Inspector General of Kemper's brigade, had written only four days before how Lee's men were "as happy and as secure in their feeling [for winning victories] as if they were already won—simply because they have an almost fanatical confidence in their cause & their leader."[11] Colonel Eppa Hunton, a former attorney who was about to be cut down, knew that his 8th Virginia men were ready for their supreme challenge. Trained at VMI (Virginia Military Institute), Hunton realized that this massive assault was about to be propelled forward by a pent-up sense of desperation: "All seemed willing to die to achieve a victory [that would be] the crowning victory and the end of the war."[12]

However, mismanagement and dysfunctional subordinate leadership, including at the corps level, intervened so that what was about to be launched was "the weakest arrangement for battle in the history of the Army of Northern Virginia."[13] Longstreet (like his fellow corps commander Hill) had not carefully orchestrated the assault's exacting details. But to be fair to "Old Pete," he had never before managed an offensive effort on such a scale.[14] However, apathy also played a role. Longstreet later admitted how Lee "should have put an officer in charge who had more confidence in his plan."[15]

The lack of the necessary tactical care ensured "that Pettigrew's line was not a continuation of that of Pickett [to ensure that the two commands] advanced in *echelon*," once unleashed, wrote Colonel Taylor.[16] Such overall tactical blundering and leadership failures were ill-timed, because Lee was determined "to accomplish some signal result, and to end the war."[17] Meanwhile, a mood that resembled "a funeral pall" had descended upon some of Pickett's soldiers.[18]

Experienced fighting men on both sides were put on edge by the eerie silence after the cannon ceased roaring. Just northeast of the copse of trees, Sergeant Hirst, 14th Connecticut, 2nd Corps, described in a letter how "you could almost hear your heart thud in your bosom."[19] Positioned on the left of Garnett's brigade, Lieutenant George Williamson Finley watched while the "black powder smoke began to drift away from the muzzles of the guns, and it was like a curtain going up on the last act of a drama."[20]

With the surreal quiet causing anxiety, Yankees wondered if Lee would dare attack across such a wide stretch of open ground. Mary Chesnut, the South Carolina aristocrat, refused to forget an accusation from United States Senator Henry Mower Rice (of Minnesota) that the Southern people were "savages who put powder and whiskey in the soldiers' canteens to make them mad with ferocity in the fight." She proudly explained, "We do not need to be fired by drink to be brave [because] In that one thing we are Spartans"—a fact about to be demonstrated by Pickett's Charge.[21]

Many of Lee's men wore wooden canteens that had been emptied of the cool water from Pitzer's Run, while Meade's troops carried United States Army– regulation tin canteens forged by an industrialized giant: a symbolic contrast of an agrarian South battling a Northern war machine. One of Garnett's officers of the 56th Virginia wrote, "Every canteen in the regiment was empty, and every throat was parched and dry" as a bone. Another one of Pickett's officers described "Gettysburg water" as "the coldest, hardest water that ever sprung out of limestone rock." But there was now no time for soldiers to dash rearward to refill canteens at the little spring that ran down the ridge's western slope to Pitzer's Run. On one of the year's hottest days, with temperatures of near 90 degrees, however, a few fortunate 1st Virginia men utilized water from a well near the row of guns.[22]

Hundreds of young men and boys were about to earn renown as Pickett's "Spartan band." Of course, this laudatory analogy applied to the Spartans' defense of the strategic pass at Thermopylae (the Hot Gates) in 480 BC. Ominously, however, the 300 Spartans of King Leonidas's army were killed to the last man by Xerxes's invaders from across the vast Persian Empire. Some of Lee's soldiers now carried small volumes of the ancient "Greek classics," espe- cially Homer's *Iliad*, in haversacks. Symbolically, the heroics of these ancient Western warriors still inspired Lee's men.

Cemetery Ridge had gained its eerie name from the locals. Gettysburg's cemetery was located on the northern end of the ridge: another ominous por- tent, especially for superstitious Southern soldiers.[23] Some of Lee's most edu- cated men actually viewed themselves much like the ancient Greek warriors, including Achilles of the *Iliad*, providing a forgotten motivator in the assault on Cemetery Ridge. One of Lee's soldiers expressed the age-old value system of the warrior ethos in a letter to his wife: "[W]e look for nothing but victory [and] We will show the Yankees this time how we will fight."[24] "Lee's army is now the great hope of the South [and it consisted of] a terrible band of veterans," one confident Georgian gloated.[25]

At the head of about 480 38th Virginia soldiers on the left of Armistead's brigade, 34-year-old Lieutenant Colonel Powhatan Bolling Whittle, educated at the University of Virginia, personified the determination that infused Pickett's ranks. Standing at six foot, four inches when the average soldier's height was a foot less, Whittle had already lost his left arm at Malvern Hill on July 1, 1862. But with his one remaining arm, Whittle now held his ornate saber. Meanwhile, soldiers fingered crucifixes given to them by mothers, sweethearts, and sisters: sacred talismans of their spiritual faith that they hoped would save them from harm. Devout Catholics, especially the Irish, crossed themselves and nervously stroked rosaries, invoking God's mercy. Whittle, who had been wounded in the right leg at Williamsburg, was about to be shot in the right arm and left leg.[26]

Lee had done everything that he could to ensure that his men were not about to experience another Malvern Hill—hence, the massive bombardment and Stuart's cavalry striking from the rear at the most opportune moment. Indeed, this time everything was different, because the odds for success were actually now considerably stacked in Lee's favor. What was about to be decided was the future course of the American nation, culture, politics, and society, because this assault would determine the heart and soul of America. Ironically, in a tribute to Lee's stealthy preparations that masked his masterstroke, Captain Haskell wrote: "It was the opinion of many of our Generals that the Rebel will not give us battle to-day—that he had enough yesterday," on July 2.[27] Meanwhile, Lieutenant George Williamson Finley, 56th Virginia, was uneasy, lamenting how "we had wasted the whole morning" without striking a blow, allowing the opponent time for rest.[28]

Meade's Pennsylvania soldiers, especially in the targeted sector, had taken Lee's challenge very personally, because they were defending home soil. In his diary, Captain Alexander Wallace Given, 114th Pennsylvania, described the vivid dream that had prompted him to enlist, revealing a sacred revolutionary inheritance: "Genl. Washington appeared to me [and] looking me in the eye said as he raised his hand in a solemn manner, 'This country must and shall be free'."[29] One of Lee's men mocked the fact that these Yankees so revered "the father of rebellion" from Mount Vernon in Virginia.[30]

Meanwhile, Pickett's soldiers placed their faith in God and Lee's tactical skills. The four Presgraves brothers (Lieutenant John R., Privates William T. and George Washington, and Corporal James, all captured today, July 3) from the low-lying James River country, were determined to succeed at any cost. The brothers now served in Company I, which had been organized at Mount Gilead, Loudoun County, 8th Virginia, Garnett's brigade. Likewise, the four Tweedy brothers (George Dabney, Edmund, Fayette, and Smith) of Company C (the Clifton Greys), 11th Virginia, Kemper's brigade, were also ready for their greatest challenge.

This highly personalized struggle was now a holy war to save their long-suffering families back home and the fledgling people's republic. In their minds, these veterans in gray and butternut fought to preserve not only their nation-state but also their distinctive Christian civilization. They believed that they fought against the moral decay of a Northern industrialized society consisting of "the mongrel races from Europe that swelled Yankee ranks, Jacobin theories of excessive democracy and racial disorder": another reason why the esprit de corps of Lee's troops remained high, because the upcoming assault represented a climactic clash between two distinct civilizations.[31]

Because the Confederacy desperately needed divine intervention, one Southern newspaperman concluded that "a more religious war was never waged by any nation."[32] Lieutenant Benjamin Lyons Farinbolt had been born where Washington and his French allies won their October 1781 victory at Yorktown, Virginia. He now commanded Company E (Pamunkey Rifles), 53rd Virginia, Armistead's brigade. In a letter to his wife, cousin Lelia May, whom he had married in October 1860, Farinbolt often gave thanks to "our good and pious Genl. Lee."[33] On this "Beautiful" Friday, Lee felt no restrictions, because there was now literally no tomorrow for his army and nation.[34] And the only way that a great "evil," as even Lee saw it, could be destroyed was for his troops to split the Army of the Potomac in half and then systematically destroy it. To Lee's thinking, decisive victory was near because of God's will and that Stonewall Jackson's "spirit lives with us," as he confidently penned in a letter.[35]

The spirit of America's heroes and even past presidents also inspired the men of Pickett's Charge. The Carroll boys from Carroll County, Company C, 24th Virginia, Kemper's brigade, were led by Captain Martin Van Buren Shockley, who commanded other Carroll County (located in the Blue Ridge country of southwest Virginia) soldiers. In the ranks were seasoned fighting men like Privates George Washington Chappell, who was about to fall wounded, and Andrew Jackson Dalton and Francis Marion Dalton, who were brothers named after an American president and Revolutionary War hero, respectively. Most significant, such American history–inspired names of fighting men were widespread throughout Pickett's and Pettigrew's divisions. Equally symbolic, Company A (Monticello Guard), 19th Virginia, Garnett's brigade, was named in honor of the stately hilltop residence (Monticello of neoclassical architecture) of Thomas Jefferson, near Charlottesville, Virginia, the Monticello Guard of Albemarle County, Virginia.[36]

Meanwhile, two of Pickett's high-ranking officers were now prepared to march forth, despite having lost arms in previous battles. Now second in command of the 38th Virginia, Armistead's brigade, Lieutenant Colonel Powhatan Bolling Whittle, born in Mecklenburg County, Virginia, was determined to do his best that afternoon. His first name recalled Virginia's Native American heritage and the first tribe encountered by Jamestown's English settlers. Interestingly, among these Virginians, Powhatan was still a popular Old Dominion name. In the 38th Virginia, Armistead's brigade, Sergeant Powhatan B. Scruggs, Company H (Secession Guards from Pittsylvania County), who was about to be killed, and Private Powhatan J. Meakes stood in the ranks. A lawyer by training and one of 15 children, Whittle had lost his arm at Malvern Hill.[37]

Likewise, one senior officer of the 19th Virginia, Garnett's brigade, Major Charles Stephens Peyton, prepared to lead his troops forward. A 22-year-old farmer born in the Piedmont of Albemarle County, he had lost his left arm at Second Manassas the previous August. Like Lieutenant Colonel Whittle, Peyton was also about to be cut down during the great assault.[38]

Pickett's division

In one of the paradoxes of Pickett's Charge, Pickett's division was *not* considered either an elite nor crack command at this crucial moment. However, the division's most ridiculed command, Armistead's brigade, was destined to garner more laurels that afternoon than any other brigade. In a July 1863 letter to his brother, Captain John A. Herndon, a reliable company commander of Company D (Whitmell Guards), 38th Virginia, Armistead's brigade, admitted: "You know that I used to think that our brigade was not worth a cent and would not fight. . . ."[39]

Less than a year before, William Henry Cocke, 9th Virginia, Armistead's brigade, bitterly condemned: "We are in a miserable Brigade–reg't & every thing else."[40] Likewise in an April 29, 1863, letter, Private Meredith "Merit" Branch Thurman, Company C, 14th Virginia, Armstead's brigade, described how, during the recent Suffolk Campaign in southeast Virginia, "two men Run over to the yankeys from the 57th [Virginia and] a good many of our men is gone to the yankeys since the army [Longstreet's corps] is bin down hear and a good many more is talking about going."[41] In a March 1863 letter, Thurman, who was fated to die in this war, wrote of the glum mood in Pickett's division, because of the ever-growing realization that this was a rich man's war and a poor man's fight: "I think all the men is getting disheartened and it is a nough to dishearten any boddy to think how poor men has to suffer hear [in the army] and there familys suffering at home and greaving the selves to death."[42] For such reasons in early 1863, so many men—at least 60—were absent without leave in the 9th Virginia, Armistead's brigade, that a reward of $1,800 was issued for their capture.[43]

The predominant role of Pickett's division in the upcoming assault was actually symbolic within the overall context of the contours of American history. At Jamestown, Virginia, in 1619, "American democracy and American slavery first put down their roots within weeks of each other" on American soil.[44] And on July 3 in Adams County, Pennsylvania, thousands of fighting men who represented those two contradictory institutions were about to determine which institution ultimately prevailed. Symbolically, Corporal Robert (Bob) Tyler Jones, a teenager of his "Charles City company" (Company K), now served as the 53rd Virginia's color-bearer. He had enlisted at Jamestown, where English settlement in America began, on June 25, 1861. This idealistic, young man was the grandson of former President John Tyler (1841–1845).[45]

Lee also felt supremely confident because Pickett's division was his army's only fresh division. However, casualties had been unexpectedly high (more than 500 men) in the bombardment. In addition, the relative freshness of the division hid weaknesses that were not obvious at first glance. After having missed the first two days of fighting, a strange fate seemingly had now placed Pickett's division (the army's only division consisting of troops from a single state) in a vital role as essentially Lee's strategic reserve. Consequently, Pickett's division was now saddled with the mission of spearheading and guiding Lee's greatest assault. Ironically, Lee's decision to rely so heavily upon Pickett's division had only developed because the command had ingloriously brought up the army's rear on the march to Gettysburg.

Not only because of its small size and lack of combat experience, Pickett's division also had brought up the rear partly because of an overlooked factor: Lee had lost faith in Pickett. Pickett had too often placed his personal life ahead of his military duties and responsibilities. To be in the arms of his teenage lover who lived near Suffolk, Pickett had routinely departed from his command at night. Pickett's lengthy absences from his troops, his negligence of daily responsibilities, and especially his heavy drinking had reached Lee's ears. Consequently, Pickett had fallen out of Lee's good graces, which was glaringly evident by Pickett's unanswered missives to Lee's headquarters.

As the army's final ace in the hole and strategic reserve due to circumstance, Pickett's division was ready for the challenge, after its belated arrival on the field. If Lee had lost faith in Pickett, he retained full confidence in his Virginia troops, especially Pickett's old "Gamecock Brigade." Destiny itself had seemingly ordained that this Virginia command was now Lee's last fresh division, after having missed the brutal slugfest of the first two days.[46]

Pickett's division had been notably absent on the second day because of Lee's own decisions. After a grueling 22-mile march east, Pickett's troops had been within easy reach of the battlefield on the afternoon of July 2 to have supported Longstreet's assault on Meade's left. However, Lee ordered Pickett's division to rest when the command was only several miles west from Gettysburg. In overrunning the Peach Orchard and smashing through Meade's left-center on the second day, Barksdale's Mississippi brigade, Longstreet's corps, had narrowly missed delivering a decisive knockout blow primarily because of the lack of support troops. Pickett's division could have made the decisive difference if hurled forward behind Barksdale to exploit the Mississippians' significant gains. Longstreet regretted having been forced to unleash his second day's assault without Pickett's division. One Pennsylvania soldier captured at the Peach Orchard, Lieutenant Frank E. Moran, Company H, 73rd New York Volunteer Infantry, Excelsior Brigade, recalled how, when among his captors, one complaint was especially prevalent: "[T]he absence of Pickett's division was commented upon among the privates" in gray.[47]

For a variety of reasons, Pickett now possessed a chance to redeem himself. Displaying qualities that had ensured he graduated dead last in his West Point class, General Pickett had been basically put on the shelf until this key moment, because of his negligence of duties, poor performances, drinking, bouts of temper, and most recently having placed his obsessive love interest before responsibilities. Ironically, Pickett's division had been designated to spearhead and guide the assault, despite ample evidence that the long-haired general "was losing his stomach for war."[48]

Just before reaching the battlefield late on July 3, Pickett's soldiers had been encamped near sycamore-lined Marsh Creek, a fairly wide, slow-moving creek, several miles in Lee's rear west of Gettysburg. For Pickett's well-educated officers, who were schooled in the ancient classics, especially Homer's *Iliad* (the Western world's first anti-war narrative), this campaign's strange twists boded ill. Pickett's men had recently escorted free blacks, whom the army's advanced units had gathered during the push through a Pennsylvania absent of slavery's horrors. On the first day of combat, Longstreet diplomatically referred to one of the campaign's greatest horrors, reminding Pickett that the "captured contrabands had better be brought along with you for further disposition," a return to slavery.[49]

But the good fortune of Pickett's division in having been spared from the murderous combat at Chancellorsville and Gettysburg's first two days was about to be reversed. Ironically, Pickett's division had not fought as a single command with Lee's army since the summer of 1862. But paradoxically, Pickett's division, consisting of only three brigades instead of the usual five, thanks to Richmond's meddling, was now only a shadow of its former self. Pickett's division was still unproven as a single unit in combat at this time. Far below its usual strength of 8,000 men, as few as 4,700 soldiers were now available in Pickett's division.

Unfortunately, two of the division's five brigades, under Generals Montgomery D. Corse and Micah Jenkins, had been left behind to safeguard Richmond, more than 180 miles directly south of Gettysburg. To placate President Davis, who was initially against the ambitious Pennsylvania invasion, Lee had been forced to significantly weaken Pickett's division to make doubly sure that Richmond was safe just in case the Army of the Potomac failed to follow the Army of Northern Virginia north: an unrealistic strategic scenario given Lincoln's wise priority of the safety of his capital rather than the capture of Richmond—as Lee fully understood. Pickett's efforts to regain his absent brigades were in vain. Consequently, thousands of Pickett's veterans remained far away, around Richmond, when the capital of the South was under no serious threat. Even after Lee had marched north toward Pennsylvania, he was still writing back to Richmond with reassurances that the capital was safe.[50]

Because Pickett's division had been stripped of two experienced brigades and its combat capabilities were therefore dramatically reduced, Major Harrison, the division's inspector general, was incensed. He was severe in his "castigation of the War Department for denying Pickett two of his brigades prior to the Gettysburg Campaign," a significant blunder that haunted Lee on July 3.[51] Pickett "was very much fretted when [these troops] were taken from him and sent south" to never return, wrote Henry Thweatt Owen to his wife, Harriet Owen, in a March 14, 1863, letter.[52] Pickett was concerned that because these two brigades were taken from him, then "his old Brigade—and rest of his Division might go to hell." Therefore, he openly expressed his anger toward Richmond's self-serving politicians, including the president: sharp criticism not approved by the ever-diplomatic Lee.[53]

Compared to Lee's other divisions, Pickett's division possessed relatively little experience in the tactical offensive. The division had even missed two of Lee's greatest victories at Fredericksburg and then at Chancellorsville within six months, when on detached service during the Suffolk Campaign. Junior in age to his three brigade commanders (Kemper, Garnett, and Armistead), Pickett possessed relatively little combat experience, especially in leading his division in action. Longstreet was well aware of Pickett's limitations. These realizations caused him to take special care of the rambunctious Virginian in an almost father-son relationship. Longstreet always "looked after Pickett [especially] to make sure he did not go astray." Perhaps partly because he had lost his own children, Longstreet "was exceedingly fond" of Pickett, who needed such a guardian angel in high places. By July 3, Pickett's division had still to prove its mettle, despite suffering heavy losses, during the Peninsula Campaign.[54]

The Green Fields of Early Summer

Contrary to the popular conceptions about the alleged elite combat qualities of Virginians, General James Johnston Pettigrew's division, consisting of mostly North Carolina troops, was more battle-tested than Pickett's division. However, Pettigrew's division was "terribly cut up on the 1st," wrote one North Carolina survivor. Pickett's and Pettigrew's divisions were significantly weaker than they appeared on paper, but paradoxically for entirely different reasons.[55]

Pickett had just lost more than 500 men: killed and wounded in the rear of the Henry Spangler farm. In Company A (Blue Ridge Rifles), 28th Virginia, Lieutenant Clifton H. Spangler, a 24-year-old former boatman who now wished to have been once again on calm waters instead of on the verge of entering Gettysburg's raging storm, was not aware that the property he laid upon was owned by a farmer with his same last name.[56]

Most of Pickett's and Pettigrew's troops, the products of an insular, xenophobic culture of an agrarian nation, believed in the invincibility of the Southern fighting man. Lieutenant John Henry Lewis, Jr., 19th Virginia, described how Lee was "determined to strike the center of Meade's army, and . . . break through and reach the Baltimore pike, then [Meade's] head would fall in the basket."[57] Pickett's relatively fresh division was not only to spearhead and guide the assault, but also to provide new energy and vitality, thanks partly to so many VMI leaders and regimental commanders in the ranks (like Lee's artillery arm).[58]

Meanwhile, Pickett's three brigades (Kemper on the right, Garnett on the left, and Armistead in the rear) remained in position on the reverse side of Seminary Ridge. Armistead hotly protested the fact that his brigade (because of the front's narrowness at this point) had been positioned in the second line behind Garnett and Kemper. Armistead asked Major Walter Harrison, on Pickett's staff, to request permission from Longstreet to be allowed to ease his brigade to the open ground on Garnett's left, where a wide gap existed between Pickett's and Pettigrew's divisions. An irritated Longstreet, discussing strategy with Lee on the crest of the ridge, informed Harrison to tell Armistead to remain in position and that the brigade could compensate by moving forward more rapidly once the assault was unleashed.

On that hot afternoon, there was something slightly surreal about the natural beauty that lay before these young soldiers: a broad expanse of ripening fields and luxurious crops of plenty as far as the eye could see. These mostly young farm boys marveled at the sight of the luxurious crops flowing eastward. The "[w]heat is elegant," penned one South Carolina soldier in a letter.[59] He also wrote back to his family back in Pendleton, South Carolina, "The country is the most beautiful I ever beheld, and the wheat and corn crops are magnificent. . . ."[60] And one incredulous North Carolina artilleryman swallowed Southern pride in writing how the "system of Agriculture here is in a more advanced state than with us" in the South.[61] These men marveled at the cultivating skills of German farmers, after most Scotch-Irish settlers (generally less patient and skilled than ever-meticulous Teutonic agriculturalists) had moved farther west, while industrious German farmers had remained behind to improve their land to a degree seldom seen.[62] General Trimble described in a letter that "the peculiarly rough and wooded character of [Virginia] in which our army was accustomed to operate, and which in some respects was unfavorable for the maneuvers of large armies [but] it was different here."[63]

Thirteen mounted officers of Pickett's division rode down the lengthy formations. They carried orders to brigade and regimental commanders to ready their troops for the advance. Pickett rode "gracefully, with his jaunty cap raked well over on his right ear and his long auburn locks, nicely dressed, hanging almost to his shoulders." In Pickett's division, the following officers were mounted: General Kemper, who rode a muscular bay; General Garnett, mounted on a high-spirited thoroughbred "black charger" named Red Eye; Garnett's aide-de-camp and former 8th Virginia private, Lieutenant John Simkins Jones, who was about to have Garnett's less favorite mount, "a bay gelding," shot from under him in the attack; Major Charles Pickett, adjutant general of Pickett's division; Captains Edward R. Baird and Robert A. Bright and Lieutenant W. Stuart Symington, who were Pickett's aides-de-camps (Pickett only had four staff officers); Captain Thomas Gordon Pollock, who was shortly killed; Captain William T. Fry, adjutant general of Kemper's brigade, West Pointer, and a VMI graduate (Class of 1862); Lieutenant George E. Geiger, Kemper's 37-year-old aide-de-camp, about to be mortally wounded; and Colonel Eppa Hunton, who, being unable to walk, rode "a little dun gelding" owned by his orderly. Commanding the 8th Virginia, Hunton was being groomed for brigade command, if Garnett was killed. Leading these veterans, who were armed with Model 1855 rifled muskets, of the 1st Virginia, was the likewise-mounted Colonel Lewis Burwell Williams, Jr., (VMI Class of 1855), who was about to be killed.[64]

A Virginia-born lawyer and devoted husband, Captain Thomas Gordon Pollock, age 24 and a Yale graduate (Class of 1858), rode his favorite mare near the mounted General Kemper. Having a premonition (true) of not surviving the charge, Pollock had kept his finest uniform (recently purchased) packed away to remain less conspicuous during the assault.[65] Two privates, now serving as couriers, were likewise mounted: 21-year-old Robert H. Irvine, a former student who served as an aide-de-camp to General Garnett, and lean Thomas R. Friend, who was detached from the 9th Virginia to serve on Pickett's staff. These two expert equestrians now galloped across the open fields to deliver orders. Irvine and Friend were fleeter than former courier George T. Walker, of Kemper's brigade, who was a large-sized Rebel known as "Big Foot."[66]

To preserve the leadership corps, Lee's orders were for officers to go into the advance on foot.[67] Upon receiving orders to lead the way while dismounted, Williams informed Captain Bright, one of Pickett's hard-working staff officers, that he was simply too ill to advance on foot. The former VMI professor begged the younger staff officer, "Captain Bright, I wish to ride my mare up." However, Bright answered curtly, "Colonel Williams, you cannot do it. Have you not heard me give the order to your general [Kemper] to go up on foot?" But the distinguished graduate (VMI Class of 1855) was intent on going into the attack mounted to inspire his men. He pleaded, "But you will let me ride; I am sick to-day." Although knowing that he might be granting the brave colonel's final wish, Captain Bright relented, "Mount your mare and I will make an excuse for you." Consequently, Colonel Williams prepared to lead the way on his favorite horse, a prized mare named Nelly of prime age, into a charge from which he never returned.

Meanwhile, Bright was the last staff officer to deliver Pickett's final orders to a brigade commander. A former artillery officer who had resigned for health reasons before joining Pickett's staff, the captain already had a close call. An iron shell fragment had struck one of Bright's spurs, turning the multipointed rowel (attached to the heel of his boot to prod the horse into a gallop) in another direction, a fact commented on with a sense of humor by Pickett.[68]

On this day of destiny, diehard veterans were stoically resolved to do or die. One soldier penned in a letter, "If we must die, for God's sake let us die on the battlefield fighting for Old Virginia."[69] These stirring words were reminiscent of when King Leonidas had informed his armor-clad Spartan warriors at Thermopylae in 480 BC to fulfill their warrior ethos's wish for "beautiful deaths" to save Sparta.[70] Meanwhile, like a homespun minister of a small country church, a devout captain now raised a favorite hymn among Pickett's men. The hymn brought memories of homes and families so far away—additional motivational fuel that inspired the Virginians to do or die.[71]

An almost-fatalistic sense of duty to God, comrades, regiments, families, and country fueled resolve. If these young men were going to get killed on the open fields before Cemetery Ridge, then at least some personal solace came with the fact that they would die a "good death." Lieutenant Colonel Rawley White Martin, age 27, described how among his 53rd Virginia troops: "The Espirit-decorps could not have been better; and the men were in good physical condition, self-reliant, and determined [and] the general sentiment of the division [Pickett's] was that they would succeed in [capturing] their objective point. . . ."[72]

General James Johnston Pettigrew's division
Contrary to the biased writing of the Virginia School of Lost Cause romance, the troops of the four brigades of Pettigrew's division were every bit as capable

as, if not more capable than, Pickett's Virginians. Most of these men were North Carolinians of middle-class status from small farms across the western and central part of the state. Not yet 25 and a well-respected VMI graduate (Class of 1860), dark-haired Colonel James "Jimmie" Keith Marshall was mounted on his finest warhorse. The handsome Marshall now led the battle-tested brigade of four North Carolina regiments. This young man of great expectations was a member of Virginia's old family aristocracy from the western "uplands," located just east of the Blue Ridge Mountains. This highland region had been settled largely by the Scotch-Irish and other Celts (Scots and Welsh), who had led America's westward expansion toward the setting sun for generations. Appropriately, one of the North Carolina brigade's popular songs was "The Campbells Are Coming."

Marshall was proud of the fact that his great-grandfather, John Marshall, had served with distinction under Washington (a distant relative). His great-grandfather (as a teenager) had early organized western frontiersmen and Indian fighters into a volunteer company known as the Fauquier Rifles (mostly Scotch-Irish) from Fauquier County. Ironically, this company of mountaineers and yeomen farmers was commanded by Captain William Pickett. Respected for his leadership ability, this Pickett was one of Richmond-born George Edward Pickett's ancestors, who had first drifted northwest from the Tidewater in search for better lands, before returning to the James River country. Much like Marshall in regard to his Revolutionary War ancestors, George Pickett took pride in "the Fighting Picketts of Fauquier County." The young colonel's middle name honored Isham Keith, who also had served in the Fauquier Rifles commanded by Captain Pickett. The sharpshooting western rifle company eventually became part of the Culpeper militia battalion, the Culpeper minutemen. They wore hunting shirts with "Liberty or Death" written across the front and wore the tails of white-tailed deer in cocked hats, while flying a colorful banner with a coiled rattlesnake and the threatening motto "Don't Tread on Me." Marshall's frontier unit became part of the 11th Virginia, which was Colonel Daniel Morgan's elite rifle regiment of Continentals. "Jimmy," the grandson of the famed United States Supreme Chief Justice John Marshall, now hoped to reap laurels in what he viewed as a comparable struggle for liberty like in 1775–83.[73]

Colonel Marshall cantered before the lengthy ranks of his North Carolinians. Perhaps he reflected upon the fact that tomorrow was the Fourth of July—the three-year anniversary of his VMI graduation. Ironically, at VMI, the young cadet's heart was never totally devoted to military life. Therefore, after graduation, this natural scholar had taught at a private school located at Edenton amid the fertile Tidewater lands of northeast North Carolina (low-lying tobacco country) before he departed to join the volunteer company (Chowan Dixie Rebels), 1st North Carolina Infantry. Marshall that day prepared to lead his veteran North Carolina brigade—formerly commanded by General James Johnston Pettigrew, who now commanded the division—to a place where few returned.[74]

Sweltering Under a Hot July Sun

Under the bright sunshine, 11 brigades, mostly of two divisions, had been selected to advance across about 1,400 yards of open ground. According to Lee's plan, Pickett's right wing and Pettigrew's left wing were to shrink their respective fronts (a challenging tactical undertaking) in order to compact their ranks to simultaneously converge on the Angle and the clump of trees. Pettigrew's division had been recently led by unpretentious Henry "Harry" Heth (West Point Class 1847), who had suffered a head wound on the first day. More than half of the attackers of Pickett's Charge were 3rd Corps troops from Upper South and Deep South states: North Carolina, Alabama, Tennessee, Mississippi, and Florida. As if to seek vengeance for his father's wounding, Heth's son, Captain Stockton Heth, now served as Colonel "Jimmy" Marshal's aide-de-camp. (Revealing the close links between leading Virginia families, General Heth was the oldest son of Pickett's aunt, Margaret Pickett Heth.)

Pettigrew's division had been in existence for only a few weeks, having joined the army only on June 1, 1863. Now deployed on Seminary Ridge's reserve slope behind the David McMillan farm and its sheltering wood lot to the southwest—and simply because of its position on the field—Pettigrew's battle-weary division had been designated as the assault's left wing. Pettigrew was untested as the commander for this seemingly ill-fated division. Worst of all, what was Lee's largest division (nearly 8,000 soldiers at the sunrise of July 1) had been reduced to only about 4,300 men.

Not only Lee, but also Hill was not fully aware of the extent of the July 1 mauling suffered by the division during the savage combat northwest of Gettysburg. After tangling in a brutal "no quarter" fight around McPherson's Grove with tough westerners of the Iron Brigade, who wore tall, black Hardee hats ("a badge of honor"), the division was in bad shape. During the attack to push the bluecoat westerners off McPherson's Ridge, Pettigrew's 26th North Carolina lost more than 70 percent of its manpower. Consequently, thanks largely to the combat prowess of the Iron Brigade, which included a young drummer boy whose drum sticks were from a British drummer who had been killed in America's struggle for liberty, unlike Pickett's division, the division had lost some confidence. Nevertheless, despite its decimation, Pettigrew's division was now still larger than Pickett's division. But the overall morale of Pettigrew's division had improved by engaging in no combat on July 2. Though its soldiers were Lee's most rested, Pickett's division (consisting of three brigades, versus Pettigrew's four brigades) was now one of the army's smallest divisions, but was saddled with the largest responsibilities.

An attorney from Charleston, South Carolina, who had served as the chief military adviser of the South Carolina governor during the firing on Fort Sumter, James Johnston Pettigrew was no ordinary division commander. Personifying a rare blend of scholar and man of action, Pettigrew was a respected man of letters. He also was a romantic idealist, with a penchant for republican and lost causes. He had volunteered to fight for Cuban rebels against monarchical Spain and in northern Italy against the Austrians. Renowned scholarly qualities caused Pettigrew to be seen unfavorably by some followers. "He appears to hold himself too much aloof from everybody," in the words of the more personable Colonel Henry K. "Harry" Burgwyn, Jr., who had been a VMI cadet at the same time as "Jimmy" Marshall. Age 21, Burgwyn now lay in a freshly dug grave under a walnut tree near the turnpike leading to Gettysburg, after having been cut down on July 1 while "bearing our colors" in leading the way.

An avid student of the art of war who had studied Napoleon's battle-fields in person, Pettigrew was also ambitious. A child prodigy, he was the son of a leading Tyrrell County, North Carolina, family, and a distinguished University of North Carolina graduate (Class of 1847) at Chapel Hill, North Carolina. Pettigrew was now the leading literary figure in Lee's army. His well-received book, *Notes on Spain and the Spaniards in the Summer of 1859*, was published in Charleston (1861). A Renaissance man, Pettigrew possessed a law certificate from the prestigious University of Berlin in Germany. The handsome Pettigrew was fluent in half a dozen languages, including Latin, Hebrew, Arabic, and Greek. His 35th birthday was the following day (July 4), if he survived to see the next sunrise. Pettigrew believed that the Yankees were more like "the English and North Germans" than Southerners, who were more like Mediterranean types.[75]

Pettigrew early on feared the horrors of total war. He had informed his brother, "This is no ordinary war [because] It is a war of peoples not of soldiers."[76] Pettigrew had long believed that the only possibility for decisive success was for an immediate northern invasion that "would have carried us through Washington [DC] to the centre of the North & brought an early and favorable peace."[77]

As he had recently written to North Carolina's Governor Zeb Vance, an excessively states' rights–minded politician, Pettigrew emphasized that "we need every man with the colors, if a peace is to be conquered this summer."[78] The "most educated of all Confederate generals," Pettigrew was not to survive this ill-fated campaign north of the Potomac.[79] The gifted Pettigrew proudly commanded his hard-fighting "Old North State" men. As Hood's Texas soldiers were inspired by the Alamo and San Jacinto during their own revolution, these North Carolinians were highly motivated because their "forefathers had fought the British at King's Mountain [where a Tory command was swiftly vanquished in October 1780] and Guilford Court House" (in mid-March 1781), which led the way to the final showdown at Yorktown, Virginia.[80] A boyhood companion from the family's Tidewater plantation, a black servant named Peter, had journeyed to Gettysburg with Pettigrew.[81]

Like Pickett, the 34-year-old Pettigrew, who wore a stylish goatee, relied on capable subordinate commanders. Forty-one-year-old Colonel Birkett Davenport Fry was one such fine leader. A member of VMI Class of 1843, Fry never graduated (leaving in early June 1841); he later did the same at West Point, which he departed in 1842. Clearly, Fry's adventuresome nature was not suited for years of studious routine. After General Archer's capture on July 1, Fry commanded the Tennessee and Alabama brigade of about 400 veterans. This command had suffered high losses during the terrible bloodletting at Chancellorsville. Then, Fry's brigade had taken a beating from a vicious flank fire unleashed from the Iron Brigade (Wisconsin, Indiana, and Michigan troops) that caused the hard-hit command to break on July 1.

A veteran of Scott's westward march on Mexico City, Fry's brigade occupied Pettigrew's far right, which was located nearest to the left flank of the companion division commanded by his former West Point classmate Pickett. Fry and Pickett had early risked their military careers by defying West Point's rules. They had slipped off academy grounds to clandestinely visit Benjamin "Benny" J. Haven's notorious tavern, a two-story wooden structure situated on a steep hillside in nearby Highland Falls, New York. There, they enjoyed an alcohol-induced night of merriment. While Pickett graduated last in the Class of 1846, Fry failed to graduate.

Despite his youth, James Keith Marshall was the brightest star among this constellation of Pettigrew's commanders. The handsome colonel now led Pettigrew's "Old North State" brigade of four regiments, after Pettigrew took divisional command. "Jimmie" Marshall was now the youngest of Pettigrew's brigade commanders at 24. In fact, he was the youngest brigade commander of all front line attackers that afternoon. The excessively modest Marshall had instilled "discipline and yet command[ed] the affections" of his men. A distant relative of not only George Washington, but also Thomas Jefferson, George Edward Pickett, and Lee himself, Marshall's upcoming death would bring tears to the eyes of even the most hardened veterans.[82]

North of Pickett's division

When Lee received his first close-up view of Pettigrew's men during a brief inspection before the attack, he was shocked. Not privy to the first day's fighting, Lee was not aware that Pettigrew's troops had taken a severe beating. Therefore, when he rode by Pettigrew's four brigades, he was "visibly shaken." Hill had failed to either report or badly understated his devastating July 1 losses. Pettigrew's ranks were now reduced by around 40 percent, to about 4,600 men. Walking wounded (with blood-stained bandages around their heads, arms, and hands) now stood stoically in line. Lee remarked with rarely shown emotion, "I miss in this [Pettigrew] brigade the faces of many dear friends." A shaken Lee commented, "Many of these poor boys should go to the rear; they are not able for duty."[83]

Understandably, many survivors were in relatively low spirits after the severe losses of July 1. However, positioned in the shelter of David McMillan's Woods, Pettigrew's division suffered less in the artillery bombardment than Pickett's division, which partly compensated for the shock of the first day's bloodletting. The toughness of these North Carolina boys had earned them the sobriquet of "pine knots." These soldiers were then motivated by Colonel Burgwyn's "memory [which] will be cherished [forever] in the hearts of the men who have followed him," wrote one soldier.[84]

Colonel Marshall's North Carolina brigade, containing companies like the Pee Dee Wild Cats from South Carolina's Pee Dee River country (the uncharted Revolutionary War haunts of Francis Marion, "the Swamp Fox"), held "the post of honor" in Pettigrew's front ranks. Marshall's brigade was situated between General Joseph Robert Davis's Mississippi and North Carolina brigade on the left and Fry's Tennessee and Alabama brigade on the division's right flank.

When Fry first learned that Pettigrew's division was to attack in conjunction with Pickett's division, he rode to Pickett's headquarters. An upbeat Pickett emphasized how the massive artillery bombardment would enable the infantry assault to "drive" the Yankees off Cemetery Ridge. Then, Fry and Pickett talked of their youthful days in Mexico, especially the assault on Chapultepec. Now at age 42, Fry was as tough as nails. He could be counted upon to be responsible of eventually linking his brigade to Pickett's left (Garnett's brigade). Hit by iron shell fragments in his shoulder, Fry suffered his fourth wound of the war. But he refused to relinquish command. He hailed from Kanawha County's mountains in today's West Virginia. And unlike Pickett, Fry possessed a solid VMI education.

After leaving an attorney position in San Francisco, California, and a wife, Martha (after only two years of marriage), he had joined William Walker, after the audacious Tennessean captured Granada, Nicaragua. Walker presented Fry with a colonel's commission. Fry then served as a top lieutenant of America's most famous filibuster. Fry first commanded the 13th Alabama, now positioned on the brigade's right-center. He was a worthy successor as brigade commander to diminutive General James Jay Archer. On July 1, the Maryland-born Archer had been tackled and then captured by a strapping Irishman named Maloney, Lee's first general to suffer such an ignominious fate. A hero of Chapultepec, General Archer was fated for a prison death. Three of Heth's four brigades were now led by new commanders, replacements for experienced leaders lost in Gettysburg's grim harvest. Colonel Taylor lamented this key miscalculation: "They were terribly mistaken about Heth's division in the planning [because] It had not recovered, having suffered more than was reported on the first day."[85]

Consequently, the overall assault was far weaker on the left than planned by Lee. But these men were tough veterans of numerous campaigns, despite the fact that many soldiers were only boys. The Civil War was "The Boys' War," with an estimated 250,000–420,000 boys serving on both sides. The average age in Lee's army was only 19. Therefore, Pickett's Charge was equally what might be described as the boys' charge of the Civil War.[86] Private John Caldwell, of Burke County, North Carolina, served in Company E, 33rd North Carolina. He was in the second line (behind Marshall's brigade) on the left flank of General James Henry Lane's North Carolina brigade, which was positioned behind Marshall's brigade. Caldwell was "a mere boy [who] had been with us but a short time," before he received his death stroke "within forty yards" of Cemetery Ridge's crest.[87] Captain William Watts Parker's "Richmond Battery,"

Alexander's Battalion, now consisted of "teen-agers ranging from fourteen to seventeen years of age."[88]

As Lee hoped, an unbreakable fighting spirit compensated for recent losses. As one Confederate officer had penned to his wife, Lee's army "thinks it can whip its weight in wild cats."[89] Another Rebel soldier swore that Pennsylvania's invaders "will make Yankeedom howl."[90] To support Pettigrew's frontline troops to compensate for the sad attrition, Lee assigned two North Carolina brigades of Major General Dorsey Pender's division, 3rd Corps: Lane's brigade and General Alfred Moore Scales's brigade (from north to south) to the second line behind Pettigrew's right. Colonel William Lee J. Lowrance, a former schoolteacher in his late twenties, now commanded Scales's brigade, after General Scales went down with a leg wound on July 1. Consisting of about 1,700 men, these two excellent North Carolina brigades (each made up of five regiments) had been part of Hill's hard-hitting "Light Division."

Riding his favorite mare, Jinny, and like a teenager itching for a fight, although age 61, Isaac Ridgeway Trimble led the brigades of Pender's division. A West Point graduate, Trimble took charge of the division only a couple of hours before the assault. He had taken the place of General Pender, age 29, who had fallen, mortally wounded on the previous day, dying on July 18 after his leg's amputation.[91] Seemingly ill-fated in part because these veteran North Carolinians had unleashed the fatal volley that dropped Stonewall Jackson in May, Lane's brigade had been decimated at Chancellorsville. "Little Jim" Lane was a Virginian (a graduate of both VMI and University of Virginia). Nevertheless, despite being better known as a mathematical professor whiz at VMI rather than for military achievements, Lane now led the brigade consisting of 7th, 18th, 28th, 33rd, and 37th North Carolina, which was in better shape than Scales's brigade. Scales's command had been "torn apart" in losing at least 900 of about 1,400 on the first day.[92]

Timely Support

Lee ordered that Pickett's division was to be supported on the south by other 3rd Corps troops. But it was left to Longstreet and Hill to orchestrate that support. Lee had ordered General Richard H. Anderson's large division of five brigades (about 8,000 veterans) and Colonel David Lang's brigade, including the army's only three Florida regiments, to advance to support the flanks, especially Pickett's right. Lee had planned for these four brigades to exploit the frontline troops' breakthrough. However, only two brigades were to advance on the south to protect Pickett's right flank. These troops were to widen the breach opened in Meade's right-center.[93]

Meanwhile, after Colonel Alexander—who correctly worried of precious time slipping away—complained how the "formation of our infantry lines consumed a long time," Lee's veterans continued to wait in their assigned positions. Meanwhile, Sergeant John W. Mosely—a former Marion, Alabama, merchant of the Marion Light Infantry (Company G of Marion), which was first organized by Captain Harry Mosely, 4th Alabama Infantry, Hood's division—knew that he was about to die. After having been hit in the assault on Little Round Top, Sergeant Mosely penned a last, pathetic letter to his "Dear Mother" back in Alabama. The 24-year-old bachelor was still confident of victory on July 3: "I am here a prisoner of war and mortally wounded. I can live but a few hours more at farthest. . . . I have no doubt of the final result [of the Battle of Gettysburg], and I hope I may live long enough to hear the shouts of victory before I die."[94]

Clearly, the next round of fighting at Gettysburg "will determine the fate of Baltimore & Washington," penned one worried Unionist in his diary.[95] Pickett's Charge was about to be unleashed to fulfill Private Mosely's last wish, before he died on July 5.[96] Almost like a final prayer offered for the salvation of his dying republic trapped in an inescapable war of attrition, Lee was heard to mutter to himself, "The attack must succeed."[97]

At one point, Longstreet walked his horse calmly before the lines as "if he was on a Sunday picnic," in one soldier's words. They feared that Longstreet would be killed while "rifle balls [from snipers] whistled past his head" and ignored the impertinent cry of "You'll get your fool head knocked off!" One of Garnett's men caught the pervasive fighting spirit, when he yelled to "Old Pete": "We'll fight without you leading us!"[98] Galloping along the line, the handsome General Garnett had so animatedly inspired his men under the shelling that he had to be persuaded to save his heroics for when the attack began.[99] Sergeant Randolph Abbott Shotwell, 8th Virginia, Garnett's brigade, emphasized how the Virginia soldiers "saw nothing of the 'rashness,' 'blind folly,' or 'uselessness' of the upcoming offensive effort, but on the contrary were in splendid spirits and confident of sweeping everything before them."[100]

Lee decided not to utilize the magic of his personal leadership to inspire his troops in their supreme offensive effort. However, one secret of Napoleon's success was leading by personal example, especially early in his career. Napoleon led the initial phase of the Imperial Guard's assault in the final bid to smash through Wellington's center at Waterloo. Lee was so confident in what his men could achieve that he felt no need to similarly inspire his troops during the advance's initial stages.[101]

Symbolically, before being fatally cut down, 21-year-old Colonel Burgwyn had been fully convinced that Lee's veterans "compare favorably with those of the [ancient] Romans or of Napoleon's Old Guard."[102] However, a North Carolinian soldier about to advance interpreted Waterloo's lessons differently: "I had read of the 'old guard' at Waterloo in its hopeless attempt to dislodge the enemy, and felt that this was equally as hopeless."[103]

Especially after having viewed Pettigrew's battered ranks, Lee placed even more faith in Pickett's division in spearheading the assault. However, the Virginians had taken a severe pounding during the lengthy bombardment, both physically and psychologically—a tradeoff that balanced out the overall equation in terms of capabilities. Perhaps the only advantage possessed by Pettigrew's men was that they now possessed better shoes than Pickett's troops, having recently stripped footwear off Yankee dead.

Pickett's division allegedly possessed a "cosmopolitan makeup," but this has been an exaggeration. The division's broad socioeconomic diversity was perhaps its most unique quality, consisting of "an admixture of farm boys from the Piedmont, clerks from the Richmond offices, tidewater fishermen, rough men who found zest in daring irrespective of the cause they were fighting for. . . ."[104]

Lee knew that he could rely on Pickett's highly qualified brigade commanders: West Pointers and Mexican War veterans Richard Brooke Garnett, James Kemper, and Lewis Addison Armistead. Organized in time for the first major battle at First Manassas on July 21, 1863, Garnett's brigade (Pickett's own command) consisted of the 19th Virginia, which had been recruited in Albemarle County; the 18th Virginia, raised in Pittsylvania County; the 28th Virginia, from Roanoke County; and the 8th Virginia, which had been recruited in Loudon County. The 56th Virginia was added to the brigade in time for the 1862 Peninsula Campaign. Pickett had led these troops in the attack at Gaines's Mill, where he was wounded in the shoulder. Pickett, although not senior in rank among his brigade commanders, thanks to Longstreet's blatant favoritism, was promoted to division commander and then to major general, after the Maryland Campaign. Garnett had then taken charge of this brigade of five Virginia regiments. Thanks to his close relationship with Longstreet and omnipresent Virginia politics, Pickett had been promoted beyond his abilities and experience level.[105] Unlike most other divisions, Pickett's division (in its present composition) had first served together as a unit barely six months before at Fredericksburg, but only in a reserve role. Therefore, as fate would have it, July 3 was the first time Pickett's regiments were about to take the offensive together as a division.[106]

Meanwhile, along the 2nd Corps's front around the copse of trees with the cessation of artillery fire, while clouds of sulfurous smoke drifted higher into a luminous blue sky, Captain Haskell wrote, "There was a pause between the acts, with the curtain down, soon to rise upon the great final act, and catastrophe of Gettysburg."[107] Sergeant Hirst, of German descent, and his veteran "Rockville boys" felt a creeping dread, because of the "terrible stillness."[108]

Black Confederates

With Company D, 14th Connecticut, Hays's 3rd Division, 2nd Corps, just north of the Angle, Sergeant Hirst was soon to see the almost unbelievable sight of the 14th Tennessee's color-bearer of the so-called Tennessee brigade, under Colonel Fry, on Pettigrew's far right. This diehard Rebel was a black color corporal named George B. Powell. He was destined to fall in the upcoming attack like another African American fighting man of the 14th Tennessee, "Boney" Smith. Smith's lanky, tall frame had bestowed his nickname.[109] Before the 18th Virginia, on Garnett's right-center, a black drummer named Austin Dix, who had enlisted on April 23, 1861, stood beside his white comrades.[110] Dix only continued the tradition of Andrew Ferguson, an African American teenager from Virginia who fought at the battle of Kings Mountain, South Carolina, on October 7, 1781, during a major turning point of the American Revolution.[111]

Black Confederates participating in the Civil War's most famous charge revealed the overlooked complexities of the Southern experience. When the black troops of the 54th Massachusetts Volunteer Infantry assaulted Fort Wagner, South Carolina, they faced another black Confederate soldier: an African American from a free black family of "model Confederates," Private John Wilson Buckner, 1st South Carolina Artillery. Hailing from the rolling hills of the South Carolina Piedmont (where the battle of Kings Mountain was fought), this "faithful soldier" of African descent, age 33, fell wounded in Fort Wagner's defense on July 12, less than 10 days after the battle of Gettysburg.[112]

Color Corporal George B. Powell was a member of today's most forgotten sizeable body of white troops of Pickett's Charge: middle-Tennessee soldiers of the Tennessee brigade, which was officially organized in March 1862. Three brigades of Pettigrew's division were positioned on the Tennesseans' left (Marshall, Davis, and Colonel John Mercer Brockenbrough, from south to north, respectively). This western brigade was to serve as "the guiding brigade of [Pettigrew's] assaulting column." In consequence and unlike Pickett's men, especially Kemper's brigade on the far south, Colonel Fry and his brigade members only had to keep their eyes focused in order to march mostly straight, east toward Meade's right-center.

The Volunteer State soldiers' baptismal fire came during the Peninsula Campaign, during which the Tennessee boys suffered high losses. These three Tennessee regiments—the 1st, 7th, and 14th Tennessee—were reliable. Student militia companies (predominately Scotch-Irish) of the Presbyterian Cumberland University, Lebanon, Wilson County, Tennessee, served as a nucleus of Companies H and K, 7th Tennessee. Lieutenant Mitchell A. Anderson, 7th Tennessee, the son of the University's reverend-president, was about to be killed. This fine regiment contained six companies from Wilson County. However, Fry's so-called Tennessee brigade also included the 13th Alabama Infantry and the diminutive 5th Alabama Battalion. The 13th Alabama consisted of 308 men (more than 50 percent became casualties in the upcoming assault) from Macon, Randolph, Wilcox, Montgomery, Elmore, and Butler counties, along with three counties distinguished by Creek names: Talladega, Coosa, and Tallapoosa.

The 7th Tennessee, which included veteran companies like the Hurricane Rifles (Company G), was composed of men mostly from four north-central Tennessee counties. Meanwhile, the 14th Tennessee, which had its own glee club, was composed of soldiers from primarily three counties: Montgomery, Stewart, and Robertson. The 1st Tennessee's ranks were most heavily represented by south-central Tennessee. These seasoned fighting men were ready to exploit gains achieved by "the fiercest cannonading known to warfare," in the words of dark-haired Captain Jacob B. Turney, Company K, 1st Tennessee. The full-bearded Turney was about to be cut down and captured, before the sun dropped over the Cumberland Mountains.[113]

Colonel Birkett Davenport Fry, who had been part of the California gold rush, commanded this spunky brigade with his usual competence. He was the former colonel of the seasoned 13th Alabama, which included resilient companies like the Tallassee Guards (Company F), which had been organized in Montgomery, Alabama (the Confederacy's first capital), in mid-July 1861.

Despite the right shoulder of his gray uniform being bloodied, which failed to diminish his fighting spirit, as if still serving under the irrepressible Walker in Central America, Fry gamely prepared to lead his troops forward.[114]

Meanwhile, the confident men of Pickett's Charge could almost envision themselves marching triumphantly down Pennsylvania Avenue in a grand victory parade with battle flags flying. These soldiers conveniently ignored the ugly reality that details now busily buried their comrades, especially of Pettigrew's division. In their view, these young men had died on the "foreign" soil of a "foreign nation" in this "rich part of Pennsylvania, where the oversized barns are finer than the houses."[115] As if the war was a thousand miles away, one North Carolina soldier marveled how "the wheat crop here is now ready to harvest," but a far greater harvest was about to be reaped in Adams County.[116] The bright sunshine and scenic setting masked dark realities: Lee's new three-corps organization structure and those leading those corps—Longstreet, Ewell, and Hill—had failed to rise to previous offensive challenges at Gettysburg.[117]

Symbolically, like the continued existence of his agrarian nation, if decisive victory was not achieved that afternoon, so Lee's life was even now slowly ebbing away. The privileged life of an aristocratic eighteenth-century Virginia gentleman and cavalier, including that of those who had governed the American nation since its birth, was fading away like the recent Pennsylvania spring (the war's third). Lee's time was passing in more ways than one. He had recently "contracted a severe sore throat, that resulted in rheumatic inflammation of the sac inclosing the heart."[118]

Arguably, one of Lee's tactical mistakes was not launching his attack in column, instead using linear formations in two wings over an overextended line that involved complex maneuvers to reach Meade's right-center. Attacking in column would literally have created a battering ram from the beginning of the assault. Instead, he employed this tactic at the end, to smash through Meade's line after sizeable losses had been incurred—a risky tactical undertaking while under fire.[119] The incomparable Marshal Michel Ney, Napoleon's most never-say-die top lieutenant, emphasized that "columns form the essential part of tactics."[120]

However, the offensive effort (a column of horsemen) from the opposite direction suffered from no comparable tactical handicaps. Lee now had his most clever tactical trick up his sleeve—not found in the military manuals or taught at military academies: Stuart's cavalry (four brigades) striking from the west to "hit the enemy's rear" when the defenders faced Pickett's Charge in front.[121] In the words of historian Thom Hatch with regard to Lee's brilliant plan: "The tactic had been brilliantly designed by Robert E. Lee as a coordinated effort with a detachment of Confederate cavalry that would simultaneously strike the Union rear from another direction and cause havoc along the lines. If this collaborative plan was successful, Pickett and his mile-wide line would smash through the blue-clad front to rout the Yankees and place the future of the Army of the Potomac and the Union itself in dire jeopardy."[122]

So far, Lee had demonstrated considerable tactical innovativeness and resourcefulness to a degree previously unseen. By relying on Stuart, he was not guilty of allowing the reluctant Longstreet to exclusively make all arrangements for the assault, increasing his chances for success. Lee also personally chose two of Hill's brigades to reinforce the assault and gave Longstreet permission to utilize the rest of Hill's 3rd Corps if necessary.[123] However, as seen by an appalled Colonel Alexander, Hill and Ewell were now "entirely unprepared to render aid" to the assault.[124]

Chapter IV

A Carefully Calculated Case of Going for Broke

Under the bright July sunshine, while temperatures steadily rose on the cloud-less day, an anomaly mocked the loftiest Confederate ambitions. For one last time, Lee and Longstreet rode together along the lines (an apparent harmony that masked their deep tactical and personal discord) to make sure "that every-thing was arranged" as the commander desired.[1] On an afternoon when every-thing was at stake, Lee represented the greatest "Hope of His Country," in one Irishman's words, while Pickett's Charge represented the final best hope of the beleaguered Confederate nation.[2] Therefore, as penned by one Rebel officer in a letter, the belief was pervasive that "[i]f General Lee can carry out what I believe are his designs he will achieve the greatest victory of the war."[3] Another soldier was so confident that he had already informed his wife that he would "be sure to write [when] we go to Washington or Baltimore."[4]

Lee was finally ready to deliver his massive blow from a formidable line that spanned nearly two miles. However, Lee had no idea that Longstreet had failed in properly organizing his assault and communicating the exact require-ments with infantry and artillery commanders, especially those of other corps (including flying artillery to protect the flanks of the assault). Longstreet was also in over his head, when close inter-corps coordination and understanding was required. As planned by Lee, the opportunity to reap a decisive victory existed as never before: the massive bombardment had succeeded in damaging and eliminating more than 30 guns on Meade's right-center, providing an even greater advantage before these Union guns could be replaced.

Lee counted on his finest soldiers from a nation that had been transformed into a warrior society, after having mobilized on a scale never seen before in American history. More than 1.3 million Southerners served (94,000 gave their lives) during the war, and the upcoming assault symbolized this massive trans-formation of Southern society. Since war was indeed only a continuation of pol-itics (as famously emphasized by Carl P. G. von Clausewitz), Pickett's Charge symbolized the omnipresent quest for a decisive political victory calculated to save the infant Confederate nation's life.

These soldiers stoically ignored the required inevitable sacrifice ordained by the god of war, just as the ancient Greeks and Romans had believed. Like pawns, they were caught up in a never-ending human activity that had given more important meaning to their lives: deep feelings elevated to new heights on the afternoon of July 3. The god of war, Mars, now demanded a frightfully high price as since time immemorial, causing one of Lee's men to write, "We can't fight many more years longer [because] The men will all be dead." Therefore, hoping to achieve a decisive victory before it was too late, these Southern soldiers were now playing their parts on the most dramatic stage during Gettysburg's climactic showdown. As Homer had believed, the god's capriciousness was the timeless force that also fueled the South's most desperate bid to win it all.[5]

Lee's soldiers understood that the close bounds of comradeship—and not Mars—was really the true motivating force that would propel their charge all the way to Cemetery Ridge. As these veterans intimately realized, all of this seemingly endless combat "with its ecstasy of destruction, its constant temptation of self-sacrifice, its evil bliss, is more about comradeship" than anything else.[6]

The fact that Ewell's attacks on the north had failed to coincide with Pickett's Charge, as envisioned by Lee, now served as no deterrent. Lee was correct in his tactical calculations because Ewell's menacing presence had ensured that Meade dispatched no sizeable reinforcements south to bolster his thinly held right-center. Therefore, when the foremost Rebels peered across the three-quarters of a mile of open terrain, covered by fields of green and gold, toward Cemetery Ridge, they saw much more than another enemy position. What Lee and his men now viewed was something that was as intoxicating as it was grandiose: "[T]he spires of Baltimore and the dome of the National Capitol were foremost upon their glad vision."[7]

In one Confederate officer's words, they knew "that on them possibly hung the success of their cause: the peace and independence of the Confederacy [and realized] that victory meant . . . to us uninvaded and peaceful under our own rule and under our own nationality. . . . With this end in view, all felt that victory was to be won at any cost. All were willing to die, if only their country could thereby triumph."[8]

Feeling almost as young as when he had carried the United States flag to the top of Chapultepec's heights more than 15 years before, Pickett remained an enigma. However, he was anything but the one-dimensional, showy simpleton, according to the popular stereotype promoted by generations of novelists and historians since. In fact, "this grand little man," in one Texan's words, was a much more complex and contradictory individual than commonly portrayed, transcending the popular image much like the great charge itself.[9]

One modern historian has recently speculated that Pickett's confidence was now nothing more than a cynical and calculated "pose."[10] But Colonel Birkett Davenport Fry described how "Pickett [was] in excellent spirits, and, after . . . a pleasant reference to our having been together in work of that kind at Chapultipec, expressed great confidence in the ability of our troops to drive the enemy" off Cemetery Ridge "after they had been 'demoralized by our artillery'."[11]

Pickett was "sanguine for success," as recorded by many observers. After having felt personally insulted by his recent assignment in bringing up the army's rear, Pickett was determined to redeem his sullied reputation and that of his men.[12]

Pickett Rises to the Challenge

Eager to finally receive orders to go forward after so much wasted time, Pickett galloped over to the 1st Corps's commander. He jauntily approached Longstreet, who was sitting on a rail fence while attempting to observe the bombardment's results through his binoculars. The two old friends who had performed heroically side by side during the attack on Chapultepec's heights were once again together on another scorching day before a great attack. To fulfill the all-important "concert of action," including that the artillery "was pushed forward as the infantry progressed," Longstreet was not doing near enough to achieve that result, however.[13] He had not bolstered the assault line to either protect or extend the front beyond Pettigrew's left and Pickett's right, ensuring the lack of much-needed support on the assault's flanks. Nor was there a second line of troops behind Pickett's division (Kemper's was only a makeshift, temporary second line) because of the absence of a strategic reserve: almost certainly the reason that Lee developed the plan for Stuart to strike in Meade's rear.[14]

In so strongly disagreeing with Lee's plan, Longstreet recalled Malvern Hill's slaughter, and might have had flashbacks of the attack just outside the gates of Mexico City, when he nearly lost his life in carrying the regimental colors.[15] He thought much like one of Pickett's disillusioned staff members, who believed that the attackers were like the unfortunate "condemned, in going to execution. . . ."[16]

After dismounting from his warhorse, Pickett walked over to Longstreet and handed him Alexander's first hastily scribbled note about 2:30 a.m.: "If you are to advance at all, you must come at once or we will not be able to support you as we ought . . ."[17] Longstreet quickly read the note, but said nothing. Although Longstreet still enjoyed the lofty standing as Lee's "Old War Horse," he was no longer that same aggressive warrior. Behind his back, soldiers mocked him as "Peter the Slow." Life's tragedies and personal losses, especially his children's deaths, had sapped his old fighting spirit—much like one of Napoleon's top lieutenants, Pierre Augereau, after he lost his wife. Instead of vigorously making final preparations to ensure the success of the assault, an apathetic Longstreet had been "as quiet as an old farmer." To be sure, he made contributions, but they were insufficient. Meanwhile, Pickett was chomping at the bit. He had already dispatched couriers three times to Colonel Alexander with the question: "Is it time to charge?" But now he directly asked Longstreet, "General, shall I advance?" The glum Georgian silently nodded his mute order. Pickett then said, "I am going forward, sir," and smartly saluted.[18]

But Pickett had no idea that his old friend had not made sure that all the troops of General Richard H. Anderson's division, 3rd Corps, and perhaps remaining units of Rodes's division, 2nd Corps, were ready to move forward in close support of the assault, especially to protect the flanks, as Lee envisioned. Such was not the case.[19]

Pickett was unknowingly about to embark upon a course that forever altered the Southern nation's future. Pickett was about to discover what cruel twists of fate that this murderous war had in store for him.[20]

Like Lee's own, Pickett was now fortunate to have the reliable services of a small, but capable, staff, a dangerous job that recently "got [the] nose shot off" of one unlucky staff officer in Longstreet's division. Lieutenant W. Stuart Symington was one of his promising staff officers. He was first cousin by marriage to Pickett. Captains Edward "Ned" R. Baird and Robert A. Bright, from Williamsburg, Virginia, also served as staff officers who Pickett now called together. These aides (mocked as "glorified couriers" by contemptuous privates) in fancy gray uniforms played key roles that afternoon. The Tidewater general's only brother, Major Charles Pickett, age 23, served as another staff officer. Major R. Taylor Scott, brigade quartermaster and aide-de-camp, was another one of Pickett's most esteemed staff officers. Scott was married to doe-eyed Fanny Carter Scott, who faithfully awaited the handsome captain's safe return to her Loudoun County, Virginia, home on the Blue Ridge's east side, "Glen Welby." Fanny was worried about the welfare of not only her husband, but also her brother, Captain Edward Carter, a Virginia Military Institute–educated officer of Company K (organized in Fauquier County), 8th Virginia, who was about to fall with serious wounds in both legs.[21]

In a tortured July 6 note that she hastily dispatched to Lee's army, Fanny asked in desperation, "Where are you, my dear husband [and] what are you doing and what is going on? . . . we are all anxious to hear more [and] I live hourly in dread of a battle . . . . Is Edward safe?"[22] Such intense anxiety among the folks on the home front—Burke County, North Carolina, in this case—had caused young "Johnny" Caldwell, 33rd North Carolina, Lane's brigade, to pen a letter to his father, Todd Robinson Caldwell, "Don't be uneasy about me": his last letter home before he was killed in the upcoming charge.[23]

A comparable devotion was shared between a father-son fighting team of Company C (the Craig Mountain Boys), 28th Virginia, Garnett's brigade, of the Spessard clan of southwest Virginia's mountains: Captain Michael Peters Spessard, age 41, and his son, Private Hezekiah C. Spessard. Appropriately, because father and son were holy warriors, Hezekiah was a biblical name that honored the 13th King of Judah (House of David). But the love between them was as strong as that between Moses and his sons Gershom and Eliezer. Captain Spessard was even more solicitous over his son's welfare because Hezekiah had only recently enlisted: the young man had signed up on January 16, 1863 at Guinea Station, Virginia, north of Richmond. A homespun product of the blue-hazed mountains that he loved, the son's enlistment at this remote place was ominous, because Stonewall Jackson had died of his Chancellorsville wounds at Guinea Station, located just south of Fredericksburg, on May 10, 1863.[24]

After staff officers relayed their orders to Pickett's anxious brigade commanders, the troops of Pickett's 15 Virginia regiments of about 5,800 troops (but perhaps as many as 6,260 according to some estimates) finally moved out from the reverse slope of Seminary Ridge. With muskets on right shoulders, they then pushed through the thick woodlands. Here, while marching up the slope that gently rose toward the crest, the shade felt refreshing cool compared to the blistering heat beyond the tall trees. Then, with disciplined precision, as if on a drill field in Richmond, the Old Dominion troops aligned at the edge of the broad expanse of open fields just beyond the crest of Seminary Ridge, while sunshine glistened off lengthy rows of muskets. Because of the front's narrowness on the right wing, two of Pickett's brigades were assigned to the front rank, while the third brigade (Armistead) was to follow close behind in a second line. Therefore, Garnett's brigade was positioned on the division's left, while Kemper's brigade, the largest of Pickett's units, was on the right. Armistead's brigade was ordered to follow behind the front two brigades once the assault began. Veterans of companies like the Black Eagle Rifles, Valley Regulators, Blue Ridge Rifles, Evergreen Guards, Franklin Fire Eaters, Rough and Ready Guards, Laurel Grove Riflemen, Mattapony Guards, and the Dismal Swamp Rangers stood ready for their greatest challenge to date.

Final Preparations For the Attack

Not long after the expansive ranks were exposed in the open, long-range shots from Union artillery hurtled their way. Mounted on an animal of outstanding stamina, Captain Bright galloped rapidly to the right, to the southern end of Pickett's line. There, Kemper's brigade of five veteran regiments, which had suffered the most severe beating of Pickett's three brigades during the cannonade, held the division's right, or southern, flank. Captain Bright reigned up before Kemper's ranks. A former Virginia politician and not the kind of man to be trifled with, Kemper was a bulky figure. His full beard (long and black) made the general look not unlike the famous pirate Edward Teach (Blackbeard).

At this time when his brigade's right lay around 1,300 yards from the crest of Cemetery Ridge, Kemper wore a cotton handkerchief under his hat. Kemper's handkerchief hung over his face for protection from the spray of the gravel and dirt kicked up by shell explosions. Mounted on his warhorse, Kemper received Pickett's directions from the captain: "dress on Garnett [on the left to the north] and take the red barn [the large Nicholas J. Codori barn just east of Emmitsburg Road and several hundred yards before the copse of trees atop Cemetery Ridge and seen from Seminary Ridge] for your [initial] objective."[25] Beyond the Codori House and barn and slightly northeast up the western slope of the ridge stood the clump of trees, a two-tier point of vision to guide the assault for Pickett's division.

Blessed with a lively wit and poetic nature, Kemper was a dynamic individual. Kemper could eliminate Yankee lives with the same ease as with quoting well-chosen lines from Shakespeare or the popular romantic works of Walter Scott. Known for his razor-sharp wit, he still recalled the retort of one of his spunky 7th Virginia men. He had silenced a jeering Union woman, who was draped in a United States flag that covered her upper torso, at Chambersburg, Pennsylvania, on June 28 with a single comment. When she refused to remove the flag and then asked why she should comply, the 7th Virginia man then threatened that "these old rebs are hell on breastworks." One of Hood's Texas colonels described Kemper as "a man of warm and quick temper, but of gracious speech and courtly manners."[26]

General Kemper had passed the word that the brigade and the entire division had been assigned to "the post of honor" in the upcoming assault. He was still motivated by the memory of when his soldiers marched toward victory at Second Manassas in August 1862. Kemper's troops, in one officer's words, "passed near Orange Court House, Gen. Kemper's mother is setting on the front porch to greet us as we go. She is bent with years and silvered are her tresses bound up in neat simplicity; but she waves her kerchief to her son's brave troops and bids them Godspeed against a relentless and unprincipled foe."[27]

Pickett emphasized to Garnett that, in regard to gaining their ultimate objective, "it's a hell of an ugly place over yonder." Garnett agreed, concluding that "this is a desperate thing to attempt." Armistead responded with resignation: "It is but the issue is with the Almighty and we must leave it in His hands."[28] With nicotine infusing a soothing calm as if back in a smoking room at the Spotswood Hotel in Richmond, Garnett finished "puffing at his cigar." He might have sensed that this was the last smoke of his life.

Extra gear already had been taken off by Garnett's and Kemper's soldiers. To ensure a swifter advance, meager personal possessions now lay in piles to the rear. Not only were cartridge-boxes full of 40 rounds, but also pant pockets were now crammed with another 20 extra rounds. With the 1st Virginia, Kemper's brigade, Lieutenant John Edward Dooley, Jr., later described, "Our artillery ha[d] ceased to roar and the enemy have checked their fury, too [and] The time appointed for our charge is come."[29]

Major Charles Pickett, 15 years younger than his brother-general and who had also been seriously wounded during the Seven Days' fighting like General Pickett, rode down the line to issue Pickett's final directives. Despite his upper-class status, Charles, or "brother Charlie," who was the general's only brother, had joined 1st Virginia at Richmond as a lowly private in the war's beginning. He had followed on the coattails of his brother's meteoric rise to divisional command.[30] Another one of Pickett's staff officers (either Symington or Baird) dashed down the lengthy lines. The courier galloped up to General Armistead, who was then "pacing up and down in front" of Lieutenant Colonel Rawley White Martin's 53rd Virginia, which contained nearly 470 men and officers.[31]

While located in a reserve position behind Garnett's and Kemper's front brigades, Armistead also barked out orders for his men to strip off all excess gear to lighten their loads so that no extra, unnecessary weight impeded movements during the upcoming advance. Tight-fitting knapsacks—either Southern-made, imported from England, or United States–made that had been stripped off Yankee dead—were quickly taken off. Soldiers also removed dirty blanket rolls wrapped across the right shoulder and white cotton haversacks that could contain tobacco, a clay or corncob pipe, perhaps a corn cake—"corn dodgers"—or kernels of raw corn, and mess gear. The metallic clatter of discarded accouterments echoed down Armistead's ranks. Excess equipment and personal belongings of Armistead's men were piled in individual clumps behind the line. Pocket Bibles and hymnbooks, including those taken from dead Yankees, remained in pockets, however. As a cruel destiny would have it, most of these little piles of personal gear would never be claimed, as their owners never returned.[32]

With the war-weariness of a veteran who hoped that his strong Catholic faith might save him in the assault, Lieutenant John Edward Dooley, Jr., with the other Irish of Company C, 1st Virginia, Kemper's brigade, wrote candidly that, "there is no romance in making one of these charges [and] the enthusiasm of ardent breasts in many cases *ain't there*, and instead of burning to avenge the insults of our country, families and altars and firesides, the thought is most frequently, *Oh*, if I could just come out of this charge safely how thankful *would I be!*[33] As revealed in a July 11, 1863, letter to his brother, Captain John A. Herndon, 38th Virginia, on Armistead's left flank, described the sight that took his breath away, after "we emerged from the cover of the woods in which we had formed we discovered the position of the enemy which was certainly the strongest for a new position I ever saw . . . the land in front being an open plain 3/4 of a mile wide with not a tree rock or variation in it sufficient to afford a man lying down concealment much less protection."[34] But the open ground nestled between Seminary and Cemetery Ridges was gently rolling terrain and even irregular at points, with an occasional rocky outcropping, and also dips, swales, and folds not readily seen (as in Captain Herndon's case) to the naked eye. In fact, this ground was so irregular that entire units could disappear from the Yankee eyes upon descending into a grassy swale or fold: yet another advantage for the attackers.[35]

Major Walter Harrison summarized how the prospect of "this direct assault on the heights of Cemetery Ridge, was quite enough in itself to turn the stomach of many a brave man."[36] However, the realization of inevitable horrors about to come was mingled with the seemingly paradoxical setting of the pristine pastoral scene that lay before lengthy formations. It was a "lovely little valley," in the words of one soldier, who appreciated nature's splendor on that radiant afternoon.[37] In this serene setting, the sheer beauty of this rolling terrain bestowed a surreal mood, almost as if the war's madness and death itself had been somehow suspended: another illusion on an afternoon of many shattered illusions.

Confidence Remains High

Meanwhile, the Virginians continued to make last-minute preparations before receiving final orders to advance. After having lain in position on the sun-baked ground of the grassy "hollow" and fields during the intense cannonade, the Old Dominion soldiers were stiff and sore. However, these men felt reenergized by the long-awaited opportunity to perhaps end the war in one masterstroke and then return home as conquering heroes, if they survived the attack.

A weakened Brigadier General Richard Brooke Garnett relied upon a prized horse out of necessity. He was in overall bad shape and still too weak to walk. Because of the early-afternoon intense heat, not wearing his favorite blue overcoat as when he had served with distinction as a United States regular, Garnett needed assistance to mount "his magnificent, thoroughbred gelding." The strange course of Garnett's life had been a twisting one. Now in his 44th year, after graduating from West Point in 1841, the handsome general was now placed at the head of a brigade in a key role. He had fought the ever-elusive Seminole and their black allies (escaped slaves and free men) in Florida's swamps and had tangled with Great Plains Indians. Life had not been easy for Garnett. But his light-hearted nature and sense of humor partly compensated for past setbacks.

Garnett's prewar opposition to the slave trade and secession (including speeches) had won him few friends in the Deep South. The lively tune "Willie Brew'd a Peck of Malt [Beer]" penned by Robert Burns in 1789, a popular Scottish drinking song, was the general's favorite. Garnett had risen from the rank of major to brigadier general in less than half a year. Known affectionately as "Dick" to his friends (including Pickett), Garnett was one of 16 officers and enlisted men of Pickett's division (two couriers, including Lieutenant John Simpkins Jones, who rode "a dark bay mare") who were now mounted.

Surgeons in gray had already "strongly advised" Garnett to remain behind. But Garnett ignored their wise words, donning his finest uniform. Still suffering from a vicious kick to the lower leg from an unhappy horse hitched to a wagon on the night of June 20 while the army crossed the Blue Ridge at Snicker's Gap, Garnett was forced to tightly grip his saddle's brass pommel. Because of his severely bruised lower leg, Garnett just hoped to stay steady on his favorite warhorse, Red Eye (a "magnificent thoroughbred gelding" and a splendid bay valued at an eye-popping $675, the second-highest-priced horse in Longstreet's 1st Corps). Born at the family's plantation known as "Rose Hill" in Essex County, Virginia, as a youth, Garnett had overcome a serious childhood illness by leading a more vigorous life, which included learning how to fence and box. Clearly, Garnett was tough, mentally and physically.

He now wanted to redeem the stain on his reputation stemming from an unfortunate incident: his arrest by Stonewall Jackson during the 1862 Shenandoah Valley Campaign. Such willpower ensured that Garnett never returned from the assault. But Garnett, who had commanded his brigade since November 1862, could not be talked out of leading his troops, despite being "scarcely able to walk." Like Armistead and Kemper, Garnett was determined to lead this "admixture of rawboned farm boys from the Piedmont, clerks from the Richmond offices, tidewater fisherman, rough men who found zest in daring irrespective of the cause they were fighting for, and chivalrous young gentleman. . . ."[38]

These soldiers from across Virginia and of such divergent backgrounds were now bound together like a band of brothers. They understood "the enormity of what was being required of them."[39] But one man in Pickett's division stood apart because of his Union sentiments: Private James M. Burchett, Company K, 8th Virginia, Garnett's brigade. Almost certainly the most unorthodox Rebel in ideological terms of Pickett's Charge, Private Burchett's uncle was Tennessee's military governor Andrew Johnson (the future 17th president after Lincoln's assassination). Therefore, Burchett was "disliked by some comrades for professing strong Union sentiments." Nevertheless, Private Burchett was about to advance beside the Old Dominion comrades, and received what at first looked to be his certain death stroke. However, Burchett survived his wounds, after his capture and left leg's amputation. He also suffered a badly dislocated shoulder, evidently from hand to hand combat with the boys in blue, who ironically thought like himself.[40]

Braving exploding shells, meanwhile, faithful chaplains in gray, including one gray-haired man of God who "offered prayer," bestowed spiritual comfort to Pickett's men. Unlike Pettigrew's chaplains who were now attending wounded soldiers in makeshift divisional field hospitals far to the rear, Pickett's chaplains moved down the lengthy lines and blessed soldiers, who were fated to never see tomorrow. Speaking words of faith and offering spiritual guidance, these dedicated men of God worked fast, with time quickly running out for such niceties. Thinking of homes and families that they might not ever see again, some men began to sing popular hymns that they had known in a more innocent time, when growing up in the Blue Ridge Mountains and the Potomac, Appomattox, and Nottoway River country.[41] Scotch-Irish Chaplain Florence McCarthy had been appointed chaplain of the 7th Virginia, Kemper's brigade, which included a troupe that sang "the old negro songs," well-harmonized gospels from the plantation, in mid-January 1862. He was described "as bold as the bravest and is to be seen in the first and fiercest battles [including Gettysburg], consoling and assisting the wounded."[42] Clearly, such devoted men of God, as one of Lee's pious soldiers penned in a letter, were "worth more than a brigade of wicked men."[43]

In the eerily silent ranks of Kemper's brigade on the right to the south, one young soldier never forgot how suddenly, "[g]reat big, stout-hearted men prayed, loudly too. . . . They were in earnest, for if men ever had need of the care and protection of our Heavenly Father, it was now."[44] Meanwhile, other fighting men were now obsessed with revenge, "thinking of their own despoiled homes, looted of everything." These veterans understood that the quickest way to end the Southern people's suffering was to now tear a giant hole through Meade's right-center.[45] A grim veteran's humor also lifted spirits. When a shell had earlier exploded in a nearby tree, Armistead casually picked up a piece of the splintered trunk. Offering a challenge, the West Pointer then turned to his men and shouted, "Boys, do you think you can stand up under that?"[46]

These veterans now realized that the fortunes of war and fate would determine if they would live or die on that afternoon. Already, Private Charles J. Winston, an ex-farmer who had enlisted in Lynchburg, Virginia, the previous July, felt fortunate. A shell fragment from a nearby explosion had just struck the leather pocketbook of this 11th Virginia soldier, "blending together two half-dollar silver pieces" like putty.[47]

An Emerald Hue

Long overlooked about the iconic story of Pickett's Charge was that the majority of its participants were of Celtic heritage (mostly generations removed from the immigrant experience) and therefore, Anglo-Celts, who were mostly

Scotch-Irish. Individuals of Irish, Scottish, and Welsh heritage had been long the South's most fundamental demographic. Thousands of these soldiers were unaware that Gettysburg and the surrounding area had been first settled by the Scotch-Irish, along with German Lutherans. Ironically, some early Celtic settlers of Gettysburg and Adams County might well have been ancestors of some of Pickett's men. During the colonial period, many Irish had migrated south from Pennsylvania in search of more fertile lands, settling in the remote backcountry of Virginia, the Carolinas, and Georgia. Mirroring their vanguard role in Pickett's Charge, Celtic-Gaelic soldiers had been at the forefront of the revolutionary war effort, serving in disproportionate numbers in the struggle for liberty, including in Washington's Continental Army.[48]

Additionally, a sizeable number of Lee's men—like the South's population in general—were Irish immigrants. The South's largest immigrant group consisted of Sons of Erin. An estimated 40,000 Irish, both Protestant and Catholic immigrants, fought for the Confederacy, and every Southern state was represented by distinctive Irish units, companies, and regiments. In consequence, the Irish were also the largest immigrant demographic of Lee's army and in the upcoming attack: one of the forgotten distinctive cultural and demographic qualities of Pickett's Charge. Nevertheless, to this day, the assault has continued to be viewed as a homogenous mass of Anglo-Saxon attackers in accordance with Lost Cause mythology.

The greatest number of Lee's men consisted of the sons, grandsons, and great-grandsons of Irish immigrants, who hailed mostly from Ulster Province in Protestant north Ireland, but also from the other three-quarters (three provinces that were primarily Catholic) of the Emerald Isle. In the 1st Virginia, Kemper's brigade, Lieutenant John Edward Dooley, Jr., was typical of the second generation Irish of Pickett's division. He was the son of John and Sarah Dooley, of Richmond, Virginia. Dooley's parents were Irish immigrants (also cousins) from Viking-founded Limerick on the Shannon River, Ireland's longest waterway.

The Dooley family made their American dream come true in the South, becoming respected members of the Richmond community. John Dooley, Sr., also rose in status by serving as leading officer of the prewar Montgomery Guard. These Irish soldiers celebrated every St. Patrick's Day, including the St. Patrick's Ball. Wearing emerald-green coats with sky-blue pants, the "Montgomeries" of Richmond had been organized among the Irish population in 1850. They wore a distinctive brass insignia on their Napoleonic-like shakos with the brass letters

"M.G.," surrounded by a wreath of Irish shamrocks, and "M.G." brass buckles that reflected Irish pride.

Later, the former Irish immigrant had organized the 1st Virginia's Montgomery Guard (Company C), which consisted of Richmond's Irish who marched to war in green uniforms. John Dooley, Sr., took command of the regiment in late 1862. These Irish Rebels continued the revolutionary tradition of not only the United States (Washington originally commanded the 1st Virginia, which included Irish soldiers), but also of Ireland. These 1st Virginia's Irish embraced the ancient Gaelic war cry of "Faugh a Ballagh!" ("Clear the Way!")[49]

The hard-fighting 1st Virginia's Irish had played a significant role in the regiment's earning the distinguished sobriquet of the "*Bloody First*, as Gen. Kemper styled us upon the eve of the battle of Fredericksburg." The Irish Confederates "had no scruples of any kind in killing as many of the northern brethren as they possibly could."[50] Ironically, the Irish Brigade, Army of the Potomac, "was almost annihilated at Fredericksburg [on] the property of Col. Marye, an officer of our [Kemper] brigade," wrote Lieutenant John Edward Dooley, Jr.[51]

Dooley and his comrades were proud that their 1st Virginia had been Washington's original command, one of America's oldest regiments. At age 14 in 1856, Dooley entered America's premier Jesuit school, Georgetown University, near the nation's capital. After eventually putting his books aside, the young man then served beside not only his father (the major) but also his brother, James Dooley, who was wounded and captured during the Seven Days' battles.[52]

The 19th Virginia, Garnett's brigade, also possessed Montgomery Guards, Company F. Organized in Charlottesville, Virginia, along with common laborers, many Emerald Islanders of this mostly Irish company were carpenters. Typical were two Herndon boys: 22-year-old Edward J., who was about to fall mortally wounded, and teenage Nicholas W., who was soon captured along with his brother. Leading Company F, Captain Bennett Taylor (about to be shot down and captured) was a 24-year-old teacher and descendent of Thomas Jefferson.[53] These Irish Confederates were some of Lee's best fighting men, which contradicted appearances. When one civilian asked the 1st Virginia Irish what regiment they represented, a Celtic-Gaelic soldier answered with typical Irish humor, "[I]t's the Bloody First, ye spalpeen . . . an didn't ye know us by our immigrant clothes?"[54] The Irish were best known for their combativeness. When Captain James Hallinan, a former laborer from Richmond who now commanded the Irish of Company C (Montgomery Guard), was angered by the reckless riding of the regimental adjutant John N. C. Stockton, an arrogant Virginia Military Institute graduate (Class of 1857), that endangered his boys, the Irishman drew his revolver. Hallinan then warned that if the transgressing adjutant "came near his company again, he would shoot him."[55]

Leading his 1st Virginia on horseback, dark-bearded Colonel Lewis B. Williams, Jr., a VMI graduate, admired his tough fighting men, Anglo-Celtic or Irish.[56] Jewish soldiers, mostly from Richmond and merchant's sons, also served in the 1st Virginia's ranks. Contrary to popular stereotypes rooted in the South's postwar history, there was relatively little anti-Semitism in Lee's army. James Beale was a Jewish Confederate of Company D, 1st Virginia. Teenage Corporal William A. Stoaber (Stober), a former Richmond salesman of Company B (Richmond City Guard) was another Hebrew soldier. Beale, along with Company C's Private Samuel H. Sloan (fated to die in a Federal prison after his capture that afternoon), was about to be cut down. Sloan was shortly to fall on property once owned by his namesake, who was the original settler of the Codori Farm over which the attackers were about to surge.[57] Major Raphael J. Moses served as one of Longstreet's most respected staff officers. His Jewish roots extended back for generations in Charleston, South Carolina, where many Jews had migrated. He was proud of his three sons, darkly handsome with black hair and eyes, who faithfully served the Confederacy and the Torah.[58] The Moses family very likely hailed from Prussia (present-day Germany), where Frederick the Great was still revered. The gifted Prussian nationalist leader had early understood that the parade ground was "nothing less than a peacetime battlefield," where tactical skills were perfected to win future victories.[59]

Drums in the Afternoon and Irish Memories

One 1st Virginia teenager, William "Willie" Henry Mitchel, Jr., cherished an especially distinguished Irish past. He was the son of the South's "premier Irish nationalist of the 19th Century," John C. Mitchel, Sr. A former Protestant minister who embraced liberation theology and Irish nationalism as one and the same, the senior Mitchel was the most famed Irish revolutionary leader (Young Ireland Movement of 1848) in the Confederacy. Escaping imprisonment for promoting open rebellion as Ireland's only solution to longtime British domination, John C. Mitchel, Sr., fled to "the land of the free" in 1853. He then settled in New York City. Born in County Derry, Northern Ireland, he hated the industrial North's exploitation of so many poor Irish immigrants.

The Mitchel family was proud of their three sons who served the Confederacy. "Willie" was the youngest and favorite son. He served as the color-bearer of the 1st Virginia, Kemper's brigade. Looking even younger than his 17 years, Willie Mitchel, dark-haired and boyish, was soon to enter a hell from which he never returned. Scholarly and introspective, the young man had been educated at a prestigious Catholic college in France. Willie remained in school until he departed with his exiled father, who just escaped British imprisonment, for America. The teenager was determined on July 3 to prove that he was worthy of the Dooley name and his Irish revolutionary ancestors. To make his father and two brothers—John, Jr., who served as a brigade staff officer, and James, who died in 1864—proud, he stood in the 1st Virginia's color guard.[60]

Willie might have pondered his destiny, which had caused him to forsake one of the finest educations (in France).[61] The dying words of Willie's brother and their father's oldest son, Captain John C. Mitchel, Jr., captured the family's revolutionary zeal: "I die willingly for the South, but oh! That it had been for Ireland."[62] A British observer marveled how these "Southern Irishmen make excellent 'Rebs,' [who sought to destroy] as many of their northern brethren as" possible.[63] Indeed, a vicious civil war among the Irish was played out in full during Pickett's Charge—one of the hidden chapters of the Civil War's most iconic charge.

Other Sons of Erin

The Irish Rebels of the Emerald Guards Company, 8th Alabama, General Cadmus Wilcox's Alabama brigade, also served in Pickett's Charge. Hailing from the port of Mobile, the Emerald Guards had first gone to war in emerald-green uniforms. They had also marched under a flowing green battle flag, which had been blessed by Bishop John Quinlan from County Cork, Ireland. This Irish flag was decorated with Irish national and revolutionary symbols, including the shamrock and the ancient Gaelic battle cries of "Erin go Bragh!" ("Ireland Forever!") and "Faugh a Ballagh!" ("Clear the Way!")[64]

A large number of Emerald Islanders also filled Company H, 11th Virginia, which was Kemper's second-largest regiment of more than 400 soldiers. Hailing from Lynchburg, in west-central Virginia, and the surrounding Piedmont, these Irish served in the Jeff Davis Guards. Located at the foot of the Blue Ridge and known as the "City of the Seven Hills," Lynchburg was a railroad center and had long served as a magnet for Irish immigrants. There, immigrant Sons of Erin had long found ample work as common laborers and railroad workers.

Captain James Risque Hutter (VMI Class of 1860) led these Emerald Islanders, until he would be shot down shortly at the stone wall. He had been assisted in molding a crack company by an Irish sergeant, Henry Doyle, age 24 and a former newspaper reporter. These Emerald Islanders made Kemper's brigade the most thoroughly Irish of Pickett's three brigades.[65]

The Emmet Guards and O'Connell Guards were other distinctive Irish companies of Pickett's division. But the 17th Virginia, Corse's brigade, was now absent on duty in the dreary Little River country above Richmond to protect the capital's northern approaches.[66] Ironically, a good many Virginia and North Carolina Rebels were destined to wear gray jackets manufactured in Ireland.[67]

German Rebels and Common Soldier Demographics

The second-largest number of foreign immigrants of Pickett's Charge, especially Pickett's division, were Germans. Many men had been born in the Teutonic homeland of numerous Germanic states ruled in feudal fashion by ancient nobility. Soldiers like Private William H. Tappey, Company A, 9th Virginia, Armistead's brigade, were born in the land that became Germany. Of German heritage and born in the Shenandoah Valley like many Germans who served in the Stonewall Brigade, Corporal George M. Setzer, a teenage former carpenter of Company F (Farmville Guards), 18th Virginia, Garnett's brigade, was about to be fatally cut down. Most of Virginia's German population, like the Irish, was located in major cities. Symbolically, Generals Kemper and Armistead were of German ancestry—"Old Germans" or Americanized Germans.[68]

Representing a wide spectrum, the about 5,800 infantrymen (with average ages between 22 and 24, but also including many teenagers) of Pickett's division hailed from regions of 40 counties across Virginia. A close look at a typical regiment of Pickett's division has revealed an exceptionally highly diversified group of individuals from the Tidewater to the Blue Ridge. These men represented the full spectrum of their Old Dominion communities, such as Portsmouth and Richmond (represented mostly in the 1st Virginia), and distinctive ethnic societies: demographics that have contradicted popular stereotypes of the simple Southern backwoods "cracker." Irish and Germans, especially in the cities, were disproportionately represented by skilled occupations such as artisans and mechanics.

The smallest regiment of Armistead's brigade, the 9th Virginia, by July 3 consisted of barely 260 soldiers. This regiment was composed primarily of men from the Chesapeake Bay region ports of Norfolk (Virginia's largest city, with many French, Irish, and German immigrants) and Portsmouth. The diversified occupations of 9th Virginia soldiers included 56 carpenters, 30 mechanics, 20 merchants, 20 students, 20 clerks, 19 ship carpenters, 18 painters, a dozen sailors/seamen and a dozen blacksmiths, seven professors, seven coppers, seven machinists, six physicians, six boat builders, six brick masons, six pharmacists, five attorneys, five shoemakers, four coach makers, four millers, four stone cutters, and four confectioners.[69] Interestingly, three 9th Virginia members each held the positions of engineer, gardener, tinner, butcher, businessman, printer, tailor, moulder, shipwright; harness-maker, plasterer, house carpenter, and cabinet-maker.[70] Other occupations included a professor (Simon C. Wells, who taught mathematics and natural philosophy at Roanoke College, Roanoke, Virginia), gunsmith, baker, dentist, editor, piano maker, grocer, judge, college superintendent, music instructor, court clerk, brass founder, bank cashier, accountant, city marshal and attorney, musician, peddler, watchman, oyster packing businessman, surveyor, music teacher, railroad conductor, morocco dresser, toll collector, policeman, etc.[71]

Such diverse occupations of 9th Virginia members, including soldiers (Company D) who were initially armed with long wooden pikes, represented the foundation of Tidewater society. Because Portsmouth (like Norfolk) was a major port and a destination for immigrants, the regiment's ranks were also represented by a good many Irish-born and German-born soldiers, and men of French heritage, whose ancestors had left the St. Domingue (Haiti) slave revolt in the 1790s. These fighting men formed tight-knit family units within companies, representing families, regional clans, and home communities, fueling high morale. Of English heritage, 13 Timberlake boys served almost exclusively in Companies B (Barhamsville Grays) and E (Pamukeny Rifles), of the 53rd Virginia, Armistead's brigade.

Born on July 28, 1831, Captain Henry Thweatt Owen, 18th Virginia (then consisting of nearly 380 men), wondered if he would live to see his 32nd birthday in only 25 days. He described how, in regard to the diversified demographics of Pickett's division, "[s]cattered through the different regiments was a sprinkling of restless, roving adventurers, seekers after excitement, whose passion, pastime and pleasure had been war and revolution for the last quarter century—some had fought under Sam Houston at San Jacinto [April 21, 1836], others with the celebrated British Legion in the Don Carlos War [also in the 1830s], others with [filibuster William] Walker in Nicaragua, and others with

[Chatham Roberdeau] Wheat and [Giuseppe] Garibaldi in Italy [and] There were men who fought under Zack[ary] Taylor from Palo Alto to Monteray [sic], and with [General Winfield] Scott from Vera Cruz to the City of Mexico" in 1847.[72]

The breadth of such varied experiences of the Virginians was matched in diversity by the North Carolina, Alabama, Tennessee, Virginia, and Mississippi troops of Pettigrew's division. A lucky survivor of Walker's Nicaraguan expedition, Colonel Fry led the Tennessee and Alabama brigade on Garnett's left. Of "brigadier-material," he earned renown for leadership ability with Walker during the zenith of the filibuster decade of the 1850s.[73]

The diverse backgrounds of Pickett's men were symbolically represented by their outward appearances. A Union prisoner, of Irish descent, never forgot the sight of these fighting men: "Pickett's division formed in line of battle, wore snapping caps and adjusting belts and all the familiar preparations of serious work were plainly visible. In spite of the marked incongruity of color and make-up of the men's uniforms, particularly in the matter of head-dress, which often bordered on the fantastic, there was no mistaking the fact that these men were disciplined and trusty veterans. . . ."[74]

Deep Hidden Weaknesses

Lee's veterans were dressed in all manner of clothing, including civilian dress and parts of Union uniforms. Indeed, "[s]ome of the men patched their clothing . . . one man having the seat of his pants patched with bright red, his knees patched with black, another with a piece of gray or a brown blanket."[75] Lieutenant George Williamson Finley, 56th Virginia, Garnett's brigade, described how his men now wore "captured Federal sky blue trousers boiled in walnut juice [for the trademark butternut color], and they varied in shade from a light tan to a dark brown—depending on how long they had been boiled in walnut juice. And calico shirts with wide suspenders and brown, gray, or black wide-brimmed, slouch hats pinned up on the side or rolled up in the front . . . our boys looked like a pack of dirty, lean, gray, brown, hungry wolves."[76]

More importantly, these Virginia fighting men possessed excellent weapons, especially their favorite .577 caliber Enfield rifle in overall good condition. They had carefully checked their well-maintained weapons before loading. Black leather cartridge-boxes and cap pouches taken from Union dead were being worn by new owners. Ironically, some soldiers now carried captured .58 caliber Springfield muskets like their opponents on Cemetery Ridge.[77]

But a closer look at Pickett's veterans showed some alarming weaknesses, revealing how the cannonade had taken a heavy toll not only in lives but also in morale. No one better than Napoleon had appreciated the value of "shock and awe" of a heavy artillery bombardment. The former Georgetown University scholar, Lieutenant John Edward Dooley, Jr., noted that when Kemper's men had risen from the reserve slope, some uninjured soldiers remained prostrate: "the men in whom there is not sufficient courage to enable them to rise, but of these last, there are but few."[78] Lieutenant William B. Taylor, Company A, 11th North Carolina (the Bethel Regiment), Marshall's brigade, was astounded by the number of soldiers who were "fainting all along the [line] before [we] started on the charge."[79]

But this situation was more than just cowardice or nerves, because other forgotten factors came into play. Private Meredith (Merit) Branch Thurman, Company C (Fluvanna Rifle Guard), 14th Virginia, Armistead's brigade, hated the war. He only wanted to return home to his young wife, Jane Rosser Humphrey. The former lowly coal miner and James River boatman from Chesterfield County, Virginia, had married the pretty teenage woman (two decades his junior) of his dreams. Now one of Pickett's most reluctant soldiers, Private Thurman only wished to be "free" of the army, because he had "tired of Souldiering." He, therefore, seriously contemplated deserting in Pennsylvania, and then bringing Jane to this new land for a new start in life. Especially class conscious because of his lowly background, Thurman was deeply troubled by the conflict's escalating social inequities, a rich man's war and a poor man's fight, eroding his once-strong Southern patriotism.

Despite only wanting to "just get out of [this] war," Thurman answered the call to duty on July 3. Therefore, Private Thurman was now about to go forward with his comrades, despite believing that the South could not win this war. As if knowing that he would not survive the war (he received his death stroke in May 1864), Merit shortly wrote a poem to his wife that prophetically emphasized: "[O]ur time is short our days are few."[80]

As part of Lost Cause romance that was the antithesis of the complexities faced by common soldiers like Private Thurman, Reverend J. Williams Jones described Lee's soldiers as representing "the very flower of the intelligence, the wealth, the education, the social position, the culture, the refinement, the patriotism, and the religion of the South."[81] But of course in truth, Pickett's division was composed of a diverse mix of backward, illiterate crackers and well-educated scholars, the societal elite and the dregs of society, saints, drunks, cowards, thieves, heroes, and sinners infected by ravages of venereal disease. Nevertheless, they were now all united as one by the single desire to reap the war's most decisive victory. However, deep fissures existed just below the surface. Even the Irish Confederates were divided by class and religion (Protestant versus Catholic). And more middle-class Irish served as officers, while the lower (or laboring) class, mostly immigrants, served in the enlisted ranks.[82]

About to fall wounded, Private James Farthing, of English and German descent, was one of Pickett's typical common soldiers in socioeconomic terms, "a poor dirt farmer," of south-central Virginia near the North Carolina border. Growing crops of corn and wheat and a small cash crop of tobacco, Farthing and his fellow lower-class and lower-middle-class neighbors—now members of Company H (Secession Guards), 38th Virginia, of Pittsylvania County (Virginia's largest)—owned no slaves. Having helped to create a disciplined regiment, Lieutenant Colonel Powhatan Bolling Whittle was the right-hand man of Lieutenant Colonel Edward Claxton Edmonds. Edmonds was a VMI graduate (Class of 1858). He had supervised his own military school (Danville Military Academy) in Danville, Virginia, before the war. Edmonds, age 28, was about to be killed in leading the 38th Virginia. On Armistead's left flank, this well-trained command was known as "the Pittsylvania Regiment" because most of its members—six companies—hailed from the fertile lands of Pittsylvania County.[83]

The Curtain Opens

In a letter, Captain Charles Minor Blackford, Longstreet's staff, scribbled down his thoughts in haste, after the most "terrible cannonading" of the war: "This will be a great day in history . . . I suppose our lines [now] are preparing to charge."[84] One of Longstreet's Georgians explained in a letter of the assault's political objective: "I hope to God [that we will] make them [the northern people] cry out 'Peace, peace' [and] With the blessing of God we will do valiant things."[85] On July 3, the South needed for "heaven [to] send us a Napoleon."[86]

Paradoxically and despite fighting in a rich man's war and a poor man's fight, these mostly lower- and middle-class soldiers of Pickett's and Pettigrew's divisions were determined to reverse the war's course. On Meade's weak right-center, Union officers had been debating about what would come next from the unpredictable Lee. After having returned to command the 2nd Division, 2nd Corps, after General Hancock took charge of the 2nd Corps, General John Gibbon had expected no attack.[87]

Of course, such complacency was Lee's best ally. Seasoned Union leadership assumed that Lee would never launch an attack over three-quarters of a mile of open ground. Therefore, Lee possessed the advantage of the element of surprise: a massive offensive effort launched in two distinct assaults (Pettigrew's left wing and Pickett's right wing) that would move toward each other in order to converge just before striking the clump of trees sector.[88] Haskell revealed that Meade "was not of the opinion that the enemy would take the center, our artillery had such sweep there, and this was not the favorite point of attack with the Rebel."[89]

However, General Hancock, who played a key role in halting Longstreet's fierce attacks of July 2, did not agree with Gibbon, who was "humorously" referred to by one fellow general as "this young North Carolinian"—a reference that would have amused Pettigrew and his North Carolina soldiers, who were shortly headed his way. Hancock correctly believed that "the attack would be upon the position of the 2nd Corps."[90]

The savviest Union leaders were now convinced that the clump of trees and Angle sector had been targeted by Lee because artillery fire had caused so much damage to Union batteries on the right center. Many Yankees had hoped that the cannonade had been merely a smokescreen to mask Lee's withdrawal back to the Old Dominion. But others had believed that Lee would never depart Pennsylvania without one last offensive thrust.[91]

Of course, this debate had ended when the seemingly endless lines of Confederates suddenly emerged from the dark woodlands of Seminary Ridge. For the first time that day, Pickett galloped forth and took center stage before his aligned troops with a Virginia cavalier's dramatic flair. Ironically, Pickett might have been the least likely of officers to have been suddenly thrust into his vital situation of spearheading and guiding Lee's most important assault with his relatively inexperienced division. After all, he had been promoted to major general well beyond his abilities. At age 37, Pickett was no longer the same man who had charged like a madman up the bullet-swept slope of Chapultepec to inspire his comrades. War-weariness, hardships from two years of active campaigning, and his burning love for his dark-haired Nansemond County, Virginia, Belle, teenage LaSalle (Sally) Corbell, had sapped the strength of Pickett's warrior ethos and martial ambitions.

He wanted to marry the enchanting Sally, and then live happily ever after. War, especially a grinding, brutal one, had lost its appeal to Pickett. The seductive appeal of winning a name for himself (a true siren's song) no longer lingered for Pickett. Pickett's West Point value system was also slipping away, passing him by like his swiftly passed youth. A host of factors had made Pickett one of the army's worst division commanders: growing apathy, war-weariness, negligence of duties, and increased drinking. But because this dandified Virginian now commanded the army's only fresh division, the commander-in-chief had no choice but to place his trust completely in Pickett, although he had failed him in the past.[92]

Rightly feeling that fast-paced events were entirely beyond his control, Pickett had recently informed General Wilcox with stoic resignation that revealed he had regained some of his old more admirable qualities: "Whatever my fate, Wilcox, I shall do my duty like a man, and I hope that . . . I shall reach either glory or God."[93] General Armistead was more fatalistic.[94] Mounted on his sleek warhorse "Old Black" (befitting its color) before his sprawling formations, Pickett unsheathed his saber. Ironically, this sword was destined to be inherited by his abandoned son, black-eyed James Tilton Pickett. He had been born in December 1857 to an Indian mother who died in giving birth. Pickett had sired "Jimmie" of a teenage woman when he had been stationed in the Pacific Northwest, the Washington Territory. Given his current obsession with Sally, Pickett obviously possessed a proclivity toward dark-featured teenage women (Indian or white). As fate would have it, had this woman not died and had Pickett decided to remain in the northwest with his Indian family, then Lee's greatest charge on July 3 would have been known by another name, and may have ended differently.

Contrary to prudish Victorian stereotypes, such recreational sexual dalliances were not unusual for West Pointers when stationed far from home and family. Illicit affairs with Indian women were not uncommon among members of the Southern planter class, including one of Pickett's own brigade commanders. In 1855 and only two years before the birth of Pickett's Indian son, Lieutenant Richard Brooke Garnett became the father of the son of an Oglala Sioux woman named Looking Woman or Looks at Him (named for her beauty) near Fort Laramie, Wyoming Territory. William "Billie" Garnett was the child's name.

Of course, such social indiscretions were nothing new among the Virginia aristocracy. Thomas Jefferson, Virginia's most famous Founding Father (after Washington), had a longtime affair with a slave mistress at Monticello, and she bore him children. While home on leave from West Point, even "Stonewall" Jackson was reported to have fathered a child, Isaiah Jackson, of a slave woman from the Beverly, Virginia area. Allegedly Jackson's mulatto son was born less than a year after the birth of Pickett's Indian son. With regard to white nine-teenth-century values, an American male fathering an Indian child was prefer-able to having children with a slave woman, although a slave child possessed economic value that steadily increased with maturity. In this sense, therefore, Pickett was not guilty of having violated the greatest social taboo of his upper-class society of the Virginia Tidewater.

Pickett's Moment in the Sun

To his great credit, Pickett rose splendidly to the challenge of July 3. At about 3:00 p.m. and in an "animated" manner to inspire his troops, Pickett dis-mounted to address his command. In a booming voice that rang over the east-ern slope of Seminary Ridge just beyond the tree line, he shouted: "Remember today that you are from Old Virginia!" Beardless drummer boys in gray began to beat the long roll. In a brief address just behind the now-silent rows of artil-lery, Pickett ordered his troops, "Advance slowly, with arms at will. No cheer-ing, no firing, no breaking from common to quick step. Dress on the center." Pickett then shouted "Forward! Guide center! March!" After having lost his first wife, who died while giving birth at a remote Texas outpost in 1851, Pickett knew the pain of personal loss that evaporated in the excitement of bat-tle. At that moment, the middle-aged Pickett was almost miraculously trans-formed, once again becoming that romantic-minded youth of Chapultepec, but only briefly.[95]

Despite being a "staunch Anglican" (the former Church of England) of the upper class of the Virginia Tidewater, Pickett still wore a silver Catholic crucifix given him by a Mexican priest not long after the battle of Chapultepec—a preference respected by his Irish Catholics, who already had crossed themselves. He revered it as a token of spiritual protection that reminded him of his many narrow escapes in two wars. Irish Catholics in Pickett's ranks, especially in the 1st Virginia, likewise wore similar crucifixes that they hoped would keep them safe from harm.[96]

Now "each regiment uncased his colors and shock them out [and] The battle flags blossomed like red [Confederate battle flags] and blue [Virginia State flags] flowers all down the Confederate line" as far as the eye could see.[97] Lieutenant George Williamson Finley described how the battle flag of his 56th Virginia "was the very soul of the regiment [and] Our color-bearer was [Corporal] Alexander Lafayette Price Williams, better known as 'Corporal

Sandy'."[98] Like so many other 56th Virginia members, the popular color-bearer was soon shot down and captured.[99]

Upon Pickett's orders to move forward and because the troops had earlier laid down in "the usual order of battle," before marching beyond the crest of Seminary Ridge, no last-minute tactical adjustments were necessary. Garnett's brigade of about 1,800 men, in the front rank on the division's left, moved out with flags flying. Meanwhile, Kemper's brigade, of about the same size, simultaneously swung forward on the division's right. To the rear of Kemper's and Garnett's brigades, Armistead's larger brigade of about 2,180 troops would be the last to advance as Pickett's second line (or reserve). With disciplined step, Garnett's and Kemper's troops marched toward "the valley of the shadow of death," in one Virginian's words.[100]

A lack of close coordination then raised its ugly head. Longstreet and Pickett failed to inform Pettigrew of the exact time of the advance. Evidently Pettigrew, who was not familiar with conducting such a large-scale assault of an entire division, had not requested the exact time to unleash his division. Also, the pocket watches of Confederate leaders were not synchronized. Therefore, relying upon eyesight alone in peering south to ascertain the assault's beginning, Pettigrew was destined to be late in getting started. Stretched in a lengthy line across the open fields, Pettigrew's division finally made last preparations to advance, but only long minutes after Pickett's division moved forward on its own.[101]

General Pettigrew, with his characteristic "bright look" on a battle's eve, galloped up to Marshall's North Carolina brigade, which occupied the division's center. Eyes were focused on Pettigrew, who was so different from most upper-class leaders. Pettigrew, in camp like the lowest private, consumed the same meager rations—tasteless hardtack and pork—despite his aristocratic background and intellectualism. Looking stylishly handsome in a neat-trimmed goatee but not wearing his finest uniform coat, he shouted to "Jimmy" Keith Marshall, "Now Colonel, for the honor of the good Old North State. Forward."

Pettigrew's troops belatedly poured out of the green woodlands of Seminary Ridge, flooding the open fields bathed in summer sunlight. Revealing their high spirits earlier than the silent Virginians, Pettigrew's veterans unleashed a spontaneous cheer that rang over the fields. The assault's left wing rolled over the expanse of wide-open fields—golden with luxurious wheat and green from rye and clover—that seemed to stretch endlessly to the eastern horizon.[102] In one of Gettysburg's many ironies, the mounted Pettigrew led his wing toward a targeted area defended by his second cousin on his mother's side, General John

Gibbon, who commanded three brigades of the 2nd Division, 2nd Corps, on the right-center. As among the Irish and Germans in blue and gray, this was the brothers' war on multiple levels.[103]

The sight presented by the advance, extending nearly two miles, was magnificent, but in fact represented "a fatal parade" because of numerous failures behind the scenes.[104] Entirely unknown to Lee, Longstreet had not properly arranged for adequate support on either flank of the frontline attackers. Therefore, the assault was no wider than Pettigrew's and Pickett's divisions, whose flanks had no protection from either infantry or artillery.[105] Nevertheless, the young men and boys continued onward with the certitude that "I expect to try to die like a brave man fighting for the right of the country, and try to die the death of the righteous" warrior, if God so deemed.[106]

Among the eight companies of the 9th Virginia, Armstead's brigade, Sergeant James Hodges Walker, from Portsmouth and a member of Company K (Old Dominion Guards), which had been organized at the bustling port in April 1861, made sure that the advancing ranks were neat and tight. He described with pride how the frontline troops of the "division advanced steadily in quick time [while a brass] band at the extreme right [Kemper's brigade] played in the same manner that it would, had the division been passing in review."[107] Virginia-born Sergeant Randolph Abbott Shotwell, Company H (Potomac Greys), 8th Virginia (around 240 men) and other "Old Bloody Eighth" soldiers felt that they were already on the golden road to Baltimore. Ironically, Shotwell, one of many teenagers in gray, had been a student at the Tuscarora Academy, Mifflin, Pennsylvania, located only about 70 miles north of Gettysburg.[108]

Anxious Boys in Blue on Cemetery Ridge

Meanwhile, the splendidly mounted Pickett was seen by the boys in blue from the ridgetop, while the lengthy formations moved relentlessly through the open fields. After the numerous batteries, especially Cushing's unit, on Meade's right-center had taken a terrible pounding, these experienced Union soldiers knew that the thin line of infantry had to hold firm at all costs. Consequently, these men hurriedly checked muskets and bayonets for the close-range combat that was sure to come. On that splendid summer afternoon, they marveled at the majestic sight of the sweeping advance with colorful banners leading the way. In the words of Private William Haines, 12th New Jersey, positioned near the center of General Alexander Hays's 3rd Division (the "Blue Birds," a name derived from the unit's insignia of a large clover leaf of blue on a white background), 2nd Corps, that was aligned along the stone wall north of the Angle: "[T]heir bayonets glisten[ed] in the sun from right to left, as fare as the eye could see." With their line on their right extending north to the high-ground dominated by the tall hardwood trees of Ziegler's Grove just south-west of Cemetery Hill and just northeast of the targeted copse of trees, these seasoned "Blue Birds" lay concealed behind the stone wall. They were made more formidable that afternoon by their capable leader, "Alex" Hays, a tough Mexican–American War veteran. A more distinguished name than the con-temptuous "Blue Bellies" and "blue bells" used by Lee's men, these feisty "Blue Birds" were determined to hold firm. As Captain Haskell, a former adjutant of the 6th Wisconsin, Iron Brigade, penned of the unbelievable sight: "Every eye could see his legions, an overwhelming resistless tide of an ocean of armed men sweeping upon us!"[109]

Another awed Federal felt heightened anxiety, if not fear, because it was clear that "[t]hey mean business [but] few of their officers are mounted" on the open ground.[110] As scribbled in his diary, one Pennsylvania soldier, William J. Burns, expressed the greatest fear, because if this assault succeeded, then it would be "all up with the USA."[111] As if still battling Mexican soldados (sol-diers) before Mexico City so long ago, the ever-flexible Hays, a hard-nosed West Pointer, developed a very good plan: he ordered his "Blue Birds" to only open fire when Pettigrew's attackers reached the fences along the Emmitsburg Road, where the dual fences on each side of the road would slow the advance. With a voice that brooked no indiscipline or insubordination, Hays shouted, "Hold your fire until they reach the fence!" Fearing the worst, Captain Winfield Scott, 126th New York, Hays's division, recited a favorite verse (Song of Solomon 6:10) out loud to calm his men: "Fair as the moon, bright as the sun, and ter-rible as an army of banners."[112] Likewise, Lee's soldiers often found solace in the hopeful words of the Book of Psalms and the identical verse.[113] As always, they also found solace in each other, because men have always fought together, out of loyalty to each other as much as abstract ideas since times immemorial.

All along Cemetery Ridge, meanwhile, the Yankees continued to make last-minute preparations for the inevitable onslaught. Frantic officers shouted orders, and veteran artillerymen prepared their guns in mechanical fashion. Fortunate to have survived the cannonade that mauled the right-center, artil-lery commanders made sure that sufficient ammunition, especially cans of can-ister, were carried forward. Canister was now piled high beside each field piece. Infantrymen in sun-faded blue placed ramrods against the stone wall to load more quickly. Then, leather cartridge-boxes were shifted to their front and flaps were opened, while extra paper cartridges were piled on the ground by their sides. Because the topsoil along the ridge was so thin and rocky (with dense shale just underneath), the Federals were unable to implant iron ramrods in the ground as usual in defending a position to quicken the loading process.

Grim-faced Union officers with years of experience in the art of killing their fellow man made sure that their six-shot Colt and Navy revolvers were loaded. To draw their weapons faster for when close-range combat erupted, Yankee officers returned their revolvers to their leather holsters without closing the flap. Enlisted men of the 14th Connecticut Volunteer Infantry were also ready, although they had not yet seen a year in service. But these New Englanders had experienced the war's bloodiest day at Antietam the previous September. Above the Angle along the low stone wall, these Connecticut soldiers were positioned near and just north of Captain William A. Arnold's Company A, 1st Rhode Island Light Artillery of "steel rifled cannon." On the open slope, the barrels of these 3-inch Ordnance Rifles reflected the July sunshine like mirrors. Some 14th Connecticut men felt greater confidence than their nearby comrades, who were armed with single-shot rifled muskets. The soldiers of two Connecticut companies now gripped breech-loading rifles, the lethal .52 caliber Sharps Rifle, appropriately manufactured in Hartford, Connecticut, which guaranteed a high rate of fire.

Basking in his wise stratagem, General Hunt must have smiled to himself, because the Confederates had taken the bait of his clever reduction of his artillery fire, which created the false impression that the Southern cannonade had been entirely effective in silencing his guns, though he was only conserving ammunition for when the Rebel infantry got near. On the 2nd Corps's front, Captain Haskell, the former attorney-turned–staff officer, described the unforgettable sound of "the click of the [musket] locks as each man raised the hammer to feel with his fingers that the [percussion] cap was on the nipple."[114] Viewing his 14th Connecticut comrades amid the heightened nervous tension, Sergeant Hirst never forgot how one soldier "is looking at the Far off Home [that] He will never see again [while] Another is looking at his Little ones [in a tintype or ambrotype taken in Washington, DC, Boston, or Philadelphia], and he mechanically empties his Cartridge Box before him determined to part with Life as Dearly as posible."[115]

Meanwhile, through the simmering heat haze that was undisturbed by the ever-so-faint breeze that felt more hot than refreshing, the Yankees watched the unbelievable sight: "The red flags wave, their horsemen gallop up and down; the arms of eighteen thousand men, barrel and bayonet, gleam in the sun, a sloping forest of flashing steel."[116]

After Pickett's formations had earlier passed through the rows of smoking Confederate guns, aligned hub-to-hub in some places of the smoke-laced ground, the men in the ranks saw that nothing but the wide expanse of open fields were lying before them. Dearing's Virginia artillerymen, including those wearing "little kepi caps trimmed in red [for artillery]," cheered the advancing infantrymen by waving their headgear to encourage them onward. In return, Pickett's men had "doffed our old, wide brimmed slouch hats" in the common soldier's salute. Then, the soot-grimed gunners went back to work, reopening their fire (although, it would have been wiser to save their ammunition for flying artillery missions to protect the infantry's flanks as Lee had ordered) to cover the advance of the soldiers, who they knew were "going to catch hell," in Longstreet's words.

Therefore, still another salvo of Confederate shells, primarily manufactured in Richmond, slammed into Cemetery Ridge, killing some of the relatively few remaining artillerymen and horses behind the stone wall around the Angle and clump of trees. From the 14th Connecticut's ranks that was positioned north of the copse of trees, Sergeant Hirst watched in astonishment: "[T]here they come a Cloud of Skirmishers in front, with two, three lines of Battle, stretched all along our Front with their Banners flying, and the men carrying their Pieces at trail Arms. It was a Glorious Sight to see, Rebels though they were [and] They seemed to as though upon Parade, and were confident of carrying all before them."[117] An amazed private of the 108th New York Volunteer Infantry (north of the 14h Connecticut), 2nd Corps, thought that these Confederates were "moving like so many automatons" and as if nothing could stop them.[118]

Early Lack of Coordination

However, this was a high-ground panoramic view from more than 1,000 yards that became the standard romanticized portrayal of a sweeping advance that appeared flawless from a distance. In truth, the Confederate advance early exhibited a host of serious flaws, especially with regard to the overall disjointed advance between Pickett's and Pettigrew's divisions and the supporting 3rd Corps units. The two assault wings were widely separated along a nearly two-mile expanse. Therefore, Pickett's right wing and Pettigrew's left wing would have to come together to simultaneously strike an overpowering blow on

Meade's right-center: a most challenging tactical requirement of an unprecedented complexity. Rather than acting in unison, the two divisions had pushed forward not only at different times (Pettigrew belatedly) but also at different speeds—hardly a promising beginning to an assault that depended on near-perfect timing for success. Because this was a complex attack plan of a broad front advance by divergent commands that had never before acted in conjunction during an offensive operation, close supervision was now needed for the proper convergence and near-perfect timing for the two divisions to simultaneously meet and then form a battering ram to smash through Meade's right-center.

But because of their personal animosity that guaranteed a lack of communication, Hill assumed that Longstreet would supervise his attack and issue specific instructions, while "Old Peter" assumed that the 37-year-old Hill would fulfill this vital role. Both generals were badly mistaken. Meanwhile Lee assumed that Longstreet was taking all necessary steps to ensure the success of the assault. Therefore, because of the lack of understanding and a fractured relationship, Longstreet and Hill were doing little, if anything, to closely coordinate the attack. Therefore, the right of Pickett's division on the south and the left of Pettigrew's division on the north continued to be entirely unprotected.

Even more, Hill was lethargic and sick (like Lee) and in overall bad physical, if not mental, shape. He was also inexperienced in commanding a corps, and in command of three times more men than ever before. Hill had been promoted beyond his capabilities (like Pickett and Ewell) primarily because he was a Virginian. Clearly, Hill let Longstreet down, and Longstreet let Lee down in a disastrous chain reaction. Incredibly, these two corps commanders were not working together, while the commander-in-chief had "not yet recovered from the [heart] attack I experienced last spring," near Fredericksburg, in Lee's words. For such reasons, a troubled Colonel Taylor lamented how Pettigrew's line continued not to be "a continuation of that of Pickett, but that it advanced in echelon" (like the July 2 assaults) contrary to Lee's plans.[119]

Ironically, doing nothing to correct the problematic tactical situation on multiple levels, Longstreet and Hill had blundered the same way with regard to the previous day's assaults. Longstreet merely assumed that Hill was directing Anderson's division to protect the assault's flanks, while Hill assumed that Longstreet was directing Anderson's division on this vital mission. And, of course, Lee assumed that Longstreet was making sure that Anderson's division provided proper support: a classic case of the blind leading the blind.[120] Little, if anything, was accomplished to protect the flanks or getting flying artillery to advance on July 3.[121] As mentioned, Lee was not monitoring Longstreet, assuming that everything was flowing smoothly.[122]

Meanwhile, in sharp contrast to the rising tide of dysfunction among Confederate leadership, the 2nd Corps's leaders were having their finest day. Near the copse of trees from his high-ground perch, Sergeant Hirst described the firm resolve of the boys in blue "behind that long, low stone Wall our own Glorious 2nd Corps [was intent on] hurling back that Rebelious Crew who brought their Polluting footsteps to our own dear North."[123]

However, what the Federals could not see was the fighting spirit of the men that made the advancing formations much more formidable. Perhaps one of Lee's soldiers said it best: "We whip the Yankees every time we catch them and we get half a chance at them."[124] One of Longstreet's men boasted in a letter, "God is surely with us, we never could have whipped them so bad" and so often in the past.[125] With more than 12,000 Rebels advancing, the "whole line of battle looked like a stream or river of silver moving towards us." However, Lee's sprawling formations consisted of an ad hoc mixture of diverse commands with varying levels of experience in terms of combat and leadership, conditions, and temperaments. While Garnett's and Kemper's brigades swung relentlessly across the open ground, Armistead's brigade, the largest in Pickett's division, belatedly prepared to advance because Pickett's front was so narrow: hence, two initial assault lines.[126] Both of Pickett's frontline brigades, Garnett on the left and Pickett on the right, moved smoothly onward because they were in good shape and were veteran units, having received their baptismal fire at First Manassas when the war had seemed like nothing more than a glorious adventure.[127]

But conditions had already taken a high toll. Lieutenant John Edward Dooley, Jr., described the effect of the day's intense heat, and mounting anxiety: "Some [1st Virginia Infantrymen] are actually *fainting* from the heat and dread. They have fallen to the ground overpowered by the suffocating heat and the terrors of the hour. Onward—steady—dress to the right—give way to the left—steady, not too fast—don't press upon the center," shouted experienced officers intent on maintaining proper alignment.[128] Some attackers, especially those educated at West Point and VMI, thought about Napoleon's great assaults. An omnipresent influence, the Napoleonic legacy even existed in the names of Pickett's men: teenage Private Napoleon B. Bowler, a former mechanic and member of Company A (Richardson Guards), 7th Virginia; Corporal Napoleon B. West, Company K (Halifax Rifles), 3rd Virginia, and who would be captured that afternoon and eventually died of disease in a Union prison; and

Private Napoleon Butler, a 20-year-old farmer of Company G (Rappahannock Guards), 7th Virginia. These little "Corsican emperors" in dirty gray and butternut now advanced in the 360-man 7th Virginia on Kemper's left-center.[129]

Armistead Takes Center Stage

After Garnett's and Kemper's brigades rolled over the open fields, "Lo" Armistead, a member of the Masonic Order, prepared to lead his five-regiment brigade forward. Armistead's brigade had received its baptismal fire at Seven Pines on June 1, 1862. Not unlike that hot day at Chapultepec as a 6th United States Infantry officer, Armistead stood before the flowing colors of the 53rd Virginia, his old regiment. The command had suffered less in the bombardment than Garnett's brigade and especially Kemper's brigade: a guarantee that morale was relatively higher in Armistead's brigade, while boding well for the assault.

The 46-year-old Virginian pulled out his 1850 foot-officer's saber from its ornate sheath. Standing before the 53rd Virginia, on the brigade's center and serving as "the battalion of direction of Armistead's brigade," General Armistead felt a dual pride not only in the Virginia soldiers but also in Pettigrew's North Carolina boys to the north. Armistead had been born in the port of New Bern, in the low-lying North Carolina Tidewater, in mid-February 1817. His mother, Elizabeth, had given birth to Lo at her family's plantation on a visit home, after having married against her father's wishes. Elizabeth's father had desired much more for his daughter than marriage to a career soldier, Walter Keith Armistead. He never forgave his daughter. Grizzled and with few, if any, illusions remaining in a life marked by an inordinate amount of tragedy that bestowed a cynical disposition, Armistead now carried a handful of raw corn kernels from a Pennsylvania cornfield in his pants pocket for subsistence.

Ironically, he was about to lead his well-honed brigade toward veteran troops commanded by his old friend and former comrade of the 6th United States, Pennsylvania-born General Hancock. Those few kernels of corn in Armistead's pocket represented more food than carried by most common soldiers. Most of Pickett's men already had gobbled down, "just like we always did," the three-days' rations cooked on the night of July 1. Having won distinction for bravery in the Mexican–American War and the Seminole War, Armistead was about to meet the veteran troops of his general-friend (a fellow mason) on the battlefield. Armistead, who wore a short beard, was not as beloved by his men as the more popular Garnett and Kemper. But he was widely respected, and Armistead's boys would follow him to hell and back if necessary.

Beside Lieutenant Colonel Rawley White Martin, the University of New York graduate who possessed a prestigious medical degree, Color Sergeant Leader C. Blackburn stood before the 53rd Virginia. Blackburn was shortly to find a final resting place in Pennsylvania soil. Armistead "took the folds of the [colors] tenderly in his hand." He then issued a personal challenge to Blackburn, who had demonstrated valor at Seven Pines: "Sergeant, I want you and your men to plant your colors on those works, Do you think you can do it?"[130] Sergeant Blackburn answered, "Sir, I'm going to try, and if mortal man can do it, it will be done."[131] All the while, the tension, fear, and the heat of day reached new heights.

Born on September 20, 1835, in Pittsylvania County in south-central Virginia, Lieutenant Colonel Rawley White Martin felt the heavy burden of command responsibility. However, he never doubted that these men could "succeed in driving the Federal line" from the right-center.[132]

The attackers continued to move smoothly across such a wide stretch of open ground that spanned for more than 1,000 yards over the broad fields to Cemetery Ridge. Young drummer boys beat a steady cadence to maintain morale and a disciplined step. On Kemper's left flank, Colonel Joseph Mayo, 3rd Virginia (about 350 men), described the landscape before him as "the plain."[133] Lieutenant George Williamson Finley, 56th Virginia, viewed "a green field of gently undulating wheat about [three-quarters of a] mile long and three quarters of a mile wide."[134] Colonel Taylor described how this expansive battlefield was the antithesis of Virginia's battlegrounds: "the peculiarly rough and wooded character of the country in which our army was accustomed to operate, and which, in some respects, was unfavorable for the maneuvres of large armies. . . ."[135]

Lee's men knew that to bring the brutal war to an end, a good deal of killing was called for that afternoon. One North Carolina officer, not long before he was mortally wounded at Gettysburg, described the weariness stemming from killing his fellow man to his mother in one of his last letters: "God alone knows how tired I am of this war [and] He alone knows when it will end."[136] Ironically, in January 1863, William Ross Stilwell, one of Longstreet's soldiers, predicted: "I think we will have peace by the fourth of July," or tomorrow.[137] A good many of Pickett's men had seen the destruction of their own communities and homes. They now took that searing memory and pain with them toward Cemetery Ridge, with vengeance serving as motivation. But even this passion was secondary to the burning desire of destroying Meade's army and ending the war.

Under the blazing sun, 29-year-old Lieutenant John Henry Lewis, Jr., Company G (Portsmouth Rifles), 9th Virginia, described how the order for the final brigade of Pickett's division (in reserve behind Garnett's and Kemper's brigades) to advance came at about three o'clock. Armistead shouted orders that broke the tension that hung as heavy as the searing heat. He described: "I shall never forget that moment or the command as given by General Louis A[ddison] Armistead [who] was possessed of a very loud voice, which could be heard by the whole brigade, being near my regiment [9th Virginia; Infantry Regiment but directly in front of the 53rd Virginia]. He gave the command, in words, as follows: 'Attention, second battalion! battalion of direction forward; guides center; march!'"[138]

Carrying the 53rd Virginia's banner in Armistead's center, Color Sergeant Leander C. Blackburn led the way, after having responded to Armistead's question-challenge (if he could plant the regimental battle flag atop Cemetery Ridge) that reflected his can-do spirit.[139] However, Armistead was more careful with regard to Sergeant Robert Tyler Jones, because he was President Tyler's young grandson, issuing no comparable stiff challenge.[140] Sergeant Jones never forgot how Armistead "unloosed his collar, threw away his cravat, and placed his old black hat upon the point of his sword and held it high in the air" for all to see.[141] Meanwhile, unlike Armistead and like their division commander, Generals Kemper and Garnett galloped before their troops contrary to Lee's orders for officers only to advance on foot. Kemper simply refused to obey the directive, while Garnett was hobbled by his leg injury. Armistead obeyed orders like a good soldier.[142]

At about three o'clock, the lengthy line of Armistead's troops surged ahead with bayonets sparkling in the sunshine. With discipline and muskets at right shoulder shift, Pickett's and Pettigrew's troops now simultaneously pushed forward. Leading the way, flag-bearers moved ahead with red and blue flags flapping in the light, sultry breeze of early summer.[143] On Armistead's far left flank and seeing to the north that Pettigrew's division had already advanced before his brigade (Armstead's command), Captain John A. Herndon, 38th Virginia, described in a letter: "We advanced in three lines of battle about 300 yards between—our Division being the 2nd line."[144]

Like so many others, Captain William Weldon Bentley, Company E, 24th Virginia, Kemper's brigade, was wrapped in his own thoughts and fears. As he had written to his mother of his greatest concern that now haunted the young VMI graduate (Class of 1860): "Oh! My Dear Mother you do not know how my heart aches & how sad I feel when I think that I may never see you all again on earth, & that my body may not rest under the sod of my own dear home but may be left to moulder on the field [north of the Potomac] probably with the bodies of the wicked" Yankees.[145]

Early Tactical Dysfunction and Breakdown on Pettigrew's Left

Because of the lack of artillery ammunition, Lee's plan "for the assaulting column to advance under the cover of the combined fire of the artillery" of all three corps was not fulfilled.[146] Even more, as if still another ill harbinger, serious problems developed almost immediately on the northern flank of the assault. When Pettigrew had ordered his advance, two brigades failed to move out of the heavy timber on the crest of Seminary Ridge. Despite being complimented by Mary Chesnut as "this clever man," the inexperienced Pettigrew failed to coordinate his units properly, but other officers were also at fault. When Pettigrew finally ordered the advance, only two of his brigades (instead of four) pushed forward, while Generals Joseph Robert Davis's and John Mercer Brockenbrough's brigades (on the far left from south to north) remained behind and immobile.[147]

On Brockenbrough's right, Davis's Mississippi and North Carolina brigade, which should have advanced in conjunction with Marshall's brigade on his right to the south, had belatedly pushed out of the shadowy woodlands crowning Seminary Ridge. Davis's inexperienced unit was in overall bad shape, after suffering high losses in the railroad cut sector on the first day's morning. As in the case of Archer's (now Fry's) brigade, the tough Iron Brigade had administrated the most damage with severe flank and front fires. Several hundred of Davis's men were forced to surrender, before Davis ordered the mauled brigade to withdraw. Archer's and Davis's brigades had been decimated (losing more than half their strength) after having learned a bloody tactical lesson: Such wide expanses of open ground of Adams County (seldom seen in Virginia) guaranteed that the flanks of massed Confederate assaults were exposed. Davis, educated at Miami University, Oxford, Ohio, lacked experience for the stiff challenges of the third day.

But the greatest problem occurred on the extreme left beyond Davis's Mississippi and North Carolina brigade. Here, even before the assault, Colonel Brockenbrough had committed the tactical mistake of dividing his Virginia brigade into two wings of two regiments each. Compared to its sister brigades, these Virginians had taken a relatively light beating (losing only about 15 percent of their strength) but lost their commander in the fighting along McPherson's Ridge on July 1. However, these Virginians had displayed a lack of fighting spirit, including failing to advance in conjunction with other commands.

Colonel Robert Murphy Mayo, 47th Virginia, officially commanded the left wing of the brigade, while Brockenbrough led the right wing next to Davis's brigade. The Virginia brigade was initially nowhere to be seen, to the astonishment of advancing troops to the right, when the advance began about 3:00 p.m. After all, these northernmost Virginians were to have moved out when the brigade on its right (Davis's brigade) pushed forward. After having arrived late on the field and not having properly aligned next to Pettigrew's other units, Brockenbrough's right wing finally moved out belatedly, but without its left wing. Colonel Mayo was nowhere to be found, adding to the confusion.

With the rest of his division moving relentlessly onward, Pettigrew was not surprised by the dysfunction because of the poor reputation of Brockenbrough's brigade. Nevertheless, despite its leadership problems and ·shaky record, Brockenbrough's command now served as the northernmost anchor on the front line of Pettigrew's left wing—a crucial position. Even more, this Virginia brigade was far too small for the key role of protecting the assault's extreme left flank, because of the higher leadership's failure to reinforce the Virginians and to extend the assault column north by adding artillery and extra support troops.

This rather bizarre placement of Brockenbrough's brigade in one of the most vital positions—the extreme left flank of the assault—has been one of the great paradoxes of Pickett's Charge. This strange placement of the worst brigade in the assault has long baffled historians. However, only one logical explanation can possibly explain this situation. The fact that the weakest (in all respects) and least reliable brigade of Pickett's Charge occupied the extreme left flank (instead of the largest brigade: Pettigrew's old North Carolina command) and without second line support was so tactically egregious that it simply could have been neither an accident or gross error as long assumed. After all, the lack of dependability and ineffectiveness of this Old Dominion command was well known among top leadership.

In fact, this Virginia brigade was long considered "virtually of no value in a fight." Because Lee's plans called for convergence of attackers at the clump of trees, a weak unit on the far left flank to the extreme north actually made tactical sense: If and when this Virginia brigade broke (only a matter of time), then this collapse would not be sufficient to jeopardize the primary attackers to the south to sabotage the greater goal (rather than the safety of the northern flank) of hitting Meade's right-center. Again, Pettigrew's attackers were to ease south and converge with Pickett's division to strike at the copse of trees. This overall tactical objective also explained why the two brigades (General James H. Lane and Colonel William Lee C. Lowrance—Scales's brigade—in the second line, north to south, behind Pettigrew) on the left were also the weakest and least dependable units in the assault, after Brockenbrough's brigade. Consequently and most importantly, these weak-link units would inevitably take the worst punishment (from artillery enfilading fires from Cemetery Hill) instead of the best combat units to the south that would form the battering ram to smash through the clump of trees sector. Like so many other brigades, especially Davis's command on Brockenbrough's left in the first line, Scales (command now under Lowrance in the second line) had suffered badly from tangling with 1st Corps's troops on July 1, especially from a flank fire on the left, including salvoes of canister. General Scales was cut down during this bombardment.

At long last, the late-arriving Virginians of Brockenbrough's left wing finally emerged from the dark woodlands to enter the open fields, bathed in sunlight. But Brockenbrough's Virginians trailed behind the foremost ranks to the southeast, and far from the advancing left flank of Marshall's North Carolina brigade. However, the early failing of this Old Dominion Brigade (a frontline unit) on the far north was an ominous development.[148]

Stretching more than one and a half miles in length, Lee's 11 brigades of seasoned veterans, with muskets on right shoulders, surged onward through the luxurious fields of early summer. What had been unleashed was a superior killing machine. An eerie quiet (except the trod of thousands of feet) hovered over the advancing ranks. Meanwhile, two heavy lines of experienced skirmishers in gray and butternut surged forward about 300 yards before the assault formations. Orders had been issued that not a man was to fire a shot or unleash the "Rebel Yell" until ordered by officers when close to their strategic objective: a true test of nerves and discipline even for veterans.[149]

Unlike during past assaults, the advancing Rebels were primarily focused on maintaining alignment. Silent prayers recalled from childhood days were said to themselves. The Color Corporal of the 7th Virginia on Garnett's left-center, David Emmons Johnston, never forgot how "[m]en prayed on that field that never prayed before."[150] Leading Company K (Harrison Guards), 56th Virginia, on Garnett's far left, Lieutenant George Williamson Finley, of Irish descent, felt reassurance because he had placed his small pocket Bible "inside my old gray, frockcoat [and] inner coat pocket just over my heart" for divine protection. Finley carried his well-worn Holy Bible: "[M] y wife gave it to me [and] because nothing will give you greater spiritual comfort than a New Testament [and because] absolutely nothing will stop a minie ball better than a New Testament! With luck, that rifle ball will enter at the first chapter of Matthew and stop somewhere short of the last chapter of Revelation."[151]

Pushing Forward with Flags Flying

As they fully realized, these attackers from the west (Tennessee) to the east coast (Virginia and North Carolina) to the Gulf of Mexico (Alabama) needed God's mercy that afternoon in hell. Major Charles Stephens Peyton, commanding the 19th Virginia, which contained around 425 men and advanced in Garnett's center, described how the "ground was open, but little broken, and from 800 to 1,000 yards from [Cemetery Ridge's] crest, keeping up its line almost perfectly, notwithstanding it had to climb" the first of three post-and-rail fences dividing the farmer's lush fields.[152] Major Peyton's estimations were slightly incorrect: Garnett's and Armistead's brigade would have to march across around 1,200 yards to reach Meade's right-center, while Kemper's brigade would have to traverse about 1,500 yards.[153] However, besides an occasional exploding shell, the relative calm was shattered when skirmishing escalated to new heights, crackling like firecrackers. Initially advancing about 300 yards before Pickett's and Pettigrew's divisions, Rebel skirmishers blasted away at their stubborn counterparts, who were deployed in a seemingly endless skirmish line of blue.[154]

To the rhythmic pounding of beating drums, the initial descent of Pickett's division through the open fields was deceiving to the eye. Although the terrain before the attackers seemed mostly level at first glance, the ground dipped slightly to create a shallow depression before rising to another and more commanding rise—which hardly appeared like a rise from Seminary Ridge—about 500 paces beyond the open crest of the Ridge. Beyond this rise, the large red barn of Nicholas J. Codori, "a well-known butcher" who had migrated as a bright-eyed teenager to America, loomed like a beacon (therefore, now used for guiding the attack along with the clump of trees to its rear, or east) on the horizon to the left, or just to the northeast, along the Emmitsburg Road. Located on high-ground just northwest of the head of Plum Run and just on the east side of the road, this huge, red barn (easily seen from Seminary Ridge) was a natural aiming point for the attackers, pointing the way (especially for the right and left wings' convergence) toward their ultimate objective of the copse of trees just beyond on the distant eastern horizon.

Meanwhile, the Southerners had no idea that they were steadily approaching the small farm owned by a free black agriculturalist, Maryland-born Abraham Brien. An industrious farmer who raised wheat and barley, Brien was the proud father of Pennsylvania-born children. He was descended from Irishman Sydney O'Brien. Brien's two-story, wood-frame house was situated on commanding ground at the southwestern edge of crescent-shaped Ziegler's Grove, consisting of tall oaks, hickories, and chestnuts, at the northern end of Cemetery Ridge. Dominating the open crest north, Ziegler's Grove was situated between the Brien House and Cemetery Hill to the north, while the Brien barn stood just west of the low stone wall that ran from the Angle to just past the small wooden barn.

Overlooking a wide expanse of the shallow valley to the west, the white-washed and tidy Brien House, located on the crest about 250 yards north of the Angle and higher up the ridge, served as General Hays's headquarters. Brien's children attended public school, unlike their former slave father. Gettysburg was the home to a free black population of nearly 200, including some African-Americans who had long lived on the northern end of Cemetery Ridge. Many of Gettysburg's blacks or their descendants had escaped the slave state of Maryland (less than a dozen miles to the south) where the Mason-Dixon Line separated two very different world views and societies.

Commanding a Georgia regiment in William Tatum Wofford's Peach State brigade, Colonel Goode Bryan knew that Abraham Brien (despite being in his late fifties) and his wife, Elizabeth, would fetch a hefty price in the South's slave market. A tall, independent-minded free black woman in her midthirties named Margaret "Mag" Palm, and her family, rented a house, owned by Brien, located just east of the Emmitsburg Road almost directly west of the Brien House and slightly northwest of the barn. The troops of Pettigrew's left flank were about to shortly march past the Palm House without ever knowing that their occupants were of African heritage.

Unknown to the attackers, Meade's headquarters was then located at the white-washed farmhouse of Widow Lydia Leister. Located along the Taneytown Road, the two-room Leister House stood almost directly east and just southeast of the Abraham Brien barn, northeast of the Codori Farm. Most importantly, the ultimate target of the assault, the copse of trees southwest of Meade's head-quarters and south of the Brien barn, lay directly ahead of Pickett's division's left.

Farther north, the Brien House and barn, built in 1856, stood atop Cemetery Ridge before Pettigrew's advancing ranks.

On the eastern horizon to the attackers' view, the virgin timber of Ziegler's Grove rose up at the highest point of Cemetery Ridge, while the clump of trees to the south stood on lower ground farther down the ridge. A lengthy stretch of open ground (the gently descending ridge) spanned south from the extensive grove of the industrious German farmer to the copse of trees. Behind Cemetery Ridge ran the Baltimore Road, which led southeast to the major port city ripe for the taking.

At the head of the 19th Virginia (Garnett's center) was the regimental color guard, consisting of Color Corporals William Black and John Harvey, a carpenter. Harvey's lowly status among his peers had been considerably elevated by his decision to protect the sacred flag with his life. Meanwhile, Color Sergeant William O. Thomas carried the colorful banner of the 8th Virginia, which consisted of men from Dunmore, Augusta, Berkeley, Fincastle, Culpeper, Hampshire, and Frederick counties. Advancing on the left, or southern, flank of Garnett's brigade, Colonel Eppa Hunton's regiment ("the Bloody Eighth") provided a solid anchor.

Only about five minutes after the beginning of the advance, an even more wide-open view was provided to Pickett's troops upon reaching the top of the grassy rise (the first time that the true commanding height was fully realized) of an open plateau, that extended like a broad, grassy shelf east beyond the crest of Seminary Ridge. Pickett and his officers could see all of their advancing line, moving "rapidly and grandly" in one soldier's words; it was an awe-inspiring sight. Now, the entirety of the Codori House and its prominent red barn, positioned on high-ground of the Emmitsburg Road ridge, to the left (slightly northeast) was once again seen from this commanding perch, from where the land sloped downward in every direction. This rise was quickly passed by the briskly moving ranks of gray and butternut that seemed to span endlessly through the brightly colored fields.

From this commanding rise, the foremost Virginians looked down the open slopes that led east to the Emmitsburg Road, which ran along lower ground of the Plum Run's pristine upper valley, although situated on a north–south running ridge: the Emmitsburg Road ridge. More significant, from this high point (the crest of the rise) that overlooked the shallow valley, not only the Emmitsburg Road and ridge (not fully perceptible to the eye) but also Cemetery Ridge's expansive length could be now seen. Ironically, to the naked eye of the attackers, Cemetery Ridge no longer appeared exceptionally high, from this elevated point. Therefore, the view from this grassy rise presented a deceiving illusion, because Cemetery Ridge looked less high than was actually the case. In this sense, the attackers were in for a nasty surprise once they eventually crossed the Emmitsburg Road and when the ground (Cemetery Ridge's western slope) began to gradually rise toward the crest.

All the while, the clump of bright-green oak trees now stood out like an umbrella-shaped beacon on the heat-hazed horizon of Cemetery Ridge. Lieutenant John Edward Dooley, Jr., 1st Virginia, Kemper's brigade, described: "steady—keep well in line—there is the line of guns we must take—right in front—but how far they appear! . . . Upon the center of this we must march."[155] A thin cloud of dust slowly rose from thousands of marching feet, moving in almost perfect step like a well-oiled machine. This dusty haze hovered above and slightly to the rear of the lengthy formations "like the spray at the prow of a vessel" on the ocean, wrote Sergeant Randolph Abbott Shotwell, Company H (Potomac Greys), 8th Virginia, on Garnett's far right.[156]

The Most Majestic Advance of this War

As mentioned, one of the popular misconceptions about Pickett's Charge was that the attackers marched over almost perfectly flat terrain: a core tenet of the alleged supreme folly of Lee's assault. However, the gently rolling terrain, with dips and folds in the land that hid movement and provided protection, was anything but the stereotypical flat landscape that automatically ordained a failed assault. On Pickett's right flank, the terrain before Kemper's brigade and leading to the copse of trees was basically divided into three swales. Meanwhile, two swales, on either side of the William Bliss Farm, lay along the advance of Pettigrew's right. Generally, the attackers between the right and left flanks faced less rolling terrain, "the multitudinous rows" of farmer's split rail fences, and an occasional low hedgerow.[157] Meanwhile, Pettigrew's troops continued to advance at "right-shoulder-shift" as if on a parade ground in Charlotte, Tallahassee, or Nashville, but along a wider front than Pickett's surging ranks. Riding his thoroughbred "dapple-gray," Pettigrew led the way and inspired his troops.[158] Pettigrew felt self-satisfaction in having successfully thwarted a young relative's efforts to join his staff. The enthusiastic novice had been under the illusion that he would find "a safe place" on the general's staff. Pettigrew had convinced the youth otherwise, emphasizing, "I assure you that the most unsafe place in the Brigade is about me!"[159] Pettigrew now remained true to his word.

Major Raphael J. Moses, a witty, 53-year-old Jewish soldier in gray, watched the sweeping advance from Seminary Ridge. From the Pentateuch (Torah), he never forgot the severe trials of an ancient people's struggle for survival by heroically persevering for centuries, despite slavery, persecution, and exile. Blessed with a wry sense of humor, he was the father of three sons in gray: Israel Moses Nunez, Raphael J. Moses, Jr., and Albert Moses Luria. Perhaps taking inspiration from the great Jewish victory when more than 5,000 prime fighting men of the famed Roman Legions were destroyed at the Beth Horon Pass in the Province of Judea in 66 AD, Moses now served as the chief commissary officer of Longstreet's corps. Moses described that "the charge of Pickett's division was not exceeded in valor by the charge of the six hundred" during the Light Brigade's attack on October 25, 1854 in the Crimean War.[160] Captain James E. Poindexter, Company H (Secession Guards), 38th Virginia, marveled how Garnett's and Kemper's brigades moved smoothly over the open ground "like waves of the sea."[161]

A Pennsylvania prisoner captured during Barksdale's charge that had overwhelmed the strategic high-ground of the Peach Orchard on July 2, Lieutenant Frank E. Moran, of Irish descent, described the drama from an eerily silent Cemetery Ridge: "What a thrilling sight! As the column advanced over the open plain and began to descend the gentle slope in [the] front, . . . a chilling fear possessed me for those agonizing minutes that our army had abandoned Cemetery Hill, the [Cemetery] Ridge and Round Tops, and that all was lost [but] The Union batteries opened almost immediately" to break the haunting silence.[162]

Amid the exploding shells, Pickett's men fell in clumps to stain the green grass with splashes of red. One soldier of the 14th Virginia (then containing about 480 men), Armistead's brigade, described in a letter to his wife: "Now & then a man's hand or arm or leg would fly like feathers before the wind."[163] Ignoring the horror, the Rebels continued onward with discipline, stepping over the increasing number of bodies. After surviving so many bloody campaigns, these veterans had been thoroughly "calloused." In one soldier's words from a letter: "We don't mind seeing a dead man" at all. They now even ignored the deaths of relatives who dropped around them.[164] In the 24th Virginia, Kemper's brigade, Captain William Weldon Bentley envisioned the decisive success so "that God would in His infinite goodness bring about a speedy peace."[165]

With their .577 caliber Enfield rifles on right shoulders, two Fluvanna County, Virginia, brothers advanced in Company C (Fluvanna Rifle Guard),

14th Virginia, on Armistead's far right. Thirty-four-year-old Colonel James Gregory Hodges, an ex-physician from Portsmouth, led the 14th Virginia in his last charge. Meanwhile, the two Ross brothers (Privates James Eastin Ross and William David Ross, the sons of James Ross and Frances Hudson Loving Ross, of Wilmington, Fluvanna County, Virginia) marched side by side with their Fluvanna comrades. Neither brother returned from the attack alive.[166]

To lift spirits, the brass regimental band of the 7th Virginia, Kemper's brigade, played "in the same manner that it would, had the division [Pickett's] been passing in review."[167] Chief Musician Richard Hughes led the young musicians (the oldest musician was 25) from Companies A and C, who advanced instead of remaining behind as usual. These musicians in gray included teenagers James F. Melton, an ex-farmer who had enlisted at Culpeper Country House in April 1861, and William H. Gaar, an 18-year-old former student. Francis Marion Burrows was another musician, having enlisted barely a year before at Richmond. Like many other young Rebels, Burrows had been named in honor of South Carolina's famed guerrilla fighter, the "Swamp Fox," of the American Revolution.[168]

Tantalizing Visions Add Fuel to the Relentless Advance

Soldiers advanced faster because they knew that Washington, DC (like Baltimore) lay over the low range of bluish hills on the southeastern horizon. If everything went according to Lee's plan, then a triumphant march all the way to the Yankee capital would be easy because the land gradually dropped to the Tidewater's lowlands and to where the Potomac River waters became tidal. In the 8th Virginia's ranks on Garnett's right flank and adjacent to Kemper's left, Private James P. Boss advanced barefoot. Known as "Little Jimmie," he had been hobbled by the "broken rock of the McAdamized turnpike" on the march to Gettysburg. His mother's words reminded him "to get himself a pair of new boots in Baltimore." However, "Little Jimmie," was advancing stoically to his death. Having sensed as much, this ill-fated young man had just handed his journal to a comrade to send back to his mother upon his death—a timely last wish of Private James P. Boss.[169]

All the while, thousands of soldiers advanced relentlessly while "see[ing] the mouth of the gaping cannon waiting for us to get in range," wrote North Carolinian Captain Louis Gourdin Young, who rode beside Pettigrew.[170] The North Carolina troops (14 regiments) of Pettigrew's division continued onward through shell explosions from the long-range artillery fire, including soldiers of the Jeff Davis Mountain Rifles (Company A), 26th North Carolina. These men hailed from the picturesque Blue Ridge of western North Carolina. In the same regiment, Lieutenant John R. Emerson, Company E, had already prepared for the worst. He had made a will that "bequeath[ed] to my wife [Martha] all my property of all and every kind."[171]

In the 1st Virginia's surging ranks, which consisted mostly of city boys and a large number of Richmond Irish who advanced in the center of Kemper's brigade (the extreme right flank of the southern wing of the assault), Lieutenant John Edward Dooley, Jr., marveled, "how gentle the slope!"[172] Another Confederate remarked, "Before us stood Cemetery Heights, of which we could get glimpses through rifts in the clouds of powder-smoke which enveloped them."[173]

Leading his 3rd Virginia (on Kemper's left flank) onward, Colonel Joseph Mayo carried a grim reminder of the cannonade that had pounded Seminary Ridge's reverse slope. He ignored the shattered blood and brains of "two poor fellows" of Company D (Southampton Greys, organized in the Tidewater town of Jerusalem, today's Courtland, Virginia: the first strategic target of the most successful slave revolt in American history, Nat Turner's August 1832 insurrection in Southampton County). One victim of an exploding shell had "flaming red hair," and his blood stained Colonel Mayo's gray uniform at the shoulder.[174] Major Edmund Berkeley, meanwhile, advanced before his 8th Virginia with the blood and brains of Private Albert J. Morris of Company D, Champe Rifles (who had been decapitated by a shell) on his hat.[175] On Kemper's far right, the young "regimental drummer" of the 24th Virginia, James O. Bussey, led the way with the color-bearer. The rhythmic cadence of Bussey's drum helped to keep these disciplined men in near perfect step and inspired confidence, while moving relentlessly through the knee-high grass and fields of summer.

Few sights of this war were more breathtaking than the spectacle of so many brigades, with a seeming endless number of red and blue (Virginia and North Carolina state flags) waving above formations, while rolling onward over these picturesque farm lands. Thousands of soldiers pushed relentlessly toward Cemetery Ridge, as if nothing in the world could stop them. In the first line, 10 blue flags of Virginia (equally divided between Garnett's and Kemper's brigades) fluttered in the faint summer breeze, blowing gently from the west to the attackers' backs.[176] With the 2nd Corps, a mounted Captain Haskell marveled how "they move, as with one soul, in perfect order . . . magnificent, grim, irresistible."[177] Advancing in the 14th Virginia's ranks, Private Meredith (Merit)

Branch Thurman, a strong-armed former coal miner, fulfilled a promise to his wife Jane as penned in a letter: "I promust you that . . . I never intend to act a coward."[178] Near the clump of trees, West Pointer General Alexander Hays, age 44, watched the splendid advance, which was "as steady as if impelled by machinery."[179] General Hooker's on-target estimation of Lee's army held true, because it "had, *by discipline alone*, acquired a character for steadiness and efficiency unsurpassed, in my judgment, in ancient or modern times."[180]

However, the awesome appearance of thousands of well-trained veterans advancing smoothly onward at about one hundred yards per minute, through the green (clover and grass) and gold (wheat) fields that filled the broad length of the shallow valley, scoured by ancient glaciers, between the two parallel ridges, was deceiving. After moving farther down the gentle slope toward the Emmitsburg Road and with Codori's red barn a dominant feature of the landscape to Pickett's left, Cemetery Ridge began to look increasingly higher to the attackers. But in fact, Cemetery Ridge rose to only about 40 feet higher than the lowest point between Seminary and Cemetery Ridges.

Flying Artillery Crisis

In what might have been expected of an army in its first battle, no one seemed to have noticed that the flying artillery had already faltered badly. Besides infantry support, it should have been sent forward to protect the flanks and behind the first line troops. The nine howitzers, positioned before Pickett's division, that were to have advanced with the infantry as Lee desired, were not moving forward. When Colonel Alexander dispatched messengers to hurry up the reserve guns under Major John B. Richardson, they could not be located. As envisioned by Lee, all guns were to have advanced as flying artillery to "keep up with the infantry" to protect the open flanks of the assault. However, these field pieces were now either too low on ammunition or had suffered too heavy losses in men and horses. Captain Joseph G. Blount's Virginia battery (Lynchburg Artillery, Dearing's battalion, Longstreet's corps) had lost five gunners and 41 out of 48 horses during the bombardment. Because of the comedy of errors, Richardson's guns were "delayed beyond expectation," in Pendleton's words, in advancing as flying artillery on Pickett's right to protect the southern flank. Ironically, because Dearing and other artillery commanders had been under the correct impression that the bombardment was planned for only about 15–20 minutes, the replenishing ammunition limbers had not been a priority. Alexander was now unable to utilize the highly mobile Virginia guns of four veteran batteries of Dearing's Virginia battalion, because most of its rounds had been so rapidly expended.

Considering this early sabotaging of the Confederate chances for success, Pendleton should have remained a minister back in Lexington, Virginia. Another clog in this ultra-democratic army of revolutionaries, Pendleton was openly mocked as "Parson" and "Granny" Pendleton. Pendleton had lingered in command of Lee's artillery like a sacred religious relic of a martyred Christian saint in an ancient French Cathedral in Lyon or Reims. He only belatedly discovered that "the anticipated advance of the artillery, delayed beyond expectation, I found [a good] many batteries getting out of or low in ammunition . . . . Frequent shell endangering the 1st Corps [Longstreet] ordnance train in the convenient locality I had assigned it, it had been removed farther back [upon his orders]. This necessitated [the] longest time for refilling caissons [but] What was worse, the train itself was very limited, so that its stock was soon exhausted, rendering requisite demand upon the reserve train, farther off."[181]

With his artillery battalion of four batteries out of ammunition, Major Dearing belatedly "sent back my caissons . . . for a fresh supply, but they could not get it."[182] Indeed, the 1st Corps's artillery train had been moved farther to the rear by Pendleton to escape the falling shells that even caused havoc at the field hospital of Pickett's division. Then, Pendleton failed to inform his battery commanders of the new location of the ordnance train. Rebel cannoneers, therefore, now stood idly by silent guns instead of providing fire support as flying artillery.[183]

But the greatest crisis continued to exist on the extreme left wing of the assault. Here, Brockenbrough's Virginians, after having failed to advance from Seminary Ridge on time, which had then left the extreme northern flank (Davis's Mississippi and North Carolina brigade) exposed, faltered before the assault even began, because of a disastrous mix of dysfunction and communications failures. Mayo's left wing only finally caught up with the brigade's other half, the right, wing under Colonel Brockenbrough, after the Virginians raced forward on the double-quick. However, this much-belated unity made little difference because of the brigade's overall inherent weaknesses and poor leadership.

Unseen by Pettigrew but deciphered by the men of Trimble's two brigades (General James H. Lane and Colonel William Lee J. Lowrance of Pender's division from north to south) advancing in a second line in the rear of Pettigrew's division (then under Marshall), Brockenbrough's Virginia soldiers, individually and in small groups, early began to fall back, heading rearward across the open fields in an early flight that dismayed onlookers.[184] Advancing with the 7th North Carolina, Lane's brigade, Major J. McLeod Turner, who was soon wounded and captured, could hardly believe his eyes, because "crowds of stragglers [were now] coming to the rear."[185]

But to be fair, Brockenbrough's ill-fated soldiers of the smallest brigade (perhaps not even 500 men) in the assault suffered from the artillery fire's severity. They had been victimized because the extreme left flank was now "dangling in the air" without support or protection, especially from flying artillery. Therefore, the Virginians' vulnerable left flank had been swept early by "the full force" of 31 artillery pieces under Major Thomas W. Osborn, atop Cemetery Hill. Osborn had wisely conserved ammunition during the bombardment for the express purpose of mauling infantry exposed in the open. While the Confederate guns had been successful in weakening Meade's right-center with regard to artillery but not infantry support, the Union artillery on the flanks, especially Cemetery Hill to the northeast, had been mostly ignored. Therefore, the far left of Pettigrew's line—Brockenbrough's Virginia brigade, which advanced perpendicular to the Union guns atop Cemetery Hill—was cut to pieces early. Osborn was amazed by the sheer destruction delivered by his murderous oblique fire: "The whole force of our artillery was brought to bear . . . and the havoc produced upon their ranks was surprising."[186] Another Yankee officer watched as "[a]rms, heads, blankets, guns and knapsacks were thrown and tossed into the clear air."[187]

The flight of increasing numbers of Virginians on the extreme left flank and the lack of flying artillery support on the far north led to an early crisis. With Brockenbrough's Old Dominion boys faltering badly, Davis and his Mississippi and North Carolina brigade to the right (or south) became more vulnerable on its left flank. An ever-mounting list of blunders from miscommunication and the lack of coordination early sabotaged Lee's planned vital artillery support on the left flank.

Flying Artillery's Ultimate Failure

Major William Thomas Poague was shocked by these fast-paced developments. A graduate of Washington College (today's Washington and Lee University in Lexington, Virginia) in 1857, 28-year-old Major Poague now commanded an artillery battalion, Pender's division, 3rd Corps. Poague's batteries of 10 cannon, including Captain Graham's 1st North Carolina Battery (Charlotte Artillery), were aligned in the "best" position in the rear of the right of Hill's division and the rear of Pettigrew's division.[188] Major Poague revealed his lack of understanding of the required flying artillery, because his "orders were to open on the enemy's position in front . . . and that as soon as our infantry, in the charge to follow, reached the crest, to proceed as rapidly as possible to the summit with all my guns [but] Not a word was said about following the infantry as they advanced to the attack."[189]

Therefore, unknown to Lee and with Longstreet not rectifying the situation, Poague's guns failed to fulfill the crucial role of flying artillery to provide all-important fire support to protect the vulnerable northern flank of the assault.[190] Likewise, after having expended too much long-range ammunition and without sufficient rounds remaining in ammunition chests, Dearing's Virginia battalion was unable to fulfill the vital flying artillery role on the opposite, or right, flank, as envisioned by Lee.[191] When Longstreet had finally learned that Major Richardson's guns could not be located and that ammunition was low, he belatedly made his final attempt to cancel the assault (through Alexander) until additional artillery ammunition could be secured. But Alexander explained to the lieutenant general that this would take too much time, allowing the enemy ample time to bring up replacement guns and ammunition to negate what the cannonade had achieved on the right-center.[192]

Even worse, at a time when the Confederate cannonade had been successful in eliminating so many guns in the targeted sector, Anderson's division, Hill's 3rd Corps (most of which had been spared the slaughter on bloody July 2) had not aligned either behind or on the flank of Pickett's division to act as a mobile strategic reserve. Besides flank protection from Anderson's division, Lee had also planned for about 4,000 troops to advance 300–400 yards in Pickett's rear—an ideal position to exploit any breakthrough. Meanwhile, with regard to the other half of Anderson's troops, two brigades (Wright and Posey) were to protect Pickett's right flank that hung in midair. But Longstreet failed to hurry Anderson's troops forward.

Because Lee had also bestowed Longstreet with the authority to utilize the four brigades of Heth's (by then Pettigrew's) division and two brigades from Pender's division, this delegation called for close cooperation between Hill and Longstreet. To be fair, Longstreet, 1st Corps's commander, was not familiar with 3rd Corps commanders and units. For a host of reasons, the much-needed cooperation was not forthcoming. Therefore, no guns were advanced as flying artillery to support Hill's attackers on the north. Sadly, Longstreet and Hill failed to correct this disastrous situation by either communicating or working closer. Hill was performing way below expectations partly because of health problems he faced, much like Lee and unlike Longstreet, as well as war weariness. He was partly incapacitated with a bad case of gonorrhea from a New York City prostitute, while a naive cadet in the 1840s.

Because this was Longstreet's assault, Lee was less active than usual in seeing that his orders were carried out to the letter. Longstreet was even less active than Lee, but for entirely different reasons. Saddled with two untried corps commanders (Hill and Ewell) and another (Longstreet) who opposed the assault's launching, Lee was largely on his own. He assumed that his top lieutenants were working closely together in harmony. In a dismal repeat performance of July 2, Longstreet or Hill failed to ensure that the 8,000 men of Anderson's division (four brigades) promptly moved up to protect the flanks.[193]

Lee was unable to personally make sure that Longstreet was doing his job partly because, as revealed in his own summer 1863 words to President Davis: "I am becoming more and more incapable of exertion and am thus prevented from the personal examinations, and given the personal supervision to the operations in the field which I feel to be necessary. I am so dull that in making use of the eyes of others I am frequently misled."[194] Colonel Taylor lamented the overall tactical situation, after the "given signal, the movement began, b[ecause] the plan agreed on [by Lee and Longstreet] was not carried out."[195] General Wilcox, hesitant to advance and not believing that the assault would succeed like Longstreet, failed to push his Alabama brigade forward either in the rear or to Pickett's right.[196]

Unfortunately for Lee, "neither Longstreet nor Hill did anything to coordinate the attack, strengthen its support, or create a diversion [and therefore] The infantry was left alone" to do or die.[197] Longstreet's July 3 failures mirrored those of the previous day's offensive effort. An angry General Lafayette McLaws lamented the missed opportunities of July 2, describing to his wife in a July 7 letter: "Longstreet is to blame . . . I consider him a humbug—a man of small capacity. . . ."[198]

In the past, Lee had always made sure to encamp close to Longstreet and maintain close contact, because it was "necessary [to] plod him into action." Not only with regard to Anderson's division, Lee also expected Longstreet to hurl McLaws's and Hood's divisions on the right forward to exploit any initial breakthrough. Longstreet later admitted how Hood's and McLaws's divisions were to "spring the charge as soon as the breach at the centre could be made," but failed to act in accordance to Lee's overall plan.[199]

Much like Hood's and McLaws's divisions on the comatose right, "A.P. Hill who had a large force nearby remained largely unengaged" instead of supporting the assault at the rear or flanks.[200] After having taken a "slight wound" at Chancellorsville and suffering from illness, Hill (in his first battle as a corps commander and promoted beyond his abilities) was at his worst that day, like Longstreet.[201]

Longstreet (South Carolina–born but raised in northern Georgia) was convinced that Ambrose Powell Hill (a Virginian) owed his rapid promotion to the 3rd Corps commander more to omnipresent Virginia politics than ability.[202] Clearly, Lee had made a serious mistake in promoting Hill to command the 3rd Corps over two senior commanders, Generals McLaws, a capable West Pointer, and Daniel Harvey Hill, Stonewall Jackson's brother-in-law. A highly qualified West Point graduate, Daniel Harvey Hill had headed the North Carolina Military Academy (a state-operated institution established in 1859) in Charlotte, North Carolina.[203]

Therefore, as originally envisioned by Lee, vital factors were already missing from the formula for decisive victory, especially the lack of troops to protect flanks from supporting infantry and artillery and as a strategic reserve to exploit any initial success.[204] Captain Graham, 1st North Carolina Artillery, lamented the early problems in a July 30 letter to his father: "The Infantry were to have charged through the dense smoke immediately upon the cessation of our fire, but by some mismanagement there was quite a delay, until everything became settled, and the Enemy had time to prepare for the charge."[205]

Meanwhile, on Meade's line at the right-center, Captain Haskell described the hectic activity along the crest: "The battery men .... were handling ammunition boxes and replenishing those that were empty."[206] Because of General Hunt's timely efforts, Union gunners had saved most of their ammunition for when the advancing infantrymen grew close.[207]

Ominous Signs

Of course, all of these ominous developments in regard to a complex battle plan already gone awry were unknown to Lee. With nearly twice as many troops in the front ranks compared to the second line, the attackers continued onward with a will of their own. Inspiring his troops, General Armistead continued to lead the way with grim resolve, because all that now mattered to the West Pointer was to achieve decisive victory at any cost.[208]

Lieutenant John Henry Lewis, Jr., described how Armistead, a North Carolinian born in the Tidewater like Pettigrew, steadily advanced "about twenty paces in front of his brigade [although] His place was in the rear, properly."[209] However, Armistead was actually in overall bad physical shape, weak and wracked by fatigue, mental and physical. For stimulation, therefore, the general now carried a flask of brandy in a satchel that hung from a leather strap from his shoulder. Color Corporal David, "Davy," Emmons Johnston, 7th Virginia, was shocked that fatalistic Virginia soldiers had earlier bid farewell to their comrades, "Good bye, boys! Good bye!"[210] Indeed, "right before us stood Cemetery Heights in awful grandeur."[211]

As revealed in a letter, Captain Graham, commanding the 1st North Carolina Artillery, early ascertained weaknesses among some of Pettigrew's veterans: "It was a very oppressive day, and our troops were much fatigued by the work of the two days previous [and] I feared then I could see a want of resolution in our men. And I heard many say, 'that [this] is worse than Malvern Hill,' and "I don't hardly think that position can be carried,' etc., etc., enough to make me apprehensive about the result" of the attack.[212] Major Thomas W. Osborn, who commanded nearly fifty XI Corps's artillery pieces on Cemetery Hill, viewed the assaults at Malvern Hill and Fredericksburg as "criminally foolish." But contrary to popular stereotypes, such was not the case in regard to Pickett's Charge.[213] Without realizing Lee's plan to strike via Stuart's cavalry from the rear, Captain Henry Livermore Abbott, commanding the 20th Massachusetts Volunteer Infantry, Gibbon's 2nd Division, Hancock's 2nd Corps, was confident that they "would give them Fredericksburg."[214]

Wavering resolve at the attack's beginning only revealed how this first modern war had been transformed into a nightmare for the long-suffering common soldiers, who had become little more than cannon fodder.[215] Veterans were ever-mindful of the slaughters at Malvern Hill and Fredericksburg.[216] Captain Graham, a University of North Carolina graduate, and others, had early ascertained what was the early lack of resolve on Pettigrew's left flank: disturbing evidence of the "want of resolution" that revealed the Achilles' heel of Pickett's Charge.[217]

Nevertheless, without adequate support and protection on either side that guaranteed even greater problems, the assault continued rolling over the open fields. Symbolically, with regard to analogies to ancient military history, Sergeant Achilles H. Burnett (like many soldiers with classical first names) surged onward in Company H (Secession Guards), 38th Virginia, on Armistead's left.

Determined to emulate an ancient warrior ethos, the men of Company B, of Colonel Stuart's 56th Virginia, were known as the Mecklenburg Spartans in honor of the most celebrated ancient warriors of western civilization.[218]

Another astute observer who had been wounded in the first day's combat, General Alfred Moore Scales, a former United States congressman in his midthirties—whose North Carolina brigade was located in the second line (to Lane's right, in support of Pettigrew's division)—was also disturbed by fast-paced tactical developments on the north. Still reeling from the "slaughter" of July 1, he detected early on an inexplicable sluggishness. A University of North Carolina man and former attorney, Scales wrote how the left wing's advance "was not characterized by that dash and enthusiasm which usually attends an infantry charge of shorter duration."[219] This should have come as no surprise because Lee had informed General Trimble that many of "these poor boys should go to the rear" for treatment.[220]

A valuable tactical lesson had been learned the hard way on July 1. Archer's and Davis's brigades had been decimated in their assaults because the open ground of farmer's fields guaranteed that their unprotected flanks were easily enfiladed and cut to pieces. Clearly, the old ways of attacking as in Virginia (where woodlands most often protected flanks) were no longer tactically viable on this rolling terrain around Gettysburg. Therefore, Lee had prudently ordered that the flanks were to be protected by ample artillery and infantry, but his subordinates had failed him.[221]

However, the problems developing on Pettigrew's left wing perhaps could be partly solved by inspired leadership of experienced commanders, who led by example rather than remaining safely to the rear. Reverend J. Williams emphasized one secret to the army's remarkable successes: "Personal devotion to their leaders was also an important element in their discipline and *morale*."[222] Fortunately, Pettigrew's division possessed many resolute officers. When Pettigrew first learned of the failure of Brockenbrough's small Virginia brigade, he merely stated how it actually "would not matter," because thousands of his hardened veterans south of the collapsing extreme left flank still continued onward. Contrary to conventional wisdom, Pettigrew's tactical analysis was actually correct. The general's cynical words have provided additional proof that this small Old Dominion brigade (placed there by Pettigrew, which partly revealed North Carolina bias—Virginia over Tar Heel) had been utilized as little more than cannon fodder. Indeed, this small Virginia brigade, with its longtime poor performance record, was most likely deliberately sacrificed for a greater good: a tactical situation—the extreme left's tactical problems actually helped to guarantee the stability of the center and right of the assault—that allowed Pettigrew's best troops to continue toward Meade's right-center without a break. Pettigrew, therefore, nonchalantly declined the timely offer of a vigilant staff officer to ride north to assist to Brockenbrough's hard-hit unit.

Embracing a lifelong devotion to the Bible's verses of wisdom of ancient Hebrew scholars, this dashing general known as "Johnston Pettigrew" to the Richmond elite and "earnest student of the scriptures" believed that God's will would lead his attackers to the most remarkable Confederate success to date. Pettigrew's men were convinced that they "will go through your damned Yankee line" like a knife cutting through butter. These Tar Heels were as tough, if not tougher, than the Virginians. When some Alabama officers wrote a disparaging report about Pettigrew's North Carolina boys at Suffolk, Virginia, the colonel and major of the 55th North Carolina (positioned on Davis's left-center) had challenged two Alabama captains to a duel. Such representative fighting spirit ensured that the 55th North Carolina soldiers reached the stone wall.[223]

Captain Edward Fletcher was one such dependable 55th North Carolina officer. Twenty-six-year-old Captain Fletcher wore a dark, Hardee-style hat— ironically like the Iron Brigade men. He possessed a University of North Carolina degree (Class of 1858), and had practiced law in Roxboro, north-central North Carolina. Fletcher hoped to marry Jennie Pearson, whom he would never see again, as he would meet his Maker that afternoon.[224]

Most importantly, Pettigrew's battle-hardened attackers possessed true shock power, because they were well trained, were led by experienced officers, and possessed well-honed discipline. Consequently, Lee's men continued to advance with orders to not fire until close to their opponent and then rely on the bayonet.[225]

Despite being in bad physical shape overall, Armistead's decision to lead his Virginians into the vortex of the storm revealed his mettle. For his performance at Seven Pines on June 1, 1862, Armistead had been highly complimented by his division commander, General Daniel Harvey Hill. Hill had marveled how, with only a handful of men, "that gallant officer [Armistead] maintained his ground against an entire Brigade" of Yankees.[226] However, a tragic fate in his personal and professional life haunted Armistead, whose wives and close friends (even when young) always seemed to die. At Malvern Hill, Lee had chosen Armistead to begin the attack in his last attempt to destroy the Army of the Potomac.[227] In the 9th Virginia's ranks, meanwhile, Lieutenant James Francis

Crocker, who had suffered three wounds at Malvern Hill, advanced at the head of his troops, after mastering his fears like Armistead.[228]

The disastrous "Charge of the Light Brigade" at Balaclava on the Crimean Peninsula on the Black Sea still haunted Colonel George T. Gordon. He commanded the 34th North Carolina, the left-center regiment of Lowrance's (Scaless) North Carolina brigade, on July 3. A former British marine of imposing size, he was a gambler by nature, taking as many risks on the gaming table as on the battlefield. Distinguished by red hair and whiskers, Gordon soon fell wounded in the attack.[229]

A gentlemanly Englishman, Gordon was the very antithesis of the rough-and-tumble Irish Confederates. However, Gordon's own fighting spirit was comparable to the Irish. This combativeness was revealed when Scotch-Irish Sergeant Major Robert McCandlish Jones, a 22-year-old enlisted leader of the 1st Virginia and a former schoolmate of Captain Robert A. Bright, Pickett's staff officer, had barked to the captain: "Bob, turn us loose and we will take" Cemetery Ridge.[230]

Garnett's Vindication

Amid the sweltering heat, meanwhile, Brigadier Generals Garnett, Kemper, and Armistead continued to lead their brigades onward through the exploding shells. No longer confined to an ambulance, where he had been for the past two weeks and as late as on the morning of July 3, "Dick" Garnett, age 45, rose to the challenge. He had limped out of a rickety army ambulance just to lead his brigade during its greatest charge, ignoring the pain of his disabling injury and the danger of leading the way. Although Pickett advanced in the rear of his division's center and played a role in hurrying couriers to implore Longstreet to dispatch support, he remained safely at the rear, unlike his brigade commanders.[231] Major Walter Harrison respected Garnett because he "was really in no condition, physically, to have been upon the battlefield, but it was impossible to dissuade him from leading his brigade" forward.[232]

Garnett was still haunted by a seemingly ill-fated past. His twin brother, William, had died tragically in 1855 while attempting to save lives during a yellow fever epidemic in Norfolk, Virginia, from where many of Pickett's men hailed. The Garnett family's tragic losses dealt severe blows to the general. Exile from surviving family members led to a lonely life for him as a bachelor in the prewar United States Army, except when he (like Pickett) took a common-law Indian wife. He had served in the remote corners of the West, including the

Dakotas, California, and New Mexico. Therefore, Garnett never permanently settled down.[233]

Life's unpredictable ups and down had taken a toll on Garnett. Leading his troops onward through the expansive fields of wheat, rye, and clover now offered a redemptive moment to his mental anguish. Shaped by Southern society's values of manhood and high expectations, Garnett was psychologically vulnerable because of his "peculiar sensitiveness" in matters of honor, in Major Walter Harrison's words.[234] He had clashed with Stonewall Jackson, resulting in his arrest over a relatively minor incident in 1862. That humiliation still stung Garnett deeply. As Major Harrison explained: "This was at most, perhaps, but a matter of temper, which might have been readily passed over and forgotten; yet to the brave, proud, and sensitive spirit of Garnett, it was a cruel blow, from the effect of which *his* heart was never relieved. . . ."[235] Ironically, Garnett had no need to prove his courage, but was "ever thereafter anxious to expose himself" in battle. Therefore, "all lamented his entertaining the morbid feeling" that he carried with him toward Cemetery Ridge.[236] Major Harrison described how "this ever-pressure upon his mind drove him into the jaws of death," although Garnett "was unable to walk, and scarcely able to sit on his horse, in fact physically unfit to go into the fight."[237]

Like the debonair Garnett, Armistead also should have been in a hospital instead of leading his troops in the attack. Not even his only son, Lieutenant Walker Keith Armistead, who had served as his aide-de-camp since April 30, 1863, had been able to ease his father's mental anguish because of life's tragic twists and turns. Although he "suffered much from over-exertion, want of sleep, and mental anxiety within the last few days," Armistead continued to lead the way, encouraging everyone onward by his inspiring example.[238]

Much like Pickett and Kemper, Garnett was also haunted by May 12, 1863, when a national hero was buried with full military honors, after the "accursed miscue" of fratricide in Chancellorsville's forests. Pickett, Garnett, and Kemper had served as pallbearers when the embalmed body of "Old Jack" was carried from the governor's mansion to the "Capitol of the new Republic." Symbolically, Pickett's hand-picked troops had served as the honorary military escort for the hearse that carried Stonewall Jackson's coffin draped in a Confederate flag, drawn by four white horses. At that time, Garnett had lamented, "Who can fill his place?" That day's memory reminded Pickett, Kemper, and Garnett (who manfully put aside plenty of ill will to serve as Jackson's pallbearer) that the presence of the lamented Jackson (instead of Longstreet) was needed on July 3 as never before.[239] Lee had embraced the only tactical formula that could possibly save the fledgling nation: "Stonewall's tactics were the best—hard knocks, blow after blow in rapid succession. . . ."[240]

Colonel William Dabney Stuart, age 32, also refused to remain behind in a safe position. He helped to fill the void left by Pickett's uninspired leadership in commanding the 56th Virginia, Kemper's brigade. Major Poague recalled how Stuart was confident for success.[241] With humble roots stemming from his lowly Irish immigrant grandfather, he represented a true American success story. Stuart was on the fast track to a brigadier general's rank. Educated at the Staunton Academy at Staunton, in northwest Virginia, the town (county seat of Augusta County) where he had been born, Stuart was a former assistant professor of mathematics and instructor of tactics at VMI from 1850 to 1853 who then became the headmaster of a classical school at the old tobacco port town of Georgetown, District of Columbia. Symbolically, Georgetown was the home of Francis Scott Key, who wrote the national anthem after watching Fort McHenry's spirited defense orchestrated by General Armistead's uncle. Stuart had then headed a classical school in Richmond, Virginia, just before the war erupted. Ironically, Colonel Stuart was only one day (July 4) removed from the anniversary of when he had graduated with honors (third overall in his class) from VMI in 1850, but he was destined to suffer a mortal wound by the time of the arrival of that anniversary. Colonel Stuart risked losing a promising future, a beautiful wife named Frances who loved his intelligence as much as his striking good looks, and two daughters and a son. Nevertheless, Stuart led the way with his ornate VMI saber and confidence.[242]

On Garnett's left flank, the 56th Virginia consisted of about 480 men from eight counties scattered across Virginia. Stuart had graduated first in his VMI Class in infantry tactics, and he instilled the 56th Virginia with superior training and warrior ethos. Colonel Stuart's regiment contained one Mecklenburg County unit, Company A (Mecklenburg Guards). In Company A were two brothers, Privates William H. and John H. Dedman, who had already lost another brother, Private Thomas J. Dedman, who was fatally cut down at Antietam. Despite missing young Thomas, Private William H. Dedman now steadily marched to his death, and Private John H. Dedman was about to receive a terrible wound that resulted in the amputation of his leg.

Located on the North Carolina border in southeast Virginia, Brunswick County was represented by Company E, the Ebenezer Grays. Five Jones brothers, including Private Isham ("Cham") Jones, who was about to be cut down with a nasty right arm wound, represented the close-knit family in Company E. But Private William Burch Short, known as Sambo, was the most notable target in Company E's ranks. Sambo was the company's tallest man, with his size mocked by his last name. Private Short's height was partly responsible for soon earning him a serious wound that, when, combined with disease, brought upon his death before summer's end. Short's wife, whose nickname was "Babie," had been long rightly worried about the safety of one of the 56th Virginia's tallest soldiers.

Symbolically, Private Short was the descendant of a Declaration of Independence signer. Sambo knew that a decisive victory that afternoon would almost certainly cause Philadelphia, where the historic declaration had been signed, to drop into Lee's hands like a ripe plum. Private Short instead was about to become a prisoner in another shrine to America's liberty: Fort McHenry.

Carrying distinctive cultural aspects of their Virginia Tidewater homeland with them, these young Brunswick County soldiers especially enjoyed "Brunswick stew." But few of these advancing men ever again tasted the spicy, tomato-based, vegetable gumbo-like dish with chicken and pork.[243] These Brunswick boys continued onward in the hope of reversing the hands of fate. They feared that, unless Meade's line was split in two, then "we [are] going to get beaten—as Cortez did the Mexicans—by superior weapons."[244]

On Garnett's left, Company D, 56th Virginia, was known as the Buckingham Yancey Guards. These men hailed from Buckingham County, nestled between Richmond and the Blue Ridge. A savvy Mexican–American War veteran, Private James H. Eads, was about to suffer a nasty wound that broke his arm, nearly costing him his life.[245] Meanwhile, Lieutenant Robert Stapleton Ellis, Jr., known as "Tump" to the boys, led Company C (Louisa Holliday Guards of Louisa County, Virginia), 56th Virginia. Born on a plantation in Orange County, Virginia, Ellis had been educated at the University of Pennsylvania's Medical School and then graduated from the Woodland Academy, Charlottesville, Virginia. "Tump" Ellis, a model officer, advanced at the head of his experienced soldiers, like Sergeant Thomas B. Estes, who felt almost like a wealthy man with $76 in his pocket. But the sergeant never spent a single cent of his hard-earned pay, because he was about to be fatally cut down.[246]

Meanwhile, leading Company K (Harrison's Guards), of Hanover County which was located just north of Richmond, Virginia, Lieutenant George

Williamson Finley was well-educated at today's William and Mary College. He worried that he might never again see his wife, Margaret Elizabeth Booker, whom he had married in May 1859. Finley was destined to encourage his Hanover County troops all the way to the stone wall, where he was cut down and captured. His miraculous escape from certain death on July 3 caused a thankful Finley to become a minister after the war.[247]

With his Holy Bible in his pocket to spiritually strengthen him, Captain James C. Wyant made sure that the alignment of his Company H, 56th Virginia, was tight. But nothing could protect the captain, who was shortly struck by a projectile in the face. He died of his wounds before the end of July, after the onset of disease. Some men of Company H (White Hall Guards) of Albemarle County, where Jefferson's Monticello stood on its secluded hilltop, were more sinners than saints. Like other sexually adventurous boys in the ranks, Private Nehemiah Lane had been in the hospital with syphilis. The infection might have been caught from one of Richmond's many busy houses of prostitution, such as the popular Anna Thompson whorehouse. Nehemiah, an Old Testament biblical name, was brought before a court martial for having gone AWOL. To restore honor to the tarnished family name, Robert Carson Lane, a farmer on Albemarle County soil, moved steadily onward in Company H's ranks. Private Robert Carson Lane never again saw his wife, Cordella A. Lane, as he was killed in action at Gettysburg.[248] "Cohen is a high name among Jews," wrote Mary Chesnut, which applied to not a single soldier of Pickett's division. However, a Hebrew Rebel named Samuel H. Sloan, 1st Virginia, was about to be wounded, captured, and die in prison, excelling in the Jewish warrior tradition.[249]

Commanded by Captain Henry Clay Michie, who had been born in Bel Air, Albemarle County, Company H, 56th Virginia, was a reliable unit on July 3. Of Scottish heritage and familiar with Celtic ways, Michie hailed from the plantation "The Meadows." He had been educated at the University of Virginia until the outbreak of the war ended his scholarly ambitions. A bachelor with an eye for pretty ladies, Captain Michie eventually reached the stone wall, suffering grievous wounds that guaranteed his capture. Two other Michie boys had served as Company H officers after first learning the ways of war from VMI educations.[250]

A "very handsome man" who made the girls swoon, noted a jealous artillery officer, Colonel Stuart was now ably assisted by top subordinates, including young Adjutant Richard Goode Wharton. A physician's son born in early February 1842, he had received his initial training at VMI beginning in 1858.

Colonel Stuart had attempted to gain permission for Wharton to depart the regiment to complete his VMI studies, but pressing war requirements ended those pursuits.[251]

Meanwhile, at the targeted right-center, General John Gibbon, a Pennsylvanian like Meade and Hancock, rode along his division's line. A West Pointer (Class of 1847), the native Pennsylvanian instilled confidence among his troops like Armistead, Garnett, and Kemper. Gibbon "cool and calm, and in an unimpassioned voice . . . said to the men, 'Do not hurry, men and fire too fast, let them come up close before you fire, and then aim low and steadily.'" These veterans in faded blue proudly wore the trefoil that designated their hard-fighting corps: the club of a deck of cards. These tough 2nd Corps soldiers were about to justify their popular boast, "Clubs are trumps!"[252] North of the Angle, Sergeant Hirst, 14th Connecticut, described in a letter: "We must hold this Line to the Last Man [because] The Fate of the whole Army now rests" upon the depleted 2nd Corps.[253] With full cartridge-boxes and plenty of water from nearby Rock Creek and other freshwater sources in tin canteens, these seasoned Yankee "doodles," as they were contemptuously called by the Rebels, continued to prepare for the hardest fighting that they had ever seen.[254]

Armistead Inspires His Followers

Armistead continued advancing ahead of his troops. Unlike Pickett, who decided to supervise the advance from a rearward position, a division commander's proper place under normal circumstances (which this wasn't), he ignored the haunting memory of an ugly wound suffered at Antietam when his foot was hit by a bounding cannonball. Lieutenant John Henry Lewis, Jr., described Armistead's inspirational role: With "his [plumed] hat on the point of his [1850 Foot Officer's] sword, [he] held it above his head, in front of him [while] he led his brigade, being in front of it, and cheering it on. His men [all] saw his example [and] They caught his fire and determination, and then and there they resolved to follow that heroic leader until the enemy's bullets stopped them [and] It was his example, his coolness, his courage that led that brigade over that field," while surging ever closer to Cemetery Ridge.[255]

In part because of the death of two wives and two children that had torn his heart apart, Armistead's fighting spirit now seemed to provide a psychological remedy. His reputation for feistiness had been first earned when he crashed a plate over the head of his fellow West Point cadet Jubal Anderson Early (Lee's most hard-bitten general), who the usually circumspect Lee referred to as "my bad old man."[256]

In Kemper's center, meanwhile, 175 soldiers, including the Irish of the Montgomery Guard (Company C), 1st Virginia, pushed on over the open fields. The 1st Virginia was now Pickett's smallest regiment, reminding these men that they needed to outdo themselves to compensate. An ex-sergeant of Company G who had risen through the ranks, Maryland-born Major Francis H. Langley, a 31-year-old former carpenter from Henico County, Virginia, led the 1st Virginia's survivors steadily toward the high-ground. Instead of in a hospital bed, where he probably belonged due to sickness, Langley implored his troops over the fields, until felled by a wound.[257] In Company B (Richmond City Guard), 1st Virginia, young drummer boy Thomas Acre, who had enlisted at Richmond near the end of June 1863, had yet to shave. He continued to beat his drum. A spunky Irish lad named James O'Keeffe, a Company G "musician," who was also recruited in Richmond a month before Acre's enlistment, likewise pounded away, knowing the steadying effect of the fast-paced cadence of his drum beats.[258]

Armistead's example inspired the 9th Virginia troops on the brigade's right center. But the 9th Virginia's soldiers had another strong motivation to do their best that day: these 9th Virginia soldiers were determined to wipe away the stain from an embarrassing episode at Seven Pines. Virginia officers had mistakenly believed that Southerners had fired upon them instead of New Yorkers, leading to confusion. These Tidewater soldiers, trained to a razor-sharp edge by high VMI standards, were now highly motivated to redeem their regiment's honor.[259]

Ironically, these 9th Virginia men had once lusted to shoot down an especially stern VMI martinet major, who had long made their lives miserable. Private William H. Cocke, who was fated to die in a Yankee prison in 1865, hated Major Mark Benard Hardin. The major was a former VMI professor and Stonewall Brigade veteran. Cocke described him as "a tyranical little puppy from Lexington." The angry private admitted that the major "would have been riddled with bullets and not yankee ones either," whenever the right opportunity emerged. But now these men fully understood the true meaning behind hard training, because iron discipline now might make the difference between victory and defeat.[260]

The fact that Lee had correctly targeted the right spot offering the best possibility for success was verified by Captain Haskell and others at the 2nd Corps's front. Haskell emphasized how Lee had wisely picked the weakest position (right-center) to strike his concentrated blow. Here, the bluecoats fully realized "the disparity of numbers between the assailants and the assailed; that few as were our numbers we could not be supported or reinforced until support would not be needed or would be too late."[261]

On Meade's vulnerable right-center, the lengthy stone wall continued to pay dividends for the infantrymen. Despite its low height, the stone wall hid the troops laying low in their advanced positions on the lower-lying forward (west) slope just below the crest. The veterans of two full brigades of General Alexander "Sandy" Hays's division, Hancock's 2nd Corps, quietly held their positions just before the crest of the ridge. Here, they crouched low behind the limestone wall, which was made only slightly stronger at only relatively few points by adding fence rails on top for extra protection.

Hays's men were now inspired by their spunky Irish leader. Possessing Mexican–American War experience, Hays kept up spirits by informing his followers to get ready to meet Pettigrew's troops, because they were about to "see some fun!" Then, farther to the south down the lengthy ridge that gradually descended, the low stone wall was still sufficiently high enough to provide the dual advantages of disguise and protection to the forward troops of Webb's Philadelphia Brigade. However, the Confederate bombardment had the overall effect of considerably wearing down the defenders' nerves and morale. Napoleon fully understood the powerful moral and psychological effect of a massive artillery bombardment on defenders, and Lee had exploited these lessons to the fullest.[262]

Meanwhile, Pettigrew's troops continued to push onward over the flowing fields. Officers shouted, "Steady, men, steady!" When they encountered the first post-and-rail fence that ran perpendicular to the sweeping advance, the flimsy barrier was quickly knocked down "by hand" and bayonets, allowing the troops to surge over the scattered split rails like a steamroller. All the while, the lengthy line of Confederate skirmishers continued to blast away at opposing forces. One of Pettigrew's soldiers described how the "line moves forward over fences, across fields" of green and gold.[263] Leading his 3rd Division, 2nd Corps, General Hays marveled how Pettigrew's formations moved "steady as if impelled by machinery."[264]

A Forgotten Horror

These soldiers were not only gambling with their lives in the bid to win it all for the Confederacy, but also chances for future procreation: a horror not previously explored by historians who have glorified the assault. About to endure unspeakable pain and lose the chance of ever having children, the following unfortunate men were about to receive severe wounds to the groin and testicles: Corporal Hugh H. French, a teenage former clerk of Company E (Black Eagle Riflemen), 18th Virginia; 35-year-old Private John J. Fore, Company H (Appomattox Greys), 18th Virginia; Captain William T. Johnson, also Company H (Appomattox Greys), age 23 and an ex-farmer; Private Samuel B. Huse, Company K (Botetourt Guards), 57th Virginia, Armistead's brigade, who had a musket ball "carrying away the right testicle"; Private James M. McCommac, a member of the same company and regiment, who was "shot in the right testicles"; and 22-year-old Lieutenant Hopkins Harden, Company C (The Scottsville Guards), 19th Virginia, who was hit by a lead ball that went "through his privates." William H. Hodges, a teenage private and ex-farmer of the 57th Virginia, was "shot in the right groin." Likewise, in leading his 9th Virginia, Armistead's brigade, 33-year-old Major John Crowder Owens, who was assisted by one VMI officer (Captain George Chamberlain) on his personal staff, was also about to be mortally wounded "in the groin."[265]

From the smoke-laden heights before Pettigrew's division, meanwhile, one of General Hays's men, of Major Theodore Smyth's 2nd Brigade, Charles D. Page, 14th Connecticut, behind the low stone wall north of the Angle, concluded how the majestic "advance seems as restless as the incoming tide [and it] was the last throw of the dice in this supreme moment of the great game of war."[266] Surging onward with the Appomattox Greys (Company H), 18th Virginia, veterans from the Piedmont's rolling hills of Appomattox County, including Captain William T. Johnson and at least 25 of his men, hoped to prevent what eventually happened—the army's surrender—in their own homeland at Appomattox Court House in less than two years.[267]

Meanwhile, these young soldiers continued to push onward with no idea that they were on their own because of a host of aforementioned Confederate leadership failures at the highest levels. Clearly, Lee's directives to enhance the chances of a successful assault were left glaringly unfulfilled.[268]

Oblivious to such disturbing tactical realities, Pickett's attackers relentlessly moved onward in part because they had been motivated by in inspiring words of faith from Chaplains Thomas Hume, Jr., 3rd Virginia; Florence McCarthy, 7th Virginia; George William Harris, 8th Virginia; John C. Granberry, 11th Virginia; Peter Tinsley, 28th Virginia; Ransel W. Cridlin, 38th Virginia; and James R. Waggoner, 56th Virginia. These were the forgotten spiritual players who helped to fuel Pickett's Charge. These pious chaplains had prepared Pickett's soldiers "to meet their God as well as to meet their foe."[269]

Age 24, Lieutenant George Williamson Finley, Company K, 56th Virginia, commanded Company K, Harrison's Guards, on Garnett's left. He recalled the words from a favorite verse in the Book of Psalms that provided spiritual comfort: "The Lord is my light and my salvation. Whom shall I fear?"[270] In the 14th Virginia's surging ranks and in the same brigade (Armistead's) as the 56th Virginia, Private Meredith (Merth) Branch Thurman had written to his wife in a June 1863 letter: "[Y]ou must pray for me [as] I might be killed."[271]

As Lee's attackers pushed ever closer to Cemetery Ridge, meanwhile Stuart led his four cavalry brigades of veteran horse-soldiers onward on his most important mission during the most forgotten phase of Pickett's Charge. Indeed, "Stuart must be in precisely the right position to . . . improve the opportunity by hitting the Union rear [and this powerful] one-two punch would, in Lee's estimation, ultimately result in an overwhelming Confederate victory."[272]

Chapter V

Running the Artillery Gauntlet

Meade's forces possessed nearly 200 artillery pieces of which more than half would play a role in punishing the attackers.[1] The natural setting of this "artilleryman's paradise" could not have been more aesthetically appealing to the eye: a pastoral landscape overflowing with new life nourished by ample sunlight and rain. This was primarily wheat country, and the soil and terrain were ideal for the growing of this main staple of life since time immemorial. One Confederate described how this picturesque setting was "covered with clover as soft as a Turkish carpet."[2]

With consummate skill, Meade's chief of artillery, 44-year-old General Henry Jackson Hunt, had created a defensive "long arm" masterpiece. This situation had been inadvertently created by the Confederates themselves, because they had failed to capture the strategic high-ground of Cemetery Ridge on July 2 and then failed to focus their cannonade on Cemetery Hill, at the north, and Little Round Top, to the south. These key high points at opposite ends of Meade's line now bristled with artillery not damaged by the bombardment.

An extremely capable West Pointer who had been decorated for Mexican–American War heroics and served on a prewar board to improve light artillery tactics, Hunt now commanded 36 batteries. He had understood early on that the true role of his guns was not to duel with Confederate artillery, but to conserve ammunition for his massed firepower to greet the opposing infantry. Hunt's ace-in-the hole was McGilvery's 39th Artillery Reserve, 1st Brigade, guns (virtually untouched by the cannonade) situated below the clump of trees: a key high-ground position that dominated the open fields of the upper valley of Plum Run. From there, because the range of the field pieces extended so far south, McGilvery's reserve guns could enfilade Pickett's exposed right flank (Kemper) from the southeast. Hunt had McGilvery's reserve batteries respond to the cannonade belatedly (15 minutes after the first Union cannon opened fire) so that sufficient rounds remained to greet the assault at close range.

What Hunt had orchestrated at Malvern Hill (another defensive master-piece of more than 100 guns) was now dwarfed by having so skillfully deployed nearly 40 batteries of 163 guns. In three massive artillery concentrations, these field pieces were aligned mostly along Cemetery Ridge, anchored on Cemetery Hill (and to the south, Ziegler's Grove, at the northern end of the ridge, to a lesser extent), and Little Round Top: a nearly two-mile stretch of high-ground lined with 87 guns. Perched atop Little Round Top, half a dozen "rifle-guns," (Company D, 5th United States Artillery under Lieutenant Benjamin F. Rittenhouse) in Hunt's words, dominated the open fields. Significantly, Hunt had skillfully placed his guns to create "an artillery cross-fire." With Union bat-teries perched atop Cemetery Hill and Little Round Top, Lee's troops advanced between the two commanding high-ground artillery bastions from where the deadly crossfire raked the attackers' flanks. Equally important and as mentioned, Hunt also made sure that his gunners fired slowly, husbanding ammunition to ensure that a sufficient amount remained when the infantry advanced closer.[3]

Major Thomas W. Osborn, commanding the XI Corps Artillery Brigade on Cemetery Hill, had been the first officer to suggest that a reduction of fire would cause the Rebels to prematurely launch an assault before they were truly ready, a strategy that helped to sabotage Lee's flying artillery plan and timely support troops from venturing forth. Hunt had agreed with Osborn's clever plan. Therefore, he had then deliberately ordered batteries to stop firing not only to consume ammunition but also to trick Longstreet (Colonel Alexander in this case) into ordering the assault too early. Therefore, the attackers had been prematurely forced to make the first move to force mis-takes.[4] To inflict maximum damage, Union artillery facing west on Cemetery Ridge had opened fire *except* the circumspect guns of Hancock's 2nd Corps, which defended the clump of trees sector. These rows of silent 2nd Corps guns were ordered to fire only when the Rebels got closer—about halfway across the open fields.[5]

Therefore, Lieutenant Colonel Norborne Berkeley, 8th Virginia, Kemper's brigade, a member of the Virginia Military Institute (VMI) Class of 1848, stared ominously at the "blackened mouths of numerous [2nd Corps] artillery [now] awaiting to deal destruction to us."[6] After having pushed to the top of the grassy plateau that overlooked the Emmitsburg Road to the east and then the wide upper valley of Plum Run on the east side of the road, Pickett's three brigades continued to pour across the level ground of the Seminary Ridge pla-teau and then straight east down the open slope. Rebel skirmishers had torn down large sections of fence along the front, while remaining portions of the manmade barrier were pushed down or hurriedly climbed over.

Two separate advancing wings, with lengthy lines of skirmishers out in front, steadily surged across the fields of "these Thirty German Farmers," in one admiring Virginian's words. Lieutenant John Henry Lewis, Jr., estimated, "We had about one mile [three-quarters] to go before reaching the Federal lines."[7] In still another example of this being a brother's war, General Garnett was about to see hundreds of his men killed and wounded by an artillery storm orchestrated by old friend, General Hunt.[8]

About 300 yards ahead of Pickett's formations, Rebel skirmishers (one company from each regiment) hurled back their fast-firing counterparts. Meanwhile, on the right-center before Garnett's brigade, ironically, a number of recent recruits advanced in the ranks. These novices were Marylanders, who had joined the army in Maryland. Proving "excellent soldiers," the Maryland boys served as skirmishers of Company G (Nottoway Greys), 18th Virginia, which consisted of around 100 men. Most of these Marylanders were cut down that afternoon. Sergeant William M. Hamilton, an ex-agriculturalist at age 38 (that made him a father figure to teenage soldiers) and one of the best men of the Nottoway Greys, was fatally struck that day. The three Tunstill boys—John, James, and Josephus M.—also advanced in Company G's ranks. Symbolically, Lieutenant Archer Campbell, a 23-year-old former carpenter of this same company who took ancestral pride in the Celtic Campbell clan of the Scottish Highlands, fell wounded during the hot skirmishing.[9]

Sergeant Randolph Abbott Shotwell, 8th Virginia, Kemper's brigade, made an appropriate Celtic-Gaelic analogy about how the busy Rebel skirmishers were now "firing on Paddy's rule in a 'skirmage'."[10] At times, the opposing skirmish lines were so close that animated Rebels shouted insults and taunts at the boys in blue. Like his comrades, Corporal Christopher Mead, 12th New Jersey, Hays's division, watched the Union skirmishers continue to give ground before Pettigrew's surging ranks with increasing unease.[11]

Leading the 1st Virginia skirmishers, Company D (Old Dominion Guard), before Kemper's advancing ranks, 18-year-old Lieutenant Adolphus Blair, a former clerk who had been born in Petersburg, Virginia, on the Appomattox River, was cut down in the escalating skirmishing. However, the skirmishers of Lieutenant Blair, of Anglo-German heritage, were fortunate, because the Yankees preferred to fire at the easier targets presented by the main formation on higher ground behind the skirmishers.[12] The skirmish company of the 11th

Virginia, just to the 1st Virginia's right, likewise benefitted from the Union skirmishers' diverted attention in firing over their heads. Led by the Lieutenant John Thomas James, VMI Class of 1863, the skirmishers of Company D (Fincastle Rifles) performed with a skill that made their commander, Captain David Gardiner Houston, Jr., proud. The captain, a former attorney in his midtwenties, was about to fall mortally wounded.[13]

Meanwhile, the Federal skirmishers battled back with stubbornness, especially before Garnett's formations north of Kemper's brigade. Here, Yankee skirmishers blasted away from a high post-and-rail fence. In the broad fields north of the Codori House, spunky skirmishers of the 72nd, 106th, and 69th Pennsylvania (Webb's brigade), respectively from north to south, stubbornly held their ground. These seasoned skirmishers of the Philadelphia Brigade, which defended the copse of trees sector, banged away at Garnett's Virginians, firing at not only the foremost Rebel skirmishers, like Company H (Potomac Greys), 8th Virginia, but also at the main line. These city boys from Philadelphia, only 140 miles to the east, stood their ground.

Garnett was in for a nasty shock, when a lengthy blue line of skirmishers suddenly rose up from the "tall grass" that served as hay for farmer's horses and cattle. They unleashed a scorching volley at a range of only 50 yards. In encountering what he described as the first Union line, Garnett was forced to halt his advance. He then ordered a volley fired to drive back these Yankees in the mini-battle that raged through the open fields. These skirmishers slowed Garnett's onslaught and bought extra time for the main line defenders, fulfilling their mission in splendid fashion—forgotten heroics of Pickett's Charge.

Bullets from experienced Pennsylvania skirmishers cut down young Private Hezekiah C. Spessard. The teenage skirmisher was hit twice, taking ugly wounds in the groin and thigh. Horrified by the sight of the young man's fall while leading the roughhewn mountaineers of Company C (the Craig Mountain Boys), 28th Virginia, Garnett's brigade, Captain Michael Peters Spessard rushed over to his fallen son. Age 41 and an ex-farmer from the Craig's Creek region of Craig County, amid southwest Virginia's mountains, Captain Spessard saw that the blood-stained Hezekiah was mortally wounded.

Ambitious Colonel Eppa Hunton, who commanded the 8th Virginia and occasionally Garnett's brigade in the general's absence, admired the spirited performance of Company H's (Potomac Greys) skirmishers. When he rode north from the brigade's right flank, Hunton never forgot the heart-wrenching sight: A grieving Captain Spessard, who now felt more pain than even when he was wounded at Gaines's Mill, was shaken by the fall of his first son borne of his first wife, Elizabeth, who had died when Hezekiah was about nine. Michael looked up at Hunton in anguish. In tears, the captain cried out: "Look at my poor boy, Colonel." Then, pulling himself together because duty called, Spessard paid his last respects to his fallen son, a former merchant's clerk in happier times. Destined to earn a major's rank in 1864, Captain Spessard kissed his dying son on the forehead. He then gently rested Hezekiah's head on the ground. The rawboned captain quickly stripped off his canteen and laid it by his son's side.

Now infused with a burning desire for vengeance that overwhelmed his personal pain, Captain Spessard surged back into action. He dashed over to his Craig County boys, who hailed from the southwest Virginia's mountains, including heavily forested Craig Mountain, which rose more than 2,000 feet above sea level. Before his company's line, he yelled, "Forward, boys!" Waving his saber, the rejuvenated captain led the Mountaineers onward over the sun-baked fields. Spessard's attackers included young men with patriotic names (reflected in every regiment of Pickett's Charge) such as Sergeant George Washington Webb, an ex-farmer who was captured that afternoon, and Private Andrew Jackson Huffman, a 29-year-old agriculturalist who was killed in the assault.[14] As Spessard's men realized, it took an iron will for the grieving captain to continue leading his men and perhaps toward his own death: a fate now of relatively little concern to him after his son's fall. Captain Spessard somehow ignored the overpowering urge to return to attend to Hezekiah. In a battle that had suddenly become more personal and horrible, he was now motivated to wreak havoc. As penned in one of his few surviving letters that revealed a holy warrior's motivations, Spessard fought against those who sought to "invade our home [and] confiscate our property."[15]

Likewise, the Union skirmishers who fired briskly before Kemper's brigade, to Garnett's south, proved as equally tough as those before Garnett's brigade. Commanding Company G (Lynchburg Home Guards), 11th Virginia, 22-year-old Captain John Holmes Smith, a former merchant about to be cut down, was astounded by his opponent's tenacity. He wrote: "[O]ur skirmishers had been brought to a stand [still] by those of the enemy; and the latter only gave ground when our line of battle had closed up well inside of a hundred yards of our own skirmishers."[16]

But the defiant stand of the bluecoat skirmishers before Kemper's brigade was only temporary. With thousands of Rebels drawing ever closer, larger numbers of Yankee skirmishers finally broke rearward before being overpowered by the gray and brown tide: an alarming sight that continued to cause growing consternation among Cemetery Ridge's increasingly nervous defenders. Corporal Mead, 12th New Jersey on the 2nd Corps's far right just south of Ziegler's Grove, watched Pettigrew's relentless push that drove hundreds of bluecoat skirmishers back "like so many frightened sheep."[17]

While steadily marching toward Cemetery Ridge, a grim humor rose to the fore. They dealt with the prospect of immediate death by mocking or taunting it. When Private Daniel Bird was hit in the arm by a bullet, a sergeant yelled to a nearby officer of Company D, 9th Virginia, Armistead's brigade, "Lieutenant they have winged our Bird." Private Bird had enlisted in Nansemond County, Virginia, on April 30, 1863, barely two months before. Bird survived his wound but died of disease in April 1864, before the one-year anniversary of embarking upon his short military career.[18] Meanwhile, inspiring the 9th Virginia troops onward, Color Sergeant Joshua M. Grimes, a 20-year-old ex-farmer, headed toward a cruel fate: a serious wound and a miserable existence in a northern prison camp.[19]

Two Assault Wings Begin to Come Together

According to Lee's complex plan for his attackers (a separate left wing [Pettigrew] and right wing [Pickett], which first began their respective marches when about 400–500 yards apart), the troops were to advance across a wide front of nearly two miles, before compacting for a simultaneous convergence at a single point. This required one of the most unusual and difficult of maneuvers of any assault: a stealthy indirect approach of Pickett's division that required a shift north in order to catch their opponents at the weakened right-center by surprise. The position of Pettigrew's division, closer to the targeted area and the Emmitsburg Road than Pickett's troops, called for more of a straight march (especially Fry's brigade—Pettigrew's right flank—on Garnett's left) east to the clump of trees than Pickett's division.

Consequently, for the wide gap between the two wings to narrow and then come together in the open fields of the west side of Plum Run's upper valley before the Emmitsburg Road, the Virginians were required to gradually shift to the left (toward the red Codori barn) in a sliding movement, and then turn east once again for the final charge on the clump of trees sector. Meanwhile, Pettigrew was to march east, then gradually shift south to unite with Pickett's left (Garnett), and then turn east once again, after Pettigrew's right (Fry's Tennessee and Alabama brigade) had linked with Pickett's left to arrive at the same point to simultaneously unite to create a battering ram (or "wedge") to punch through Meade's right-center. According to plan, three of Pettigrew's brigades began to shift to the right or south, after advancing about 600 yards (or about halfway to their objective).

Except for Kemper's brigade of five regiments on the far south, Pickett's troops (beginning with Garnett and then Armistead) continued the time-consuming process of gradually shifting left to eventually fulfill Lee's grand design of funneling the attackers to create a wedge-shaped battering ram. Therefore, units on the right of Pettigrew's division began to push over the open fields to the right in the southeast direction, while Garnett's and Kemper's troops eased northeastward to close the gap that existed between the two widely separated divisions, while under artillery and skirmish fire. As planned, Lee's carefully calculated assault would eventually come together along a narrow front in the form of a trapezoid that allowed for a concentrated force of veteran attackers to strike at a single point. A troubling sight to the Yankee onlookers, neither wing of attackers gradually moving toward each other stopped to realign.[20] In the words of one Union soldier at the targeted right-center, "It was a terrible sight to us [because] we did not suppose we could repulse them."[21]

Ironically, in an unintentional fortunate tactical development, Pettigrew's late advance compensated for the extra time it took for Pickett's troops to move the longer distance to the left, to ease closer to uniting with Pettigrew's right, upon gradually nearing the Emmitsburg Road.[22] After Garnett's and Armistead's brigades began to shift to the left (north), hundreds of Union gunners—especially the southernmost guns of Lieutenant Colonel Freeman McGilvery's Artillery Reserve—south of the copse of trees were presented with the vulnerable right flanks of the advancing lines. These gunners hurriedly shifted dozens of field pieces to the right and opened up a murderous enfilade fire.[23] One of Meade's finest command decisions that day was in ordering Hunt to bring up his Artillery Reserve, which had been withdrawn rearward to recuperate and make repairs after the previous day's combat.[24]

At a point nearly halfway to Cemetery Ridge and about 400 yards just southwest of the Codori House and barn, after they'd advanced less than 10 minutes, a swale before Pickett's division provided an opportunity to briefly align ranks amid the gently rolling terrain of tall grass before the Emmitsburg Road. Here, in the swale's depth of about 15–20 feet, Garnett's brigade first aligned, and then Kemper dressed on Garnett's right. After the ranks were quickly re-formed, and despite the long-range shell-fire that continued to cause damage, Pickett's division shifted northeastward and closer to Pettigrew's right (Fry's brigade).[25] During these disciplined movements, the Union artillery punishment only increased. One shell exploded in the ranks of Captain Timolean Smith's Company C (Louisa Holliday Guards), 56th Virginia, taking 16 men out of the formation.[26]

Then, after turning east once again, the troops surged deeper into the teeth of the fire from the lengthy alignment of about 150 artillery pieces spanning north from Little Round Top, along Cemetery Ridge, and up to Cemetery Hill: the masterful handiwork of the highly effective Meade and Hunt team. Hunt's 2nd Corps artillerymen had carefully husbanded their ammunition to greet the attackers at closer range. With ample ammunition and plenty of extra guns in reserve unlike Lee's artillery arm, Hunt's artillery was well prepared.

While other Cemetery Ridge guns facing west continued to fire, the artillery in Hancock's 2nd Corps sector remained silent. These veteran artillerymen demonstrated a disciplined patience, allowing their doomed targets to ease well into a murderous range. In the words of one Union gunner in the targeted sector: "The rebel lines advanced slowly but surely [until] half the valley was passed over by them before the guns dared expend a round of the precious ammunition remaining on hand."[27]

Nothing slowed the rapid fire of Lieutenant Rittenhouse's guns, Battery D, 5th United States Artillery, positioned on Little Round Top. With iron barrels that were lighter than bronze and hence more easily rifled to maximize accuracy, the 10-pounder Parrott rifled cannon (Model 1861) on Little Round Top's summit inflicted havoc. Commanding the 19th Virginia, Garnett's brigade, Major Charles Peyton described how from the blazing battery "posted on the mountain, about 1 mile to our right, which enfiladed nearly our entire line with fearful effect, sometimes as many as 10 men being killed or wounded by the bursting of a single shell."[28] Little Round Top's guns steadily inflicted casualties, including one unlucky soldier who trudged rearward with his "entire mouth & chin . . . carried away" by a 10-pounder Parrott shell.[29]

The 56th Virginia (Garnett's left flank) continued to suffer high losses. Lieutenant George Williamson Finley never forgot the horror: "The third shell struck on the extreme right of Company H [White Hall Guards]—the largest company in the regiment—37 men [and] All 37 men were swept away by a single shell, [but survivors] scrambled to the feet and resumed their place in line. . . ."[30] Leading the White Hall Guards, Captain James C. Wyant was a respected company commander with a mere $3 (inflated Confederate currency at that) in his pocket along with his well-worn "Testament." He was married to Samantha A. Wyant, who managed the family farm in his absence. Captain Wyant, along with the two Estes boys (Privates Robert G. and W. Joe Estes), who were soon to be killed, implored his sweating soldiers onward under the intense fire. He was about to take a wound from a bullet in the face, which proved fatal before the end of July.[31] Multiple direct hits severely plummeted the 56th Virginia's ranks that still solidified Pickett's extreme left flank.[32]

Meanwhile, morale continued to drop among the defenders watching the onslaught. One anxious Yankee of Hancock's Corps penned: "It seemed as they advanced on us that it would be impossible to stop them."[33] While monitoring the alignment of Company H (Potomac Greys), 8th Virginia on Garnett's right, Sergeant Randolph Abbott Shotwell was horrified when an "officer's head is blown off by a round shot—the men stepping over his body."[34] This unlucky victim was very likely Captain Alexander Grayson, who commanded Company F (Blue Mountain Boys).[35] Next to the 8th Virginia on the right-center, the 18th Virginia was also enfiladed by the long-ranged artillery (deadly Parrott rifles) roaring from Little Round Top. This flank fire knocked down handfuls of men, including color-bearers.[36] Lieutenant George Williamson Finley, 56th Virginia, described how the shells from Little Round Top's cannon "poured down upon us, and as they descended they shrieked and screeched and hissed like frightened birds [and knocked down men] like so many rag dolls."[37]

At Armistead's center after having shifted north with Garnett, meanwhile, the 53rd Virginia was also enfiladed by the artillery on Little Round Top's rocky crest. Rittenhouse's Parrott rifles swept the right of Company H (Mattapony Guards), toppling a dozen victims. One unfortunate soldier was cut entirely in two by the direct hit by a 10-pound elongated shell.[38] But the fire from the six rifled pieces of Lieutenant Charles E. Hazlett's Battery D, 5th United States Artillery (Hazelett had been killed by a sniper on July 2, which allowed Rittenhouse to take command) on Little Round Top's crest was less lethal compared to what was about to come.

All hell broke loose when the 2nd Corps's artillery unleashed their fiery wrath just after Pickett's lengthy formations reached the halfway point amid the open fields. In the words of Lieutenant John Henry Lewis, Jr.: "Suddenly about fifty pieces of artillery opened on our lines [and] The crash of shell and solid shot, as they came howling and whistling through the lines, seemed to make no impression on the men. There was not a waver; but all was as steady as if on parade. Forward was the command, and steady, boys, came from the officers, as we advanced."[39]

A good many 56th Virginia soldiers, in the words of an ex-farmer who employed an analogy that revealed his agrarian background, "were falling from the ranks as a cart spills meal on the road. . . ."[40] In a letter, one 14th Virginia attacker spared none of his wife's sensibilities by describing: "Now & then a man's hand or arm would fly like feathers before the wind," when shells tore "[g]reat gaps" in the line.[41] But the 14th Virginia soldiers remained steady partly because many men had been early trained by VMI officers and cadets.[42] This "lovely little valley," in the words of one New York soldier on Cemetery Ridge from a letter, was being transformed into a grim killing field and hell on earth.[43]

In the same regiment of Armistead's brigade, Private Meredith (Merit) Branch Thurman, the Company C poet, might have briefly thought back upon the recent words that he had written to his teenage wife, Jane: "I hope and trust if the[re] is a just god he will spare us to come together" once again, and "I will come back except [if] I die."[44] Thurman gamely continued onward with the Fluvanna Rifles of Company C, 14th Virginia. The independent-minded private now possessed more reason for hating "this wicked war." He was thoroughly disgusted because so many "[r]ich men" stayed at home, while "the poure men [including those of Pickett's Charge were] getting killed and starving to save their negroes," as he recently penned.[45] Ironically, Thurman was now among the attackers perhaps only because his wife's letter to dissuade him from marching north into Pennsylvania failed to arrive in time.[46]

The sight of the mighty assault waves rolled relentlessly onward, causing one of Hancock's men to conclude: "We expected to be whipped."[47] Meanwhile, long-range rifled guns steadily blasted away from the high-ground, while the smooth-bore artillery pieces were fired at shorter range. Enfilading the attackers' right flank, especially Kemper's brigade, Rittenhouse's long-range artillery atop Little Round Top bellowed "with remarkable accuracy," wrote Hunt. Major Thomas W. Osborn enjoyed his finest day, like Hunt. He had early informed his gunners of nearly 50 field pieces to not waste ammunition in the long-range dual with Confederate guns, but wait to fire on the advancing infantry, from their "small space of Cemetery Hill." Facing southwest, Osborn's vicious enfilade fire continued to sweep Pettigrew's left flank (and Pickett's left to a lesser degree) with a vengeance.

Roaring from Cemetery Hill to the north and Little Round Top to the south, this lethal cross fire wreaked fearful havoc. Fiery explosions knocked clumps of soldiers out of ranks, but these gaps were then hurriedly closed up by disciplined veterans. Direct hits practically vaporized victims. Anticipating as much, some of Pickett's soldiers now wore homemade (since the army issued none) identification disks. Other enterprising 56th Virginia men (such as 21-year-old bachelor and Louisa County farmer Private John William Barret) had fashioned their own identification tags by smoothing out coins with hammers and inscribing names. Therefore, these young men felt solace that their final remains could be identified if they suffered a direct hit.[48] One shell slammed into the 53rd Virginia, Armistead's brigade, blowing more than a dozen soldiers out of line, while comrades ignored the horrors around them and pressed on.[49]

Below the copse of trees, nearly 40 cannon of the Artillery Reserve, under Lieutenant Colonel Freeman McGilvery, the tough-talking former sea captain from Maine, punished Kemper's brigade without mercy. McGilvery, of Scotch-Irish descent, was Hunt's right-hand man. Having just suffered the highest losses of Pickett's division during the pre-assault cannonade, Kemper's five regiments (originally consisting of nearly 1,800 men) continued to take a beating from multiple directions: a frontal fire from Rorty's Company B, 1st New York Artillery, McGilvery's accurately firing guns of the First Volunteer Brigade, Artillery Reserve, and Rittenhouse's six long-range rifled pieces on Little Round Top, from north to south.[50]

Meanwhile, General Alexander Hays, a bulky six-footer who commanded the 3rd Division, 2nd Corps, inspired his troops along the stone wall that stretched from north of the Angle to Zeigler's Grove. He was a "true son of the Emerald Isle, who don't fear the devil." To instill confidence, he ordered some of his troops to stand up and then perform the manual of arms atop the open crest of the ridge: a defiant message that told the Southern boys that they were about to meet some very good fighting men who were as determined as themselves.[51]

In Kemper's center, Lieutenant John Edward Dooley, Jr., described how frantic officers shouted, "Close up! Close up the ranks when a friend falls, while his life blood bespatters your cheek or throws a film over your eyes!"[52] Likewise, facing the fire of Cowan's New York battery positioned below the clump of trees, General Garnett yelled, "Steady men, Steady. Save your strength for the end," while "men were falling like stalks of grain before the grim reaper. . . ."[53] To Garnett's right-rear, Armistead implored, "Steady, men! Steady!" while shell explosions tore "fearful gaps in our advancing lines," wrote a horrified Color Corporal Robert Tyler Jones of the presidential pedigree.[54]

The commander of one of McGilvery's reserve batteries, the 5th Massachusetts Battery, possessed "a spectacular view of Kemper's men" and blasted away at targets that made the mouths of the bluecoat gunners fairly water. A recent Harvard graduate, Captain Charles Phillips, a lawyer by profession, described how the hot fire from his three 3-inch Ordnance Rifles "must have sickened the rebels of their work [and] I never saw artillery so ably handled, or productive [as] It was far superior even to Malvern Hill [because] the shot ploughed through the rebels ranks most terrifically."[55] Besides McGilvery's reserve delivering punishment upon Kemper's brigade, the guns stretching from Meade's left-center to Little Round Top, including Rorty's New York battery (firing rapidly south of Cowan) unleashed a head-on fire with their 10-pounder Parrott rifles (like those on Little Round Top), inflicting carnage to Kemper's 24th Virginia, 11th Virginia, 1st Virginia, 7th Virginia, and 3rd Virginia, from south to north.[56]

But the worst was still to come. Hancock's 2nd Corps veterans, like the artillerymen, had "learned the importance of waiting until the enemy came with short range before opening fire."[57] Leading the 53rd Virginia, Armistead's brigade, Lieutenant Colonel Rawley White Martin described "the hissing, screaming, shells break in [our] front, rear, on [our] flanks, all about them, but they press forward, keeping step to the music of the battle."[58] On Pickett's right, Kemper's brigade suffered the most. Kemper's soldiers steadily dropped from the frontal fire erupting from McGilvery's nearly 40 reserve guns. During the morning, these field pieces had been placed in neat rows by Meade in the right place below the clump of trees south of Cowan's and Rorty's Empire State batteries. Lieutenant John Edward Dooley, Jr., was sickened by the effectiveness of Little Round Top's Parrott rifles: "To the right of us and above the guns [on Cemetery Ridge] we are to capture, black heavy monsters from their lofty mountains belch forth their flame. . . ."[59]

On Armistead's extreme right, the 14th Virginia was hit the hardest by the artillery pounding from Little Round Top. One shell exploded in the midst of Company H (Meadville Greys). The fiery explosion not only killed the company's revered leader, Captain Richard Logan, Jr., an ex-farmer in his early thirties and a member of VMI's Class of 1849, but also knocked down nine other members of the Halifax County company. A Company I (Chester Grays) soldier, Sergeant William B. Robertson, a former agriculturalist in his late twenties, was caught amid the exploding shells that even set the grass on fire. Ragged iron fragments cut through Robertson's leather waist belt, ripped his gray jacket with sergeant's chevrons on the shoulder, and "frazzled" (as he informed wife, Mattie, in a letter) the skin on one hip. Momentarily stunned by the shell explosion, Sergeant Robertson then dashed ahead and caught up with Company H's surging ranks. As if nothing had happened, he then pushed onward until another shell explosion soon knocked him entirely off his feet.[60]

Pettigrew's division's left was harder hit than even Pickett's right, because the exposed flank on the far north presented such a splendid target to Osborn's gunners. Cemetery Hill's experienced cannoneers had shifted more than 40 artillery pieces to face southwest, delivering a devastating left enfilade fire. With glee, one Yankee described how the hail of "shells burst in their lines, and it looked as though they had all been cut down, but they would close up the gap and come on again."[61] North of the attackers' left flank, one 8th Ohio soldier, just west of the Emmitsburg Road, watched the slaughter at close range: "I saw shells burst among them and men were blown twenty feet into the air by the explosion."[62] The awful destruction caused by the exploding shells fired from Cemetery Hill to the northeast caused the hard-hit troops on the left to crowd and ease farther south in the vain hope of escaping this terrible punishment.[63]

The Crisis Grows on the Extreme Left

On the far north, dark-haired Lieutenant Colonel Franklin Sawyer, educated at Norwalk Academy and Granville College and hoping to see his 38th birthday in 10 days, boldly confronted the left of Pettigrew's sweeping advance through the tall grass of the farmers' fields. Members of Hays's division of "Blue Birds," Sawyer's men of the diminutive 8th Ohio (barely 250 soldiers), held the army's most advanced skirmish position several hundred feet west of the Emmitsburg Road. These sturdy Buckeyes stood perpendicular to Pettigrew's left flank. Pettigrew's troops approached the dusty road later than Pickett's division, because it angled and ran northeast toward Gettysburg. The combination of Osborn's artillery fire (that had opened fire immediately on Brockenbrough's exposed left, unlike Hunt's 2nd Corps guns—which had delayed their fire—to the front before Pickett) and the Ohioans' close range volley into the Virginians' left flank at only around 100 yards, was understandably too much for the remaining members of Brockenbrough's brigade.

Swept from scorching infantry and artillery fires from two directions, larger numbers of Brockenbrough's survivors fled rearward in the "wildest confusion." After suffering from two destructive fires (musketry and cannon-fire on the flank) and taking more punishment than any other command, the Virginia brigade on the extreme left flank (the most vulnerable position of the attack) continued to steadily fall apart before reaching the Emmitsburg Road. To the right (south) of Brockenbrough's brigade, Davis's brigade (especially on its left—on Brockenbrough's right—on the north) also took a severe pounding from Osborn's artillery fire from the northeast and Sawyer's flank fire from the north. Additional numbers of Brockenbrough's hard-hit men began to retire, including all the way back to Seminary Ridge! To compensate for the collapsed extreme left, "Little Jim" Lane's brigade (on the extreme left on the second line) shifted slightly northward.[64]

Meanwhile, south of Brockenbrough's mauled brigade, the assault was progressing as planned. Pettigrew's officers admired the fruits of their labors in having created superior discipline by endless training seemingly for just this opportunity to strike a lethal blow. With officers keeping their eyes on proper alignment by focusing on the Codori House, the farmer's large red barn, and the clump of trees farther to the east like Pickett and his officers, Pettigrew's more direct eastward advance called for less extensive adjustments or maneuvers—like in Pickett's division. Pettigrew's division suffered less than Pickett's division, despite the punishment pouring over the left flank, where the batteries of Cemetery Hill and the Cemetery Ridge (especially on the north) had concentrated their fire.

To maintain proper alignment and to shift ever closer to Pickett's division, colonels, majors, and captains shouted, "Guide right!" Pettigrew's troops moved at "quick-time" through the open fields under a "murderous" artillery fire, in one 26th North Carolina private's words. Then, after shifting south, they again continued east toward Hays's division north of the clump of trees. Without stopping to return fire in adhering to strict orders, Pettigrew's troops continued onward, after having surged past the 10-acre William Bliss Orchard of apple trees and then taking the Ohioans' flank fire. They then pushed down the gentle, grassy slope and toward the Emmitsburg Road and the slight ridge upon which the dusty road ran toward the southern edge of Gettysburg.[65]

"Jimmy" Lane's brigade—on the second line's far left and to Lowrance's left likewise—steadily took casualties from the shell-fire, especially from Cemetery Hill. One lieutenant from 33rd North Carolina, on Lane's left flank, "was blown to atoms by a cannon shot."[66] However, not only Lane's but also Scales's brigades of North Carolina troops (10 regiments and from Pender's old division now commanded by Trimble) moved up to provide support for the mauled left

(Brockenbrough), bolstering Davis's Mississippi and North Carolina brigade, which was also swept by heavy flank fire.[67]

Unfortunately for the attackers, they benefitted relatively little from the scattered Confederate artillery fire (because most batteries possessed too little ammunition to provide much-needed flying artillery roles) hurled over their heads. As penned in a July 1863 letter, Captain Graham, 1st North Carolina Artillery, described how the attackers "had to advance [while] exposed all the time to the Enemy's fire [because] most of our Artillery Ammunition then expended. . . ."[68] Atop Cemetery Ridge with the 2nd Corps, Captain Haskell was perplexed by this development, writing how after the great cannonade, "the enemy [artillery] hereafter during the battle was almost silent, we know little" why.[69]

The lack of much-needed artillery fire support played a role in unnerving additional attackers on Pettigrew's battered left. Captain Graham, thankful that there were not North Carolinians, lamented how "some [of Brockenbrough's Virginia troops] did not go more than 150 yds."[70] What Graham saw on the open ground was caused not by cowardice, but the accurate shell-fire from Major Osborn's XI Corps's artillerymen of the long arm brigade poised atop Cemetery Hill. After initially overshooting, these veteran gunners had readjusted their aim to now pinpoint targets with deadly precision. Even Marshall's North Carolina brigade—sandwiched between Davis's Mississippi and North Carolina brigade on the far left, or northern flank, and Fry's Tennessee and Alabama brigade on the right, or south—was hit by this fire sweeping from the northeast. Under the pounding, meanwhile, additional "squads" of unnerved soldiers, mostly of Brockenbrough's Virginia brigade, fell back without orders, heading for the rear.

By that time, the music of regimental bands no longer inspired these northernmost men now caught amid a fiery hell. The afternoon heat was so intense that soldiers of Davis's brigade (2nd, 11th, and 42nd Mississippi Regiments and the 55th North Carolina Regiment), especially the 11th Mississippi, dropped from sunstroke. Out in front and leading his troops toward the Brien Barn atop Cemetery Ridge, 24-year-old Colonel James Keith Marshall attempted to rally these panicked troops, when an exploding shell knocked him off his horse. Marshall was down but not out. The young man of high expectations gamely ordered an aide-de-camp to assist him back into the saddle. Then, Marshall continued onward with drawn saber, leading his lengthy formations of North Carolinians deeper into the storm.[71]

Meanwhile, the right of Kemper's command continued to suffer from the devastating flank fire on the south, but the veteran brigade did not break. Kemper's left was equally hard-hit. Commanding the 1st New Hampshire Battery, McGilvery's 1st Brigade, Artillery Reserve, Captain Frederick M. Edgell, born in 1829 and a "teenage hero" of the Mexican–American War like Pickett, wrote, "I fired obliquely . . . upon the left of the attacking column with destructive effect."[72]

But the steadfastness of Kemper's troops was not duplicated on the far north. The devastating enfilade artillery fire on the north had a ripple effect even a good distance to the south. From near the right-rear of Pettigrew's brigade, Pickett was astounded by the shocking sight of the "stampede" of panicked men heading rearward. He ordered two staff officers, Lieutenant W. Stuart Symington and Captain Edward R. Baird, to ride north in an attempt to stem the escalating crisis. However, Symington's and Baird's efforts were in vain. Consequently, they departed the chaotic scene in disgust. Davis's most exposed and hence battered regiment, the 2nd Mississippi (on the brigade's far left, or northern, flank) experienced the spreading panic that had first infected Brockenridge's Virginians, leaving Davis's brigade as the extreme left flank on the first line by default. A good many men, including 42nd Mississippi soldiers (also hard hit by flank artillery fire) to the south also fled for safety, but the vast majority continued onward through the leaden storm.

Pettigrew also dispatched a staff officer, Lieutenant William B. Shepard, to steady the wavering men, but it was too late to stem the rout that had infected troops south of Brockenbrough. Pickett then dispatched Captain Robert A. Bright rearward to relocate Longstreet and inform him that he believed that his troops could take the high-ground, but the Tidewater Virginian needed reinforcements to hold it once captured—a correct assessment. The systematic rout of Brockenbrough's brigade and other troops to a lesser degree just to the south shrank the line's northern end (or extreme left flank) by about 600 feet.[73]

Receiving a severe shock, Captain Thomas Jefferson Cureton, 26th North Carolina, Marshall's brigade, described the deteriorating situation on the left: "We were still pressing quickly forward when a cry came from the left and I looked and saw the right regiment of Davis' Mississippi brigade" grow shaky.[74] Under the merciless artillery pounding on the flank, some North Carolina boys of at least one regiment of Pettigrew's old brigade (then under Colonel Marshall) likewise caught the panic, with its enfiladed left hanging in midair.[75]

Union artillery, especially McGilvery's reserve guns positioned below the clump of trees that unleashed a frontal and flank fire, bellowed from Cemetery Ridge and Little Round Top to especially punish Pickett's brigade under Kemper. Here, the two southernmost regiments, the 24th Virginia (on the far right flank of Kemper's brigade and Pickett's division) and the 11th Virginia, from right to left (or south to north), took a beating. Inspirational officers, such as 20-year-old Captain Andrew M. Houston, Jr., formerly a medical student, led the way through the exploding shells. Meanwhile, the captain's brother, Lieutenant Thomas D. Houston, who later fell wounded and was captured, also encouraged the Company K (Valley Regulators) men forward through the din. Still another brother, 23-year-old Captain David Gardiner Houston, Jr., of Company D (Fincastle Rifles) likewise continued onward. After having earlier declared that "it would require a very bloody battle to win the battle," the fatalistic captain shortly fell mortally wounded in the tempest. This accurate shell-fire, especially from lethal rifled guns, unnerved Virginians as thoroughly as non-Virginians, while inflicting equal damage with a wholly democratic lethality regardless of class, educational levels, and nativity.[76]

Because of the losses of Pettigrew's extreme left wing, the division's real strength was embodied in the steamrolling right wing, where veterans under Fry (on the far right) and Marshall (to Fry's left) surged onward with grim determination. To escape the enfilade fires and to correspond with the gradual shift to the south to link with Pettigrew's division, the troops of Lane's and Davis's brigades steadily eased south, making Pettigrew's formation more compact in preparation for inflicting an even more powerful blow. Fortunately for Pettigrew, the grizzled Fry and young Marshall made a hard-hitting team.[77]

All the while, Pickett's division maintained its own, advancing in better shape and with less overall problems than Pettigrew's division. Pickett's surging ranks remained taut and relatively neat, after closing up quickly following each deadly explosion. As they did when recently crossing the Shenandoah River, when the disciplined Virginians had employed close teamwork to cross by "hold[ing] to each other," so they remained tightly packed while moving onward with drill field-like precision.[78] Lieutenant John Edward Dooley, Jr., wrote that "at every step a gap must be closed and thus from left to right much ground is often lost."[79] Leading Company K (Charles City Southern Guards), 53rd Virginia, Armistead's brigade, 30-year-old Captain James H. Lipscomb, a former lumber merchant, was killed in one shell explosion. Lieutenant James

A. Harwood, "having heard that Captain Lipscomb was killed, [I then] turned around and saw that brave soldier fall to rise no more."[80]

Just south of Lieutenant Dooley's 1st Virginia, the 24th Virginia that anchored the right flank of Kemper's brigade also took a heavy pounding, because of its exposure to the artillery fire from Little Round Top to the southeast. Private Nathaniel Law, who had enlisted in October 1862, had his "face burned by a shell burst" that exploded in the air just before him.[81]

It was no accident that Pickett's three brigades poured over the wide fields with such a high degree of order and discipline: the enduring legacy of the early, widespread influence of so many VMI leaders in the ranks. To the amazement of men on both sides, Pickett's units surged onward with the precision of the VMI's Corps of Cadets' mock charges across the grassy parade ground.[82] Riding before Kemper's formations despite his illness, VMI graduate and former instructor Colonel Lewis Burwell Williams, Jr., mounted on his favorite mare, continued to lead the 1st Virginia. Dooley never forgot how Williams, age 30, galloped "cooly and deliberately in front of the regiment," inspiring everyone onward.[83]

In now marching toward so many Irishmen in blue, the Confederate Irish had no idea that General Meade possessed Irish immigrant roots. Meade's great-grandfather, Robert Meade, had migrated from the Emerald Isle. Ironically, the Meade family of Philadelphia might not have succeeded in America without selling slaves. A good many lower- and middle-class Irish, without ever owning slaves, now surged onward in the hope of destroying an army commanded by a man whose family of Irish antecedents had benefitted from slavery: still another one of the forgotten paradoxes of Pickett's Charge.[84]

Some evidence has revealed that a father-son team advancing in one Virginia regiment was actually a husband-wife team of Pickett's division. Their mutual love and devotion was destined to carry them to the hellish Angle and a cruel fate.[85]

So far that day, Pickett felt pride in his division's performance. Rigid VMI–like training and discipline served as a fundamental propellant behind the majestic advance, including the closing of the gap between Pettigrew's right (Fry's brigade) and the left of Garnett's brigade just west of the Emmitsburg Road. As mentioned, Garnett's men had eased to the left at a 45-degree angle for nearly 300 yards, before nearing Fry's right near the road. Garnett had succeeded in skillfully sliding his troops to the left and "dressing on," in the general's words, Fry's Tennessee and Alabama ranks: the all-important linkage of the left of Pickett's division with the right of Pettigrew's division. Therefore, about 5,000 Virginians, 3,600 North Carolinians, more than 1,000 Mississippians, about 550 Tennesseans, and about 500 Alabamians moved together as one, after the uniting of the assault's right and left wings: a remarkable tactical achievement of primarily Lee's far-sighted vision and the common soldiers' discipline and courage.[86] Increasingly nervous under the broiling sun, sweating 2nd Corps troops "waited in almost breathless suspense for the enemy who was moving on toward us like a vast avalanche."[87]

An Epiphany

In watching the precision of these veterans' smooth tactical movements, Longstreet realized that Lee was correct after all, because it appeared that this overpowering assault was going to succeed, especially after the uniting of the assault's two wings.[88] However, fast-moving bluecoat artillerymen had already prudently brought up a large supply of canister (the infantryman's ultimate nightmare), stacking them in ever-higher piles beside artillery pieces. Everything had been made ready for when the Southern infantry eased to well within close range.[89] Now that Pickett's and Pettigrew's divisions were linked together in one lengthy line that spanned across the open fields, Rittenhouse's guns on Little Round Top were presented with an even more lucrative target. The six roaring Parrott rifles atop this elevated firing platform of the treeless crest (unlike Big Round Top), which offered a sweeping panoramic view, continued to take more lives.[90]

Although more directly facing the target of the clump of trees than Pickett's division, Pettigrew's division possessed the longest distance to advance (although it had the shortest distance to advance east of the northeast-running Emmitsburg Road). This situation guaranteed the taking of artillery-fire and then shortly musketry from the New York, Delaware, New Jersey, Rhode Island, Ohio, and Connecticut troops, of General Hays's division on the right of the command's center, for a longer period. Having gained command of Company B after his company captain was cut down on July 1, newly appointed Captain Thomas Jefferson Cureton, 26th North Carolina Infantry, described in a letter: "We saw a ridge [before] us, a High and elevated position with a Beautiful Valley covered with grass and a long fence stretching through rather diagonally across [and] No trees or anything, not even a hill, to protect a charging line from artillery etc—only the long fences."[91]

Captain Cureton felt pride at how the North Carolina troops continued onward "in splendid fashion."[92] Along an expansive front, Virginia and North

Carolina regiment flags of blue (a total of 10 in the first line [Garnett and Kemper] and five in the second line [Armistead] of Pickett's division) inspired the common soldiers onward over the mangled bodies of comrades.[93] The 1st Virginia's color guard continued to lead the way in Kemper's center. Irish Sergeants Patrick Woods, age 25 and an ex-laborer, William M. Lawson, a former clerk, and John Q. Figg, an ex-wood turner at age 21, carried colorful flags of silk through the shell-fire. Color Corporals Theodore R. Martin and William "Willie" L. Mitchel were other regimental color guard members. All of these Richmond men were about to be either killed or wounded.[94] To the 1st Virginia's right, Charles W. Jones, a 25-year-old private of Company C, 11th Virginia, encouraged his comrades with the battle cry, "Come on, boys, let's [now] drive away those infernal Yankees." This ex-farmer of the Clifton Greys would not live to see July 4.[95]

While faithfully obeying orders that there would be "[n]o cheering, no firing, no breaking from common to quick step," these veterans pushed steadily ahead for "God and Country." One Confederate summarized the self-sacrificing determination: "[M]y first desire should be not that I might escape but that my death should help the cause of the right to triumph."[96]

To the boys in blue, it appeared that yet another Confederate triumph was in the making. As he had penned in his diary, William W. Burns, who now defended his native home soil, was convinced that if the assault succeeded, then it would be "all up with the USA" once and for all.[97] Another Yankee watched "this mass of men approaching our position [and] thought that our chances of kingdom come [now] were very good."[98]

As the seemingly endless formations of Pickett's division neared the Emmitsburg Road, the shell-fire became more accurate. Lieutenant Lewis wrote: "Crash after crash came the shot and shell [and] Great gaps were being made in the lines, only to be closed up; and the same steady, move forward."[99] Leading the Montgomery Guard (Company C), which had been commanded by his father at the war's beginning, Lieutenant John Edward Dooley, Jr., described how officers shouted to compensate for the gaps blown into the surging ranks: "Dress to the left or right, while [additional men] are sinking to rise no more! Still onward! . . . Still we press on—oh, how long it seems before we reach those blazing guns [that] hurl these implements of death in our faces. . . ."[100]

Thirty-year-old Private George Washington Eubank, a former carpenter, simply wanted to see his home again. A shell-shocked Eubank "deserted in the face of the enemy," living to see another day, unlike so many of his 1st

Virginia comrades.[101] Despite an illness, Colonel Eppa Hunton, the ex-militia brigadier general, continued to lead the 8th Virginia through the hail of lead. The mounted Hunton now "willing to die to achieve a victory there, which it was believed would be the crowning victory and the end of the war."[102] Complementing the "Bloody Eighth" of Garnett's brigade, General Kemper had bestowed the appropriate sobriquet of the "*bloody First*" on the 1st Virginia, because of its combat prowess and past sacrifices.[103]

Leading the 38th Virginia, on the northern, or left, flank of Armistead's brigade, Color Corporals Joseph Singleton and John R. Bullington were in the forefront.[104] Losing confidence in holding firm before such a massive onslaught, the infantrymen of Cemetery Ridge waited patiently under the searing sun. They sensed that these attackers had been "personally selected by General Lee to command and lead the flower of his army in whom was centered all his hopes on this field—they were to him like Napoleon's body [Imperial] guard at Waterloo."[105]

Colonel Joseph Mayo, Jr., commanding his troops on Kemper's left, described how the "spotless stars and bars," of new silk encouraged "[o]ur dear old Third" Virginia toward the heights now aglow with flames.[106] Mayo had just recently displayed admirable chivalry in ordering his men not to cut down a high-ranking Union officer, mounted and in the open when commanding skirmishers.[107] Now an easy target before his surging formations, like the Union officer whom he had just saved, Colonel Mayo gave thanks when a projectile just narrowly missed its mark, whizzing so close to his nose that he instinctively ducked. Not long thereafter, the VMI–educated colonel (Class of 1852) was knocked off his feet. This explosion in the 3rd Virginia's ranks felled other victims, causing a gory red spray of "splinters of bone and lumps of flesh" to descend over the half-dazed colonel.[108]

Kemper's brigade continued to be hit by multiple artillery fires: the longest-range enfilade fire from Little Round Top; from Captain James McKay Rorty's battery, Company B, 1st New York Artillery, which unleashed a shorter-range, head-on attack just southeast of the clump of trees; and from several of McGilvery's reserve batteries positioned below Rorty's guns. Sandwiched between the 15th Massachusetts Volunteer Infantry and the 19th Maine Volunteer Infantry, General William Harrow's 1st Brigade, Gibbon's 2nd Division, 2nd Corps, Rorty's 10-pound Parrott rifles were now commanded by Lieutenant Robert Rogers, after the Irish battery commander (Rorty) had been mortally wounded in the cannonade. Meanwhile, north of Kemper, Garnett's brigade took head-on fire from Captain Andrew Cowan's five New York guns that were positioned north of Rorty and just south of the copse of trees.[109]

After surging down the slope and through a pristine meadow, cut by a grassy ditch that was jumped by the attackers, meanwhile, Pettigrew's Tennessee, Alabama, North Carolina, and Mississippi troops advanced at "quick-time." Pettigrew's North Carolina men moved relentlessly toward a broad field of near-ripe wheat. This wheat field stretched up the western slope of the Emmitsburg Road ridge like a golden carpet and all the way to the dirt-lined artery. After barreling down still another wooden fence, these North Carolina veterans advanced at a good pace through the tall stalks of golden wheat. With a remarkable discipline that awed the defenders, these seasoned men moved "steady and as regular as if on a parade," despite exploding shells spreading carnage.[110]

After the right wing (Pickett) had eased to the left (all except for Kemper's brigade) toward Pettigrew's division, Lieutenant John Henry Lewis, Jr., of Armistead's brigade, described how the "line was shortened, but as steady as ever, the gallant Armistead still in the lead [and] He seemed to be as cool as if on drill [when] We were nearing the Emmitsburg road [where] there were two fences at that road. . . ."[111]

Perhaps now wishing that he was still a student in his carefree Georgetown College days, Lieutenant Dooley penned, "So many men have fallen now that I find myself within a few feet of my old Captain [21-year-old George F. Norton, VMI (Class of 1860) who led Company D, Old Dominion Guard]. His men are pressing mine out of place. I asked him to give way a little to the left, and scarcely has he done so than he leaps into the air, falling prostrate" with a serious wound.[112] Meanwhile, additional 2nd Corps soldiers along Cemetery Ridge felt that the end had come, and that death "or Libby Prison" lay in store for them.[113]

Hoping to move across the deadly ground as fast as possible, Garnett's overeager men began to move too fast, getting ahead of Fry's Alabama and Tennessee brigade to their left and Kemper's brigade to their right. Like a wise father cautioning a wayward son, Garnett immediately reined in his boys with a sharp admonishment: "Don't double quick. Save your wind . . . for the final charge!"[114] Occupying Garnett's right flank despite the brigade's smallest regiment (only about 240 men), the 8th Virginia's advancing ranks were made steadier by the efforts of the four Berkeley brothers. The Berkeley clan was such an early inspirational influence that the command became known as the "Berkeley Regiment." The Berkeley brothers hailed from the Virginia Piedmont in the northwest corner of Prince William County in northern Virginia. This agrarian community had been burned down by Union troops in early November 1862, fueling desperation among Haymarket's sons on July 3.

While Colonel Eppa Hunton, who was still mounted on "his orderly's little dun gelding," in leading the way, 35-year-old Lieutenant Colonel Norborne Berkeley, served as Hunton's top lieutenant. Major Edmund Berkeley was then the "Old Bloody Eighth's" third-highest-ranking officer. Major Berkeley was the patriarch of the plantation known as "Evergreen," which lay at the foot of the Bull Run Mountains in the Potomac River country. He had been educated at William and Mary College, Williamsburg, Virginia. Berkeley had inherited Evergreen from his father. Married to a pretty Tennessee woman named Mary Lawson Williams-Berkeley, the major had first marched off to war as the company commander of the appropriately named Evergreen Guards (Company C, also known as the Bull Run Rangers), 8th Virginia.

Major Berkeley and his brothers had transformed the 8th Virginia into one of Garnett's best regiments. Captain William Noland Berkeley led Company D (Champe Rifles) forward, with Lieutenant Charles Fenton Berkeley's assistance. He was the youngest of the four Berkeley brothers at age 29. When near Lee's strategic objective, all of the Berkeley boys, along with their regimental commander, Hunton, were destined to be cut down and then captured.[115]

Meanwhile, the swarming Rebel skirmishers, loading and firing at a brisk pace, continued to hurl the stubborn Union skirmishers rearward. At the Emmitsburg Road, the last large contingent of Yankee skirmishers on the north and center steadied muskets on rail fences and blasted away. After firing, the skirmishers then turned and dashed up the slope in the hope of gaining the main line. Gradually rising up from the Emmitsburg Road, the western slope of Cemetery Ridge was open all the way up to the stone wall. The flight of the last Yankee skirmishers allowed the Rebel skirmishers to fire on mounted Union officers, exposed against the eastern skyline, along the crest of Cemetery Ridge.[116]

Eager to strike back after losing so many men, Pettigrew ordered his soldiers to return a volley without halting or realigning to waste any precious time. After all, he needed to keep his alignment linked to Pickett's left. Union soldiers on the north were stunned by their skirmishers' wild flight, feeling the same kind of shock that had been experienced by Pettigrew's men at the unbelievable sight of Brockenbrough's collapse. However, the rolling volley that erupted with "a terrific crash" from Pettigrew's lengthy ranks before the Emmitsburg Road had overall little effect. Thousands of veteran Federals of Hancock's 2nd Corps were hunkered down under the secure cover of the stone wall, just waiting for the order to rise up and return punishment.[117] Hancock's men of Webb's division had a nasty surprise in store for the attackers under Garnett, who had once served with Hancock in the 6th United States Infantry, and Armistead.[118]

As the lengthy ranks neared the Emmitsburg Road, the Rebels finally reached an especially lethal point well within rifle range of thousands of veterans along the stone wall. As ordered, the greatest number of infantrymen in the targeted sector still held their fire even while the initial wave of attackers reached the road that angled northeast toward Gettysburg and through the farmer's fields. The last knots of panting and sweating bluecoat skirmishers, who had departed from their advanced positions around the Emmitsburg Road on the double, finally gained the safety of the stone wall, after racing up the slope under the blazing sun.

First Volleys

With the lengthy front finally free of bluecoat skirmishers, the patient infantrymen could now open fire with rifled muskets. On the south, the first of Gibbon's men before Pickett's ranks began to fire even before the Rebels reached the Emmitsburg Road southwest of the Codori House, while Hays's troops (about 1,200 muskets) north of the Angle waited until Pettigrew's men gained the road. Rising up from the stone wall below the Angle and farther south down the ridge, veterans armed with Model 1861 .58 caliber Springfield rifled musket (the standard weapon, which possessed an effective range at 300–400 yards, but could kill at 1,000 yards) and other weapons unleashed a stream of fire.

Leading the 53rd Virginia troops before Gibbon's front, Lieutenant Colonel Rawley White Martin wrote how "the distance between the opposing forces grows less and less—suddenly the infantry behind the rock fence poured volley after volley into the advancing ranks. The men fell like stalks of grain before the reaper, but they closed the gaps and pressed forward, through that pitiless storm" of projectiles.[119] Advancing with the Irish of Company C (Montgomery Guard) on Kemper's right, Lieutenant John Edward Dooley, Jr., described the awful destruction: "Our men are falling faster now, for the deadly musket is at work [and] Volley after volley of crashing musket balls sweeps through the line and mow us down like wheat before the scythe."[120]

On Garnett's far right, and leading the 8th Virginia, riding his "dun gelding," Colonel Eppa Hunton was the division's first regimental commander wounded. A bullet struck his leg and went completely through the horse owned by his orderly. Nevertheless, the warhorse, although having suffered a mortal wound, carried its bloodied rider, who felt disgust that Pickett was not now leading the troops at the forefront, rearward to safety.[121] In the center of the same brigade, Colonel Henry Gantt (VMI Class of 1851) continued to implore his troops onward while leading the way on foot, until cut down by wounds to the face and left arm.[122]

Before his 1st Virginia boys, shouting orders, Colonel Lewis Burwell Williams, Jr., galloped onward into the midst of the hail of projectiles. Like Garnett, Williams had something to prove. As a martinet, he had become unpopular with his ultra-democratic men and now wanted to redeem himself in their eyes. Riding his spirited mare, Nelly, before his troops, bullets shattered the colonel's shoulder and struck his spinal column. Nevertheless, he remained mounted. Upon nearly reaching the Emmitsburg Road southwest of the Codori House, Colonel Williams finally toppled off his "little brown mare." He then "fell on his own sword." But the 1st Virginia soldiers ignored the fall of their leader from the VMI Class of 1855, while continuing to do their duty as he had always ensured by his discipline.[123] One officer lamented how the colonel had ridden "coolly and deliberately in front of the regiment [a] most conspicuous target. . . . Poor Williams! His spinal bone is broken, the shot . . . striking at the neck joint and running down the spinal column."[124] Williams was Kemper's first regimental officer to be fatally cut down.[125]

As if beckoning the remainder of Kemper's brigade onward, the fallen colonel's terrified mare continued in a wild dash straight east. The frightened animal then "went up riderless almost of the stone wall," wrote Captain Bright of Pickett's staff.[126] Watching Williams fall to rise no more, Private Jacob R. Polak, age 23 and a former clerk of Company I, 1st Virginia, might have felt a sense of guilt, because he had brought the high-spirited Nelly to the colonel for him to lead the attack.[127]

A sergeant of the 143rd Pennsylvania Volunteer Infantry, Patrick DeLacy watched the decimation of "that magnificent line."[128] The 111th New York's colonel, Clinton D. MacDougall, of Scotch-Irish descent, rose to the challenge. Despite a bullet wound in the arm, he encouraged his men. His New York regiment had been positioned by Hays just north of the 12th New Jersey and behind the stone wall just below the Brien barn.[129] General Hays was "happiest" when now about to order the destruction of large numbers of Rebels.[130]

Despite the severe punishment inflicted upon Pickett's division before Webbs's brigade, Pettigrew's and Trimble's troops were about to receive an even greater storm of musketry in Hays's front that extended south to the Angle. Here, Hays had ordered his men to gather as many extra muskets on the field from the previous day's combat. Therefore, between the Brien House to the north and the Angle to the south, the 14th Connecticut, 1st Delaware, and 12th New Jersey (the largest regiment with about 400 men), from south to north, had stock-piled a massive amount of firepower—an urgent necessity because of the man-power shortage. The 1st Delaware had only about 200 men in the ranks, and the 14th Connecticut possessed less than 110 soldiers. Now the stone wall provided another benefit: loaded muskets were lined up in neat rows and ready for fire. Fortified by courage and pocket Bibles from the American Tract Society, Hays's troops calmly waited for Pettigrew's and Trimble's troops to get closer (unlike in Pickett's front to the south) before firing, ensuring greater destruction.[131]

To the rear of Pettigrew's front line, dark-haired Colonel John Decatur Barry, age 24 and destined to die not long after the war from wrecked health due to arduous campaigning, led the 18th North Carolina, on the brigade's left-center, onward, despite "feeble health and ought not to have crossed the Potomac," wrote one of his men. Barry rode his "shaved-tail sorrel horse" through the rain of projectiles. He eventually reached the stone wall—a rare feat for a mounted officer this afternoon.[132]

Meanwhile, four miles to the east, General Stuart was about to run into stiff resistance from hard fighting Union cavalry during his vital "mission of the utmost importance to reach the Union rear [and now] at the same instant that Pickett and thirteen thousand Confederate infantrymen were streaming across the field [toward Cemetery Ridge]. If there was any conceivable hope of sup-porting Pickett, he needed to reach the Union rear, three miles away, as soon as possible or the day could be lost of the Confederacy. Stuart [was about] to initiate his own version of Pickett's charge on horseback and force the Yankees from the pathway to his objective."[133]

In the face of the onslaught, these hard-nosed defenders of the right-center displayed considerable fighting spirit. One feisty New York color-bearer even stood up and waved the colors, shouting for the Rebels to come on and issuing the supreme insult and challenge.[134] Besides the sheets of musket fire pouring down the slopes in Gibbon's sector south of the Angle and while Hays's men north of the Angle held their fire until the Rebels reached the road, the artil-lery punishment became more severe. Massed stockpiles of canister were now utilized at close range. The shotgun-like canister of iron projectiles (like shotgun pellets) were the infantrymen's ultimate nightmare. Lieutenant Alonzo Hersford Cushing's gunners of Battery A, 4th United States Artillery at the Angle opened with canister on Garnett's brigade. To ensure a more deadly effect and at his insistence, Cushing had advanced his last remaining two guns down the slope to just behind the stone wall. Meanwhile, Captain Rorty's New York guns situated just below the clump of trees and on lower ground than Cushing, who was higher up the ridge to the north, unleashed canister upon Kemper's surging ranks. Rorty's guns were located just south of Cowan's six field pieces of the New York Light Battery, including one gun firing north of the copse of trees.[135]

Commanding the right section of the smoothbore, bronze 12-pound Napoleons of the battery (Battery I, 1st United States Artillery) of Lieutenant George A. Woodruff, which was located on the commanding perch on the edge of Ziegler's Grove on the right of Hays's division, Lieutenant Tully McCrea rose to the fore. After delivering a devastating flank fire from the northeast on Pettigrew's left, Lieutenant McCrea, of Scotch-Irish heritage, had prepared a harsh greeting for Pettigrew's troops. He had ordered his artillerymen, eager for revenge because they had suffered during the cannonade, to hold their fire with canister until the lengthy lines of gray and butternut advanced closer. Knowing that the position of their Company I, 1st United States Artillery was crucial (near the northern end of Hays's line) for holding the defensive line, Woodruff's officers yelled for their gunners, who had already expended all of their long-range rounds in punishing the attackers, to open fire with canister that had been stockpiled by New York infantry volunteers and artillerymen.

For these 2nd Corps gunners, this was payback time. With 40 rounds of canister per gun, the half-dozen bronze Napoleons of Woodruff's battery I, 1st United States Artillery, unleashed a devastating fire upon Pettigrew's troops from their 12-pounders, after having been pushed down the slope for better firing positions. Likewise, the 3-inch Ordnance Rifles of Captain William Arnold's 1st Rhode Island Light Artillery, Battery A (originally five guns positioned on high-ground—farther north up the ridge above the clump of trees—just northeast of Cushing's battery and above the northeast corner of the Angle, where the low stone fence turned north) also delivered canister into Marshall's and Davis's brigades, Pettigrew's division.

Firing around two rounds per minute from their high-ground perch northeast of the Brien barn, Woodruff's gunners, including Lieutenant John Egan, who commanded the battery's right section, marveled at the terrible destruction: the "storm of grape and canister tore its way from man to man, and marked its track with corpses straight down the line."[136] Meanwhile, with its guns positioned at the stone wall just below the clump of trees, Cowan's battery (a most timely reinforcement) hurled canister mostly into Kemper's ranks and to a lesser degree (from the northernmost guns), Garnett's brigade. Advancing in Company C (Carroll Boys from Carroll County), 24th Virginia on Kemper's far right, two Shockley brothers, William and Richard, were cut down. Private William Shockley dropped with a fatal wound in the neck.[137]

Canister from Cushing's and Cowan's batteries raked Garnett's brigade, to Kemper's left, with a vengeance. Attempting to instill confidence under the pounding, General Garnett shouted, "Steady, men!" Lieutenant George Williamson Finley, 56th Virginia on Garnett's extreme left, described: "Canister turns a cannon into a giant shotgun on wheels [and it was] so devastating that the soldiers . . . called it 'canned hellfire'."[138] The explosions of canister knocked officers off their horses, including Colonel Mayo, 1st Virginia, who described how "everything was a wild kaleidoscopic whirl" of a living nightmare.[139]

Through the canister and rifle fire, Garnett's and Kemper's ranks (from north to south) continued to roll onward without firing or raising the traditional battle cry as usual in obeying orders. Meanwhile, out of instinct, veterans' heads were slightly bowed against the hail of canister. Eyeing the long, gentle slope leading up to the crest of Cemetery Ridge and knowing that his alignment must remain as closely connected as possible to Pettigrew's right (Fry's brigade) now swept with fire from Arnold's guns, Garnett continued to instill confidence and warn his troops not to move too fast: "Save your Strength!"

Worst of all for Confederate fortunes, this attacking force was now much smaller than originally planned by Lee. As Colonel Taylor emphasized, Pickett's division "continu[ed] the charge without supports," while General Pickett remained behind his troops. Meanwhile, Pickett set his sights (where Garnett's left was descending) on the Codori House and the large red barn, where he planned to seek shelter from the storm after his troops moved up the slope.[140] Indeed, during "one of the pivotal epochs of the war, he elected not to accompany his troops" during most of the attack. Clearly, Pickett wanted more protection than just wearing the crucifix given him by a Mexican priest after the assault on Chapultepec had afforded him.[141] Meanwhile, the defenders were now "burning to pay off the old scores" of Fredericksburg.[142] A 14th Connecticut soldier, on the left of Irish-born Colonel Thomas A. Smyth's 2nd Brigade, Hays's 3rd Division near the Brien barn, was determined to "pay back [the Rebels] with *Interest,* for our defeat at Fredericksburg."[143]

Drummer boys continued to beat their drums, while additional comrades died beside them and their beautiful war flags were ripped to shreds by canister and bullets. Company A (Blue Ridge Rifles) of the 28th Virginia, on Garnett's left-center was distinguished by the eight-man Obenshain clan of Botetourt County, Virginia. The Obenshain boys advanced not far from the regimental color guard: Sergeant John J. Eakin, and Color Corporals Dexter S. Britts, Lindsey S. Creasey, and James H. Hamilton. Two of the clan's youngest members, 14-year-old Peter M. and Zebulon T. Obenshain, age 13, had been discharged because of their youth in 1861. But now musician Daniel D. Obenshain played a high-pitched fife, and drummer boy Martin Van Buren Obenshain continued the family's martial musical tradition. James P. Obenshain and 19-year-old Joel B. Obenshain, also of the Blue Ridge Rifles, were both destined to be shortly hit and captured. Meanwhile, the clan's twin boys, age 18, Samuel S. Obenshain, an ex-farmer, and William R. Obenshain, continued to surge over the open fields.[144]

Morale and Discipline Remains High

Pickett's men were still under orders not to unleash the "Rebel Yell" as in previous attacks until they were immediately upon their opponent. Meanwhile, Colonel Fry's Tennessee and Alabama boys on Garnett's left were under no such restrictions. Therefore, while Pickett's Virginians maintained their silence, a resounding "Rebel Yell" erupted from Fry's brigade. Even then, this yell "started much farther from the enemy than usual," penned "Jack" H. Moore, 7th Tennessee, which advanced on Fry's left-center.[145]

Meanwhile, the 69th, 70th, 71st, and 106th Pennsylvania, Webb's 2nd "Philadelphia" Brigade, 2nd Division, 2nd Corps, defended the copse of trees sector and north (higher up the ridge) up to the Angle that was becoming the eye of the storm. Webb, West Point Class of 1855, commanded the Philadelphia Brigade on its finest day. Ironically, these Philadelphia men had gone to war in gray uniforms. Resilient Irish-born soldiers filled the 69th Pennsylvania's ranks. These Sons of Erin revered their regimental flag of emerald green with Celtic-Gaelic pride. This banner was distinguished by the gold coat of "Arms of Ireland" on one side. Traditional Gaelic and nationalist Irish symbolism of the Irish wolf hound, round tower, and sunburst graced the other side of the banner. As cruel fate would have it for Pickett's large number of Celtic-Gaelic soldiers, the 69th Pennsylvania Irish lay low behind the stone wall directly before the clump of trees: the tactical situation that shortly guaranteed the eruption of savage hand to hand combat among a disproportionate number of Sons of Erin.

Despite being weak in numbers with the 106th Pennsylvania now assigned to Cemetery Hill's defense to the north, the 862-man Philadelphia Brigade (mostly city boys—a rare demographic for an entire brigade on either side—of whom half were about to become casualties) was in overall good shape. So far, the brigade had suffered only about 50 casualties at this targeted sector during the cannonade. Behind the stone wall standing "not more than two feet high," the 69th Pennsylvania was positioned on the south before the clump of trees. Eight 71st Pennsylvania companies were positioned behind the low stone wall, running north, to the right, or northwest of the copse of trees to the right of Cushing's two guns and all the way to where the stone wall turned east at a 90-degree right angle (the Angle about 250 feet northwest of the clump of trees), before turning once again north to Hays's sector along steadily ascending ground and just below the crest of Cemetery Ridge.

Before the cannonade caused extensive damage, Cushing's four guns of Battery A, 4th United States Artillery had been sandwiched (holding a 274-foot gap) behind the two pieces near the stone wall between the veteran 69th and 71th Pennsylvania. Artillery caissons, two-wheel carts carrying two ammunition chests, were positioned about 20 paces behind the four guns, which stood atop the plateau about 20 paces from the crest. Webb also had his 72nd Pennsylvania positioned in reserve on higher ground (closer to the crest) behind the clump of trees, just in case the Rebels overran the stone wall, which ran north–south about 85 paces west of the crest of the ridge. The Pennsylvania boys were more heavily armed than usual, after having scoured the field for extra muskets from the previous day's fallen soldiers.

Morale was high among the Pennsylvanians, thanks to defending home soil and the inspired leadership from Webb, a former West Point instructor, and the hard-fighting Irish colonel of the 69th Pennsylvania, Dennis O'Kane. O'Kane had been born in Tireighter Townland Park Village, County Derry, Ireland. The Celtic-Gaelic colonel implored his Sons of Erin with words from past revolutionary struggles on Irish soil: "Let your work this day be for victory or to the death!" Concerned that they might not be able to hold firm under the steamrolling onslaught, these Emerald Isle fighting men trusted that God was on their side.

Most importantly, Webb had early personally taken the initiative to convince Captain Andrew Cowan to depart Cemetery Hill *without* orders to move his guns south and realign his 1st New York Battery to defend the key sector just below the copse of trees. In timely fashion, Cowan had come to the rescue of the frantic 2nd Corps brigade commander. Cowan, whose New York Light Battery was part of the 6th Corps, had taken the initiative at considerable personal risk to his career, if anything went wrong. Therefore, just in time, he had hurriedly set up his five cannons north of Lieutenant Fred Brown's 1st Rhode Island Light Artillery, Battery B, 2nd Corps, artillery—which had been withdrawn after having been mauled during the cannonade—on high-ground just below the crest, while another one of Cowan's guns was aligned north of the copse of trees.

O'Kane was a devoted father and strict Catholic. He had long worshiped at St. Mary's Catholic Church in Ireland and then St. James Church in west Philadelphia. With thousands of Confederate veterans heading his way with fixed bayonets, the dark-haired O'Kane, who had a wife and a pretty daughter, Mary Ann, who said prayers for his safe return, provided inspirational leadership. He ordered his Irishmen to hold their fire until they could plainly see the "whites of their eyes." O'Kane's words echoed those heard at Bunker Hill (Breed's Hill, where General Israel Putnam issued the famous order) on June 17, 1775.[146]

Meanwhile, rejoicing in the grim destruction delivered upon Pickett's men by his roaring guns, Captain Cowan watched "[a]s gaps opened in their lines [but] they closed to their left and kept a splendid front [and] Their direction was oblique, and it seemed that they were marching to this copse of trees, as indeed they were."[147]

Most significant, the West Pointer whose Philadelphia Brigade held the targeted right-center, General Webb had his men ready. He had early realized that the "concentration of the [Confederate] artillery fired . . . upon the ground around the clump of trees had made known to us that there was to be the point of attack," and therefore took all precautions to meet the assault. Rising to the fore like Webb and another West Pointer, General Gibbon, who commanded the division (2,150 men) that occupied the thin defensive line along the stone wall below the Angle, bestowed invaluable leadership. He had ridden along the lines and "cautioned the men not to fire until the first line crossed the Emmitsburg Road."[148] Gibbon, whose front (the Angle and clump of trees) had been primarily targeted by Lee, had prepared a lethal surprise for the attackers.

No doubt the West Pointer prayed that none of his three brothers who wore the gray were about to be killed because of his well-calculated orders to fire when the attackers were close.[149]

Meanwhile, General Kemper felt consternation not only because his seemingly ill-fated brigade had suffered disproportionately during the pre-assault bombardment, but also his right flank was enfiladed by Little Round Top's cannon and simultaneously hit by McGlivery's reserve guns in front. Nevertheless, Kemper's troops continued onward through it all, while the casualty list spiraled higher. General Kemper also became alarmed because a wider gap opened between him and Armistead to his rear. Kemper, consequently, rode up to Armistead, still leading on foot, and yelled, "Armistead, hurry up, my men can stand no more!" Armistead immediately ordered his men to double-quick to catch-up. On the double, the disciplined troops of the 14th Virginia, 9th Virginia, 53rd Virginia, 57th Virginia, and 38th Virginia, left to right (or north to south) surged through the tall grass to remedy the problem.[150]

Despite the losses and early collapse on the extreme left, Lee's tactical plan was actually working to perfection with regard to his frontline troops, who steadily neared their target. Because of the superior discipline and training, and after adjusting to the left by Pickett and to the right by Pettigrew to draw closer together, the assault of so many different units was succeeding as envisioned. Up ahead, the Emmitsburg Road, where the Nicholas J. Codori House and red barn stood just to the east side of the road like a beacon, stood as the next key objective. This highly visible point continued to serve as an initial guide to show the way for the attackers to strike the vulnerable right-center.[151]

At this point so near the road, the Confederates could more clearly see the long strip of white rocks of the stone wall that lined the high-ground just below the crest of Cemetery Ridge. Even then, the ridge did not appear imposing as an elevation, because of its gentle, open western slope. Other than the fast-working artillerymen, no bluecoat infantrymen could be seen defending the strategic crest to Rebel eyes! This unbelievable sight alone brought a sense of excitement to the surging ranks, because decisive victory seemed to be looming just ahead. Of course, what the attackers had no way of knowing was that the stone wall was certainly low, but still sufficiently high enough to hide thousands of waiting Federal infantrymen.

Almost as if hoping that the legendary "Rebel Yell" might be enough to scare the Yankees off their high-ground defensive perch (a tactic that had worked in 1861 and 1862), some of Garnett's more undisciplined men had earlier unleashed a chorus of high-pitched screams when they were about 800 yards (less than halfway) before the smoke-wreathed crest—a spontaneous release of pent-up tension. But they had been quickly quieted by officers in accordance with Pickett's orders, restoring the division's silent advance through the flowing fields. Therefore, Garnett's soldiers advanced in silence, while they neared the Emmitsburg Road north of the Peter Rogers House, just southwest of the Codori House and on the slight grassy rise of what was left of the Emmitsburg Road ridge that descended toward Gettysburg. But despite the losses, these veterans still believed that Lee had bestowed them with an infallible battle plan. However, some overeager attackers shouted in vain to officers to allow them to open fire on their high-ground tormentors.[152]

Just up ahead on higher ground of the Emmitsburg Road ridge, the left of Pickett's troops neared the two-story Codori House, of dark red brick, located just on east side of the road. As usual with German farmers in this region of immense agricultural productivity, the Codori brighter-red barn was even larger than the nearby house. Irish immigrants in gray and butternut now received a closer view of the fine house of another hard-working immigrant, who liked fast horses. Codori had journeyed to America in 1828 from Alsace with the same hopes as the immigrant Irish.[153]

Despite its second-line position, Armistead's brigade also suffered severely. Color Corporal Robert Tyler Jones described how the 53rd Virginia's Color Sergeant Leander C. "Blackburn soon fell, and then another and another of the [color] guard. The flag lay prone upon the field, shot from some gallant hand, when I took it up and shook its folds in the air [and] Still onward we went, amid the storms of shot and death. . . ."[154]

In a letter, Captain John A. Herndon, 38th Virginia, Armistead's brigade, described with pride how the field "was raked by the most galling fire of musketry and artillery, but over it we went slowly and steadily and made the prettyiest, most splendid assault I ever saw or ever expect to see. I speak of our Division and especially our brigade [Armistead] . . . No troops upon drill ever moved more splendidly and steadily than they did. . . ."[155] Thirty-year-old Private William G. Monte, a former barber of Company G (Portsmouth Rifles), 9th Virginia, Armistead's brigade, also admired the disciplined advance: "What a sublime sight!" Glancing at his pocket watch, Private Monte, of French Huguenot heritage, was heard to say, "We have been just nineteen minutes in coming" not long before he was killed by canister.[156]

But the absence of flying artillery and the failure of Confederate guns, thanks to a lack of ammunition following the lengthy cannonade on Seminary Ridge to unleash a high volume of fire over the attackers' head (as originally planned by Alexander), meant that the defenders remained safe from incoming artillery rounds. Even more, Longstreet should have placed troops of Anderson's division on the flanks of the assault for protection, but that was not the case.[157]

The last stretch of open ground before the road was swiftly passed by the fast-moving ranks. After Pickett's troops surged over the grassy swale about 400 yards before the Emmitsburg Road, and moved through the lower ground of open fields, they finally descended upon the road. Another parallel and companion swale, both which drained water south from Plum Run's Upper Valley, stood on the east side of the road. These open swales lay before Gibbon's front (faced by Pickett's division) just below the Angle, but they posed no obstacles to the fast-moving ranks. In fact, these grass-covered depressions were sufficiently deep to hide and protect the attackers.[158]

But despite the differences in terrain that allowed for an overall easier advance for Pettigrew's men, Pickett's and Pettigrew's divisions managed to converge and approach the Emmitsburg Road at almost the exact same time: a remarkable tactical development under the most challenging circumstances. Just southwest of the Codori House, Garnett's and Armistead's brigades, from north to south, began the difficult maneuver of turning to advance in a northeast direction and, pushing roughly parallel to the road, reaching a point from which to attack straight east the clump of trees. Clearly, Lee's plan was working well (except on the extreme left flank) with regard to the frontline attackers who were going for broke as never before.[159]

Chapter VI

The "Vortex of Fire" along the Emmitsburg Road

So far during the lengthy advance across the open fields of early summer, almost all fences previously encountered had been split rail ("worm") fences, as found across the South. Merely temporary barriers because they had been easily constructed by hand, these fences were easily knocked down by soldiers without slowing the assault waves. Therefore, while steamrolling onward, the attackers were in for an unpleasant surprise when they encountered an entirely new kind of fence: sturdy post-and-rail fences (standing about five feet high) on both sides of the Emmitsburg Road. These post-and-rail fences consisted of solidly implanted vertical posts linked by crossbeams nailed securely to posts. Lieutenant George Williamson Finley, Company K (Harrison's Guards), 56th Virginia, described the shock: "When we got to the fence at the Emmitsburg Road, we discovered to our horror that what we thought was going to be another worm fence was–instead–post-and-rail. That Pennsylvania Dutch farmer had dug post holes alongside the road, sunk upright posts in the holes, cut slots in the tops of the posts, and fitted them with shlatted boards!"[1] One frustrated North Carolina soldier described how these were "well built fences [of] boards nailed on Black Locust post [which] will last for many years."[2]

While Garnett's and Armistead's brigades, after swinging northeast through the fields west of the road and paralleling it for a good distance, reached the road north of the Codori House and barn, Kemper's brigade gained the road farther south below the Codori House near the Rogers House. These post-and rail fences extended along both sides of the Emmitsburg Road, which was around 300 yards (in Pickett's sector) from the whitish-colored stone wall. The time it took for the Confederates, especially Pettigrew's men, who encountered more intact fences than Pickett's soldiers (thanks to Virginia skirmishers who had torn down sections and remained at the road for their comrades to catch up to them), to get across the most "formidable" barrier yet encountered on the long trek from Seminary Ridge, was far more costly than anticipated—still another unpleasant surprise.

This imposing barrier consisted of the two parallel chestnut rail fences lining both sides of the road resulted in a slaughter: a "death trap." Less-sturdy rail fences encountered earlier—little more than flimsy property markers rather than to keep hogs and small herds of cattle of subsistence farmers from slipping through—had been pushed down without difficulty. With larger posts dug deeper, the fences along the road were far sturdier and higher at a height of five rails, or about five feet. Unfortunately for the Rebels, these obstacles were encountered when they were at their most weary.

Consequently, this post-and-rail fence on the west side of the road and the post-and-slab fence now presented a most daunting obstacle. All along the line, the veteran 2nd Corps infantrymen, especially soldiers who had so enthusiastically "enlisted to kill rebels" in one bluecoat's words, lusted for the order to open fire to unleash their most concentrated volley. This was now the most vulnerable time for the attackers: not only in climbing the fence but also after they scaled the fence and then took time to re-form their ranks once on the other side of the road. In this exposed situation, the stationary Rebels provided ideal targets. General Gibbon penned how when Pickett's Rebels "paused a moment to reform [then] My division [behind the stone wall below the Angle] from the low stone wall on each side of the angle every gun along it sent forth the most terrific fire." Lieutenant John Henry Lewis, Jr., Company G, 9th Virginia, Armistead's brigade, wrote how at "this point the crash of musketry was added to the roar of artillery [and the] Men were falling in heaps."[3] But it was not all young men and boys who were cut down: unknown to Lieutenant John Henry Lewis, Jr., and his comrades, at least one female Rebel, whose hair had been either clipped short or tied up under her slouch hat, fell seriously wounded along the Emmitsburg Road.[4]

However, firing before Hays's soldiers north of the Angle, Gibbon's men inflicted the most damage on Garnett's and Kemper's troops, who were still ahead of Armistead's brigade as frontline troops. The soldiers of Gibbon's 13 2nd Division regiments (four from Pennsylvania, three from New York, three from Massachusetts, one Minnesota, one Michigan, and one from Maine) unleashed a murderous volume of fire, after rising as one from the stone wall and standing up in neat rows. A product of Harvard College, Boston-born Lieutenant Sumner Paine was shortly fated to be killed after yelling out his last words: "Isn't this glorious!" Before dying, he implored his men to fire more rapidly. Firing from a lengthy line (just below or south of the 69th Pennsylvania) that extended south along the stone wall, just southwest of the clump of trees, this veteran killing machine cut down Virginia officers in front, color-bearers, and a good many young men with businesslike efficiency.[5]

Lieutenant George Williamson Finley, 56th Virginia, described the nightmarish ordeal: "We had to climb the fence to get the enemy [but] Men were falling all around us, and cannons and muskets were raining death upon us [and] The 56th [Virginia] was being torn to pieces. . . ."[6] General Kemper was worried that he would never again see his native Madison County, in northern Virginia's Piedmont, after his troops entered into a lethal "vortex of fire,"[7] especially since he was mounted.

The high post-and-rail fence that stood on the west side of Emmitsburg Road became a scene of slaughter. The fences had been constructed in the typical manner of German farmers, whose much-improved agricultural lands and fences possessed a superior quality (typically Teutonic) generally unseen in the largely Celtic South. Because these farmers had made sure that no livestock wandered out of pastures or were easily stolen by a neighbor or stranger passing along the road, a death warrant unknowingly had been long ago signed for a good many Virginians. These chestnut rail fences stood about three times higher than the low stone wall now lined by bluecoats, who overlooked the lower ground of the Emmitsburg Road that ran along the narrow, open ridge.

One of Armistead's soldiers described the bloody ordeal: "The moments of anxious suspense and the length of time it seemed to climb up to the top of the fence, tumble over it, and fall flat into the bed of the road. All the while, the bullets continued to bury themselves into the bodies of the victims and sturdy chestnut rails" like hail on an April morning.[8] While his fast-firing men blasted away to send a sheet of lead pouring down the slope, Gibbon took satisfaction in the fact that a good many "men fell from the top [fence] rails" to rise no more.[9]

Encountering more intact fences, especially before Hays's front that extended north from the Angle, than Pickett's men, hundreds of Pettigrew's exhausted soldiers tumbled into the relative shelter of the wide roadbed to save themselves. At the stone wall immediately north of the Angle, the 14th Connecticut, Hays's division, men calmly waited until Pettigrew's boys began to climb the fence. Hays's first bluecoats to unleash a volley in this sector, the seasoned New Englanders, jumped to their feet and opened a blistering volley with their .58 caliber Springfield rifles.

Large numbers of killed and wounded men tumbled off the fence. But larger numbers of Pettigrew's men were saved because they had "sank to the ground" from weariness and well-honed survival veteran instincts, while bullets zipped overhead and the fence was splintered by the stream of projectiles. Here, the fences were more intact than in Pickett's sector, where some sections had been previously torn down. Private "Jack" H. Moore, 7th Tennessee, on Fry's left-center, described how the "time it took to climb to the top of the fence seemed to me an age of suspense. It was not a leaping over; it was rather an insensible tumbling to the ground in the nervous hope of escaping the thickening missiles that buried themselves in falling victims, in the ground, and in the fence, against which they rattled with the distinctiveness of large rain-drops pattering on a [tin] roof."[10] One Yankee marveled at the slaughter, writing how Pettigrew's soldiers "dropped from the fence as if swept by a gigantic sickle. . . ."[11]

At that bloody point, the well-worn Emmitsburg Road was much wider than typical country roads seen in the South. The distance between the fences on each side of the dusty road was wide. In fact, the road was as wide as main thoroughfares in major northern cities, including Washington, DC There, in the slightly sunken road (just deep enough to afford protection), large numbers of soldiers—frightened, feeling faint, with racked nerves, and sickened by the horror—caught their collective breath under the salvoes that seemed to have no end. A cloud of choking dust rose between the two fences, while bullets kicked up spouts of dust. In this hellish situation, survivors steeled themselves for the final push with fixed bayonets toward the flaming stone wall and Cemetery Ridge crest. Meanwhile, less-stalwart men had made up their minds that they would budge no further.

The lengthy expanse of roadbed became clogged with dead and wounded men. Fallen soldiers screamed and moaned in pain, asked for God's deliverance, and begged for assistance. Frantic officers, including those separated from their companies while crossing the fatal fence, bellowed orders for everyone to get up and go over the next fence. After his horse was shot from under him, Pettigrew was now on foot, waving his sword and shouting orders. Animating his men unlike Pickett at the rear, General Pettigrew was out in front, attempting to sort out the confusion. Companies and regiments had become mixed, especially where Fry's left met Marshall's right.[12]

So murderous was the musketry and blasts of canister that a good many of Pettigrew's soldiers never even attempted to climb the first post-and-rail fence.

Instead, they lay low in the ditch before the west side of the fence. Carnage-numbered survivors attempted to regain their nerve to continue onward into the face of the most vicious fire that they had ever seen. However, a good many of Pettigrew's men were finished fighting for the day, never advancing beyond the road, which was rapidly piling up in bodies.[13] But thanks to officers' efforts, including the unhorsed Pettigrew, the vast majority of the left wing's soldiers eventually crossed over the second fence. In the words of one of Pettigrew's survivors, "The time it took to climb to the top of the fence seemed [like] an age."[14]

Meanwhile, far fewer of Pickett's men took cover in the slightly sunken roadbed because of greater cohesion of units and sections of the fence (including one 20-yard-wide gap) had been knocked down, a guarantee that more momentum was sustained. Among the young men caught between the fences on the east and west sides of Emmitsburg Road were the Timberlake boys. Hailing from New Kent County, in the Chickahomy, York, and Pamunkey River country, the Timberlake clan was part of the 53rd Virginia on Armistead's center. These soldiers were the lucky survivors of the 13 Timberlake boys at the war's beginning. But they were caught in a bad fix because of the "very great obstacles," in the words of Major John Corbett Timberlake, speaking of the fences. A New Kent County farmer, Corporal Benjamin N. Timberlake, age 28 of Company E (Pamunkey Rifles), suffered a fatal thigh wound, while Sergeant Harry Timberlake, a University of Virginia man, went down with a serious wound.[15] Despite being recently sick with dysentery in a Richmond hospital, blue-eyed Major John Corbett Timberlake, from New Kent County and in his late thirties, led his boys, including relatives. He was thankful that Private Albert Timberlake, regimental butcher who had gone AWOL, now missed the nightmarish slaughter along the Emmitsburg Pike.[16]

Describing the crisis, Major Timberlake wrote of what initially seemed like good fortune without realizing that many Yankees had trained their muskets at a gap in the fence that allowed Pickett's soldiers easier passage compared to Pettigrew's men. When "Discerning a break in the fence, the command was give to 'pass obstruction' and in doing this, we all had to pass through this narrow space, where many of our best and bravest" were cut down.[17] The major was fated to be captured that afternoon.[18] Likewise, Lieutenant Colonel Rawley White Martin, 53rd Virginia, described how "large numbers were shot down on account of the crowding at the openings where the fences had been thrown down. . . ."[19]

Perhaps at this gap in the fence, the band of four Ammons boys, including a father-son fighting team, of Company K (Charles City Southern Guards), 53rd Virginia, Armistead's brigade, were cut down. Having enlisted at Jamestown, Corporal George W. Ammons, Sr., an ex-farmer, fell with wounds to his thighs, while his son, Private George W. Ammons, Jr., an 18-year-old former agri-culturalist, was killed. Other Charles City Southern Guards from Virginia's Tidewater were fatally cut down, such as Private James Bowery, an ex-architect. Three Binns brothers of Company K were also hit: Private Benjamin Franklin Binns (named after the Philadelphia author of *Poor Richard's Almanac*), age 28; Private Charles D. Binns; and Private Major E. Binns, who went down mor-tally wounded.[20] In addition, another father-son team, ex-farmers of Amherst County, Virginia, might well have been hit along with so many comrades along the body-strewn Emmitsburg Road: Privates George Washington Mays, Sr., and George Washington Mays, Jr., age 21, of Company H (Southern Rights Guards), 19th Virginia, Garnett's brigade.[21]

East of the Post-and-Rail Fences

After crossing two stout parallel fences, the most stalwart survivors of Pickett's and Pettigrew's divisions hastily re-formed their ranks with a mechanical pre-cision that spoke highly of their courage and discipline. There, just northeast of the Codori House, the open expanse of the upper valley of Plum Run (a shallow valley that narrowed farther northeast, toward Pettigrew's division) began to rise more sharply, but still along a gradual slope, up the western slope of Cemetery Ridge to the copse of trees that dominated the eastern horizon.

Lower-grade officers, including an Italian Rebel (like Private Horace Mangrove Giannini, 57th Virginia) from Petersburg, Virginia, named Canazio Fraetas, age 30 and a lieutenant of Company E (Cockade Rifles), 3rd Virginia, on Kemper's left, managed to get their men lined up in a tight formation on the road's east side, while under a heavy fire. Men tumbled around them with shrieks of pain or fell silently in death on the east side of the road while the ranks were shredded by musketry and artillery-fire from the crest less than 200 yards distant up the open slope.

On the west side of the Angle, where the Confederate barrage had inflicted the most extensive damage, only two guns of Lt. Alonzo Hersford Cushing's bat-tery A, 4th United States Artillery, were in action. These two 3-inch Ordnance Rifles, now positioned about ten feet above the stone wall, blasted away just northwest of the clump of trees. There, just behind the stone wall, Cushing's

Major General George Edward Pickett, West Pointer and division commander. *(Author's collection.)*

This depiction of Pickett's Charge is believed to be the only visual account by an eyewitness to the battle, rendered by artist Alfred Waud, on assignment for *New York Illustrated News*. (*Author's collection*)

Colonel Waller Tazewell "Taz" Patton (Virginia Military Institute Class of 1855) commanded the 7th Virginia Infantry, Kemper's brigade, Pickett's division. In leading his regiment during Pickett's Charge, Colonel Patton was struck in the jaws and lungs by projectiles, then captured. Patton died in a Federal hospital on July 21, 1863. "Taz" was the grand uncle of World War II American General George Patton. *(Courtesy of the Virginia Military Institute Archives, Lexington, Virginia.)*

Colonel William Dabney Stuart (Virginia Military Institute Class of 1850) was mortally wounded in Pickett's Charge, while leading the 56th Virginia Infantry, Garnett's brigade, Pickett's division. He died on July 30, 1863. *(Courtesy of the Virginia Military Institute Archives, Lexington, Virginia.)*

Confederate General Lewis Addison Armistead led his brigade over the stone wall, his hat perched on the end of his sword, giving his men a focal point. He was wounded multiple times at what was to be known as the High Water Mark of the Confederacy, and died from his wounds two days later. *(Author's collection)*

Lieutenant John Edward Dooley, 1st Virginia Infantry, Kemper's brigade, Pickett's division. The son of Irish immigrants, Dooley was wounded and captured during Pickett's Charge. *(Author's collection.)*

Colonel James "Jimmie" Keith Marshall, top left, with his Virginia Military Institute buddies. In leading Pettigrew's North Carolina brigade in the assault, Colonel Marshall — at age 24, the youngest brigade commander of Pickett's Charge — was shot off his horse and killed instantly "within 50 yards" of the Union lines, north of the Angle. *(Courtesy of the Virginia Military Institute Archives, Lexington, Virginia.)*

Brigadier General Richard Brooke Garnett, West Pointer and brigade commander of Pickett's division. Garnett was killed while leading his brigade during the attack. *(Author's collection.)*

Lieutenant Colonel John Thomas Ellis was a member of VMI Class of 1848, second in command of the 19th Virginia Infantry, Garnett's brigade, and was previously cited for Valor. He was mortally wounded by a cannonball to the face during the artillery bombardment before the assault. He died in the field hospital of Pickett's division on July 3. *(Courtesy of the Virginia Military Institute Archives, Lexington, Virginia.)*

Brigadier General James Johnston Pettigrew, division commander. Having survived leading his division during Pickett's Charge, he was later mortally wounded at the end of the Gettysburg Campaign, dying on July 14, 1863. *(Author's collection.)*

Lieutenant Edward Glenn McGehee, 22nd Virginia Infantry battalion, Brockenbrough's Virginia brigade, Pettigrew's division. McGehee, of Scotch-Irish heritage, enlisted at age 17 in his father's company. He was wounded at Chancellorsville, but returned in time to participate in Pickett's Charge. *(Author's collection.)*

Unidentified soldier of the 11th Virginia Infantry, Kemper's brigade, Pickett's division. *(Courtesy of Liljenquist Family Collection, Library of Congress, Washington, DC)*

Unidentified soldier of Company E (Lynchburg Rifles), 11th Virginia Infantry, Kemper's brigade, Pickett's division. *(Courtesy of Liljenquist Family Collection, Library of Congress, Washington, DC)*

Private John W. Anthony, Company B (Southern Guards), 11th Virginia, Kemper's brigade, Pickett's division. Anthony enlisted in Campbell County, Virginia, as a teenager. He was wounded at the battle of Seven Pines, Virginia. *(Courtesy of Liljenquist Family Collection, Library of Congress, Washington, DC)*

Corporal John Wesley Edmunds, Company B (Southern Guards), 11th Virginia Infantry, Kemper's brigade, Pickett's division. *(Courtesy of Liljenquist Family Collection, Library of Congress, Washington, DC)*

Private Archibald D. Council, Company K, 18th North Carolina, Lane's division. *(Courtesy of Liljenquist Family Collection, Library of Congress, Washington, DC)*

Private James W. Millner, Company K (Cascade Rifles), 38th Virginia Infantry, Garnett's brigade, Pickett's division. *(Courtesy of Liljenquist Family Collection, Library of Congress, Washington, DC)*

1879 photograph of the Angle and the copse of trees (to the right, or south, of the Angle) on the eastern horizon from the lower ground just to the east side of the Emmitsburg Road. This winter 1879 image shows the trees without full foliage of July 3, 1863. *(Author's collection.)*

Early twentieth-century view of the copse of trees, in full summer foliage. *(Author's collection.)*

Early artistic depiction of Pickett's Charge. *(Author's collection.)*

Another artistic depiction of Pickett's Charge. *(Author's collection.)*

"Harvest of Death" photograph taken by Timothy H. O'Sullivan for Alexander Gardner, following the battle. This graphic photo is of dead soldiers who lay in the open fields immediately east of the Emmitsburg Road. During his famous Gettysburg Address, President Abraham Lincoln eloquently honored and paid a lasting tribute to the many "brave men, living and dead, who struggled here." (*Library of Congress.*)

two remaining guns dominated a wide area of open ground, delivering death in wide swaths.

Not long after crossing the road and out of a pressing tactical urgency, still another movement began for Kemper's brigade. Now southwest of the Codori House and barn, Kemper moved to the left to align with Garnett and Armistead, who had already shifted to the left on the west side of the road. Therefore, Kemper's regiments marched in a parallel northeast direction through the open fields of Plum Run's upper valley and parallel to the Emmitsburg Pike, to gain proper alignment in order to face directly east.

Like its two sister brigades to the northeast on the east side of the road, Kemper's troops hustled northeast through the open fields to gain a new position in alignment with Garnett's right and from where they could then turn directly east to face the Angle sector, before the final rush up the slope. Hardly believing their eyes, bewildered Union troops watched in amazement, while the fast-moving ranks of the 3rd Virginia, 7th Virginia, 1st Virginia, 11th Virginia, and 24th Virginia (from north to south) surged briskly northeast and parallel to the road—the most "unusual" tactical aspect of Pickett's Charge. With muskets on right shoulders, Kemper's veterans pushed on the double northeast in a movement that cost precious time (a lengthy move not toward but parallel to the Union line), sapped their strength—if not morale—and caused even more sweat to pour down already-worn men. Farther south than any other Rebel troops, Kemper's soldiers surged northeast toward the Codori House and barn, while Zeigler's Woods stood on the distant horizon behind the structures situated amid the fields.

Taking full advantage of the opportunity, hundreds of Federal infantrymen—General William Harrow's Massachusetts, Maine, New York, and Minnesota soldiers, and Colonel Norman J. Hall's Massachusetts, Michigan, and New York men (Gibbon's 2nd Division) from north to south and below Cowan's New York guns—fired into the swiftly moving mass distinguished by five blue Virginia flags leading the way. Meanwhile, Rorty's and Cowan's gunners also blasted away with canister at the Old Dominion troops shifting parallel to their front. The Union line unleashed a blistering fire like a large warship delivering broadsides on the ocean waters during the Age of Sail.

But the most devastating artillery fire came from all of McGilvery's Artillery Reserve batteries (a concentration of nearly 40 guns), which had escaped the Confederate bombardment that had so severely pounded the clump of trees and Angle sector. These reserve guns now raked the right flank of Kemper's fast-moving men with salvoes. Having conserved ammunition by not wasting it during the lengthy artillery duel, the sweeping fire of McGilvery's guns now ensured a good many men would never see Virginia again. McGilvery described how "we had a raking fire [on them that was] terrible." Some of McGilvery's guns also turned northeast to hit the rear of Kemper's last regiment, the 24th Virginia, under "Old Buck" Terry, who commanded men from Franklin, Henry, Pulaski, Floyd, Giles, Mercer, Carroll, and Patrick counties in southeast Virginia. Additional soldiers of Company E (the Pulaski Boys) and F (the New River Rifles) were cut down.

The fire was so devastating that some of Kemper's men turned around and fled to escape. Equally ominous in Harrow's and Hall's sectors below the clump of trees, small groups of fighting men, led by noncommissioned officers and lieutenants and captains, and even entire regiments now took the initiative. They moved northeast at the double-quick higher up the ridge and toward the copse of trees, where it was obvious that Kemper's fast-moving men were headed to link with Garnett and Armistead. Cowan's New York and Cushing's United States guns now blasted away with double loads of canister, raking Pickett's ranks. At this time, Garnett's brigade was still maintaining solid alignment, as solid as a wedge. Kemper's troops raced at the double-quick under fire from Hancock's units, progressively from south to north, about 400 yards to the east, after passing the Rogers House and then the Codori House and barn, which had split the brigade on the move. Then, after sweeping past the Codori buildings, following Garnett's and Armistead's brigades and crossing the road to the northeast, Kemper's men continued the left oblique movement proper (at a sharp angle) to hurriedly link with Garnett's right that faced east, while Armistead was still advancing in a second line but mostly behind Garnett's brigade. Meanwhile, after a final alignment, Kemper's left was slightly behind Garnett's right and before Armistead's troops.

After shifting northeast and forming opposite the Angle and the position of two guns of Cushing's battery just behind the stone wall and the clump of trees, all three brigades of Pickett's ranks faced east. Before Pickett's troops, the open western slope of Cemetery Ridge was not sufficiently steep to pose an obstacle. In fact, after crossing the Emmitsburg Road, Pickett's men now had a far easier avenue by which to approach Meade's right-center than Pettigrew's soldiers to the north because of the natural glacis that lay immediately before the high-ground position of Hays's division. The defenses and artillery support were stronger north of the Angle than in Pickett's sector, thanks to the effectiveness of the bombardment in knocking out artillery. Ironically, the situation was now reversed: while Pettigrew's men had the easier time in reaching the road than Pickett's troops, who had spent much effort and lives in moving to the left to permanently link with Pettigrew's right, they seemingly now had to pay a high price in a cruel compensation.

As if having met with more intact fences in crossing the Emmitsburg Road than Pickett's men was not problematic enough, Pettigrew's troops faced more disadvantageous terrain than Pickett's division. Pickett's men had a larger stretch of the open fields of Plum Run's upper valley to cross (because the road ran northeast) than Pettigrew's division (minus Brockenbrough's Virginia brigade). Pettigrew's men faced the highest point—about six feet higher than where Pickett's division attacked to the south, where the ridge gradually descended toward the clump of trees and farther south—on the right-center (Hays's front north of the clump of trees and the Angle). Compared to Pickett's soldiers, Pettigrew's troops also faced the steepest ground—as the ridge rose steadily north before this natural glacis, as described by Captain Louis Gourdin Young, Pettigrew's aide-de-camp, before Hays's 3rd Division. The stone wall "receded" in their front and ran along higher ground, because the ridge steadily rose toward Zeigler's Grove, than in Pickett's front. Therefore, Pettigrew's men faced a more formidable natural obstacle.

Therefore, a gradual ascent from the road to the crest of Cemetery Ridge meant that the ground was still gentle (unlike Little Round Top or Cemetery Hill, which Lee prudently avoided) and not sufficiently steep or rugged to thoroughly exhaust Pickett's attackers, compared to Pettigrew's men, as they surged up the slope.[22]

To Garnett's rear, meanwhile, Armistead's 14th Virginia men, on the far right, heard the order: "Now Boys, try them with your bayonet!"[23] On Pickett's immediate left, Colonel Fry was convinced that victory had been all but won after crossing the body-strewn road.[24] This was no exaggeration, because a concentrated volley from Pettigrew's men had cut down most cannoneers of not only Woodruff's battery near Zeigler's Grove, but also Arnold's battery just north of the Angle. One of Hays's stunned men could hardly believe how "[o]ur cannon then stood silent," after the scorching volley.[25]

To inspire his troops, meanwhile, General Armistead yelled to Color Corporal Robert Tyler Jones, carrying the colors, "'[R]un ahead, Bob, and cheer them up' [and] I obeyed and passed him, and shook the flag over my head. Then the 'wild charge' began."[26] Unleashing the "Rebel Yell" in unison, the rejuvenated Southerners surged east up the open slope that ascended beyond the other side of the road. Private Albert Emmell, 12th New Jersey, Hays's division, described in a letter how Pettigrew's attackers "came [on] trying to strike terror into Yankee hearts with unnatural shrieks and yells."[27] Leading his Tennessee and Alabama troops to Garnett's left after they had realigned on the east side of the road, and with most of Arnold's and Woodruff's smoking guns standing silent, Colonel Fry implored his troops onward to the cry of "Go on; it will not last five minutes longer!"[28]

The Assault's Renewed Vigor and Momentum

Consequently, with renewed momentum, the assault of all three now-united brigades steamrolled up the slope carpeted in green. To the rear of Garnett's and Kemper's brigades, Armistead's troops had "remained within the roadbed but a few seconds before leaping again atop the five-rail fences that enclosed the roadway, leaving behind scores of dead and wounded comrades in the dust of the road," that had become a grim killing ground.[29]

Indeed, the assault was much weaker because so many soldiers had been "dropped from the fence as if swept by some powerful force of nature" in the manmade tempest. But this was largely negated by the fact Pickett's three brigades were together and delivering a united blow.[30] Believing decisive victory was near, Pettigrew's men also surged onward with a determination that caused Trimble, who led the two brigades to the read of the division, to exclaim how "those fine fellows are [bound to be] going into the enemy's line." Performing well beyond expectations, General Pettigrew, with drawn saber, led the way up the grassy slope east of the road. Additional precious ground was easily gained because Woodruff's and Arnold's batteries (except for one gun), from south to north, had been silenced. All the while, larger numbers of Pettigrew's troops—Tennessee, North Carolina, and Alabama boys—continued to fall. On Hays's right just southwest of Ziegler's Grove, which dominated the high-ground northeast of the Angle, the fast-firing men of the 14th Connecticut, two entire companies of the regiment (14th Connecticut) anchoring the left flank of Colonel Thomas Smyth's 2nd Brigade of Hays's 3rd Division, blasted away at Pettigrew's onrushing troops with breech-loading Sharps rifles that blazed like lightning along the stone wall.[31]

Lieutenant George Williamson Finley, on the extreme left of Garnett's brigade and aligned next to Fry's brigade after Pickett's sliding northeastward movement was completed, described the ground on the road's east side: "[T] he ground rose up gently to . . . Cemetery Ridge [where] There was a long stone wall or fence that ran along the top of the ridge [and] It varied in height from about three to four feet. In the center of the line the wall made a sharp right angle turn [the Angle and] There was a grove of umbrella shaped trees inside the angle," which was defended by Battery A, 4th United States field artillery under Lieutenant Cushing, who now provided inspired leadership.[32] Just before he was struck "on his left side, and he sank to his knees," Colonel William Dabney Stuart pointed his Virginia Military Institute saber at the flaming stone wall and yelled, "Men, you see that wall there? It's full of Yankees [and] I want you to help take it."[33]

Substituting for Colonel Stuart's loss, Corporal Alexander Lafayette Price Williams ("Corporal Sandy") helped to fill the void. He held the regimental colors high in leading the 56th Virginia troops onward up the gradual slope. He "could feel the little tugs as the minie balls tore through our battle flag," while "bullets buzzed around our ears like angry hornets," wrote one 56th Virginia soldier.[34]

After having shifted northeast until his left was behind Garnett (Armistead was still to the rear in a second line) and performing at a high level that gave no hint of having been a career politician, Kemper rose in the stirrups of his warhorse. He then pointed his saber and yelled, "There are the guns, boys, go for them!"[35] Following their commander, Kemper's troops charged straight east toward the roaring guns. Leading Company K (Charles City Southern Guards), 53rd Virginia, Armistead's brigade, Lieutenant Robert R. Ferguson, a 26-year-old farmer of Scotch-Irish descent, fell when his left thigh bone was shattered. Attempting to take Ferguson's place and that of Captain James H. Lipscomb, who had been cut down, Lieutenant James A. Harwood saw "his little brother, whom he had loved and sheltered in many a hard fought battle before, fall" to the ground. Diminutive Private Christopher E. Harwood, age 19 and a former teacher, was hit by two bullets, falling mortally wounded. In the words of his horrified brother who ran up to assist him, but it was too late, "the little fellow exclaimed: 'Brother James, go back to [the head of] your company; I am not hurt much and you are now in command" of Company K. Lieutenant Harwood concluded: "But it was not long ere this brave little soul, who was then shot through by two minie balls, found a soldier's grave [on August 15, 1863 in a Richmond hospital] and went to the God he had so faithfully served."[36]

Leading the Montgomery Guard (Company C), 1st Virginia, Kemper's brigade, Irish Captain James Hallinan, age 21, was fatally cut down, but the Sons of Erin continued onward with fixed bayonets. Having long studied *Hardee's Tactics* for this challenge, Lieutenant Dooley took "his place" at the head of his onrushing men.[37] Despite a premonition of receiving his death stroke, Colonel Waller Tazewell Patton, a dark-haired Virginia Military Institute (VMI) graduate, implored his 1st Virginia men farther up the slope. While directing his regiment, a musket ball tore through the colonel's jaw. The soft lead projectile mushroomed upon impact, shattering bone and spraying blood in every direction. The bullet carried the colonel's lower jaw "entirely away." In addition, a bullet passed through Patton's lungs at the same time, inflicting a fatal injury to this ancestor of World War Two's General George S. Patton, Jr..[38]

At the 1st Virginia's head, meanwhile, teenage "Willie" Mitchel had recently picked stems of wild chicory and might have thought of how the green rye fields of Adams County reminded him of Ireland's beauty. In the Mitchel family, the love for the ancient Celtic-Gaelic homeland still exerted a powerful emotional appeal and psychological spell. When the family patriarch and Irish patriot died, his tombstone read, "I could not fight for Ireland, so I chose to fight for the South." This republican sentiment was fully shared by teenage Willie.

The youngest son of this dynamic Irish clan now carried the 1st Virginia's flag. Willie was shortly hit in the lower stomach, falling northeast of the two-story Codori House. But the young man refused to go rearward as ordered. He was determined to continue onward to inspire his comrades, although "Willie clasped his hand over his abdomen, showing he had been wounded fatally." Despite the painful injury and his slight frame, he somehow continued onward with the regimental banner in the 1st Virginia, advancing in Kemper's center. However, the luck of the young son of one of America's most famous Irish immigrants finally ran out. Willie Mitchel fell on the western slope with a mortal wound. A staff officer of Kemper's brigade, a surviving brother, Captain James Mitchel, who had long commanded Company C, Montgomery Guards (mostly Irish Rebels from Richmond), might have seen his younger brother's fall. But if so, he was powerless to assist the young man of so much promise, because nothing could save Willie.[39]

Ironically, revealing the horrors of this forgotten mini–civil war among the Irish, Kemper's Emerald Islanders were now punished by a good many Irish artillerymen and infantrymen in blue. Irish volunteers, with last names like Corrigan, Dougherty, and McGiveran, of the 19th Massachusetts Volunteer Infantry, Colonel Norman Hall's brigade, Gibbon's division, 2nd Corps, volunteered to serve Cowan's Empire State guns just southeast of the clump of trees.[40] Ironically, one Federal infantryman firing upon the Irish attackers was a "Yanko-Irish soldier [who] had been a soldier under John Mitchel in '48" back in Ireland in an earlier failed revolutionary struggle for liberty.[41]

Meanwhile, despite its second line position, Armistead's brigade continued to suffer severely. Captain John A. Herndon, Company D, 38th Virginia, wrote in a letter how the "line was shortening so fast from killed and wounded that I began to think there would be none left by the time we reached the enemys works [while] Genl Armistead lead them as gallantly as Julius Caesar could have done."[42]

Armistead's life was safer because he had obeyed Lee's orders to advance on foot: a wise choice that the hardheaded Kemper earlier decided to ignore. Mounted officers, such as Kemper and Garnett, became more conspicuous targets while riding ever nearer to the stone wall. When "within 100 yards of the clump of trees," Garnett's aide-de-camp, a mounted Lieutenant John Simpkins Jones, was hit by iron fragments from an exploding shell.[43]

The animated colonel of the 38th Virginia, on Armistead's left, was one of the most inviting nonmounted targets of Pickett's division because of his height of six foot, four inches. He was wounded in the left thigh and right arm. However, Colonel Edward Claxton Edmonds, VMI graduate (Class of 1858) and former principal of the Danville Military Academy, continued to lead the 38th Virginia (the "Pittsylvania Regiment"), Armistead's brigade, onward as best he could. However, the never-say-die colonel was soon dropped by a fatal wound. Edmonds never saw his 29th birthday.[44]

Along with their leaders, some of the finest 38th Virginia's enlisted men were cut down. Private Benjamin Boothe dropped when an iron canister ball smashed through his forehead, killing him instantly. Private Joseph H. Hodges was another member of Company C (Laurel Grove Riflemen) who suffered a horrendous wound. He was struck in the forehead, then the bullet tore through his eye socket and passed into his brain. And in Company F (Jeff Davis Rifles) of the same regiment, Captain Lafayette Jennings's handsome face was torn almost beyond recognition by canister that ripped his face apart.

Swept by the Leaden Storm

The attackers were caught in the vortex of a raging storm. Bluecoat gunners continued to fire canister on the Rebels while surging east of the Emmitsburg Road.[45] In addition, on the right-center of Colonel Thomas Alfred Symth's 2nd Brigade, Hays's 3rd Division, 2nd Corps, the patient

12th New Jersey veterans (nestled between the Brien House to the north and the 1st Delaware to the south) demonstrated nerves of steel by obeying orders when about to deliver the most devastating punishment. Unfortunately for Pettigrew's troops, these New Jersey soldiers were the only of Symth's men armed with .69 caliber smooth-bore muskets loaded with lethal buck & ball. Therefore, they waited longer than any Yankees to fire, after units like the 14th Connecticut had already opened fire. Standing firm before Pettigrew's onslaught, Symth had been born on Christmas Day 1832 in Ballyhooly, County Cork, in southern Ireland, migrating in New York City in the summer of 1854. The adventuresome Irish man had served with William Walker like Colonel Fry.

Under the Irishman's steady influence, Symth's troops, crouched behind the stone wall, resisted the almost overwhelming urge to open fire. But orders were to allow the Confederates to get as close as possible, before the Yankees unleashed still another surprise upon the attackers. They tightly held "muskets-turned-shotguns" that were especially lethal at close range.[46]

For attacking Confederates at close range, no small-arms fire was more dreaded than loads of buck & ball, which guaranteed the unleashing of a massive amount of firepower. With smoothbores loaded with buck & ball, frontline defenders, not only the 12th New Jersey (before Pettigrew) but also a good many Philadelphia Brigade (before Pickett) soldiers, now prepared to release a great explosion of thousands of balls and iron pellets.[47] Indeed, the Irish veterans of the 69th Pennsylvania, positioned behind the stone wall directly before the copse of trees and southwest of the 12th New Jersey on higher ground just southwest of Ziegler's Grove, were ready to unleash their close-range destructive fire. They had gathered the muskets and cartridge-boxes of Wright's Georgians who had been repulsed the previous day. Rebel cartridges, including those made in Birmingham, England, and run through the Union naval blockade, had been ripped open and loaded in spare smoothbores. Consequently, extra loads of buck & ball (up to a dozen balls) were crammed into a large number of additional smooth-bore muskets (only recently carried by Rebels) now stacked against the stone wall for quick usage.[48]

Nevertheless, faith in their leaders and God helped to keep the Confederates charging up the slope with red and blue battle flags leading the way toward the fiery crest. The most fatalistic attackers must have felt like this one holy warrior colonel, educated at the University of Virginia, who had been fatally cut down at Fredericksburg: "Tell Generals Lee and Jackson that they know how a Christian soldier should *live*; I only wish they were here to see a Christian soldier *die*!"[49]

In the ranks of Company B (Washington Grays), 7th Virginia on Kemper's left-center, Privates James O. Elliotte, age 19, and William ("Bill") Elliotte, his older brother, were both hit. James received a mortal wound, while William was shot in the thigh. "Bill" narrowly survived amputation and a premature burial in Adams County soil like his unluckier teenage brother.[50] The attackers of Company C, 7th Virginia, Kemper's brigade, likewise suffered irreplaceable losses, including Lieutenant Charles W. Moore, age 24, a former carpenter and a VMI man (Class of 1864). The young lieutenant was shot down, along with two fellow lieutenants, 20-year-old Nathan T. Bartley, an ex-farmer, and George Smith, a former tailor of age 30, who fell with multiple wounds.[51]

Incredibly, despite being ill, and still hobbled by a painful leg injury from the horse kick that bruised the bone, General Garnett somehow remained mounted on his thoroughbred Red Eye, while riding toward the Angle. One 56th Virginia soldier, 19-year-old Lieutenant Frank W. Nelson, of Company A (Mecklenburg Guards), believed that the Yankees' "firing was bad [in over-shooting which partly] was proved by the fact that General Garnett, a very tall man, mounted on a horse" was still not struck.[52] Clearly, as ordered, most Federal infantrymen were aiming low to make sure that targets were hit. But in the excitement of battle, some Yankees continued to overshoot in firing down-hill.[53] Twenty-four-year-old Corporal John P. Daniel, an Irish "day laborer" of Company H (Jeff Davis Guard), 11th Virginia, could testify that this was not always the case: he went down with bullets in both ankles, resulting in amputation of both legs and then a painful death.[54]

Meanwhile, scores of 56th Virginia soldiers, on Garnett's left, were cut down like wheat before the scythe. In Company G (Ladies Guard) from the Pigg River country of Franklin County in southwestern Virginia, three Bird brothers fell. After having lost a brother, mortally wounded in the charge up Malvern Hill, Corporal Obadiah W. Bird, a 27-year-old farmer, was wounded in the left leg, and Private Wilson T. Bird was killed. And in Company C (the Franklin Fire Eaters from Franklin County, located in the Blue Ridge Foothills), Private Samuel W. Bird was fatally cut down. However, the regiment's most devastating loss was was about to be good-looking Colonel William Dabney Stuart. Stuart was to desperately cling to life against the odds until July 30, when he breathed his last.[55]

The regiment on the left of Kemper's brigade, the 3rd Virginia, was likewise severely punished. Organized at the popular Hargrove's Tavern, Nansemond

County (named after a Native American tribe) in southeast Virginia's Tidewater, in late April 1861, Company F (Nansemond Rangers) was especially hard hit. Captain C. Crawley Phillips, a 26-year-old former "professor," was killed, along with some of his reliable fighting men: Corporal Benjamin Franklin Ames, age 28 and an ex-farmer, who fell mortally wounded when shot in the stomach, and 22-year-old Corporal William Thomas Lancaster, who was shot in the hand and right side of the head. Lancaster suffered a fractured skull. He lingered on in anguish until dying on August 11, 1863. A number of Nansemond Rangers' privates were likewise cut down, such as John Chappel Jordan, a former student of "professor" Phillips, who suffered a mortal wound when "hit by a round shot in the thigh."[56] The mostly former workers of the Gosport Navy Yard in Portsmouth, Virginia, suffered less severely. And now the mostly lower-class men of the Portsmouth National Greys (Company H), 3rd Virginia, surged toward the crest of Cemetery Ridge.[57]

Meanwhile, to Garnett's left, Pettigrew's troops likewise steadily gained more ground partly because so many field pieces (Woodruff's and Arnold's batteries) had been silenced after gunners were shot down or driven off. All the while, Pettigrew led the way on foot, after his horse was shot down. Surging ahead through the drifting smoke, shouting encouragement for his men to follow him toward the Angle, and ignoring the fall of friends, relatives, and comrades, Garnett continued to lead by personal example while wearing his finest uniform. One of the few high-ranking officers still mounted and inspiring his troops of the 11th, 26th, 47th, and 52nd North Carolina of Pettigrew's old brigade, Colonel "Jimmy" Marshall also continued to defy fate. Leading the way toward the Brien House and barn, the dashing Marshall had commanded the North Carolina brigade for only a precious few hours (ultimately his last), after Pettigrew had taken divisional command.[58]

Garnett's troops prepared to unleash a volley (Pettigrew's men had already fired their first return volley to cut down Yankee cannoneers). Symbolically, Garnett's brigade was Pickett's old command, the "Gamecock Brigade." Although Pickett's men waited longer than Pettigrew's troops before firing, in part because the Virginians had easier terrain to charge across, Lieutenant John Henry Lewis, Jr., wrote of the chain reaction, when within an estimated "300 yards of the Federal works Garnett's brigade give their usual yell and strike the double-quick [and then at] 100 yards they deliver their fire and dash at the works with the bayonet."[59] Ironically, Lieutenant George Williamson Finley, leading Company K (Harrison's Guards), 56th Virginia, described how the order to unleash return fire was given by no general or colonel: "When we reached a point about 100 yards from the stone wall, a junior officer couldn't stand it any longer, and he gave the order we had all been waiting for: 'Take good aim, aim low, 'fire!' We fired one time, and then he said, 'Now let's holler!' The Rebel Yell rent the air for the first time that day [and] We screamed like fiends and demons from hell, and it was awe inspiring" on that day of destiny.[60]

Then, as if on cue, and while a mounted General Kemper shouted encouragement, his veterans to Garnett's right continued farther up the slope, until they halted and delivered their own rolling volley. From Kemper's neatly aligned ranks, an explosion of gunfire poured toward the stone wall from where bluecoats, with rifled-muskets, blasted away with a desperate rapidity. Nicknamed "Gentleman Jack" by the more homespun members for his refined qualities and prestigious Georgetown College education (including fellow Irish) of Company C (Montgomery Guard), 1st Virginia, Lieutenant John Edward Dooley, Jr., described how "the remnants of our brave [command] pour in their long reserved fire; until now no shot had been fired, no shout of triumph had been raised" as yet.[61]

However, to the rear, Armistead's troops kept surging up the slope, never stopping to fire a volley because too many Rebels (Garnett and Kemper) were in front and so as to not lose any built-up momentum in charging up the slope. In a letter to his brother, Captain John A. Herndon, 38th Virginia on Armistead's far left on the north, wrote with some amazement, "The Brigade never haulted to take breath" during the steamrolling assault.[62]

Meanwhile, on the south, Kemper's brigade was swept by explosions of canister from Rorty's and Cowan's blazing guns, and a frontal and flank fire from the lengthy row of McGilvery's reserve batteries. The entire color guard of the 7th Virginia, on the left-center of Kemper's brigade, fell: Color Sergeant George Washington and Color Corporal Jesse B. Young (destined to be captured that day) dropped, while Color Corporal David "Davy" Emmons Johnston had been cut down earlier in the cannonade.[63] To the right, or south, of the 7th Virginia, the 11th Virginia was likewise hard hit. Commanding the regiment, Major Kirkwood "Kirk" Otey, age 32 and a VMI graduate (Class of 1849), had earlier fallen wounded on the blood-soaked ground of the Codori Farm with an iron shell fragment in the shoulder, near the decimated color guard, which lost Sergeant Martin Van Buren Hickok, a 24-year-old former clerk, and Corporal Charles W. Simpson, a teenager. As in Kemper's other regiments, the 11th Virginia's ranks were riddled. After Otey went down, senior captain

James Risque Hutter, the leader of Company H (Jeff Davis Guard) who had been employed by the United States Postal Department, took over regimental command.

Some of the best and brightest soldiers of the 11th Virginia fell, including Captain Robert M. Mitchell, Jr., a teenager leading Company A (Lynchburg Rifle Grays), and a Catholic Rebel, Private Edmund Duval, born in Paris, France, dropped with wounds. Lieutenant James D. Connelly, a 25-year-old farmer of Irish descent and leading Company C (Clifton Greys) was killed before his men. The Blankenship brothers–Charles T. and Leslie C.–were cut down. Private Lineous Jones, a 24-year-old ex-farmer, of the Clifton Greys, was fatally shot in the throat. Captain David Gardiner Houston, Jr., a former attorney of age 23, was mortally wounded in the abdomen, while leading the Botetourt County, Virginia, soldiers of Company D (Fincastle Rifles). English-born Private John Maier, Company E, (Lynchburg Rifles) was killed. Thirty-year-old Private William H. Agnew, a former teacher of Company G, had his jaw shattered by a projectile, and Captain Andrew M. Houston (David's brother), age 20 and a medical student before the war, fell with a serious wound that was thought fatal, while leading Company K (Valley Regulators), 11th Virginia. Likewise, Lieutenant Thomas D. Houston (also of Company K) fell with a bad wound, joining clumps of bodies lining the slope.[64]

But ignoring their fallen companies, survivors continued onward with fixed bayonets and war cries. The onslaught of Garnett's brigade fueled Kemper's soldiers to greater exertions to the south. "Kemper's brigade takes up the yell [from Garnett's troops], and dashes at them with the bayonet [while] Armistead, who is a little to the left and rear, catches the enthusiasm, joins the yell, and, on the run, Armistead fell back to the rear to give his brigade a chance to fire. They fire and rush at the works and to the assistance of Garnett and Kemper," wrote Lieutenant Lewis of the resurgence of momentum.[65]

Lieutenant John Edward Dooley, Jr., a sensitive, intellectual type whose lofty idealism had been shattered by the horrors of war, described how "as the cloud of smoke [after the first delivered volley] rises over the heads of the advancing divisions [while the] battle cry which marks the victory gained or nearly gained bursts wildly over the blood stained field. . . ."[66] On the left of Garnett's brigade, Lieutenant George Williamson Finley, Company K (Harrison's Guards), 56th Virginia, and soon to be captured at the stone wall, described, "On and up the slope to[ward] the stone wall the Regiment [56th Virginia] steadily swept" through the torrent of projectiles.[67]

Steel Bayonets Glistening in the Sun

At this critical moment, the headlong charge now relied upon Napoleon's secret weapon: the sheer shock power of the bayonet. The glistening rows of "cold steel" were intimidating even to bluecoat veterans. Feeling increasingly alone (without support) and beginning to sense that the day was lost, defenders realized that Lee had concentrated a compact and massive array (the wedge or battering ram) of infantry to strike the clump of trees sector. Confirming Lee's tactical wisdom, they also began to understand that their ranks were too thin to hold the weak right-center against this concentrated onslaught of too many attackers to count.[68]

As envisioned by Lee with regard to delivering a concentrated blow, Garnett's, Kemper's, and Armistead's brigades charged toward Meade's weakest point of the Angle and clump of trees, "guaranteeing great depth [of penetration] at the crucial point."[69] Lieutenant John Edward Dooley, Jr., described how the reinvigorated 1st Virginia troops swarmed ever closer to the strategic crest, while animated officers shouted, "On! men, on! [and then] the guns are ours."[70]

Larger numbers of Federals grew shaky as so many Rebels charged ever nearer, as if nothing could stop them. After all, they occupied a defensive line that contained too few troops and too little working artillery, after the effectiveness of the bombardment devastated the artillery on Meade's right-center. Therefore, overall resistance at the Angle and copse of trees was relatively light and weak, verifying Lee's decision to unleash a great cannonade and then to strike this vulnerable position that then offered the best odds (eight to one) to be overrun with Pickett's and Pettigrew's divisions converging at this weak point.[71] Meanwhile, the 2nd Corps's defensive position grew steadily weaker with each passing minute. The charging Rebels were encouraged by the invigorating sight of many "Yankees [who] tucked their tails between their legs and ran for the rear like sheep" in Garnett's front.[72] One jubilant Confederate yelled, "Stop, you Yankee devils," because it appeared that Lee's master plan of demoralizing the defenders was working.[73]

While the onrushing Confederates' war cries reached a crescendo, the Yankees also heard the words of frantic Southern officers. Near the copse of trees, Sergeant Hirst described in a letter how "the Rebels seemed to me to be within 150 yards of us, and we could hear their Officers pressing them on to the charge."[74] Just north of the Angle, the sergeant of the 14th Connecticut, which had been organized in Hartford in August 1862, wrote how those men armed with buck & ball still held their fire for Pettigrew's howling Rebels to get close. Then, commands erupted down the New England line: "Fire, Fire, Fire all along our Line. There opened upon them such a Storm of Bullets, Oaths and Imprecations . . . Give them Hell . . . Now We've got you. Sock it to the Blasted Rebels."[75]

Seasoned bluecoats aimed their weapons at Southern officers, who were inspiring their men by waving hats and sabers. The ever-diminishing group of the original 16 mounted officers and enlisted men (couriers) of Pickett's division continued to be systematically cut down. After having been shot off his horse while leading his 1st Virginia, Colonel Lewis Burwell Williams, Jr., lay in a bloody heap. As if to reap revenge, Williams's troops charged onward with a determination to come to grips with the defenders.[76]

Because of the loss of so many experienced officers, surviving Southern leaders attempted to fill the gap. A University of Virginia product, Major Robert Henry Poore was one such inspirational leader. Poore had earlier refused to retire to a safer place behind the line. Knowing that every officer was needed for this supreme effort, a sickly Major Poore, a former lawyer from Fluvanna County, in north-central Virginia, led his 14th Virginia troops up the slope. He surged ahead beside Colonel James Gregory Hodges, while encouraging his boys onward. Major Poore fought by the axiom that "so long as he could move to the front he should *advance*, that officers should give the example to their men; that the soldier's path of duty was *onward*."[77]

But he was shortly cut down when projectiles mangled one thigh and cut into the other in horrific fashion. Although Poore was left behind with mortal wounds, the major's last words implored his 14th Virginia troops (on the right flank of Armistead's brigade) onward.[78] Colonel John Bowie Magruder's 57th Virginia (Armistead's largest regiment, which had more than 500 men in the assault) suffered more severely in consequence than its four sister regiments. Nevertheless, like Armistead in encouraging the brigade onward, this VMI–trained commander led the way up the slope as taught in military textbooks at Lexington, Virginia.[79]

To the north, another Magruder (Captain William T. Magruder), who had worn a blue uniform of a cavalry officer as late as October 1, 1862, led the survivors of the 22nd North Carolina, Scales's brigade, Pender's division, 3rd Corps (which followed Pettigrew's frontline men, Fry's and Marshall's brigades, from south to north). Magruder encouraged his Tar Heels onward by reminding these young "Old North State" soldiers why they fought: "Men, remember your mothers, wives, and sisters at home, and do not halt here."[80]

A remarkable success for the onrushing Rebels in overrunning the weak right-center then seemed inevitable, the nightmarish scenario consuming so many 2nd Corps men. By that time, all that could be seen by Armistead's attackers, in the words of Private Erasmus Williams, Company H (Meadville Greys), 14th Virginia, who was soon cut down, was "only smoke and flame," as they neared the stone wall and the clump of trees, where the fondest Confederate dreams could be realized in the next few minutes.[81]

Pettigrew's Dilemma: Escalating Crisis on the Left Flank

On the far north and quite unlike what was happening to the south, the assault was continuing to fall apart. Unknown to Pickett's men, who felt that they were on the verge of victory, only one of Trimble's two brigades crossed the Emmitsburg Road, before heading rearward despite having been positioned protectively behind Marshall's and Fry's brigades. To be fair, they had suffered so much punishment on the left flank, especially from Osborn's artillery on Cemetery Hill, that these men (still reeling from the brutal July 1 fighting) could take no more.[82] Most importantly, Pettigrew's old North Carolina brigade (Marshall) and the tough brigade under the old Central America filibuster Fry had earlier linked with Garnett's left (as Lee planned) to unite the two divisions. Upon the uniting of Garnett's and Fry's troops to fulfill Lee's tactical ambitions at this key point upon nearing the right-center, one Virginia officer had just recently pointed to the stone wall and declared, "Virginia and Tennessee will stand together on these works today!"[83]

Surging ahead as if nothing could stop them—partly because Arnold's (except for one cannon) and Woodruff's guns had been silenced—Pettigrew and his attackers were encouraged. As Pettigrew later informed Captain Joseph Graham of a crucial tactical development in a July 30, 1863 letter: "Gen'l Pettigrew told me that . . . he could see their Artillery [Arnold and Woodruff] limbering up[,] their guns to retire from the works."[84]

All the while, Pettigrew's division (except the left) headed toward Hancock's weak right of the 2nd Corps—the right of Hays's division—at Ziegler's Grove, just northeast of the copse of trees and where Woodruff's battery had been silenced. As Lee planned, the odds were increasingly in favor of the attackers north of Pickett's division. More than 6,000 attackers of Pettigrew's and Trimble's commands (two brigades) steadily pushed toward Hays's division of barely 2,000 men: highly favorable odds for punching through the sector north of Pickett's division. The North Carolina, Alabama, Mississippi, and

Tennessee attackers continued to gain additional ground in charging up the slope. Unknown to Pickett's troops, the collapse of Pettigrew's left (a case of falling dominoes) continued to threaten their deep penetration well beyond the Emmitsburg Road, however.

As mentioned, the systematic collapse of Brockenbrough's Virginia brigade had been primarily due to severe artillery enfilade fire, especially from Osborn's Cemetery Hill's guns and Woodruff's bronze 12-pounders before Zeigler's Grove. Then, the opportunistic 8th Ohio west of the Emmitsburg Road and almost directly west of Ziegler's Grove inflicted additional damage with a withering flank fire. Instead of withdrawing to the main line before Pettigrew's sweeping advance, these Ohio soldiers demonstrated homegrown innovation and tactical flexibility. They shifted to a new position behind a rail defense, an excellent defensive position located far in advance of Hays's right flank. There, the Ohioans, including a good many Irish (Company B, Hibernian Guards) from Cleveland, Ohio, had unleashed a vicious enfilade fire from the north into the left flank of what little remained of Brockenbrough's Virginians and the rapidly collapsing extreme left. The Ohio soldiers had then enfiladed the next line of frontline attackers (Davis's Mississippi and North Carolina brigade) farther south, after the Virginians fled. Because no flying artillery—on either flank—was employed, these advanced Ohioans had inflicted maximum damage at close range. Without flying artillery sweeping away the Ohio boys out of the open fields, the left of Pickett's Charge continued to suffer.

Lieutenant Colonel Franklin Sawyer, on his finest day that earned him a promotion to brigadier general, had mauled the left flank of Davis's brigade—new left flank of Pettigrew's division and the entire assault. The Ohioans, perpendicular to the Emmitsburg Road, had raked Davis's left flank, while Hays's "Blue Birds" on Cemetery Ridge blasted away in front. Despite suffering an ever-rising rate of losses, Davis's brigade, containing stalwart men like Lieutenant David A. Coon, 11th North Carolina, who shortly fell with nine wounds, persevered. In fact this command had been the first brigade of Pettigrew's division to reach the Emmitsburg Road almost simultaneously with Pickett's division—no small tactical accomplishment while suffering from hot fire from two directions. Demonstrating their mettle, the Magnolia State and Old North State soldiers of Davis's brigade then clamored over the rail fences along the road, before continuing up the slope.

After having been dispatched by Trimble to bolster the left flank and Davis's Mississippi and North Carolina brigade (the left wing of Trimble's division),

Lane's Old North State brigade, consisting of the 7th, 18th, 33rd, 37th, and 38th North Carolina, also performed well. A master tactician thanks to his VMI education, Lane bolstered the left flank and united with Davis's hard-hit men. General Hays had hurried two New York regiments to add their firepower to the flank fire to inflict even more damage from the north. Despite the enfilade punishment from more than 400 Ohio, New York, and Massachusetts veterans, Pettigrew's assault on the left had gamely continued onward in conjunction with Pickett's division. A confident Lieutenant Thomas L. Norword, 37th North Carolina, Lane's brigade, and his jubilant men were "thinking the day was ours." Norword's mind shortly changed because the 1st Delaware and the 12th New Jersey were about to open fire into mostly Marshall's and Davis's brigades at close range (after the 14th Connecticut had already opened up to their south).

Meanwhile, the vast majority of Pettigrew's division continued onward up the slope just north of the Angle, surging farther into the biting teeth of the fire streaming from the smoke-wreathed stone wall. After having sent his wounded horse to the rear, Pettigrew continued to lead his boys on foot. He ignored a painful hand wound from canister, with his hand wrapped in a white silk hand-kerchief. A VMI man who had sworn to never become a prisoner, Colonel Fry led his brigade higher up the slope with grim determination as if still fighting under William Walker in Central America.

Because of his collapsing left, Pettigrew continued to implore his troops onward in what was essentially a desperate race to gain the stone wall before too many of his men were cut down. Despite Fry's brigade, just to Garnett's left and Marshall's brigade to Fry's left, steadily descending upon the stone wall, Pettigrew's division was now much weaker because of the collapse of the left. After losing about 700 North Carolina boys, the hard-hit division lacked its former knockout power. Nevertheless, Pettigrew was determined to exploit the advantage gained from the silencing of Woodruff's and almost all of Arnold's guns (from south to north), as if no collapse to the north had ever occurred on his left flank.

Because of the smoky haze of battle, Pickett's troops (in a desperate race of their own) never saw the full extent of the collapse, which guaranteed a lack of support at the most crucial moment. But contrary to the popular myth formulated by the postwar Virginia School, Pettigrew's troops were not responsible for the eventual repulse of Pickett's division.[85]

Commanding Company B, 26th North Carolina (destined to suffer nearly 72 percent losses at Gettysburg), Thomas Jefferson Cureton in a letter described the chain-reaction disaster that befell Pettigrew's division, after crossing the Emmitsburg Road: "We pressed quickly forward and when we had reached within about Forty yards of the works our regiment had been reduced to a skirmish line by the constant falling of the men at every step. But still they kept closing to the colors. We were still pressing quickly forward when a cry came from the left and I looked and saw the right regiment of Davis's Mississippi brigade, our left regiment, driven from the field [and now] the entire left of the line was gone [and in consequence] We were then exposed to a front and enfilade fire."[86]

With Davis's brigade breaking because of a vicious enfilade and frontal fire, Pettigrew dispatched Young to order Trimble to bolster the left, and Lane's North Carolinians took the place of Davis's hard-hit brigade on the extreme left. Without adequate support—especially without flying artillery, which was never hurried forward by Longstreet to protect the left flank—the severity of the tactical problems experienced by Pettigrew's division on the north were all but inevitable. Tragically, the nine howitzers and other guns, especially from Poague's battalion, had failed to advance to provide close support and protect the left flank.[87]

In a most revealing July 30, 1863, letter, North Carolinian Captain Graham, battery commander of Hill's 3rd Corps, described the disaster on Pettigrew's left: "[T]he front line gave way [and] Our second line was 100 yards from the first, and of course not near enough to support it. This being the case, the first was completely routed, and broke through the second, spoiling the whole affair. I saw the whole charge [and] General Joseph Robert Davis' Miss[issippi] Brigade was the first to give way."[88] (Actually Brockenbrough's Virginians were the first to give way when occupying the extreme left.) But in truth and performing with courage, a good many Magnolia State troops [the 2nd, 11th, and the 42nd Mississippi], under the nephew of President Davis, continued charging up the slope toward Hays's line with fixed bayonets and determination.[89]

Ascertaining the dire tactical developments to Pickett's left and with his guns not moving forward in support, Major Poague wrote, "I watched with intense interest and anxiety the advance of the infantry on both sides of me [and] When about two-thirds of the way to the crest, there was confusion and giving away in Hill's troops, most of them turning back, though some went on apparently to within a very short distance of the enemy's lines."[90]

Pickett's division Goes for Broke

During the final surge up the slope, the troops of Garnett's brigade served as the "point of the wedge," or battering ram, that was to pierce Meade's right-center exactly where Cushing's battery had been decimated to leave a wide opening in the thin line. Providing strength exactly when and where needed the most, Armistead's brigade advanced just to Garnett's right-rear.[91]

On the extreme left of Garnett's brigade, meanwhile, Lieutenant Robert Stapleton Ellis, nicknamed "Dr. Tump," continued to lead Company C (Louisa Holliday Guards, which had been organized at Louisa Court House, Louisa County), 56th Virginia. He had been born on the Ellis Plantation, Orange County, Virginia, and attended the Pennsylvania Medical School, Philadelphia. Ellis envisioned Confederate flags flying over the Philadelphia that he knew so well. Instead, he was about to be killed.[92] Likewise, the Gibson boys—once a clan of 15 soldiers from Louisa County— advanced and prayed for the fall of major northeastern cities. Private Linnear Churchwell Gibson, also of the 56th Virginia, suffered horrible arm and wounds to both legs, resulting in one leg's amputation.[93]

After having been recently reduced in the ranks by a court martial, Private William T. Guill now had something to prove. He was killed while carrying the 56th Virginia's colors up the slope. A Company I (Charlotte Greys) member, Corporal Alexander Lafayette Price Williams picked up the flag. He was destined to carry the silk colors all the way to the enemy's line, where he fell and was captured. The tallest 56th Virginia soldier, Private William Burch Short ("Sambo") who had enlisted in Company E (Ebenezer Grays), 56th Virginia, only in February 1863, was about to be cut down and taken captive. Short was fated to die of scurvy as a prisoner in early September 1863.[94]

All the while, Pickett's troops continued up the slope "without supports" in the rear and southern flank. But with each yard gained in charging toward the clump of trees, more of the best and brightest fell to rise no more. In the 11th Virginia's ranks, on Kemper's right-center, Color Sergeant Martin Van Buren Hancock, a 24-year-old former clerk, and Color Corporal Charles W. Simpson, age 19, fell among the blood-stained bodies. On the right flank of the brigade, Color Sergeant Henry Taylor, an 18-year-old former saddle-maker, was more fortunate in carrying the 24th Virginia's colors, waving the colorful banner back and forth for the boys to see amid the drifting smoke.

Pettigrew's most determined troops, especially Fry's Tennessee and Alabama brigade on Garnett's immediate left, also steadily pushed up the slope with rebel yells. However, because of the collapsed left, and since larger numbers of men remained under the relative protection of the Emmitsburg Road instead of advancing up the slope, the odds for success steadily decreased for Pettigrew's division. This situation was partly negated by the advantages posed by the silencing of Arnold's (the vast majority) and Woodruff's guns. Colonel Taylor lamented how "our own troops [now] experience[ed] that sense of weakness which the known absence of support necessarily produced [but] In spite of all this, it steadily and gallantly advanced to its allotted task."[95]

Behind Pettigrew and after replacing Davis's brigade, Lane's troops on the far north (the new extreme left flank) likewise continued onward, but ominously "there were [now] no troops on Lane's left in the charge."[96] Even worse, a good many troops of Lane's brigade never advanced beyond the Emmitsburg Road, because of the same blistering enfilade fire that had wreaked havoc on Davis's brigade. This was the case of the 7th North Carolina, which left behind about half of the shell-shocked regiment's members in the roadbed. Meanwhile, a fiery Celtic warrior named Lieutenant Archibald W. McGregor led Company F (known as "the Scotch Boys" for their Celtic heritage), 18th North Carolina, Lane's brigade, up the slope with the ringing Celtic war cry "Hurrah for Dixie! Follow me, boys. Let us show them what we can do." But "our noble Archie," did not get far, taking a fatal bullet through the chest.[97] Colonel John Decatur Barry, who "ought not to have crossed the Potomac" due to illness, continued to lead the 18th North Carolina deeper into the leaden storm. Because of weakness from his illness, Barry rode a frisky sorrel named Shaved Tail, which proved "hard to manage under fire by a well man." Nevertheless, Colonel Barry provided an inspirational example that encouraged the yelling North Carolinians higher up the slope, as if to redeem the name of Pettigrew's division because of the left's systematic collapse.[98]

Meanwhile as tactical developments on Pettigrew's extreme left continued to plummet, an escalating crisis worsened on Pickett's far right flank, because of the most advanced Federal position just east of the Codori House and just above the head of Plum Run: the high price paid for Longstreet's failure to make sure that Pickett's right flank was adequately protected by both infantry and artillery. Positioned about 100 yards west of the main line and northwest of McGilvery's reserve batteries after Kemper had shifted to the left, General George Jerrison Stannard's 13th and 16th Vermont Volunteer Infantry Regiments, of the large 3rd Vermont Brigade, unleashed a blistering fire upon Kemper's vulnerable right flank. This enfilade fire that raked Kemper's brigade guaranteed that the command continued to be Pickett's most constantly punished command. After having been punished by the artillery flank fire from Little Round Top and from McGilvery's reserve batteries both front and right flank, and rear, Kemper's 1st, 3rd, 7th, 11th, and 24th Virginia were also swept with an enfilade fire of musketry from the Vermonters on the south.

These New Englanders had answered "Father Abraham's" call for troops in early August 1862, signing up for nine months. As rookies, they were held in contempt (part of the soldiers' natural rivalry) by the army's seasoned three-year veterans. The Vermonters were also looked down upon because they included quite a few Irish (mostly Catholics of the "Irish Company": Company A, 13th Vermont Volunteer Infantry) and even French-Canadians from north of the border. These Vermonters wore new uniforms, a sight that ensured catcalls from grizzled veterans.

West of the main line in the army's most advanced position on the south (like the 8th Ohio men and their reinforcements on the north) and striking as on the previous day, when they had devastated the southern flank of Wright's Georgia brigade's assault on the copse of trees sector, these Green Mountain State soldiers were in the right place at the right time. With muskets resting on the top of a rail fence for "perfect aim," the New Englanders unleashed a withering oblique fire. After having narrowly escaped a parting volley fired from Kemper's men, before the Virginians pushed northeast toward the clump of trees, the Vermont soldiers "delivered by a few volleys before the enemy moved by the flank to their left" and northeast parallel to the Emmitsburg Road and through farmer Codori's open fields (in Colonel Wheelock Veazey's words). The 16th Vermont's colonel had marched off to war after impregnating his "My own Angel Wife," who worried if her child would ever have a father.[99]

Armistead's right, especially the 14th Virginia on the flank, suffered from the Vermonters' scorching flank fire. After his December 2, 1862, marriage to the Virginia woman of his dreams, Private Meredith Branch Thurman, 14th Virginia (on Armistead's right flank), might have wondered if he had recently gotten his teenage wife pregnant. He now surged onward with Company C (Fluvann Rifle Guard) without knowing if Jane was expecting their first child. To ease her fears, he had informed his wife in a May 10, 1863, letter: "[Y]ou need not be fred of me geting shot [because] I hav had thousands of balls shot at me sence I saw you" last.[100] Private Thurman had recently written heartfelt words and almost prophetically to his wife: "I am coming to se you again after a while if I am killed for it [because] I am willing do die for you. I know I couldent die in a better cause because I know the never would be no more peace for me if I never could se you" again."[101]

General Pickett's Glaring Absence

After his command had crossed the Emmitsburg Road and surged up the western slope of Cemetery Ridge, Pickett should have played a more active role in inspiring his troops onward to their crucial strategic objective—one of the great paradoxes of Pickett's Charge. Pickett performed more like a "holiday soldier" than inspirational leader. When his troops needed his presence, Pickett was nowhere to be seen, as during the cannonade when he took shelter behind a large oak tree. At that crucial moment, the stereotypical image of Pickett leading the most famous charge in American history was a myth.

Pickett's absence was glaring, especially with regard to the crisis on the division's south with the serious threat on his right flank posed by the Vermont troops. This "dapper little fellow" was not found on the field by Longstreet's staff officers. Described as "a graceful horseman" while mounted on Old Black, Pickett remained safely out of harm's way. "Well before his troops went forward, he appears to have made a decision to direct them not from the front line but from a position well to the rear, out of harm's reach."[102] In fact, Pickett was the only general "who failed to move forward with his troops" to lead the way in the attack named in his honor.[103]

This proper Virginia gentleman of the Old Dominion elite freely allowed his mostly lower- and middle-class soldiers to fight and die on their own when they most needed his leadership example. Clearly, Pickett possessed other priorities on July 3. Like a lovesick teenager, Pickett was obsessed with a Virginia belle, while going through a middle-age crisis, which combined with a war weariness. He was to be married to a young (barely 15) dark-haired beauty named LaSalle, or Sallie, Corbell. The totally smitten Pickett was more consumed with "the sweetest, loveliest flower that ever blossomed," her "beautiful, soul-speaking eyes," and "wonderfully musical voice" than in leading the way.[104] Allegedly, he had penciled a final note "of good-bye and God bless" to her before the attack, but this melodramatic touch is almost certainly postwar romanticism.[105] Quite simply, Pickett had "elected not to accompany his troops" in their greatest challenge.[106]

To the shock of the enlisted men, the much-celebrated "leader of the charge," as portrayed in the earliest accounts of Pickett's Charge, was not leading the way. After riding only to within about 400 yards of Meade's right-center, he took cover around the Nicholas J. Codori House and red barn. Pickett had let his common soldiers down, as if an upper-class patrician utilizing lower-class individuals mostly as cannon fodder. Reports that Pickett was once again succumbing to his well-known weakness of drinking were so numerous that his wife later sought to refute them. Manifesting "a strange mix of femininity and masculinity," Pickett was not up to the challenge. As a strange fate would have it, he had only been admitted to West Point because of a recommendation from Lincoln's law partner. Ironically, he had ridden longer distances from his Suffolk headquarters to his teenage lover's home in Nansemond County, Virginia, for nightly trysts—which annoyed Longstreet—than from Seminary Ridge to Cemetery Ridge during the war's most important assault. Unfortunately for his hard-charging troops, Pickett was now more of a lover than a fighter.

Instead of leading the way to encourage his troops beyond the Emmitsburg Road and while they steadily died, Pickett was situated at a "whiskey wagon" in the rear, as if back on the family estate of a First Family of Virginia on Turkey Island in the James River. Retiring rearward after taking a wound from a shell fragment, Major Kirkwood "Kirk" Otey, a VMI graduate (Class of 1849), a former banker, and the 11th Virginia's leader, saw the disturbing truth. Pickett's drinking was verified in writing by other witnesses. When Major Otey passed the "whiskey wagon" while heading rearward to the field hospital, he saw members of Pickett's staff (including younger brother Major Charles Pickett) drinking. Here, Pickett was safe from "that infernal slaughter-pen." Pickett and his staff escaped unscathed (unlike General Garnett and Armistead, who were killed, and General Kemper, who suffered what seemed like a mortal wound; two of his staff officers were also killed). Otey emphasized how Pickett "did not take part in the immoral performance of his division."[107]

The respected VMI major lamented how he "never heard a positive statement as to where General Pickett was in that charge; never heard him located or placed."[108] Otley's views were echoed by Colonel Eppa Hunton, who led the 8th Virginia: "No man who was in that charge has ever been found . . . who saw Pickett during the charge."[109] Historian George Stewart concluded that Pickett was "wholly useless" as a division commander.[110] However, Stewart's opinion is unfair, because Pickett went most of the way in the assault and inspired his troops onward with the cry, "Boys, give them a cheer!" before taking refuge around the Codori House and barn—allegedly to monitor his division's progress from the rear, which was the traditional role of a division commander in theory.[111] However, under the special circumstances of July 3, Pickett should

have made the supreme effort—like everyone else, including his brigade commanders—to continue leading his troops beyond the Emmitsburg Road to
enhance the chance of winning a decisive victory.

Even General Thomas Rosser asked the key question in regard to the crisis
on Pettigrew's left that actually more applied to Pickett's right flank: "If Gen'l
Pickett were there [in the attack then], why did he not make a change of front,
with at least a portion of his command to meet this flank attack?"[112] Rosser
lamented the fact that Pickett (unlike General Pettigrew, who led the way) was
"detained in the rear . . . and was not on the field, near enough to command the
attacking column, when the enemy was reached."[113]

Major Poague, who commanded the artillery battalion (that had still
not advanced) of Pender's division, described when Pickett's troops neared
Cemetery Ridge: "At this very moment General Pickett himself appeared on
the line of my guns on horseback and near one of them looking intently to the
front [and] Nobody was with him."[114] Another Confederate had earlier seen
Pickett reposing behind the Codori barn, while his men died in unprecedented
numbers to the east.[115] Later, a Union veteran, who was captured at Gettysburg
and learned details from his captors, wrote, "Pickett himself went no farther
east than to the Emmitsburg Road."[116] Pickett was perhaps deserving of a court
martial, as suggested by some indignant Confederates. Rumors of his incompe-
tence and cowardice were widely circulated after the battle.[117]

But if Pickett was guilty at the very least of apathy and a bad case of cold
feet, then Longstreet was guilty of criminal negligence. Longstreet (either deliberately or subconsciously) was the ultimate obstructionist to the fulfillment of
Lee' battle plan. Longstreet did little to ensure proper infantry or artillery support for this attack. He prematurely concluded that the attack was a failure,
despite his 20-year friendship with Pickett. Longstreet led no troops forward
like the day before. Colonel William Calvin Oates, 15th Alabama, declared that
"Longstreet deserved to have been arrested and dismissed from service" for his
failures.[118]

With Longstreet failing to properly orchestrate the assault that was his
responsibility, the attack had gone awry from the beginning.[119] However,
although staying to the rear, Pickett attempted to do his best. Pickett had earlier
directed his aide Captain Robert Bright first to Longstreet to request support
and then to Dearing, who commanded Longstreet's artillery battalion, to hurry
his guns forward as flying artillery. He emphasized with regard to Dearing's
Virginia battalion, which lacked ammunition: "They have orders to follow up

the charge and keep their caissons filled; order them to open with every gun and break that [Union] column and keep it broken."[120] However, at the most crucial moment after his troops crossed the Emmitsburg Road, Pickett was not near the front, when Longstreet's couriers attempted to locate him.[121]

Meanwhile, two physically ill commanders, who should have been in a field infirmary, instead filled the void left by Pickett: Colonel Williams, 1st Virginia, and General Garnett. Trying hard to remain on the back of Red Eye after crossing the Emmitsburg Road before the Angle, Garnett (like the mounted Kemper and Armistead on foot) continued to lead the way toward the Angle, while Pickett remained far behind. Orderly Private James W. Clay, Company G (Nottoway Greys) 18th Virginia, who went down about 100 yards before the copse of trees when a shell fragment grazed his forehead, described Garnett as having "almost [having] the gentleness of a woman." Revealing what deterred him from going beyond the Emmitsburg Road, Pickett had warned Garnett that "you are going to catch hell."[122] And, by way of sheer willpower, Garnett continued to gamely lead his troops onward toward the flaming heights, despite his illness.

Every general of Pickett's division led their troops steadily toward their objective except Pickett. Serving as no deterrent in leading the way, Pettigrew was not consumed by the thought of never again seeing Bonarva Plantation, near Lake Phelps, North Carolina's second-largest lake. Pettigrew might have realized that he would never celebrate his 35th birthday on July 4. Despite the painful wound in his left hand, Pettigrew continued to perform in splendid fashion.[123] Meanwhile, in contrast, Pickett made sure that he would see a good many future birthdays.[124] On his finest day, Armistead's actions also proved to be the antithesis of Pickett's subpar performance. Lieutenant John Henry Lewis, Jr., 9th Virginia explained Armistead's inspirational role: "It was his example, his coolness, his courage that led the brigade . . . through shot and shell" and hell itself.[125]

But far more than Pickett's absence, a greater factor in the overall equation for the success of Pickett's Charge was the lack of artillery support from Seminary Ridge's guns, especially with regard to flying artillery. In a classic case of the lack of coordination between Confederate infantry and artillery, hundreds of veteran gunners stood impotent beside their guns, while the foot soldiers advanced without close artillery fire support, because of the lack of ammunition and Longstreet's failures to coordinate support. As described in a July 7, 1863, letter, General Wright asked: "And our guns, will they not . . .

re-open [their fire on Cemetery Ridge and] Is there no succor for those brave spirits who are so nobly and steadily bearing their country's flag in that terrible fight? Surely our artillery will help them now," but this was not the case.[126]

The costly mistakes of Confederate leaders at all levels ensured the key to a successful assault—close fire support of flying artillery to protect the vulnerable flanks and the hurrying forward of support troops—was not forthcoming.[127] Partly because Lee or Longstreet lacked the necessary artillery background and young Alexander lacked Mexican–American War flying artillery experience, these leaders failed to provide timely and proper artillery support, especially with regard to the ammunition supply, rate of fire, and artillery to protect the attackers. Because of his extensive artillery background, Napoleon possessed not only the thorough knowledge that Lee, Longstreet, and Pickett lacked but also what the army now missed to properly support the assault: "the practice of retaining a reserve of guns under his own control in order to concentrate their fire at the climax of the battle. . . ."[128]

Failures on the Right

Wilcox's and Lang's brigades, Anderson's division, Hill's 3rd Corps, had been early positioned in support of Alexander's batteries to Armistead's rear: the best position to advance to support Pickett's right to deter any flanking movement from the south that threatened the southernmost flank of the assault. But with Pickett's troops charging up the slope east of the Emmitsburg Road, these brigades were still unengaged, providing no support.[129]

From Alexander's vantage point from the Peach Orchard's high-ground, Pickett's most important contribution (because of the Vermonters raking his right flank), although belatedly, came when "he was riding with his staff in rear of his division," in the colonel's words. Pickett ordered Captain Bright to ride back to Longstreet to order Wilcox's brigade of five seasoned Alabama regiments forward to protect the exposed right flank. In total, Pickett had dispatched three couriers to prod the Alabamians into action. Therefore, a reluctant Wilcox only belatedly advanced, after the arrival of these "three staff officers in quick succession" and "support of Pickett's division." Wilcox received word from Pickett after 15–20 minutes had passed since the charge's beginning, when the attackers neared the Emmitsburg Road or had just crossed it: far too late. Then, Wilcox committed the error of advancing straight ahead (directly east) and *below* the Vermont troops (whose left flank was temptingly exposed) who had enfiladed Pickett's right flank. He had not compensated for the fact that Pickett's division had moved northeast to gain a position before the clump of trees. And Pickett, Lee, and Longstreet failed to place Wilcox on the proper course northeast instead of pushing east—basically the wrong direction.

Like Longstreet, Wilcox was hesitant to go forward, because he "was not satisfied with having lost one-half his brigade the day before." When "Old Billy Fixin" finally advanced, it was only a tentative movement so far to the right, or south, that it was "largely out of the zone of Pickett's assault." Colonel Alexander explained that by the time that "there came from the rear Wilcox's fine Ala. brigade . . . but was not *in the column* [and] alone . . . It was at once both absurd and tragic." Then, in the splitting of the overall assault effort instead of making an oblique left movement to become part of Pickett's effort, Wilcox pushed straight ahead. Therefore, Wilcox left Pickett's attackers on their own, especially on the right before the Vermonters. Without artillery support, Wilcox's tentative effort was doomed to failure from converging fires of musketry and artillery coming from two directions, especially from the flank. "Too late, too small, and not aimed in the right direction," Wilcox and Lang, consequently, never came close to supporting Pickett's right to fulfill their urgent mission, especially with regard to hitting the Vermonters on their exposed left flank and pushing them aside.[130]

After having received Pickett's urgent request, Longstreet had awakened from his seemingly comatose state to "belatedly" order Wilcox's and Lang's brigades, Anderson's division, forward, but he shortly changed his mind. Longstreet then countermanded orders for the advance of Anderson's other brigades, believing this effort "useless." Lee had planned for all of Anderson's division to join a maximum offensive effort. Believing that the assault was doomed, Longstreet also ordered no units of Hill's corps on the north to advance to protect the assault's left flank. When he finally ordered Wright and Posey's brigade forward, it would be too late.[131] If Longstreet had earlier ordered Wilcox's brigade forward to closely follow on Pickett's heels, then these veteran Alabamians could have pushed aside the green Vermonters, who were vulnerable to a flank attack from the west: a missed tactical opportunity. Indeed, Wilcox's battle-hardened troops could have easily "turned the flanking attack of the Vermonters into a bloody shambles."[132]

Also, the five guns of Eshelman's Washington Artillery Battalion that were sent forward as flying artillery about 400 yards on the right were not only ineffective, but also soon out of ammunition—just another inept effort. Therefore, these guns were shortly withdrawn from their advanced position, leaving Pickett's division without any artillery support on the right.[133]

Even worse, no swarms of Confederate cavalry struck the rear of Meade's right-center in a great surprise attack as envisioned by Lee. More than 6,000 of Stuart's troopers were to have smashed into Meade's rear around the clump of trees with slashing sabers, blazing revolvers, and rebel yells. But now the open fields that dominated Cemetery Ridge's eastern slope remained entirely empty of Confederate horse-soldiers.[134]

Stuart had much to prove after the largest cavalry clash of the war at Brandy Station on June 9, 1863, when "the yankeys whiped our [cavalry]men badly," as penned by one of Pickett's men in a letter. Stuart's recent lengthy raid almost to the gates of Washington, DC, had worn out men and horses to significantly reduce combat capabilities for striking Meade's rear. Therefore, only several miles behind Pickett's Charge when Stuart confronted two Union cavalry brigades of the 2nd Division under General David M. Gregg, the Rebel troopers were in overall bad shape for a final showdown. The four Southern brigades were also short of ammunition. To the rear of Cemetery Ridge, Stuart fought "the last great saber battle of the Civil War," which helped to ensure that he never gained Meade's right-center. But it was the rapidly firing Spencer carbine fire that truly saved the day. Ironically, Stuart's ambitious plan would have almost certainly worked in 1861 or 1862, but not on that July 3. Stuart's troopers were hit by a fierce counterattack of fresh troopers: "wild furious men" of the crack Michigan Brigade, now attached to Gregg's 5,000-man command. These cavalrymen were commanded by the ever-aggressive George Armstrong Custer, the army's youngest general. Known as the "Boy General of the Golden Lock," Custer led the 7th Cavalry forward with "Come on, you Wolverines!" There, about several miles east of Pickett's Charge (today's East Cavalry Field), "the hardest Battle of the war" was fought. Stuart was forced to retreat. Had Stuart's four brigades of more than 6,000 troopers smashed into the rear of Meade's right-center when Pickett's Charge delivered its lethal blow, then these veteran cavalrymen "could have changed the course of the battle."[135] While attackers continued to die at a rapid rate before Cemetery Ridge, Yankee cavalry had "saved the day for the Union"—the most-forgotten chapter of Pickett's Charge.[136]

Clearly, Stuart had missed his greatest opportunity by failing to fulfill his "hopes of thundering into the rear of Meade's army."[137] Indeed, signaling the passing of the dominance of Lee's legendary cavaliers, Union cavalrymen completely thwarted "the attempt of Stuart to pass into our rear while Pickett attacked us in front," penned Colonel James C. Biddle.[138] Meade concluded that, "during the time of Lee's assault, General Gregg [actually Custer] had won an extremely important cavalry engagement with General Stuart on the right of the Union line of battle."[139]

But of course, Stuart was only one of a long list of Lee's top lieutenants who failed him on July 3.[140] Besides the nine howitzers not advancing as flying artillery, Major Poague still patiently waited to advance his four (two Virginia, one Mississippi, and one North Carolina) batteries of Hill's corps, but only *after* the crest was gained by the infantry, which was far too late.[141] And after expending most of its ammunition, the four batteries of Dearing's Virginia battalion remained immobile, failing to advance on the right as Lee desired and as Pickett had implored.[142] Consequently, despite only ineffective flying artillery support from a mere five guns that advanced beyond Alexander's line and were almost immediately swept by the hot fire of Stannard's 2nd Vermont Brigade on Pickett's right flank, the infantry attackers continued to be on their own to do or die without adequate infantry and artillery support on the flanks.[143]

Therefore, the surging right (Pickett) and left flanks (Pettigrew) continued to hang in the air.[144] Meanwhile, to continue the comedy of Confederate tactical errors, the belated advance of Wilcox's Alabama brigade "was doomed from the outset, and helped seal the fate of Kemper's brigade because he was not there to support it and protect its right flank in absence of Alexander's and Dearing's artillery batteries."[145]

Charging Further East of the Emmitsburg Road

Commanding Hancock's 2nd Division, John Gibbon encouraged his troops with an appropriate order: "The fate of the whole army now rests with you . . . We must hold this line *to the last man!*"[146] Inspirational leadership was needed, because in the words of one of Hancock's men who confirmed the wisdom of Lee's plan: "I looked at our small force, not one tenth of theirs [and] I almost felt that we were gone."[147]

Indeed, in Gibbon's sector, Pickett's troops were heading toward the gap where Cushing's battery had been thoroughly decimated at the Angle. With Garnett on the left and serving as "the guiding light of the division," Kemper on the right, and Armistead in a second line mostly behind Garnett's brigade to the right-rear, the attackers continued to surge up the gentle slope with fixed bayonets. At this key moment, another factor fueled the resolve of the 9th Virginia boys (sandwiched between the 53rd Virginia to the north and the

14th Virginia to the south). Members of Armistead's brigade, these Tidewater soldiers included the Old Dominion Guards (Company K) and the Portsmouth Rifle Company (Company G) of Portsmouth and a teenage drummer boy named James Brown.

These fighting men burned with revenge because their homeland, including Portsmouth and Norfolk, had early fallen into Union hands. These soldiers had been transported north to defend Richmond during spring 1862, which made their hometowns, especially Portsmouth, more vulnerable. Therefore, Portsmouth, where some Irish in gray had recently worked at the Portsmouth Naval Yard and Norfolk, fell easily. Many Portsmouth and Norfolk soldiers were fighting and dying on northern soil, although their home ports had long grown rich from doing commerce with cities like Philadelphia. Fueling a maximum effort from these soldiers, Portsmouth and Norfolk would be liberated from Yankee occupation if they split Meade's army in half.[148] In consequence, they were bent on "making history and more graves" in the cynical words of Lieutenant William Henry Lewis, Jr., Company G (Portsmouth Rifles), 9th Virginia.[149]

In the 9th Virginia's ranks, Portsmouth men like teenager Private William B. Bennett, a plasterer, and 21-year-old, blue-eyed Sergeant John Chandler Niemeyer, a former Portsmouth clerk who had attended VMI, received their death strokes.[150] Other 9th Virginia Portsmouth soldiers, including Adjutant James Francis Crocker, continued onward. Born in the Isle of Wright County, Virginia, on January 5, 1828, Adjutant Crocker had been practicing law in Smithville, Virginia, since 1854, when he was admitted to the Virginia bar. Crocker, a bachelor, had served in the Virginia General Assembly from 1855 to 1856.[151]

Ironically, with personal history coming full circle, Crocker possessed fond memories of his youth spent at Gettysburg. This young former attorney and Madison College professor (1851–53) had many friends in Gettysburg. Now wearing blue uniforms, they had been former classmates in more innocent days. Crocker had been educated at Pennsylvania College (today's Gettysburg College, where one Company A, 9th Virginia, soldier [Simon C. Wells] had graduated in 1850). On September 19, 1850, he was the class valedictorian at the college established by anti-slavery theologian Samuel Simon Schmucker in 1832.

On that day during the college's 16th commencement, a prayer had opened the program. Crocker presented the valedictory address, after the confirmation of degrees. Perhaps the adjutant now recalled that the prophetic words of his speech had been heard by President Henry L. Baugher, whose own son in blue fell in this war: "Who knows, unless patriotism should triumph over sectional feeling but what we, classmates, might in some future day meet in hostile battle array." But Crocker never suspected that this "hostile battle array" would become a nightmarish reality at the very town where he had graduated first in his class.[152]

While leading his troops farther up the slope, Crocker fell with an injured right leg. But these well-trained 9th Virginia veterans, led by VMI officers, such as blue-eyed Lieutenant John Chandler Niemeyer, age 21 (VMI Class of 1863)—who would be killed by a shot in the head while leading Company I (Craney Island Light Artillery)—pushed on without stopping to assist the fallen adjutant.[153] After having charged to well within 200 yards of the blazing stone wall, an even greater concentration of massed volleys and canister from artillery smashed into Pickett's attackers. In the ranks of Company A (Danville Blues), 18th Virginia, Private William H. C. Brown, a teenage former clerk, was shot in the right foot and leg left, while also falling to an exploding shell that sent one jagged iron fragment that tore across his scalp. Captain Haskell described how despite the blasts of "canister, without wavering or halt, the hardy lines of the enemy continue to move on" into the cauldron.[154]

All the while, volleys continued to ripple along the stone wall. Before Pettigrew's onslaught, General "Fighting Elleck" Hays exhorted his soldiers north of the Angle "to stand fast and fight like men" to the bitter end, especially after Arnold's (except for one gun) and Woodruff's cannon were silenced. Hays, educated at Allegheny College before attending West Point, where he became friends with Ulysses S. Grant, described how: "Four lines [fired] from behind our stone wall" to unleash a tremendous rate of fire.[155] One Union soldier never forgot how the projectiles tore through the onrushing ranks: "A moan went up from the field distinctly to be heard amid the storm of battle."[156]

In Pickett's sector, the salvoes of canister caused the most damage, mowing down attackers in sickening clumps. A seasoned Federal gunner described how "canister was thrown with terrible effect into their ranks."[157] Leading the 28th Virginia troops (sandwiched between the 56th Virginia and the 19th Virginia, Garnett's brigade), Major Nathaniel Claiborne Wilson, age 23, shouted for his troops to "put your trust in God, and follow me!" shortly before he was fatally cut down in the hail of canister.[158]

Marshall's North Carolinians of Pettigrew's old brigade continued onward with the determination of pushing Hays's thin blue line off their high-ground perch. They were especially inspired by 24-year-old Colonel Marshall, who somehow remained mounted amid the torrent of lead. The good-looking young man, whose future had never seemed brighter when he was selected by VMI classmates to present the final class oration (like Adjutant Crocker) when he graduated on July 4, 1860, never lived to see the third anniversary of his graduation. An ambitious bachelor, Marshall had served as the principal of a private school at Edenton, North Carolina, and studied law. Marshall was fated to never again see his beloved home Carrington, where he had been born near Markham, Virginia, at the foot of the Blue Ridge in the fertile Piedmont of Fauquier County, Virginia. Everything had happened so fast for young Marshall in a heady swirl of adulation and advancement, including gaining a colonel's rank.[159]

After having advanced higher up the slope and at closer range, Pickett's attackers finally gained a better opportunity to return punishment of their own. Colonel Joseph Mayo, commanding the 3rd Virginia on Kemper's left flank, described, "Receiving their fire until they had approached within a hundred yards of his works, our men poured into the enemy one well-directed volley and then at the command of Gen. Kemper rushed with a cheer upon the works, closely followed by the brigades of Garnett and Armistead."[160]

After the final 1st Virginia color-bearer was cut down, Private Jacob R. Polak, in his early twenties and of German heritage, took his place. The initiative of the common soldiers like Private Polak continued to fuel the momentum of the assault, after so many officers had been killed or wounded. After Colonel Williams had been shot off his horse, Maryland-born Major Francis "Frank" H. Langley, a former carpenter in his early thirties, was dropped, and then his successor, senior Captain George F. Norton, age 21 and a member of VMI Class of 1860, who led Company D (Old Dominion Guards), also shortly fell. The last 1st Virginia officer still standing, Captain Thomas Herbert Davis, a 25-year-old schoolteacher of Company B (Richmond City Guard), likewise went down. Without receiving an order, Private Polak dashed out of Company I's ranks and picked up the battle flag. He then raced ahead, inspiring his comrades onward up the bullet-swept slope. Once every 1st Virginia officer was down, and despite being on their own, the enlisted men continued forward.[161]

But the worst was still to come for the attackers. Unlike the 14th Connecticut, which had been the first to fire from Hays's ranks, the division's regiments to the north saved their fire until Pettigrew's men got even closer. Positioned behind the stone wall just southwest of Ziegler's Grove and below the Brien House, which stood on higher ground than the Angle area, the 12th New Jersey's veterans (the largest regiment of Smyth's brigade) were aligned on the brigade's right-center. These Garden State soldiers were armed with .69 caliber smooth-bore muskets. Lying low, they waited behind the stone wall, with the 1st Delaware Volunteer Infantry, to the south, and the 111th New York, to the north on the right flank. After having collected extra muskets, these New Jersey soldiers waited until Marshall's North Carolinians, and also (but to a lesser degree) Fry's Tennessee and Alabama troops farther south, reached a point only 40–50 yards distant.

Upon receiving orders, the New Jersey soldiers and a lesser number of Delaware men (just to the south) with smoothbores suddenly rose up as one and stood shoulder-to-shoulder behind the stone wall. With a thick set of whiskers disguising his young age, dark-haired Major John T. Hill screamed, "Aim low!" The New Jersey soldiers, who had not fired a shot while their comrades on each side had been firing their rifled-muskets for some time, unleashed one of the day's most terrible fires upon Pettigrew's attackers. Marshall's North Carolina men, and what remained of the right of Davis's Mississippi and North Carolina soldiers to the north and Fry's Alabama and North Carolina men on the left, were caught in a "slaughter pen," in one man's words, when New Jersey commanders shouted, "Fire!" What the New Jersey boys and a smaller number of Delaware men poured forth was a deadly hail of buck & ball at close range. Rejoicing at the decimation, Hays screamed, "Give them hell boys."

Murderously effective within 200 yards but unbelievably destructive at less than one-quarter of that distance, loads of .69 caliber ball and three buckshot in each round exploded simultaneously from more than 400 New Jersey smooth-bore muskets. Thousands of iron pellets were unleashed in a shotgun-like effect of a lethal spray. The hail of iron shot caused fearful havoc that dropped Marshall's Old North State soldiers and Fry's men in piles. Armed with the only .69 caliber smooth-bore muskets in the entire division, these Garden State veterans had ripped open many other cartridges to cram muskets full of 10–25 pieces of lead buckshot to create an especially deadly load.

Sickened by the slaughter of so many young men and boys hailing from across North Carolina, Alabama, and Mississippi (Marshall's, Fry's, and Davis's brigades) within only 40–50 yards of the stone wall, a New Jersey officer simply described, "It was murder." Though one of the myths of Pickett's Charge was that it was doomed to failure from the beginning because of the superior lethality of rifled musket, actually close-range musketry caused the greatest damage. As mentioned, the popular "attack and die" thesis, in which long-range musketry had made defensive positions impregnable, was simply not applicable to Pickett's Charge, because training, élan, and esprit de corps were more important in determining winner from loser. In fact, hundreds of smooth-bore muskets unleashing blasts of buck & ball were far more lethal than the rifled musket on a smoke-covered field when within close range of the stone wall. Nevertheless, survivors continued to charge ahead as if there was no tomorrow precisely because there was none for the hard-pressed Confederacy.[162]

But it was not just Marshall's North Carolina boys who were cut down by the lethal blasts of buck & ball. To the south beyond Fry's right, Garnett's brigade, especially on the left where the 56th Virginia occupied the left flank and the 28th Virginia to its right (or south) also suffered from the volleys of buck & ball unleashed by 69th Pennsylvania troops positioned on the Philadelphia Brigade's left: one of two regiments defending the 500-foot stretch of the stone wall before the clump of trees. Colonel O'Kane's 69th Pennsylvania had gathered around 400 extra muskets, which guaranteed an eruption of massive firepower from these Sons of Erin.

This close-range fire from shotgun-like blasts that raked their left flank was simply too much punishment for Garnett's men. To Garnett's rear in the 38th Virginia's ranks (on Armistead's left flank) and commanding Company D, a shocked Captain John A. Herndon penned in a letter to his brother: "I reckon you want to know what became of the line which advanced in front of us [Armistead's brigade]. When they had reached within about 150 yards of the enemy's works they broke and fled in the wildest confusion running back through our line but even that did not create any confusion in our ranks." The 53rd Virginia troops, in Armistead's center, were also swept by explosions of buck & ball. The 69th Pennsylvania Irish alone unleashed at least 600 shots (perhaps more) within the first deadly minute, thanks to extra muskets. Like so many of Garnett's troops in the front line on the left flank, Private William D. Meador, of Company F (Edmunds Guards), went down with buckshot in the lower third of the left thigh.[163]

Other 53rd Virginia attackers, including Halifax County, south-central Virginia, boys of Company A (Halifax Light Infantry) and Company C (Edmunds Guards), fell in large numbers. Irish-born Sergeant John McLees, a stone mason who had suffered facial wounds at Seven Pines, surged ahead, after mastering his fears of suffering another disfiguring wound.[164] In the same brigade as the 12th New Jersey "Blue Birds," positioned just below the small Brien barn, who wreaked so much havoc among Pettigrew's men, two companies of the 14th Connecticut soldiers on the brigade's left near the Angle continued to devastate Marshall's right, Fry's brigade, and Garnett's left with their Sharps repeating rifles. These repeaters were fired so fast that they literally became too hot to handle. Connecticut soldiers poured water from tin canteens on overheated barrels, before they resumed delivering death in massive doses.[165] Captain George Bowen, 12th New Jersey, described the decimation of Davis's North Carolina and Mississippi boys and Marshall's men on the left: "They fell like wheat before the garner. . . ."[166] Without support on the left, the punishment delivered by the 12th New Jersey and 1st Delaware was so severe that large numbers of Davis's brigade, without support on the left following Brockenbrough's collapse, failed to advance any distance east of the Emmitsburg Road.[167]

In the 14th Connecticut's front just above the Angle, Hays shouted, "Boys, don't let 'em touch these [artillery] pieces." On Marshall's far left, to the right of what relatively little remained of Davis's brigade, the 26th North Carolina's ranks were unmercifully culled with men going "down in bunches," until nothing remained of the regiment but "a thin skirmish line." Waving the flag before the 26th North Carolina, 22-year-old Private Daniel Boone Thomas continued to lead the way as the regiment's last surviving color-bearer. Thomas was one of the few standing men of Company E (Independent Guards) led by Captain Andrew Stephens, age 27, who was cut down like his top subordinate, 24-year-old Lieutenant John Emerson, who fell mortally wounded when shot in the left arm. Drummer boy Thomas Hackney survived the decimation that left the slope carpeted in bodies. Thomas eventually reached the stone wall just north of the Angle, along with 26th North Carolina men, such as Sergeant James Brooks, age 22.[168]

Meanwhile, Marshall's North Carolinians fought back with spirit, returning an accurate fire. These veteran North Carolina soldiers proved deadly, shooting down four color-bearers of the 111th New York just south of the Brien House and on higher ground than the 12th New Jersey. Commanding the New York brigade (which confronted Davis's brigade and Marshall's left) on the far right behind and including the 111th New York, Colonel Eliakim Sherrill, a former New York congressman riding a "nearly white" horse, went down. He suffered a mortal wound, and the 111th New York also lost its commander, Colonel Clinton D. MacDougall, who was shot down in the hot return fire. In this embattled sector, battery commander Lieutenant George A. Woodruff also received a mortal wound.[169]

On the right of Garnett's brigade, the 8th and 18th Virginia, from right to left (or south to north) were swept by a close-massed volley. They were especially hard hit by the Philadelphia Brigade's defenders: the 69th Pennsylvania and the 71st Pennsylvania (from south to north), positioned on either side of Cushing's two roaring guns of Battery A, 4th United States Artillery at the stone wall. These soldiers included a good many Irish, especially in O'Kane's 69th Pennsylvania. They relied upon the highly effective 12th New Jersey's tactics of rising up at the last minute and firing a close range volley into the attacker's faces—an eerie repeat of how the famed Imperial Guard had been decimated by disciplined redcoat regulars at Waterloo when Napoleon unleashed his last offensive gamble.

Sergeant Randolph Abbott Shotwell, Company H, 8th Virginia, on Kemper's right flank, described the nasty surprise when within only "40 paces" of the Union line: "No sign of the foe. Three hundred! Can he have fled? Two hundred!—(passing the sunken road) and, with a shout we start to run up the slope. Lo! From behind the breastworks on the crest arises a dense rank of blue coats [and] then bursts forth a puff, a blinding, withering, wasting blaze, a long sheet of lightening, as if from the summit of the hill had suddenly sprung a vomiting volcano [and] At 40 paces it was almost impossible for the poorest of the Yankee marksmen to avoid hitting some one of the advancing throng."[170]

General Hays then yelled to his remaining men with smoothbores, "Up Vols. and at them!" In his diary, the assistant surgeon of the 108th New York (placed by Hays in a position before the southwest corner of Zeigler's Grove to defend Woodruff's battery on the south), Francis Moses Wafer, described what was essentially an ambush of sorts when the troops of the 3rd Division, 2nd Corps, let loose with devastating fire when the attackers were within 50 feet: "Our line of infantry which had lain flat under what slight cover some piles of rails & stones gathered from the field afforded, in order to escape observation & to avoid as much as possible the storm of iron poured up on them, now simultaneously rose to their feet–reminding one of the British [regulars] at Waterloo."[171]

Attacking without shouting, unlike Kemper's and Armistead's troops, the veterans on the center and right of Garnett's brigade mustered their last remaining reserves of strength for the bitterest fighting that lay ahead once they gained the crest of Cemetery Ridge. Leading the 19th Virginia (Amherst, Nelson, and Albemarle County soldiers) in Garnett's center, Colonel Henry Gantt, VMI Class of 1851 and an ex-farmer in his early thirties who was married to a Virginia girl named Pattie Eppes, was hit in the left arm and face. He lost an entire row of teeth that had been "neatly extracted" by the bullet that tore through his mouth. Meanwhile, the screaming Irish of the Montgomery Guards (Company F, 19th Virginia) from Charlottesville continued onward with abandon.[172]

Lieutenant Colonel Henry Alexander Carrington's 18th Virginia, advancing on Garnett's right-center, was riddled. Among the Cumberland County boys of Company E, 18th Virginia, two Cocke brothers of Company E (Black Eagle Riflemen) were struck: 20-year-old Captain Edmund Randolph Cocke, who was downed when a bullet grazed his head, and Lieutenant William F. Cocke, age 24 and an ex-farmer like his brother, was killed.[173] Leading Company F (Farmville Guards), 18th Virginia, Garnett's brigade, 27-year-old Captain Zachariah Angel Blanton, a tobacconist, was hit square in the face by a bullet. Blanton received the ugliest of wounds, falling with shattered facial bones and fractured upper and lower jaws, while his tongue was ripped by the lead ball. Other good fighting men of the Farmville Guards were fatally down, including the German Rebel Corporal George M. Switzer.[174]

Sensing that he was the verge of reaping a decisive victory (as many Yankees also then believed) if only enough men could get safely across the killing ground to smash through Meade's right-center, Garnett rode back and forth before the Angle, imploring his troops onward up the slope, "Faster, men! faster!"[175] Meanwhile, fast-working blue gunners, especially Cushing's surviving artillerymen, continued to rapidly fire from their two guns located not far from behind the stone wall. Thanks to the Rebel cannonade's effectiveness, four of Cushing's guns to the rear were no longer operable at their high-ground position just below the crest.[176]

Also favoring chances of a dramatic breakthrough, Union batteries in and around the Angle, especially Cushing's battery, had taken such a severe beating that they had been virtually eliminated. The 2nd Corps's chief of artillery, Captain John Hazard, described the crisis: "Battery B, First New York Artillery, was entirely exhausted; its ammunition expended; its horses and men killed and disabled; the commanding officer Capt. J[ames] M[cKay]. Rorty [in command of the four-gun battery of Onondaga County, New York, gunners for only one day], killed [and] The other batteries [of the 2nd Corps] were in similar condition [nevertheless] canister was thrown with terrible effect [Lieutenant T. Fred Brown's] Battery B, 1st Rhode Island Light Artillery [now under Lieutenant Walter S. Perrin and located just to the left of the clump of trees], had expended every round [4th United States, A] battery [under Cushing, who was mortally wounded] was exhausted, their ammunition gone, and it was feared the guns would be lost if not withdrawn. At this trying moment the two batteries were taken away," before it was too late.[177] The fall of so many leading artillerymen, especially fine officers like Captain Rorty, an Irish Fenian nationalist dedicated to liberating Ireland from British rule by force of arms, enhanced the odds for a decisive breakthrough. The same advantageous situation favored Pettigrew's attackers because of the silencing of Arnold's (all except one field piece) and Woodruff's guns north of the Angle, and the cutting down of so many bluecoat artillerymen. For good reason, therefore, one amazed Yankee was convinced that the steamrolling attackers "believed themselves invincible" and the day won.[178]

However, the excellent 6th Corps battery under 21-year-old Captain Andrew Cowan, educated at Madison College (the school's first to enlist), Hamilton, New York, continued to punish Kemper's Rebels. After having waited for Pickett's troops on the south to get within 200 yards before opening with canister because he lacked long-range ammunition, Cowan's five guns blasted away from the commanding high-ground behind the stone wall just below the copse of trees and west of the open crest of the ridge. Meanwhile, Cowan's sixth gun fired from the other (north) side of the clump of trees in line with Cushing's four now-inoperable field pieces to the north, but nearer to the chestnut oak trees. Fortunately for the right-center's defense, this New York Light Battery was not lacking in firepower capabilities at this crucial moment, after having arrived in the nick of time to relieve Lieutenant Evan Thomas's hard-hit Battery C, 4th United States Artillery (Brown's battery). Union artillerymen, especially those of Cowan's newly arrived 1st New York Independent Battery, remained working their iron field pieces, firing them as fast as possible in a desperate bid to stop Kemper's onslaught.

Fortunately for the Union fortunes, Cowan had evacuated his Cemetery Hill position in timely fashion at Webb's urging and in deciding to obey one of Hunt's frantic staff officers in reinforcing the right-center. Therefore, this capable 6th Corps officer, who had personally recruited his Cayuga County, New York, boys, was not about to abandon another defensive position. This feisty Celtic battery commander, who had been born in Ayrshire, Scotland, in late September 1841, was every inch of a fighter. Cowan had won recognition for cool, quick thinking in emergency situations on past battlefields. With his 3-inch Ordnance Rifles that he had secured from the Navy Yard, Washington,

DC, Cowan needed a stirring performance to circumvent forthcoming charges for disobedience to orders from his 6th Corps superiors. Most of all, the tall, handsome battery commander was fueled by the desire that "we may conquer," as penned in a letter. Therefore, unlike other battery commanders in this crucial sector around the clump of trees, Cowan had smartly conserved ammunition by firing slowly (to Hunt's delight) so that they could devastate the attackers at close range with ample rounds.

Representing his beloved Scotland, Cowan and his high-spirited men, including Irish gunners such as two McGinnis boys and a "Wild Irishman named Michael Smith," worked their guns at a brisk pace in killing even more of Kemper's men. Cowan's Cayuga County (named after a tribe of the powerful Iroquois Confederacy), west-central New York, gunners of the 1st New York Independent Battery, fought magnificently. However, an increasing number of New York cannoneers fell under a hot fire from Kemper's soldiers, who shot down Yankee artillerymen with veteran skill. With canister whizzing around them, these Virginians on the south had instinctively taken shelter behind a rocky, "little elevation, covered with bushes" (which deflated some iron canister balls) located just southwest of the copse of trees about 75 yards before Colonel Norman J. Hall's Massachusetts, Michigan, and New York brigade, Gibbon's 2nd Division, 2nd Corps. Here, at this slight knoll about 30 paces from the stone wall and in Cowan's words, a "few hundred Virginians [of the 11th and 24th Virginia] opened on us [from the southwest, however] the large[st] body of them [Garnett and Armistead], to their left, rushing forward in the direction of the Angle, to the right of the trees."[179]

Barely perceptible, this low, rocky outcropping (not plowed by farmers and therefore covered with underbrush) of this slight knoll was about 30 yards wide.[180] Along with the fast-firing guns of Rorty's New York battery just to the south, Cowan's five cannon "inflicted the most damaging artillery casualties on the brigades [especially Kemper] after they cleared the Emmitsburg Road" and then surged up the open slope.[181]

But these soldiers, mostly of Kemper's extreme right, of the 11th Virginia and 24th Virginia, who had taken cover at the brushy knoll (the roughest ground situated amid the open fields immediately before the stone wall) were a minority, and the division's only stationary troops. To the north, Kemper's surviving officers continued to implore their troops, especially the 3rd Virginia, 7th Virginia, and 1st Virginia, from north to south, onward up the exposed slope. Along with other surviving officers, a mounted Captain Thomas Gordon

Pollock, a respected member of Kemper's staff, encouraged Kemper's troops on the left, center, and right-center (the previously mentioned three regiments) onward, challenging these tough fighting men to "behave like Southern soldiers." Galloping along the surging ranks of the Giles County boys of Company D (Giles Volunteers), 7th Virginia, Captain Pollock was shot off his warhorse. The Pollock family's bodyservant, Richard, had "accompanied the brigade during the assault," until ordered rearward (which he protested) by an officer of higher rank than his own master.[182]

Ignoring the fact that the division's right flank was hard hit and Kemper's brigade had suffered grievously, General Armistead continued to lead his troops up the slope, which gradually became steeper. Armistead's troops had been the last of Pickett's men to unleash a volley because of their second-line position. Up ahead stood the copse of trees, dominating the eastern horizon skyline along the open crest. The never-say-die Mexican–American War veteran and brigade commander acted like a man possessed. Seemingly nothing could now deter Armistead and his onrushing veterans from gaining the copse of trees that stood so tantalizing before them.[183]

On the far right of Armistead's brigade, meanwhile, Colonel James Gregory Hodges, age 33, led his 14th Virginia troops (Halifax, Bedford, Amelia, Fluvanna, Mecklenburg, and Chesterfield County boys) toward the low stone wall held by the 69th Pennsylvania and Cowan's lethal New York guns, just southeast of the Philadelphia boys, who were blasting away from higher ground just below the crest to the Irish regiment's left-rear. Encouraging companies like the Mount Vernon Guard (Company G) and the Clarksville Blues (Company E), Hodges was determined to do or die. Like so many others, Portsmouth's ex-mayor was about to pay a high price for his bravery.[184]

Just as Lee had envisioned with tactical clarity, his bold plan of smashing through Meade's right-center was working well with regard to the frontline attackers, with the target area becoming gradually more vacant of mauled artillery units (both north and at the Angle) and held by increasingly depleted infantry regiments of a thin blue line. Even a good number of Union infantry and artillery veterans who had never run before had taken flight.[185] In the targeted sector, Captain Haskell was horrified when he saw a shocking sight that sent chills down his spine: "The larger portion of Webb's brigade . . . there by the group of trees and the angles of the wall, was breaking from the cover of their works, and, without orders or reason [now] was falling back, a fear-stricken flock of confusion! The fate of Gettysburg hung upon a spider's single thread!"[186]

Elite fighting men of humble origins from the Virginia Piedmont (such as the Piedmont Rifles—Companies B, 8th Virginia, and D, 28th Virginia—and the Piedmont Guards—Company E, 19th Virginia) and men who were proud of their agrarian home towns (like Richmond Grays—Company H, 1st Virginia—and the Richmond City Guard—Company B, 1st Virginia) continued up the slope with screams to make their native regions proud, attempting to punch through the Union line.[187] Meanwhile, additional Yankees became increasingly worried about their ability to hold their deteriorating positions. In the words of one Federal: "We looked about for reinforcements but they were not to be seen."[188]

However, at that crucial moment with decisive victory in sight, the Virginians desperately needed far more men in their culled ranks. As never before, Pickett's division needed to have the 800 soldiers (in the estimation of Randolph Abbott Shotwell) who had fallen in the pre-assault bombardment and at least another 132 men who had died from sunstroke and heat exhaustion during the grueling march to Pennsylvania even before the last week of June 1863—enough good fighting men to fill an entire brigade. But most of all, the attackers needed Stuart to strike from the rear. General Stuart and his cavalrymen were not coming to anyone's assistance on that ill-fated afternoon of destiny, however.[189]

Chapter VII

Overrunning the Angle

Ironically, while Stuart had failed to strike from the rear, the least-admired general of Pickett's division was now playing the most inspiring role. In leading the way for his brigade, General Armistead now performed as if to compensate for Stuart's shortcomings. Less than a year before, one of his own officers angrily criticized in a letter how Armistead "is full enough of saying 'Go on boys' but [he] never said 'come on' when we are going into a fight."[1] Armistead was now demonstrating that he was the very antithesis of this harsh evaluation.[2]

The well-formed wedge of Virginians surged toward Cushing's position inside the Angle with more concentrated might than Pettigrew's assault, thanks to Armistead and his brigade's second-line (reserve) position, its relatively fresh status, and more experienced officers in the ranks (which had not been decimated on July 1 like Pettigrew's division)—which all combined to then fuel their powerful momentum. The most concentrated mass of attackers, Armistead's and Garnett's brigades and Kemper's northernmost troops, descended upon the Angle with fixed bayonets. Located about 250 feet just north of the clump of trees, the Angle was now the epicenter of the raging storm. Here, the attackers were presented the best opportunity of splitting Meade's army in two. Because the low (only two to three feet high) east–west running stone wall of the Angle that jutted west, about 80 feet from the north–south defensive line to the northeast and lay between Hays's division to the north, and Gibbon's division to the south, overrunning the Angle would drive a wedge between Hancock's two divisions and outflank the defenders along the north–south running stone wall to the south: the recipe for decisive victory.

At this time, this vital sector along Webb's depleted front was especially vulnerable, because the open, gentle slope (unlike the rougher ground on Hall's front southwest of the clump of trees and the less favorable ground—the "natural glacis"—in Pettigrew's sector to the north) was ideal for the attackers to swarm up to achieve a dramatic breakthrough at Meade's right-center. Most importantly, there were relatively few defending infantry at the target point because batteries (Cushing inside the Angle, Arnold just north of the Angle, and Cowan on the south—except for one gun just above the copse—and separated from the other two batteries to the north by the copse of trees) took up a good deal of open space where larger numbers of infantry should have been placed to prevent a breakthrough. In addition, all but one of Arnold's and two of Cushing's guns had been knocked out, presenting a greater opportunity.

Even more, Cushing's mauled battery had not been replaced with a fresh battery (like Brown's was with Cowan's). After having been earlier moved down the slope to nearly the stone wall just northwest of the copse of trees, Cushing's two guns of Battery A, 4th United States Artillery, had not been enough to protect this crucial sector, which was at its weakest with regard to both artillery and infantry. Likewise, Rorty's hard-hit New York battery, below the clump of trees, had not been replaced. In a striking paradox, what little was left of the two decimated batteries that most needed replacement on either side of the copse of trees (Cushing to the north and Rorty to the south) were not to receive succor in the most crucial sector, where Lee had targeted his attack.

Clearly, "the Angle was not strongly held" (especially after the cannonade) by either infantry or artillery, nor were Cushing's and Arnold's guns (mostly silenced) in and around the Angle adequately protected, because less than 400 infantrymen were poised along a 500-foot front of low stone wall. In this relatively small space, therefore, far more attackers (at least eight-to-one odds) had converged at this vital point to focus on breaking through the battered right-center: Meade's ultimate nightmare. Favoring the Yankees to a far lesser degree than could be expected, both the cannonade and the recent northward movement of Pickett's troops to directly confront the Angle had telegraphed Confederate ambitions at this most vital point. However, nothing could now compensate (along with Kemper's northernmost troops) for Garnett's and Armistead's momentum and concentrated might.[3]

Of all 2nd Corps's batteries, Cushing's guns of the Battery A, 4th United States Artillery, were located to the most strategic high-ground point on the battlefield: inside the Angle, which had become the eye of the storm, north of the copse of trees. The greatest mass of attackers (Armistead, Garnett, and Kemper to a lesser degree) converged on this point as planned by Lee. No longer operable, four of Cushing's guns stood inside the Angle about 80 feet from where the stone wall turned east, while the battery's limbers were aligned in a neat row higher up the slope (about 40 feet east of the stone wall) and the caissons in a third line (about 50 feet east of the stone wall) near the crest. Nevertheless, no 2nd Corps commander had placed infantrymen before Cushing's artillery, located just south (or inside) of the Angle and north of the clump of trees, after the four guns were disabled—a tactical error that left the 274-foot gap between the left of the 71st Pennsylvania (except for two companies to the northeast aligned on the left, or south, of Arnold's guns) and the 69th Pennsylvania's right. Sergeant Frederick Fuger, Cushing's battery, described this crucial position exposed on dominant ground of a small, level, and open plateau running off, and just west, of Cemetery Ridge's crest: "The guns were on the highest point of the ridge called the [western] extension of the Cemetery Ridge."[4]

Just rushed to the Angle in the nick of time, the 71st Pennsylvania was especially vulnerable, with its right dangling in midair immediately north of the Angle's stone wall after it turned to run east–west, just before again turning north–south, to where Arnold's guns were located and the ridge ascended northward. Consequently, the advance of Fry's Tennessee and Alabama troops into the Angle's north side was in a position to shortly outflank the Pennsylvanians on the right.[5]

Ironically, the lack of Union infantry in this key sector—none before Cushing to provide an open field of fire—had provided an opportunity early ascertained by Cushing. General Webb had earlier agreed with the young lieutenant (West Point Class of 1860) to move two of the artillery pieces by hand off the small, but commanding, plateau and down the ascending ground to the north–south running stone wall. Webb then made sure that the bulk of the 71st Pennsylvania (except two companies positioned on the left of Arnold's southernmost gun just to the northeast) was in a good position behind the stone wall, just north of Cushing's two field pieces. From this elevated point, Cushing's two advanced guns had a panoramic view toward the Codori House, a vast amphitheater of open fields framed against the blue-hued Cumberland Mountain Range that dominated the far western horizon. These fields east of the road were filled with a tide of howling Rebels. Yankees firing into the Confederates charging across this bowl-like setting of green and gold was almost like shooting fish in a barrel.

However, near the stone wall, Cushing's two 3-inch Ordnance Rifles had become more vulnerable because they had been positioned on lower ground 283 feet before the open crest, especially now because the guns stood before Garnett's and Armistead's (and Kemper's northernmost troops) concentrated might. They had early drawn a more concentrated fire from Confederate guns that caused havoc among hard-hit Pennsylvania infantrymen on either side of

Cushing's two guns. The sight of two Pennsylvanians literally losing their heads to a screaming shell unsettled soldiers of the 71st, whose right flank hung in midair beyond the east–west running stone wall of the Angle. Therefore, this elevated perch that commanded a wide area like an ancient Greek open air theater was now largely vacated of artillery in the Angle sector and along the crest (Cushing's original position and Arnold's position just north of the Angle after his damaged guns—the majority—were evacuated) at the exact point targeted by Lee.[6]

While Garnett's and Armistead's yelling Rebels swarmed ever closer, Cushing's gunners of the two field pieces near the stone wall busily fired in defending the Angle with businesslike efficiency, while their dead and wounded comrades lay around them. Then, the nightmare scenario occurred when Cushing's gunners discovered that nearly all ammunition had been expended at the most critical moment. The Wisconsin-born Lieutenant Cushing, who already had been hit in the shoulder, refused to leave the hard-pressed battery and his surviving gunners in the day's greatest crisis situation.

With the low stone wall providing only slight cover, Cushing then took a nasty wound "in the testicles." Nevertheless, the 22-year-old Cushing, born in Delafield, Wisconsin, continued to direct the fire of his guns while screaming Rebels closed in with fixed bayonets. He yelled, "Fire!" and his two guns rocked back violently from the greater-than-usual recoil after unleashing triple loads of canister. Almost immediately, the young lieutenant was "shot through the mouth [and] instantly killed" when the Virginians were practically atop the two lonely guns. But the young man's leadership emboldened his artillerymen to hold firm, earning him a Medal of Honor officially bestowed by President Obama 151 years later. After expending their last rounds of triple loads of canister that cut down swaths of attackers, Cushing's resourceful veterans loaded smoking barrels with anything that they could get their hands on. Then, unorthodox projectiles—pieces of broken shells, even part of a bayonet, gravel, and stones—which were deadly at such close range, were hurled from the two cannon's mouths.[7]

Although Garnett's and Armistead's attackers and Kemper's northernmost soldiers before Cushing's guns were slowed by the triple-load canister, swarming Rebels on the flanks rushed ahead to curl around the two isolated guns. They then turned on Cushing's gunners, sweeping the artillerymen with a deadly cross fire. The Virginians converged on Cushing's two advanced field pieces at the stone wall and the four guns atop the little plateau-like elevation, just west of the ridge crest, at the Angle. Consequently, Armistead's and Garnett's regiments, and Kemper's northernmost men, could taste decisive success as never before. With their crucial objective so near, the attackers' desperate efforts were fueled to new heights. Color Corporal David Emmons Johnston, 7th Virginia, Kemper's brigade, fully realized that "in their hands [now] rested the destiny of the Republic."[8]

A high-spirited rivalry existed among Pickett's onrushing brigades, which helped to propel the attack up the slope. Commanding the 19th Virginia, which anchored the center of Garnett's surging line, one-armed Major Charles Peyton described the dramatic moment when "the three lines [including Kemper's left and center], joining in concert, rushed forward with unyielding determination and an apparent spirit of laudable rivalry to plant the Southern banner on the [stone] walls of the enemy."[9] Envisioning a repeat performance, the large number of Irish Rebels might have recalled the battle of Fontenoy (Belgium), when the famed Irish Brigade (which included some of its descendants in Pickett's division) of the French Army smashed through the English lines with a bayonet charge to the vengeful war cry, "Remember Limerick!"[10]

Encouraging his soldiers of Company H (Jeff Davis Guard), 11th Virginia, on Kemper's right-center, young Captain James Risque Hutter (Virginia Military Institute Class of 1860), was shot "across the chest near the stone wall." After Captain Andrew Jackson Jones (named for the seventh president), an ex-farmer of age 30, had been hit, the boys of the Rough and Ready Rifles were encouraged onward by surviving lieutenants and noncommissioned officers.[11] Meanwhile, Armistead's brigade steadily lost more good men during the final mad sprint toward the stone wall. Private Joel A. Beggerly, Company I (Pittsylvania Life Guards), 57th Virginia, was hit and lost his right eye, while nearby Corporal Levi J. Gammon, in the same company, was also struck in the face.[12] And on Garnett's left, Captain James C. Wyant, leading Company H (White House Guards), 56th Virginia, "was shot in the face and writhed in pain as he fell in front of the wall."[13] Meanwhile, Colonel William Dabney Stuart, the ambitious grandson of an Irish immigrant who had graduated third in his VMI Class of 1860, continued to implore his 56th Virginia soldiers toward the clump of trees.[14]

Mirroring the spirited performance of their animated general, Kemper's staff officers also performed magnificently, including 37-year-old Lieutenant George E. Geiger, Kemper's aide-de-camp since the previous November. When Geiger's horse was shot from under him, he continued forward on foot, encouraging the troops onward with a waving sword, before he went down with a mortal wound.[15] To Kemper's left, meanwhile, Lieutenant Colonel Henry Alexander Carrington (VMI Class of 1851) continued to carry the 18th Virginia's colors on Garnett's right-center, inspiring his men up the slope covered with clover.[16]

Leading his troops toward the Philadelphia Brigade and somehow still mounted before the Angle, Garnett shouted orders above the tumult. But the din of musketry was so loud that nothing could be heard in the roaring tempest. More importantly, Fry's regiment (1st Tennessee) on the far right still maintained relatively good alignment with Garnett's regiment (56th Virginia) on the left: the vital juncture of Pickett's and Pettigrew's divisions for the descent upon the Angle sector, where most of Arnold's and Cushing's guns had been silenced. However, the alignment was far from perfect, because of escalating losses. Just before the final sprint up the slope, therefore, Garnett had hurriedly dressed his men closer to Fry's right. Under the circumstances, Fry and Garnett performed exceptionally well in maintaining contact as much as possible. Garnett had recently ridden up to Fry on his division's crucial right flank, and shouted, "I am dressing on you!"[17]

Because he was mounted and led the way, Garnett's good fortune continued for most of the distance up the slope. Hoping to kill as many Rebels as possible before they reached the crest, bluecoat veterans overshot in their eagerness to cut down Garnett, without sufficiently compensating for firing downhill.[18] As they closed in, Garnett and his men set their sights on Cushing's two guns near the stone wall. To his horror and from just north of the Angle, Captain Arnold looked to the southwest and watched the Rebel tide descending like an avalanche upon what little remained of Cushing's mauled battery. He screamed for his surviving Rhode Island gunners, assisted by volunteers of the 99th Pennsylvania Volunteer Infantry, to depart their stone wall position and drag five of their six guns (disabled from the cannonade) higher up the slope to the crest's relative safety, before it was too late.[19]

Tragedies among Brothers

On the opposite flank to the south, meanwhile, Garnett's far right regiment, next to Kemper's left, was led up the slope by two of four Berkeley brothers, Lieutenant Colonel Norborne Berkeley and Major Edmund Berkeley. The Berkeley brothers were another example of how Pickett's Charge was very much a family affair. Captain William Noland Berkeley was the first brother to fall, going down when iron fragments ripped through his thigh to cause blood to flow "in a stream," while leading the Champe Rifles (Company D), 8th Virginia.[20] The same drama was played out among groups of brothers in all Pickett's regiments: kinship groups were represented in Hancock's defending regiments but to a lesser degree. In the close-knit ranks of Company K (Charles City Southern Guards), 53rd Virginia, in Armistead's center, Lieutenant James A. Harwood continued up the slope, although he had left behind his dying teenage brother, Private Christopher E. Harwood.[21] Meanwhile, two sets of 8th Virginia brothers advanced side by side: Privates John L. Bailey and Edwin S. Bailey of Company D (Champe Rifles, which included other Bailey relatives in the charge: Privates George H., and Thomas B. Bailey), and Corporal Benjamin R. Lunceford and Private Evans O. Lunceford, both of whom enlisted in the summer of 1861 at Leesburg, Virginia, of Company C (Evergreen Guards).[22] Two Baily brothers were hit, "with Edwin falling dead on top of his brother," John.[23]

All the while, the fast-moving troops of the spearhead (or wedge) of Pickett's and Pettigrew's divisions, especially Fry's brigade on Garnett's left, continued to surge up the grassy slope, heading for the Angle. At this time when Trimble's two brigades (Lane and Scales) lagged too far rearward to provide assistance, as many as 3,000 men (a high estimate) of Pettigrew's division charged onward with the hope of delivering a knockout blow in conjunction with Pickett's attackers.[24]

Under the hottest fire that he had ever faced that came primarily from the 14th Connecticut, the southernmost regiment of Hays's division just above Arnold's guns and the embattled Angle, Colonel Fry continued to lead the way up the slope. Exposed in the open, he was cut down, when a bullet ripped through his thigh. Ironically, the colonel might well have been hit from the fire of men under the command (2nd Brigade, Hays's 3rd Division, 2nd Corps) of Irish-born Thomas Alfred Smyth, the former coachmaker from Wilmington, Delaware, who also had served with Fry as one of William Walker's volunteers in Nicaragua. Feeling "confident of victory" despite the losses, Fry went no farther up the slope, ending the old filibuster's burning ambition of leading his troops over the crest of Cemetery Ridge in triumph.

While Fry's Tennessee and Alabama troops (mostly the 1st Tennessee and the 13th Alabama, from south to north) advanced toward the Angle just to Garnett's left, especially the 56th Virginia on the brigade's northern flank, Marshall's North Carolina brigade (to Fry's left) surged toward the stone wall north of the Angle. Perhaps as many as 1,200 of Fry's Alabama and Tennessee and Marshall's North Carolina charged up the slope before the fast-firing men of Hays's 3rd Division of mostly New York troops, but also New Jersey (14th), Delaware (1st), and Connecticut (14th) regiments, behind the stone wall. There, the ground gradually rose higher toward Zeigler's Grove, where an occasional ancient sycamore stood amid the tall oaks.

Now "bent on victory or death," in Captain Jacob B. Turney's words, Fry's Tennessee men surged onward. Fry's fighting spirit was still intact although his bleeding body had failed him. Remembering his glory days that included the September 1847 victory at Chapultepec, where he had fought (like Pickett and Longstreet) in a blue uniform, Colonel Fry continued to implore his onrushing men with shouts of "Go on! It will not last five minutes longer." Fry watched while his Tennessee and Alabama soldiers dashed up the slope with flashing bayonets and wild shouts.[25] With Major Newton J. George already shot down, Captain Turney took charge as the 1st Tennessee's senior captain. While bleeding heavily, Colonel Fry ordered Turney, "Captain, take command of the regiment [and] don't stop to fire a gun."[26]

Twenty-four-year-old Captain Stockton Heth, the son of Jacob Heth of Montgomery County, Virginia, a descendant of one of Washington's 1st Virginia officers in America's struggle for liberty, and brother of General Heth, had just spoken to Colonel Marshall, while bullets whizzed around them. Knowing that his chances for survival were slim, 24-year-old Colonel "Jimmy" Marshall, shouted above the din, "[W]e do not know which of us will be the next to fall," just before the division's rising star "dashed on with his cool courage for which he was so remarkable," as penned in a October 6, 1863 letter.[27] The inspired leadership of handsome Colonel Marshall, the young VMI man of promise, stirred his men's admiration.[28]

Leading his Company C (his father's old Irish command of the Montgomery Guard) of 1st Virginia, located in Kemper's center and not far from mounted General Kemper, Lieutenant John Edward Dooley, Jr., continued the distinguished legacy not only of the ancient Gaelic warriors but also of Washington's old 1st Virginia. The lieutenant and former Georgetown College student from Richmond described the dramatic moment when victory was seemingly within the attacker's grasp: "Thirty more yards and the guns are ours."[29]

The ground rose gradually to be come more steep, but still offered a relatively gentle slope for onrushing men sweating heavily under a scorching sun. Meanwhile, Sergeant Fuger and Gunner Christopher Smith remained under cover beside Cushing's two remaining guns. One of Garnett's officers on the brigade's left explained another bitter surprise: "[W]hen we reached a point about 50 yards from the wall there were only two gunners left able to function in Cushing's battery. They both dropped down on their stomachs and watched us come through a crack in the wall. Each had his hand on a lanyard, and each lanyard was attached to a three inch rifled gun triple shotted with canister."[30]

Closing In on the Copse of Trees and the Angle

Despite the losses and the fact that the 11th and 24th Virginia battled the Vermonters to the southwest, the remaining three regiments of Kemper's brigade—the 1st Virginia (in the center), 7th Virginia, and 3rd Virginia (from south to north)—still presented a formidable strike force. At the time, prospects for success never seemed brighter before Armistead's, Garnett's, and Kemper's northernmost troops (mixed with Garnett's right by that time) with additional 71st Pennsylvania troops, just north of Cushing's two guns, taking flight (also thanks to Fry's men outflanking them on the north) from the low stone wall. A triumphant Lieutenant Dooley was elated because "all that line of guns is [about to be] ours." In addition, before Kemper's center and right (consisting of attackers on the right of the 1st Virginia and the left of the 11th Virginia—detached by the center and right of the 11th and 24th Virginia facing the Vermont threat to the south), large numbers of the 59th New York Volunteer Infantry, Hall's brigade below the clump of trees, took flight. Some New Yorkers had been unnerved earlier by the sight of their skirmisher comrades killed by Kemper's Rebels, who had not realized that they were attempting to surrender.

Lieutenant Dooley was cut down only 30 yards just southwest of Cushing's two guns near the stone wall. Falling beside him were other fine 1st Virginia officers, including Irish Lieutenant William Henry "Pete" Keiningham, of Company D (Old Dominion Guard) age 19 and an ex-clerk from Richmond.[31] Perhaps in Kemper's brigade, which contained the largest number of Sons of Erin in Pickett's division, the Irish of Dooley's Montgomery Guard (Company C), 1st Virginia, and the Jeff Davis Guards (Company H), 11th Virginia, raised the old Gaelic war cry, "Faugh a Ballagh!," or "Clear the Way!" Perhaps intimately known to County Cork–born General Thomas Alfred Smyth whose men of his 2nd Brigade, Hays's division, blasted away from behind the stone wall, this famous Irish battle cry spurred the Irish Confederates onward to storm the high-ground.[32]

Leading the way for the 1st Virginia as a color-guard member, 25-year-old Sergeant Pat Woods, Company C (Montgomery Guard), was described by one comrade as "a most reckless, daring Irishman.[33] The regimental color guard had been cut to pieces: Private Theodore R. Martin, Sergeants John Q. Figg and William M. Lawson, who lost his right arm at the shoulder from a wound that resulted in amputation, dropped to the blood-stained grass. All the while, as written by Captain John Holmes Smith, 11th Virginia, Kemper's elated troops on the left and center "rushed the works, running . . . almost at full speed" with fixed bayonets and ear-piercing shouts.[34]

The Irish Rebels had no idea that they were descending upon a large number of Philadelphia Brigade Irish, especially the 69th Pennsylvania, aligned on the southern flank of Cushing's two guns poised on higher ground to the north. In the onrushing ranks of Company H (Jeff Davis Guard), 11th Virginia, which consisted of a large percentage of Irish common laborers and railroad workers, a number of Sons of Erin were cut down. Sergeant Henry Doyle, a former newspaper reporter, and Private Cyrus Fitzgerald, age 22, were among these fallen Emerald Islanders.[35]

In the Montgomery Guard (Company C), 1st Virginia, additional Irishmen dropped from the merciless fire streaming from the stone wall below the clump of trees. With their steel bayonets flashing, the Irish continued onward with Rebel Yells, despite the death of their popular Celtic-Gaelic leader, Captain James Hallinan. As fate would have it, the Irish Rebels charged toward the green flag of Ireland that inspired the 69th Pennsylvania Irish to load and fire faster at their fellow countrymen. Meanwhile, Sons of Erin of Company C, 1st Virginia, falling to rise no more included Sergeants Edward Byrnes, a 38-year-old mechanic, and Charles Kean, a saddler in his midthirties. Mortally wounded Irish included Private Richard E. Giles of Company C.[36] Meanwhile, on his brigade's right to the south, a mounted Kemper encouraged his troops to race faster up the slope: "There are the guns, boys, go for them."[37] Ironically, in a forgotten civil war among the Emerald Islanders during the bloody showdown at the Angle, the Irish of Company A, 1st Virginia, had no idea that their 11th Virginia and 24th Virginia comrades (mostly the latter on the extreme right and including Irish soldiers), from north to south (or left to right), were falling to the blistering fire of 13th Vermont Irish of Stannard's 3rd Vermont Brigade.[38]

Garnett's and Armistead's men received their most severe punishment from Cushing's two remaining gunners, who were German immigrants, Fuger and Smith. They were about to cut down a good many fighting men, perhaps including fellow German immigrants in gray and butternut. One of Garnett's officers described how when the howling Virginians were practically atop the guns, Cushing's most defiant two artillerymen "jerked the lanyards simultaneously, and the two cannons rocked back from the wall with a splitting report. They fired their last shots [of triple-shot canister] full into our faces and so close to me that I distinctly felt the flame of the explosion against my left cheek. Their last shots cut a bloody swath in our ranks to my immediate left about 50 feet wide. No one in that path of that swath could possibly have lived."[39]

When within only 20 paces of the stone wall, veterans on Garnett's right advancing before Kemper's left (3rd Virginia), the 8th Virginia (Garnett's right flank) and 18th Virginia (next in line to the north), who had either not fired in the initial volley or had reloaded on the run, were ready to unleash their first return fire. Sergeant Randolph Abbott Shotwell, Company H, 8th Virginia, described when the Virginians unleashed their most concentrated fire at close range to inflict the most extensive damage so far: "At twenty paces from the works, those who had not fired their muskets in the confusion of the first volley, poured a fusillade upon the Yankees with so much effect that I [th]ought the day was ours, as whole companies [71st Pennsylvania at the Angle] ran back towards the upper line" around Cushing's surviving two guns defending the Angle.[40] In one Rebel's estimation, the embattled stone wall "will last for ages" unlike the lives of the dwindling band of defenders.[41]

Additional Federals were unnerved by the onslaught that could not be stopped. Leading Company G, 11th Virginia, on Kemper's right-center and marveling at Adjutant Hilary Valentine (known as "Val") Harris's heroics in picking-up the fallen battle flag after another bearer was killed, Captain John Holmes Smith's eyes widened at the amazing sight of what lay before him. Upon nearing the stone wall, Smith felt the thrill of victory when: "I could see, first, a few, and then more and more, and presently, to my surprise and disgust, the whole line break away in fright."[42] In a letter, Captain Charles Minor Blackford described with awe, "Val Harris [a former banker, age twenty-two, and fated to be killed in April 1865] covered himself with glory. When the color-bearer of his regiment [11th Virginia on Kemper's right-center] was shot down he seized the flag and, with it in his hand, [was about to] le[a]d the regiment over the breastworks from which they had driven the yankees."[43]

Meanwhile, onrushing soldiers, especially on Garnett's left, were invigorated by the sight of the flight of even more defenders, when increasing numbers of 71st Pennsylvania men broke from the Angle north of Cushing's two guns.

This panicked flight became so widespread that the regiment's deteriorating position, entirely outflanked on the right (north) by Fry's Tennesseans and Alabamians swarming toward Arnold's Rhode Island guns, was compromised. But just south of Cushing's two field pieces, meanwhile, the stalwart 69th Pennsylvania men continued to gamely unleash volleys at close range upon Garnett's and Armistead's attackers and Kemper's northernmost soldiers.[44]

Besides losses, Pickett's overall strength had been reduced by the fact that, in Sergeant Randolph Abbott Shotwell, 8th Virginia, on Garnett's far right, a "portion of the division did not go farther than the road, being terribly cut up and scattered by a severe flanking fire."[45] Meanwhile, Major Nathaniel Claiborne Wilson, who had been trained at VMI and educated at the University of Virginia, continued to lead the 28th Virginia, Garnett's brigade, onward behind the mounted General Garnett, until canister inflicted a mortal wound on him from one of Cushing's blasts. The ill-fated major was about to gain a final resting place in a pretty meadow under a walnut tree, where Wilson finally found the peace that had escaped him in life.[46]

Contrary to the mythical image that the South was a homogeneous region devoid of extensive ethnic diversity to represent Anglo-Saxon purity, Pickett's Charge was as heavily ethnic in composition as the South itself. The largest number of soldiers in the assault was of Scotch-Irish descent, or Anglo-Irish, from north Ireland. However, a good many attackers Rebels were of German heritage, including Generals Armistead and Kemper, who were Americanized Germans. Because the South was largely Celtic in heritage, cultural, and demographics, if these men managed to win it all that afternoon, then it would be largely an Anglo-Celtic success, reflecting the South's predominant demographics, roots, and heritage.[47]

Escalating Vermont Threat on the Right Flank

Still in the most advanced position of any Federal troops (about 100 yards west of the main line) to the south on Pickett's right flank, Union leadership, especially General George Jerrison Stannard, who commanded the 3rd Brigade, 1st Corps, prepared to unleash his Vermont regiments to strike the Virginian's exposed right flank. After continuing to advance north, the Vermonters were in a position to serve as the "agents of the destiny of a nation."[48] Fortunately for the Union, these excellent fighting men now played a vital role only because the government had wisely exercised its right to keep the Vermonters in service longer (from the original nine months to July) to meet the national crisis of Lee's invasion. In disbelief because they (like Lee) thought that Wilcox's Alabama brigade and the other brigades of Anderson's division would advance to protect their right flank, the Virginians on the south were attacked by a "line of men at right angles with our own, a long, dark mass, dressed in blue, and coming down at a 'double quick' upon the unprotected right of Pickett's men."[49]

After delivering punishing volleys with a vicious oblique fire on Kemper's southernmost troops, the 13th and 16th Vermont of Stannard's 3rd Vermont Brigade had maneuvered from facing west to north by a pivot in a right-wing wheel. After the Green Mountain Boys "swung out squarely on Pickett's flank," in one officer's words, the 13th Vermonters, on the right, or east, of the 16th Vermont, counterattacked north and fired into Kemper's vulnerable right flank, the 11th Virginia and 24th Virginia, from north to south. Leading company B, 1st Virginia, and in his mid-twenties, Captain Thomas Herbert Davis - who had attended Vermont's Norwich College - might have been cut down by Vermonters whom he might have known.[50]

Marveling at the number of fallen bodies left from the New Englanders' brutal flank fire, Colonel Veazey, commanding the 16th Vermont, described, "Very many of the enemy were killed."[51] However, in advancing north, the Vermonters paid dearly for their audacity when nearing the rough, brushy ground of a little knoll around 100 paces southwest of the clump of trees, and before the stone wall defended by the 19th and 20th Massachusetts, 7th Michigan, and the 59th and 42nd New York, Hall's brigade, southwest of the copse of chestnut oaks. Held by Kemper's veterans, who had not continued up the slope like on the brigade's left and center after they had peeled off from the main force to reload and catch their breath, this advanced position provided good cover amid the wide open fields.

Here, Kemper's veterans had some protection from low-lying slabs of smooth rocks and underbrush—an advanced position that offered ideal firing positions for Kemper's men to blaze away at the gunners and horses of Cowan's New York battery just to the northeast beyond the stone wall. Situated on a slight knoll, this rugged ground provided excellent firing positions for sharp-eyed Virginia veterans, who turned to fire south on the Vermonters. Sergeant George Scott described how the Vermont rookies suffered severe punishment from "[a] body of rebels [in] a clump of bushes in front and poured into our ranks a murderous fire. Our men are dropping all long our lines."[52]

Then, General Stannard ordered the 16th Vermont, on the 13th Vermont's left, to join in the counterattack for a combined northward thrust of about 900 troops. Commanding fresh men, dark-haired Colonel Veazey, 16th Vermont and a Dartmouth College (Class of 1859) graduate, described how "we charged forward on the enemy [and] Very many of the enemy were killed. . . ."[53] In frantic haste, soldiers on Kemper's right returned fire with spirit, after having refused their line on its southern end. But this fire was not sufficient to stop the Vermonters, especially after they were bolstered by a third regiment, 14th Vermont. Among these 14th Vermont reinforcements, Private Eden Bailey, Jr., wore an identification tag dedicated "To Mary and Burtie": his wife and two-year-old son, who had died of disease in February 1863. About 1,500 Vermont men on Pickett's vulnerable right flank unleashed volley after volley at almost point-blank range "into the mass of men on which every bullet took affect," wrote Lieutenant George Grenville Benedict.[54]

While Vermonters on the south flank inflicted severe damage on Kemper's right, because no Rebel flying artillery or infantry had advanced to hurl these Green Mountain boys back, the surging 1st Virginia, 7th Virginia, and 3rd Virginia, from south to north, continued up the slope, while the 24th Virginia and 11th Virginia blasted away at close range at the troublesome Vermonters. Thanks in no small part to General Kemper's inspiring example, meanwhile, the three regiments continued to pour onward as if nothing could stop them.[55]

Sandwiched between mounting dual pressure on the northern and southern flanks, because no Confederate flying artillery or infantry support was there to push back these escalating threats, Pickett's Charge was gradually being squeezed by the Vermonters on the right flank from the south and the 8th Ohio and 126th New York and other left flank troops on the north. In consequence, Garnett's attackers were slightly more advanced than Kemper's men on the right in part because of their close-range confrontation with the Vermonters and the enfilade artillery fires, while Armstead's troops, after moving at the double-quick, had already closed up and gained the rear of Garnett's brigade and Kemper's northernmost troops. Because Garnett's left had been so hard hit by that time, Armistead's left, especially the 38th Virginia, packed the greater punch on Pickett's northern flank directly before the Angle. But the flank punishment delivered upon Kemper's extreme right by the Vermonters had diminished the assault's overall striking power at a crucial moment: a high price to pay for leadership failures at the highest levels with regard to the lack of artillery or infantry support on the south to protect the extreme right flank.[56]

General Kemper Goes Down

Feeling close to achieving decisive success, two of Pickett's brigade commanders were in the eye of the storm. From their high-ground perch, excited Yankees had been overshooting, allowing Generals Garnett and Kemper to escape unscathed, despite being mounted in front of their troops. Kemper had been organizing resistance to the Vermont attackers on the south, before resuming the effort to overrun the stone wall farther north. Riding his "mettlesome sorrel" before his troops while heading toward the gap and the weakening left flank of the 69th Pennsylvania, Kemper was cut down. He was shot off his ride near the stone wall just to the south of where Garnett was about to fall, only 25 paces from the wall but farther north. A bullet "entering his groin" to cause an "excruciatingly painful" wound and then turned upward into his lower body. In his words from a September 7, 1863 letter, General Kemper wrote, "I was shot from my horse severely wounded and was insensible [unconscious] and supposed to be dying for two days thereafter."[57]

Because of a relatively sweet spot between the fire of Cowan's and Rorty's guns, Kemper had been spared from blasts of canister. However, the general's bullet wound initially appeared mortal. After falling from his "handsome bay," Kemper wondered if he would ever again see his beloved wife, Cremora (Belle) Cave Kemper, whom he had married on July 4, 1853—and would survive to see that 10-year anniversary the following day. He "was to shout no more commands at the head of his men" on this afternoon. Former Speaker of the Virginia House of Delegates and the ex-president of the board of visitors for VMI, Kemper described his close brush with death, when he "was shot from my horse [when] I was near enough to the enemy's line to observe the features and expressions of the faces of the men in front of me, and I thought I observed and could identify the soldier who shot me."[58] Upon Kemper's fall after having been "terribly mangled" by the bullet, Colonel William Richard "Old Buck" Terry, VMI graduate (Class of 1850), a former merchant, and the 24th Virginia's commander in his midthirties and destined for a brigadier general's rank, took command of the brigade, which still possessed plenty of fighting spirit and momentum.[59]

General Garnett's Finest Hour

To the attackers' eyes, the clump of trees loomed on the eastern horizon with no ground to the rear (east) visible. Lee had targeted one of the highest points on Meade's right-center, providing visibility to the onrushing troops.[60] North of where Kemper went down, an animated General Garnett implored his followers further up the slope. Knowing that each second cost additional lives, he shouted, "Faster, men! Faster!" Handsome "Dick" Garnett, wearing his finest uniform, then disappeared into choking swirls of whitish smoke that shrouded the slope before the Angle, while riding his prized Red Eye, the "bay gelding" valued at $675. Waving his artillery officer's sword, Garnett headed straight for the clump of trees. Ignoring death on all sides, the West Pointer (Class of 1841), who wore his black hair "rather long," presented a most inviting target as he neared the stone wall.[61]

Against all odds for survival and wearing a resplendent gray uniform recently purchased in Richmond (in June), Garnett progressed farther up the slope than any mounted officer in the attack. He made it almost all the way to the stone wall before the Angle, while riding his thoroughbred "black steed," after having guided his horse through a gap torn in the Emmitsburg Road fence. A seasoned member of the Nottoway Greys, Private James W. Clay, Company G, 18th Virginia, on the brigade's right-center, had earlier gone down when hit by shell fragments about 100 yards before the clump of trees that rose up like a green beacon atop Cemetery Ridge.[62]

The Virginia private saw an unbelievable sight—looking like an apparition—through the drifting smoke: Garnett leading the way for his charging men, now the "guiding light of the division," up the slope immediately before the copse of trees. The general rode at the forefront of the battering ram and toward the center of the line, held by the city boys of the 69th Pennsylvania, Philadelphia Brigade: "The last I saw of General Garnett he was astride his big, black charger in the forefront of the charge near the stone wall, just beyond which is marked the farthest point reached [and] I remember that he wore a black felt hat with a silver cord [and his] sword hung at his side."[63]

The dark-bearded Seminole War veteran, who ironically carried an 1850 United States artillery sword inscribed "R. B. Garnett, U.S.A.," reached "25 paces from the stone wall" just southwest of Cushing's two guns near the stone wall. With his brigade serving as "the point of the wedge" of the division's assault, Garnett's inspirational example astride his horse continued to propel his soldiers ever closer to the stone wall, where the remaining 69th Pennsylvania soldiers just south of Cushing's two guns loaded and fired as fast as possible.

In the 28th Virginia's ranks on Garnett's left-center, one of the regiment's best officers was John Abbott Independence Lee, a name that honored a distinguished revolutionary heritage that the Confederacy now embraced as its own. He inspired his Craig Mountain Boys (Company C) from southwest Virginia to greater exertions, after picking up the regimental colors after still another flag-bearer was cut down.[64]

Garnett and Armistead continued to lead their troops closer to decisive victory.[65] North of Garnett's and Fry's brigades, meanwhile, Colonel Marshall encouraged his North Carolinians ever nearer to the stone wall now covered with a smoky haze.[66] On Fry's left flank, next to Marshall's right, advanced the 5th Alabama Battalion. This command of shrinking numbers consisted of companies like the Daniel Boone Rifles from Mobile County, the White Plains Rangers from the Coosa River country of Calhoun County (northeast Alabama), and the Calhoun Sharpshooters. Of its 98 men, 43 were cut down in the desperate bid to gain the crest.[67]

At last, after suffering severely from blasts of triple-shot canister from two of Cushing's cannon, the first of Garnett's soldiers on the far left reached the stone wall. There "[s]ome of the [71st Pennsylvania men at the Angle's northwestern tip] Yankees put up their hands and shouted, 'Don't shoot! We surrender!' For the next few minutes, there were no bluecoats in front of our regiment," the 56th Virginia on Garnett's far left: an exhilarating moment of triumph.[68] But this amazing success in pushing the Philadelphia Brigade soldiers aside was expensive. With Company K, 56th Virginia, Lieutenant George Williamson Finley suddenly "looked back and saw General Garnett ride up to the wall" in triumph.[69]

Young Lieutenant Frank W. Nelson, 56th Virginia, on Garnett's left, described how the mounted Garnett, wearing his exquisite, tailor-made new uniform, nearly reached the stone wall, when he was suddenly "shot in the forehead." Toppling off his horse that he had just turned to ride to the left, the West Pointer was killed (not by canister, as commonly thought) instantly near the stone wall (the 69th Pennsylvania's center) just southwest of Cushing's two guns and immediately before the clump of trees. One of the most inspirational officers of Pickett's division now lay on a blood-soaked field of clover, where General Garnett breathed his last.[70]

While targeting the gap that existed between the 69th Pennsylvania to the south and the collapsing 71st Pennsylvania to the north while riding near the line's left, Garnett had been felled by the close-range fire from the 69th Pennsylvania positioned before the copse of trees. About to suffer the same tragic fate, clean-shaven Colonel Marshall (VMI Class of 1860) continued to lead his North Carolina troops ever closer onward up the slope north of the Angle.[71] Lieutenant George Williamson Finley saw Garnett "on horseback [when he] took a minie ball right between the eyes and toppled off his horse stone dead." The general's "magnificent" thoroughbred, with a "huge" shoulder wound, galloped alone through the battle smoke back to our lines" in the rear.[72] But the 69th Pennsylvania Irish paid a high price for cutting down General Garnett. Incensed by the general's fall, Garnett's Virginians unleashed a renewed fire into the Pennsylvanians.[73] Somehow, Private Robert H. Irvine, Garnett's courier, survived the same withering volley that cut down the general, but his horse, which fell over the general's body, was shot from under him.[74]

Meanwhile, on Garnett's left, the Tennesseans and Alabamians of Fry's brigade poured up the slope with rebel yells from the Blue Ridge. Commanding the 1st Tennessee, Captain Jacob B. Turney, the former Boon's Creek Minutemen (Company K) captain, described: "Onward swept the columns, thinning now and weakened, the dead behind, the foe in front, and not thought of quarter" on the most important day of the war.[75]

First Bloody Struggle for the Stone Wall

With Generals Kemper and Garnett shot down, and as a result of going into the attack on foot to verify Lee's wisdom of saving officer's lives, Armistead was left to fill the vital leadership void at the most critical moment. With knowledge of the ancient classics, including Caesar's *Gallic Wars* (58–51 BC), that chronicled the Roman Legion's struggle primarily against the Gauls in today's France, Captain John A. Herndon, Company D, 38th Virginia, in a letter marveled at Armistead leading his troops "as gallantly as Julius Caesar." As Pickett's only surviving brigade commander, Armistead's role became more crucial. This "sentimental" widower performed like the heroic young soldier that he had been during the Mexican–American War.

Thanks to the fact that Garnett's and Kemper's brigades in front had initially received the brunt of the punishment, especially canister, because his brigade had advanced in a second line, Armistead was Pickett's only surviving brigade commander, still leading his troops toward what increasingly appeared the greatest Confederate success to date. About 20 paces before his formations, Armistead had somehow miraculously escaped harm after numerous close calls. He had long felt himself lucky. Armistead had escaped serious injury in the attacks on Churubusco and Chapultepec.[76]

Besides Armistead's efforts, other indispensable leaders inspired his troops ever farther up the slope. Thirty-three-year-old Major John Crowder Owens led the 9th Virginia before suffering a mortal wound in the groin. After numerous color-bearers of the 28th Virginia, on Garnett's left-center, were systematically cut down, Colonel Robert Clotworthy Allen (VMI Class of 1855) picked up the battle flag to fill the void. Likewise, Lieutenant Colonel Henry Alexander Carrington, who had been educated at VMI and the University of Virginia, demonstrated outstanding valor. He carried the 18th Virginia's colors deeper into the maelstrom and all the way to the stone wall.[77]

After having advanced for about 20 minutes across open ground, it was about 3:30 p.m. at the Angle and the clump of trees that had now become ground zero for Pickett's Charge. The flow of adrenaline and the sweet taste of victory continued to drive Armistead onward up the slope. The North Carolina native now provided timely assistance to Garnett's troops and Kemper's north-ernmost men as they converged on the stone wall. At exactly the right moment and right place, Armistead filled the leadership void left by Garnett's and Kemper's fall.

Not far to the south of where Garnett had fallen, Armistead led the mixed body of his own and Garnett's troops toward the widening gap that had opened up between the 71st Pennsylvania, on the north, and the 69th Pennsylvania, on the south. By that time, the flight of additional 71st Pennsylvania soldiers widened this gap. A sight that fueled Rebel efforts to new heights, this 274-foot gap (from where Cushing's two guns had fired the last two shots of triple-shot canister from before the stone wall about 50 paces down the slope from the crest) loomed invitingly. Most importantly, this ever-widening gap at the Angle promised to grow wider when additional troops of the outflanked left of the 71st Pennsylvania to the north gave way. Therefore, the opportunistic Armistead was quick to exploit this increasingly favorable tactical situation, heading straight for the hole torn into the buckling lines of blue.

Having been cited for valor at Malvern Hill, where he fell wounded, and about to receive still another leg wound, fair-haired Lieutenant James Wyatt Whitehead, born in 1838, never forgot how Armistead led the way "15 or 20 steps in front of his Brigade all the [while] cheering all the time and calling on his men to follow him" all the way to the stone wall.[78] Clearly, Armistead could no longer be criticized for "saying 'Go on boys' but never [saying] 'come on' . . ."[79]

After spying the eye-popping tactical opportunity, the West Pointer targeted the 274-foot gap between the two Philadelphia Brigade regiments (the

71st Pennsylvania on the north and the 69th Pennsylvania) to the south, setting the stage for a bloody showdown between mostly city boys from the City of Brotherly Love versus country boys from rural Virginia. By that time, Armistead had become the very focal point of the most determined bid to tear a gaping hole through Meade's collapsing right-center. The tactical opportunity was a golden one, with the ever-widening gap between the two increasingly hard-pressed Pennsylvania regiments. All Yankee artillerymen in Lee's targeted sector had been either cut down or fled the attackers. Seeing that his command was in a bad fix, the 71st Pennsylvania's commander prepared to order his heavily pressed companies to retire to the crest, where a good many regimental members had already fled. At that key moment, the strength of Pickett's onslaught was now largely on the north with Armistead's and Garnett's units, while gradually decreasing in strength southward to Kemper's less-powerful effort on the right, because two regiments—the 11th and 24th Virginia—were still battling the Vermonters to the southwest.

Armistead was consumed with the single obsession of winning decisive victory to save his nation's life. Perhaps Armistead hoped to divert the tragic course of his own life, with a decisive victory promising to change everything for the better. Cholera had taken his first wife, who presented him with his first child. What Armistead had loved the most (wife and daughter) had died of disease within only seven months of each other. Then, Lewis's next wife, Cornelia, (whom he married in 1853) bore him a son. But illness had also taken them both away. These misfortunes took a heavy toll on Armistead's heart and soul. By the end of 1854, while only in his thirties, Armistead had lost two wives and two children. Armistead, wearing a closely cropped beard, was now doing everything in his power to ensure that another life that he loved—the Confederacy in its infancy—would not also succumb to a tragic demise. The army was Armistead's home and family.[80]

Astounded Yankees could hardly believe the attackers' hysterical determination, especially that of Armistead, to smash completely through Meade's right-center and win it all. Like a good many Irish of his regiment, and especially after seeing 71st Pennsylvania soldiers to the north retiring, Captain William Davis, 69th Pennsylvania (now left alone to defend the embattled Angle), which held its ground unlike its neighboring unit to the north), was convinced that "no power could hold them in check."[81] Major Edmund Berkeley encouraged his cheering 8th Virginia soldiers onward on Garnett's right—now mixed with elements of Kemper's left (but in general Garnett's brigade was more advanced than Kemper's, especially those on the far left that had gained the stone wall). He was an avid poker player, involved in the highest stakes game of his life. Berkeley nearly reached the stone wall when hit by "a nearly horizontal shot." The shot struck him above the knee, with the soft lead of "the ball running 20 inches beneath the skin" before stopping upon hitting bone. Although downed, Major Berkeley felt a greater personal anguish, because his three brothers had already fallen: Norborne, who had his left foot shattered by a projectile near the Codori House, Charles Fenton, and William Noland, who was hit in the thigh (but by an exploding shell) like Edmund.[82]

To the south in Kemper's brigade, Lieutenant Hilary Valentine Harris, the regimental adjutant who served on the general's staff, and was born on the Mill Quarter Plantation, Powhatan County, implored his 11th Virginia troops forward on the brigade's right center while their comrades fought Vermonters to the south, after several color-bearers had been cut down. Age 22 and a former private of Company G (Lynchburg Home Guard), "Val" Harris charged toward surviving Philadelphia Brigade soldiers, while carrying the flowing colors. As the adjutant revealed in a letter about this "bloodiest battle of the war [he felt] shielded through greater dangers than I have every undergone before.[83]

In a desperate final effort to stop the murderous fire—from Yankee infantry behind the stone wall to the rear—large numbers of Rebels halted, formed up, and delivered punishing volleys of their own upon the 69th Pennsylvania. Two blistering Confederate fires brought immediate results at the vital gap of the Angle where Cushing's four guns (behind the two near the stone wall and on higher ground than at the stone wall and the clump of trees) stood near the west edge of the plateau that extended west from the crest. Higher up the gradually ascending slope, these four guns were aligned about 50 paces behind Cushing's two frontline cannon. Slightly more advanced than Kemper's men, especially on the far right that had been attacked by the Vermonters, and when near the stone wall, a close-range volley from Garnett's men swept the front and right of the 69th Pennsylvania Irish. Meanwhile, on Garnett's left flank, Lieutenant George Williamson Finley wrote how his soldiers "fired obliquely at the Yankees on the left" flank to the north—the last remaining and most stalwart Yankees remaining of the 71st Pennsylvania.

Simultaneously, targeting Cowan's five New York cannon situated near the crest just south and slightly to the left-rear of the copse of trees, Kemper's veterans continued to return a hot fire. Kemper's men maximized the advantage of good firing positions along the rough ground of the knoll, just southwest and about 30 paces from the stone wall in front and 100 paces from the clump of trees to the northeast. From the natural vantage point (brushy, rocky, and the only slightly elevated ground of a small knoll that offered protection before antagonists defending the stone wall) and despite being located on lower ground than their opponents at the lengthy row of stone, hundreds of Kemper's veterans of mostly the 11th and 24th Virginia continued to blast away from prone and kneeling positions. From this advantageous point southwest of the clump of trees, they poured a hot oblique fire into the exposed and wavering left flank of not only the 69th Pennsylvania on higher ground, but also a flank fire on the few remaining cannoneers around the leftmost guns of Cushing's battery (behind the two guns at the stone wall) on higher ground to the regiment's northeast with a flank fire.

Kemper's veterans focused on Cowan's artillerymen in the front just to the northeast on higher ground, blasting away at the defiant New York gunners, who now fired double-shot canister from barrels depressed to their lowest level, to spray the open fields filled with desperate men. These southernmost Virginians also fired at the Pennsylvania, New York, and Michigan troops of Hall's brigade who were exposed above the low stone wall just southwest of Cowan's guns. Meanwhile, to the north and with Armistead's troops close behind, the attackers of Garnett's 19th Virginia, 28th Virginia, and the 56th Virginia, from south to north, made a dash in a determined bid to capture Cushing's guns, targeting the gap between what was left of the two Philadelphia Brigade regiments: the wavering 71st to the north and the 69th to the south.[84]

Watching Cowan's devastating salvoes of canister and with Kemper's attackers so close that he admitted to his wife that the unnerving sight of all of the "Secesh Battle flags was splendid and scary," General Hunt was in for the fight of his life. Shouting to Cowan, he emptied his revolver at the howling tide of Old Dominion soldiers. But the sight of a high-ranking Union officer mounted so near the stone wall caused the Virginians to turn their muskets on Hunt. The general's horse was shortly riddled with nearly half a dozen bullets.[85] With his New York battery swept by a hail of bullets, Captain Cowan described the horror of facing dual threats, from the front and from Kemper's fast-firing men, just southwest of the clump of trees: "There was a little elevation, covered with bushes. A few hundred Virginians [of the 11th and 24th] fell down behind that brush-covered knoll and open fired on us [while] the large[st] body of them, to their left, rushed forward in the direction of the Angle, to the right of the [copse of] trees."[86]

Fearing the day lost, Cowan's support troops, the 59th New York (consisting mostly of New York City boys and Upper New York State men), 2nd Corps, who were just southwest of the New York guns, headed rearward, leaving Cowan on his own.[87] Meanwhile, even more panicked Yankees fled from the Angle. With the rebel yell from the elated Virginians rising higher, the remaining hard-hit survivors of the 71st Pennsylvania, just northwest of the copse of trees and manning the stone wall that spanned north to where it turned about 130 paces north of the western edge of the clump of trees and angled east, also broke in panic.

The Pennsylvanians fled for their lives, heading toward the crest and leaving the Angle wide open and free of defenders. For all practical purposes, the 71st Pennsylvania was eliminated from the struggle for possession of the Angle. This rout left the sturdier 69th Pennsylvania, consisting of hardy Irish less inclined to be pushed aside, outflanked on the north. It was left largely to the 69th Pennsylvania to hold the Angle in the face of Garnett's and Armistead's onslaughts and Kemper's northernmost men.[88] Sergeant William J. Burns, 71st Pennsylvania, fled along with his comrades, after a savage contest that "was awful [and] We had to retreat."[89]

To Webb's horror, as penned in a letter, the fast-firing Virginians "shot my men with their muskets touching their breasts."[90] Then, after the 71st Pennsylvania had been swept aside, it was the turn of the 69th Pennsylvania, outflanked on the north or to the right, to suffer such a severe pounding that an appalled teenaged private thought that "it looked as though our regiment would be annihilated."[91]

Hurling aside hundreds of Yankees came at a frightful cost. Waving the 28th Virginia's colors, Colonel Robert Clotworthy Allen was "killed close to the stone wall," while still tightly gripping the flag staff. Near the left flank of Garnett's brigade, the silk banner was grabbed by Lieutenant John Abbott Independence Lee, Company C (Craig Mountain Boys), who sprinted through the sulfurous smoke that covered the slope like a white blanket. He dashed farther ahead than any other flag bearer of the entire division. Hailing from the picturesque Blue Ridge Mountains of Craig County in southwest Virginia, Lee reached the stone wall near Cushing's two advanced guns.

At last fulfilling the loftiest of Confederate ambitions, consequently, the first audacious flag bearer of Pickett's division to reach the stone wall was not an esteemed member of a regimental color guard, because all such protectors had been already cut down. Lieutenant Lee, an ex-farmer and leader of hunters, woodsmen, and yeomen farmers of Company C (Craig Mountain Boys), was the first flag bearer to gain the stone wall. Feeling almost as if he were standing atop the world at this commanding elevation that overlooked the vast expanse of farmlands to the west, the young lieutenant stood atop the wall. In a triumphant moment to the 56th Virginia's right on the brigade's left flank, he waved the 28th Virginia's flag in triumph. A regimental adjutant scribbled in Lee's service record how the 23-year-old lieutenant was "the first man of Pickett's division to cross the stone wall."[92] Within seconds, a bullet hit the flagstaff, hurling the regimental colors back to the stone wall's west side. While projectiles made the air sing, Lieutenant Lee retrieved the bullet-shredded banner. John Abbott Independence Lee was shortly shot, and then endured the war's remainder in a Federal prison.[93]

Just to the 28th Virginia's left and with Colonel Stuart already cut down, the 56th Virginia soldiers gained and then clung to their forward position at the stone wall, where they rapidly loaded and fired. There, among the dead and dying Federals, the colors of not only the 28th Virginia, but also of Garnett's other four regiments (Pickett's 1st Brigade to gain the stone wall), were planted triumphantly atop the low row of stone. Meanwhile, knots of half-dazed Philadelphia Brigade prisoners were sent rearward. But most importantly, the momentum and "the field" then "belonged to the men of Garnett's brigade" (like the division in general) on the north—a remarkable tactical feat that would have made their handsome general, now lying dead just before the embattled stone wall, proud, because his legacy had been faithfully perpetuated in overrunning the stone wall.[94]

Carrying the regimental flag like an ordinary color corporal or a lowly private detailed from the ranks for color guard duty, Lieutenant Colonel Henry Alexander Carrington also gained the stone wall, but shortly after fell wounded. But more importantly, Carrington had fulfilled his role in getting the 18th Virginia, on Garnett's extreme left flank, all the way up the slope to the stone wall relatively intact.[95] Surging onward just to Garnett's rear and even leading the attack on the left flank where Garnett's boys had broken through and gained the stone wall, Armistead's troops had been relatively spared the worst punishment because of the brigade's second-line position.[96]

While leading the way for 57th Virginia soldiers from companies like the Franklin Sharpshooters (B), the Galveston Tigers (D), and the Rivanna Guards (H), Armistead's brigade, VMI–trained Colonel John Bowie Magruder was cut down. The former teacher was "shot in the left chest and upper right arm

[when] within 20 steps of Cushing's [two] guns" at the stone wall. Magruder's top right-hand man, Lieutenant Colonel Benjamin H. Wade, a former physician, went down mortally wounded, and Major Clement R. Fontaine, was also hit. Still another father-son team went down, too. Along with Sergeant John R. Seay, both Private William S. Seay, Sr., and Private William S. Seay, Jr., of Company A (Jeff Davis Guard), 57th Virginia, were killed in attempting to make the loftiest Confederate dreams come true.[97]

Major Harrison described the amazing triumph: "Like a narrow wedge driven into a solid column of oak, they [had] crushed the inner rind of defence, and penetrated even to the heart."[98] Meanwhile, inspired by the breakthrough to the north and after having caught their breath, the Virginians (11th and 24th men of Kemper's right) southwest of the clump of trees prepared to charge from the cover offered by the brushy knoll. Before them, Cowan's five New York guns positioned just below the copse of trees posed the most tempting target. Especially after the 59th New York, along the stone wall just to his southwest, broke and fled, Captain Cowan knew that Kemper's men would inevitably launch an attack to link with their comrades to the north and then tear even a larger gap in Meade's crumbling right-center.[99] Therefore, a frantic Cowan yelled to his gunners of his five field pieces, "Load with double canister."[100]

Armistead's Finest Hour

Feeling that the most decisive victory of the war had been won, Garnett's troops, slightly ahead of Kemper's troops, remained at the stone wall, holding tight to their significant gains. There, these sweat-drenched veterans, sucking hot air, caught their breath while hurriedly reloading muskets. Garnett's veterans, who sensed decisive victory within their grasp, were poised before the initial 274-foot gap, which had been considerably widened by that time, between the two mauled Philadelphia Brigade regiments. After gaining the stone wall, Garnett's soldiers unleashed a cheer that echoed over body-strewn Cemetery Ridge, announcing that the Union right-center had been broken and the Army of the Potomac's life was now more seriously threatened than ever before: the initial fulfillment of Lee's plan for the assault column to concentrate the greatest mass of attackers at the most damaged and weakest point, where Cushing's battery and its support had been eliminated.

Not far behind Garnett's and Kemper's men, General Armistead and his troops, elated by the dramatic success, descended upon the stone wall at the

Angle. Leading the 14th Virginia on Armistead's far right, Colonel James Gregory Hodges almost made it to the stone wall. But he fell mortally wounded to a bullet fired by a 69th Pennsylvania soldier, when the colonel was within only "4 feet of the enemy line" at the stone wall. On Garnett's left, "General Armistead arrived at the head of the remnants of his brigade," whose timely appearance, combined with the withering volley from Garnett's men from the stone wall, was sufficient to hasten the departure of the remaining city boys (Philadelphia) of the 71st Pennsylvania.

As mentioned, Armistead and his men were in overall better shape than the troops of the other two brigades, because of their second-line role. Because he advanced behind Garnett's and Kemper's brigades, that had offered somewhat of a shield from the worst punishment; Armistead's chances of not only gaining the stone wall, but also of continuing onward to gain Cemetery Ridge's crest, were thus greater. Therefore, the final rush of Armistead's troops who gained the stone wall was the timely reinforcement that served as the key catalyst that infused new life to Garnett's troops and Kemper's left at the stone wall. Decisive victory seemed inevitable because Pickett's division represented more than 4,500 men (with the greatest concentration at the Angle, because of Armistead's second-line's role at that point to form a battering ram) who had gained the stone wall, after having lost about 1,300 men during the advance, while more than 1,000 of Pettigrew's soldiers descended upon the stone wall north of the Angle.

At the stone wall, where Armistead's troops linked with Garnett's men, Armistead's dynamic leadership rallied survivors around him. Cited for bravery during the Second Seminole War and winning distinction in the Mexican–American War, Armistead was about to outdo all those stirring performances. He was emboldened, following the capture of two of Cushing's guns near the stone wall and the hurling back of the 71st Pennsylvania (outflanked on the north by Fry's Tennessee and Alabama soldiers), thus making the Angle the most vulnerable sector of Meade's collapsed line. Armistead wanted to exploit these tactical gains to the fullest, take additional cannon, and widen the gaping hole in Meade's right-center.

As planned in the traditional role of reserve (second-line) troops, the arrival of Armistead's cheering men rejuvenated Garrett's soldiers, who had been hard hit on the far left, which had caused some 56th Virginia men to flee. Most importantly, sufficient strength remained among the victors to still achieve far more dramatic gains. A horrified General Webb saw that his brigade's line was now "gone." As General Lee had envisioned, this timely concentration of converging troops at the Angle gave them the added advantage of eight-to-one odds at the key moment. But the odds were actually higher, counting Fry's soldiers, especially the 1st Tennessee, on Pettigrew's far right. These Alabama and Tennessee veterans on the brigade's south merged with the Garnett's left at the Angle in timely fashion.

With Garnett and Kemper shot down, Armistead "leaped onto the stone wall right at the colors of the 56th Virginia." Armistead's black slouch hat, with its large plume that resembled what had been worn by Napoleon's generals at Borodino, had now "worked its way down the blade and right over his hand." Armistead had suddenly emerged out of the swirling smoke to the astonishment of the disbelieving Pennsylvanians, who saw him leading his cheering soldiers to the stone wall. As fate, luck, and raw courage would have it, Armistead was the only Confederate general who reached the stone wall. Ironically, he commanded these tough fighting men who had been more disparaged and ridiculed than any others of the division. Even more ironic, he had once shared a deep prewar friendship with the man whose troops he was bent on destroying, General Hancock.[101]

Armistead knew that the key to victory was to keep moving and completely overrun the Angle; he also realized that time was precious. Clearly, the attack could not stop at the stone wall. Indeed, every tactical gain had to be exploited to the fullest. First and foremost, this situation meant pushing further up the open slope in a final bid to gain the crest of Cemetery Ridge. After his men and Garnett's soldiers on the left had reloaded their muskets and caught their collective breath, Armistead turned to these veterans, who were united as one.

With his hat still held aloft by his saber, Armistead then yelled his greatest challenge when time was of the essence: "Come forward, Virginians! Come on, Boys, we must give them the cold steel; who will follow me?"[102] A wild cheer erupted across the body-strewn slope, sending chills down the spine of surviving bluecoats. Armistead's booming words were "electric," fueling a resumption of the attack farther up the slope and toward Cushing's four other field pieces positioned on the high-ground just below the crest. Knowing that it was now or never, Armistead led the way deeper into the Angle with about 300 elated followers during the most desperate offensive effort of the war, like King Leonidas's numbers of Greek warriors at Thermopylae against the Persians.[103]

A sergeant major of the 71st Pennsylvania, William S. Stockton, never forgot the unnerving sight at "a great boulder which formed a sort of stepping stone and made it easy to get over the wall, and they appeared to mass at this place it being easier to get over, and [they] came over the wall in overwhelming numbers."[104] This advantage allowed for many men to cross easily over the stone wall. While the stone wall generally stood at a height of only about three feet in most places, the situation was different where Garnett's men gained the wall, because at their position the ancient stones were piled higher. Fortunately for the Army of the Potomac, this four- to five-foot barrier of stone at this point prevented larger numbers of Garnett's exhausted men from crossing over and heading toward the smoke-lined crest. Instead, in the confusion, most Virginians below Armistead's wild surge into the Angle remained behind this more formidable barrier to return fire with the 69th Pennsylvania boys in their front while also being hit with an enfilade fire from the Vermonters to the southwest, which discouraged an advance farther up the open slope.[105]

Moving forward to link with Armistead's final push up the slope were some of the best fighting men of the 18th Virginia, on Garnett's right, just like soldiers on Kemper's left: Adjutant Richard Ferguson, an ex-farmer of age 22, and Sergeant Major James C. Gill, a teenager of Scotch-Irish heritage and a former student.[106] Lieutenant George Williamson Finley initially hesitated to follow Armistead's charge, which meant forsaking the safety of the stone wall. But then Finley remembered the last words that he had read from his well-worn, "little pocket Testament . . . 'I know whom I have believed and am persuaded that He is able to keep that which I have committed unto Him against that day'" July 3, 1863.[107] Emboldened by his strong faith amid this manmade hell, the lieutenant of Irish descent wasted no time in heading for the strategic crest: "I too jumped the wall, and I landed in the worst fight I have ever been in my life!"[108] With hundreds of rejuvenated Rebels pouring "over the fences, the army of the Potomac was nearer being whipped than it was at any time of the battle," in General Webb's words, which revealed the extent of the disaster.[109]

Inspiring the common soldiers as much as Armistead and other leaders, including in the noncommissioned ranks, were flag bearers, including those who carried the silk colors of the 14th Virginia, on the brigade's far right, not far from Armistead. The 53rd Virginia's veterans, in Armistead's center, were emboldened by frenzied efforts of their color guard, all of whom were cut down: Color Sergeant Leander Blackburn fell mortally wounded; Color Corporal John B. Scott was killed; and Color Sergeant Thomas T. Carter was shot in the shoulder and later captured. Most symbolically, the 53rd Virginia's color followed the animated Armistead, who continued deeper inside the Angle and through Meade's collapsed right-center, leading the way toward the crest of Cemetery Ridge.[110]

Meanwhile, the struggle for possession of the Angle below Armistead's breakthrough was tenacious, especially against the 69th Pennsylvania Irish. Knowing what was at stake, desperate men used clubbed muskets far more than bayonets. One survivor, Private James Clay, estimated that this intense fighting lasted for 15 minutes.[111] Leading Company G (Portsmouth Rifles), 9th Virginia, on Armstead's right just to the north of the 14th Virginia on the extreme right, Lieutenant John Henry Lewis, Jr., described the horror: "Men fell in heaps, still fighting, bleeding, and dying."[112]

North of Armistead's dramatic breakthrough of Meade's right-center, the Tennesseans—obeying the final order of Colonel Fry, who was now lying wounded after his adamant refusal to be carried rearward—unleashing their first return volley of the day. Additional seasoned Volunteer State soldiers, like Captain James W. Lockert, Company K, 14th Tennessee, went down. He was known as "Old Ironclad" because of his uncanny ability to always emerge from battle unscathed, but no amount of luck could save him then. Now commanding the 1st Tennessee on Garnett's left, Captain Turney described how "we continued to charge and not until we were within about fifteen steps of the stone wall did I give the command to fire. The volley confused the enemy [so] I then ordered a charge with bayonets, and on moved our gallant boys."[113] To Fry's left, to the north, meanwhile, Marshall's North Carolinians likewise unleashed another close range volley at Hays's men. Of all Marshall's North Carolina regiments, the fire of the 26th North Carolina soldiers was the most effective, because, in Pettigrew's words, these lethal marksmen "shot as if shooting squirrels" back in North Carolina pine forests. These veterans targeted bluecoat officers, who presented ideal targets on horseback while silhouetted against the eastern skyline, causing serious damage among Hays's veteran officer corps.[114]

Soldiers, even near Garnett's left, failed to follow Armistead's push farther up the slope, because of the intensity of frontal and flank fires. Leading the Nelson County soldiers of a decimated Company G (Nelson Grays), 19th Virginia, Garnett's brigade, an 18-year-old ex-farmer, Captain Waller F. Boyd (VMI Class of 1863), went over the stone wall, imploring his men onward. But he was soon forced to return because too many comrades had been cut down and survivors refused to follow him beyond the stone wall. Boyd shortly fell, "wounded in the thigh at the stone wall," along with Private Meridith Winston

Fortune, a 38-year-old distiller who was killed, and the three Ponton boys, who were shot and later captured.[115]

Meanwhile, to Garnett's right—and although more belatedly than Garnett's soldiers on the north—Kemper's men on the left were the first members of that brigade to gain the stone wall. Like Pickett's troops to the north, they overran the high-ground, taking possession of the stone wall. This tactical achievement was no small accomplishment, because Kemper's brigade had been under the fire of sweeping U-shaped fusillade of canister from Cowan's and Rorty's Battery B, 1st New York Light Artillery (a frontal fire), and McGilvery's Artillery Reserve batteries (a flank fire from the southeast)—severe punishment that had slowed the advance, while also partly explaining why Armistead was able to break through farther north: because he faced less artillery fire than Kemper's troops.

New York gunners blasted away as rapidly as possible, as if to avenge the loss of their fallen commander, Captain Rorty. These Empire State guns fired from lower ground than at the Angle, before rising steadily north to the plateau-like ground where Cushing's guns stood. There the five guns of Cowan's New York battery roared just to the left-rear of the clump of trees. Kemper's attackers had lost more heavily than Garrett's men farther north (especially on the left before the Angle where the attackers faced less cannon fire), because they suffered from a direct frontal fire from Rorty's and Cowan's batteries (also the bloody fate of Armistead's right). Garnett's brigade and Armistead's left and center had only faced Cushing's two guns at the stone wall. Firing double-shot canister, Cowan's and Rorty's guns decimated all of Pickett's brigades, but mostly Kemper's soldiers, which ensured that they gained the stone wall later than Garnett's and Armistead's soldiers at the Angle.[116]

As mentioned, the Vermont attackers to the south had also slowed Kemper's advance, especially on the south, with their blistering enfilade fire. On Kemper's right, because the 18th and 24th Virginia troops had confronted the attacking Vermonters on their exposed right flank, and because of the devastating effects of double-shot canister from Rorty's and Cowan's guns, from south to north, the final surge of Kemper's men in this sector caused them to literally fight on two fronts. Meanwhile, the survivors of Colonel Waller Tazewell "Taz" Patton's 7th Virginia on Kemper's left-center, reached the stone wall, while still another color-bearer, Color Corporal Jesse B. Young, who had grabbed the banner from the fallen Sergeant George Washington Watson, was shot down at point-blank range.

All of a sudden, one Union officer rose from behind his side of the stone wall and carefully sighted his revolver on Young. Corporal Young held up his hand in desperation to shield his face. The bullet only entered Young's elbow, saving his life. Twenty-one-year-old Private John N. Tolbert, Company B (Washington Grays), grabbed the fallen banner, and then raised it at the stone wall. But he was almost immediately cut down when a bullet grazed his head, stunning the young man. After Tolbert fell, the 7th Virginia's flag was snatched by a Yankee who then fled rearward with his comrades: the first Confederate battle flag captured during Pickett's Charge.[117]

As mentioned, Colonel Patton was not able to see the capture of the flag. He fell with horrendous wounds when a bullet tore away his lower jaw and shredded his tongue, leaving him splashed with blood and unable to speak. He was about to be captured, dying at the makeshift hospital at "the Pennsylvania College," where young minds had once been enlightened about the folly of war.[118]

Meanwhile, charging up the slope with bayonets like Garnett's victorious men just to their right, the 1st Tennessee attackers on Fry's right surged up to the stone wall with wild yells. There, they fought hand to-hand in a vicious struggle for possession of the obscure rock wall that was now the bone of contention. Many defeated Federals retired toward the crest. Captain Turney described the desperate struggle "for the possession of the stone wall [now] the sole barrier between the combatants. Each man seemed to pick his foe, and it fell to my lot to struggle with a stalwart Federal officer, who made a vicious thrust [with his sword] at my breast [but] I parried it just in time."[119]

Second Struggle for the Stone Wall: Union Counterattack

Far greater gains had been achieved just to the Tennesseans' south. After the 71st Pennsylvania—positioned just north of Cushing's two guns along the stone wall to where it turned east—had been swept aside from the Angle, the southern end of the Union line to the northeast beyond the Angle (the now vulnerable southern flank of Hays's 3rd Division) was exposed to the surging Rebel tide to the south. If the Confederates gained additional ground inside the Angle and turned north, they could roll up that exposed Union left flank, now hanging in midair, by charging up (or north) the ascending ridgetop. All the while, the crucial gap of wide, open ground that had allowed Cushing's guns to fire through (just below where the 71st Pennsylvania had defended the stone wall and north of where the 69th Pennsylvania had once held the stone wall) was opened even wider by Armistead's breakthrough.

Webb had earlier "to cover the space vacated by" Cushing's guns, ordered forward his reserve regiment, the 72nd Pennsylvania (his last support troops)—who were positioned behind the copse of trees—to plug the fast-widening gap between the 71st and 69th Pennsylvania. With the 71st Pennsylvania hurled aside by Armistead's breakthrough, the right of the 69th Pennsylvania, south of Cushing's two guns, had been left hanging. Therefore, the northern end of the Irishmen's line (two companies: A and I) had been hurriedly moved to face the breakthrough with the howling Rebels only a few feet away, because the stone wall no longer offered protection to the enfilade fire sweeping south down the line. The 69th's thin blue line was now enfiladed from the north, becoming untenable. This deteriorating situation caused a larger number of 69th men to break rearward, especially Company F, which had been ordered to refuse its line with the two other companies, but was unable to do so. Consequently, most of Company F was overrun and captured, with Armistead's attackers exploiting the tactical opportunity when the hole opened in the 69th Regiment's line.

Especially vulnerable on the right flank after Company F was swiftly eliminated by the onrushing Rebels, the remaining 69th Pennsylvania soldiers, who were still busily blasting away at the southernmost of Garnett's men (like the 8th Virginia, on the extreme right flank, and 18th Virginia), and the northernmost of Kemper's soldiers (especially the 3rd Virginia on the brigade's left), the 72nd Pennsylvania's troops arrived in the nick of time. Suddenly appearing out of the thick layers of sulfurous smoke that blanketed the crest, and after the 71st Pennsylvania fled up the slope for the safety of the crest, the 72nd Pennsylvania charged down the slope. Believing that decisive victory had been won, one of Garnett's men was astounded by the sight, writing that all of a sudden "the 72nd Pennsylvania came over the hill on the other side of the wall." Then, hundreds of veteran Pennsylvanians "level[ed] their muskets as one," and fired "a terrible volley" downhill and "straight into" the midst of Garnett's men, who had joined Armistead's troops in overrunning the stone wall and pushing the 71st Pennsylvania aside.[120]

In the 56th Virginia's ranks on Garnett's far left, Lieutenant George Washington Finley, Company K (Harrison's Guards), and leading the Harrison County boys to the stone wall vacated by the 71st Pennsylvania, described: "[S]uddenly a terrific fire burst upon us from our front, and looking around I saw close to us, just on the crest of the ridge, a fresh line of Federals [the 72nd Pennsylvania] attempting to drive us from the stone fence, but after exchanging a few [volleys] with us they fell back behind the crest, leaving us still in possession of the stonewall," after the Pennsylvanians suffered heavily.[121]

A good many Philadelphia Brigade soldiers, the 72nd Pennsylvania and the right of the exposed 69th Pennsylvania, which lost most of its Company F as prisoners and even had Rebels in their rear before heading up the slope, were pushed aside. In fact, the onrushing Confederates had enveloped the 69th Pennsylvania, which included father-son fighting teams, on three sides before it retired to escape certain destruction.[122]

Armistead Unleashed

Everything then depended upon Armistead's penetration into the Angle with about 300 elated men who believed that decisive victory had been won. However, a host of factors now conspired—other than attrition and the fact the stone wall was higher (up to four to five feet) in some sectors—to limit the momentum of Armistead's thrust.[123] Lieutenant George Washington Finley was fortunate to have survived the fire of Cushing's last two gunners, who had refused to retire up the slope in order to deliver one final fire. Finley, of Scotch-Irish descent, experienced exhilaration when the southernmost contingent of Fry's 1st Tennessee soldiers (including men from the Boon's Creek Minutemen of Company K and the Mountain Boys of Company C) arrived to link with the 56th Virginia's left at the northern edge of the Angle, gaining the point where the 71st Pennsylvania had been pushed aside north of Cushing's two guns. This uniting of the clans added greater impetus to Armistead's penetration into the Angle in a crucial final linkage of the flanks of two divisions at the exact point of penetration, in a wedge at the stone wall from which the red and blue battle flags of Pickett's and Pettigrew's divisions flew in triumph.[124]

By that time, Armistead's troops, such as the 38th Virginia on the far left flank and the next regiment in line, the 57th Virginia, were united with Garnett's men, including with elements of Fry's brigade, especially the 1st Tennessee soldiers, during the dramatic breakthrough. The 53rd Virginia had advanced in Armistead's center as the brigade's guide regiment just behind the brigadier general as the regiment of direction. The 53rd represented a dozen Tidewater counties of south and southeast Virginia. Color Corporal James L. Carter, Jr., was cut down before reaching the stone wall. Colonel William Roane Aylett, the distinguished great-grandson of Patrick Henry, had been hit by shell-fire to leave Lieutenant Colonel Rawley White Martin in command.

Close beside Armistead during the push deeper inside the Angle, a contingent of 53rd Virginia soldiers advanced mostly in the center. Armed with a revolver, teenage Color Corporal Robert Tyler Jones, grandson of President

John Tyler (America's 10th) charged toward the clump of trees.[125] Lieutenant Hutchings Lanier Carter, Color Corporal James Carter's brother and later killed, was one of few surviving Company I (the elite color company) officers who looked upon the intoxicating sight of the regimental flag leading the way toward the strategic crest.[126] After company commander Captain Benjamin L. Farinholt had fallen wounded "in the thigh in the Angle," Lieutenant William Harvie Bray (VMI Class of 1861) commanded Company E (Pamunkey Rifles), 53rd Virginia, and crossed over the stone wall. However, he shortly fell with a mortal thigh wound that led to amputation and a July 14, 1863 death.[127]

Ignoring the searing pain of an arm wound, young Color Corporal Robert Tyler Jones, of Company K (Charles City Southern Guards, whose members hailed from where the New York gunners of Cowan's battery had seen service during the 1862 Peninsula Campaign), 53rd Virginia, continued to perform beyond the call of duty. He was keeping the distinguished family legacy of the Tyler family alive, with former president Tyler recently dying (December 1862). He had early snatched the fallen regimental colors from the ground after the first color guard member, Sergeant Leander C. Blackburn, had been cut down with a mortal wound and then the sergeant's successors also fell. After Color Sergeant Blackburn, Corporal John B. Scott, who was killed, and Corporal James Carter, Jr., who was wounded, were all cut down, Corporal Jones reached the stone wall.

But the young man, who had enlisted at Jamestown, Virginia, not long after Southern guns fired on Fort Sumter [defended by a largely Irish garrison], presented an ideal target after he reached the stone wall. The teenager "waved [the flag] in triumphantly" back and forth in elation, while standing atop the stone wall and bullets (mostly from the 69th Pennsylvania) pinged off the lengthy row of rocks. Destined to survive like so few of his Tidewater Company (K) comrades from Charles City, the corporal of the Charles City Southern Guards, 53rd Virginia, soon fell with a serious wound that ended his flag waving, tumbling off the stone wall like a rag doll. As he penned, "faint from the loss of blood due to a shot in the head, I fell" at the stone wall. Feeling as if that he could do nothing to assist his wounded brother James, 27-year-old Lieutenant Hutchings Lanier Carter, Company I (Chatham Grays), "snatched" up the fallen colors, and dashed toward Cushing's four cannon on higher ground before the crest during Armistead's breakthrough.[128]

But many of Armistead's best men no longer followed him. After leading the 57th Virginia survivors, Armistead's brigade, 24-year-old Colonel John

Bowie Magruder led the way on foot. Elated when the Virginians overran Cushing's two cannon and pushed all Pennsylvania resistance aside, Colonel Magruder yelled, "They are ours!" Magruder was then hit by multiple bullets. One bullet plunged deeply into the left side of his chest, while another lead ball tore through his upper right arm. Magruder had dropped from fatal wounds with the University of Virginia graduate within "twenty steps of Cushing's guns." Born in Scottsville, located on the upper James River in central Virginia, the 23-year-old Colonel Magruder, who wore a new uniform coat that cost $110 in Richmond (known for its highly inflated prices)—where he spent every cent as if having had a dark premonition about his Gettysburg death—realized his tragic fate. The stoic colonel had earlier believed with prophetic resignation: "I will never leave this Northern land alive."[129]

However, Magruder was not the only regimental commander of Armistead's brigade who never surged into the Angle. Leading the 14th Virginia, on Armistead's far right—delayed in gaining the stone wall because of the fire of Cowan's and Rorty's guns—33-year-old Colonel James Gregory Hodges, who possessed a "manly and handsome form," and the ex-mayor of Portsmouth, was killed "within 4 feet of the enemy's line" to make a widow of his wife and his sons orphans.[130] The entire top leadership tier of the 14th Virginia, on Armistead's extreme right, was cut down in the last volley fired by 69th Pennsylvania Irish on the southern end of their line, while retiring toward the crest. Struck by the same volley that swept the ranks when they were all within four feet of the stone wall, former attorney Major Robert Henry Poore, educated at the University of Virginia, and Adjutant John Summerfield Jenkins, another ex-lawyer, fell in a twisted heap with their former physician-colonel. At the moment of success, the bodies of these three promising officers lay closely intertwined in death as in life.[131]

After having followed Armistead into the Angle, Color Corporal James L. Carter never forgot how "over the wall the remaining few went" up the slope in a desperate charge to gain the strategic crest of Cemetery Ridge, while Lieutenant Hutchings Lanier Carter waved the 53rd Virginia's flag for survivors to see.[132] Colonel Rawley White Martin also led his surviving soldiers deeper into the widening gap of the Angle, following closely behind Armistead. Shouting in elation, the Confederates continued to surge farther beyond the stone wall. Displaying his typical bravado that resulted in seventeen bullet holes through his clothing, Lieutenant Carter swung the bullet-tattered colors of the 53rd Virginia back and forth, while followed by only seven or eight men, as if to honor the memory of his fallen brother.[133]

All the while consumed by the thrill of success, Armistead continued to lead the way up the gentle slope toward the crest with nothing but a luminous blue sky behind it, encouraging his attackers (about 300 men) farther into the open gap torn into the Angle and the very heart of Meade's collapsed position. All of Cushing's gunners had been either cut down or had fled by that time, leaving a wide open gap in Meade's right-center. The 69th and 71st Pennsylvania had been swept from the Angle. To escape capture, some Yankees dropped to the ground, feigning death. They lay quietly among the dead artillery horses and fallen men in blue that blanketed the Angle. The surging Rebels headed toward the four guns of Cushing's but all abandoned battery (the second line positioned higher up the slope behind the lieutenant's two captured guns near the stone wall), while they sensed decisive victory as never before. Lieutenant Carter held the 53rd Virginia's banner high in the smoke-wreathed air to encourage survivors toward the crest—the deepest penetration of any Confederate battle flag during Pickett's Charge.

Taking a good many prisoners from the Keystone State, especially of Company F, the 69th Pennsylvania had also limited the number of attackers who surged into the Angle with Armistead. Seventeen-year-old Sergeant Drewry B. Easley, Company H (Meadville Greys), 14th Virginia, on Armistead's far right, had been shocked by still another sign that revealed the extent of the success. He described how, during the charge, he suddenly "saw a gap in our line to the right and hurried through it and unexpectedly I ran into a whole line of Yankees. I brought down my bayonet, but soon saw that every man had his arms above his head [and then] struck the stone fence in a battery of brass pieces" of Cushing's battery. He had then "mounted the [stone] fence and got one glance up and down the line, while General Armistead mounted it just to my left, with only a brass cannon between us"—an exhilarating sight.

Along with other red battle flags and blue state banners, the bullet-shredded colors of the 14th Virginia, Armistead's extreme right flank regiment, near the West Point–educated general, continued farther up the slope. Fueled by a resurgence of energy and desperation, the dramatic breakthrough of Meade's right-center fulfilled Lee's tactical vision, verifying his wisdom in having targeted this strategic point. Most importantly, the breakthrough threatened to achieve far greater tactical gains: the splitting of Meade's army in two, and then a rolling up of blue lines to the north or south. About 150 Yankees of the 69th Pennsylvania and the 71st Pennsylvania had been swiftly overwhelmed around the Angle and taken prisoner by the surging tide that had a life of its own. Armistead's attackers were propelled by a heady cocktail of adrenaline and the intoxicating conviction that the greatest Confederate dream was about to be realized at long last: a view shared by many Yankees. The 71st Pennsylvania, which had held the northwest corner of the Angle, had been routed to a degree that shocked General Webb and others.

Meanwhile, "Lo" Armistead continued to lead several hundred of his elated soldiers, including some of Pettigrew's men (Tennessee and Alabama boys of Fry's brigade and especially the 1st Tennessee), who were now mixed up with the Virginians on the north. After the elimination of most of Arnold's Rhode Island guns just north of the Angle and Cushing's guns inside the Angle, an inviting open avenue now lay before Armistead and his attackers surging through the smoke-shrouded Angle. The victors continued onward in a determined bid to not only capture the strategic crest but also additional artillery poised before them on higher ground.

All that Armistead and his onrushing troops had to do was to push aside the final defenders, the repositioned (by Webb) 72nd Pennsylvania, who were behind another low stone wall along the crest behind the Angle to cover the gap left by Cushing's battery, before a complete victory was realized. Armistead, like his men, instinctively knew that it was now or never. Emboldened by the capture of Cushing's two guns near the stone wall and smashing through Meade's right-center in one gallant rush, these swarming attackers, with Rebel battle flags clumped together in front, surged ever higher up the gentle slope of the grassy plateau. Attacking with abandon, these veterans carried not only .577 caliber Enfield rifles (Model 1853 at nine and a half pounds), with 20-inch bayonets fixed, but also the greatest hopes of the Southern people. In the words of Sergeant Easley, an ex-student who was shortly captured, "We went [toward] the second line of artillery," Cushing's four guns positioned just below the strategic crest.[134]

Meanwhile, additional cheering troops continued to pour over the stone wall and surge farther up the open slope, following the day's deepest penetration and Armistead's desperate bid to win it all. At that critical moment, Lieutenant Lewis described, "I had followed Armistead [into the Angle although now] being the only officer" of the 9th Virginia.[135] Indeed, some of the finest officers, including Colonel Robert Clotworthy Allen (VMI Class of 1855), who was killed "close to the stone wall" while leading the 28th Virginia, Garnett's brigade, continued to go down.[136]

Within only 15 feet of the never-say-die Armistead, Private James M. Kirkland was one Company H member (Mattapony Guards), 53rd Virginia, to reach the stone wall, but he was soon cut down. The small Bible in his breast pocket saved his life when a bullet struck it. However, the lead projectile still broke a rib to leave a painful injury. "Jimmy" Kirkland was hit by another lead ball, which tore into his right leg. But the most gruesome wound came when a bullet struck the unlucky private in the mouth, and "split his tongue." With his face and mouth splattered and red with blood, Private Kirkland was down, but somehow miraculously survived.[137] Charging farther up the slope than Private Kirkland and near Armistead, Captain Robert McCulloch, of Scotch-Irish descent and leading the Danville Grays of Company B, 18th Virginia, surged deeper into the hellish Angle. There, near Cushing's second line of guns and ignoring a previous wound, Captain McCulloch fell with a more serious wound "at the Angle," when hit by a bullet.[138]

In his diary, VMI graduate (Class of 1862) Captain George K. Griggs, leading Company K (Cascade Rifles) of the sizeable 38th Virginia, on Armistead's left, described how "we moved steadily forward, driving them from their strong position. . . ."[139] An 1858 VMI graduate and one of the seven VMI–educated colonels who fell that afternoon, Colonel Edward Claxton Edmonds, the 38th Virginia's commander, was not alive to see the significant gains achieved by his onrushing men, especially in overrunning Cushing's artillery pieces.[140] To the north and left of Garnett and Armistead, Fry's Tennessee and Alabama soldiers added fuel to the penetration after pouring over the stone wall, including attackers on the right who had joined Armistead's final push. Colonel Fry described: "All of the five regimental colors of my command reached the line of the enemy's works, and many of my men and officers were killed or wounded after passing over it."[141]

Meanwhile, south of Cushing's battery—whose six field pieces stood in silence after the last gunners had been killed, wounded, or captured—the rejuvenated Rebels continued toward the strategic crest with a chorus of shouts. This remarkable success was not yet duplicated on the lower ground (farther south down the gradually descending ridge) to the south, where Cowan's and Rorty's New York cannon continued to unleash double-shot canister with devastating effect. Kemper's right (unlike his left, which had mingled with Armistead's right) on the far south had not gained the stone wall. There, the 11th and 24th Virginia soldiers, lusting for the opportunity to capture the fast-working guns of Cowan's and Rorty's New York batteries just below the crest, continued to fire at the bluecoat artillerymen, while blasting away from the cover of the brushy knoll amid the open field southwest of Cowan's guns.

Before the stone wall just southwest of the clump of trees, one Old Dominion officer, perhaps even an enlisted man, provided the spark to resume the assault by the 11th Virginia and 24th Virginia, on Kemper's far right, up the slope. Kemper's attackers, primarily "country-raised men" compared to the mostly city boys (Richmond) of the 1st Virginia, charged to the right (south) of Armistead's penetration in a desperate bid to overrun the stone wall and then pour up the ascending ground to eliminate the cannon. However, with all Federal infantry in his front having been either killed, wounded, or captured, or having shifted north to meet Armistead's threat, Rorty's New York artillerymen had depressed their field pieces as low as possible. In this emergency situation, Rorty's gunners hurriedly crammed the barrel of one field piece with its most lethal possible load: triple-shot canister. The terrific force of the eruption completely overturned the gun. However, the great blast was effective, causing the considerable damage among the onrushing Virginians on Kemper's right and a lesser number of Garnett's southernmost soldiers.

But nothing could stop these determined men, especially with the sight of coveted artillery prizes so close and well within reach. Battling against the cresting Rebel tide, the New York gunners of Rorty's battery relied with spirit. Gunners went down in a flurry of swinging sponge-staffs, rammers, revolvers, and fists. One Virginia captain scrambled atop a field piece, waving the regimental colors and shouting, "Those guns are ours!" Sergeant Louis Darveau, of French descent, screamed back, "Not by a damned sight!" while taking a mighty swing with a handspike that struck the officer across the forehead. The Rebel was knocked off the gun that the feisty sergeant cherished like a summertime lover. Existing evidence from Virginia muster rolls has revealed that he was not a captain, but actually a lieutenant of Company C (Clifton Greys), 11th Virginia: James D. Connelly, an ex-farmer of Irish descent in his midtwenties.[142]

But north of Rorty's guns, Captain Cowan and his 1st New York Independent Battery, situated just below the copse of trees, faced the greatest threat, because the combined troops of Garnett, Armistead, and Kemper had broken through to the north on the gunners' right flank. Therefore, with the breakthrough perpendicular to his north–south row of guns, Captain Cowan believed the day lost, especially after his support troops, the 59th New York at the stone wall just to the southwest, took flight. Cowan described the belated charge of the several hundred of Kemper's resurgent Virginians, who previously "had found shelter behind that little rock knoll covered with brush, rush forward toward our uncovered front."[143] With the New Yorkers low on artillery rounds, the situation became so desperate that some of Cowan's gunners picked up rocks and hurled them at the onrushing attackers.[144]

Thinking fast in the crisis situation, Cowan ordered his men to stand their ground with all five guns crammed with their last loads of double canister. The Scotland-born captain waited for Kemper's Virginians to get even closer (all the way to the stone wall just vacated by the panicked 59th New York) before he gave the order to fire.[145] After watching the capture of Cushing's two guns near the stone wall with the attackers surging farther up the slope on the other side (north) of the clump of trees, the "Wild Irishman" Mike Smith, of Cowan's battery, decided to get out before it was too late. However, the Irishman suddenly saw the emerald-green flag of the 69th Pennsylvania, which was carried by Sergeant David Kaniry, age 23, from County Cork, Ireland, on higher ground to the north. The precious banner of green was protected by the Irishmen of Company C (The Emmett Guards)—the elite color company that contained the regiment's most diehard Irish nationalists. The sight of 69th Pennsylvania Irishmen gamely battling back instantly restored the Irish artilleryman's fighting spirit. Inspired by the emerald banner that represented his native homeland so far away, he cried, "Hurrah for the Ould Flag" of Ireland. Cowan, despite a bullet tearing through his frock coat, and his Empire State gunners, including Smith and especially other Irishmen, somehow managed to hold firm, while more artillerymen fell.[146]

Significant Gains and a Dramatic Success

Despite the heavy losses, the attackers on Pickett's left and Pettigrew's extreme right (Fry) at the Angle had smashed through Meade's right-center. They had succeeded in driving hundreds of Yankees rearward, while capturing artillery and a large number of prisoners. At that moment, the Army of the Potomac was effectively split in two, and decisive victory seemed to be well within Lee's grasp. But these significant gains still had to be fully exploited and the breakthrough had to be widened, especially with regard to rolling up the Union line's flanks to left (north) and right (south). All that was needed was the arrival of support troops to exploit the tactical gains already achieved. In a letter, Colonel Taylor described the breathtaking success, because so many stone wall defenders had been unable to "resist Pickett [as long as possible] but fled before him" in panic.[147]

In a letter to his wife, General Webb, whose 2nd Brigade troops had been mauled in attempting to hold the Angle and clump of trees sector, admitted how at this crucial moment, "the army of the Potomac was nearer being whipped than it was at any time of the battle."[148] Commanding the 2nd Corps's artillery, Captain John Hazard revealed, "All seemed lost, and the enemy, exultant, rushed on."[149] Soon to be wounded, General Gibbon was stunned by the catastrophe, after peering north and "calling the attention of the officers and men to the large numbers [of Yankees] falling back from the assaulting party. . . ."[150]

Webb had been shocked by the unbelievable sight of hundreds of his 71st Pennsylvania soldiers fleeing from Armistead's breakthrough. He described to his wife in a letter, "When my men fell back I almost wished to get killed [because] I was almost disgraced." In fact, sharp-eyed Confederate officers were attempting to do just that: directing their men to fire at Webb, when the general "stood but thirty-nine paces from them." Indeed, the capable Webb needed to be eliminated as soon as possible, because his efforts earned him the Medal of Honor.

Instead of saving the day, as Webb had hoped from his last reserves, the 72nd Pennsylvania had only taken a severe beating. The regiment had lost more than 50 men in the first volley unleashed by Garnett's and Armistead's men, before additional Pennsylvania soldiers were cut down in subsequent volleys fired at close range. Consequently, the 72nd Pennsylvania's survivors had flooded back toward the crest behind the Angle from where they had just come. Beside the north side of the copse of trees, Webb frantically attempted to rally the 72nd Pennsylvania, which had retired to the open crest while still under a sharp fire from Rebels at the stone wall and from Armistead's attackers.

But despite the best efforts of Webb and other officers, these hard-hit Federals from the Keystone State refused to counterattack as ordered. Meanwhile, victorious Confederates penetrated into the clump of trees that began about 40 paces east of the stone wall, easing their way through the underbrush and chestnut oaks. They gained good cover and firing positions to enfilade the flanks of bluecoat infantry and artillery to the north and the south. At the Angle and the copse of trees, Pickett's veterans were masters of the field, having torn a gaping 100-yard-wide hole (ripped open between the hurled back 69th Pennsylvania companies and the left of the 106th Pennsylvania, both regiments of Webb's hard-hit brigade) near the crest. A few more yards of precious ground gained in surging uphill and after pushing the last Federals off the crest, then the victorious Rebel could turn south to enfilade and sweep Hall's and Harrow's brigades, from north to south below the clump of trees, off the high-ground, and then turn Hays's left flank to the north. Back on Seminary Ridge and much to his surprise, meanwhile, Longstreet received a round of hearty congratulations for having orchestrated a successful assault that had reaped a most impressive victory.[151]

Indeed, like Cushing's battery, Webb's brigade had been vanquished. Chances for success increased when General Hancock swayed in the saddle when hit by a bullet, fired by one of either Kemper's or Garnett's men, that tore into his groin. The 69th Pennsylvania had been dealt with harshly. After Armistead's troops had reached Garnett's men at the stone wall to create a united front, the combined force of hundreds of soldiers had then continued up the slope to ensure that "the hill must fall," outflanking and even gaining the 69th Pennsylvania's rear on the right. Meanwhile, the 69th's left farther south was then turned by the left of Kemper's attackers, including a good many Irish soldiers in gray and butternut, who methodically shot (especially with a flank fire) down Irishmen in blue, including their commander from County Derry, Ireland, Colonel Dennis O'Kane. At that point, the rampaging Confederate Irish finally saw the green flag of Ireland (the same one that emboldened Cowan's Irish artillerymen to the south on the opposite side of the clump of trees) carried by the 69th Pennsylvania. Stubbornly, the 69th Pennsylvania Irish were pushed ever farther up the slope by the surging Confederate tide that included a good many Irish Rebels, who must have stared in disbelief at the green Irish banner. A civil war among the Irish added to the nightmarish qualities of the breakthrough combat. Most importantly, for the Rebels to hurl these stubborn Pennsylvania Irish aside would open up the door for enfilading and rolling up the Union line to the north and south.[152] Like his 69th Pennsylvania comrades and while shouts of "Surrender!" rose higher among the victors, Anthony W. McDermott admitted: "I was afraid we were going to get whipped" and badly.[153]

During one of the most dramatic moments of the Civil War: "Now they pour in volleys of musketry—they reach the works—the contest rages with intense fury—men fight almost hand to hand [and] The Yankees flee . . . Pickett's men deliver their fire at the gunners and drive them from their pieces. I see them plant their banner in the enemy's works. I hear their glad shout of victory!"[154] Lieutenant James Wyatt Whitehead, Jr., Company I (Chatham Grays), 53rd Virginia, which had advanced in Armistead's center, never forgot the sense of exhilaration: "We had driven the Yankees from behind the stone wall, captured all artillery in front of Armistead's brigade, and the victory up to this point was complete."[155]

While Cushing's battery was engulfed by the surging tide of elated Rebels, Captain Cowan's guns of the 1st New York Independent Battery to the south were ready for the inevitable onslaught, while hundreds of Kemper's men continued to charge as one from behind the "brush-covered knoll." Pickett's southernmost attack to overwhelm the stone wall also rejuvenated Garnett's troops, at the stone wall on their immediate left, and Kemper's men on the center to a lesser degree. Kemper's timely reinforcement fueled a resurgence of momentum that propelled the final push to overwhelm Cowan's five guns. Timing was the key, because the desperate assault was launched when Cowan's guns were the most vulnerable, when the sweat-stained gunners busily reloaded and after the 59th New York had fled. Most importantly, Kemper's renewed attack on the south complemented Armistead's breakthrough just to the north, promising to open a wider breach in Meade's collapsed right-center with the delivering of a solid one-two punch. Farther north, the 18th Virginia, on Garnett's right-center, were among the foremost attackers of this well-timed dash, attempting to overrun the northernmost New York guns before they could be reloaded.

Hoping to cut down as many bluecoat cannoneers as possible to ensure that the guns could not be reloaded in time, Old Dominion marksmanship proved deadly, with head shots instantly killing men like Gunner James A. Gray. With yelling Confederates pouring up the open, ascending slope and through the tall grass just east of the brushy knoll located about 100 paces southwest of the clump of trees, Cowan's men busily reloaded. Kemper's and Garnett's men blasted away, hoping to kill every gunner before they unleashed their lethal blasts of canister: literally a race with death between desperate young men who wanted to destroy each other—a Darwinian struggle of survival of the fittest.

Teenage Jake McElroy, one of Cowan's gunners of Irish descent, fell with "three bullets holes in his face," while Cowan and his few surviving men, including Irishman Corporal "Little Aleck" [Alexander] McKenzie who went down with a wound, faced the onslaught. He never forgot the unnerving sight: "I saw a young officer, waving his sword, leap the wall, followed by a number of men, and heard him shout: 'Take the gun' . . . closest to the trees. They were within 10 yards when I shouted 'Fire!' My last [dis]charge literally sweep the enemy from my front."[156] Indeed, some "220 chucks of lead from each" of Cowan's 3-inch guns slaughtered the onrushing Virginians.[157] The daring battery commander had not the luck of the Irish, but the luck of the Scots with him. Captain Cowan was the only battery commander around the clump of trees to survive the nightmarish combat.[158] He wrote to his Scotland-born mother without exaggeration, "We occupied the hottest place, in the center, and our loss was awful. How I wish I could tell you of the acts of our brave boys, they stood to their pieces when the enemy were 15 yards from the muzzles" of his New York cannon.[159]

However, the New York guns were especially vulnerable also because so many of Hall's and Harrow's troops (from north to south), who had been positioned south of Cowan, had shifted at the double-quick north in an attempt to reinforce the collapsing clump of trees sector to leave the battery to the south vulnerable. To exploit this opportunity, Pickett's southernmost attack consisted of Kemper's men and the right of Garnett's troops, including the 18th Virginia. The 18th Virginia troops followed the regimental colors now carried by another flag-bearer, after Lieutenant Henry Alexander Carrington had been cut down at the stone wall.

Cowan screamed, "Fire!" when the howling Virginians in this southern sector below the copse of trees began to pour over the stone wall. From their two 10-pound Parrott Rifles, the New Yorkers unleashed double-shot canister that literally blew the foremost attackers to pieces. Then, Rorty's artillerymen turned their guns northwest to enfilade Kemper's exposed right flank, while the 13th New York Volunteer Infantry and the 151st Pennsylvania Volunteer Infantry played key roles in thwarting Kemper's breakthrough just below the clump of trees. Some of Kemper's men charged so close to Cowan's guns that they were burned by explosions of fire from the cannon's barrel. During the bitter struggle, "the hands of the foe were laid upon" the 10-pounders, including allegedly those of a brave Virginia mayor. However, none of Pickett's majors fell before Rorty's New York guns that roared south of Cowan's field pieces. Maryland-born Francis "Frank" H. Langley, 1st Virginia, a former carpenter and an ex-sergeant, was the only major falling in this sector, but he was only wounded.[160]

Therefore, the unidentified young Virginia officer who was cut down between the stone wall and crest below the clump of trees was most likely only a captain. This Rebel officer "left behind his sword as a physical reminder of his anonymous heroism." In a token of respect, Cowan later buried the brave officer with honor: a final resting place in a solitary grave near Captain Rorty instead of a mass burial trench.[161] Cowan also eventually ordered the erecting of a proper headboard inscribed with a heartfelt tribute from a Scotland-born officer in blue: "A Rebel major, killed while gallantly leading the charge near this spot, July 3, 1863."[162]

On the far south, young Private Nathaniel C. Law, Company D, 24th Virginia, charged so close to Cowan's last remaining cannon that when the final discharge exploded, he was burned by the blast. Nevertheless, Law survived his burns, but not a hellish northern prison. He never again saw his home and mother, Sally, dying in September 1863—the tragic fate of 191 of Pickett's men captured that afternoon.[163]

Widening the Hole Torn in Meade's Right-Center

After eliminating the southernmost threat, Cowan looked north and was horrified by the sight of so many Federals fleeing from the Angle sector. Irishman Joseph McKeever described the breakthrough after the 69th Pennsylvania "fell back just as they [the attackers] were coming in to the inside of the [clump of] trees and they made a rally, and then they were coming in all around, but how they fired without killing all our men I do not know."[164]

With Armistead leading the way, the Confederates steadily widened the breach, while surging through the gap ripped through the right-center and pushing up open ground—the commanding plateau—of the Angle. Larger numbers of Webb's men were cut down. One Keystone State soldier was convinced: "We thought we were all gone." Meanwhile, the hard-hit 72nd Pennsylvania still refused to counterattack. Webb was utterly astounded that the command "failed to move," in his words. Although in the eye of the storm, General Webb continued to be targeted, including by one bullet that grazed the general's thigh.[165]

Armistead's success was partly the product of the tactical flexibility of leadership at all levels, including noncommissioned officers. Lieutenant Charles Fenton Berkeley, commanding Company D (Champe Rifles, 8th Virginia), filled in for his brother Captain William Noland Berkeley, who had been cut down by an exploding shell while leading the company to the stone wall.[166]

Captain Michael Peters Spessard was one of the premier fighting men who helped to drive back the defenders from the stone wall. A member of the 28th Virginia, he fought like a demon to reap vengeance for his teenage son Hezekiah's mortal wounding. Ignoring a burning thirst after having left his canteen with his dying son, the last assistance that he ever bestowed upon Hezekiah, Captain Spessard fought like a man possessed. He "was particularly conspicuous," wrote Major Charles Peyton, who then commanded the 19th Virginia. Destined to be the only remaining field officer of Garnett's brigade left standing at day's end after narrowly surviving the most "terrific fire" that he had ever seen, one-armed Peyton had led his troops to the stone wall.

After his son was fatally cut down, Spessard led Company C, the Craig Mountain Boys, 28th Virginia, "to the [stone] wall, which he climbed, and fought the enemy with his sword in their own trenches until his sword was wrestled from his hands by two Yankees."[167] However, he ignored the summons of three Federals to surrender. Instead Captain Spessard did what the Yankees least expected: picking up stones and driving off the three bluecoats with a strong arm. He then charged into the embattled Angle in search of additional victims to vent his rage, waging his own personal war for his fallen Hezekiah.[168]

Of Scotch-Irish descent and from Craig County, southwest Virginia, Private James R. McPherson, Company C (Craig Mountain Boys), 28th Virginia, described the incident: "My captain, M. P. Spessard [with an empty revolver], encountered three Yankees at the works, who had hid there. One of them wrung the sword from Spessard's hand and ordered him to surrender, but, instead, he ran the Yankees from the works with stones. . . ."[169] Amid the close-range combat swirling out of control, Captain John A. Herndon, leading Company D (Whitmell Guards), 38th Virginia, Armistead's brigade, quickly emptied his revolver at the Yankees. Then, as penned in a letter, "I had my pistol shot to pieces in my belt when I had but just placed it after firing it. It was an instrument in the hands of Providence to save my life."[170]

To Garnett's right, meanwhile, Kemper's men, especially on the center and left where they were not punished by Stannard's Vermonters like on the extreme right, were ecstatic. Like Armistead's soldiers to the north, they felt that decisive victory had been won, especially after capturing Rorty's New York guns, 10-pound Parrott Rifles of Company B, 1st Rhode Island Artillery. After Kemper was shot off his horse, Colonel Mayo commanded the brigade. Mayo described the tactical situation: "The entrenchments were carried, the enemy were driven from his guns."[171]

Meanwhile, to Garnett's left, elements of the 1st Tennessee (on Fry's right flank) and other of Pettigrew's troops—such as 13th Alabama soldiers just to the Tennesseans' left, on the right of Fry's brigade—also gained the stone wall (including in the Angle sector) with a triumphant shout. Fry's Tennesseans and Alabamians on the left and Marshall's North Carolinians, mixed together in the rush to gain the strategic crest, were exposed on the "natural glacis" of the open slope: a natural killing ground. Arnold's Rhode Islanders, who had been assigned to protect the left wing of Hays's division northeast of the Angle and just north of Cushing's four guns, attempted to limber up their four guns to escape.

With the Rebels closing in, Arnold's four cannon were in the process of being withdrawn up the slope, which was higher than the clump of trees area, to the southwest, and even higher than the generally level ground of the plateau (extending west from the crest) upon which Cushing's guns of Battery A, 4th United States Artillery were perched inside the Angle. Arnold's four guns were positioned higher up the ridge just northeast of Cushing's guns and parallel to his ammunition limbers to the south. The victorious Rebels now focused on Arnold's and Cushing's guns farther up the slope with lustful eyes, and raced onward to secure the prizes to exploit the dramatic breakthrough.

Pettigrew's division Goes for Broke

More than 1,000 of Pettigrew's troops descended upon the stone wall, including just north of the Angle, where Fry's Tennessee and Alabama brigade struck, including soldiers who had charged into the Angle with Armistead.[172] With Pettigrew's southernmost attackers having descended on Arnold's Rhode Island lone cannon (now the only operable field piece) and outflanked the 71st Pennsylvania's right from the north to provide invaluable assistance to Armistead's breakthrough just to the south, Private William C. Barker, Number 4 gun, kept his nerve. He had just seen Armistead and his men capture Cushing's two cannon at the stone wall, just before the low barrier of limestone rocks turned east at 90 degrees to form the Angle, to the southwest. Despite little ammunition remaining, Barker stayed beside his gun positioned just north of the Angle, where the stone wall continued in a north–south direction, before Arnold's withdrawing four guns.

All the while, Barker allowed Fry's men and the North Carolina Rebels of Marshall's brigade, especially the 26th North Carolina on the far left, or northernmost, flank after Davis's brigade to the north had been hurled back, to get as close as possible. Barker calmly held the lanyard. Just northeast of the clump of trees and on higher ground, he wanted to kill as many Rebels as possible. Therefore, Private Barker was intent on allowing many North Carolinians, who were now led by the 13th color-bearer after a full dozen flag-carriers already had been cut down, to charge within killing range. Demonstrating patience and courage, Barker waited for what seemed like an eternity. Finally, when the 26th North Carolina boys were within only 20 yards, Barker finally jerked the lanyard.

The New England artilleryman described the explosion of double-shot canister: "[T]he gap made in that North Carolina regiment was simply terrible."[173] North of the Angle before Arnold's foremost gun, 26th North Carolina bodies were literally blown apart by the fiery blast that exploded in their faces: the bloody "high tide" of the 26th North Carolina. Captain George Bowen, at the southern end of the 12th New Jersey's line, never forgot when "one confederate jump[ed] on one of the [Arnold's disabled] guns, wave his flag and give a cheer," just before being cut down by a Rhode Island gunner.[174] So desperate was the close range combat in this bloody sector that some soldiers, perhaps including Irishmen like Sergeant Frank Riley, mostly from southern New Jersey, had no time to reload muskets. They picked up rocks and hurled them at the Tar Heels only a short distance away. Ironically, fellow Princeton classmates, where large numbers of Southern boys had been educated, traded fire, while perhaps even recognizing a former classmate.[175]

Like the Virginians to the south, meanwhile, small groups of soldiers on Pettigrew's center and right either neared or gained the stone wall. About 150 11th North Carolina attackers surged to within 50 yards of the fence line until stopped by musketry. Groups of Marshall's desperate men gained the stone wall or reached points within only 12–15 yards away. In overrunning the stone wall, some 26th North Carolina men had united with the left of Fry's brigade, delivering a combined blow in the bloody sector held by Arnold's guns. There, Major John Thomas "Knock" Jones, commanding the 26th North Carolina, and about 60 other Old North State soldiers were elated, after nearly reaching the wall north of the Angle. Major Jones "thought victory was ours. . . ."[176]

Farther to the south in another united effort, numbers of Garnett's Virginians on the left (or north) had mixed with the right of Fry's Upper South (Tennessee) and Deep South (Alabama) soldiers to overrun the stone wall. Fry's troops, especially the 1st Tennessee on the extreme right, had merged with Garnett's left in penetrating the smoke-filled Angle. With the loss of so many officers, common soldiers led the way. They battled on their own, surging onward in a desperate bid to gain the strategic crest, where hopes and dreams could be realized.

Meanwhile, Lieutenant Colonel John R. Graves led about 150 soldiers of the 47th North Carolina to an advanced point within 40 yards of the blazing fence, before ordering them to the ground to escape the stream of bullets. North of the Angle and long after linear formations had melted away from the sheets of flame, the stone wall was gained by small groups of Pettigrew's most determined veterans who naturally bunched together out of a survival instinct: the "high-water mark of Marshall's brigade."[177] Colonel James Keith Marshall, age 24, went down "within 50 yards" of the stone wall and the Abraham Brien barn.[178] As revealed in a letter, "Jimmy" was killed *instantly* [as] he was shot in the forehead and expired immediately."[179]

Although Colonel Marshall and other leaders had been cut down, the most stalwart North Carolinians continued onward. Private Daniel Boone Thomas, age 22, still headed toward the stone wall with the colors, while comrades from the Haw and Eno River country in the Piedmont of Chatham County and other counties followed close behind. They charged up the slope to within around 40 yards of the wall. But Marshall's men were on their own, because a disastrous chain of events doomed their best efforts. Larger groups of survivors of Lane's North Carolina brigade and Davis's Mississippi and North Carolina brigade (most of which had already withdrawn) headed rearward to escape the vicious frontal and flank fires. Sapping offensive capabilities, these troops—first Davis and then Lane to the rear—had already suffered terribly not only from frontal, but also the 8th Ohio's flank fire. The Ohioans had been strengthened by skirmishers of the 111th New York and then the entire 126th New York, adding to the punishment. Nevertheless, despite the flank fire, the only ones among Davis's troops who continued toward the wall were diehard 11th Mississippi attackers.

After having retired down the slope, many soldiers had then attempted to realign upon gaining the relative safety of the Emmitsburg Road. Effectively flanked on the left, Pettigrew's troops remained in place instead of continuing the attack east of the road. Pettigrew had dispatched a staff officer, Lieutenant William B. Shepard, to order hundreds of men, including soldiers who had not even advanced from the slightly sunken roadbed, to move up the slope. But by that time, large numbers of North Carolinians of Lowrance's brigade, on Lane's right, were also falling back. About half of the 7th North Carolina's survivors continued onward. Therefore, General "Jimmie" Lane, his warhorse so badly wounded he was on foot, was about to order "my brigade back."[180]

Consequently, at a crucial moment, Pickett's division lost even more support on the far left. Pettigrew's left continued to take an unmerciful pounding to the point of "annihilation," according to a 14th Connecticut officer, who led two companies of men firing Sharps repeaters that roared.[181] Nevertheless, some of Lowrance's resolute men continued onward like the 38th North Carolina on the far left, reaching the stone fence north of the Angle. But the 16th North Carolina soldiers made the most significant gains on the brigade's far right, or south, even mingling with Fry's 1st Tennessee in the Angle itself.

Incredibly, two of the foremost attackers on Pettigrew's far left were somehow spared. Private Daniel Boone Thomas and Sergeant James M. Brooks, both age 22 and 26th North Carolina members, defied the odds. Impressed by the courage of the two boys from the North Carolina Piedmont, the 12th New Jersey Yankees (who knew of vibrant Southern sentiment in their own south New Jersey homeland) held their fire after they had belatedly opened up when the North Carolinians first advanced to within 40 yards away. A single shot from a 12th New Jersey musket, loaded with buck & ball, could have swiftly eliminated Thomas and Brooks at such close range. A compassionate Garden Stater at the stone wall shouted above the din, "Come over to this side of the Lord!" The North Carolina boys crossed over the stone wall, and Private Thomas relinquished the 26th North Carolina's colors to the 12th New Jersey victors.[182]

North of the 26th North Carolina, the last of Lane's men, including of the 7th and 37th North Carolina, continued to advance to meet grisly ends on the open slope, while their hard-hit Tar Heel brigade retired. While leading 33rd North Carolina soldiers, Lane's brigade, one officer "was blown to atoms by a cannon shot."[183] Captain George Bowen, 12th New Jersey, described the fate of Marshall's left south of the 33rd North Carolina: "[B]ut still on they came until they were within a dozen feet of us when those that were left threw down their guns and surrendered."[184]

With the left flanked and mauled, Pettigrew's most significant gains were made to the south. Here, soldiers on the right and left of Fry's brigade not only overran the stone wall but also continued onward, raising a hearty shout. Ironically, the collapse of Pettigrew's left and the Ohioans' flank fire now paid dividends for delivering the maximum blow, having forced additional troops (more as individual groups than units) south to escape the punishment. Closer to Pickett's division, a fortunate coincidence maximized the strength of the offensive punch at the most vulnerable sector: These men, including even 16th North Carolina soldiers (Lane), had then joined Fry's brigade (especially the 1st Tennessee), giving it extra strength, including at the Angle to add fuel to Armistead's breakthrough. Captain Jacob B. Turney, 1st Tennessee, Fry's brigade, described how after overrunning the stone wall "one triumphant shout was given as the Federals in our immediate front and to our right [when Garnett's men had broken through and gained the stone wall] yielded and fled in confusion I now mounted the rock wall and found everything successful on my right, while the center and left of Archer's [Tennessee and Alabama] brigade had failed From my position to the right the works were ours" and decisive victory seemed assured.[185]

Some powder-stained soldiers on Fry's left, especially the 7th Tennessee, also gained the stone wall north of the Angle. Captain Turney ordered his Tennessee boys to align beyond the stone wall, and then to turn north and fire into the exposed left flank of those Yankees behind the stone wall, where the center of Fry's brigade had failed to penetrate, unlike Fry's left (farther north) and right (at the Angle). This flank fire that raked the Federals, who were now sandwiched between Fry's right and left—after the brigade's center (due to the "horseshoe shape" of the advancing line) had still not reached the stone wall—was effective in creating considerable "confusion" among the defenders, while widening the breach to the north.[186]

Sergeant Randolph Abbott Shotwell, 8th Virginia, described the savage combat to the north: "At their head was the noble Marshall . . . who fell within a few feet of the Yankee bayonets, and . . . His horse was ridden off by a Tennessean showing how the two States were mixed" in the surge over the stone wall north of the Angle.[187] Combined with Armistead's breakthrough to the south, Pettigrew's men made such extensive gains in reaching the stone wall that Private William J. Burns, of the 12th New Jersey, Smyth's 2nd Brigade, Hays's division, was convinced that "it was all up with us."[188]

Meanwhile, north of Marshall's brigade, the groups of soldiers of the 2nd, 11th, and 42nd Mississippi and the lone 55th North Carolina of Davis's brigade, on the far left, had possessed relatively little hope of making significant gains (unlike Marshall's and Fry's brigades to the south), because of the early collapse of the extreme left, which left them with no support on the north, after Brockenbrough's Virginia brigade on the far left had vanished. Therefore, large numbers of Magnolia State and North Carolina soldiers of Davis's brigade had remained in the relative safety of the Emmitsburg Road instead of going forward.

However, isolated contingents of Davis's Rebels continued the attack on their own. Indeed, although most of Davis's men had withdrawn, the 11th Mississippi surpassed its sister regiments in going for broke. The 11th Mississippi, thanks partly to the fact that it was Davis's only regiment that had been spared from the July 1 bloodletting, outperformed all other brigade regiments. As usual, the Irish Rebels were also in the forefront in this sector. After four color-bearers had been shot down, a "never-flinching little Irishman," in the words of Lieutenant William "Billy" Peel, 11th Mississippi, named George

Kidd led the way up the slope. He had been born in Ireland in 1836 and migrated with his family to Baltimore, Maryland, in 1852. His older brother William, age 28, had been wounded in carrying the flag at Antietam. Even more symbolic, Irish-born Private William O'Brien, age 34, had been killed while holding the colors aloft in crossing the Emmitsburg Road, where Kidd had first picked up the flag. Then, with his fellow Mississippians following, Kidd surged up to the stone wall. There the young Irishman was cut down with wounds in both hands. Ironically, this Son of Erin who led one of the deepest penetrations north of the Angle was fated for confinement in Fort McHenry, Baltimore, in a community that he still called home.[189]

After sweeping aside opposition and ripping a hole in Meade's line, decisive victory would be secured if only reinforcements arrived to widen the breach in the collapsed right-center. At the point where the 11th Virginia on Kemper's right-center overran the works lined with bluecoat bodies, Captain John Holmes Smith, age 22, described the intoxicating sense of success: "We thought our work was done, and that the day was over, for the last enemy in sight we had seen disappear over the hill in front, and I expected to see General Lee's army marching up to take possession of the field."[190]Like his men of Company G (Portsmouth Rifles), 9th Virginia, Lieutenant John Henry Lewis, Jr., was elated by the heady tactical success: "[A]t [this] point, Meade's army was whipped."[191]

Finally, the foremost attacker of Pickett's Charge was killed near the open crest of so much strategic importance, after catching sight of the broad open fields—over which Stuart's cavalrymen were to have charged west to strike Meade's rear—that flowed endlessly to the east. To this day, no one knows the name of this brave common soldier who went farther than anyone else. He charged beyond Cushing's second line of artillery and nearly gained the strategic crest. Colonel Mayo described: "Twenty paces beyond [these guns] the foremost hero of them all, a humble private, without a name, bit the dust."[192]

No Support

In a discussion with Colonel Alexander before the assault, General Wright had emphasized the key to reaping a decisive success: "[I]t is mostly a question of supports."[193] Longstreet and Hill failed to properly support the breakthrough. With attacking units decimated and Pickett's men worn out from the lengthy advance, most survivors had halted at the stone wall to catch their wind, regrouped at the wall below the Angle, and reloaded for the inevitable next round of bitter fighting. By this time resistance had strengthened among resurgent 69th Pennsylvania Irish, and Armistead's several hundred attackers (including Garnett's soldiers and Kemper's northernmost men, and even a handful of Fry's Alabama and Tennessee boys) found themselves on their own in their penetration beyond the stone wall and into the Angle.

While these common soldiers prayed for timely support, top Confederate leadership failed them in their greatest hour of need. Longstreet failed to properly ensure that both flanks were properly supported. Lee also was a nonfactor, because he had handed the job of orchestrating the assault to Longstreet. Pickett was far to the rear, somewhere behind the Codori House. Tragically for so many young common soldiers, Longstreet, Pickett, and even Lee (to a lesser degree) let them down, leaving them to die on their own by way of miscalculations and egregious errors.

Longstreet or Hill continued to fail to act "in concert," in Lee's words, to support the attack. As planned by Lee and along with other troops, the 8,000 men of Anderson's division of Hill's 3rd Corps had not advanced 300–400 yards behind in close support of the flanks of the assault because of not only breakdowns in communication, but overall leadership failures. Then, Longstreet only belatedly sent two brigades of Hill's corps forward: General Wilcox's about 1,000 Alabamians and Colonel Lang's three small regiments of only about 400 Floridians. However, these two brigades were in overall bad shape, having suffered severely in the attacks of July 2. "Old Billy Fixin" Wilcox had lost his fighting spirit on July 2, believing like Longstreet that the assault was doomed. Lang protested his advance order, while more resolute men fought and died at the Angle.

Seeing no chance for success in a self-fulfilling prophecy and after having ordered the two units forward, Longstreet then ordered Anderson to stop the advance of Posey's Mississippi and Wright's Alabama brigades (on the north flank and south flank, respectively). Two of Anderson's brigades (Wilcox's and Lang's) on the Alabamians' left failed miserably to protect Pickett's right flank. And on the far right, neither McLaw's or Hood's divisions advanced as Lee had planned, because Longstreet failed to order them forward.

Although Wilcox's Alabama brigade, which should have served as the all-important right "flank guard" for Pickett's Charge, finally advanced, it was 20 minutes too late—about the time that it took for the attackers to reach their objective. As mentioned, these reinforcements advanced too far south across the open fields of the upper section of the shallow Upper Plum Run Valley and well below and southwest of the Codori House, while on a course straight east and far below the clump of trees sector, where they were needed. All in all, Wilcox's and Lang's Florida troops, carrying Springfield rifles refitted in Richmond, advanced too late to provide timely assistance. Tragically, if Wilcox had not attacked belatedly and too far south, then the Alabamians could have easily outflanked the Vermont troops (facing north) on the left flank attack.

Longstreet and Hill failed to hurry available brigades forward to fulfill vital roles. Like Longstreet had posed resistance to Lee, so Longstreet's subordinates balked. Wilcox early made up his mind to "not again lead his men into such a deathtrap," and only under protest while obeying orders. Therefore, no one (not Lee, Longstreet, or Pickett) ensured that the assault was properly supported.[194] Unfortunately, for the foremost attackers, top leaders of Hill's corps, reflecting the superior's defeatism, were early convinced that "what Anderson's division had failed to do on the 2nd, Pickett could not do 24 hours later. . . ."[195]

Although these units were "in position to offer a great deal of help", Longstreet countermanded the orders for the advance of two support brigades on the left that desperately needed reinforcements: not only Posey's Mississippi brigade but also General William "Billy" Mahone's sizeable, fresh Virginia brigade, as Lee had planned.[196] Clearly, as Colonel Taylor explained with considerable understatement, "the plan agreed on was not carried out."[197]

Indeed, to adequately support the first-line attackers, Lee "expected all of Anderson's troops [five brigades] and perhaps Robert Rodes's remaining units to move in support of the main attack."[198] Anderson reported, "I was about to move forward Wright's and Posey's brigades, when Lieutenant General Longstreet directed me to stop the movement. . . ."[199] In his diary, Trimble, who was then commanding Pender's division and who was shot in the left leg (which was later amputated) during the attack, described the crisis on the left: "I took in 2 N.C. Brigades, [Scales's] & Lane's, as the supporting force [and] reached a point some 200 yards from the breast works—here the men broke down from exhaustion & the fatal fire & went no further but walked sullenly back" to the rear.[200]

Colonel Taylor, shocked that Lee's battle plan had imploded, lamented: "Much can be said in excuse for the failure of the other commands to fulfill the task assigned to them."[201] Even one Union soldier concluded, "Lee had ordered that Pickett should be strongly supported, but it was impossible to find in his army supports who had not been there before, many of them more

than once on this same field or nearby, and it was not strange that their enthusiasm was not at the white heat that seemed to burn in the hearts of Pickett's
men."[202]

Describing the golden opportunity, Major Walter Harrison, the inspector
general and acting adjutant of Pickett's division, concluded how just like "a
narrow wedge driven into a solid column of oak, they [broke] through the
outer barriers of resistance, crushed the inner rind of defence, and penetrated
even to the heart [and] touched the vital point [but they were] not sufficiently
strong."[203]

Expecting timely and sizeable reinforcements, large numbers of
exhausted Virginia soldiers had taken positions behind the stone wall south
of the Angle to await assistance. Higher up the slope near the smoky crest,
there was still another stone wall, where Yankees had rallied and returned
fire: an additional reason why large numbers of Armistead's, Garnett's, and
Kemper's men halted at the stone wall below the Angle. Survival instincts
had risen to the fore, because the north–south running stone wall, the only
protection on the open slope, offered protection. Rebel leaders were sadly
lacking to mount an organized effort for the attack's continuation below the
Angle, because so many had been shot down. Few men had seen Garnett fall
from his horse amid the swirling dust and smoke. However, Garnett's body
had been found by his courier, Robert H. Irvine, who then secured the general's pocket watch to send back to the family. Symbolically in a final tribute,
the general's artillery saber was left by Garnett's side in the ancient Spartan
warrior tradition.[204]

At that crucial moment, Major Harrison lamented the recent interference
of bungling Richmond politicians, including the president, that had resulted
in the absence of the two of Pickett's five brigades that had been left behind to
safeguard the Richmond area because, "With them we might have held on to
the grip. Two lines of guns had been already taken, two lines of infantry had
been driven back, or run over in this headlong assault; but the enemy still had
a dense body in reserve. The critical moment for *support* had arrived to his little
band of so-far victors. Another wedge must be driven in. . . . Where then were
their supports? where were those two lines that were to follow up this glorious
burst of valor?"[205]

With Kemper cut down, Colonel Mayo, now leading the 500-man brigade
before the attack, described: "At this critical juncture when seconds seemed
more precious than hours of any former time, many an anxious eye was cast

back to the hill from which we came in the hope of seeing supports near at hand and more than once I heard the desperate exclamation, 'why don't they come!'"[206]

In the same brigade on the south, young Captain John Holmes Smith, who commanded Company G (Lynchburg Home Guard), 11th Virginia, also thought the day was won. Along with surviving comrades like Private J. M. "Blackeyed" Williams, who had enlisted in March 1862 and eventually fell wounded like Smith, he looked rearward expecting to see reinforcements. But Williams "could see nothing but dead and wounded [and] my heart never in my life sank as it did then." In desperation, therefore, surviving 11th Virginia officers dispatched a "long-legged, big-footed fellow," Private George T. Walker, appropriately nicknamed "Big Foot," to dash down the slope to request reinforcements, but such efforts were too little, too late.[207]

Lieutenant John Henry Lewis, Jr., described how the foremost Virginia Rebels, "with scarce any officers" left standing, continued to anxiously "look back over the field for assistance that should have been there; but there are no troops in sight; they had vanished from the field, and Pickett's division, or what is left of it, is fighting the whole Federal center alone."[208]

Proving now to be a most prophetic name, Cemetery Ridge had been transformed into a ready-made graveyard. Hundreds of soldiers continued to die to hold an obscure ridge. With what little remained of the 53rd Virginia, which suffered nearly 50 percent losses, Lieutenant James Wyatt Whitehead, Jr., Company I (Chatham Grays), 53rd Virginia, lamented how he saw "reinforcements arriving from the enemy and none for ourselves [now began to ensure] that was the end of our dearly bought victory."[209] In the words of Lee's faithful adjutant as written in a July 17, 1863, letter in regard to this critical moment when opportunity beckoned for reinforcements as never before, "If we had had 10,000 more men, we would have forced them back" and achieved a decisive victory as planned by Lee, if the designated support troops would have arrived.[210]

But Lee's words were in the fact more significant: "[I]f they had been supported as they were to have been—but, for some reason not yet fully explained to me, were not—we would have held the position and the day would have been ours."[211] Lee shortly informed General John Daniel Imboden, a former Virginia legislator, of the same opinion."[212] Quite correctly, Lee later emphasized that decisive victory would have been won if only "one determined and united blow [could] have been delivered by our whole line."[213]

Despite the fact that he had been assigned to orchestrating the overall assault—especially the close coordination of infantry and artillery—Longstreet had failed to dispatch "a second wave of attackers to support and exploit" to bolster the assault's vulnerable flanks and to fully exploit the significant breakthrough on Meade's right-center. Quite simply, "Lee might well have won Gettysburg and the war, had Longstreet augmented Pickett's charge with strong supporting units."[214] As mentioned, when things began to go wrong in the attack, Pickett had dispatched a staff officer to beg Longstreet for "vigorous and immediate support," but this was not enough.[215]

Almost all of the Confederate artillery remained far to the rear, with precious few, including five guns of the Washington Artillery on the south, advancing as flying artillery to protect the attackers, especially on the left flank. Artillery leadership, especially Lee's Chief of Artillery Pendleton and his battalion commanders of each corps, failed to coordinate their efforts. On the north, Major Poague believed that he possessed orders to advance his four batteries (two Virginia, one Mississippi, and one North Carolina) to support the attackers after they secured the crest—far too late. Like most batteries, the four batteries of Virginia guns of Major Dearing's Virginia battalion were entirely out of rounds. More than 170 Southern field pieces, especially the nine howitzers that Alexander had planned to push forward, remained entirely ineffective and without sufficient ammunition. What Alexander sent forward individually to protect the right lacked numbers and concentration of firepower, in violation of Napoleon's most basic artillery principles. These guns, including Company A, 38th Virginia Artillery Battalion, which possessed only three rounds of solid shot left after the cannonade and could not be utilized after Pickett dispatched Captain Bright to secure support to dislodge the Vermonters on the south, were unable to assist the attackers.[216]

After Pickett dispatched Bright to hurry forward the guns of Dearing's battalion as flying artillery, the major only then discovered that his Virginia batteries possessed too little ammunition. In a pathetic response, four batteries of Dearing's battalion contributed but three cannon blasts "from my rifled guns," in the major's glum words, to support Pickett's division on the right.[217]

Major Poague's words revealed the comedy of errors: "As soon as Pickett's men reached the crest I gave the order to limber to the front [and] prepare to advance" about 1,400 yards to Cemetery Ridge's crest, "but before starting I began . . . seeing small bodies of men coming back and the number increasing every moment until the awful truth began to force itself upon me that the attack had failed." Upon spying Pickett in the most rearward of places for a division commander at such a key moment, Poague galloped over on a fresh mount (his "little sorrel" had been "torn to pieces by a shell") to the division commander. The major informed Pickett, who had already returned to the Confederate guns of Seminary Ridge by that time, while his men continued to die on their own: "General, my orders are that as soon as our troops get the hill I am to move as rapidly as possible to their support. But I don't like the look of things up there." Peering eastward upon a sight nearly a mile away, Pickett "made no reply."[218] Meanwhile, in striking contrast to Pickett's absence and despite suffering what appeared to be a mortal wound from a bullet that remained in place to pain him for the rest of his life, Kemper was still on the field, barking out orders. He had earlier directed "Big Foot" Walker to find Longstreet on Seminary Ridge and implore him to send reinforcements. But it was already too late. Kemper was rescued by Sergeant Leigh M. Blanton, who carried the general rearward on his back.[219]

Because of the failures of Dearing and Poague (battalion commanders of Pickett's division and Pender's division, respectively) to advance their guns as flying artillery, young Lieutenant James F. Crocker, the Phi Beta Kappa man from Gettysburg College and the 9th Virginia's adjutant, lamented how "the batteries [were to have been] pushed forward as the infantry progressed, to protect their flanks and support their attack. The attack was not made as here ordered" by Lee.[220]

Major Harrison described how two lines of infantry had failed to come up to support the men who had gained the stone wall and overran the Angle, because "the *second* and *third* places had been too hot for them [and] Midway they wavered, and from midway they fell back in disorder [although] these other troops were ordered to support them [but] it is quite as well known they did *not*. These troops had behaved most gallantly on other occasions. They had been already seriously engaged [unlike Pickett's troops] on the two days previous, and had lost many valuable officers, in whom the men had confidence and were accustomed to follow."[221]

But the true culprit was higher up: Longstreet had failed to properly organize and hurl forward a second wave of larger numbers of troops or adequate support—infantry or artillery—especially on the flanks, to exploit tactical gains.[222] Colonel Alexander lamented the lack of support: "What we did, under all our disadvantages, with only 9 brigades in the storming column surely justifies sanguine anticipations of what might have been done by 22, at a more favorable locality & with more artillery."[223] Longstreet had been so negligent that "Stonewall Jackson would have placed him under arrest on the spot and that Napoleon would have had him shot" for sabotaging chances for success.[224]

The same could be said of Hill in terms of failing to properly support the assault. However, Lee had fundamentally committed the sin of delegating the exact details of the orchestration of the assault "to Longstreet and Hill, and neither of these old antagonists took control. Longstreet would not, and Hill, assuming Longstreet to be in charge of the offensive, could not. Thus, Hill's 3rd Corps troops became a sort of orphan force, left to tag along as best they could."[225]

Ironically, while the ever-dwindling band of surviving soldiers looked rearward toward where the sun would set over the bluish-hazed mountains, they should have been looking in the opposite direction for Stuart and his cavalrymen, but they were not aware of Lee's intended surprise. Like reinforcements from the west, so these horsemen never arrived from the east. In a classic understatement, one Federal soldier, the son of an Irish-born farmer, mused that if Stuart "had reached the rear of our infantry and charged in conjunction with Pickett, he could have hurt us much."[226]

Escalating Crisis to the South

Meanwhile, without adequate flying artillery, especially from Dearing's Virginia battalion, to provide protection on the right flank and because Longstreet had not ordered Wilcox's Alabama brigade to follow closely behind Pickett in support, the crisis intensified on the south in Kemper's battered sector. In their advanced position about 100 yards west of the main line, about 1,500 Vermont troops of three regiments applied greater pressure. Pushing north to create a protruding bulge that pointed like a dagger to pierce Pickett's right flank, the Vermonters steadily unleashed volleys that toppled additional Virginians, including mounted officers, who were exposed on higher ground.

So far that afternoon, the Vermonters' escalating threat on Codori's open fields had been met only in disorganized fashion in part because Kemper and others initially believed that the force to the south was Wilcox, where he should have provided flank protection. Therefore, at first, only small groups of Kemper's veterans (11th and 24th Virginia troops) turned to the right, or south, to blast away at General George Jerrison Stannard's troublesome men. The fire from the

Green Mountain Boys was devastating. In the words of a 9th Virginia captain of Armistead's brigade: "Under this terrible cross-fire the men reeled and staggered between falling comrades, and the right came pressing down upon the centre, crowding the companies into confusion" before gaining the stone wall. In desperation to galvanize the most organized Confederate resistance to the south to counter the escalating flank threat, since there was no advance by Wilcox or flying artillery, Colonel Mayo faced a vexing tactical dilemma. Filling in for the fallen Kemper, he described the desperate situation on the line's southern end: "Our right flank was entirely exposed & but for the promptness with which a small portion of the 11th and 24th Regts were thrown back at right angles to our line, under the direction of Col. Terry and Capt. Fry the enemy would have gained our rear."[227]

Indeed, Colonel William Richard Terry, a capable VMI graduate (Class of 1857) in his midthirties and born in Bedford County, Virginia, had his 24th Virginia, on the far right, or southernmost, flank of Kemper's brigade, facing the Vermonters, after turning south. Captain William T. Fry, Kemper's staff officer since June 1862, the adjutant of Kemper's brigade, and a recent graduate of VMI (Class of 1862), provided timely assistance. Covered in blood from his horse, which had been shot in the neck, Captain Fry took command of the 11th Virginia after "Old Buck" Terry had "sent him to stop the rush to [the] left," duplicating Colonel Terry's achievement in turning the regiment to face their new threat.

Fortunately, for Kemper's southern flank, Terry was tactically astute (destined for a brigadier general's rank) and he possessed capable top lieutenants, such as Major Joseph Adam Hambrick (VMI Class of 1857) and Adjutant William T. Taliaferro (VMI Class of 1845), who was affectionately nicknamed "Tell." Colonel Mayo and Lieutenant Colonel Henry Alexander Carrington, a married man since 1856 and University of Virginia graduate of the 18th Virginia, along with Captain William W. Bentley, 24th Virginia and a Class of 1860 VMI graduate, also played key roles in meeting the Vermonters' ever-growing threat. Therefore, just in the nick of time with the advancing Vermonters threatening to gain Kemper's rear, this "small band" of Virginians laid down a scorching fire, after refusing their line in timely fashion.[228]

The fighting grew in intensity. Colonel Mayo described: "[E]verything was a wild kaleidoscopic whirl . . . Seeing the men as they fired, throw down their guns and pick up others [of the dead and wounded] from the ground, I followed suit, shooting into the flock of blue coats that were pouring down from the right, I noticed how close their [United States and state] flags were together."[229] A blistering fire from the Vermont men continued to sweep the Virginians' southern flank southwest of the Angle. To his horror, Colonel Mayo noticed the "splinters of bone and lumps of flesh sticking to my clothes" from nearby Adjutant Taliaferro, 24th Virginia. Named in honor of the famous Seminole (born a Creek) leader who had died in 1838 defying United States encroachment, the handsome "boy lieutenant" Osceola T. White, a former student, was hit. Simply called "Ocey," White staggered when a bullet grazed his head. The Company A (Dismal Swamp Rangers from southeast Virginia), 3rd Virginia, officer survived the wound. However, a principal source of Ocey's youthful vanity was lost when the bullet "carried away one of his pretty flaxen curls" to raise a "whelk on his scalp."[230]

Before he was sent back down the slope in a futile effort to secure reinforcements to exploit the breach in Meade's right-center, Private George "Big Foot" T. Walker, whose horse had been shot from under him while serving as Kemper's orderly and who was described as "ungainly, hard-featured, [and] good-natured," was shocked. He asked Colonel Mayo in frustration: "Oh! Colonel, why don't they support us?"[231]

To the north, the same scenario was played out. Captain "June" Kimble, 14th Tennessee, and his comrades of Fry's brigade, likewise "prayed for support" before it was too late.[232] But the greatest flank crisis among Pickett's men took place in this overlooked fight on the extreme right in the open fields southwest of the clump of trees. There, on the far right, Kemper's Virginians loaded and fired as fast as possible, keeping the aggressive Vermonters at bay. One Old Dominion captain described, "Muskets were crossed, as some men faced to the right and others to the front, and the fighting was terrific, far [*] beyond all experience, even of Pickett's men."[233]

However, the foremost Rebels who had broken through Meade's right-center could hardly realize the grim reality that, in the words of delight from one of Cushing's gunners, "of all those rebels that came over the wall not one got back."[234] And the principal reason why they never returned was because the infantry and "artillery support so vital to the success of General Lee's plan of attack had now vanished completely [and precisely when Pickett's troops] most desperately needed it to press their momentary advantage" to exploit the dramatic breakthrough.[235] Twenty-two-year-old Captain John Holmes Smith, Company G (Lynchburg Home Guard), 57th Virginia, looked around and

"I expected to see General Lee's army marching up" to reinforce the frontline attackers, but such was not the case.[236]

Despite the lack of support from the rear, General Armistead continued to lead his attackers farther up the grassy slope with battle flags flying, going for broke on that day of destiny.

Chapter VIII

Capturing Additional Union Cannon

During their desperate rush to cut the Army of the Potomac in two, Armistead and several hundred attackers hoped to exploit their dramatic breakthrough to the fullest. Making Virginia Military Institute (VMI) proud, Captain Robert McCulloch, Company B (Danville Greys), 18th Virginia, Garnett's brigade, surged ahead with Armistead, leading surviving Danville boys farther into the deepest penetration of the day. Armistead was determined to gain the ridge's strategic crest, which was still ripe for the taking.

Lying before Armistead and his attackers, along with some of Fry's soldiers (especially the 1st Tennessee) and Garnett's men, the slope gently ascended to the open crest. With his plumed slouch hat held aloft by his sword, Armistead continued to yell "Follow me!" in his booming voice. Near Armistead and the 56th Virginia's colors, Private Robert B. Damron, Company D (of the Buckingham Yancey Guards, which had every one of its 23 members killed, wounded, or captured), 56th Virginia, on Garnett's far left—whose leader, Colonel William Dabney Stuart, already had been cut down—followed Armistead toward the strategic crest. Damron continued onward up the slope until hit in the shoulder when near one of Cushing's abandoned guns at the stone wall. Likewise, a good many 14th Virginia soldiers, on Armistead's far right, also followed their animated brigadier like a good many 9th Virginia men. On the 14th Virginia's left, these 9th Virginia soldiers were no longer led by Major John Crowder Owens, after he fell mortally wounded before the stone wall.

During Armistead's breakthrough, most veterans remained in position behind the stone wall in part because of its greater height of four to five feet in the sector near Garnett's left and farther south, below the clump of trees (mostly of Kemper's center and Garnett's right), while providing fire support. After Armistead's surging tide of several hundred men finally reached the second row of four artillery pieces located on higher ground behind Cushing's two guns near the stone wall, the triumph had seemed nearly complete. But this "second line" of artillery also consisted of one of Arnold's remaining guns (in line with Cushing's four field pieces) to the north just above the Angle.

Arnold's battery was located on higher ground along the crest slightly northeast of Cushing's four field pieces of the second line, situated about 100 paces east of the stone wall. Despite Arnold's frantic efforts to remove his guns back to the crest, these field pieces were still vulnerable to Armistead's breakthrough just to the southwest. In fact, the removal of the first three guns, from right to left, left the southernmost three guns ripe to the attackers pouring through the Angle to outflank any field pieces on their left. After gaining the second line of artillery (Cushing's four guns directly south of Arnold's battery)—about halfway between the stone wall and the strategic crest with Armistead—Private Erasmus Williams, Company H (Meadville Greys), Armistead's brigade, wrote that Armistead, "who possessed a very loud voice," screamed in this key situation, "Turn the guns!"[1]

Amid the confusion surrounding the Angle, ironically, Generals Webb and Armistead came close to literally meeting each other face to face: a situation that might have resulted in an interesting personal grappling match between the two generals, as if in the ancient showdown between Achilles and Hector outside Troy's walls from the immortal pages of Homer's *Iliad*. In a letter to his wife, Webb penned how with "all my artillery in their hands . . . General Armistead, an old army officer, led his men, came over my [stone] fences and passed me with four of his men."[2]

Meanwhile, the Angle became even more of a killing zone with each passing minute, with the 69th Pennsylvania Irishmen putting up stiffer resistance. Attempting to turn one gun as directed by Armistead, Captain Benjamin L. Farinholt, who led Company E (Pamunkey Rifles), 53rd Virginia, was hit in the thigh and went down.[3] Twenty-one-year-old Lieutenant Thomas C. Holland, an ex-farmer now leading the Bedford County boys of Company G (Patty Layne Rifles), 28th Virginia, was "shot in the cheek and neck in the Angle," but survived his horrific wounds. Half a dozen Creasey boys of Holland's company were hit.[4]

After having enlisted belatedly in May 1862, the Meadville Greys private now found himself in the eye of the storm. Erasmus Williams, Company H, 14th Virginia, suffered from a badly bruised wrist struck by a shell fragment. But obeying Armistead's last order, Williams described: "I caught hold of one of the enemy's cannon. We got the gun turned towards the enemy [to the east on the open plateau along the crest], and I was in a few feet of Gen. Armistead [and Lieutenant] Col. R[awley] W[hite] Martin, of the 53rd of our brigade, was also within a few feet of Armistead."[5] Already wounded in the left foot by a shell fragment, Martin attempted to do his best in what seemed to be an impossible situation.[6] In attempting to turn the gun to face east, Williams also suffered a cut on the forefinger of his left hand.[7] Meanwhile, along the crest, General Webb's heroics in trying to stem the Confederate tide continued to pay dividends, while, in the general's words: "I stood but thirty-nine paces from them. Their officers pointed me out [for their men to fire at], but God preserved me."[8]

A veteran sergeant of the Meadville Greys (Company H), 14th Virginia, Drewry B. Easley, described how he "stepped off the [stone] fence with [Armistead and continued onward toward the crest, and then] We went up to the second line of artillery" just below the crest.[9] Armistead and his foremost soldiers were swept by volleys when attempting to turn Cushing's captured guns of the second captured artillery line to rake the blue legions descending upon them. In his early twenties, Captain Thomas C. Holland, Company G, (Patty Layne Rifles) 28th Virginia, was hit when a bullet smashed through his cheek and neck.

Forty-six-year-old Armistead was on borrowed time. He had advanced farther and deeper into the Union position than any general of Lee's army. Sergeant Frederick Fuger, who had taken charge of Cushing's battery after its commander's death, described the vicious close-range combat, before he retired: "I fired at Armistead with my pistol." Other Yankees took careful aim at the conspicuous Armistead. Pouring from three directions, the storm of bullets began to rapidly cut down the Rebels around Cushing's captured guns. Blasting away at Armistead, Colonel O'Kane's resurgent 69th Pennsylvania division, armed with Springfield and Enfield rifles, was filled with Irish nationalists that included father-son teams and brothers, determined to hurl the Rebels back across the stone wall. These resilient Irishmen accomplished more in now saving the day at the Angle than any other troops.

There, on the left of the row of four iron 3-inch guns of Battery A, 4th United States Artillery, General Armistead was hit by two "rifle balls" in the fleshy part of the arm. He also took a more serious injury when a bullet tore into the leg just below the knee. The resplendently uniformed general fell next to Cushing's No. 3 gun, dropping within a stone's throw of the strategic crest. A 69th Pennsylvania Irishman, Anthony W. McDermott, saw Armistead's fall, which was highly symbolic: "We poured fire upon him . . . until Armistead received his mortal wound [and he] made two or three staggering steps, reached out his hands trying to grasp at the muzzle of what was then the 1st piece of Cushing's battery, and fell. I was at the time the nearest person to him," when the general was cut down.

Compared to Captain Holland who had been hit in the face, Armistead was relatively fortunate, having taken less serious wounds. Hoping to regain the Angle like the 69th Pennsylvania, the 72nd Pennsylvania fought back with tenacity. A regimental file closer, Sergeant Easley described the volley that downed Armistead: "A squad of from twenty-five to fifty Yankees [of Webb's 72nd Pennsylvania] around a stand of colors to our left [north] fired a volley back at Armistead and he fell forward, his sword and hat almost striking a gun. I dropped behind the gun and commenced firing back at them. . . ." Colonel Martin and Lieutenant Carter also fell amid the torrent of bullets, along with the 53rd Virginia's battle flag that he had carried. Eight of the regiment's 10 color-bearers, who had followed Armistead, were killed on the field.[10] Color Corporal Robert Tyler Jones described the surreal nightmare of the day's deepest penetration: "In the excitement of the hour I only knew that I had reached the fortifications, when, faint from the loss of blood due to a shot in the head, I fell. My flag was found grasped in the hands of Gen. Armistead, who fell within the enemy's works among his own guns."[11]

Of Scotch-Irish descent and christened with the most American of first and middle names, Lieutenant George Williamson Finley, Company K (Harrison Guards), 56th Virginia, had charged into the Angle with Armistead up the slope of no return. He described the decimation because relatively "[f]ew of us" were now left standing at the point of the day's deepest penetration.[12] Nevertheless, some attackers, such as Lieutenant Thomas C. Holland, 28th Virginia, continued onward against the odds. Surging higher up the slope and ever closer to the strategic crest, the young lieutenant, not yet in his midtwenties, waved his hat and shouted, "Come on, boys," after Armistead was cut down. Holland was shortly felled with a shot through the cheek and one in the neck.[13] Ironically some of Garnett's men let Armistead down at that crucial moment. When teenaged Captain Waller M. Boyd, Company G (Nelson Guards), 19th Virginia and VMI Class of 1863, had leaped over the stone wall and implored his men to follow, no one ventured forth. Boyd was shortly felled with a bullet in the thigh.[14]

Lieutenant Frank W. Nelson, leading the Mechlenburg Guards, 57th Virginia, saw Armistead go down. He described how the brigade commander, just before he was hit, looked to the rear and sides and was shocked to see no reinforcements. Armistead then "shook his head, as if to say it could not be done. About this time he fell."[15] Sergeant Easley described Armistead's fatal wounding, when the attackers "went up to the second line of guns almost as close together as if we had been marching in ranks. . . . The squad that killed Armistead was [evidently from] the 71st Penn[sylvania]." Ironically, this sergeant was also at war with one of his comrades in arms. When Sergeant Easley encountered a soldier feigning a wound and lying low to avoid combat, he "clubbed the musket and started to burst his head with it . . . raising it as high as I could dropped it on the back of his head [and] he growned" as though "a shell struck him."[16] Meanwhile, other dependable leaders fell along with Armistead, including Robert McCulloch (VMI Class of 1864). Recently promoted to captain to lead the Danville Greys of Company B, 18th Virginia, McCulloch dropped inside the Angle with two wounds.[17]

Meanwhile, Armistead's survivors, like Sergeant Drewry B. Easley, 14th Virginia, continued to fight on against too many Yankees to count.[18] Color-bearers of the 14th Virginia, the 57th Virginia (Armistead's old regiment), and the 53rd Virginia (all of Armistead's brigade and fated to be captured along with the 9th Virginia's flag), when held by Lieutenant Hutchings Carter before he fell. Then, still another flag-bearer, having run a gauntlet of bullets, also reached the second line of captured guns. Four battle flags stood at the second row of Cushing's captured guns in defiance amid the hail of bullets.

Sergeant Easley felt pity for the courageous brigadier, who had led the way to the second line of artillery: "General Armistead did not move, groan, or speak while I fired several shots practically over his body; so I thought he had been killed instantly and did not speak to him."[19] Lieutenant George Washington Finley, 56th Virginia, described, "I went up to Gen. Armistead as he was lying close to the wheels of the gun on which he had put his hand, and stooping, looked into his face, and I thought from his appearance and position that he was then dead," which was not the case.[20] However, the advanced position of the 53rd Virginia's colors beside a captured gun, which had been finally turned toward the crest, of the second artillery line completed the color guard's thorough decimation. To achieve the ambitious goal of placing the regimental flag at the point of the deepest penetration of Meade's right-center, eight out of the 10-man color guard were killed and the other two wounded.[21]

Meanwhile, below the Angle and clump of trees, the majority of Virginia men (especially Kemper's center and left and Garnett's right), who were too intent on firing, too exhausted under a searing sun, or simply failing to see Armistead's final surge because of the thick battle smoke, remained in position behind the stone wall. They busily loaded and fired until rounds in cartridge-boxes ran out. Sergeant Major William S. Stockton, 71st Pennsylvania, blasted away at "the rebels [who] knelt along the wall as far as I could see to our left; kneeling down, firing over the wall."[22]

Captain John W. Jones had his surviving men of the Mecklenburg Spartans of Company B, 56th Virginia, Garnett's brigade, loading and firing as fast as possible. They believed that the day had been won.[23] But harsh realities dictated otherwise. They began to realize that they could not possibly hold out against the overpowering odds, an unkind fate, too many comrades lost, incompetent Confederate leadership, and the lack of reinforcements. Lee's best and brightest had become little more than sacrificial lambs, because no reinforcements were forthcoming. Many soldiers bitterly "blame[d] General Pickett for not getting us the order to fall back" to save themselves. Indeed, at the most critical moment, Pickett was nowhere to be seen.[24]

Clearly, sizeable reinforcements would have made a significant, if not decisive, difference in the outcome, especially in gaining either the Angle or the area below the clump of trees to rejoin the Virginians to enfilade Webb's sector from the south. Indeed, this vital point presented "the greatest danger to Union forces . . . because the advanced location of Webb's line exposed it to a cross fire, especially on the right. . . ."[25]

The Third and Final Struggle for the Stone Wall's Possession

Any chance of attacking north to roll up the Union line from the south—to relieve Pettigrew's foremost men pinned down before Hays's division so that they might resume the attack with those soldiers who had gained the stone wall—ended when the precarious position of Arnold's vacated battery, just northeast of the Angle on higher ground, was replaced by a fresh Union battery just in the nick of time: Lieutenant Gulian Weir and his Battery C, 5th United States Artillery. On what he described as "a small open plain," and despite his horse having been shot from under him, Weir deployed his six 12-pound Napoleons of the Artillery Reserve (once again proving invaluable in a vital situation). Then, these bronze smoothbores opened fire with double-shot canister on Pettigrew's men (Fry's Tennesseans and Alabamians and Marshall's North Carolina boys) and Pickett's soldiers (on the extreme north) who threatened to overrun this new battery.[26] Lieutenant Homer Baldwin, Weir's battery, wrote in a letter to his father not long after the battle that the "flashes of our pieces would scorch and set fire to the clothing of those that lay in front of us. I have seen many a big battle [but] I never saw the likes as this one."[27]

Near where Armistead went down at the second row of cannon of Cushing's battery, close to the crest (now roughly in line with Weir's guns just to the north above the east–west running stone wall of the Angle), Lieutenant Colonel Rawley White Martin commanded what little remained of the 53rd Virginia. The man who had dedicated his life to saving fellow human beings before the madness of the war had descended upon the land described the no-win situation this way: "By this time the Federal hosts lapped around both flanks, and made a counter advance in their front. . . ."[28] About to engage in a "general melee," wrote Webb, the rejuvenated 72nd Pennsylvania was finally ready to surge down the slope from the crest in a bid to reclaim the stone wall.[29]

By then the only regimental commander of Pickett's division beyond the stone wall still on his feet, Martin was one of the last of the foremost Rebel officers to fall around the captured guns of the Battery A, 4th United States Artillery. He was hit by three bullets, shattering his leg. In Martin's words: "I was disabled at Armistead's side a moment after he had fallen, on the Federal side of the rock fence" at the end of a vicious struggle in which "we tried to destroy each other. . . ."[30]

The sons of a respected Chatham County, Virginia, judge, the Tredway boys found themselves caught in the vortex of the storm whirling over the bloody Angle. Martin's "good friend," Sergeant Thomas Booker Tredway, Company I (Chatham Grays), 53rd Virginia, "ran to his assistance [but he] was shot and fell across his body." The sergeant had entered VMI in late January 1862, but took a 10-day furlough, joined up with his brother, and "did not return" to the Institute. Indeed, "not yet twenty years" of age, Tredway was captured and fated to die in a Gettysburg field hospital on July 13. His 24-year-old brother, Captain William Marshall Tredway, a married man who wondered if he would ever be reunited with his wife, was "Shot in the Angle."[31]

Besides an artillery piece of Cushing's decimated battery and its dead 22-year-old commander inside the Angle, Armistead lay in pain near the bodies of his fallen men. After having suffering three wounds, Armistead listened while bullets pelted off the captured iron guns, whose barrels glistened in the sun. Armistead feared that he would never again see his beloved boyhood home near the picturesque northern tip of the Shenandoah River country.[32]

Cut down about 30 yards before the second row of Cushing's guns, Lieutenant John Edward Dooley, Jr., 1st Virginia, described how by "my side lies Lt. Kehoe [Keough, a fellow Irishman], shot through the knee. Here we lie, he in excessive pain, I fearing to bleed to death, and dead and dying all around . . . We seem to have victory in our hands; but what can our poor remnant of a shattered division do if they meet beyond the guns an obstinate resistance? There—listen—we hear a new shout, and cheer after cheer rends the air. Are those fresh troops advancing to our support? No! no! That huzza never broke from southern lips. Oh God! Virginia's bravest, noblest sons have perished here today and perished all in vain!"[33]

Now back at the stone wall, after retiring back down the slope from where Armistead had fallen about halfway between the stone wall and the strategic crest, Lieutenant George Washington Finley, 56th Virginia, described "our men in line [at the stone wall] and encouraged them to look for support [but] then the Federals advanced in heavy force. The bullets seemed to come from front and both flanks . . . and soon the sharp[,] quick huzza!"[34] In the ranks of Company G (Portsmouth Rifles), 9th Virginia, Lieutenant John Henry Lewis, Jr., wrote that the survivors "with scarce any officers, look back over the field for the assistance that should have been there; but there are no troops in sight. We see ourselves being surrounded. The fire is already from both flanks and front; but yet they fight and die."[35]

Meanwhile to the north, among the band of 14th Tennessee soldiers and other men of Fry's left (while the 1st Tennessee on the right had penetrated the Angle), who had gained the stone wall and were "in the center [of the penetration and defiantly] held the works," Private "June" Kimble described how "for five, perhaps ten, minutes, we held our ground and looked back and prayed for support. It came not. . . ."[36]

But the unity between Pettigrew's soldiers on the far right with Pickett's men on the far left was permanently severed by the blistering fire from the guns of Weir's newly arrived battery, which had just filled the gap left by Arnold's cannon just northeast of the Angle. At close range from their elevated perch that overlooked such a wide area of open fields, the guns of Battery C, 5th United States Artillery, unleashed double-loads of canister. Because of the luxury of having an artillery reserve (unlike Lee), these roaring guns were now in the right place—just above the Angle at the northern edge of Armistead's breakthrough—at exactly the right time. Combined with rippling volleys from Hays's nearby infantrymen, this "Hellish fire" from Weir's pieces when the attackers were only

20 feet away "cleared the slope" in murderous fashion. Indeed, these double loads of canister left the ground covered with dead, moaning, and twisting men, the elite of their units. The withering blasts from Weir's guns also turned Pickett's northernmost men (either Garnett's or Armistead's boys, or both) south and back toward the Angle, especially its inner wall of stone, to escape the fire sweeping down the grassy slope.[37]

When the weary Virginians glanced back in the hope of catching sight of the reinforcements, they only saw the broad, open fields, framed by the long range of blue-hazed mountains on the western horizon. These fields were now filled with the seemingly endless number of bodies of dead and wounded comrades instead of advancing reinforcements. Beside Armistead's fallen body, Private Erasmus Williams, 14th Virginia, described the ultimate nightmare scenario for the men who had overrun the second line of artillery near the crest: "As we looked over the field we could see now the enemy advancing in front and on our left and right at the same time, and when we looked back we could see that no reinforcements were coming. If either Wilcox's brigade or any other body of good troops could have arrived at this time, I think we could have held our ground" and won the day.[38]

Even more, the eastern slope of the ridge behind the Angle was open and not steep but gentle (like the western slope), which would have allowed an easy advance (especially by Stuart's cavalry from the east) and deeper penetration to split Meade's army in two, if only the long-awaited reinforcements arrived in time. Meanwhile, Private Williams and other survivors fought from the relative safety of the stone wall now raked by bullets. They continued to blast away at their increasing number of antagonists, especially the 69th Pennsylvania Irish, who seemed to be coming from every direction. The fighting Irish of the 69th were determined to regain the Angle. Symbolically, Armistead, near the strategic crest and within sight of his great goal, was left behind by the relatively few survivors. This unavoidable abandonment of the day's most successful Confederate leader later induced considerable guilt among survivors for not having carried Armistead rearward.[39]

In his diary, Captain Griggs, 38th Virginia, whose commander, VMI graduate (Class of 1858) Colonel Edward Claxton Edmonds, age 28 and the former principal of the Danville [Virginia] Military Academy, was killed, explained the ugly realities once the momentum of the assault was spent, after they "capture[d] all their guns but we had lost too many to hold our trophies & having no reinforcements & the enemy being on our flanks & rear" to make the situation of those who had surged across the stone wall more precarious than ever before.[40] As in every regiment, some of the 38th Virginia's finest leaders were lost by that time. Having led his 38th Virginia boys with his usual skill, despite having lost his arm at Malvern Hill in the previous July, Lieutenant Colonel Powhatan Bolling Whittle, standing at six foot, four inches, had been cut down with multiple wounds.[41]

As revealed by the words of Colonel Edmonds, the captured six guns of Cushing's battery, and at least one of Arnold's guns, were prized "trophies" that had to be abandoned, including one that had been turned on the Yankees. However, one band of Rebels, perhaps obeying one of Armistead's final directives, attempted "to drag off a gun & were actually rolling it down the slope," wrote one incredulous Federal in his diary.[42] There would have been no need to attempt to push the field pieces rearward had Stuart's horsemen arrived to strike from the rear as Lee planned. But Stuart and thousands of his cavalrymen were nowhere to be seen in the open fields on the eastern slope of Cemetery Ridge: a bold tactical vision and dream deferred.[43]

Savage Hand-to-Hand Combat at the Copse of Trees

The men who had gained the stone wall and the clump of trees continued to inflict damage on the resurgent Yankees, especially the 69th Pennsylvania. One Rebel excelled in the grisly art of killing his fellow man. He was an expert marksman who almost never missed a shot. Firing through a narrow gap in the stone wall where piled-up stones had been either knocked down or deliberately removed, Private James D. Lunceford, of Company F (Blue Mountain Boys), 8th Virginia, on the far right of Garnett's brigade, blasted away through this ideal firing position that provided protection. Meanwhile, comrades, including a brother, hurriedly hand-loaded and passed muskets to Lunceford in an assembly line of death. Because of the density of the encroaching blue ranks, some of Lunceford's well-aimed bullets dropped two men with a single shot, with the bullet whizzing completely through the foremost Federal to find another victim immediately behind him. From this vantage point, this especially young Blue Mountain Boy "killed more men than any other during the assault."[44]

However, Lunceford fell wounded and was captured. He was fated to die a captivity prisoner in a filthy northern prison, earning a shallow grave in New Jersey soil in 1864. James paid the ultimate price for "getting two [Yankees] at a crack."[45] However, like a Greek tragedy that mocked man's folly because the gods always punished prideful individuals—especially those who underestimated an opponent or situation but never themselves—the ever-dwindling band of survivors battled against a cruel fate. Lieutenant George Washington Finley, 56th Virginia, saw the inevitable: "I saw that we could not hold the [stone] fence any longer."[46]

All the while, Colonel Norman J. Hall's men, including the 19th Massachusetts Volunteer Regiment and the 42nd New York Volunteer Infantry, and General William Harrow's troops (all 2nd Division, 2nd Corps men) steadily converged on the Angle and the clump of trees from the south, where they had been originally positioned. From the south to stem the breakthrough and recapture Cushing's guns, Harrow's and Hall's troops charged north up the ascending ground leading to the copse of trees then filled with fast-firing Rebels. The 15th Massachusetts Volunteer Infantry, Harrow's Brigade, exchanged volleys with Kemper's 11th and 24th Virginia on the south. These close-range exchanges of musketry were so costly to the Yankees (including de-horsing and wounding General Hancock) that one New England private yelled, "[T]hey'll kill us all if we stand here." Bolstered by the arrival of fresh artillery, Hall's, Webb's, and Harrow's troops decided not to withdraw but to advance, closing in on the surviving Confederates with fixed bayonets.

A timely arrival, these fresh blue waves gave new life to Webb's battered troops, including rallied 71st and 72nd Pennsylvania troops, providing a most timely reinforcement. The Philadelphians surged down the slope in a jumbled "fighting mass" of men (basically a "mob" without order). The hard-fighting 69th Pennsylvania Irish were also part of the sweeping counterattack from the crest. In the words of Captain Robert McBride, 71st Pennsylvania, "[W]e charged right down to the wall . . . and I captured the colors of a rebel standard" in the melee. Along the stone wall, savage hand to hand combat erupted, especially around red and blue battle flags that represented homes, families, and homelands far away.

Men, whose uniforms were burned by blasts fired from muskets at close range, fought desperately over their colors. Despite having lost all of their field officers, the Irish of Colonel Dennis O'Kane's 69th Pennsylvania, Webb's brigade, fought furiously as if to redeem a subjugated Ireland's reputation on their finest day. These Emerald Islanders struggled hand to hand with Garnett's soldiers on the north and Kemper's men on the south, and Armistead's surviving Rebels as well. One Irish captain in blue was slashed over the head by a saber in a Virginia officer's hand. In a true "donnybrook," an Irish sergeant wrote that "we battered the 'rebs' on the head with our guns." One Son of Erin had his head smashed by a rifle butt swung by one of Kemper's men. Likewise, the nightmarish contest in Kemper's sector below the 69th Pennsylvania was especially vicious, with the soldiers "fighting pretty much at will." Major Edmund Rice, 19th Massachusetts, described how the "men now suffered from the enfilading fire of the enemy who were in the copse" of trees, where a last stand was made. The 7th Michigan Volunteer Infantry and the resurgent 59th New York, which was followed by the 20th Massachusetts (all of Hall's brigade), and the Harrow's regiments struck the right flank of Kemper's fast-firing men.

In Major Rice's words: "All the time the crush toward the enemy in the copse of trees was becoming greater [while the] men in gray were doing all that was possible to keep off the mixed bodies of men who were moving upon them swiftly and without hesitation, keeping up so close and continuous a fire that at last its effects became terrible [and the copse of trees] was fairly jammed with Pickett's men, in all positions, lying and kneeling. Back from the edge [of the copse] were many standing and firing over those in front."[47] Such a hot fire was concentrated on the copse defenders that the chestnut oak trees "were soon to be stripped of their bark by the bullets" of a perfect hail.[48]

Perhaps a shot fired by an Irish Rebel from Virginia struck a fellow countryman of the 69th Pennsylvania square in the chest. However, Corporal John Cassidy was momentarily saved because the bullet hit his prayer book, *The Manual of the Christian Soldier*, positioned before his heart. Nevertheless, a mortal wound had been inflicted upon the young Irish-born corporal.[49] Battling with what little remained of the Portsmouth Rifles (Company G, 9th Virginia), Lieutenant John Henry Lewis, Jr., lamented how by this time all other Southern troops (Pettigrew) "had vanished from the field, and Pickett's division, or what is left of it, is [now] fighting the whole Federal center alone."[50]

The sweeping counterattack of the jumbled blue ranks that had rolled down the body-strewn slope hit the exhausted Rebels exceptionally hard. Assisted by the advantage of charging across a gently descending slope, this final offensive effort to hurl back the once-elated soldiers who had gained possession of the Angle and copse of trees was very much an instinctive one led from veteran enlisted men, after so many officers had been cut down. Perhaps Sergeant John Plummer, one reinforcing bluecoat, wrote: "[E]very man fought on his own hook [as] few officers were left. Each man acted as though he felt what was at stake [and] did all in their power to drive the enemy, without regard to officers [while] Regiments all mixed up together. . . ."[51]

Echoing the sergeant's words, a 1st Minnesota soldier, Private Daniel Bond, explained that "we knew how to defend our hills" to the bitter end.[52] In meeting the breakthrough head-on, Bond explained, "We wanted no command but moved to our right to meet them sending bullets into them as fast as we could load and fire [and after] they planted their colors on two pieces of Battery A [and here] they . . . mass[ed] on that point and we had them with a thin semicircle [of fire]. They could never lift their colors from these guns so deadly was our fire [with] Every man fighting on his own hook."[53] But enough fighting spirit remained among the Virginians to present a united front in the face of hundreds of onrushing Federals. With the 56th Virginia's survivors on Garnett's left, Lieutenant George Washington Finley wrote that the "Federal line pressed on until our men fired almost into their faces."[54]

And even when out of ammunition, some desperate boys in blue hurled stones. In the words of William Lochran, 1st Minnesota, Harrow's Brigade, "The bayonet was used for a few minutes, and cobble stones [now] filled the air, being thrown by those in the rear over the heads of their comrades," including those Minnesota soldiers who captured the battle flag of the 28th Virginia, on Garnett's left, in the Angle around Cushing's second row of guns.[55] Wiping the stain from their earlier flight from the Angle, the 71st Pennsylvania soldiers "fought our way down to the wall," with frantic men cursing, slashing with sabers, firing muskets, and thrusting bayonets on their bloody way through worn Rebels, whose momentum had been spent.[56] Despite their color-bearer having been cut down, the 72nd Pennsylvania charged in a "maddened" crowd, which "rolls to the walls [where] flesh meets flesh. . . ."[57] One of Pickett's men, E. C. Wilson, described how he "[w]as wounded twelve times . . . Received two saber cuts on the back of the head, had end of thumb shot off, wounded in knee, and several small wounds [but] we drove the enemy forty feet and we had a hard hand to hand fight."[58]

Captain John D. S. Cook, 80th New York, noted an especially horrible feature of the intense hand to hand combat: "A curious thing about this fighting was that although all the men were armed with bayonets, no one seemed to be using them. Those nearest clubbed their muskets and beat each other over the head. . . ."[59] This perception of the bloody struggle in and around the Angle was seconded by Confederate survivors of the most vicious combat that they had ever seen.[60] James Wilson, Company F, 72nd Pennsylvania struggled against Rebels, who made their last stand on the open slope just east of the stone wall: "[W]e fought hand to hand and clubbed guns, any way at all; each man picked out his man, that last a very short time and they fell back, what was left of them."[61] Most symbolically in a mini civil war of Irish in blue, especially the men of the 69th Pennsylvania, once again meeting Irish in gray amid a savage flurry of hand to hand combat, Irish Sergeant Thomas Murphy, Company G, carried the 72nd Pennsylvania's colors over the stone wall and in the recapture of Cushing's two advanced guns, while his cheering Irish comrades followed.[62]

Beside the last band of his surviving men of Company I (Chatham Grays), 53rd Virginia, Captain William Marshall Tredway, Jr., was "[s]hot down in the Angle," along with his top lieutenant, Hutchings Lanier Carter, who was felled (as mentioned) and captured, along with the company's father-son Tidewater team, Privates John H. Meadows, Jr., and John H. Meadows, Sr., both of whom had enlisted in Suffolk, Virginia, in late March 1862.[63] Meanwhile, among the final defenders at the stone wall, at least one known (certainly there were more) brother team fought tenaciously to defend their advanced position against the odds. As mentioned, defiant soldiers like Private James D. Lunceford, Company F (Blue Mountain Boys), 8th Virginia, stood their ground. Before he fell wounded, Lunceford fired rapidly, thanks to his brother, Corporal Benjamin R. Lunceford, busily loading and capping muskets for him. Another Lunceford clan member fired nearby from a nearly empty cartridge-box, Private Evans O. Lunceford, Company C (Evergreen Guards), 8th Virginia.[64]

Near the body-strewn Angle amid the blinding smoke not blown away by any breeze, Lieutenant John Henry Lewis, Jr., Company G (Portsmouth Rifles), 9th Virginia, described the bitter end of the loftiest Southern dreams: "The men fought with desperation, cool and courageous[ness], until surrounded on all sides."[65] Thanks to good cover, some surviving Rebels continued to defend the clump of trees to the bitter end, while the thicket was covered with "wounded and dead."[66] Even when Virginia boys ran out of ammunition, they continued to fight back in desperation, finding stones to hurl at the encroaching Yankees in last acts of desperate defiance.[67]

Just south of the clump of trees, the 80th New York, consisting of mostly men from Ulster County (named after Ulster Province, Northern Ireland, a place that had special meaning to the Irish Virginians) surged northwest toward the stone wall. They tangled with Kemper's survivors, who faced a hot fire from the south that raked their right flank and front. In his diary, Major Walter A. Van Rensselaer, of Dutch descent that reflected the early Dutch settlement of New York City (then known as New Amsterdam), described: "Near a slash of timber [copse of trees], I discovered a Rebel flag behind the fence in the hands of an officer [Colonel William Richard Terry, 24th Virginia]—I demanded its surrender—he replied 'not by a damned sight' and fired at me with his revolver, wounding me in the small of the back. I lunged at him with my saber when he fired again, the ball striking my saber scabbard—five or six of my boys came to the rescue and he surrendered, following by his whole regiment [the 24th Virginia on Kemper's far right and the 11th Virginia, which had advanced on Kemper's right-center with just over 400 men]—they came over the fence like a flock of sheep—think we captured, at least, 1500 prisoners."[68] The largest regiment of Kemper's brigade, and hence its key position on the brigade's right flank, the 24th Virginia had entered the attack with around 450 men, and more than half of these men were cut down.[69]

But many of Kemper's soldiers on the mauled right escaped, falling back in small groups to minimize targets. After picking up muskets from the fallen comrades, officers in gray gamely fired back in desperation, but nothing could alter the outcome of the battle. In a letter, young Lieutenant John Thomas James (VMI Class of 1863) of Company D (Fincastle Rifles) described: "Some of the men had taken possession of the cannon, when we saw the enemy advancing heavy reinforcements. We looked back for ours, but in vain; we were compelled to fall back and had again to run as targets to their balls. Oh, it was hard, too hard to be compelled to give way for the want of men, after having fought as hard as we had that day. We gained nothing but glory and lost our bravest men."[70] And they also lost precious battle flags, including four regimental colors of Armistead's brigade, the 9th Virginia, 53rd Virginia, 14th Virginia, and 57th Virginia in the Angle.

Meanwhile, to the north, one of the last remaining regimental banners of Pickett's division was carried off the crest and toward Seminary Ridge until captured on the north by a sergeant of the 8th Ohio, which continued to advance south to outflank the fleeing Rebels and inflict additional damage.[71] But it was no easy chore to capture the tattered battle flag of the 19th Virginia, Garnett's brigade, to the south. A corporal of Hispanic descent from Boston named Private Joseph H. De Castro swung the flagstaff of the banner of the 19th Massachusetts (which launched a counterattack northwest toward the eastern edge of the clump of trees) and toppled the Virginia color-bearer with a mighty blow. He became the first Hispanic to win the Medal of Honor.[72]

Because Longstreet had only belatedly sent Wilcox's Alabama brigade and then stopped Wright's and Posey's brigades from supporting Pickett on the right to eliminate the growing Vermont threat, Stannard's Vermont troops continued to surge north through the wide, open fields of the Upper Plum Run Valley on the Codori Farm. These New Englanders steadily punished Kemper's Virginians, especially the 11th Virginia and 24th Virginia boys, with sweeping volleys that cut down Johnny Rebs like "wheat before a reaper," in one Yankee's words. The rampaging Vermonters also scooped up additional prisoners, and even the flag of the "Old Bloody Eighth" Virginia, Garnett's brigade. Despite no hope for success or even salvation, some die-hard Virginians remained defiant to the bitter end. Private Edward Freeman described the horror of the high cost of Rebel defiance against the odds: "My comrade shot a rebel right in the head because he would not give up his gun."[73]

But without infantry or artillery support, the vast majority of Kemper's men, especially those on the right that had been especially hard-hit by the Vermonters' flank fire, retired to save themselves. With their fighting blood up, some Vermont soldiers persisted in the ugly business of killing. At least one Rebel was shot down—a "dastardly act" condemned by his comrades—after having surrendered.[74] In a rare admission that revealed the forgotten horrors of Pickett's Charge, Sergeant John Plummer, 1st Minnesota, "We took revenge for what they had done to our poor fellows the day before [in part because] we never had had such a chance before."[75]

But in truth, the systematic killing of Rebels could have been much more extensive. When one Virginia lieutenant was hesitant in complying with a shouted demand to surrender his sword, the scholarly Lieutenant Stephen F. Brown, Company K, 13th Vermont, took an extreme step. Hardly resembling the former part-time schoolteacher since age 16 and a lover of Greek and Latin, the 20-year-old Brown raised "a common camp hatchet" instead of his "elegant Sword" that had been taken away when recently arrested. He was just about to strike with the unorthodox weapon "as it glistened in the sun," until the shocked Old Dominion officer quickly unbuckled his sword belt and handed over to Lieutenant Brown. Brown had meant business, like an Abenaki warrior (allied with the French) raiding an isolated New England settlement on a wintery dawn during the French and Indian War.[76] Ironically, upon having been presented his handsome sword by the people of Montpelier, Vermont, Lieutenant Brown had solemnly sworn: "It shall be used to strike terror into the hearts of traitors . . . in the maintenance of the best government that the light of the sun ever shone upon."[77]

The Last of Pettigrew's Men Fall Back

Meanwhile, Pettigrew's men likewise fell back at nearly the same time that Pickett's soldiers retired. Too many good soldiers, especially officers, had been cut down, such as David A. Coon, known as "Honest David" of the 11th North Carolina, Pettigrew's brigade. He was hit nine times "in less than nine minutes." One 26th North Carolina officer of the same brigade, Major John Thomas "Knock" Jones, described how, after gaining the stone wall, "we received a murderous fire upon our left flank [because] we were completely upon our left, not only by infantry, but artillery [because] one of the brigades of our division [Brockenbrough] had given way, the enemy had seized upon the gap, and now poured a galling fire into our left, which compelled the troops to give way in succession, to the right. At the very moment I thought victory ours, I saw it snatched from our hands."[78] On the left (or north) of the 26th North Carolina, Lieutenant William B. Taylor and his battered 11th North Carolina also fell back. Out of the 30 soldiers in Taylor's company, only eight men were left standing, while the lieutenant had bullet holes through his uniform and a dent in his scabbard from a lead ball.[79]

In a letter to a fellow officer written in early 1864, Captain Louis Gourdin Young, one of Pettigrew's aide-de-camps who survived Gettysburg's nightmare to eventually find success in the family's cotton business, summarized the bitter end: "Subjected to a fire even more fatal than that which had driven back the brigade [Brockenbrough] on our left, the men listening in vain for the cheery command of officers who has, alas! fallen, our [North Carolina under Marshall, who had been killed] brigade gave way likewise, and simultaneously, with the whole line."[80]

Streaked with dirt and blood after having his horse shot out from under him and an iron canister smashing into his left arm, Major "Knock" Jones (a childhood nickname for his youthful combativeness) knew that the end had come at last, after surveying the field strewn with North Carolina bodies. A promising son from the fertile Yadkin Valley of western North Carolina and a student of University of North Carolina at Chapel Hill, the major had been luckier than most high-ranking fellow officers on that bloody afternoon in hell. Knowing that discretion was the better part of valor, the 22-year-old Jones ordered around 60 surviving "pine knots" (a complimentary term for North Carolina toughness) rearward around the same time that Pickett's Virginians began to fall back.[81] Major Jones's order saved the last few survivors of the 26th North Carolina, which suffered the highest losses (687 men) of any regiment during the three days at Gettysburg, at about 85 percent.[82]

Private "Jack" Moore, 7th Tennessee, described the bitter end for the survivors of Fry's brigade: "[A]s victory was about to crown our efforts, a large body of troops moved resolutely upon our left flank, and our extreme right at the same time began to give way, as did our left. Still we in the center held the works, but finally, being unsupported, we were forced to fall back [because] Those of the second line who reached the Emmitsburg road never moved beyond that point to our assistance."[83] Contrary to popular perceptions and myths about the lack of determination and valor of Pettigrew's division, the command lost more attackers than Pickett's division.[84]

The Last Virginians Depart Cemetery Ridge

The opportunity to exploit the breach in Meade's right-center gradually faded away like a soft summer evening. The confident troops who had swarmed over the stone wall with such high hopes had waited in vain and "for fully twenty minutes," as emphasized by Captain John Holmes Smith, 11th Virginia, on Kemper's right-center.[85] Just to the left, or north, of the 11th Virginia, the band of 1st Virginia survivors had dwindled to almost nothing by that time. A lowly lieutenant commanded what little was left of the decimated regiment of mostly Richmond and Henrico County soldiers: Edward P. Reeve, Company D (Old Dominion Guard). A former clerk from Richmond, Lieutenant Reeve had seen his immediate commanding officer, Captain George F. Norton (VMI Class of 1860) fall.

All other company commanders had been killed or wounded, and the regiment's leader, Colonel Lewis Burwell Williams, Jr., and his top lieutenants, such as Major Francis H. Langley, likewise had been cut down. Captain William Fry, Kemper's adjutant, had earlier given Reeve orders to advance the regiment in a final bid to gain Cemetery Ridge's crest, but only about a dozen survivors of the "Old First" rose up from the stone wall and formed into line for the final challenge. When these relatively few men started to drop from a hot fire, a frustrated Lieutenant Reeve yelled out in anguish that there was no regiment left to obey the last order. Nevertheless, Lieutenant Reeve had led a handful of soldiers forward until cut down in the last advance of Pickett's division. Surviving men of the 1st Virginia, which suffered the highest percentage loss (62 percent) of Kemper's brigade, then retired down the grassy slope choked with bodies. They unknowingly left behind the regimental colors where they had fallen at the stone wall, where Private Jacob Polak, Company I, had been cut down.[86] Captain Alphonso N. Jones, 7th Virginia, on Kemper's left center and just to the 1st Virginia's left, and an ex-farmer, described the final struggle: "Heavy reinforcements were moved upon us by the enemy, and the sanguinary conflict was renewed with redoubled violence; and after fifteen minutes we were driven from the enemy's works."[87]

On the far left flank, the 3rd Virginia was the last regiment of Kemper's brigade to retire, after the brigade's other mauled regiments to the south withdrew from the smoky cauldron. Commanding the 3rd Virginia, 29-year-old Colonel Joseph Mayo, Jr., was the luckiest regimental commander of Pickett's division: a VMI graduate (Class of 1852), he was the only regimental commander not killed or wounded. Mayo, therefore, commanded what was left of Kemper's brigade. He also was the sole remaining representative of VMI, after seven VMI colonels had been killed or wounded.[88]

Anguished by the non-arrival of reinforcements, the saddened colonel had seen his regiment cut to pieces. Company F (Nansemond Rangers), on the regiment's far right, lost 24 out of 25 men killed or wounded. Among the victims, Captain C. Crawley Phillips, the scholarly "professor" who went from enlightening young minds to destroying as many Yankee lives as possible, was killed, and his top lieutenant, Azra P. Gomer, a former clerk in his midtwenties, was cut down at the stone wall.[89]

Just to the north on Kemper's left and despite Virginians either falling back or remaining under cover of the stone wall to surrender, one defiant sergeant of the 8th Virginia, on Garnett's far right, was still full of fight. Sergeant Randolph Abbott Shotwell looked north in the hope that the breach was widened in Pettigrew's sector: "Thinking the North Carolinians had secured a lodgment on the crest, I picked up a musket and started to move towards the left. But on firing the gun (which probably had three charges rammed down one upon the other, as was common in the excitement of battle) it kicked so violently as to nearly cause me to turn a somersault. When I recovered myself the enemy was pouring a terrific volley into the retreating Confederates and all was over."[90]

Lieutenant John Abbott J. Lee, who still possessed plenty of fighting spirit like other Craig Mountains Boys (Company C), 28th Virginia, Garnett's left-center, was proud of the fact that he had been the first soldier of Pickett's division to gain the stone wall. Lee, therefore, was not finished fighting. When the blue tide finally descended upon him from three sides, and taking a wound, Lieutenant Lee knew that the bitter end had come. Symbolically, when he fell near one of Cushing's 3-inch Ordnance Rifles, so dropped the regimental colors that he had planted on the stone wall, when it appeared that a decisive victory had been won. But the young lieutenant still held tightly to the flagstaff. Lee was horrified at the thought that he would be forced to surrender his saber. As best he could with a wound dripping blood, Lieutenant Lee tried to break his sword blade in two. But a "big, burly German" officer, who faced Virginia Rebels of German heritage in a forgotten Teutonic civil war, demanded Lee's saber. Lee felt thankful when a comrade rushed over in the nick of time and thrust his bayonet into the midsection of the oversized Teutonic officer.[91]

While most of their comrades retired on the double back down the gory slope, the most never-say-die Rebels still remained in advanced positions. They were still hoping against hope that some kind of divine intervention might still prevail. Instead, these powder-stained soldiers who remained at the stone wall were quickly taken prisoner.[92] Meanwhile, survivors of the carnage headed back down the slope in the running of a deadly gauntlet. Lieutenant George Washington Finley, on Garnett's left, described the death of Confederate ambitions: "I again looked back over the field to see the chances of withdrawing. The men who had begun to fall back seemed to be dropping as they ran, like leaves . . . It seemed foolhardy to attempt to get back[.] I ordered the few men around me to 'cease firing' and surrendered."[93] Despite the hopeless situation, not everyone was as ready to surrender as Lieutenant Finley. After having carried the 53rd Virginia colors and despite bleeding from two wounds, including in the arm, teenaged Color Corporal Robert Tyler Jones, was not giving up. Therefore, with a drawn revolver, he threatened to shoot down anyone who attempted to surrender.[94] In his diary, Sergeant Levin Christopher Gayle summarized the inglorious finale: "[W]e charged the works and tak [sic] A section of them and holde [sic] them 20 minutes and then the first thing that I knew they had me [surrounded and] hemed [sic] up and carried me to the rear" as a prisoner of war.[95]

Bloody Finis

Colonel Clinton MacDougall, of Scotch-Irish descent and the 111th New York Infantry's commander, described the unbelievable sight: "When the smoke cleared away . . . The high tide of the Rebellion had been reached and the fate of the CONFEDERATE STATES OF AMERICA was sealed."[96] A Confederate artilleryman felt the same: "many of us shed tears at the way in which our dreams of liberty had ended" on the body-strewn open fields of

Adams County.[97] Indeed, Cemetery Ridge's defenders of the 2nd Corps had "fought and dug Secession's grave" in the fertile soil of Adams County.[98]

But perhaps a saddened Lieutenant Colonel Rawley White Martin, 53rd Virginia, who received multiple serious wounds during the charge through the Angle and was now a prisoner of war, said it best in a letter to his father in a sad lament to an infant republic that had received a mortal wound on July 3: "Oh, my country, my country."[99] One of Lee's surviving Irishmen also used his favorite phrase by invoking Ireland's patron saint because of the cruel twist of fate that ensured a bloody repulse: "Holy Saint Patrick."[100]

Near the copse of trees with his victorious 14th Connecticut, Sergeant Hirst described in a letter: "the Exhultant [sic] Shouts of our Brave Boys as the while Rebel force gave way in utter confusion [while] leaving thousands and thousands of Killed, Wounded and Missing in our hands. What a sight it was, where but a short time before had stood the Flower of the Rebel Army in all the Pomp of Pride and Power was now covered with Dead in every conceivable Posture. Our [2nd] Corp[s] alone Captured 30 Stand of Colers [sic] our Division taking 13 of them, 6 of which were captured by our own little Regt, besides this we took more Prisoners then we numbered men."[101] After having been cut down with wounds in both thighs within around 30 yards of the strategic crest, Lieutenant John Edward Dooley, Jr., 1st Virginia, described the anguish: "Virginia's bravest, noblest sons have perished here today and perished all in vain!"[102]

Just to the north, the Connecticut regiment's sister regiment of the brigade, the 12th New Jersey's survivors, positioned along the stone wall just below the Brien barn, were sickened when "the smoke lifted [and then] what a horrible sight [because Pettigrew's] Dead and dying everywhere, the ground almost covered with them" as far as the eye could see.[103] Feeling fortunate to have survived the slaughter, especially after having seen Confederate officers pointing him out for marksmen to cut down during the close-range combat at the Angle, General Webb wrote in amazement to his wife that Armistead "was killed within 40 feet of me & in my rear."[104]

Meanwhile, on Seminary Ridge, Major Poague, who was ready to obey his orders to go forward with his artillery, rode up to General Pickett, who was "looking intently to the front," and asked, "General, my orders are that as soon as our troops get the hill I am to move as rapidly as possible to their support." Pickett refused to look at the impatient major, but only "continued to gaze with an expression on his face of sadness and pain."[105]

Pickett and Poague simultaneously realized that it was over when they saw the most sickening sight of all. In Major Poague's words, "At that instant a [dark blue] Virginia flag was borne rapidly along and in the rear of the stone wall by a horseman. . . ."[106] On the body-strewn crest, Captain Haskell watched the Yankees celebrate their success by tossing around the most cherished objects of the vanquished. Haskell wondered, "Are these red cloths that our men toss about in derision the 'fiery Southern crosses' thrice ardent, the battle flags of the rebellion that [recently] waved in defiance at the wall?"[107]

Meanwhile, the last flurries of combat for the possession of flags continued while the survivors retired down the body-strewn slope. On the far north, the eyes of a sergeant of Company G, 8th Ohio, widened when he spied the flag of the 34th North Carolina, Scales's brigade (under Colonel Lowrance), and a handful of weary guardians. A shell exploded above the band of men, knocking the dazed color-bearer to his knees. "Covered with dust, the blood trickling from a gash on his forehead." A young North Carolina officer, despite being wounded, grabbed the flag before it touched the ground to avoid the ultimate disgrace. The Ohio sergeant demanded the colors from the injured officer, who was alone and with an empty revolver. The wounded officer refused, and then dodged a bayonet thrust "with great dexterity." Sergeant John Miller then demanded, "Surrender, or I'll shoot you." Instead, the Tar Heel officer made his own thrust with his saber that cut the sergeant's wrist. Now "Miller had to shoot [and] The Southern[er] fell backward upon his banner [and] So tight was his grasp on the staff that Miller had to tear off the flag."[108] But no amount of heroics could save these prized banners, then shredded by bullets. Garnett's brigade lost every one of its (five) regimental flags.[109]

Back on Seminary Ridge, meanwhile, Major Poague informed Pickett, "Our men are leaving the hill," but the general again made no reply.[110] Poague was now horrified by the sight of "a Virginia flag [that] was borne rapidly along and in rear of the stone wall."[111] This Old Dominion flag might have been the one taken from a defiant flag bearer, an officer, who had to be subdued by half a dozen rough-and-tumble New York soldiers in order to secure the prized banner.[112] Like Achilles, the legendary warrior of the ancient Greeks, dragging the body of Hector around Troy's walls behind his chariot, General Hays, mounted on his third horse after the first two animals had been shot from under him, continued to drag the battle flag behind him, while galloping down the line. And as with Achilles, so the angry gods of war were destined to strike Hays down in less than a year, because of his contemptuous gesture that revealed hubris: in early May 1864, Hays was shot in the head and killed at the Wilderness, Virginia, where the 26th North Carolina's beloved commander, Major John "Knock" Jones was also killed.

Taking their cue, Hayes's young aides joined the fun. They also dragged other captured Confederate battle flags in the dust of Cemetery Ridge, after pulling them out of grotesque piles of bodies. The "Blue Birds" of Hays's division (New Jersey, Delaware, Connecticut, and New York boys) cheered wildly and threw their kepis in the smoke-laced air. They celebrated not only the repulse but also the greatest harvest of Rebel banners in the army's history.[113] Meanwhile, the victors busily gathered additional trophies, especially officers' sabers that were scattered across this grim field of harvest. One Yankee cut off the three stars insignia from both sides of General Garnett's gray collar, guaranteeing that his body would never be identified. Garnett, therefore, was destined to be thrown into a shallow burial trench with his hard-fighting common soldiers, whom he loved like his children.[114]

Rebel survivors now realized that had Lee's top lieutenants, especially Longstreet, only performed like Stonewall Jackson, then decisive victory would have been reaped. As Pickett penned in a July 8, 1863, letter to his wife: "We were ordered to take a height [and] We took it. . . ."[115] Contrary to the romance of Lost Cause mythology, Pickett's Charge was indeed a very close thing. If the attack had been properly supported in a timely manner, Lee would have certainly achieved his most decisive victory of the war.

As mentioned, Longstreet failed to utilize the troops of Anderson's division to protect the flanks of the attack. Then, too little, too late and attacking too far south, Wilcox's and Lang's attack of two brigades, about 1,400 Alabama and Florida men, respectively, was easily outflanked. Longstreet had failed to ensure that these two brigades attacked on Pickett's heels to exploit the breakthrough. Then, they had marched straight east into the face of the terrible fire of McGlivery's reserve batteries instead of northeast (to compensate for Pickett's move to the left to face the clump of trees), effectively splitting the assault in two. Without having been easily pushed aside by Wilcox and Lang by a flank attack, Stannard's inexperienced Vermont soldiers on the south wreaked havoc on Kemper's southern flank, charging farther north to deliver a flank attack that played a key role in compromising Pickett's Charge. Then, the 16th Vermont smashed into the flank of Perry's Floridians, Lang's brigade, and quickly hurled them rearward, capturing most of the 2nd Florida and its colors. Its sister regiment, the 14th Vermont, not only also inflicted severe damage, but also captured five battle flags of the Florida boys.

Young Private Lewis Thornton Powell, Company I (Jasper Guards), 2nd Florida, was one Florida soldier (known as "Flowers" for their subtropical homeland) of the hard-fighting little brigade that suffered the highest loss, 62 percent, of any comparable command in the Gettysburg Campaign. Although wounded and captured, the Alabama-born Powell, age 19 and raised in Jasper, Florida, survived the final tragic phase of Pickett's Charge. Disillusioned by the bloody repulse, Powell later became a follower of John Wilkes Booth and one of the Lincoln assassination conspirators. Ironically, Powell's young life ended in Washington, DC, which was Lee's ultimate target had Pickett's Charge succeeded. When Powell was hanged on July 7, only four days after the second anniversary of Pickett's Charge, he no doubt still regretted the repulse of Lee's greatest attack and the loss of the 2nd Florida's colors. Until the very end, Powell felt pride of having been a member of the Florida brigade's "Old Guard."[116]

Unknown to his men at the time, Lee's last opportunity to deliver a mortal blow to the Army of the Potomac had passed forever. As one Texas survivor lamented: "the fate of the Confederacy was sealed, but we never knew it then."[117] In a July 11, 1863, letter to his brother, Captain John A. Herndon, 38th Virginia (Armistead's extreme left) was bitter about the collapse of Garnett's far left and the lack of any support from the rear when most needed for decisive victory: "The line in front and rear of us having both failed to prove of any assistance to us [therefore] we were compelled to fall back with our scanty" band of survivors.[118] Herndon's haunting words were echoed by a captured Rebel officer who could hardly believe his eyes, lamenting, "My God!, if we only had had another line, we could have whipped you."[119] To his life's end, Lee agreed with this common soldier's evaluation. However, some Rebels still refused to concede the awful reality of defeat. After gaining Seminary Ridge, a "wild mountaineer" from the Blue Ridge and now the latest flag bearer of the 24th Virginia, which included men from Rocky Mount, Franklin County, Virginia, waved the banner back and forth to rally the troops. The spunky mountain boy yelled to Lee, "General, let us go it again!"[120]

During the height of the attack, a young Virginia lieutenant had yelled to his men, imploring them to greater exertions: "Remember, home is over beyond those hills."[121] After the repulse, one Union officer hoped to assist "a handsome youngster; a Virginian, of Kemper's brigade," but the man was dying.

The Virginian's last words immediately before he died focused on the universal theme that had become an obsession to the attackers of Pickett's Charge: "I'm going home. Good-bye."[122]

The sad irony for hundreds of young men and boys was that the only "home" which they gained on July 3 was a shallow burial trench. A great dream was buried with them, because Lee "realized he would never get his invincible army to Washington" to fulfill the greatest of Confederate ambitions.[123] General Webb simply concluded that "had Pickett broken through my lines this army would have been routed."[124] Therefore, one Union soldier emphasized with relief: "The Glorious Fourth and we are still a Nation, and . . . for centuries to come."[125] Charles C. Coffin reported late on July 3 in the *Journal*, Boston, Massachusetts: "[T]he power of the Confederacy broken [and now] a country redeemed, saved, baptized, consecrated anew to the coming ages."[126]

But perhaps one veteran of the 9th Virginia, which lost 185 out of 200 men (including 23 of 24 officers), emphasized the most appropriate historical analogy, when he penned on the muster rolls of Private Samuel L. Williams, of Company D, how Gettysburg was the South's Waterloo.[127] Ironically, General Pickett's family traced its origins back to France, where its name had been Picquett. Pickett's favorite foreign language had been French, which he had learned at the Richmond Academy—the educational advantage that had allowed him to excel in French at West Point (Class of 1846) and narrowly graduate.[128]

Much like Lee on July 3, Napoleon had attempted to win it all by hurling his prized troops, the Imperial Guard (his strategic reserve) forward into a frontal assault to pierce Wellington's center at Waterloo.[129] Therefore, Lieutenant John Edward Dooley, Jr., compared the Virginians' assault to "the Old Guard of Bonaparte."[130] A 24-year-old private of the 13th Vermont, Ralph Orson Sturtevant, who hailed from Fairfield, Vermont, described how Pickett's men "were to [Lee] like Napoleon's body guard at Waterloo."[131]

General Kemper viewed his men were "as dauntless as the Imperial Guard, [which] knows how to die but not to surrender."[132] Likewise embracing popular analogies, Sergeant James H. Walker, Company K (Old Dominion Guards), 9th Virginia, Armistead's brigade, emphasized how the great assault will forever be "remembered by future Americans, as the English remember that of the "Light Brigade" and the French that of the "Old Guard."[133] Meanwhile, the *Philadelphia Inquirer* printed an eye-catching headline that crowed, "Waterloo Eclipsed!"[134]

Lieutenant William Richardson Bond, who served as an aide-de-camp in Pettigrew's brigade, thought that Lee had failed to achieve decisive success on July 3 because his "army was too weak numerically to afford him the luxury of having a body of troops who were always to be held in reserve for extraordinary occasions, or for rounding up his victories like Napoleon's Imperial Guard."[135] Bond was correct in his analysis in regard to artillery and infantry, because Lee had not designated or assigned any troops as a strategic reserve. Because Pickett's division had brought up the rear of Longstreet's 1st Corps and missed the first two days of battle explained why the command became Lee's acting strategic reserve more by accident than preplanned design. Therefore, Pickett's fresh division was employed much like the Imperial Guard at Waterloo in Napoleon's last-ditch bid to win it all.[136]

However, comparing Lee's defeat to Waterloo was most appropriate because Napoleon's greatest victory, Austerlitz, had been won by smashing through his opponent's left-center with a frontal assault at the Pratzen Heights to capture strategic high-ground and to win the day.[137] As Lee fully understood on July 3, Napoleon's brilliant success at Austerlitz proved "that the counterattack or tactical offensive is the true key to defense."[138]

Significantly, far more than the famed "Old Guard" at Waterloo, Pickett's Charge came much closer than acknowledged by today's armchair historians, who have continued to deride Lee's folly for launching his massive assault. As realized by those brave men who broke through Meade's right-center, Lee's decision to launch his greatest assault was not folly, tactical error, or an insane leadership decision.[139] Captured Rebels were shocked by the lack of manpower on the battered right-center, asking their captors, "Where are all of your troops?"[140] And one equally dismayed Confederate officer swore to one Yankee, "If I had known that this was all you have, I would not have surrendered."[141] Unfortunately for him and his troops, Lee faced the highly competent Meade and an army on their finest day on July 3.[142]

Contrary to the view of today's historians, Captain Joseph Graham, the North Carolina physician-turned-artilleryman, emphasized in a July 30, 1863, letter to his father: "Gen'l Lee's plan was excellent, but *some one* made a botch of it indeed. Had we carried those Heights, that Army [of the Potomac] would have been ruined."[143] Longstreet's failure to ensure that the flanks of the assault were properly reinforced and to send forward a second wave of support troops— especially all five brigades of Anderson's division and Wilcox's Alabama brigade (which Pickett's staff officers [first Baird, then Symington, and the Bright] had attempted to belatedly hurry forward)—in timely fashion was fatal. Longstreet did little, and then only belatedly, to ensure that 8,000 attackers of Anderson's division were advanced to exploit the breach torn into Meade's line.[144]

After having been taken prisoner at the Angle, Lieutenant John Henry Lewis, Jr., saw first-hand the extent of the lost golden opportunity on July 3: "In passing to the rear of Meade's army I saw that which, if it had been known to Lee, even then the battle might have changed. In fact at that point Meade's army was whipped. Worse, it was demoralized, and to a large extent."[145] Pickett was correct in boasting in his letter to his wife how his division had been ordered "to take a height [and] We took it."[146] Ensuring that hundreds of men died in vain, Lee was denied decisive victory by the multiple failures to properly support the flanks of the assault and send forward the second wave of attackers close to exploit the dramatic breakthrough.[147] Lieutenant John Edward Dooley, Jr., 1st Virginia, perhaps revealed as much: "But a little well timed support and Gettysburg was ours [and] The Yankee army had been routed" to all but bring the war to an end.[148]

Then, Stuart's failure to strike the Union right-center from behind completed the lengthy list of Confederate failures. Of course, the vulnerability of Meade's rear at the time of Pickett's Charge was exactly why Lee had targeted it to be struck from the east by Stuart's cavalry. As demonstrated by Napoleon's greatest successes in which the close coordination of all three branches (infantry, cavalry, and artillery) was the true key to decisive victory, a massive infantry assault in front and cavalry simultaneously striking in the rear would have shattered the Meade's right-center. In the end, "Stuart had to watch his hope of thundering into the rear of Meade's army frustrated," like Lee, who had watched the repulse of Pickett's Charge.[149]

The undeniable reality of the closeness to achieving the war's most decisive success on July 3 has revealed the invalidity of the popular "attack and die" thesis that emphasized how every Civil War assault was automatically doomed to failure, because of the advances in modern weaponry (rifled-musket) had outpaced tactics by 1863.[150]

As lamented Adjutant Crocker, 9th Virginia, Armistead's brigade, Lee's assault, as he envisioned it, "was to be made in the [early] morning [of July 3] with the whole of Longstreet's corps, composed of the divisions of Pickett, McLaws and Hood, together with Heth's division, [including] two brigades [Wright and Pender] and that the assaulting column was to advance under the cover of the combined fire of the artillery of the three corps, and that the assault was to be the combined assault of infantry and artillery—the batteries to be pushed forward as the infantry progressed, to protect their flanks and support their attack closely. The attack was not made as here ordered. The attacking column did not move until 3 p.m., and when it did move it was without McLaws' and Hood's divisions and practically without Wilcox's brigade and without accompanying artillery."[151] Lee's military secretary, Colonel Armistead Lindsay Long, who graduated from West Point in 1850, described how during the field conference on the morning of July 3, "it was decided that General Pickett should lead the assaulting column, to be supported by the divisions of McLaws and Hood [but] Hood and McLaws were not moved forward" by Longstreet.[152]

These crack troops, if unleashed by Longstreet, might well have succeeded in achieving a decisive breakthrough. But Longstreet had thought otherwise, compounding his "biggest failure [which] was in not properly arranging for support on either side of the attack column."[153] Colonel Walter Herron Taylor bitterly lamented how "Hood and McLaws were not moved at all [but] Had Hood and McLaws followed or supported Pickett and Pettigrew and Anderson been advanced, the design of the Commanding General would have been carried out."[154] In fact, if only Brockenbrough's Virginia brigade on the assault's extreme left flank had "advanced on Hays's thin line, this portion of the battle might have gone differently."[155]

In a July 4 letter to his wife, Captain Charles Minor Blackford described the high price paid for leadership failures: "[O]ur men made a charge which will be the theme of the poet, painter, and historian of all ages . . . The loss is especially great among the officers, and those from Virginia particularly. Your cousin [Colonel] Jimmy Marshall, was killed leading a North Carolina [brigade and I] saw [Major] Kirk[wood] Otey [11th Virginia and] Kirk is wounded in the arm by a piece of shell. [Captain] Jno. Holmes Smith [ex-merchant of age 22] has a bullet hole through his [right] thigh. . . ."[156]

After his division's decimation, Pickett was in tears, lamenting "We've lost all our friends."[157] Informing his sister of the horror, one fortunate survivor in gray summarized: "The slaughter on both sides was terrible & exceeds anything of the war."[158] In a Fourth of July 1863 letter to his wife, Adjutant Charles M. Blackford, a member of Longstreet's staff born in Fredericksburg and educated at the University of Virginia (Class of 1855), penned, "Our loss in men and officers exceeds anything I have ever known" in this war.[159] A North Carolina soldier, who contemptuously called the Yankees "blue birds," scribbled in his diary of the universal sentiment among Lee's survivors: "Oh how many of our comrades have we left behind us! We can never forget this campaign."[160] A Michigan Yankee was shocked by the gory scene after the repulse, but felt much better when he realized that "it was Rebel blood so it did not seem so bad."[161]

Narrowly escaping death while carrying the regimental colors of the 53rd Virginia, young Color Corporal Robert Tyler Jones wrote his disbelief: "Out of sixty five men in the Charles City company [Company K, Charles City Southern Guards], to which I belonged, but five escaped death or capture."[162] After the repulse, the clover, oats, rye, and yellow wheat fields were covered with bodies—a scene from Dante's Inferno. Confederate dead lay in a gory repose on the blood-stained soil of Adams County, after their most cherished dreams had died.[163] Pickett's division suffered 2,400 casualties for a 45.4 percent loss, while Pettigrew's division lost 41.7 percent.[164] One historian estimated that Garnett suffered the highest percentage loss (48.9 percent), followed by Armistead (48.3 percent) and then Kemper at (38.1 percent). But Armistead lost the most men (1,057); then Garnett (905), and Kemper (678).[165] Presenting the most accurate analysis of losses, historian Earl Hess tabulated a 2,655-man loss (42.4 percent) for Pickett's division, with Garnett (65 percent), Armistead about the same, and Kemper (43 percent). Meanwhile, Pettigrew's division suffered a higher loss at 2,700 men, representing a 62 percent loss.[166] Total losses for Pickett's Charge came to 6,555 killed, wounded and captured: a 55.4 percent loss. Private John R. Morris, 57th Virginia, penned in a letter how: "Pickett's Division got cut to peases [and family member Private] John W. Morris [14th Virginia] has not bin seean sence the fight." John had been captured, and was fated to die in prison before the end of 1863.[167]

In a July 9, 1863, letter to his wife Jane, Private Meredith (Merit) Branch Thurman, 14th Virginia, Armistead's brigade, emphasized: "[W]e had a big fight in pensilvania and more then half of pickets division was killed and wounded [and of the] seventy five [men of Company C] went in the fight and only nine came out Safte with my self . . . all the officers in the 14th and 57th was killed nearly and a great many privates."[168] Of the 32 field officers of Pickett's division in the assault, only one returned without injury. These leaders went down with not only their commands but also their battle flags: only two banners of the entire division were saved from becoming trophies in Northern state capitals.[169]

An estimated six million pounds of human and animal carcasses were strewn in the broad fields, meadows, wood-lots, and hilltops. Some 22,000 wounded men, filling every house, shed, and barn, and the town's eight churches, all hoped to survive Gettysburg's nightmare.[170] Volunteer nurse Elizabeth W. Farnham, who shortly died as the result of disease from attending the sick and wounded, penned in a July 7, 1863, letter of the ordeal some men of Pickett's Charge at a filthy 2nd Corps field hospital on the Jacob Schwartz farm. There, she found Colonel Fry, who "was shot through the ankle [shoulder and thigh], but seems well and very resolute. There is a man and his son lying beside him, each having lost a leg; other men [perhaps Private John P. Daniel, 11th Virginia] with both legs gone."[171]

However, for nearly 10,000 men in blue and gray, all of their suffering and pain had already ended forever in shallow graves and hastily dug burial pits.[172] In his diary, one of Armistead's men penned of the decimation: "I do not know who is living."[173] Likewise stunned by the horror, Private Thurman, 14th Virginia, penned in a letter to his wife: "I cant begin to tel you all [who] was killed."[174] One mind-numbed Union medical officer merely wrote that he saw "the greatest amount of human suffering known in this nation since its birth."[175]

With a grim gallows humor combined with mockery, an Adams County, Pennsylvania, citizen named Jacob Hoke looked upon the piles of dead Southern soldiers without pity: "They boasted that in coming into [Pennsylvania] they had got back into the Union—many who thus boasted [were now dead]. Their boasting had met a fearful verification."[176] In a classic understatement, one Virginia private described in a letter how he "[h]ad a good time till we got to Gettysburg."[177] Private Thurman, Armstead's brigade, caught the representative mood in a letter: "I was sorry after I got to pensilvania that I ever left Virginia. . . ."[178]

Not far from the tree-lined banks of Marsh Creek, 19-year-old Private George Dabney Tweedy, Company C (Clifton Greys), 11th Virginia, died in the field hospital of Pickett's division late on July 3. George failed to survive his leg's amputation. George was buried "in the corner of a field at the edge of the woods and on the south bank of Bream's Mill Dam" at tree-lined Marsh Creek, by his three surviving older brothers: Privates Smith P. Tweedy, Jr., a 20-year-old ex-farmer, Edmund A. Tweedy, age 20 and a man of the soil like George, and Fayette B. Tweedy, an ex-agriculturalist in his midtwenties.[179]

Like other fortunate survivors, thankful VMI graduate (Class of 1862) Captain George K. Griggs, Company K (Cascade Rifles), 38th Virginia, Armistead's brigade, praised God for his mercy. With a sense of relief tinged with sadness, he penned in his diary at 8:00 p.m. on July 3: "I have just gotten through one of the most terrible ordeals of my life. Thank God I am alive thought [sic] I have a severe flesh wound in my right thigh [as] a minie ball having passed" through it. During the assault, "we had no protection [and] had to climb two fences [along the Emmitsburg Road with] the enemy throwing shell [,] grape & all kinds of missiles of death at us, but we moved steadily forward, driving them from their strong position . . . our loss was heavy & do not know now what Col. [Edward Clayton] Edmonds & Capt. [Daniel C.] Towns [who commanded Company A] are reported killed [which was the case for both]. Al [sic] my Lieuts are wounded [and] 20 of my Co. [K] are wounded & 17 missing . . . I carried 49 muskets in [the] fight."[180]

Private Robert P. White, 14th Virginia, survived the slaughter, but embarked upon the anguished ordeal of attempting to find the bodies of his two cousins who had fallen. The two brothers hailed from Wilmington, Fluvanna County in the Piedmont of central Virginia. White's search for the two young brothers of Company C (Fluvanna Rifle Guard), 14th Virginia (which had advanced on Armistead's far right flank) was in vain. From Fluvanna County ("Anne's River") and the James River country, Privates James Eastin Ross, a former carpenter in his late twenties, who had enlisted in Richmond in May 1862, and 24-year-old William Daniel Ross, an ex-farmer manager, were killed during the charge.[181]

Tragic End for Some of the Best and Brightest

Union soldiers on burial details scoured the sun-baked killing fields before Cemetery Ridge, gathering hundreds of dead Rebels. Most Southern dead, with legs tied together by burial details to more efficiently move bodies into hastily-dug burial pits, were unceremoniously thrown into too-shallow (only around three feet deep) burial pits.[182] Haunted by the memory of so many comrades left behind, one grieving Confederate survivor lamented how "the worst of all was we did not get to bury our dead."[183]

Meanwhile, mortally wounded men were more concerned about what would happen to their mortal remains when so far from their Southern homes and families. Writing his last words, one dying Mississippian prayed only "to be buried . . . deep . . . so the beasts [dogs, wolves, and buzzards] won't get me."[184] A wounded Captain Griggs, 38th Virginia, offered a heartfelt prayer in his diary on July 3: "Kind Heavenly Father we would humbly pray Thee to Comfort those who lay wounded from two days work & soon restore them to health [and] to the many distressed families & enable them to bear their losses without Complaint."[185]

Lieutenant John Edward Dooley, Jr., described the suffering of his regimental commander of the 1st Virginia, mortally wounded Colonel Lewis Burwell Williams, who should have not been in the attack because of illness: "Poor Williams! His spinal bone is broken. He suffers continual and intense agony."[186]

As reported in the July 13 issue of the *Richmond Daily Dispatch*: "There is but one officer in the regiment [1st Virginia] who was not killed or wounded, and that was Lieut. [Henry C.] Ballou [Ballow, a 25-year-old former carpenter of Company I], who now commands it. Col. L. B. Williams went into action on horseback and was instantly killed. He fell forward on being shot, and did not speak afterwards. His horse was hit three times."[187]

Confederates, from colonels to lowly privates, died side by side from botched operations and amputations gone wrong. Lieutenant Giles H. Cooper, who had his leg amputated at the lower third of his left thigh, died on July 27. He was buried "on a hill" near the hospital and "under a walnut tree."[188] A teenager, Private Samuel Parrish, 28th Virginia, informed nurse Jane Boswell Moore, who labored in a 2nd Corps hospital when he would die, "I know that before to-morrow's sun rises I shall be gone."[189] The 16-year-old, who held close the treasured ambrotype (perhaps taken in the Richmond photo gallery of Charles Richard Rees) of his beloved sister, was correct, never again seeing his native Botetourt County, Virginia.[190]

Only age 24, Colonel John Bowie Magruder, 57th Virginia, knew his end was near. In the 2nd Corps field hospital, the philosophical University of Virginia graduate sadly concluded, "I am sinking . . . Some day, when peace is restored, my friends in old Virginia will carry my bones to the ancestral burying ground. But I will never more join the family or social circle [because] Death is creeping up on me . . . I feel that my race is run [and] I have faced my duty as I saw it like a man, and I have no regrets. . . ."[191]

A member of Company A (University Greys consisting of young men— all of whom were hit during the attack—from the University of Mississippi, Oxford, Mississippi), 11th Mississippi, Davis's brigade, Corporal Jeremiah Gage, from Holmes County, Mississippi, had been horribly mangled by an exploding shell. The dying University of Mississippi ("ole Miss") graduate penned a final letter, stained with his blood, to his mother, Patience W. Gage, Richland, Holmes County, Mississippi: "This is the last you may ever hear from me. I have time to tell you that I died like a man. Bear my loss best you can. Remember that I am true to my country and my greatest regret at dying is that she is not free . . . you must not regret that my body can not be obtained. It is a mere matter of form anyhow . . . I can not write more."[192] Such commitment and stoicism revealed the very best in the American fighting man, who rose to the challenge of Pickett's Charge in magnificent fashion during what was truly the *Iliad* of the Civil War.

Meanwhile, a wounded Private William Taylor Bradley, Company B, 7th Tennessee, thought of the bitter irony of having been captured by his own brother-in-law, Private William Petrie, of a Pennsylvania regiment, who was married to his sister Mary Violet Bradley-Petrie. She shortly became a widow and just another forgotten casualty of America's bloodiest war.[193]

Thousands of captured men of Pickett's Charge (3,750 captives, the largest ever lost by Lee's army) were herded together at bayonet point into lengthy columns for transport to northern prison camps. Many of Pickett's men, including Lieutenant Lewis, were imprisoned at the latter-day American shrine known as Fort McHenry. There, General Armistead's uncle, Major George Armistead, had successfully defended the masonry fort when the British fleet bombarded it and threatened to capture Baltimore.[194] For Pickett's captive men, that hallowed shrine to America liberty now became a hell on earth, after they were "cast into the black hole of Fort McHenry," which no longer symbolized freedom to these unfortunate survivors.[195]

Armistead, age 46, was taken to the XI Corps (smashed by Stonewall Jackson's flank attack at Chancellorsville) makeshift infirmary at the George Spangler House on Cemetery Hill. Here, in Spangler's huge wooden barn, resting on a stone foundation, Armistead was treated by Union surgeon Daniel Garrison Brinton. He was encouraged by Armistead's chances of survival because "neither of [the bullet wounds were] of a serious character [and] His prospects of recovery seemed good." However, Armistead died "like a soldier" on the hot morning of July 5, after having remained defiant to the end. Among Armistead's final words to the Union surgeon, who treated him well, came when he pulled out a few kernels of raw corn from his pocket, "Men who can subsist on raw corn, can never be whipped."[196] As revealed in his service record, Armistead "died of exhaustion at 9 AM 5 July."[197] General Armistead's body was taken to Baltimore by relatives and St. Paul's Cemetery, of St. Paul's Church. In the city's oldest cemetery, the North Carolina–born Armistead found the peace that had long eluded him in life in the family crypt beside the body of his revered uncle and childhood hero of Fort McHenry, Major George Armistead.[198]

In the most bitter of ironies, hundreds of the young men and boys of Pickett's Charge died in Union hospitals in Philadelphia, Harrisburg, Baltimore, and Washington, DC, where they had once envisioned Confederate battle flags (now in their opponent's hands) flying in triumph.[199] Captive Sergeant Levin Christopher Gayle, 9th Virginia, Armistead's brigade, described in his diary of the prisoners who would "stop at Fort Mc Henry [and] then start to that Hell on Earth called Fort Deleware [sic]. Oh what a place."[200] In the dreary months ahead, survivors of the great attack witnessed hundreds of comrades, including brothers, sons, cousins, and even fathers, die of disease, while a lesser number were shot by guards.[201]

Surviving brigade members were long tormented by July 3. A horrified Private Thurman, Company C, 14th Virginia, concluded in a letter that "evrything is at a loss [because] the[re] is So many of our men killed and gone."[202] Captain Charles Minor Blackford lamented in a letter: "I grieve deeply over Pickett's division, in which I had so many friends. Three of its brigades were absent but the three remaining lost thirty-nine hundred killed, wounded and missing and almost all their officers. Poor Virginia bleeds again at every pore. There will be few firesides in her midst where the voice of mourning will not be heard when the black-lettered list of losses is published [but] The residue of the army did not suffer proportionately. . . ."[203]

Indeed, as explained Colonel Walter Herron Taylor: "There were nine divisions in the army; seven were quiet" on July 3 when Lee went for broke and needed his top lieutenants to perform capably and in unison.[204]

Chapter IX

Requiem for an American Tragedy

Quite simply, "the plan for Pickett's charge as devised by Lee was nothing short of brilliant [because] the coordinated effort of Pickett and Stuart would have been devastating [but] [i]t has always been assumed that the role of Jeb Stuart's cavalry on this final afternoon was to disrupt Union supply lines and chase fleeing Yankees after Pickett routed them from the lines. Although Lee never produced actual orders that confirmed his plan to send Stuart's cavalry against the Union rear, solid evidence exists that this was his intention."[1]

What has been most overlooked by historians was exactly how close Pickett's Charge actually came to succeeding. Wounded and taken prisoner on July 2 and at a XII Corps hospital, a 4th Texas officer, Decimus Et Ultimus Barziza (known as "Pinney"), whose last name reflected his Italian roots (rare in Texas), described the opportunity for Stuart to charge into Meade's rear: "Great anxiety was discernable among the Federals [and] soon came streams of ammunition wagons, ambulances and disable artillery, driving frantically to the rear; thousands of soldiers rushed back . . . the scene was that of a routed and panic-stricken army. We, Confederates, who were at the hospital, were buoyant, and strained our eyes to see the grey backs rushing across the open fields."[2]

Here, as explained by this well-educated Texan, was the golden opportunity that Stuart's cavalrymen could have exploited to the fullest by charging west through the open fields behind Cemetery Ridge to strike Meade's right-center from the rear as Lee had envisioned with clarity.[3] Knowing how close Lee had come to winning it all, General Webb concluded how "had Pickett broken through my lines this army would have been routed."[4]

In his July 8, 1863, letter to his wife, Pickett described the remarkable achievement of tearing a hole in Meade's right-center, but "Alas! Alas! No support came, and my poor fellows who had gotten in were overpowered."[5] In his July 11, 1863 letter to his brother, Captain John A. Herndon, Company D, 38th Virginia, wrote bitterly: "The line that was to have come up behind us—the 3d line never came up at all. I don't know what troops they were and I don't wish to know."[6] Colonel Walter Herron Taylor realized that had Lee's planned supports been advanced, then "the world would not be so at a loss to understand what was designed by throwing forward unsupported against the enemy's stronghold so small a portion of the army."[7]

Pickett was partly to blame for the fiasco—a blame shared by Lee, Longstreet, Stuart, Hill, and other leaders in high places. Top Confederate leadership had failed the common soldiers, who had fought with their hearts.[8] With regard to the 3rd Corps commander: "Hill's role in the planning and preparation was virtually nonexistent" during the war's most important assault.[9]

Meanwhile, General Pettigrew blamed the failure not only on the lack of support from the rear but also from the early collapse of the left. He emphasized to Colonel John Jones: "My noble brigade had gained the enemy's works, and would have held them had not [Brockenbrough's] Brigade, on the left, given way."[10]

George Washington Booth, from Baltimore, Maryland, witnessed the assault and concluded that "the fearful lack of prompt, energetic obedience on the part of those occupying the high places, tell the story of the failure" of Pickett's Charge.[11] Right on target, Colonel William Allen emphasized the high cost of no support on the flanks: "Pickett was overwhelmed not by troops in front but by those on his flanks. . . ."[12]

Generations of Southerners sincerely believed "that the stars had fought against [Lee] in Pennsylvania."[13] But instead of the capricious dictates of the gods of war, the true culprits of Confederate defeat were at headquarters. Lee's battle plan began to fall apart long before the repulse at the Angle, beginning with the failure of the army's long arm. Quite simply, the bungling of top Confederate leadership guaranteed that July 3 was the Army of Northern Virginia's worst day.

A battle-hardened Louisiana Tiger, men who were considered "some of the [army's] wildest, coarsest soldiers," William J. Seymour, concluded how "we should have gained the day but for a want of cannon ammunition."[14] However, this statement was especially appropriate with regard to guns that might have been employed to closely support the infantry as flying artillery. For obvious logistical reasons, Lee's artillery arm brought too little ammunition to Pennsylvania, and too much had been expended during the first two days of battle (about 130–150 rounds per gun) and during the pre-assault bombardment. Therefore, at the most critical moment, Dearing's artillery battalion and other guns were unable to advance (like Anderson's brigades and other units) to protect Pickett's right flank because of the lack of ammunition. The relatively few guns that were advanced by Alexander on the right belatedly pushed ahead without coordination or sufficient rounds for massed fire.[15] As planned by Lee, the assault was to have been a combined infantry–artillery attack in close coordination, especially for flying artillery to advance in close support and protect the flanks.[16]

Long before the assault was launched, the forgotten cause of the Confederate artillery dysfunction that ensured the overall ineffectiveness of its flying artillery role lay in defective organizational structure: the elimination of the army's artillery reserve before the northern invasion. In addition, a single guiding officer of ability was badly needed to orchestrate the army's artillery like General Hunt. Therefore, without centralized management and control, the ineffectiveness of the Southern artillery arm was guaranteed at the most critical moment: the epitome of the Army of the Potomac's success was the magnificent performance of Hunt and his artillery, especially McGilvery's Artillery Reserve.[17]

A full "two-thirds of Lee's artillery remained idle or improperly employed" at the most decisive moment.[18] Major Poague never advanced his guns.[19] Likewise, Dearing's Virginia battalion, the longtime guardians of Pickett's division, was unable to advance to protect the assault's right flank, because so much ammunition had been expended during the bombardment to negate its vital role as flying artillery.[20] Only five guns of the Washington Artillery advanced on the south to provide inadequate close fire support for the attack.[21] In a pathetic display to protect the attackers' southern flank, these five "lonely pieces" were "all that was left of General Lee's original grand design of his artillery closely supporting " his most important offensive effort.[22] And on the north to protect the attackers' left flank, "none of [the] guns [were run out] in time to support Hill's infantry in the assault."[23]

Longstreet failed to ensure that the artillery possessed ample ammunition and faithfully followed on the infantry's heels (as in not sending Anderson's division forward and other units to protect the attack's vulnerable flanks) because he believed "the charge hopeless." Longstreet even failed to apprise Lee of the serious artillery ammunition shortage, until it was too late.[24] In the end, the Confederate masterful battle plan was "thwarted by an almost complete lack of coordination by these three corps commanders [especially in regard to coordinating artillery and infantry]. Certainly the fates were less than kind to General Lee that day" of destiny.[25]

Emphasizing the lost possibilities, Lieutenant John Edward Dooley, Jr., Kemper's brigade, concluded: "But a little well timed support and Gettysburg was ours [and the] Yankee army had been routed. . . ."[26] To his dying day, Lee was correctly convinced that decisive victory could have been achieved on July 3 "if all things could have worked together" as planned by him.[27] Meanwhile, the failure of Pettigrew's division was explained to his mother in a July 8, 1863, letter by Lieutenant William Calder, 2nd North Carolina: "[T]he finest charge of the war and had Pickett's division been supported we could have held the field but Heth's division [actually only Brockenridge's brigade and other brigades to a lesser degree but certainly not Pettigrew's division proper] failing to come up as it should have done. . . ."[28]

A former Virginia lawyer and ex-staff officer on Stonewall Jackson's staff, Lieutenant Henry Kyd Douglas lamented how Pickett's Charge failed because it "was left unsupported and was slaughtered. Much has been said of Longstreet's failure to do his duty. That there was a lamentable failure of co-operation in the Confederate attacks, and that somebody blundered there can be no question."[29] Lee's hope that "the spirit" of Stonewall Jackson had imbued his top lieutenants and corps commanders was dashed on the final day.[30] Therefore, after the war, Lee openly admitted in private "that if Jackson had been at Gettysburg [then he] would have gained a victory" during the most important battle of the war.[31]

The *Southern Illustrated News*, Richmond, Virginia, explained the great assault's failure on August 2, 1863: "Owing to the absence of two brigades, the division [under Pickett] did not exceed five thousand in number, yet this little body of men advancing steadily over half a mile [three-quarters of a mile] of broken ground, charged and carried the most formidable entrenchments . . . and would have maintained the position but for the failure of the supports which they should have received. . . ."[32]

But Lee said it best: if Pickett's Charge had been properly "supported as they were to have been" then Gettysburg would have represented the most dramatic victory of the Civil War.[33] In a bitter July 23, 1863, letter to his future young wife Sally (LaSalle Corbell, whom he married in early September 1863), Pickett emphasized: "If the charge . . . had been supported, or even if my other two Brigades [left to safeguard Richmond] had been with me [then] we would have been in Washington and the war ended."[34]

Angry over the missed opportunity, an embittered General Wright, Anderson's division, whose Georgia brigade was halted on Longstreet's orders, explained in a July 7, 1863, letter to his wife, Mary Savage-Wright, why Pickett's Charge had failed: "I cannot understand why Ewell's [2nd] corps and all of A. P. Hill's [3rd Corps] were not engaged in this day's fighting. I am satisfied that if they had been [sent in support of Pickett then], our victory would have been complete."[35] Although he commanded half of the attackers, Hill remained comatose to the extent that one dismayed observer wrote that the lieutenant general only watched the assault and "looked at me as if he were dazed, if not confounded at the scene before him."[36]

Pickett's Virginians often blamed the attack's failure on the ineffectiveness of the troops to the right, Wilcox's Alabama brigade, to protect their right flank. Indeed, Wilcox's large brigade provided only belated, insufficient support. In the end, the attack of Wilcox's Alabamans and Lang's Floridians was still another wasted effort. Lieutenant John Edward Dooley, Jr., wrote: "Farther to our right [was] posted [Anderson's] division [which] should have charged simultaneously or immediately following us, thus overlapping our flank (right) and preventing our force from being surrounded in that direction. Unfortunately, owing to bad management (I am sure not to want of bravery) they were of no assistance to us in the charge; and either advancing in the wrong direction or when too late, two thousand of them fell into the enemy's hands."[37] In his diary, Jedediah "Jeb" Hotchkiss, Lee's top cartographer and topographer, simply concluded, "[W]e drove the enemy from their works, but our supports were not near enough," dooming the assault.[38]

Most Virginians laid blame for failure on non-Virginia troops: the foundation for the enduring myth that Pettigrew's division had failed Pickett's division. But in truth, Pettigrew's attackers were handicapped by more formidable terrain after leaving the Emmitsburg Road and their targeted defensive position was naturally stronger than in Pickett's sector.[39] William Henry Cocke, Pickett's division, wrote in a July 11, 1863, letter about the chronic lack of support as a source of shame: "[T]hanks to Gracious they were not Va. troops."[40] However, Virginia troops had been the first to collapse, jeopardizing the assault, when Brockenbrough's brigade broke on the extreme left.[41]

The son of a Charleston, South Carolina, reverend with an undying faith in "the good God," Captain Louis Gourdin Young, of Pettigrew's staff, explained the correct blameworthy scenario in a wartime letter how "the Brigade [Brockenbroughs] on our left, reduced almost to a line of skirmishers, gave way [and they] were blameable [in no small part for the attack's repulse] having retired without orders."[42] Even General Pettigrew exclaimed on the field in disgust: "My noble brigade had gained the enemy's works, and would have held them had not [Brockenbrough's] brigade . . . on the left, given away."[43]

In a February 1864 letter, Pettigrew's aide-de-camp and "warm friend," the Grahamville, South Carolina–born Young, laid blame where it was rightly due: "The supports under Maj. Gen. Trimble did not advance as far as we [Pettigrew's division] had."[44] Colonel Taylor lamented the lost golden opportunity because of the widespread miscarriage of Lee's battle plan. He rhetorically asked, "[W]e here are the supports to reap the benefit of their heroic efforts, and gather the fruits of a victory so nobly won? Was that but a forlorn hope, on whose success, not only in penetrating the enemy's lines, but in maintaining its hold against their combined and united efforts to dislodge it, an entire army was to wait in quiet observation? Was it designed to throw these few brigades—originally, at the most, but two divisions—upon the fortified stronghold of the enemy, while, full half a mile away, seven-ninths of the army, in breathless suspense, in ardent admiration and fearful anxiety, watched, but moved not? I maintain that such was not the design of the commander general," Lee.[45]

Indeed, Colonel Taylor summarized the key to the assault's repulse by emphasizing that too few troops had been hurled forward only because "the plan [of General Lee] agreed on was not carried out."[46] This tragic scenario of a miscarried plan haunted Lee to his life's end.[47] After all, the most fundamental of Napoleon's axioms was to concentrate all available numbers of every branch of his army at the major point of decision to deliver the decisive knockout blow.[48]

Most of all, "Lee's plan hinged partially on reinforcements following Pickett's men [but] Wilcox's and Lang's brigades [Anderson's division] did step off toward the ridge, but were too little, too late, and without clear directions of where they were supposed to go [and then] Anderson had Wright's and Posey's brigades in motion, but upon Longstreet's order, pulled them back."[49] Likewise, Hood's and McLaw's Divisions, the army's finest troops, were to have attacked "as soon as the breach at the centre" was opened.[50] Quite simply, if all support troops had been utilized for the offensive effort as Lee envisioned, then "some 25,000, and perhaps closer to 30,000 men," in total, would have made the decisive difference.[51]

Modern historians, benefitting from hindsight, have long derided Lee's tactics as absolute folly.[52] But in striking contrast, Colonel Taylor emphasized that Pickett's Charge failed not because of a faulty tactical plan, but because support troops assigned to following the attack either never moved out or only advanced when it was too late. Taylor summarized that Lee's masterful battle plan was not at all responsible for the repulse of the assault, because when the attack was launched "the plan agreed on was not carried out." He concluded, "Much can be said in excuse for the failure of the other commands to fulfill the task assigned them" according to Lee's plan.[53]

In a letter to his mother, teenage Lieutenant William Calder, 2nd North Carolina, who possessed prewar military academy training in North Carolina, explained that Lee's final bid to win it all was "the finest charge of the war and had Pickett's division been supported we could have held the field but Heth's division failing to come up as it should have done. . . ."[54]

Like close infantry support, Lee knew that without adequate artillery support advancing with his foot-soldiers, his infantry attack was "doomed without it."[55] Therefore, Lee correctly emphasized: "[I]f they had been supported as they were to have been—but, for some reason not yet fully explained to me, were not—we would have held the position and the day would have been ours."[56] As penned Private Alexander McNeill in a July 7, 1863 letter to his wife of the ultimate tragedy: "We did the best we could with them under the circumstances and our brave boys now sleep in a cold and silent grave upon the enemy's soil."[57]

As revealed in his July 8, 1863, letter to his future wife, LaSalle Corbell, Pickett lamented the thorough decimation of his division: "My grand old division, which was so full of faith and courage then, is now almost extinguished. But one field officer of the whole command escaped . . . Your uncle, Colonel Phillips, behaved most gallantly—was wounded, but not seriously. Your cousins, Captain Cralle and C[rawley] Phillips, [a 26-year-old "professor" who led Company F (Nansemond Rangers), 3rd Virginia] are among the missing . . . how any of us survived is marvelous, unless it was by prayer. My heart is very, very sad. . . ."[58] Pickett's surviving men saw the flood of "tears" from their anguished commander when he attempted to speak about what happened to his division on a single afternoon in hell.[59] But in truth, Pickett had other reason to shed tears: quite simply, this "was Pickett's worst day" of his military career.[60]

No Glory, Only Ugly Reality

In one of the great understatements that mocked the so-called glory of Pickett's Charge, which generations of novelists and historians have endlessly emphasized in an incessant myth-making process distinguished by excessive romanticism, Lieutenant John Edward Dooley, Jr., revealed the unvarnished truth: "I tell you, there is no romance in making one of these charges."[61] Contrary to recent books devoted to Pickett's Charge with titles and subtitles that have emphasized the word "glory" (merely a path to the grave), the true reality was altogether different, because these soldiers had been to hell and back. Only a few survivors were convinced that "Uncle Robert will get us into Washington yet."[62]

The awful attrition of July 3 told of a horror that had nothing to do with an abstract word like glory. In a July 11, 1863, letter, Captain John A. Herndon, Company D, 38th Virginia, was sickened by what little was left of "our scanty remanent but oh the melancholy sight the division presented. It was nearly annihilated. Every Brigade Genl killed except Genl. Armistead and he was wounded and taken prisoner. 4 Colones in our Brigade [Armistead] killed and the others one wounded [and] 2 Lieut Colonels killed—Rawley [White] Martin being our—and the other three wounded . . . Our regiment went in with 350 men and have not since been able to muster more than about 125 of that number [and now] Genl Pickett cant speak of the affair without tears. He says that he had rather been killed himself than for his division to have been so cut up."[63] Surgeon Charles Edward Lippitt, 57th Virginia, penned in his diary: "Every field officer of our Brigade [Armistead] was either killed or wounded [and] Every officer command a co[mpany] in the 57th Va was killed, wounded or taken prisoner."[64]

As mentioned, the dying continued for Pickett's captured men who succumbed to the ravages of disease (nearly 200 men) in prison camps across the North well into 1865. A member of Company G (Portsmouth Rifles), 9th Virginia, Private Jordan W. Grant, age 23 and a ship carpenter from Portsmouth, Virginia, languished at Point Lookout Prison Camp in southern Maryland. In a sad, final letter to his mother, Private Grant scribbled, "I am sick with chronic Diarhhoea [sic] have had it five months [and I am now] a mere skeleton [and] am unable to help myself, there is no medicine here . . . they say I can not last this winter."[65] Another one of the many forgotten victims of Pickett's Charge, Private Jordan W. Grant died on New Year's Day 1864.[66] In Grant's regiment (the 9th Virginia) alone, 16 comrades, who had been captured in the assault, died of disease (primarily smallpox) in nightmarish Union prisons.[67] Meanwhile, Virginia soldiers wounded in the grand assault continued to die as late as May 1864 in Southern hospitals.[68]

Captain Benjamin Lyon Farinholt, Company E (Pamunkey Rifles), 53rd Virginia, Armistead's brigade, survived the infamous prison camp on Johnson's Island, Sandusky, Ohio. Ironically, Farinholt had been born near Yorktown,

Virginia, where George Washington and his French Allies secured the victory that led to a new nation's independence, while defeat at Gettysburg sealed another republic's fate. In a letter to his wife, Lelia May Farinholt, the captain, who had been wounded and captured inside the Angle, described how Gettysburg "was the bloodiest fight of the war. Nearly a hundred of my Regt.[,] including officers and privates[,] were captured with me and largely over a hundred left dead on the field. . . ."[69] In his diary, a 53rd North Carolina survivor of Gettysburg's horrors, James T. Morehead, concluded on July 13: "We are now, thank God, on Confederate soil, but oh, how many of our dear comrades have we left behind. We can never forget this campaign" north of the Potomac.[70] A saddened Lieutenant John Edward Dooley, Jr., who had been wounded and captured, lamented how his 1st Virginia lost 120 of 155 attackers.[71]

Named after Yorktown's Virginia-born victor, George Washington Ammons, Jr., a teenage farmer of Company K (Charles City Southern Guards), was among the 53rd Virginia's dead. George Washington Ammons, Sr., who was wounded in both thighs and captured, lost his son on bloody July 3.[72] Likewise, Captain Michael P. Spessard, Company C (Craig Mountain Boys), 28th Virginia, Garnett's brigade, lost his teenage son Hezekiah. After much suffering, the young man died on July 19 in a 3rd Corps hospital on Jacob Schwartz's farm from two wounds. Far from his mountainous homeland in southwest Virginia, Private Hezekiah Spessard might have died while still clutching the canteen—now a reminder of home and family—that his father had handed him before continuing to lead his Craig Mountain Boys to the stone wall, where the captain had swung his saber at every Yankee in sight. Sadly, the captain's personal tragedies were only beginning in this most murderous of America's wars. Both his second wife Anna (the first Elizabeth and mother of Hezekiah had died) and young daughter died back in Craig County, southwest Virginia, in 1864, while he fought his country's battles far from home.[73]

The regimental chaplain and former Company I private, Peter Tinsley, who was captured at Gettysburg, penned a letter to his stepmother, Anna, back in Craig County, informing the family how young Hezekiah had lingered "with two wounds, one in the groin and [the] other in the thigh."[74] Ironically, Anna's late-July letter finally enlightened Captain Spessard, who still had not learned of his son's tragic fate because Hezekiah had been transported to a 3rd Corps field infirmary. He had engaged in a heartbreaking, but futile, search for his son, after the assault.[75]

The commander of the 33rd North Carolina, Lane's brigade, Colonel Clark M. Avery, wrote an anguished letter on July 18, 1863, to Todd Robinson Caldwell, a future North Carolina governor, to break the tragic news of his son's death. John Caldwell, who was described by a comrade as "very young, and had not long been with the army," had been killed near the stone wall. He described: "[W]e advanced to within forty yards of the Enemy's work[s] and it was here that my little friend Jonny fell. The loss of my little friend is to me one of the most distressing incidents of the war . . . To console a Father for an only son is a difficult task. You may have the satisfaction to know that he fell where we would all wish to fall (if it be God['s] will) with his face to the enemy."[76]

For the assault's traumatized survivors, they were left to wrestle with the omnipresent demons and nightmares of the assault's horrors. In one of the saddest letters ever written by him, General Kemper, who narrowly survived his own wounds, wrote to Nannie L. Pollock, about the death of her brother, Captain Thomas Gordon Pollock, who ironically had been appointed the Adjutant and Inspector General of Kemper's brigade only on June 7, 1863, in a classic case of bad timing: "While advancing in line of battle, I ordered Capt. Pollock to the rear of the line to superintend certain movements and rode myself to the front [where] I was shot from my horse . . . your brother was seen to fall suddenly from his horse—apparently lifeless. In the loss of your brother, I mourn the loss of a cherished friend and comrade—an accomplished, chivalrous and noble soldier and gentleman."[77]

Ironically, even more revealing than General Kemper's previously unpublished letter to the grieving sister of Thomas Gordon Pollock, a Yale man (Class of 1858), was a letter from the black bodyservant, Richard, of the deceased captain. Because the captain's body was never found, his wife wrote Richard to inquire about Thomas's final burial and the whereabouts of his final affects. On March 30, 1863, the Pollock family's black servant, who thereafter served as the bodyservant of Colonel Joseph Mayo, Jr., 3rd Virginia, Kemper's brigade, a VMI graduate (Class of 1852), wrote in a long letter: "You ask me to tell you all I know of my late dear Master . . . The last I saw of him was just before the battle commenced at Gettysburg. He then left me and I saw him no more. I was informed that he had been wounded by a shell and wounded in three places, in the head, arm, and breast. He fell from the mare he was riding [which was wounded but was retrieved and survived, unlike its owner] and we were forced to leave him on the field. I would have gone back if I could, but I could not and even if I had gone, I could not have done any good as his spirit had fled and his soul [had] gone up to Him who gave it. I need not tell you my dear young mistress how I felt. I loved him so much having been with him so long. I could not for a long time bring myself to believe that he was gone, but at last the reality burst forth, and I felt lonesome indeed."[78]

In one of the greatest ironies of Pickett's Charge, the luck of gifted General Pettigrew, who somehow survived leading his division at the forefront with only a left arm wound, ran out not long after the assault. During Lee's withdrawal out of Maryland and back to Virginia, he was back in action with his rearguard division. Buying time at the Potomac River crossing known to locals as Falling Waters, located just below Williamsport, Virginia, Pettigrew was still fighting on July 14, only two weeks after his 35th birthday on the Fourth of July—the most disastrous one in the Confederacy's history because of the Gettysburg reversal and Vicksburg's surrender on the "Father of Waters."

When General George Armstrong Custer's Michigan troopers suddenly charged as if to repeat their performance in stopping Stuart from striking into Meade's rear, Pettigrew was at a disadvantage with his arm in a splint. During close quarter combat, Pettigrew fell when his horse was shot from under him. In an exchange of revolver fire at close range, Pettigrew received a fatal wound in the stomach. A North Carolina private, who loved Pettigrew like a brother, ran down the fleeing Yankee trooper, who had shot the revered general. Catching up to the exhausted Michigan cavalryman, the enraged private beat him to death with a rock.

Pettigrew lingered in a nearby farmhouse until dying on the morning of July 17 far from his native Tyrrell County, North Carolina. The handsome Pettigrew spoke his last words to his aide-de-camp that morning, Captain Louis Gourdin Young, "It is time to be going," almost as if one of the South's leading scholars only wanted to return home to escape the horrors of the war.[79] General Pettigrew finally returned home but not as he had imagined had Pickett's Charge succeeded. This "brightest star of the galaxy" of North Carolina's sons in the Army of Northern Virginia no longer shined brightly. Pettigrew's body was interred at the family's graveyard at Tidewater plantation, Bonarva, where he had been born.[80]

Bitter End

During this last bitter campaign of the war, no general officer of Lee's army was more tortured than Pickett. When Lee saw Pickett, he asked in dismay, "Is that man still with this army?"[81] Pickett was only a shadow of former self, having left much of his heart and soul at Gettysburg.[82]

Contrary to the almost universal condemnation of Lee's tactics by historians, Colonel Taylor described the truth of Pickett's Charge in a December 20, 1863 letter: "The "Reports" of the battle of Gettysburg show how *very near* we came to conquering Peace there [Pickett's Charge] and the *next time*, God willing and helping, we'll not only come very near to, but we *will* have a glorious victory and perhaps peace."[83] Lieutenant John Edward Dooley, Jr., 1st Virginia, thought much the same, writing how if only "a little well timed support and Gettysburg was ours."[84]

Pickett's Charge displayed not only the outstanding heroics of the American fighting man, but also a good deal of folly, cowardice, ineptitude, and errors long disguised by the romanticism and glorification. A seasoned Florida officer at Gettysburg penned in a July 22, 1863, of the forgotten side of Pickett's Charge, said: "I see the Richmond papers gave all credit of the hard fighting in the Centre to Pickett's division of Virginians, a more cowardly set of fellows near disgraced our uniform than the 2d & 3rd Lines of that Division that went in Battle on the 3d of July . . . Genl Lee himself tried to rally Pickett's division and could not. When the Secret history of the war is Known, then we will get justice I hope."[85] Of course, this "Secret history" included Stuart's planned cavalry strike into Meade's rear.[86]

Perhaps a 53rd Virginia survivor best summarized the true meaning of the great assault: "And when the sun [of July 3, 1863] went down on the shattered and broken columns of Pickett's division in the final charge on Cemetery Hill . . . the Southern Cross and all we fought for was as decisively lost as was the Crown of Napoleon when the Imperial Guards bearing the Eagles of France went down in the magnificent charge of Ney at Waterloo."[87]

Lee's complex battle plan on July 3 was more brilliant than Napoleon's at Waterloo. While Napoleon sought to win the day by unleashing a frontal assault with the revered Imperial Guard, Lee unleashed a sophisticated and complex, three-part tactical plan to split the Army of the Potomac in two.[88] Despite the failure of Stuart's cavalry to charge into the rear of Meade's right-center, and the lack of Longstreet's and Hill's coordination of the offensive effort as Lee bitterly reflected for the rest of his days, the attack had nearly succeeded nevertheless. Indeed, "a little well timed support" and Gettysburg would have been the most impressive Confederate victory of the war.[89]

Nevertheless, the stereotype that Lee's largest attack was nothing but absolute folly of the first magnitude has persisted to this day as a core tenet of Civil War historiography: Gettysburg's greatest myth. In a recent book that perpetuated the same old tired stereotypes, one author emphasized the oldest stereotype and a simplistic analogy: "Pickett's Charge should be seen as a vastly magnified version of the Charge of the Light Brigade at Balaclava in the Crimean War—as an act of lunacy or perversity. . . ."[90]

But the greatest "perversity" was that thousands of additional men on both sides were slaughtered in vain after Gettysburg. This grim reality was the very reason why Lee had risked it all on July 3 to break the lethal grip of a fatal war of attrition. Instead of being condemned by modern historians for foolishly wasting his men's lives for nothing like a reckless gambler, Lee was actually trying to preserve the lives of a far larger number of men who were slaughtered during the remainder of the war.

One cynical journalist of a Richmond newspaper reflected a truism of the human experience which called for average men to leave civilian pursuits to slaughter each other too often only because they wore uniforms of different colors, spoke with different accents, or had been born on the opposite sides of a mountain range or an abstract, manmade boundary line. On assignment from "this Babylon of the James," he presented a solemn mid-July 1863 tribute to Southerners who died at Gettysburg: "How sad to think that after men have done all that men could possibly do by their valor, won for themselves an immortal name, that some mismanagement should rob them and their country of their fruits of their heroic deeds . . . There is fault to be attached [for the sacrifice] to someone, let our high officers, the proper ones, say to whom."[91]

In a rather remarkable development, no one was held responsible for Confederate defeat at Gettysburg. Rumor had it in Richmond that Lee had suggested court martial proceeding against leading officers, who had been "delinquent" in their duties at Gettysburg, but President Davis had refused for the sake of national unity. In the wake of such a bitter Confederate defeat, the South needed no scapegoats but heroes. Therefore, Lee wrote in a letter to President Davis with regard to defeat at Gettysburg: "I am alone to blame"—in essence a cover-up for the overall national good. On July 3, Lee had failed in his best efforts to finally stop the frightful loss of five times more soldiers than the number of Americans lost during the Vietnam War, which was far more disproportionate because of the relatively small Southern population.[92] Indeed, the most tragic figures of America's "strange, sad war," in the words of poet

Walt Whitman, were the forgotten young men and boys, mostly lowly privates of humble origins, from North Carolina, Virginia, Tennessee, Alabama, and Florida, who fell during Pickett's Charge.[93]

The best and brightest "of a whole entire generation," wrote one of Pickett's men, Lieutenant Christian S. Prillaman of the 57th Virginia, in a letter before the dramatic Gettysburg showdown (where he fell wounded) of young Americans were slaughtered in this war for what they believed was right. The tragic failure of American political leadership resulted in a frightfully high price to be paid in full by mostly young farm boys (both sides) of the yeoman class. The tragic symbolism of young Americans of essentially the same historical and cultural antecedents became hauntingly clear in regard to the mortally wounded Lieutenant John T. Burton, Company E (Ebenezer Grays), 56th Virginia. He pleaded for a young cannoneer of the 11th New York Independent Battery of Light Artillery, to assist him, while leaning against the stone wall around fallen comrades. The Federal captain who helped the dying Virginian possessed the same name, John Burton. The rebel from the Meherrin River country of south central Virginia "seemed to be shot through both cheeks." With gentleness, the kind Captain John Burton, in blue, kneeled down and assisted John T. Burton, in gray. Knowing that he had suffered a mortal wound, the blood-splattered Confederate asked the Yankee captain to take a final message to his mother. The Union officer pulled out an envelope and pencil, and then handed it to the young Virginian. The bluecoat captain shook his enemy's hand and said that he "hoped this would not prove fatal [while] the Confederate only shook his head," knowing the sad truth. The lieutenant knew that he would never see his far-away home in the Piedmont and tobacco country of south central Virginia. Without long to live, John T. Burton scrawled his final tragic words to this mother, whom he knew that he would never see again, on the piece of paper that the New York officer eventually presented to the deceased Virginian's mother in Brunswick County, on Virginia's southern border. He also hoped that the Union officer would "Tell my mother I died trusting in the Lord."[94]

Like the tragic fate of Private Burton, it was the common soldiers who paid the highest sacrifice for so many Confederate leadership blunders and failures. A South Carolina soldier of Scotch-Irish descent penned of a tragic reality in a July 7, 1863, letter to his wife that "thousands of our brave boys are left upon the enemy's soil and in my opinion our Army will never be made up of such material again. . . ."[95] And a lucky Georgia survivor, sickened by the horror, described Gettysburg in a letter as "the hardest fought battle of the war. It was terrible."[96]

But perhaps the most fitting final tribute to the attackers who fell on July 3 was presented by Colonel Joseph Mayo. He commanded the 3rd Virginia at the beginning of Pickett's Charge, but ended the fight in command of Kemper's brigade. Never forgetting the sight of an unknown Confederate soldier who had believed that victory had been won, Mayo paid a final tribute to him: "Twenty paces beyond the spot which is marked to tell where stout Armistead fell, the foremost hero of them all, a humble private, without a name, bit the dust."[97]

In the end, the greatest tragedy of Pickett's Charge and the slaughter of so many young soldiers of lower-class origins was the fact that they had died because they had been led into America's most horrific war by the wealthy planter class and other slave-owning interests. The unsettling realization that this was a "rich man's war, poor man's fight" affected fighting spirit and resolve: a forgotten factor that helped to sabotage Pickett's Charge.[98]

Indeed, the "economic greed of a few [had] pre-ordained their defeat" in the end.[99] The Machiavellian greed of self-serving Southern politicians and the wealthy planter class that had led the poor and middle-class whites into the brutal conflict against a vastly more powerful nation resulted in a failed war effort partly because of, in one Confederate's words, "those poor men who deserted us, saying they would not fight for the *rich*."[100]

As usual, the lowly common soldiers paid the highest price. After somehow miraculously surviving Pickett's Charge, 30-year-old former railroad agent Captain Henry Thweat Owen, Company C (the Nottoway Rifle Guards), 18th Virginia, Garnett's brigade, was tormented by the attack's horrors. He wrote to his wife only four days before Christmas 1863 and explained in his most vivid nightmare: "Far away to the front, I saw the dim outlines of lofty hills, broken rocks and frightful precipices which resembled Gettysburg. As we advanced further I found we were fighting that great battle over again. . . ."[101]

Noncombatants across the South also suffered severely because of Pickett's Charge. Mary Chesnut long remembered a tormented Virginia mother's anguish in Richmond with the arrival of a trainload of recently exchanged Southern prisoners that pulled into the nation's capital near the end of March 1864: "Yesterday we went to the capitol grounds to see our returned prisoners . . . The president joined us first, and then Mr. [John C.] Mitchel, the Irish patriot [who had lost his youngest son "Willie" Mitchel, 1st Virginia, during Pickett's Charge] . . . We walked slowly up and down until Jeff Davis was called upon to speak to the prisoners . . . these men were so forlorn, so dried up, shrunken, such a strange look in some of their eyes . . . others again, placidly vacant, as if they had been dead in this world for years. A poor women was too much for me. She was hunting her son [who very likely had been killed in Pickett's Charge]. He had been expected back with this batch of prisoners. She said he was taken prisoner at Gettysburg. She kept going in and out among them, with a basket of provisions she had brought for him to eat. It was too pitiful. She was utterly unconscious of the crowd. The anxious dread—expectation—hurry and hope which led her on showed in her face."[102]

Most likely, this unfortunate woman's son had been killed at Gettysburg or died in prison. Mary Chesnut lamented with sadness in regard to the South's sacrificed sons: "The best and the bravest of one generation swept away! . . . There is nothing to show they ever were on earth."[103]

Perhaps no one felt the searing pain of losing a young son more than Sarah Jane Mitchel. Jane and her Irish-born husband, John C. Mitchel, Sr., grieved over the loss of their youngest son, 17-year-old Willie, 1st Virginia. In the July 13, 1863, edition of the *Richmond Daily Dispatch*, the news was first reported that "Wm. Mitchell [sic], son of John Mitchell [sic], in command of the color guard of the regiment, is wounded and missing."[104] Therefore, hope had initially remained among the Mitchel family and Richmond's Irish community (which lost many sons) that the naive teenager survived, and might still turn up in a hospital or a northern prison camp.

But the awful truth was soon forthcoming: Willie had fallen near the stone wall while carrying the regimental colors. As she revealed in a letter to her son James, who also had served in Company C (Montgomery Guard), 1st Virginia, the Irish-born Sarah Jane had been informed by his comrades who had "found Willie rolled in a blanket pinned with three pins [and] his face had been washed and there was a slip of paper pinned to his blanket with his name 'W. J. Mitchel' son of Irish patriot—with the help of a colored man they dug a grave on the banks of a small cabin so close that no plow would ever disturb it—and laid him there and took the paper and fastened it to a piece of cracked board and hammered it there at the head of the grave."[105]

Revealing how Willie's tragic fate had been of concern to the Irish community across the nation, especially New York City, the *Irish-American* of New York City reported on August 29, 1863 under the headline of JOHN MITCHEL'S YOUNGEST SON: "We have received with sincere sorrow the intelligence that William Mitchel, the youngest of John Mitche's sons, fell mortally wounded on the battle-field of Gettysburgh, shot through the lower part of the abdomen. He was the color-bearer of the 1st Virginia regiment, and fell near the breastworks . . . in the last desperate charge. . . . He was a young lad of the highest promise, and never failed to endear himself to those with whom he brought in contact, by the sterling goodness of his disposition and the many excellent traits of character he displayed [as he was a] bright, open-hearted boy."[106]

But the searing memory of teenage Willie, especially his childlike innocence and love for life, never died in Sarah Jane Mitchel's grieving heart. Although she, an Irish immigrant, was well aware of not only her son's death but also his burial, Sarah Jane had long believed that her youngest son would return home one day. As she penned in her sad letter to her surviving son James, "I would like to find that grave. It was years before I gave up the hope that he would someday appear. I got it into my head that he had been taken prisoner and carried off a long distance but that he would make his way back [to home and family in Richmond] one day—this I knew was very silly of me but the hope was there nevertheless."[107]

Lieutenant Colonel John C. L. Mounger, 9th Georgia, was mortally wounded at Gettysburg, and died before his two sons, Thomas and John Mounger, who served in the same regiment. In a July 18, 1863 letter to his "Dear Mother," the respected officer, who was killed at the Wilderness in May 1864, described how, "Tom took good care of dear dear Pa until he died, but he only lived a few minutes after he was shot . . . Dear Mother we tried to carry him to Virginia before we burried [sic] him but it was impossible as the Yankeys [sic] were all around us . . . Dear Mother let us all try and meet him in Heaven, Tom & myself will try and be better boys" in the future and "Tom kept the stars on his coat and a lock of his hair. . . ."[108]

The news of the tragic deaths of so many brothers, cousins, sons, and relatives sent shock waves reverberating across the South. Pickett's Charge had created thousands of widows and orphans. F. Lewis Marshall, Colonel "Jimmy" Keith Marshall's brother, wrote a sad October 6, 1863, letter to his uncle to inform the family of the death of the 24-year-old colonel and one of Virginia Military Institute's finest, while leading his troops while mounted almost to the stone wall: "It becomes my painful duty to inform you, and my dear Aunt, [that] Jimmy was killed *instantly* on the 3rd day's fight at Gettysburg. [Lieutenant J. C.] Warren [52nd North Carolina] says [in a letter] that he was killed near him and that he was shot in the forehead . . ." Lieutenant Warren himself was hit, and "lay wounded on the field for *three days*" without care. F. Lewis Marshall offered some consolation to the grieving family that some scant information was soon forthcoming about "where Jimmy's grave was" located.[109]

Few relatives ever received any accurate information about the tragic fates of loved ones who fell in the great attack. One of Lee's anguished soldiers, who himself was fated to die in this war, offered heartfelt words to his sister, who had lost the love of her life: "Your husband is gone to a world of rest where there is no tumult of war [and] He will suffer no more hunger or thirst [because] your loss is his gains. He died an honorable death: he gave his life, a sacrifice for his country's rights."[110]

In a fitting epitaph, Captain Richard Irby, 17th Virginia, described another one of the tragedies of Pickett's Charge: "[A]ll of the killed and wounded were left in Pennsylvania, and no one knows their graves, if buried [and their bones] have whitened and mingled into dust on the field where they fell, which now the plow-boy, whistling as he plows, turns over a common earth, unconscious that his plowshare is stirring sod hallowed by the blood of as brave men as the continent has ever known."[111]

Irby's words were prophetic. Even before the end of July, the shallow burials of Pickett's young soldiers were already desecrated by the ravages of nature. Near the Angle and "copse of trees" area, nurse Jane Moore described her "walk along the low stone wall or breastwork" in a July 26, 1863, letter. She was horror-struck by the sight of "the hillock of graves–the little forest of headboards scattered everywhere . . . Oh how they must have struggled along that wall" of stone, and "beyond it two immense trenches filled with rebel dead, and surrounded with grey caps, attest the loss to them. The earth is scarcely thrown over them, and the skulls with ghastly grinning teeth appear, now that the few spadefuls of earth are washed away."[112] One astonished visitor to the final resting places of Pickett's soldiers saw "skeletons which had been plowed up and now lay strewn about the surface" around the angle and stone wall.[113]

For decades, the scattered remains of Pickett's men were discovered by generations of farmers plowing their fields. In 1886, one farmer "residing on the [Nicholas J.] Codori Farm on June 5, plowed up the remains of a soldier in the field over which Pickett charged and [discovered] a piece of skull with a bullet protruding at both sides [and] the remains were probably one of Pickett's men."[114] As late as 1996, the scattered remains of the men of Pickett's Charge continued to be discovered on Gettysburg's hallowed ground.[115]

The most forgotten tragedy of Pickett's Charge was not only the fratricidal conflict between fellow Americans but also between ethnic groups, especially the Irish, Germans, and Hispanics. The Virginians' romanticized Lost Cause version of Pickett's Charge emphasized the heroic Anglo-Saxon Virginia cavalier at the expense of these forgotten ethnic soldiers. Consequently, the story of the Irish and Germans who fought on both sides at Gettysburg has been a forgotten story of Pickett's Charge. However, the Latino role at Gettysburg has been ever lesser known. Hispanic soldiers in gray, especially in Lang's Florida regiments (which represented the "Land of Flowers"), fought Hispanics in blue during Pickett's Charge. Cubans were represented on both sides. Lieutenant Joseph De Castro became the first Hispanic to win the Medal of Honor for heroics as the color-bearer of the 19th Massachusetts, 2nd Corps. The Latino officer knocked down and captured a Confederate flag-bearer and the 19th Virginia's banner.[116] The Florida brigade brought 742 men (including those of Latino descent) to Gettysburg, and only 461 survived the slaughter, suffering the highest percentage casualty loss of any brigade.[117]

All differences of race, class, education, and culture among the slain men of Pickett's Charge were forgotten when they lay together in common graves. In one of the war's strange paradoxes, a good many soldiers of companies like the Appomattox Greys of Company H and the Farmville Guards of Company F, 18th Virginia, who fought around the stone wall where their regimental flag was captured, saw the war finally end at their own Appomattox River County in central Virginia.[118] Even at this time, the Allan family of Richmond was still grieving. In an April 5, 1865 letter, one Richmond lady wrote with sadness how "the Allan home [was still] closed to all the world since poor John fell at Gettysburg."[119]

Feeling "perfectly lost" by the absence of so many friends who had been cut down during the assault, William Henry Cocke, 9th Virginia, Armistead's brigade, was tormented about the tragic fate of Adjutant John Summerfield Jenkins, a 28-year-old lawyer from Portsmouth. As Cocke penned in a letter that revealed his torment about "poor [John Summerfield] Jenkins—no one knows what has become of him [and] I am afraid he was killed—he has told me several times that he wouldn't be taken a prisoner."[120] Adjutant Jenkins, 14th Virginia, Armistead's brigade, remained true to his word, fulfilling his promise never to be captured by the Yankees. He had been killed with Colonel [James Gregory] Hodges within four feet of the enemy line."[121]

Perhaps the greatest irony of Pickett's Charge was the fact that it has been long generally perceived as primarily a Virginia assault by the so-called "flower" of Lee's army: a creation of the power of influential Virginia's Lost Cause mythology that won the second war in regard to popular memory, thanks to generations of prolific Virginia writers and historians. In truth and in a striking paradox, the brigade of Pickett's division that performed the most magnificently was in fact the one that had been most ridiculed before the assault, Armistead's brigade. Virginia's winning of the literary battle resulted in the permanency of the Virginia version of Pickett's Charge, which led to the tarnishing of Pettigrew's division and thousands of North Carolina, Florida, Mississippi, Alabama, and Tennessee soldiers.[122] However, the truth of what really happened on July 3 was better seen in the words of a frustrated 7th Tennessee soldier who survived Lee's greatest assault: "I can't understand why the Virginians, as a rule, make the statement that Heth's [Pettigrew's] Division retreated or fell back first. The truth is that the center, including the left of Pickett and the right of Heth, were the last to abandon the field. The right and left retreated first because they were flanked. When . . . I left the field the extreme right of Pickett was . . . in rapid retreat."[123]

Epilogue

A lucky survivor of the assault, teenage Sergeant Randolph Abbott Shotwell, 8th Virginia, Company H (Potomac Greys), perhaps best placed the most enduring myth of Pickett's Charge (the popular misconception that Lee's greatest offensive effort was doomed from the beginning) in a proper perspective: "It is easy to say *now* that this was an impracticable undertaking—that the Federal position and forces were too strong, and that the attacking column altogether too weak for any such task."[1]

In truth and contrary to conventional wisdom and time-worn stereotypes about the alleged folly of Lee's final assault at Gettysburg, Pickett's Charge (with roughly one-third of his entire force instead of the planned far greater percentage) was Lee's best and last opportunity to save the Confederacy's life: one final desperate effort that came far closer to succeeding than generally realized. While historians have long condemned the bold decision to attack on July 3, Lee correctly emphasized in a letter to President Davis: "I thought at the time that [winning decisive victory] was practicable. I still think if all things could have worked together it would have been accomplished. But with the knowledge I then had, & in the circumstances I was then placed, I do not know what better course I could have pursued."[2] In truth and as mentioned, Pickett's Charge was indeed the best last chance to achieve a decisive success at Gettysburg to conquer a peace, before it was too late for the Army of Northern Virginia and the Confederacy.[3]

But as he diplomatically hinted, Lee's top lieutenants had badly let him down in not supporting Pickett's Charge to exploit its success: Ambrose P. Hill and Ewell (new corps commanders promoted well beyond their limited capabilities), Stuart's failure to strike from the east, and Longstreet, who was in charge of the assault—who failed not only Lee but also the men of Pickett's Charge. From beginning to end, the personal failures and flaws of Lee's top lieutenants doomed the great attack.[4]

Lee possessed "some 25,000, and perhaps closer to 30,000 men, available to press the Federal lines," and he had meant to use all of these troops to reap a decisive result.[5] Colonel Walter Herron Taylor, the commander-in-chief's highly competent adjutant, emphasized in a July 17, 1863, letter that the "charge was the handsomest of the war . . . and though it carried the works and captured a number of guns, it was not well supported by the division on its left, which failed to carry the works in its front & retired without any sufficient cause, thereby exposing Pickett's flank [and] The enemy then moved on Pickett's left & forced him to retire."[6]

Born on Christmas Day 1843 and destined to be the last survivor of Pickett's division (dying in late 1936), Frank W. Nelson, Company A (Mechlenburg Guards), 56th Virginia, perhaps said it best in explaining the repulse: "Our failure to a great extent can be laid to General Lee's one fault—he left too much to his subordinate officers."[7] In a repeat of his typical leadership style in which his "battlefield control was minimal" that had worked so well with Stonewall Jackson, Lee failed to keep his subordinates on a tight leash to ensure that his orders were carried out to the letter.[8]

During the most important assault of the war, Lee's "remaining hopes therefore lay in the hands of an officer [Longstreet] utterly opposed to it."[9] As mentioned, Longstreet's and Hill's failures to ensure that the flanks of the attackers were adequately protected and supported were fatal.[10] Likewise, Pickett was of relatively little help in fulfilling Lee's grand vision of achieving decisive victory, because he kept himself "quite close to the rear of his division much of the time," when proactive leadership was most needed.[11]

Stuart, another favorite, also let General Lee down on July 3. Several miles east of Gettysburg, Stuart's miserable failure to push aside the blue troopers to fulfill Lee's orders by striking into Meade's rear also doomed the attack. While Longstreet has been long derided for having lost the Battle of Gettysburg primarily because of postwar feuding among veterans, the South's premier cavalryman, Stuart, the idolized Virginia cavalier who was killed in 1864, failed to strike in conjunction with Pickett's Charge.[12] In consequence, Lee's ambitious vision of Pickett and Stuart coming together and "shaking hands" atop the crest of Cemetery Ridge crest to have all but guaranteed the Army of the Potomac's destruction was not to be.[13]

What cannot be denied was that Lee's great assault would have succeeded only if all three arms—artillery, infantry, and cavalry—had performed in a closely coordinated manner: Napoleon's classic formula for success. Only one of these arms fulfilled Lee's expectations, however. Therefore, two-thirds of Lee's battle plan failed. Long overlooked by historians who had condemned the assault as absolute folly, Lee had planned to utilize this timeless tactical formula for victory: the classic and "careful coordination of cavalry, infantry and guns into one continuous process of attack [in the close] inter-arm cooperation [that was the key] to victory."[14]

In his letter, Colonel Taylor emphasized, "If we had have had say 10,000 more men, we would have forced them back [and] As it was they did not resist Pickett but fled before him & had the supporting or 2nd Division [Pettigrew] performed its part as well, the result would have been different." Significantly, after Lee had already hurled roughly a third of his army forward, Colonel Taylor's estimation that an additional 10,000 men would have won the day, which was nearly the size of Anderson's division that should have advanced behind Pickett's division to exploit a break in Meade's right-center. Instead, in repeat of his dismal Malvern Hill performance, a hesitant Longstreet had only belatedly utilized Anderson's troops when it was already too late.[15]

But in fact, Taylor's estimation of an extra 10,000 men might have been too high to guarantee success. Ironically, the additional troops that could have been utilized to achieve a decisive success had been those of Pickett's own division. What historians, who had declared that the assault was doomed from the beginning, have forgotten was the fact that the failed attack "bore little resemblance" to what Lee had planned. Failure also lay in the White House of the Confederacy with regard to the two brigades that had been detached by the War Department to guard Richmond from a threat that never came. Virginia Military Institute–trained Major Walter Harrison, the inspector general of Pickett's division, well understood how this drastic reduction in strength of Pickett's division had doomed the assault: "The nerve and spirit to strike was there; but the [small] force; the force to hold was impotent. Where then should have been Corse and Jenkins. Oh! For those four thousand veteran and brave Virginians and South Carolinians, led on by the tough old bullterrier Corse, and the gallant, ardent Jenkins!"[16]

Major Harrison explained the disastrous decision made by the War Department and President Davis: "Pickett earnestly and repeatedly asked that these two brigades, numbering nearly four thousand men, should be permitted to rejoin him; and Gen. Lee strongly urged the application, but to no avail, with the War Department. . . . With these two brigades, Pickett's division, in its celebrated charge at Gettysburg, would have been over eight thousand instead of only forty-seven hundred strong." As the inspector general of Pickett's division, Harrison realized that these "two large brigades, of as good and proved fighting material as any in the army" would have made a decisive impact on July 3.[17]

In addition, Lee's overly "calm assurance" of July 2 that Pickett's division would not be needed at Gettysburg until the following day might well have indicated that the commander-in-chief had overlooked the fact that two of Pickett's brigades were far away in the Richmond area.[18] Indeed, perhaps the battle of Gettysburg was actually lost the moment when Lee almost casually informed Major Harrison on July 2: "Tell Gen. Pickett I shall not want him this evening, to let his men rest, and I will send him word when I want them."[19] In this regard and even before the first shot of the battle of Gettysburg had been fired in anger, perhaps the real culprit for defeat on July 3 was the War Department.[20]

General Wright was puzzled about the assault's failure: "I cannot understand why Ewell's corps and all of A. P. Hill's were not engaged . . . I am satisfied that if they had been, our victory would have been complete."[21] Nevertheless and as revealed by participants, Pickett's Charge had been a very close thing.[22] Indeed, "[h]ad southern artillery managed to provide adequate support to the infantry, and had additional infantry quickly and effectively moved to support the flanks, the charge might have succeeded."[23] Colonel Armistead Lindsay Long, Lee's military secretary and a graduate of West Point (Class of 1850), concluded, "Had Hood and McLaws [and their crack troops] followed or supported Pickett, and . . . Anderson been advanced, the design of the commanding general would have been carried out" with success.[24]

Knowing that the failure of the assault was due to the lack of timely support, an embittered General Fitzhugh Lee concluded, "A consummate master of war such as Lee would not drive en masses a column of fourteen hundred thousand" attackers toward Cemetery Ridge, while "giv[ing] his entering wedge no support. Why, if every man in that assault had been bullet proof, and if the while of those fourteen thousand splendid troops had arrived unharmed on Cemetery Ridge, what could have been accomplished? [and] there would have been time for the Federals to have seized, tied, and taken them off in wagons, before their supports could have reached them. Amid the fire and smoke of this false move these troops did not know someone had blundered."[25]

Colonel Taylor emphasized the undeniable truth about exactly how close Pickett's Charge actually came to succeeding. As he explained in an August 8, 1863, letter to his beloved Bettie: "I fear that you all in Richmond do not understand our campaign [and] of how near we came to accomplishing what would have surprise the world for its brilliancy and of the shallowness of the Yankee claims of victory" at Gettysburg.[26]

Equally as revealing after learning even more of the intimate tactical details of Pickett's Charge, Colonel Taylor marveled in a letter "how very near we came to conquering Peace" on the third day.[27] In a July 30, 1863, letter to his father, North Carolinian Captain Joseph Graham, of Hill's corps, summarized how a great tactical opportunity was nearly exploited in full: "Gen'l Lee's plan was excellent, but someone made a botch of it indeed. Had we carried those Heights, that Army [of the Potomac] would have been ruined. There were only two avenues of escape, and Ewell had one, and Longstreet the other. So that they must have surrendered or been cut to pieces, and entirely ruined. They would have been scattered over the whole country, and we must have had Washington City [Washington, DC], and Baltimore. And I hoped a speedy peace. But the fortune of war was otherwise."[28]

Before the postwar romantic glorification of Pickett's Charge, Major Harrison concluded how, "if the desperate attack made upon his centre had been fully sustained, as Gen. Lee intended it, the line would have been thoroughly broken through at that point; and the army of the Potomac cut in half."[29] Harrison additionally emphasized how, had Pickett's men "been supported by one or two more good brigades, that portion of the lines [at the copse of trees] would have been fully carried."[30] Lieutenant Colonel Rawley White Martin, 53rd Virginia, was correct when he concluded, "Somebody blundered at Gettysburg but not Lee. He was too great a master of the art of war to have hurled a handful of men against an army."[31] But Lee said it best when concluding in 1868 how decisive victory could have been won by Pickett's Charge, if this "one determined and united blow [could] have been delivered by our whole line."[32]

Because the South was caught on a downward spiral that was rapidly leading to not only his army's but also to his nation's eventual extinction, and without the supplies and ammunition remaining to continue a campaign of maneuver, Lee had no choice but to go for broke on the final day. If Lee's well-laid plan had been carried out as envisioned, then Pickett's Charge would have altered the course of not only American history but also world history: a true turning point for the American people.

Like the Southern nation that was on the road to certain extinction by the red-streaked sunset of Gettysburg's bloody third day, the attackers of Pickett's Charge were sacrificed for the greatest of Southern national sins of slavery, hubris, and secession. Perhaps the extensive failures of Lee's subordinates to provide timely and full compliance to his orders when most needed had been ordained by the stars from the beginning. No matter who was at fault for the fiasco, the troops who died in the great charge became little more than cannon fodder and sacrificial lambs in the end. The words of the famous Thomas Gray poem "Elegy Written in a Country Churchyard" only too fittingly applied to the central tragedy that was the Pettigrew–Trimble–Pickett charge: "The Paths of Glory Lead But to the Grave."

This Judgment Day ensured that nothing would ever be quite the same after the repulse of that climactic assault. In a letter to his father as a wounded prisoner, Rawley White Martin wrote this final dirge for his Southern Republic: "Oh, my country, my country." Perhaps the final tribute to the death of an Irish Confederate, 17-year-old Willie Mitchel, the diminutive Irish nationalist who fell while carrying the regimental colors, best symbolized one of the most iconic tragedies in the annals of American history:

Bright in his genius and bright in his youth
Gone to his grave!
Died with his banner encircling his head,
The staff by his side!
No tall marble shaft adorning his grave
Speaks of his fame.[33]

E. C. Wilson, Pickett's division, was left with a far greater wound that cut more deeply into his soul. Wilson was lucky, surviving with a dozen wounds, including two cuts on the back of his head from a Union officer who defended the Angle sector. In Wilson's anguished words that told of the family tragedy: "I lost my father and four brothers that day," July 3, 1863.[34]

Like other survivors, 18-year-old Lieutenant William A. Miller, Company F (Farmville Guards), 18th Virginia, long felt a sense of grief, because he could never escape the haunting realization that "many of those noble faces that I have been accustomed to See" would never be seen again, because they "are sleeping their last-Sleep on the blood Stained field of Gettysburg."[35]

But perhaps the most poignant reminder of what might have been and exactly how close Pickett's Charge had come to succeeding came from Lee himself on his deathbed. On the afternoon of October 10, 1870, Lee slipped into a coma. Among Lee's last words uttered as he relived a final battle in his mind, "Tell [A. P.] Hill he *must* come up!"[36]

Even to the last moment of a life marked by an inordinate amount of tragedy and triumph, Lee was perhaps thinking of how the war could have been won, if Hill had only advanced to support Pickett's Charge. For ample good reason, Lee felt that "he had been ill served at Gettysburg, as indeed he had been," and his last struggle might well have been in attempting to get not only Hill, but also Longstreet and Ewell to "act in concert" on July 3.[37] In the words of the 6th Corps's commander, who emphasized how Lee's assault "should have won: More men should have been put into it, at least on division from Ewell, more [and] Longstreet should have gone with it."[38]

Perhaps in the end, the true cause of Pickett's Charge's failure was actually the one most overlooked by historians. Given that the infant Southern nation betrayed the most progressive values of the day by keeping four million slaves in bondage by perpetuating the ugliest anachronism of a bygone age (an inheritance from ancient Greece and Rome), then perhaps one of Lee's men understood the true cause of the repulse of Pickett's Charge: "God must have ordained our defeat."[39] The devout William Ross Stilwell, Longstreet's division, felt the same, writing in a letter how "it is not right for us to invade their country [because] God has showed his displeasure every time we go over there [including the 1862 Maryland invasion] and has never bless[ed] our arms with such success as he has in our own country."[40]

Indeed, the repulse of Pickett's Charge sounded not only "the death knell of slavery," but also "the second birth of Freedom in America," in the words of a *New York Times* journalist, Samuel Wilkeson. A divine providence certainly seemed to "have taken a direct hand" in the great battle's final outcome, especially on July 3.[41] In a letter to his wife, an officer of General Henry Lewis "Old Rock" Benning's Georgia brigade knew that a successful Pickett's Charge meant that slavery "is established for centuries" to come.[42] A Protestant Union soldier of Irish descent captured at Gettysburg simply concluded how "not only in the Gettysburg campaign, but in the whole war, we were on God's side and Lee was not."[43] The chaplain of the 14th Connecticut Volunteer Infantry wrote with firm conviction how "the highest, mightiest surge of the slave holders' rebellion was shattered and overcome at the stone wall front of the Second Army Corps. . . ."[44]

After all if everything had gone right in a closely coordinated assault with adequate support of thousands of troops as planned by Lee and flying artillery to protect the flanks, then "we would have been in Washington and the war ended," as Pickett revealed in his July 23, 1863, letter.[45] But as fully realized by Lee to his dying day, General Marsena Rudolph Patrick said it best to the captured Major John Corbett Timberlake, 53rd Virginia, "A few more men, Major, and you would have gained your independence right here."[46]

Like so many other relatives across the South, the family of Sergeant Thomas (Tom) Booker Tredway, Company I, 53rd Virginia, Armistead's brigade, who was mortally wounded at the stone wall, waited in vain for Tom's return: "We never knew the particulars of his death, but heard afterward that the fatal bullet struck him while bending over the body of his wounded colonel [Rawley White Martin] whom he was endeavoring to assist. . . . My mother spent long days and nights awaiting his return, and even after some kind friend had sent home his testament, ring, and other little trinkets, every footstep on the porch outside her door and every unusual voice in the night made her think it was her 'Tom' coming home."[47]

But like so many other young men and boys of Pickett's Charge, Tom was never coming home. Ironically, after the attack was repulsed, a Union lieutenant might have actually encountered Sergeant Thomas Booker Tredway: "Nearby I saw a handsome youngster, a Virginian. I knelt beside him, and wondered if perhaps he was sleeping, he was so calm and still . . . I asked him where he was wounded. He drew a hand slowly to his breast. I asked him if he was afraid to die. He whispered, 'No' "A spasm of pain closed his lids. I shall never forget [his] sweet, trusting look that spread over all his face as he said to me . . . 'I am going home. Good-bye.'"[48] In much the same way, so a final good-bye now applied to the Southern experiment in becoming its own sovereign nation, and also a good-bye to institutionalized slavery, after the repulse of the most famous attack in American history, Pickett's Charge.

About the Author

Phillip Thomas Tucker received his PhD in American history from St. Louis University, St. Louis, Missouri, in 1990. Tucker has authored many books, especially about Gettysburg and the Civil War. He has written about some of the most iconic moments in American history, including *George Washington's Surprise Attack: A New Look at the Battle That Decided the Fate of America* (Skyhorse Publishing, 2014).

Notes

Chapter I

1. Earl J. Hess, *Pickett's Charge, The Last Attack at Gettysburg* (Chapel Hill: University of North Carolina Press, 2001), p. 36; David H. Donald, ed., *Why the North Won the Civil War* (New York: Collier Books, 1973), p. 32.
2. Edwin B. Coddington, *The Gettysburg Campaign, A Study in Command* (New York: Charles Scribner's Sons, 1984), p. 443.
3. Robert L. O'Connell, *The Ghosts of Cannae, Hannibal and the Darkest Hour of the Roman Republic* (New York: Random House, 2011), pp. 3–4, 13, 132–169, 261–266; Hess, *Pickett's Charge*, p. 385; Carlos Canales, *Hannibal's Army, Carthage against Rome* (Madrid: Andrea Press, 2005), pp. 40–43; Nic Fields, *Carthaginian Warrior 264–146 BC* (Oxford: Osprey Publishing, 2010), pp. 24, 26; John Keegan, *A History of Warfare* (New York: Vintage Books, 1994), p. 271.
4. John W. Finley, "Bloody Angle," *Buffalo Evening News*, Buffalo, New York, May 28, 1894.
5. Jonathan North, trans. and ed., *With Napoleon's Guard in Russia, The Memoirs of Major Vionnet, 1812* (Barnsley, UK: Pen and Sword Books, Ltd., 2012), p. 58; Scott Bowden and Bill Ward, *Last Chance for Victory, Robert E. Lee and the Gettysburg Campaign* (New York: Da Capo Press, 2001), pp. 423–425.
6. Coddington, *The Gettysburg Campaign*, pp. 442–444; Ron Field, *Robert E. Lee, Leadership, Strategy, and Conflict* (Oxford: Osprey Publishing Company, 2010), p. 38.
7. Coddington, *The Gettysburg Campaign*, pp. 454–459; John H. Lewis, *Recollections from 1860 to 1865* (Washington, DC: Peake and Company Publishers, 1895), p. 77; Allen Guelzo, *Gettysburg, The Last Invasion* (New York: Knopf Publishing, 2013), pp. 374–376, 386; Bowden and Ward, *Last Chance for Victory*, p. 428; Allen Barra, "One Mile of Open Ground, " *Civil War Times*, pp. 34–35; Gabor Boritt, ed., *The Gettysburg Nobody Knows* (New York: Oxford University Press, 1995), p. 124; Edward Longacre, *Pickett, Leader of the Charge* (Shippensburg, Pa.: White Mane Publishing Company, 1995) p. 116; Hess, *Pickett's Charge*, pp. 5, 51; Shelby Foote, *The Civil War, A Narrative, Fredericksburg to Meridian* (3 vols.) (New York: Random House, 1963), vol. 2, p. 521.
8. Michael Stevens, ed., *As if it Were Glory, Robert Beecham's Civil War from the Iron Brigade to the Black Regiments* (New York: Rowan and Littlefield Publishers, Inc., 1999), p. 98.
9. Hess, *Pickett's Charge*, p. 37.
10. Ibid., pp. 38–39.

11. Stevens, ed., *As if it Were Glory,* p. 98; Noah Andre Trudeau, *Gettysburg, A Test of Courage* (New York: Harper Publishing, 2003), pp. 461–462; Coddington, *The Gettysburg Campaign,* p. 459; Foote, *The Civil War,* vol. 2, p. 521; Longacre, *Pickett,* p. 116; Tim Smith, compiler, *Farms at Gettysburg* (Gettysburg, Pa.: Thomas Publications, 2007), p. 15; A. T. Cowell, *Tactics at Gettysburg* (Gaithersburg, Md.: Olde Soldier Books, 1987), p. 66.

12. Grady McWhiney and Perry D. Jamieson, *Attack and Die, Military Tactics and the Southern Heritage* (Tuscaloosa: University of Alabama Press, 1990), pp. 3–191; Carol Reardon, *Pickett's Charge in History and Memory* (Chapel Hill: University of North Carolina Press, 2003), pp. 1–213; Ralph Peters, "The Myths of Gettysburg, The Battle of Lies that Trailed the Battle of Blood," *Armchair General* (July 2013), p. 34; Coddington, *The Gettysburg Campaign,* pp. 463–464; Foote, *The Civil War,* vol. 2, p. 522; Guelzo, *Gettysburg,* p. 382.

13. Annette Tapert, ed., *The Brothers' War, Civil War Letters to Love Ones from the Blue and Gray* (New York: Vintage, 1989), p. 175.

14. Ronald Moseley, ed., *The Stillwell Letters, A Georgian in Longstreet's Corps, Army of Northern Virginia* (Macon, Va.: Mercer University Press, 2002), pp. 176–177.

15. Guelzo, *Gettysburg,* p. 31.

16. Richard N. Current, *The Lincoln Nobody Knows* (New York: Hill and Wang, 1993), p. 152; Sandburg, *Abraham Lincoln,* vol. 2, p. 352.

17. Guelzo, *Gettysburg,* pp. 32, 333–334.

18. Guelzo, *Gettysburg,* p. 32, 99, 333–334; Carl Sandburg, *Abraham Lincoln* (3 volumes), (Dell Publishing, 1965), vol. 2, p. 352; *Annals of the War, Written by Leading Participants North and South* (Edison, N.J.: Blue and Grey Press, 1996), pp. 306–307; Emory Thomas, *Robert E. Lee, A Biography* (New York: W. W. Norton and Company, 1995), pp. 292–293.

19. Bowden and War, *Last Chance for Victory,* p. 427.

20. Thomas, *Robert E. Lee,* pp. 292–293.

21. Current, *The Lincoln Nobody Knows,* p. 152.

22. Guelzo, *Gettysburg,* p. 376.

23. Stevens, ed., *As if It Were Glory,* p. 98; Coddington, *The Gettysburg Campaign,* pp. 458–459.

24. J. B. Polley, *Hood's Texas Brigade, Its Marches, Its Battles, Its Achievements* (New York: The Neale Publishing Company, 1910), p. 153; McWhiney and Jamieson, *Attack and Die,* pp. xiii–24.

25. Guelzo, *Gettysburg,* p. 18.

26. C. Vann Woodward and Elisabeth Muhlenfeld, eds., *The Private Mary Chesnut, The Unpublished Civil War Diaries* (New York: Oxford University Press, 1984), p. 196.

27. Charles Royster, *Light-Horse Harry Lee and the Legacy of the American Revolution* (Cambridge, Mass.: Cambridge University Press, 1986), pp. 13–246; Guelzo, *Gettysburg,* pp. 18, 374–376; Polley, *Hood's Texas Brigade,* p. 153; Donald, ed., *Why the North Won the Civil War,* p. 48; Barra, "One Mile of Open Ground," *CWT,* pp. 34–35; Thomas, *Robert E. Lee,* pp. 17–18, 30–31, 292; Lewis, *Recollections from 1860 to 1865,* pp. 77, 79; Trudeau, *Gettysburg,* p. 499; Coddington, *The Gettysburg Campaign,* p. 463–464;

Douglas Southall Freeman, *R. E. Lee, a Biography* (4 vols.) (New York: Charles Scribner's Sons, 1962), pp. 2–3; Dwight G. Anderson and Nancy S. Anderson, *The Generals, Ulysses S. Grant and Robert E. Lee* (New York: Knopf Publishing, 1988), p. 385; James K. Swisher, *The Revolutionary War in the Southern Back County* (Gretna, La.: Pelican Publishing Company, 2008), pp. 293–294.

28. Guelzo, *Gettysburg*, pp. 374–375.

29. *Annals of the War*, pp. 305–306; Martin Dugard, *The Training Ground, Grant, Lee, Sherman and Davis in Mexico, 1846–1848* (New York: Little Brown and Company, 2008), pp. 335–369; Trudeau, *Gettysburg*, p. 499; Jeffrey D. Wert, *A Glorious Army, Robert E. Lee's Triumph, 1862–1863* (New York: Simon and Schuster Publishing, 2012), p. 269; George R. Stewart, *Pickett's Charge* (New York: Fawcett Publications, 1963), p. 188; Clifford Dowdey, *Death of a Nation, Lee and His Men at Gettysburg* (New York: Knopf Publications, 1958), p. 257; Lockwood R. Tower, ed., *Lee's Adjutant, The Wartime Letters of Walter Herron Taylor, 1862–1865* (Columbia: University of South Carolina Press, 1995), pp. 58, 101; Jefferson Davis, *The Rise and Fall of the Confederate Government* (New York: Collier Books, 1961), p. 428; Thomas, *Robert E. Lee*, p. 299; Kent Gramm, *Gettysburg, A Meditation on War and Values* (Bloomington: Indiana University Press, 1994), p. 8; Jeffrey Record, *Beating Goliath, Why Insurgencies Win* (Washington, DC: Potomac Books, 2009), pp. 65–66; Barra, "One Mile of Open Ground, " *CWT*, pp. 32–35; Lewis, *Recollections from 1860 to 1865*, p. 77; Coddington, *The Gettysburg Campaign*, pp. 459, 463–464; Longacre, *Pickett*, p. 117; Sandburg, *Abraham Lincoln*, vol. 2, p. 352; "Quercus Prinus, " Wikipedia; Kathy G. Harrison and John R. Busey, *Nothing but Glory, Pickett's Division at Gettysburg* (Gettysburg, Pa.: Thomas Publications, 2001), p. 21; G. Howard Gregory, *53rd Virginia Infantry and 5th Battalion Virginia Infantry* (Lynchburg, Va.: Howard Publications, 1999), p. 52; Thomas, *Robert E. Lee*, pp. 289, 292, 299.

30. Emory M. Thomas, *Robert E. Lee, A Biography, (New York: Norton, 1995)*, p. 292; Freeman, *R. E. Lee*, vol. 1, pp. 249–300; Anderson and Anderson, *The Generals*, p. 388.

31. David G. Chandler, *The Campaigns of Napoleon, The Mind and Method of History's Greatest Soldier* (New York: Scribner, 1966), p. 1092; Coddington, *The Gettysburg Campaign*, pp. 454, 463–464; Guelzo, *Gettysburg*, p. 382; Trudeau, *Gettysburg*, p. 499; Wert, *A Glorious Army*, pp. 175–205; Adam Zamoyski, *Moscow 1812, Napoleon's Fatal March* (New York: HarperCollins Publishers, 2004), p. 14.

32. Richard Rollins, ed., *Pickett's Charge* (Mechanicsburg, Pa.: Stackpole Books, 2005), p. 317.

33. Gregory, *53rd Virginia Infantry and 5th Battalion Virginia Infantry*, p. 53.

34. Joseph B. Mitchell, *Military Leaders in the Civil War* (McLean, Va.: EPM Publications, Inc., 1972), p. 137.

35. William G. Piston, *Lee's Tarnished Lieutenant, James Longstreet and His Place in Southern History* (Athens: University of Georgia Press, 1997), p. 47.

36. Lewis, *Recollections from 1860 to 1865*, pp. 77, 79.

37. Gary W. Gallagher, ed., *The Third Day at Gettysburg and Beyond* (Chapel Hill: University of North Carolina Press, 1998), p. 15.

38. Wert, *A Glorious Army,* p. 230; Combined Service Records of Confederate Soldiers Who Served in Organizations from the State of Virginia, Record Group 109, National Archives, Washington, DC

39. Lewis, *Recollections from 1860 to 1865,* p. 79; *Annals of the War,* pp. 305–306; Trudeau, *Gettysburg,* p. 499; Barra, "One Mile of Open Ground, " *CWT,* pp. 34–35; Coddington, *The Gettysburg Campaign,* pp. 463–464.

40. Tapert, ed., *The Brothers' War,* pp. 160, 162; Barra, "One Mile of Open Ground, " *CWT,* pp. 34–35.

41. Guelzo, *Gettysburg,* p. 382.

42. "Gettysburg 150th Anniversary: Pickett's Charge a Deadly Mistake by Gen. Lee, " *The Macomb Daily,* July 3, 2013, Mount Clemens, Michigan.

43. Joseph Graham to William A. Graham, July 30, 1863, Papers of William A. Graham, Southern Historical Collection, University of North Carolina, Chapel Hill, North Carolina; Trudeau, Gettysburg, p. 499; Barra, "One Mile of Open Ground," *CWT,* pp. 34–35; Coddington, *The Gettysburg Campaign,* pp. 463–464.

44. Gabor S. Boritt, *Why the Confederacy Lost* (New York: Oxford University Press, 1992), p. 97; Paul Johnson, *Napoleon, A Life* (New York: Penguin Books, 2006), p. 49; Samuel Carter, *The Last Cavaliers, Confederate and Union Cavalry in the Civil War* (New York: St. Martin's Press, 1982), pp. 169–172; Tom Carhart, *Lost Triumph, Lee's Real Plan at Gettysburg–and Why it Failed* (New York: Putnam Books, 2005), pp. xi–269.

45. Chandler, *The Campaigns of Napoleon,* p. 1085.

46. *Annals of the War,* pp. 312–313; Coddington, *The Gettysburg Campaign,* p. 462; Trudeau, *Gettysburg,* pp. 461, 499; Timothy H. Smith, *The Story of Lee's Headquarters,* (Gettysburg, Pa.: Thomas Publications, 1995), pp. 1–9, 37–50, 59–62; Bowden and War, *Last Chance for Victory,* p. 429; Hess, *Pickett's Charge,* p. 5.

47. Trudeau, *Gettysburg,* p. 499; Coddington, *The Gettysburg Campaign,* pp. 443–444, 454–464; James I. Robertson, *General A. P. Hill, The Story of a Confederate Warrior* (New York: Vintage Books, 1987), p. 220; Wert, *A Glorious Army,* p. 269.

48. Hess, *Pickett's Charge,* p. 36; Stewart, *Pickett's Charge,* p. 48.

49. *Annals of the War,* pp. 312–313; Hess, *Pickett's Charge,* p. 36; Robertson, *General A. P. Hill,* pp. 197, 212; James K. Swisher, *Warrior in Gray, General Robert Rodes of Lee's Army,* (Shippensburg, Pa.: White Mane Publishing Company, Inc., 2000), p. 124.

50. *Annals of the War,* pp. 312–313; Robertson, *General A. P. Hill,* pp. 216–220; McKenzie, *Uncertain Glory,* p. 160; Wert, *A Glorious Army,* pp. 269, 274–275, 282; Tucker, *Lee and Longstreet at Gettysburg,* p. 95; Bowden and Ward, *Last Chance for Victory,* p. 428; Longacre, *Pickett,* pp. 116–117; Cowell, *Tactics at Gettysburg,* pp. 78–79.

51. Stevens, introduction, *As if it Were Glory,* pp. 98–99; Thom Hatch, *Glorious War, The Military Adventures of George Armstrong Custer* (New York: St. Martin's Press, 2013), p. 139; Cowell, *Tactics at Gettysburg,* p. 81; Carhart, *Lost Triumph,* pp. xi–269.

52. James M. McPherson, *This Mighty Scourge* (New York: Oxford University Press, 2007), p. 86; Hatch, *Glorious War,* pp. 139–159; Cowell, *Tactics at Gettysburg–* p. 81.

53. Robert L. O'Connell, *The Ghosts of Canne* (New York: Random House, 2011), pp. 3–4, 132–169, 262; McPherson, *This Might Scourge,* p. 86; Carhart, *Lost Triumph,* pp. xi–269; Cowell, *Tactics at Gettysburg,* p. 81.

54. Stevens, introduction, *As if it Were Glory,* pp. 98–99; Gabor S. Boritt, editor, *The Gettysburg Nobody Knows,* (New York: Oxford University Press, 1997), pp. 21–22; Guelzo, *Gettysburg,* p. 382; Barra, "One Mile of Open Ground, " *CWT,* pp. 32–35; Coddington, *The Gettysburg Campaign,* pp. 463–464; Longacre, *Pickett,* p. 117; *Annals of the War,* pp. 215, 313; Carter,, *The Last Cavaliers,* pp. 169–172; Carhart, *Lost Triumph,* pp. 1–269; Cowell, *Tactics at Gettysburg,* p. 81; Foote, *The Civil War,* vol. 2, pp. 521–522; Trudeau, *Gettysburg,* p. 499; Hess, *Pickett's Charge,* pp. 6–11; Stewart, *Pickett's Charge,* p. 48; Stevens, ed., *As if it Were Glory,* pp. 98–99.

55. Walter Harrison, *Pickett's Men, A Fragment of War History* (Baton Rouge: Louisiana State University Press, 2000), p. 183; Longacre, *Pickett,* p. 117; *Annals of the War,* p. 313; Carhart, *Lost Triumph,* pp. 1–269; Stevens, ed., *As if it Were Glory,* pp. 98–99; Trudeau, *Gettysburg,* p. 499; Hatch, *Glorious War,* p. 139; Cowell, *Tactics at Gettysburg,* pp. 76, 78–79, 81; Stewart, *Pickett's Charge,* p. 188.

56. D. Scott Hartwig, "High Water Mark, Heroes, Myth, and Memory, " Paper, Archives, Gettysburg National Military Park, Gettysburg, Pennsylvania; "Quercus Prinus, " Wikipedia; Hess, *Pickett's Charge,* p. 90.

57. Hartwing, "High Water Mark, Heroes, Myth, and Memory, " GNMP; Harrison, *Pickett's Men,* p. 183.

58. Hartwig, "High Water Mark, Heroes, Myth, and Memory, " GNMP.

59. Ibid.; Harrison, *Pickett's Men,* p. 183; Coddington, *The Gettysburg Campaign,* pp. 459, 463–464; Hess, *Pickett's Charge,* p. 174; Cowell, *Tactics at Gettysburg,* pp. 76, 81; Carhart, *Lost Triumph,* pp. xi–260, Hatch, *Glorious War,* pp. 139–159.

60. Guelzo, *Gettysburg,* p. 376.

61. Coddington, *The Gettysburg Campaign,* pp. 459, 462, 463–464; Carhart, *Lost Triumph,* pp. xi–269; Hess, *Pickett's Charge,* p. 120.

62. Harrison, *Pickett's Men,* p. 183; Carhart, *Lost Triumph,* pp. 1–269; Coddington, *The Gettysburg Campaign,* pp. 463–464; Wert, *A Glorious Army,* p. 269; McWhiney and Jamieson, *Attack and Die,* pp. 3–125, 143–169; Hess, *Pickett's Charge,* p. 90; Bowden and Ward, *Last Chance for Victory,* pp. 424–425, 430; Trudeau, *Gettysburg,* p. 499; Guelzo, *Gettysburg,* p. 382; Clary, *Eagles and Empire,* pp. 368–371; Hatch, *Glorious War,* pp. 139–159; Hartwig, "High Water Mark, Heroes, Myth and Memory, " GNMP; Cowell, *Tactics at Gettysburg,* pp. 78–79, 81.

63. Benjamin G. Humphreys to Lafayette McLaws, January 6, 1878, Lafayette McLaws' Papers, Southern Historical Society Collection, University of North Carolina Library, University of North Carolina, Chapel Hill, North Carolina; Wert, *A Glorious Army,* pp. 269, 274–275; Thomas, *Robert E. Lee,* pp. 18, 298–299; Guelzo, *Gettysburg,* p. 35; *Buffalo Evening News,* May 28, 1894; Longacre, *Pickett,* pp. 116–117; Piston, *Lee's Tarnished Lieutenant,* pp. 40–41, 59; Barra, "One Mile of Open Ground, " *CWT,* p. 35; *Annals of War,* p. 313; Kenneth Allers, *The Fog of Gettysburg, The Myth and Mysteries of a Battle* (Nashville, Tenn.: Cumberland House Publishing, 2005), pp. 146–147; Rod Gragg, *Covered with Glory, The 26th North Carolina at the Battle of Gettysburg* (Chapel Hill: University of North Carolina Press, 2000), pp. 67, 156; Swisher, *Warrior in Gray,* pp. 124–125; W. Buck Yearns and John G. Barrett, ed., *North Carolina Civil War Documents* (Chapel Hill: The University of North Carolina

Press, 1980), p. 125; Hess, *Pickett's Charge,* pp. 5–7, 36; Thomas, *Robert E. Lee,* pp. 296–299; Coddington, *The Gettysburg Campaign,* pp. 454–458, 462; Field, *Robert E. Lee,* p. 36; Phillip Thomas Tucker, *Barksdale's Charge, The True High Tide of the Confederacy at Gettysburg, July 2, 1863* (Havertown, Pa.: Casemate Publishing, 2013), pp. 95–260; Bowden and Ward, *Final Chance for Victory,* pp. 424–430; Cowell, *Tactics at Gettysburg,* pp. 78–79, 81; Foote, *The Civil War,* vol. 2, pp. 528–529; Robertson, *General A. P. Hill,* pp. 196, 207–209, 216–224; Dowdey, *Death of a Nation,* pp. 303–305; Trudeau, *Gettysburg,* pp. 367–392; *Annals of the War,* pp. 315–316; J. B. Polley, *Hood's Texas Brigade, Its Marches, its Battles, its Achievements* (New York: The Neale Publishing Company, 1910), p. 193.

64. Allers, *The Fog of Gettysburg,* pp. 146–147; *Annals of the War,* p. 313.

65. Wert, *A Glorious Army,* pp. 269, 274–275.

66. Allers, *The Fog of Gettysburg,* p. 146; *Annals of the War,* pp. 315–316; Gragg, *Covered with Glory,* p. 156; Coddington, *The Gettysburg Campaign,* p. 462.

67. Coddington, *The Gettysburg Campaign,* p. 452; Robertson, *General A. P. Hill,* pp. 193–225; Hess, *Pickett's Charge,* p. 19.

68. *Annals of War,* p. 313; Trudeau, *Gettysburg,* p. 499; Wert, *A Glorious Army,* pp. 169, 274–275; Cowell, *Tactics at Gettysburg,* pp. 78–79; Foote, *The Civil War,* vol. 2, p. 530; Thomas, *Robert E. Lee,* pp. 302–303; Robertson, *General A. P. Hill,* pp. 196, 216.

69. Robertson, *General A. P. Hill,* p. 220; Field, *Robert E. Lee,* p. 5.

70. Stewart, *Pickett's Charge,* p. 48.

71. Coddington, *The Gettysburg Campaign,* p. 462; Wert, *A Glorious Army,* pp. 274–275, 281–282; Cowell, *Tactics at Gettysburg,* pp. 78–79.

72. Bowden and Ward, *Last Chance for Victory,* p. 439.

73. Coddington, *The Gettysburg Campaign,* pp. 463–464; Stewart, *Pickett's Charge,* p. 48; Guelzo, *Gettysburg,* p. 382; Barra, "One Mile of Open Ground, " *CWT,* pp. 32–35; Reardon, *Pickett's Charge,* p. 21; Cowell, *Tactics at Gettysburg,* pp. 78–79.

74. Carhart, *Lost Triumph,* pp. xi–269; Stevens, ed., *As if it Were Glory,* pp. 98–99, 102; Hatch, *Glorious War,* pp. 139–159; Cowell, *Tactics at Gettysburg,* pp. 76, 81; Stewart, *Pickett's Charge,* p. 188.

75. Tower, ed., *Lee's Adjutant,* p. 60.

76. Ibid., p. 61; Wert, *A Glorious Army,* p. 269; Cowell, *Tactics at Gettysburg,* pp. 76, 78–79, 81; Stewart, *Pickett's Charge,* p. 188; Hatch, *Glorious War,* pp. 139–159.

77. Trudeau, *Gettysburg,* p. 499; Hess, *Pickett's Charge,* p. 7; Cowell, *Tactics at Gettysburg,* pp. 76, 78–79; Foote, *The Civil War,* vol. 2, pp. 531–532; Longacre, *Pickett,* pp. 3, 14, 26–27, 117; Hatch, *Glorious War,* pp. 139–159; Gramm, *Gettysburg,* pp. 186–188; Barra, "One Mile of Open Ground, " *CWT,* pp. 32–35; Wert, *A Glorious Army,* p. 268; Joseph Wheelan, *Invading Mexico: Mexico's Continental Dream and the Mexican War, 1846–1847* (New York: Carroll and Graf, 2007), pp. 371–373; Dugard, *The Training Ground,* pp. 335–369; Coddington, *The Gettysburg Campaign,* pp. 463–464; Lewis, *Recollections from 1860 to 1865,* pp. 77, 79; David A. Clary, *Eagles and Empire, The United States, Mexico and the Struggle for a Continent* (New York: Bantam, 2009), pp. 368–372; McWhiney and Jamieson, *Attack and Die,* pp. 27, 34, 40, 148, 153–157,

159–160, 168–169; Stevens, introduction, *As if it Were Glory,* pp. 98–99, 102; Wert, *A Glorious Army,* p. 269.

78. Johnson, *A Gallant Little Army,* p. 223; Longacre, *Pickett,* pp. 19, 26; Piston, *Lee's Tarnished Lieutenant,* p. 6.

79. Longacre, *Pickett,* p. 26.

80. Johnson, *A Gallant Little Army,* p. 223; McWhiney and Jamieson, *Attack and Die,* pp. 27, 34, 40, 134–136, 148, 153–160, 168–169; Wheelan, *Invading Mexico,* pp. 371–373; Johnson, *A Gallant Little Army,* pp. 213–226; Longacre, *Pickett,* pp. 26–27; Dugard, *The Training Ground,* pp. 335–369; Thomas, *Robert E. Lee,* p. 292.

81. Wheelan, *Invading Mexico,* pp. 371–373; Longacre, *Pickett,* pp. 26–27; Johnson, *A Gallant Little Army,* pp. 213–226; Dugard, *The Training Ground,* pp. 335–369; Chandler, *The Campaigns of Napoleon,* pp. 133–201; McWhiney and Jamieson, *Attack and Die,* pp. 27, 34, 40, 134–136, 148, 153–160, 168–169.

82. McWhiney and Jamieson, *Attack and Die,* p. 36; Chandler, *The Campaigns of Napoleon,* pp. 133–201; Coddington, *The Gettysburg Campaign,* pp. 463–464; Barra, "One Mile of Open Ground, " *CWT,* pp. 32–35.

83. Theodore J. Crackel, *West Point, A Bicentennial History* (Lawrence: University of Kansas Press, 2002), pp. 103–105, 118.

84. McWhiney and Jamieson, *Attack and Die,* p. 36; Paul Johnson, *Napoleon, A Life* (New York: Penguin Books, 2002), pp. 49, 55–56; T. E. Crowdy, *Incomparable, Napoleon's 9th Light Infantry Regiment* (Oxford: Osprey Publishing, 2012), p. 117; Hatch, *Glorious War,* pp. 139–159.

85. Johnson, *Napoleon,* p. 56.

86. Chandler, *The Campaigns of Napoleon,* pp. 133–134; McWhiney and Jamieson, *Attack and Die,* pp. 41–42; Donald, ed., *Why the North Won the Civil War,* pp. 36–49; Dugard, *The Training Ground,* pp. 335–369; Edward Stackpole, *Chancellorsville* (Mechanicsburg, Pa.: Stackpole Books, 1989), p. 368; Field, *Robert E. Lee,* p. 55; Theodore J. Crackel, *West Point, A Bicentennial* (Lawrence: University Press of Kansas, 2002), pp. 103–105, 118.

87. Trudeau, *Gettysburg,* p. 499; McWhiney and Jamieson, *Attack and Die,* pp. 27–43, 47; Dugard, *The Training Ground,* pp. 335–369; Coddington, *The Gettysburg Campaign,* pp. 463–464; Barra, "One Mile of Open Ground, " *CWT,* pp. 32–35.

88. McWhiney and Jamieson, *Attack and Die,* p. 41; Chandler, *The Campaigns of Napoleon,* pp. 133–134.

89. Chandler, *The Campaigns of Napoleon,* p. 135.

90. Bowden and Ward, *Last Chance for Victory,* p. 425; Guelzo, *Gettysburg,* p. 18; Donald, ed., *Why the North Won the Civil War,* p. 22; Thomas J. Connelly and Barbara J. Bellows, *God and General Longstreet* (Baton Rouge: Louisiana State University Press, 1995), pp. 11–12; Alan T. Nolan, *Lee Considered, General Robert E. Lee and Civil War History* (Chapel Hill: University of North Carolina Press, 1991, pp. 99–100).

91. Bowden and Ward, *Last Chance for Victory,* p. 426.

92. Johnson, *A Gallant Little Army,* p. 226; Hatch, *Glorious Victory,* pp. 139–159; Cowell, *Tactics at Gettysburg,* p. 81.

93. Gregory, *53rd Virginia Infantry and 5th Battalion Virginia Infantry*, pp. 50–51; Longacre, *Pickett*, p. 26; Guelzo, *Gettysburg*, p. 382; Coddington, *The Gettysburg Campaign*, pp. 463–464; Thomas, *Robert E. Lee*, p. 292; Barra, "One Mile of Open Ground," *CWT*, pp. 32–35; Carhart, *Lost Triumph*, pp. xi–260; Bowden and Ward, *Last Chance for Victory*, pp. 425–426; Hatch, *Glorious War*, pp. 1–3, 139–159; Cowell, *Tactics at Gettysburg*, pp. 78–79, 81.

94. Time-Life Editors, *Voices of the Civil War, Gettysburg* (Alexandria, Va.: Time-Life Books, 1995), p. 148.

95. Tower, ed., *Lee's Adjutant*, p. 101; Lewis, *Recollections from 1860 to 1865*, pp. 77, 79; Gramm, *Gettysburg*, pp. 8, 186–188; Guelzo, *Gettysburg*, pp. 18, 382; Trudeau, *Gettysburg*, p. 462; Coddington, *The Gettysburg Campaign*, pp. 458–464; Davis, *The Rise and Fall of the Confederate Government*, p. 428; Nolan, *Lee Considered*, pp. 99–100; Gallagher, ed., *The Third Day at Gettysburg and Beyond*, p. 11; Jeffery Record, *Beating Goliath, Why Insurgencies Win* (Washington, DC: Potomac Books, 2009), pp. 65–66; Timothy D. Johnson, *A Gallant Little Army, The Mexico City Campaign* (Lawrence: University Press of Kansas, 2001), pp. 213v226; Wheelan, *Invading Mexico*, pp. 371–373; Piston, *Lee's Tarnished Lieutenant*, p. 28; McWhiney and Jamieson, *Attack and Die*, pp. xiv–169; *Annals of the War*, pp. 305–306, 313, Hess, *Pickett's Charge*, pp. 9–15; Thomas, *Robert E. Lee*, p. 292; Wert, *A Glorious Army*, p. 269; Bowden and Ward, *Last Chance for Victory*, pp. 424–434; Dugard, *The Training Ground*, pp. 335–369; Robertson, *General A. P. Hill*, pp. 220–221; Bradley M. Gottfried, *Brigades of Gettysburg, The Union and Confederate Brigades at the Battle of Gettysburg* (New York: Skyhorse Publishing, 2012), pp. 467–468, 474; Time-Life Editors, *Voices of the Civil War, Gettysburg*, p. 163; Anderson and Anderson, *The Generals*, pp. 381–382; Gene Smith, *Lee and Grant* (New York: Meridian Books, 1984), p. 189.

96. Gottfried, *Brigades of Gettysburg*, p. 474; Robertson, *General A. P. Hill*, p. 221.

97. Davis, *The Rise and Fall of the Confederate Government*, p. 428; Johnson, *Napoleon*, pp. 49, 56; Thomas, *Robert E. Lee*, p. 288.

98. Coddington, *The Gettysburg Campaign*, pp. 463–464; Wert, *A Glorious Army*, p. 270; Dowdey, *Death of a Nation*, p. 257; Lewis, *Recollections from 1860 to 1865*, pp. 77, 79; Barra, "One Mile of Open Ground, " *CWT*, pp. 34–35; Trudeau, *Gettysburg*, pp. 367–421, 461–462.

99. Tower, ed., *Lee's Adjutant*, pp. 1–2, 53; Guelzo, *Gettysburg*, p. 382.

100. Coddington, *The Gettysburg Campaign*, pp. 459–464; Trudeau, *Gettysburg*, pp. 461, 490, 499; Barra, "One Mile of Open Ground, " *CWT*, pp. 32–35; Wert, *A Glorious Army*, p. 270.

101. Trudeau, *Gettysburg*, pp. 461–462, 499.

102. Ibid., p. 462; McWhiney and Jamieson, *Attack and Die*, pp. 3–4; Barra, "One Mile of Open Ground, " *CWT*, pp. 32–35; Coddington, *The Gettysburg Campaign*, pp. 459–464; Piston, *Lee's Tarnished Lieutenant*, p. 35; Wert, *A Glorious Army*, pp. 269–270.

103. Bowden and Ward, *Last Chance for Victory*, pp. 434–435.

104. Gottfried, *Brigades of Gettysburg*, p. 479.

105. Humphreys to McLaws, January 6, 1878, UNCL; Piston, *Lee's Tarnished Lieutenant*, p. 33; Trudeau, *Gettysburg*, pp. 351–396; Time-Life Editors, *Voices of the Civil War, Gettysburg*, p. 148; McWhiney and Jamieson, *Attack and Die*, p. 7.

106. Compiled Military Service Records of Confederate Soldiers from the State of Virginia, Record Group, 109, National Archives, Washington, DC; George M. Setzer to parents, December 15, 1862, Museum Quality Americana Online Sales, Internet.

107. Trudeau, *Gettysburg*, p. 499; Stewart, *Pickett's Charge*, p. 48; Guelzo, *Gettysburg*, p. 382; Gramm, *Gettysburg*, pp. 186–188; Coddington, *The Gettysburg Campaign*, pp. 463–464; Davis, *The Rise and Fall of the Confederate Government*, p. 430; Hess, *Pickett's Charge*, p. 388; Stewart, *Pickett's Charge*, p. 188; Reardon, *Pickett's Charge*, pp. 39–175; Cowell, *Tactics at Gettysburg*, p. 76; Barra, "One Mile of Open Ground, " *CWT*, pp. 34–35; Lewis, *Recollections from 1860 to 1865*, pp. 77, 79; Frank A. Haskell, *The Battle of Gettysburg* (London: Eyre and Spottiswoode, 1959), p. 100; Wert, *A Glorious Army*, p. 269.

108. Anderson and Anderson, *The Generals*, p. 415, Harrison, *Pickett's Men*, p. 182; Benjamin G. Humphreys to Lafayette McLaws, January 6, 1878, University of North Carolina Library, Chapel Hill, North Carolina; Phillip Thomas Tucker, *Barksdale's Charge, The True High Tide of the Confederacy at Gettysburg, July 2, 1863*, (Havertown: Casemate Publishing, 2013) pp. 95–260; Hess, *Pickett's Charge*, pp. 11, 15; Bowden and Ward, *Last Chance for Victory*, p. 424; Cowell, *Tactics at Gettysburg*, pp. 76, 78–79; Wert, *A Glorious Army*, pp. 269, 274–275.

109. Matthew Spruill, *Summer Thunder, A Battlefield Guide to the Artillery at Gettysburg* (Knoxville: University of Tennessee Press, 2010), p. 213; Harrison, *Pickett's Men*, p. 182.

110. Hess, *Pickett's Charge*, p. 388; Trudeau, *Gettysburg*, p. 499; Wert, *A Glorious Army*, pp. 269–270.

111. Harry W. Pfanz, *The Battle of Gettysburg, National Park Civil War Series* (Washington, DC: Eastern National Park and Monument Association, 1994), pp. 33–34; Stewart, *Pickett's Charge*, p. 48; Wert, *A Glorious Army*, pp. 269–270.

112. Joseph Graham to William Graham, July 30, 1863, SHC; Monroe F. Cockrell, ed., *Gunner with Stonewall, Reminiscences of William Thomas Proague* (Wilmington, N.C.: Broadfoot Publishing Company, 1987), p. 68.

113. Bowden and War, *Last Chance for Victory*, pp. 434, 437–438.

114. Cockrell, ed., *Gunner with Stonewall,*, pp. xvi, 70; Guelzo, *Gettysburg*, p. 376; Anderson and Anderson, *The Generals*, p. 416; Cowell, *Tactics at Gettysburg*, pp. 78–79; Trudeau, *Gettysburg*, pp. 461, 499; Joseph E. Persico, *My Enemy, My Brother, Men and Days of Gettysburg* (New York: Simon and Schuster Publishers, 1977), p. 212; Robertson, *General A. P. Hill*, p. 197; Bowden and Ward, *Last Chance for Victory*, pp. 439, 451; Hess, *Pickett's Charge*, p. 14; Wert, *A Glorious Army*, pp. 269–270.

115. *Annals of the War*, p. 313; Guelzo, *Gettysburg*, p. 376; Cowell, *Tactics at Gettysburg*, p. 76; Robertson, *General A. P. Hill*, p. 221; Wert, *A Glorious Army*, pp. 269–270.

116. Bowden and Ward, *Last Chance for Victory*, p. 439; Persico, *My Enemy, My Brother*, p. 212.

117. Zack C. Waters and James C. Edmonds, *A Small but Spartan Band* (Tuscaloosa: University of Alabama Press, 2013), pp. 70–72, 82, 184.

118. Haskell, *The Battle of Gettysburg*, p. 100; Coddington, *The Gettysburg Campaign*, pp. 463–464; John Michael Priest, *Into the Fight, Pickett's Charge at Gettysburg* (Shippensburg, Pa.: White Mane Publishing Company, 1998), p. 49; Barra, "One Mile of Open Ground, " *CWT,* pp. 34–35; Trudeau, *Gettysburg*, p. 499; Bowden and Ward, *Last Chance for Victory*, p. 428; Wert, *A Glorious Army*, pp. 269–270; Rollins, ed., *Pickett's Charge*, pp. 4–10, 16.

119. Carhart, *Lost Triumph*, pp. 1–240; Bowden and Ward, *Last Chance for Victory*, p. 428; Hatch, *Glorious Victory*, pp. 139–159; Cowell, *Tactics at Gettysburg*, p. 81; Hatch, *Glorious War*, pp. 139–159; Stevens, ed., *As if it Were Glory*, pp. 98–99.

120. Boritt, ed., *The Gettysburg Nobody Knows*, p. 114; Stevens, ed., *As if it Were Glory*, pp. 98–99; Carhart, *Lost Triumph*, pp. xi–269; Hatch, *Glorious Victory*, pp. 139–159; Cowell, *Tactics at Gettysburg*, p. 81.

121. Boritt, ed., *The Gettysburg Nobody Knows*, pp. 98–99.

122. Priest, *Into the Fight*, p. 49.

123. Harrison and Busey, *Nothing but Glory*, p. 21; Hess, *Pickett's Charge*, p. 47; Trudeau, *Gettysburg*, p. 499; Thomas, *Robert E. Lee*, p. 292; Gottsfried, *Brigades of Gettysburg*, p. 477; Wert, *A Glorious Army*, pp. 269–270.

124. Longacre, *Pickett*, pp. 3–5; Anderson and Anderson, *The Generals*, p. 417.

125. Haskell, *The Battle of Gettysburg*, p. 100; Barra, "One Mile of Open Ground, " *CWT,* p. 35; Trudeau, *Gettysburg*, p. 499; Coddington, *The Gettysburg Campaign*, pp. 463–464; Wert, *A Glorious Army*, p. 269; Stewart, *Pickett's Charge*, p. 188.

126. Rollins, ed., *Pickett's Charge*, p. 10; Bowden and Ward, *Last Chance for Victory*, p. 439; Wert, *A Glorious Army*, pp. 274–275; Cowell, *Tactics at Gettysburg*, pp. 78–79.

127. Stewart, *Pickett's Charge*, p. 188; Carhart, *Lost Triumph*, pp. xi–260; Hatch, *Glorious War*, pp. 1–3, 139–159; Bowden and Ward, *Final Chance for Victory*, p. 439; Cowell, *Tactics at Gettysburg*, p. 81.

128. Bowden and Ward, *Final Chance for Victory*, pp. 434–439; Guelzo, *Gettysburg*, p. 21; Wert, *A Glorious Army*, pp. 269, 281–282.

129. Stewart, *Pickett's Charge*, p. 188.

130. Gottfried, *Brigades of Gettysburg*, p. 464; Humphreys to McLaws, January 6, 1878, UNCL; Trudeau, *Gettysburg*, pp. 367–392; 461–462; Harrison, *Pickett's Men*, p. 183; Persico, *My Enemy, My Brother*, p. 205; Foote, *The Civil War*, vol. 2, pp. 521–522; Bowden and Ward, *Last Chance for Victory*, pp. 434–439; Wert, *A Glorious Army*, pp. 269–270; Tucker, *Barksdale's Charge, The True High Tide of the Confederacy at Gettysburg, July 2, 1863*, pp. 95–260.

131. Haskell, *The Battle of Gettysburg*, p. 72; Wert, *A Glorious Army*, p. 269; Cahart, *Lost Triumph*, pp. xi–269; Hatch, *Glorious War*, pp. 139–159; Bowden and Ward, *Last Chance for Victory*, p. 439.

132. Haskell, *The Battle of Gettysburg*, p. 73; Trudeau, *Gettysburg*, p. 499; Stewart, *Pickett's Charge*, p. 48; Trudeau, *Gettysburg*, p. 423; Wert, *A Glorious Army*, p. 269; Rollins, ed., *Pickett's Charge*, p. 62.

133. Trudeau, *Gettysburg*, pp. 442, 449; Barra, "One Mile of Open Ground, " *CWT*, pp. 34–35; Guelzo, *Gettysburg*, p. 382; Wert, *A Glorious Army*, pp. 269–270; Piston, *Lee's Tarnished Lieutenant*, pp. 96–164; Field, *Robert E. Lee*, p. 40.

134. Stephen W. Sears, *Gettysburg* (Boston, Mass.: Houghton Mifflin Company, 2003), p. 388; Trudeau, *Gettysburg*, pp. 461–462, 499; Coddington, *The Gettysburg Campaign*, pp. 463–464; Hess, *Pickett's Charge*, pp. 15–19, 32–33, 117–120; Piston, *Lee's Tarnished Lieutenant*, p. 59; Stewart, *Pickett's Charge*, p. 48; Wert, *A Glorious Army*, pp. 269–270.

135. James M. Paradis, *African Americans and the Gettysburg Campaign* (Lanham, Md.: Scarecross Press, 2012), pp. 1, 59.

136. Hess, *Pickett's Charge*, p. 118.

137. Haskell, *The Battle of Gettysburg*, p. 72.

138. Ibid., pp. 73–74; Hess, *Pickett's Charge*, p. 118.

139. Boritt, ed., *The Gettysburg Nobody Knows*, p. 129; Field, *Robert E. Lee*, p. 38.

140. Haskell, *The Battle of Gettysburg*, p. 100; Wert, *A Glorious Army*, pp. 269–270; Trudeau, *Gettysburg*, p. 499.

141. Boritt, ed., *The Gettysburg Nobody Knows*, p. 129; Haskell, *The Battle of Gettysburg*, p. 100; Trudeau, *Gettysburg*, p. 499; Cowell, *Tactics at Gettysburg*, pp. 78–79, 81; Barra, "One Mile of Open Ground, " *CWT*, pp. 32–35; Coddington, *The Gettysburg Campaign*, pp. 463–464; Wert, *A Glorious Army*, pp. 269–270.

142. Haskell, *The Battle of Gettysburg*, pp. 74, 100.

143. Ibid., p. 80; Anderson and Anderson, *The Generals*, p. 415.

144. Piston, *Lee's Tarnished Lieutenant*, pp. 58–59; Robertson, *General A. P. Hill*, p. 220; Foote, *The Civil War*, vol. 2, pp. 528–529.

145. Hess, *Pickett's Charge*, p. 389.

146. Ibid.; Trudeau, *Gettysburg*, p. 499; Guelzo, *Gettysburg*, p. 382; Barra, "One Mile of Open Ground, " *CWT*, p. 35; Tapert, ed., *The Brothers' War*, p. 162; Haskell, *The Battle of Gettysburg*, p. 100; Coddington, *The Gettysburg Campaign*, pp. 463–464; Wert, *A Glorious Army*, pp. 269–270.

147. Carhart, *Lost Triumph*, p. 171; Trudeau, *Gettysburg*, pp. 461–462; Stewart, *Pickett's Charge*, p. 94; Cowell, *Tactics at Gettysburg*, p. 76; Barra, "One Mile of Open Ground," *CWT*, pp. 32–35; Coddington, *The Gettysburg Campaign*, pp. 463–464; Wert, *A Glorious Army*, pp. 269–270.

148. Carhart, *Lost Triumph*, p. 171; Chandler, *The Campaigns of Napoleon*, p. 141; Haskell, *The Battle of Gettysburg*, p. 100; Trudeau, *Gettysburg*, p. 499; Bowden and Ward, *Last Chance for Victory*, pp. 424–425.

149. Chandler, *The Campaigns of Napoleon*, p. 141; Guelzo, *Gettysburg*, p. 382; *Annals of the War*, p. 313.

150. Chandler, *The Campaigns of Napoleon*, pp. 410–433; Dugard, *The Training Ground*, pp. 353–359; Trudeau, *Gettysburg*, p. 499.

151. Ibid.; Carhart, *Lost Triumph*, pp. 2–6, 153–269; Coddington, *The Gettysburg Campaign*, pp. 463–464; Digby Smith, *Charge! Great Cavalry Charges of the Napoleonic Wars* (Mechanicsburg, Pa.: Stackpole Books, 2003), pp. 9–12; Guelzo, *Gettysburg*, pp. 374–377; Cowell, *Tactics at Gettysburg*, pp. 76, 78–79, 81; Hess, *Pickett's Charge*, p. 365;

Foote, *The Civil War*, vol. 2, pp. 521–522; Boritt, ed., *The Gettysburg Nobody Knows*, p. 114; Trudeau, *Gettysburg*, pp. 427–442, 499; Harrison, *Pickett's Men*, p. 183; Wert, *A Glorious Army*, pp. 269–270; Royster, *Light-Horse Harry Lee*, pp. 13–54; Hatch, *Glorious War*, pp. 139–159.

152. H. C. B. Rogers, *Napoleon's Army* (New York: Hippocrene Books, Inc., 1974), p. 74.

153. Ibid., p. 75; Cowell, *Tactics at Gettysburg*, p. 81.

154. Coddington, *The Gettysburg Campaign*, p. 450; Carhart, *Lost Triumph*, pp. 3–6, 253–369; Hatch, *Glorious War*, pp. 139–159.

155. Chandler, *The Campaigns of Napoleon*, p. 363; Hatch, *Glorious War*, pp. 1–3, 139–159; Smith, *Charge!*, pp. 9–12.

156. Rogers, *Napoleon's Army*, p. 75; Carhart, *Lost Triumph*, pp. 2–269; Smith, *Charge!*, pp. 9–12; Coddington, *The Gettysburg Campaign*, pp. 463–464; Cowell, *Tactics at Gettysburg*, pp. 76, 78–79, 81; Barra, "One Mile of Open Ground," *CWT*, pp. 32–35; Wert, *A Glorious Army*, pp. 269–270; Hatch, *Glorious Victory*, pp. 139–159.

157. Bowden and Ward, *Last Chance for Victory*, p. 439; Cowell, *Tactics at Gettysburg*, pp. 78–79, 81; Carhart, *Lost Triumph*, pp. 2–6, 153–269; Chandler, *The Campaigns of Napoleon*, pp. 410–433; Trudeau, *Gettysburg*, p. 499; Smith, *Charge!*, pp. 9, 12, 46–60; Thomas, *Robert E. Lee*, p. 303; Polley, *Hood's Texas Brigade*, p. 153; Wert, *A Glorious Army*, pp. 269–270; Hatch, *Glorious Victory*, pp. 139–159.

158. Carhart, *Lost Triumph*, pp. 2–6, 153–269; Bowden and Ward, *Last Chance for Victory*, pp. 439, 424–425; Cowell, *Tactics at Gettysburg*, pp. 76, 77–78, 81; Barra, "One Mile of Open Ground," *CWT*, p. 35; Joseph Graham to Graham, July 30, 1863, SHC, UNC; Lewis, *Recollections from 1860 to 1865*, pp. 77, 79; Guelzo, *Gettysburg*, p. 382; Bishop, Randy Bishop, *The Tennessee Brigade* (Gretna, La.: Pelican Publishing, 2010), p. vii; *Annals of the War*, p. 313; Trudeau, *Gettysburg*, p. 499; Hatch, *Glorious War*, pp. 1–3, 139–159; Foote, *The Civil War*, vol. 2, p. 521; Haskell, *The Battle of Gettysburg*, pp. 72–74, 100; Wert, *A Glorious Army*, p. 269.

159. Smith, *Charge!*, pp. 9–12, 46–60; Carhart, *Lost Triumph*, pp. 2–6, 153–269; Chandler, *The Campaigns of Napoleon*, pp. 410–433; Trudeau, *Gettysburg*, p. 499; Wert, *A Glorious Army*, pp. 269–270; Hatch, *Glorious Victory*, pp. 139–159.

160. Chandler, *The Campaigns of Napoleon*, p. 145; Guelzo, *Gettysburg*, pp. 18, 374–377.

161. Guelzo, *Gettysburg*, pp. 374–377; Smith, *Charge!*, pp. 9, 12, 46–60; Carhart, *Lost Triumph*, pp. 2–6, 153–269; Chandler, *The Campaigns of Napoleon*, pp. 410–433; Coddington, *The Gettysburg Campaign*, pp. 463–464; Cowell, *Tactics at Gettysburg*, pp. 78–79, 81; Barra, "One Mile of Open Ground," *CWT*, pp. 32–35.

162. Royster, *Light-Horse Harry Lee*, pp. 16, 245; Cowell, *Tactics at Gettysburg*, p. 81.

163. Chandler, *The Campaigns of Napoleon*, p. 180.

164. Ibid., p. 1085; Cowell, *Tactics at Gettysburg*, pp. 78–79, 81; Carhart, *Lost Triumph*, pp. 2–369.

165. Crowdy, *Incomparable*, pp. 81–102.

166. Henry Lachouque, *The Anatomy of Glory, Napoleon and His Guard, A Study in Leadership* (Providence, R.I.: Brown University Press, 1962), pp. 160–163.

167. Cowell, *Tactics at Gettysburg*, pp. 76, 77–78, 81; Carhart, *Lost Triumph*, pp. 2–6, 153–269; Foote, *The Civil War*, vol. 2, pp. 521–530; Trudeau, *Gettysburg*, p. 499; Stevens, *As if it Were Glory*, pp. 98–99; Wert, *A Glorious Army*, pp. 269–270; Hatch, *Glorious Victory*, pp. 139–159.

168. Trudeau, *Gettysburg*, p. 499; Cowell, *Tactics at Gettysburg*, pp. 76, 78–79, 81; Hess, *Pickett's Charge*, p. 389; Carhart, *Lost Triumph*, pp. 2–6, 153–269; Guelzo, *Gettysburg*, p. 382; Robertson, *General A. P. Hill*, p. 220; Hatch, *Glorious Victory*, pp. 139–159; Longacre, *Pickett*, pp. 128–129; Hatch, *Glorious Victory*, pp. 139–159; Stevens, ed., *As if it Were Glory*, pp. 98–99; Harrison, *Pickett's Men*, p. 183; Wert, *A Glorious Army*, pp. 269–270.

169. Chandler, *The Campaigns of Napoleon*, p. 363.

170. Waters and Edmonds, *A Small but Spartan Band*, p. 80; Lewis, *Recollections from 1860 to 1865*, p. 77; Carhart, *Lost Triumph*, pp. xi–269; Chandler, *The Campaigns of Napoleon*, pp. 363, 1085; Thomas, *Robert E. Lee*, pp. 292–293; Bradley M. Gottfried, *Brigades of Gettysburg, The Union and Confederate Brigades at the Battle of Gettysburg* (New York: Da Capo Press, 2002), p. 478; CVSR, NA; Barra, "One Mile of Open Ground, " *CWT*, pp. 32–35; Coddington, *The Gettysburg Campaign*, pp. 463–464; Bowden and Ward, *Last Chance for Victory*, p. 425; Wert, *A Glorious Army*, pp. 269–270.

171. Guy R. Everson and Edward W. Simpson, eds., *Far, Far from Home, The Wartime Letters of Dick and Tally Simpson, Third South Carolina* (New York: Oxford University Press, 1994), p. 257.

172. Moseley, ed., *The Stilwell Letters*, pp. 84, 167.

173. Waters and Edmonds, *A Small but Spartan Band*, p. 64.

174. Gregory, *53rd Virginia Infantry and 5th Battalion Virginia Infantry*, pp. 52–53; CVSR, NA.

175. Gragg, *Covered with Glory*, pp. 4–5, 42, 141.

176. Ibid., pp. 50–51, 74; Wert, *A Glorious Army*, pp. 269–270.

177. Field, *Robert E. Lee*, p. 56; Chandler, *The Campaigns of Napoleon*, pp. 133–191, 367–376.

178. Joseph Gibbs, *Three Years in the Bloody Eleventh, The Campaigns of a Pennsylvania Reserve Regiment* (University Park: The Pennsylvania State University Press, 2002), pp. 47–48; James A. Rawley, *Turning Points of the Civil War* (Lincoln: University of Nebraska Press, 1989), p. 153.

179. Bowden and Ward, *Last Chance for Victory*, p. 74.

180. Edward G. Longacre, *The Cavalry at Gettysburg, A Tactical Study of Mounted Operations During the Civil War's Pivotal Campaign, 9 June–14 July 1863* (Lincoln: University of Nebraska Press, 1986), pp. 220–221; Hatch, *Glorious Victory*, pp. 139–159; Trudeau, *Gettysburg*, pp. 437, 440–442; Cowell, *Tactics at Gettysburg*, p. 81.

181. Hess, *Pickett's Charge*, pp. 15, 32–33, 389; Time-Life Editors, *Voices of the Civil War, Gettysburg*, p. 133; Trudeau, *Gettysburg*, pp. 430, 436.

182. Durkin, ed., *John Dooley, Confederate Soldier*, p. 102; Trudeau, *Gettysburg*, p. 436; Rollins, ed., *Pickett's Charge*, p. 73; Wert, *A Glorious Army*, p. 270; Harrison and Busey, *Nothing but Glory*, p. 15.

183. Harrison, *Pickett's Men,* p. 90; Trudeau, *Gettysburg,* p. 429; Harrison and Busey, *All but Glory,* p. 17.

184. Harrison and Busey, *All but Glory,* p. 17.

185. Trudeau, *Gettysburg,* p. 429; Hess, *Pickett's Charge,* p. 5.

186. John W. Finley, "Bloody Angle, " *Buffalo Evening News,* May 28, 1894.

187. Ibid.; CVSR, NA.

188. Harrison and Busey, *All but Glory,* p. 15; Durkin, ed., John Dooley, *Confederate Soldier,* p. 102.

189. Bishop, *The Tennessee Brigade,* pp. 83–85, 190–191, 203.

190. Trudeau, *Gettysburg,* pp. 440–441; Hess, *Pickett's Charge,* p. 389.

191. Levin C. Gayle Diary, Gettysburg National Military Park Archives, Gettysburg, Pennsylvania; Hess, *Pickett's Charge,* pp. 50–51; Trudeau, *Gettysburg,* pp. 440–442.

192. Bishop, *The Tennessee Brigade,* pp. 203–204; Joseph T. Durkin, ed., *John Dooley, Confederate Soldier, His War Journal* (Tuscaloosa: University of Alabama Press, 2005), p. 103.

193. Harrison and Busey, *Nothing but Glory,* p. 16.

194. Ibid., p. 17.

195. David S. Heidler and Jeanne T. Heildler, eds., *Encyclopedia of the War of 1812* (Annapolis, Md.: Naval Institute Press, 1997), p. 12; Wayne E. Motts, *"Trust in God and Fear Nothing, " Gen. Lewis A. Armistead, CSA.* (Gettysburg, Pa.: Farnsworth House Military Impressions, 1994), pp. 4, 7, 17, 19. 29–30; Gregory, *53rd Virginia Infantry and 5th Battalion Virginia Infantry,* p. 43.

196. Motts, *"Trust in God and Fear Nothing, "* pp. 21–24.

197. Motts, *"Trust in God and Fear Nothing, "* pp. 8–10; Oden Papers, 1755–1836, Manuscript 178, Maryland Historical Society, Annapolis, Maryland; A. J. Langguth, *Union 1812, The Americans Who Fought the Second War of Independence* (New York: Simon and Schuster, 2006), pp. 318–321; Tucker, *Lee and Longstreet at Gettysburg,* p. 144.

198. Paradis, *African Americans and the Gettysburg Campaign,* p. 2.

199. Guelzo, *Gettysburg,* pp. 243–244, 315–316.

200. Jeanne T. Heidler and David S. Heidler, editors, *Encyclopedia of the War of 1812* (Santa Barbara, Calif.: ABC-CLI0, 1997) p. 13.

201. Ibid.

202. Motts, *"Trust in God and Fear Nothing, "* pp. 26, 28; Gregory, *53rd Virginia Infantry and 5th Battalion Virginia Infantry,* p. 42.

203. Motts, *"Trust in God and Fear Nothing, "* p. 8; Langguth, *Union 1812,* pp. 319–320.

204. Anthony McDermott to John Bachelder, n.d., New Hampshire Historical Society, Concord, New Hampshire.

205. CVSR, NA; Troy D. Harman, *The Great Revival of 1863, The Effect Upon Lee's Army of Northern Virginia,* p. 112; National Park Service, Washington, DC; Harrison and Busey, *Nothing but Glory,* pp. 16—7.

206. Moseley, ed., *The Stilwell Letters,* p. 124.

207. Stewart, *Pickett's Charge,* p. 116.

208. Moseley, ed., *The Stilwell Letters*, pp. 80, 84, 186.

Chapter II

1. Coddington, *The Gettysburg Campaign*, pp. 462–463; Wert, *A Glorious Army*, p. 269; Trudeau, *Gettysburg*, p. 445.
2. Harrison, *Pickett's Men*, p. 94; Hess, *Pickett's Charge*, p. 123.
3. Haskell, *The Battle of Gettysburg*, p. 81; Trudeau, *Gettysburg*, p. 429; Foote, *The Civil War*, vol. 2, pp. 538–539.
4. Gayle Diary, GNMP.
5. John C. Granberry to John W. Daniel, March 25, 1905, John W. Daniel Papers, 1824–1914, University of Virginia Library, Richmond, Virginia.
6. Wilbur S. Nye, *Here Comes the Rebels!* (Baton Rouge: Louisiana State University Press, 1965), pp. 13–14; Jennings Cropper Wise, *The Long Arm of Lee, From Bull Run to Fredericksburg* (Lincoln: University of Nebraska Press, 1991), vol. 1, pp. 155, 373–408; Hess, *Pickett's Charge*, p. 75; Persico, *My Enemy, My Brother*, p. 212; Chandler, *The Campaigns of Napoleon*, pp. 179–180.
7. Hess, *Pickett's Charge*, p. 75; Stewart, *Pickett's Charge*, pp. 54–55; Wise, *The Long Army of Lee*, vol. 1, p. 155; Piston, *Lee's Tarnished Lieutenant*, pp. 38–41.
8. Cockrell, ed., *Gunner with Stonewall*, pp. xii, xv; Susan Leigh Blackford, *Letters from Lee's Army* (New York: A. S. Barnes and Company, Inc., 1962), p. 176.
9. Moseley, *The Stilwell Letters*, p. 163.
10. Stevens, ed., *As if it Were Glory*, p. 104.
11. Crowdy, *Incomparable*, p. 83; Hess, *Pickett's Charge*, p. 75.
12. Crowdy, *Incomparable*, p. 84.
13. Bishop, *The Tennessee Brigade*, p. 205.
14. Ibid., p. 204; John W. Finley, "Bloody Angle, " *Buffalo Evening News*, May 28, 1894; Tucker, *Barksdale's Charge*, pp. 95–244; Hess, *Pickett's Charge*, pp. 75–76, 125–126; *The Patriot*, Albany, Georgia, December 12, 1861; Coddington, *The Gettysburg Campaign*, p. 462; Foote, *The Civil War*, vol. 2, p. 539; Clark and Time-Life Book Editors, *Gettysburg*, p. 129; Humphreys to McLaws, January 6, 1878, UNCL; Stewart, *Pickett's Charge*, pp. 44–45; Piston, *Longstreet's Tarnished Lieutenant*, p. 35; Persico, *My Enemy, My Brother*, p. 199; Dowdey, *Death of a Nation*, p. 284; Trudeau, *Gettysburg*, pp. 367–392, 432, 445–446; Lesley J. Gordon, *General George E. Pickett in Life and Legend* (Chapel Hill: University of North Carolina Press, 1998), pp. 112, 115; Bowden and Ward, *Last Chance for Victory*, p. 456; Cockrell, ed., *Gunner with Stonewall*, p. xv; Rollins, ed., *Pickett's Charge*, p. 51.
15. Coddington *The Gettysburg Campaign*, p. 444; Trudeau, *Gettysburg*, p. 453.
16. Trudeau, *Gettysburg*, pp. 444–445.
17. Lafayette McLaws to wife, July 7, 1863, Lafayette McLaws Collection, University of North Carolina, Chapel Hill, North Carolina; Piston, *Lee's Tarnished Lieutenant*, pp. 39–40.
18. Hess, *Pickett's Charge*, p. 27; Harrison and Busey, *Nothing but Glory*, p. 23.

19. Joseph Graham to Graham, July 30, 1863, SHC; Cockrell, ed., *Gunner with Stonewall,* p. 69; *New Orleans Times-Picayune,* New Orleans, Louisiana, July 10, 1909; Sylvia G. L. Dannett and Rosamond H. Burkart, editors, *Confederate Surgeon, Aristides Monteiro* (New York: Dodd, Mead and Company, 1969), p. 123.

20. Hess, *Pickett's Charge,* p. 125.

21. Joseph Graham to Graham, July 30, 1863, SHC; Harrison and Busey, *Nothing but Glory,* p. 23.

22. Gragg, *Covered with Glory,* p. 168.

23. Wert, *A Glorious Army,* p. 271.

24. Gregory A. Coco, *On the Bloodstained Field, I and II, 262 Human Interest Stories of the Campaign and Battle of Gettysburg* (Orrtanna, Pa.: Colecraft Industries, 2013), p. 66.

25. Lafayette McLaws to wife, July 7, 1863, Lafayette McLaws Papers, University of North Carolina Archives, Chapel Hill, North Carolina.

26. Bishop, *The Tennessee Brigade,* p. 205; CTSR, NA.

27. Durkin, ed., *John Dooley, Confederate Soldier,* p. 103.

28. John W. Finley, "Bloody Angle, " *Buffalo Evening News,* May 28, 1894.

29. Lewis, *Recollections from 1860 to 1865,* p. 81.

30. Morris M. Penny and J. Gary Laine, *Struggle for the Round Tops, Law's Alabama Brigade at the Battle of Gettysburg* (Shippensburg, Pa.: White Mane Publishing Company, 1999), pp. 115'116.

31. *Times-Dispatch,* Richmond, Virginia, February 7, 1904.

32. Rufus K. Felder to mother, July 9, 1863, 5th Texas Folder, Gettysburg National Military Park, Gettysburg, Pennsylvania.

33. Haskell, *The Battle of Gettysburg,* p. 82.

34. Ibid., p. 84.

35. Paradis, *African Americans and the Gettysburg Campaign,* p. 60; Stewart, *Pickett's Charge,* pp. 127–128.

36. Benjamin Hirst to Sarah, n.d., Alden Skinner Camp, Sons of Union Veterans of the Civil War, Rockville, Connecticut.

37. Chandler, *The Campaigns of Napoleon,* p. 141; H. C. B. Rogers, *Napoleon's Army* (New York: Hippocrene Books, 1974), pp. 74–75.

38. Crowdy, *Incomparable,* pp. 83–84; Chandler, *The Campaigns of Napoleon,* p. 179; McWhiney and Jamieson, *Attack and Die,* pp. 60–61.

39. Wise, *The Long Army of Lee,* vol. 1, p. 155.

40. Johnson, *Napoleon,* p. 56.

41. Chandler, *The Campaigns of Napoleon,* p. 356.

42. Ibid.

43. Ibid., pp. 362–363; Trudeau, *Gettysburg,* pp. 445, 461.

44. Chandler, *The Campaigns of Napoleon,* p. 363.

45. Ibid.

46. McWhiney and Jamieson, *Attack and Die,* pp. 60–61.

47. Chandler, *The Campaigns of Napoleon,* p. 179; Trudeau, *Gettysburg,* pp. 458–461; Rogers, *Napoleon's Army,* pp. 74–75; Hess, *Pickett's Charge,* p. 76.

48. Hess, *Pickett's Charge*, p. 126.

49. Bishop, *The Tennessee Brigade*, p. 205.

50. *Carolina Watchman*, Salisbury, North Carolina, August 5, 1863; Stewart, *Pickett's Charge*, p. 46; Edward Stackpole, *They Met at Gettysburg*, (Mechanicsburg: Stackpole Books, *1959*), p. 256; Stewart, *Pickett's Charge*, pp. 129–130.

51. Harrison, *Pickett's Men*, p. 96; David Shultz, *"Double Canister at Ten Yards,"* The Federal Artillery and the Repulse of Pickett's Charge (Redondo Beach, Calif.: Rank and File Publications, 1995), p. 3; Hess, *Pickett's Charge*, pp. 76, 126.

52. Richard E. Beringer, Herman Hattaway, Archer Jones, and William N. Still, *Why the South Lost the Civil War* (Athens: University of Georgia Press, 1991), p. 14.

53. Beringer, Hattaway, Jones, and Still, *Why the South Lost the Civil War*, p. 14; Johnson, *Napoleon*, p. 56; Dugard, *The Training Ground*, pp. 359–360; Johnson, *A Gallant Little Army*, pp. 170, 220–221.

54. McWhiney and Jamieson, *Attack and Die*, p. 60.

55. Ibid., pp. 60–61, 120; Harrison and Busey, *Nothing but Glory*, pp. 19–20; Chandler, *The Campaigns of Napoleon*, pp. 363, 1088; Hess, *Pickett's Charge*, pp. 25–26, 113–116, 120, 198, 210–211, 246; Stewart, *Pickett's Charge*, pp. 55–56; Persico, *My Enemy, My Brother*, p. 205; Rollins, ed., *Pickett's Charge*, pp. 22, 46, 50–51; Trudeau, *Gettysburg*, p. 445.

56. Cockrell, ed., *Gunner with Stonewall*, pp. 73–74; Hess, *Pickett's Charge*, p. 26; Stewart, *Pickett's Charge*, p. 147.

57. Haskell, *The Battle of Gettysburg*, pp. 89–90; Hess, *Pickett's Charge*, p. 25; Trudeau, *Gettysburg*, p. 452.

58. Wert, *A Glorious Army*, p. 269; David D. Ryan, ed., *A Yankee Spy in Richmond, The Civil War Diary of "Crazy Bet" Van Lew* (Mechanicsburg, Pa.: Stackpole Books, 1996), pp. 2–51, 107–111.

59. Boritt, *The Gettysburg Nobody Knows*, pp. 24–25.

60. *Fayetteville Observer*, Fayetteville, North Carolina, March 27, 1864.

61. Stewart, *Pickett's Charge*, 137.

62. Shultz, *"Double Canister at Ten Yards,"* p. 21; Trudeau, *Gettysburg*, p. 452.

63. Haskell, *The Battle of Gettysburg*, p. 94; Stewart, *Pickett's Charge*, p. 126.

64. Coddington, *The Gettysburg Campaign*, p. 494; Stewart, *Pickett's Charge*, p. 126; Haskell, *The Battle of Gettysburg*, p. 93; Shultz, *"Double Canister at Ten Yards,"* p. 21; Trudeau, *Gettysburg*, p. 452.

65. Shultz, *"Double Canister at Ten Yards,"* p. 21; Chandler, *The Campaigns of Napoleon*, p. 1087–1089.

66. Manley Stacey to father, July 1–5, 1863, Historical Society of Oak Park and River Forest, Illinois, Oak Park, Illinois.

67. Beringer, Hattaway, Jones, and Still, *Why the South Lost the Civil War*, p. 15; McWhiney and Jamieson, *Attack and Die*, p. 121; Longacre, *Pickett*, p. 122; Harrison and Busey, *Nothing but Glory*, pp. 19–20; Freeman, *Lee's Lieutenants*, vol. 3, 179.

68. McWhiney and Jamieson, *Attack and Die*, p. 121; Baringer, Hattaway, Jones, and Still, *Why the South Lost the Civil War*, p. 15; Rollins, ed., *Pickett's Charge*, p. 22; Harrison and Busey, *Nothing but Glory*, pp. 19–20; Hess, *Pickett's Charge*, pp. 25, 27.

69. Beringer, Hattaway, Jones, and Still, *Why the South Lost the Civil War*, p. 15; Trudeau, *Gettysburg*, p. 452; Gragg, *Covered with Glory*, p. 63.

70. Haskell, *The Battle of Gettysburg*, p. 32; Shultz, *"Double Canister at Ten Yards,"* p. 21; Foote, *The Civil War*, vol. 2, p. 542.

71. Beringer, Hattaway, Jones, and Still, *Why the South Lost the Civil War*, p. 15; McWhiney and Jamieson, *Attack and Die*, pp. 59–60; Rogers, *Napoleon's Army*, pp. 74–75.

72. Gragg, *Covered with Glory*, p. 63.

73. Shultz, *"Double Canister at Ten Yards,"* pp. 21–23; Haskell, *The Battle of Gettysburg*, pp. 95–96, note 25; Foote, *The Civil War*, vol. 2, p. 545.

74. Shultz, *"Double Canister at Ten Yards,"* p. 22.

75. Hess, *Pickett's Charge*, p. 398; Spruill, *Summer Thunder*, p. 213; Joseph Graham to Graham, July 30, 1863, SHC; Haskell, *The Battle of Gettysburg*, pp. 92–93; Shultz, *"Double Canister at Ten Yards,"* pp. 21, 25.

76. CVSR, NA; Durkin, ed., *John Dooley, Confederate Soldier*, p. 103; Chandler, *The Campaigns of Napoleon*, pp. 362–363; Longacre, *Pickett*, p. 121; Stewart, *Pickett's Charge*, p. 132; Schultz, *"Double Canister at Ten Yards,"* pp. 23, 25; Harrison and Busey, *Nothing but Glory*, pp. 20, 22, 24, 27–28; *Buffalo Evening News*, May 28, 1894.

77. John A. Herndon to brother, July 11, 1863, Carl Sell, Franconia, Virginia; CVSR, NA.

78. CSSR, NA.

79. Harrison and Busey, *Nothing but Glory*, pp. 18, 22.

80. John W. Finley, "Bloody Angle, " *Buffalo Evening News*, May 28, 1894; Longacre, *Pickett*, p. 121.

81. John W. Finley, "Bloody Angle, " *Buffalo Evening News*, May 28, 1894.

82. Hess, *Pickett's Charge*, p. 154.

83. Durkin, ed., *John Dooley, Confederate Soldier*, p. 103.

84. CVSR, NA; Rollins, ed., *Pickett's Charge*, p. 107.

85. CVSR, NA; Harrison and Busey, *Nothing but Glory*, p. 48.

86. Hess, *Pickett's Charge*, pp. 154–155.

87. CVSR, NA; Harrison and Busey, *Nothing but Glory*, p. 27.

88. CVSR, NA.

89. Ibid.; Harrison and Busey, *Nothing but Glory*, p. 25.

90. Harrison and Busey, *Nothing but Glory*, p. 28; CVSR, NA.

91. Colonel Joseph Mayo Report, July 25, 1863, George Edward Pickett Papers, William R. Perkins Library, Duke University, Durham, North Carolina; Harrison and Busey, *All But Glory*, p. 17.

92. Longacre, *Pickett*, p. 121.

93. Troy D. Harman, *The Great Revival of 1863, The Effect Upon Lee's Army of Northern Virginia*, Gettysburg National Military Park Archives, Gettysburg, Pennsylvania.

94. CVSR, NA; Gragg, *Covered with Glory*, pp. 172–173; Harrison and Busey, *Nothing but Glory*, p. 24.

95. *Carolina Watchman*, August 5, 1863.

96. Coddington, *The Gettysburg Campaign*, p. 494.

97. Harrison, *Pickett's Men,* pp. 160, 200; McWhiney and Jamieson, *Attack and Die,* pp. 120–121; Rollins, ed., *Pickett's Charge,* pp. 107, 109–110; Albert F. Harris, *Fated Stars, Virginia Brigadier Generals Killed in the Civil War, 1861–1865* (Gettysburg, Pa.: Thomas Publications, 2000), pp. 93–98.

98. Priest, *Into the Fire,* p. 86; CVSR, NA.

99. CVSR, NA; Harrison and Busey, *Nothing but Glory,* pp. 20, 22; Stewart, *Pickett's Charge,* p. 132.

100. Stewart, *Pickett's Charge,* p. 132; CVSR, NA.

101. CVSR, NA; Stewart, *Pickett's Charge,* p. 132.

102. Stewart, *Pickett's Charge,* p. 132; CVSR, NA; Harrison and Busey, *Nothing but Glory,* pp. 15, 22, 29–31.

103. Hess, *Pickett's Charge,* p. 154.

104. Gregory, *53rd Virginia Infantry and 5th Battalion Virginia Infantry,* pp. 52, 143; CVSR, NA; Gregory A. Coco, *Wasted Valor, The Confederate Dead at Gettysburg* (Gettysburg, Pa.: Thomas Publications, 1990), p. 116; Eric Burns, *Virtue, Valor, & Vanity* (New York: Arcade Publishing, 2007), pp. 75–77, 153–158, 169–173; Harrison and Busey, *Nothing but Glory,* p. 31.

105. Gregory, *53rd Virginia Infantry and 5th Battalion Virginia Infantry,* pp. 52–53, 176–177; CVSR, NA; Chandler, *The Campaigns of Napoleon,* pp. 362–363.

106. Gregory, *53rd Virginia Infantry and 5th Battalion Virginia Infantry,* p. 52.

107. Gregory A. Coco, *Wasted Valor, The Confederate Dead at Gettysburg* (Gettysburg, Pa.: Thomas Publications, 1990), p. 116; Rollins, ed., *Pickett's Charge,* p. 73; Harrison and Busey, *Nothing but Glory,* p. 29; Schultz, *"Double Canister at Ten Yards, "* p. 23.

108. Trudeau, *Gettysburg,* p. 453.

109. Ibid., p. 127–128; B. David Mann, *They Were Heard From, VMI Alumni in the Civil War* (Buena Vista, Va.: Mariner Publishing, 2006), pp. 26–27; James Lee Conrad, *The Young Lions, Confederate Cadets at War* (Mechanicsburg, Pa.: Stackpole Books, 1997), p. 152; Swisher, *Warrior in Gray,* p. 6; Harrison, *Pickett's Men,* p. 38; CVSR, NA; Wise, *The Long Arm of Lee,* p. 97; Rollins, ed., *Pickett's Charge,* p. 106; Harrison and Busey, *Nothing but Glory,* pp. 5–6.

110. Donald, ed., *Why the North Won the Civil War,* pp. 36–41; Mann, *They Were Heard From, VMI Alumni in the Civil War,* pp. 7–42; Wise, *The Long Arm of Lee,* pp. 95–103.

111. CVSR, NA; Virginia Military Institute Archives, Virginia Military Institute, Lexington, Virginia; Conrad, *The Young Lions,* pp. 1–6, 151–152; Coco, *Wasted Valor,* pp. 127–128; Mann, *They Were Heard From, VMI Alumni in the Civil War,* pp. 7–42; Swisher, *Warrior in Gray,* pp. 6–7; Tower, ed., *Lee's Adjutant,* p. 2; Adam Zamoyski, *Moscow 1812, Napoleon's Fatal March* (New York: HarperCollins Publishers, 2004), pp. 130–480; Robert N. Rose, *The Jewish Confederates* (Columbia: University of South Carolina, 2000), pp. 169–171, 227–228; Wise, *The Long Arm of Lee,* pp. 95–103.

112. William C. Davis, *The Battle of New Market* (New York: Doubleday and Company, 1975), p. 47.

113. Wise, *The Long Army of Lee,* p. 99.

114. Mann, *They Were Heard From, VMI Alumni in the Civil War,* pp. 26–27; Conrad, *The Young Lions,* pp. 1–6, 152; CVSR, NA; Wise, *The Long Army of Lee,* p. 96.

115. Wise, *The Long Arm of Lee,* p. 96.

116. CVSR, NA; Davis, *The Battle of New Market,* pp. 48–49; Swisher, *Warrior in Gray,* p. 7; Tower, ed., *Lee's Adjutant,* p. 2; Wise, *The Long Army of Lee,* pp. 95–103.

117. CVSR, NA; *Buffalo Evening News,* May 28, 1894; Hess, *Pickett's Charge,* p. 48.

118. CVSR, NA; Benjamin H. Tresk, *9th Virginia Infantry* (Lynchburg, Va.: H. E. Howard, Inc., 1984), p. 3.

119. Tresk, *9th Virginia Infantry,* pp. 3, 7, 86; CVSR, NA.

120. Harrison, *Pickett's Men,* pp. vi–x, xiv–xvi.

121. CVSR, NA; *Philadelphia Times,* Philadelphia, Pennsylvania, October 21, 1882; Harrison and Busey, *Nothing but Glory,* p. 43; Susan Leigh Blackford, compiler, *Letters from Lee's Army* (New York: A. S. Barnes and Company, Inc., 1962), p. 188.

122. CVSR, NA; Mann, *They Were Heard From, VMI Alumni in the Civil War,* pp. 26–28; Barra, "One Mile of Open Ground, " *CWT,* pp. 34–35; Conrad, *The Young Lions,* p. 152; Davis, *The Battle of New Market,* pp. 46–49; Wise, *The Long Arm of Lee,* pp. 95–103; Swisher, *Warrior in Gray,* pp. 6–7.

123. CVSR, NA; Gregory, *53rd Virginia Infantry and 5th Battalion Virginia Infantry,* pp. 59–60; Compiled Military Service Record of Confederate Soldiers from the States of North Carolina, Record Group 109, National Archives, Washington, DC

124. *Philadelphia Times,* October 21, 1882.

125. CVSR, NA.

126. Durkin, ed., *John Dooley, Confederate Soldier,* p. 104; Hess, *Pickett's Charge,* p. 27; Longacre, *Pickett,* p. 121.

127. CVSR, NA; Hess, *Pickett's Charge,* p. 155.

128. Longacre, *Pickett,* p. 122; Rollins, ed., *Pickett's Charge,* pp. 22, 109–110; Hess, *Pickett's Charge,* pp. 26–27; Harrison and Busey, *Nothing but Glory,* pp. 32–33.

129. Rollins, ed., *Pickett's Charge,* pp. 109–110.

130. Cockrell, ed., *Gunner with Stonewall,* pp. 73–74; Hess, *Pickett's Charge,* p. 154.

131. John W. Finley, "Bloody Angle, " *Buffalo Evening News,* May 28, 1894.

132. Wert, *A Glorious Army,* p. 271..

133. Tapert, ed., *The Brothers' War,* p. 162; Longacre, *Pickett,* p. 119; Rogers, *Napoleon's Army,* pp. 74–75; Hess, *Pickett's Charge,* p. 27; Foote, *The Civil War,* vol. 2, pp. 542–543; Rollins, ed., *Pickett's Charge,* p. 46; Webb Garrison, *Civil War Stories, Strange Tales, Oddities, Events and Coincidences* (New York: Promontory Press, 1997), p. 251.

134. McWhiney and Jamieson, *Attack and Die,* p. 120; Compiled Service Records of Confederate Soldiers from the State of Louisiana, Record Group 109, National Archives, Washington, DC

135. Joseph Graham to Graham, July 30, 1863, SHC; Philip A. Katcher, *The Army of Robert E. Lee* (London: Arms and Armour Press, 1994), p. 227; Wert, *A Glorious Army,* p. 271.

136. Joseph Graham to Graham, July 30, 1863, SHC.

137. Longacre, *Pickett,* p. 122; *Carolina Watchman,* August 5, 1863, Harrison and Busey, *Nothing but Glory,* pp. 32–34.

138. Stewart, *Pickett's Charge*, p. 138; Haskell, *The Battle of Gettysburg*, pp. 84, 92–93; Wert, *A Glorious Army*, pp. 269–271; Hess, *Pickett's Charge*, pp. 96, 141–143; Shultz, "*Double Canister at Ten Yards,* "p. 24; Coddington, *The Gettysburg Campaign*, p. 494.

139. Haskell, *The Battle of Gettysburg*, pp. 87–88.

140. Shultz, "*Double Canister at Ten Yards,* "pp. 21–22.

141. Haskell, *The Battle of Gettysburg*, p. 92; Hess, *Pickett's Charge*, p. 27; Harrison and Busey, *Nothing but Glory*, p. 32.

142. Haskell, *The Battle of Gettysburg*, p. 96, note 25; Hess, *Pickett's Charge*, pp. 25, 141–145; Wert, *A Glorious Army*, pp. 271–272.

143. Captain Graham to Graham, July 30, 1863, SHC.

144. Haskell, *The Battle of Gettysburg*, p. 95, note 25; Shultz, "*Double Canister at Ten Yards,* "p. 3.

145. Hirst letter to Sarah, n.d., ASC.

146. Longacre, *Pickett*, p. 122; Hess, *Pickett's Charge*, pp. 160–160.

147. Hess, *Pickett's Charge*, pp. 160–161.

148. *Annals of the War*, pp. 95–95, note 25, 214; Hess, *Pickett's Charge*, p. 161; McWhiney and Jamieson, *Attack and Die*, pp. 115; Rollins, ed., *Pickett's Charge*, pp. 46, 109–110.

149. *Annals of the War*, p. 214; Haskell, *The Battle of Gettysburg*, pp. 95–96, note 25; Foote, *The Civil War*, vol. 2, p. 550; Wert, *A Glorious Army*, pp. 271–272.

150. Hess, *Pickett's Charge*, pp. 141–144; Persico, *My Enemy, My Brother*, p. 212; Haskell, *The Battle of Gettysburg*, pp. 92–95, note 25.

151. Haskell, *The Battle of Gettysburg*, pp. 92–93; Hess, *Pickett's Charge*, pp. 160–161.

152. Wert, *A Glorious Army*, p. 271; Hess, *Pickett's Charge*, pp. 141–144.

153. Haskell, *The Battle of Gettysburg*, p. 93.

154. Ibid.

155. Hess, *Pickett's Charge*, pp. 160–163; Shultz, "*Double Canister at Ten Yards,* "pp. 21–22; Haskell, *The Battle of Gettysburg*, pp. 92–95.

156. Haskell, *The Battle of Gettysburg*, p. 94; Rollins, ed., *Pickett's Charge*, pp. 46, 109–110; Harrison and Busey, *Nothing but Glory*, pp. 32–34.

157. Rogres, *Napoleon's Army*, pp. 74–75.

158. William A. Fletcher, *Rebel Private Front and Rear, Memoirs of a Confederate Soldier* (New York: Meridian Books, 1997), pp. 1, 3, 81; Wert, *A Glorious Army*, pp. 271–272.

159. Boritt, ed., *The Gettysburg Nobody Knows*, p. 20.

160. Moseley, ed., *The Stilwell Letters*, p. 165.

161. Longacre, *Pickett*, pp. 120–121, Sandburg, *Abraham Lincoln*, vol. 2, p. 355.

162. Haskell, *The Battle of Gettysburg*, pp. 59–60; *Annals of the War*, pp. 206–208, 213; Sandburg, *Abraham Lincoln*, pp. 351–352, 354; Thomas, *Robert E. Lee*, p. 293; Archer, *Civil War Command and Strategy*, p. 168; Foote, *The Civil War*, vol. 2, p. 539; Gordon, *General George E. Pickett in Life and Legend*, pp. 77, 98–100, 113; Longacre, *Pickett*, pp. 120–121; Wert, *A Glorious Army*, p. 270; Moseley, ed., *The Stilwell Letters*, p. 153.

163. Hess, *Pickett's Charge*, pp. 133–134; Carhart, *Lost Triumph*, pp. xi–260; Bowden and Ward, *Last Chance for Victory*, p. 439; Hatch, *Glorious Victory*, pp. 139–159.

164. *Annals of the War*, p. 213.

165. Haskell, *The Battle of Gettysburg,* pp. 80, 95; Hess, *Pickett's Charge,* pp. 137–139.

166. Thomas, *Robert E. Lee,* pp. 298–299.

167. Wert, *A Glorious Army,* pp. 269–270; Hatch, *Glorious Victory,* pp. 139–159; Carhart, *Lost Triumph,* pp. xi–260; Bowden and Ward, *Last Chance for Victory,* p. 439; Cowell, *Tactics at Gettysburg,* p. 81.

168. Thomas, *Robert E. Lee,* p. 299; Haskell, *The Battle of Gettysburg,* p. 100; Barra, "One Mile of Open Ground, " *CWT,* pp. 34–35; Rollins, ed., *Pickett's Charge,* pp. 2–3, 22; Foote, *The Civil War,* vol. 2, pp. 526–528; Boritt, ed., *The Gettysburg Nobody Knows,* p. 124; Johnson, *Napoleon,* p. 49; Wert, *A Glorious Army,* pp. 269–270.

169. *Augusta Daily Constitutionalist,* Augusta, Georgia, July 23, 1863; Harrison and Busey, *Nothing but Glory,* pp. 32–34; Stewart, *Pickett's Charge,* pp. 138, 145–146.

170. *Carolina Watchman,* August 5, 1863.

171. Coddington, *The Gettysburg Campaign,* p. 499.

172. CVSR, NA; Harrison and Busey, *Nothing but Glory,* p. 52.

173. Walter Brian Cisco, *Wade Hampton, Confederate Warrior, Conservative Statesman* (Washington, DC: Brassey's, Inc., 2004), p. 120.

174. Wert, *A Glorious Army,* p. 270; Carhart, *Lost Triumph,* pp. xi–260; Hatch, *Glorious War,* pp. 1–3, 139–159; Hess, *Pickett's Charge,* pp. 141–145; Stewart, *Pickett's Charge,* pp. 138, 145–146.

175. Earl Schenck Miers and Richard A. Brown, *Gettysburg* (Armonk, N.Y.: M. E. Sharpe, 1996), p. 164; Carhart, *Lost Triumph,* pp. xi–260; Bowden and Ward, *Last Chance for Victory,* p. 439; Hatch, *Glorious War,* pp. 1–3, 139–159.

176. Bowden and Ward, *Last Chance for Victory,* p. 11.

177. Moseley, ed., *The Stilwell Letters,* p. 132.

Chapter III

1. Longacre, *Pickett,* p. 117.

2. Coddington, *The Gettysburg Campaign,* p. 512; Stewart, *Pickett's Charge,* p. 148.

3. Wert, *A Glorious Army,* p. 269; Hess, *Pickett's Charge,* p. 77.

4. Hess, *Pickett's Charge,* pp. 133–134, 141–143; Foote, *The Civil War,* vol. 2, p. 543; Stewart, *Pickett's Charge,* p. 46.

5. Harrison, *Pickett's Men,* p. 94.

6. John W. Finley, "Bloody Angle, " *Buffalo Evening News,* May 28, 1894; Hess, *Pickett's Charge,* pp. 141–143.

7. Blackford, ed., *Letters from Lee's Army,* p. 179.

8. CVSR, NA; Hess, *Pickett's Charge,* p. 52.

9. Gragg, *Covered with Glory,* p. 62.

10. Moseley, ed., *The Stilwell Letters,* p. 176.

11. CVSR, NA; Mark Alden Branch, "The Yale Men Who Died at Gettysburg, " *Yale Alumni Magazine,* July 3, 2013, online; A. D. Pollock Papers, 1794–1944, Call No. 00865, The Southern Historical Collection, Louis Round Wilson Special Collections, University of North Carolina, Chapel Hill, North Carolina.

12. CVSR, NA; Hess, *Pickett's Charge*, p. 54.

13. Hess, *Pickett's Charge*, pp. 13–19, 32–33; Cowell, *Tactics at Gettysburg*, pp. 78–79; Dowdey, *Death of a Nation*, p. 276.

14. Wert, *A Glorious Army*, pp. 269, 274–275; Hess, *Pickett's Charge*, pp. 15–19, 32–33; Dowdey, *Death of a Nation*, p. 276; Robertson, *General A. P. Hill*, pp. 220–224.

15. Hess, *Pickett's Charge*, p. 13.

16. Ibid., p. 77; *Annals of the War*, p. 313.

17. Thomas, *Robert E. Lee*, p. 292; Hess, *Pickett's Charge*, pp. 15–19, 32–33; Wert, *A Glorious Army*, pp. 269–270, 274–275.

18. Foote, *The Civil War*, vol. 2, p. 549.

19. Hirst letter to Sarah, n.d., ASC.

20. John W. Finley, "Bloody Angle, " *Buffalo Evening News*, May 28, 1894.

21. Woodward, ed., *Mary Chesnut's Civil War*, p. 416.

22. John W. Finley, "Bloody Angle, " *Buffalo Evening News*, May 28, 1894; Hess, *Pickett's Charge*, p. 53; Miers and Brown, *Gettysburg*, p. 14; Francis A. Lord, *Civil War Collector's Encyclopedia, Arms, Uniforms, and Equipment of the Union and Confederacy* (New York: Castle Books, 1965), pp. 71–73; Time-Life Editors, *Echoes of Glory, Arms and Equipment of the Confederacy*, (Alexandria, Va.: Time-Life Books, 1991), pp. 208–209; Harrison and Busey, *Nothing but Glory*, p. 120; Harrison, *Pickett's Men*, p. 95; Stewart, *Pickett's Charge*, p. 140.

23. Miers and Brown, *Gettysburg*, p. 8; Ernle Bradford, *Thermopylae, The Battle for the West* (New York: Da Capo Press, 1993), pp. 21–143; *Annals of the War*, p. 194; Gordon, *General George E. Pickett in Life and Legend*, p. 155; Woodward, ed., *Mary Chesnut's Civil War*, p. 416.

24. Gragg, *Covered with Glory*, p. 62.

25. Wert, *A Glorious Army*, p. 280.

26. CVSR, NA; Rollins, ed., *Pickett's Charge*, p. 41; Harrison and Busey, *Nothing but Glory*, pp. 6, 115.

27. Haskell, *The Battle of Gettysburg*, p. 70; Bowden and Ward, *Last Chance for Victory*, p. 439; Carhart, *Lost Triumph*, pp. xi–260; Hatch, *Victorious War*, pp. 1–3, 139–159; Wert, *A Glorious Army*, pp. 269–270; Stewart, *Pickett's Charge*, p. 188; Cowell, *Tactics at Gettysburg*, pp. 78–79, 81.

28. John W. Finley, "Bloody Angle, " *Buffalo Evening News*, May 28, 1894.

29. William W. Given Diary, Alexander W. Given Collection, Civil War Library Museum, Philadelphia, Pennsylvania.

30. Moseley, *The Stilwell Letters*, p. 118.

31. Connelly and Bellows, *God and General Longstreet*, pp. 11–12; Henry Lee Curry, III, *God's Rebels, Confederate Clergy in the Civil War* (Lafayette, La.: Huntington House, Inc., 1990), pp. 1–6; Coco, *Wasted Valor*, p. 116–117; Lewis, *Recollections from 1860 to 1865*, pp. 77, 79.

32. *Richmond Dispatch*, Richmond, Virginia, June 12, 1862.

33. Gregory, *53rd Virginia Infantry and 5th Battalion Virginia Infantry*, pp. 39, 158.

34. Gayle Diary, GNMP.

35. Connelly and Bellows, *God and General Longstreet*, pp. 11–12; Wert, *A Glorious Army*, pp. 269–270; Rollins, ed., *Pickett's Charge*, p. 23.

36. CVSR, NA; CNCSR, NA.

37. CVSR, NA; Harrison and Bussey, *Nothing but Glory*, p. 115.

38. CVSR, NA.

39. Herndon to brother, July 11, 1863, CS.

40. William Henry Cocke to parents, July 14, 1862, Cocke Family Papers, 1794–1981, Virginia History Society, Richmond, Virginia.

41. Robert H. Crewdson, *Love and War, A Southern Soldier's Struggle Between Love and Duty* (Buena Vista, Calif.: Mariner Publishing, 2009), p. 77.

42. Ibid., pp. 56, 65.

43. Ibid., pp. 52, 55.

44. David A. Price, *Love and Hate in Jamestown, John Smith, Pocahontas and the Heart of the New Nation* (New York: Faber and Faber Limited, 2003), p. 194.

45. CVSR, NA; The Weider History Group, Gettysburg, (150th Anniversary Issue, 2013), p. 72.

46. Hess, *Pickett's Charge*, pp. 14, 36, 51; Harrison and Busey, *Nothing but Glory*, p. 1; Harrison, *Pickett's Men*, pp. 88–89; CVSR, NA; Gordon, *General George E. Pickett in Life and Legend*, pp. 87, 98–105.

47. Eric A. Campbell, "Hell in the Peach Orchard, " *America's Civil War* (July 2003), p. 43; Humphreys to McLaws, January 6, 1878, UNCL; Trudeau, *Gettysburg*, pp. 367–392; Longacre, *Pickett*, p. 115.

48. Gordon, *General George E. Pickett in Life and Legend*, pp. 91–105; Hess, *Pickett's Charge*, p. 14.

49. *Franklin Repository*, Chambersburg, Pennsylvania; Nolan, *Lee Considered*, p. 17; Piston, *Lee's Tarnished Lieutenant*, pp. 4, 18; Hess, *Pickett's Charge*, pp. 15–18; Longacre, *Pickett*, p. 115; Boritt, ed., *The Gettysburg Nobody Knows*, p. 137.

50. Hess, *Pickett's Charge*, pp. 36, 401; Harrison and Busey, *Nothing but Glory*, pp. 1–2; Davis, *Jefferson Davis*, pp. 504–505; Guelzo, *Gettysburg*, p. 81; Dowdy, *Death of a Nation*, p. 251; Thomas, *Robert E. Lee*, pp. 290–292; Gragg, *Covered with Glory*, p. 156; Harrison, *Pickett's Men*, pp. xxv, 56–63, 78–79, 98.

51. Harrison, *Pickett's Men*, pp. xxi, 98.

52. Henry T. Owen to Harriet Owen, March 14, 1863, Owen Papers, Virginia Historical Society, Richmond, Virginia.

53. Ibid.

54. Harrison and Busey, *Nothing but Glory*, p. 1; Donald, ed., *Why the North Won the Civil War*, pp. 17–18, 79–90; Foote, *The Civil War*, vol. 2, pp. 532–533; Gordon, *General George E. Pickett in Life and Legend*, pp. 97, 100; Piston, *Lee's Tarnished Lieutenant*, p. 35.

55. *Fayetteville Observer*, March 27, 1864 and April 18, 1864; Gragg, *Covered with Glory*, p. 156; CVSR, NA.

56. CVSR, NA; Coco, *Wasted Valor*, p. 116; Wert, *A Glorious Army*, p. 270.

57. Lewis, *Recollections from 1860 to 1865*, p. 79; Wert, *A Glorious Army*, p. 270.

58. Harrison and Busey, *Nothing but Glory*, pp. 1–2; Conrad, *The Young Lions*, p. 152; Mann, *They Were Heard From, VMI Alumni*, pp. 26–27; Davis, *The Battle of New Market*,

pp. 47–49; Barra, "One Mile of Open Ground, " *CWT,* pp. 34–35; Schultz, *"Double Canister at Ten Yards, "* p. 25; Hess, *Pickett's Charge,* p. 14; Thomas, *Robert E. Lee,* p. 295; CVSR, NA.

59. Everson and Simpson, eds., *Far, Far from Home,* p. 249.

60. Ibid., p. 250.

61. *Carolina Watchman,* August 5, 1863.

62. William R. Reynolds, *Andrew Pickens, South Carolina Patriot in the Revolutionary War* (Jefferson, N.C.: McFarland and Company, Inc., Publishers, 2012), p. 10; Grady McWhiney, *Cracker Culture, Celtic Ways in the Old South* (Tuscaloosa: University of Alabama Press, 1988), pp. 16–20.

63. *Raleigh Observer,* Raleigh, North Carolina, November 30, 1877.

64. *Times-Dispatch,* February 7, 1904; Edmund Berkely, "Rode with Pickett, " *Confederate Veteran,* vol. 22 (1915), p. 175; Coco, *Wasted Valor,* p. 127; Hess, *Pickett's Charge,* p. 47; Mann, *They Were Heard From, VMI Alumni in the Civil War,* pp. 26–27; Conrad, *The Young Lions,* p. 152; Tucker, *Lee and Longstreet at Gettysburg,* pp. 131–133; Harrison and Busey, *Nothing but Glory,* p. 137; CVSR, NA; Katcher, *The Army of Robert E. Lee,* p. 261; Longacre, *Pickett,* p. 122.

65. Pollock Papers, UNC; CVSR, NA; Charles Kelly Barrow, J. H. Segars, and R. B. Rosenburg, "Forgotten Confederates, An Anthology About Black Southerners, " *Journal of Confederate History,* vol., 14, p. 33; Longacre, *Pickett,* pp. 11, 119; Rollins, ed., *Pickett's Charge,* p. 107.

66. CVSR, NA; Edmund Berkeley, "Rode With Pickett, " *Confederate Veteran, vol. 23* (1915), p. 175; Harrison and Busey, *Nothing but Glory,* p. 137; Rollins, ed., *Pickett's Charge,* p. 107.

67. Coco, *Wasted Valor,* pp. 124, 127.

68. CVSR, NA; *Times-Dispatch,* February 7, 1904; Harrison and Busey, *Nothing but Glory,* p. 26; Tucker, *Lee and Longstreet at Gettysburg,* pp. 107–108, 131.

69. Gregory, *53rd Virginia Infantry and 5th Battalion Virginia Infantry,* p. 11.

70. Bradford, *Thermopylae,* p. 139; Drew Gilpin Faust, *The Republic of Suffering, Death and the American Civil War* (New York: Vintage Books, 2009), pp. 7–14.

71. Stewart, *Pickett's Charge,* p. 156.

72. Faust, *The Republic of Suffering,* pp. 5–7; Gregory, *53rd Virginia Infantry and 5th Battalion Virginia Infantry,* p. 53.

73. Hess, *Pickett's Charge,* p. 61; Gragg, *Covered with Glory,* p. 175; Jean Edward Smith, *John Marshall, Definer of a Nation* (New York: Henry Holt and Company, Inc., 1966), pp. 41–52; Reardon, *Pickett's Charge,* pp. 154–175; Longacre, *Pickett,* pp. 3–5; McWhiney, *Cracker Culture,* pp. 5–22; Archie K. Davis, *Boy Colonel of the Confederacy, The Life and Times of Henry King Burgwyn, Jr.* (Chapel Hill: University of North Carolina Press, 1985), pp. 281, 316.

74. Gragg, *Covered with Glory,* pp. 175–176.

75. Hess, *Pickett's Charge,* pp. 36, 54–59; Clyde N. Wilson, *The Most Promising Young Man in the South, James Johnston Pettigrew and His Men at Gettysburg* (Abilene, Tex.: McWhiney Foundation Press, 1998), pp. 17–32, 50–62; Cockrell, ed., *Gunner with Stonewall,* p.

70; *Fayetteville Observer,* July 20, 1863; Hess, *Pickett's Charge,* p. 32; *Annals of the War,* pp. 194, 312–313; Harrison, *Pickett's Men,* pp. 99–100; Davis, *Boy Confederacy of the Confederacy,* pp. 312–315, 336; Gragg, *Covered with Glory,* pp. 50, 141–142, 175–176; *Carolina Watchman,* July 27, 1863; Wert, *A Glorious Army,* pp. 269–273; Longacre, *Pickett,* pp. 13, 120–121; David McMillan Farm, Stone Sentinels, Internet; Trudeau, *Gettysburg,* p. 453; Wert, *A Glorious Army,* p. 271; Donald L. Smith, *The Twenty-fourth Michigan* (Harrisburg: Stackpole Company, 1962), pp. 10, 41.

76. Wilson, *The Most Promising Young Man in the South,* p. 36.

77. Ibid.

78. Ibid., pp. 51–52; Gragg, *Covered with Glory,* p. 11.

79. Wilson, *The Most Promising Young Man in the South,* pp. 76–77; Robertson, *General A. P. Hill,* p. 196.

80. *Charlotte Daily Observer,* Charlotte, North Carolina, July 4, 1903; David K. Wilson, *The Southern Strategy, Britain's Conquest of South Carolina and Georgia, 1775–1780* (Columbia: University of South Carolina Press, 2005), pp. 262–266.

81. Paradis, *African Americans and the Gettysburg Campaign,* pp. 72–73; Lewis, *Recollections from 1860 to 1865,* p. 56.

82. *Fayetteville Observer,* March 27, 1864; Wilson, *The Most Promising Young Man in the South,* pp. 13, 47, 64–70; Hess, *Pickett's Charge,* p. 60; Swisher, *Warrior in Gray,* p. 124; Longacre, *Pickett,* pp. 11–14, 119; VMI's Civil War Generals, "Birkett D. Fry, Class of 1843, " Biographical Sketch, Archives, Virginia Military Institute, Lexington, Virginia; Davis, *Boy Colonel of the Confederacy,* pp. 301–303.

83. Anderson and Anderson, *The Generals,* p. 417; Gragg, *Covered with Glory,* pp. 148, 155–156; Dowdey, *Death of a Nation,* p. 279; Foote, *The Civil War,* vol. 2, p. 535.

84. *Fayetteville Observer,* July 20, 1863; *Carolina Watchman,* September 15, 1887; Gragg, *Covered with Glory,* p. 146; Stewart, *Pickett's Charge,* pp. 132–133.

85. Rollins, ed., *Pickett's Charge,* p. 79; Hess, *Pickett's Charge,* p. 60; Gragg, *Covered with Glory,* pp. 155, 160; CNCSR, NA; Longacre, *Pickett,* p. 14; Stephen Dando-Collins, *Tycoon's War, How Cornelius Vanderbilt Invaded a Country to Overthrow America's Most Famous Military Adventurer* (New York: Da Capo Press, 2008), pp. 117–120, 127, 207–208, 254, 257–260; Hugh F. Rankin, *Francis Marion, The Swamp Fox* (New York: Thomas Y. Crowell Company, 1973), pp. 52–284; Foote, *The Civil War,* vol. 2, p. 535; Coddington, *The Gettysburg Campaign,* p. 491; Smith, *The Twenty-fourth Michigan,* p. 126; Swisher, *Warrior in Gray,* p. 125; Anderson and Anderson, *The Generals,* p. 417.

86. Wert, *A Glorious Army,* pp. 269, 275; *The News and Observer,* Raleigh, North Carolina, September 24, 1887; Jim Murphy, *The Boys' War* (New York: Clarion Books, 1990), pp. 1–2; Persico, *My Enemy, My Brother,* p. 200; CVSR, NA; CNCSR, NA.

87. CNCSR, NA; *The News and Observer,* September 24, 1887; Tod Robinson Caldwell Papers, 1801–1890, Southern Historical Society Papers, Chapel Hill, North Carolina.

88. Dannett and Burkart, eds., *Confederate Surgeon,* p. 121.

89. John Rozier, ed., *The Granite Farm Letters, The Civil War Correspondence of Edgeworth and Sallie Bird* (Athens: University of Georgia Press, 1988), p. 108.

90. Moseley, ed., *The Stilwell Letters,* p. 180.

91. Reardon, *Pickett's Charge in History and Memory*, p. 8; Hess, *Pickett's Charge*, pp. 64–65, 68–70; Stewart, *Pickett's Charge*, p. 212.

92. Reardon, *Pickett's Charge*, pp. 8, 36; Hess, *Pickett's Charge*, pp. 67–68; Wert, *A Glorious Army*, pp. 194–195.

93. Robertson, *General A. P. Hill*, p. 223; Hess, *Pickett's Charge*, pp. 15–19, 32–33, 70–72; McKenzie, *Uncertain Glory*, p. 160; Cowell, *Tactics at Gettysburg*, pp. 78–79; Foote, *The Civil War*, vol. 2, p. 530; Tucker, *Lee and Longstreet at Gettysburg*, p. 95; Wert, *A Glorious Army*, pp. 269, 274–275.

94. Jeffrey D. Stocker, ed., *From Huntsville to Appomattox, R. T. Cole's History of the 4th Regiment, Alabama Volunteer Infantry, C.S.A., Army of Northern Virginia* (Knoxville; University of Tennessee Press, 1996), pp. 15, 115; Compiled Military Service Records of Confederate Soldiers from the State of Alabama, Record Group 109, National Archives, Washington, DC

95. Rollins, ed., *Pickett's Charge*, p. 50; Gragg, *Covered with Glory*, p. 149.

96. CASR, NA; Stocker, ed., *From Huntsville to Appomattox*, pp. 15, 115.

97. Anderson and Anderson, *The Generals*, p. 417.

98. John W. Finley, "Bloody Angle, " *Buffalo Evening News*, May 29, 1894.

99. Hess, *Pickett's Charge*, pp. 156–157.

100. Rollins, ed., *Pickett's Charge*, p. 74.

101. Chandler, *The Campaigns of Napoleon*, pp. 155, 1087.

102. Gragg, *Covered with Glory*, p. 42.

103. *The News and Observer*, Raleigh, North Carolina, March 24, 1887.

104. Longacre, *Pickett*, p. 121; Gragg, *Covered with Glory*, p. 156; Swisher, *Warrior in Gray*, p. 133; Glenn Tucker, *Lee and Longstreet at Gettysburg* (Dayton, Ohio: Morningside Press, 1982), p. 102.

105. Gordon, *General George E. Pickett in Life and Legend*, pp. 92–93, 97; Harrison, *Pickett's Men*, pp. 18–33; Foote, *The Civil War*, vol. 2, p. 533; Longacre, *Pickett*, pp. 60, 92.

106. Harrison, *Pickett's Men*, p. 70.

107. Haskell, *The Battle of Gettysburg*, p. 95.

108. Hirst letter to Sarah, n.d., ASC.

109. Priest, *Into the Fight*, pp. 128, 130–131.

110. CVSR, NA.

111. Robert M. Dunkerly, *The Battle of Kings Mountain, Eyewitness Accounts, The Battle that Turned the Tide of the American Revolution* (Charleston, S.C.: The History Press, 2007), p. 46.

112. Michael P. Johnson and James L. Roark, *Black Masters, A Free Black Family of Color in the Old South* (New York: W. W. Norton Company, 1984), pp. 306–307, 317.

113. Bishop, *The Tennessee Brigade*, pp. 17–30, 54, 57, 63–101, 204–206, 211, 217; William C. Floyd and Paul Gibson, *The Boys Who Went to War from Cumberland University, 1861–1865* (Gettysburg, Pa.: Thomas Publications, 2001), pp. 6, 12, 28, 42, 180; Stewart, *Pickett's Charge*, p. 171; Compiled Military Service Records of Confederate Soldiers Who Served from the States of Alabama and Tennessee, Record Group 109, National Archives, Washington, DC

114. Bishop, *The Tennessee Brigade*, p. 205; CASR, NA.

115. Rollins, ed., *Pickett's Charge*, p. 98; Moseley, ed., *The Stilwell Letters*, p. 174; Gragg, *Covered with Glory*, p. 156.

116. *Carolina Watchman*, August 5, 1863.

117. Swisher, *Warrior in Gray*, pp. 140–141.

118. Robert E. Lee, Jr., *Recollections and Letters of General Robert E. Lee* (New York: Garden City Publishing Company, Inc., 1924), p. 434.

119. Hess, *Pickett's Charge*, pp. 69–70.

120. Chris McNabb, *Armies of the Napoleonic Wars, An Illustrated History* (Oxford: Osprey Publishing, Ltd., 2009), p. 61.

121. Cisco, *Wade Hampton*, p. 120; Carhart, *Lost Triumph*, pp. xi–290; Hatch, *Glorious War*, pp. 1–3, 139–159; Cowell, *Tactics at Gettysburg*, p. 81.

122. Hatch, *Glorious War*, p. 1; Carhart, *Lost Triumph*, pp. xi–290; Cowell, *Tactics at Gettysburg*, p. 81.

123. Hatch, *Glorious War*, pp. 1, 139–159; Carhart, *Lost Triumph*, pp. xi–290; Cowell, *Tactics at Gettysburg*, p. 81; Hess, *Pickett's Charge*, p. 20.

124. Cowell, *Tactics at Gettysburg*, p. 72.

Chapter IV

1. Wert, *A Glorious Army*, pp. 270–271.

2. Nelson D. Lankford, ed., *An Irishman in Dixie, Thomas Conolly's Diary of the Fall of the Confederacy* (Columbia: University of South Carolina Press, 1988), p. 52.

3. Blackford, ed., *Letters from Lee's Army*, p. 175.

4. Moseley, ed., *The Stilwell Letters*, p. 172.

5. Chris Hedges, *War Is a Force that Gives Us Meaning* (New York: Public Affairs, 2002), pp. 10, 12, 29; John Keegan, *A History of Warfare* (New York: Vintage, 1994), pp. 27, 360–361; Hess, *Pickett's Charge*, pp. 15, 30–33, 77; Cowell, *Tactics, at Gettysburg*, pp. 68–70, 72, 78; Moseley, ed., *The Stilwell Letters*, p. 188; Stewart, *Pickett's Charge*, p. 148.

6. Hedges, *War Is a Force that Gives Us Meaning*, p. 115.

7. Robert E. Lee, Jr., *Recollections and Letters of Robert E. Lee* (Old Saybrook, Ct.: Konecky and Konecky, 1998), pp. 415–416; *Charlotte Observer*, July 7, 1902; Haskell, *The Battle of Gettysburg*, p. 135; Wert, *A Glorious Army*, p. 270; Moseley, ed., *The Stilwell Letters*, p. 180; Foote, *The Civil War*, vol. 2, p. 538; Thomas, *Robert E. Lee*, p. 299.

8. Gragg, *Covered with Glory*, pp. 157–158.

9. Reardon, *Pickett's Charge in History and Memory*, pp. 1–4; Gordon, *General George E. Pickett in Life and Legend*, pp. 1–2; Longacre, *Pickett*, pp. ix–x; John W. Stevens, *Reminiscences of the Civil War, A Soldier in Hood's Texas Brigade, Army of Northern Virginia* (Hillsboro, Tex.: Hillsboro Mirror Print, 1902), p. 182.

10. Longacre, *Pickett*, pp. 119–120.

11. Rollins, ed., *Pickett's Charge*, p. 79.

12. Ibid.; Longacre, *Pickett*, p. 119; Gordon, *General George E. Pickett in Life and Legend*, p. 110; Joseph Graham to Graham, July 30, 1863, SHC.

13. Gordon, *General George E. Pickett in Life and Legend,* p. 97; Piston, *Lee's Tarnished Lieutenant,* pp. 6–7, 60–61; Wert, *A Glorious Army,* pp. 269, 274–275; Hess, *Pickett's Charge,* p. 15; Dowdey, *Death of a Nation,* p. 300; Cowell, *Tactics at Gettyburg,* p. 68; Longacre, *Pickett,* pp. 14, 25–26.

14. Hess, *Pickett's Charge,* pp. 15–16, 20–21; Carhart, *Lost Triumph,* pp. xi–260; Hatch, *Glorious War,* pp. 1–3, 139–159; Cowell, *Tactics at Gettysburg,* pp. 72, 78–79, 81.

15. Longacre, *Pickett,* p. 26; Hess, *Pickett's Charge,* pp. 9, 11; Piston, *Lee's Tarnished Lieutenant,* pp. 59–61.

16. Foote, *The Civil War,* vol. 2, p. 539.

17. Longacre, *Pickett,* p. 121.

18. R. F. Delderfield, *The March of the Twenty-Six, The Story of Napoleon's Marshals* (South Yorkshire: Pen and Sword Books, Ltd., 2004), p. 115; Cowell, *Tactics at Gettysburg,* pp. 72, 78; Foote, *The Civil War,* vol. 2, pp. 550–551; Longacre, *Pickett,* pp. 121–122; Rollins, ed., *Pickett's Charge,* p. 184; *Times-Dispatch,* February 7, 1904; C. Van Woodward, ed., *Mary Chesnut's Civil War* (New Haven, Conn.: Yale University Press, 1981), p. 495.

19. Wert, *A Glorious Army,* pp. 269, 274–275; Cowell, *Tactics at Gettysburg,* pp. 72, 78–79; Hess, *Pickett's Charge,* pp. 15, 32–33.

20. Longacre, *Pickett,* pp. 2–4.

21. Guelzo, *Gettysburg,* p. 13; Time-Life Editors, *Voices of the Civil War, Gettysburg,* p. 156; CVSR, NA; *Times-Dispatch,* February 7, 1904; Harrison and Busey, *Nothing but Glory,* p. 49; Field, *Robert E. Lee,* p. 56; James C. Olson, *Stuart Symington: A Life* (Columbia: University of Missouri Press, 2003), p. 3; Moseley, ed., *The Stilwell Letters,* p. 154.

22. Guelzo, *Gettysburg,* p. 13.

23. John Caldwell to Tod Robinson Caldwell, June 22, 1863, Tod Robinson Papers, 1801–1890, SHC.

24. CVSR, NA; Wert, *A Glorious Army,* p. 208.

25. *Times-Dispatch,* February 7, 1904; CVSR, NA; Hess, *Pickett's Charge,* pp. 38, 77; Tucker, *Lee and Longstreet at Gettysburg,* p. 107; Robert E. Lee, *Blackbeard the Pirate* (Winston-Salem, N.C.: John F. Blair Publishing, 2000), pp. 113–125.

26. Robert M. Powell, "With Hood at Gettysburg, " *Times Weekly,* Philadelphia, Pennsylvania, December 13, 1884; Hess, *Pickett's Charge,* pp. 14, 43; Blackford, ed., *Letters from Lee's Army,* p. 185; Stewart, *Pickett's Charge,* p. 149.

27. Durkin, ed., *John Dooley, Confederate Soldier,* p. 8; Hess, *Pickett's Charge,* p. 52.

28. Armistead Biography Information, ECU; Rollins, ed., *Pickett's Charge,* p. 199.

29. Durkin, ed., *John Dooley, Confederate Soldier,* p. 104; Gregory, *53rd Virginia Infantry and 5th Virginia Battalion,* p. 53; Stewart, *Pickett's Charge,* p. 47; Rollins, ed., *Pickett's Charge,* pp. 11, 199.

30. Harrison, *Pickett's Men,* pp. 29–32, 70, 191; Longacre, *Pickett,* pp. 4, 54, 91–93; Tucker, *Lee and Longstreet at Gettysburg,* p. 107; Rollins, ed., *Pickett's Charge,* p. 200.

31. Gregory, *53rd Virginia Infantry and 5th Battalion Virginia Infantry,* p. 53; Tucker, *Lee and Longstreet at Gettysburg,* p. 107; CVSR, NA.

32. Margaret S. Creighton, *The Color of Courage, Gettysburg's Forgotten History, Immigrants, Women, and African Americans in the Civil War's Defining Battle* (New York: Perseus

Books Group, 2005), p. 124; Gregory, *53rd Virginia Infantry and 5th Battalion Virginia Infantry*, p. 53; Henry Steele Commager, *The Blue and the Gray* (2 vols.) (New York: Penguin Books, 1973), vol. 2, p. 292; Philip Katcher, *American Civil War Armies (1), Confederate Artillery, Cavalry and Infantry* (London: Osprey Publishing, 1989), pp. 36–37; Motts, *"Trust in God and Fear Nothing,"* p. 48; Moseley, ed., *The Stilwell Letters,* p. 156; Rollins, ed., *Pickett's Charge,* p. 74.

33. Durkin, *John Dooley, Confederate Soldier,* pp. 104–105; CVSR, NA.

34. John A. Herndon to brother, July 11, 1863, CS.

35. Reardon, *Pickett's Charge,* p. 13; Hess, *Pickett's Charge,* pp. 76–79.

36. Harrison, *Pickett's Men,* p. 100.

37. Anderson and Anderson, *The Generals,* p. 421.

38. Rollins, ed., *Pickett's Charge,* p. 73; *Buffalo Evening News,* May 28, 1894; Berkeley, "Rode with Pickett," *CV,* p. 175; Hess, *Pickett's Charge,* p. 47; "Willie Brew'd a Peck O'Malt," National Galleries, Edinburgh, Scotland; Rod Gragg, *The Illustrated Gettysburg Reader* (Washington, DC: Regnery Publishing, Inc., 2013), pp. 330–334; Persico, *My Enemy, My Brother,* p. 229; Tucker, *Lee and Longstreet at Gettysburg,* pp. 102, 131–132; Foote, *The Civil War,* vol. 2, p. 526; CVSR, NA; Coco, *Wasted Valor,* p. 127; Dowdey, *Death of a Nation,* pp. 296, 300.

39. *Times-Dispatch,* February 7, 1904; Harrison and Busey, *Nothing but Glory,* p. 137; Tucker, *Lee and Longstreet at Gettysburg,* p. 102; Foote, *The Civil War,* vol. 2, p. 553.

40. CVSR, NA.

41. Anderson and Anderson, *The Generals,* p. 420; Hess, *Pickett's Charge,* p. 62; Foote, *The Civil War,* vol. 2, p. 551.

42. CVSR, NA; Durkin, ed., *John Dooley, Confederate Soldier,* pp. 58–59.

43. Moseley, ed., *The Stilwell Letters,* p. 203.

44. Dowdey, *Death of a Nation,* p. 294.

45. Tucker, *Lee and Longstreet at Gettysburg,* p. 104.

46. Armistead Biographical Information, ECU.

47. CSRV, NA; William H. H. Winston Account, John W. Daniel Papers, Box 23, Library of Virginia, Richmond Virginia.

48. CVSR, NA; Guelzo, *Gettysburg,* pp. 4, 104; Phillip Thomas Tucker, *How the Irish Won the American Revolution, A New Look at the Forgotten Heroes of America's War of Independence* (New York: Skyhorse Publishing, 2015), pp. 1–339; Creighton, *The Color of Courage,* p. 35; McWhiney, *Cracker Culture,* pp. xiii–145, 268–271; James Haltigan, *The Irish in the American Revolution and Their Early Influence in the Colonies* (Washington, DC, James Haltigan Publisher, 1908), pp. 28–34, 85–128; Thomas Fleming, *Washington's Secret War, The Hidden History of Valley Forge* (New York: HarperCollins Publishers, 2005), pp. 141–142, 259–260, 285.

49. John E. Dooley, SJ, Papers, Special Collections, Georgetown University, Georgetown, Virginia; Durkin, ed., *John Dooley, Confederate Soldier,* pp. ix–xv; Thomas G. Rogers, *Irish-American Units in the Civil War* (Oxford: Osprey Publishing, Ltd., 2008), pp. 29, 40–41; McWhiney, *Cracker Ways,* pp. xii–145; CVSR, NA; CNCSR, NA; Kelly J. O'Grady, *Clear the Confederate Way! The Irish in the Army of Northern Virginia* (Mason

City, Iowa: Savas Publishing Company, 2000), pp. iii–vi, xvii, 256; Ella Lonn, *Foreigners in the Confederacy* (Chapel Hill: University of North Carolina Press, 2002), pp. 4–13, 23–32; James P. Gannon, *Irish Rebels, Confederate Tigers, The 6th Louisiana Volunteers, 1861–1865* (Campbell, Calif.: Savas Publishing Company, 1998), pp. ii–iii; Edith Moore Sprouse, *Mount Air, Fairfax County, Virginia* (Fairfax, Va.: Fairfax County Office of Comprehensive Planning, 1976), pp. 7, 13; David T. Gleeson, *The Irish in the South, 1815–1877* (Chapel Hill: The University of North Carolina Press, 2001), pp. 23–54.

50. Durkin, ed., *John Dooley, Confederate Soldier,* p. 177; Lonn, *Foreigners in the Confederacy,* p. 55; O'Grady, *Clear the Confederate Way!,* p. 256.

51. Durkin, ed., *John Dooley, Confederate Soldier,* pp. 116–117.

52. Durkin, ed., *John Dooley, Confederate Soldier,* pp. xiv–xv, 1–2, 224–229, 233; Harrison Clark, *All Cloudless Glory* (Washington, DC: Regnery Publishing, Inc., 1995), pp. 73–139; CVSR, NA; Anderson and Anderson, *The Generals,* p. 420; Harrison, *Pickett's Men,* p. 74.

53. CVSR, NA; O'Grady, *Clear the Way!,* p. 258.

54. Harrison, *Pickett's Men,* p. 74; Tucker, *Lee and Longstreet at Gettysburg,* p. 108.

55. Durkin, ed., *John Dooley, Confederate Soldier,* pp. 75–76; CVSR, NA.

56. CVSR, NA; Coco, *Wasted Valor,* pp. 127–128.

57. Robert N. Rosen, *The Jewish Confederates* (Columbia: University of South Carolina Press, 2000), pp. xii–xiii, 169; Harrison and Busey, *Nothing but Glory,* p. 47; CVSR, NA; Smith, comp. , *Farms at Gettysburg,* p. 15.

58. Piston, *Lee's Tarnished Lieutenant,* p. 35; Rosen, *The Jewish Confederates,* pp. 2–3.

59. David Stone, *Fighting for the Fatherland, The Story of the German Soldier from 1648 to the Present Day* (Washington, DC: Potomac Books, Inc., 2006), p. 63.

60. CVSR, NA; Tucker, *Irish Confederates,* pp. 90–94; Gleeson, *The Irish in the South, 1815–1877,* pp. 132, 155; Coco, *Wasted Valor,* p. 141; Durkin, ed., *John Dooley, Confederate Soldier,* pp. 142–143; McWhiney, *Cracker Culture,* pp. xii–145; O'Grady, *Clear the Confederate Way!,* pp. xiii, 35–37.

61. John E. Dooley, SJ, Papers, Special Collections, Georgetown University, Georgetown, Virginia; Durkin, ed., John Dooley, *Confederate Soldier,* p. 142; Harrison, *Pickett's Men,* p. 74.

62. Gleeson, *The Irish of the South,* p. 156; Tucker, *Irish Confederates,* pp. 91–92.

63. Gleeson, *The Irish of the South,* p. 156.

64. O'Grady, *Clear the Confederate Way!,* pp. 25, 249; Lonn, *Foreigners in the Confederacy,* p. 96.

65. CVSR, NA; O'Grady, *Clear the Confederate Way!,* pp. 256–257.

66. CVSR, NA; Rodgers, *Irish-American Units in the Civil War,* p. 41; Harrison and Busey, *Nothing but Glory,* p. 2.

67. Time-Life Editors, *Echoes of Glory, Arms and Equipment of the Confederacy* (Alexandria, Va.: Time-Life Books, 1991), p. 139.

68. CVSR, NA; James I. Robertson, Jr., *The Stonewall Brigade* (Baton Rouge: Louisiana State University Press, 1963), pp. 12–13; Lonn, *Foreigners in the Confederacy,* pp. 2–4, 31.

69. CVSR, NA; Harrison and Busey, *Nothing but Glory,* p. 4; Lonn, *Foreigners in the Confederacy,* pp. 2–4, 31; Thomas C. Parramore, *Norfolk, The First Four Centuries* (Charlottesville: University Press of Virginia, 1995), pp. 102–208.

70. CVSR, NA.

71. Ibid.

72. Henry Thweatt Owen article (September 26, no year) from *Philadelphia Times,* Philadelphia, Pennsylvania, Clippings Book, I, Gettysburg National Military Battlefield Park Archives, Gettysburg, Pennsylvania; Biographical Sketch of Henry Thweatt Owen, Henry Thweatt Owen Papers, 1822–1929, Library of Virginia, Richmond, Virginia; CVSR, NA; Katcher, *The Army of Robert E. Lee,* p. 263; Parramore, *Norfolk,* pp. 102–198.

73. Stewart, *Pickett's Charge,* p. 52; Dando-Collins, *Tycoon's War,* pp. 331–333.

74. Campbell, "Hell in the Peach Orchard, " *ACW,* p. 43; CMSR, NA.

75. Gragg, *Covered with Glory,* p. 46.

76. John W. Finley, "Bloody Angle, " *Buffalo Evening News,* May 28, 1894.

77. Ibid.; Gragg, *Covered with Glory,* pp. 46, 63, 176; CVSR, NA.

78. Durkin, ed., *John Dooley, Confederate Soldier,* p. 105; Rogers, *Napoleon's Army,* p. 74; Andrew Uffindell, *Napoleon's Immortals, The Imperial Guard and its battles, 1804–1815,* (Spellmount Publishing, Limited, 2007) p. 56.

79. William B. Taylor to family, July 29, 1863, William B. Floyd Collection, copy in Robert L. Brake Collection, United States Army Military History Institute, Carlisle, Pennsylvania.

80. Crewdson, *Love and War,* pp. x–66, 106; CVSR, NA.

81. *Annals of the War,* pp. 191–192.

82. Ibid; CVSR, NA; Thomas G. Rodgers, *Irish-Americans in the Civil War* (New York: Osprey Publishing, Ltd., 2008), pp. 3–4.

83. CVSR, NA; Carl L. Sell, Jr., *"Thank God He Survived Pickett's Charge"* (Alexandria, Va.: Private printing, 2011), pp. 2, 4, 6, 72–73; James Farthing, Franconia, Virginia, to author, March 11, 2015 email.

84. Blackford, ed., *Letters from Lee's Army,* p. 187.

85. Moseley, ed., *The Stilwell Letters,* p. 180.

86. Woodward, ed., *Mary Chesnut's Civil War,* p. 103.

87. Haskell, *The Battle of Gettysburg,* pp. 80, 95.

88. Reardon, *Pickett's Charge,* pp. 13, 20; Cowell, *Tactics at Gettysburg,* p. 76; Johnson, *A Gallant Little Army,* pp. 150, 270.

89. Miers and Brown, *Gettysburg,* p. 172.

90. Haskell, *The Battle of Gettysburg,* p. 80; Miers and Brown, *Gettysburg,* p. 180; Trudeau, *Gettysburg,* pp. 244–245.

91. Coddington, *The Gettysburg Campaign,* p. 494; Haskell, *The Battle of Gettysburg,* p. 95; Shultz, *"Double Canister at Ten Yards, "* p. 17; Stewart, *Pickett's Charge,* p. 138.

92. Gordon, *General George E. Pickett in Life and Legend,* pp. 77, 91–105; Wert, *A Glorious Army,* p. 273; Hess, *Pickett's Charge,* p. 14; Rollins, *Pickett's Charge,* p. 219.

93. Stevens, *Reminiscences of the Civil War,* p. 182; Gordon, *General George E. Pickett in Life and Legend,* p. 110.

94. John W. Finley, "Bloody Angle, " *Buffalo Evening News,* May 28, 1894.

95. John W. Finley, "Bloody Angle, " *Buffalo Evening News,* May 28, 1894; Gordon, *General George E. Pickett in Life and Legend,* pp. 49–53, 77, 92–113, 169–170; David Jonathan Sawyer, *My Great-Grandfather Was Stonewall Jackson, The Story of a Negro Boy Growing Up in the Segregated South* (Baltimore, Md.: Publishing Concepts, 1994), pp. ix, 265–275; Hess, *Pickett's Charge,* p. 37; Foote, *The Civil War,* vol. 2, p. 551; Elise Lemire, *Miscegenation, Making Race in America* (Philadelphia, Pa.: University of Pennsylvania Press, 2002), pp. 1–86; Gallagher, ed., *Third Day at Gettysburg & Beyond,* p. 104; Longacre, *Pickett,* p. 2; Richard G. Hardorff, compiled and edited, *Indian Views of the Custer Fight* (Norman: University of Oklahoma Press, 2005), p. 34, note no. 2.

96. Longacre, *Pickett,* pp. 3–4, 27; CVSR, NA.

97. John W. Finley, "Bloody Angle, " *Buffalo Evening News,* May 28, 1894.

98. Ibid.; CVSR, NA; BibleGateway, Internet.

99. CVSR, NA.

100. CVSR, NA; John W. Finley, "Bloody Angle, " *Buffalo Evening News,* May 28, 1894.

101. Hess, *Pickett's Charge,* p. 184.

102. "Ancestor in a Little Blue and a Lot of Gray, " Pettigrew Family, November 29, 2012, Pettigrew Family Blog, Internet; Hess, *Pickett's Charge,* p. 184; Gragg, *Covered with Glory,* pp. 176–178; Time-Life Editors, *Echoes of Glory,* p. 104; Coddington, *The Gettysburg Campaign,* p. 503.

103. "Ancestor in a Little Blue and a Lot of Gray, " Pettigrew Family, November 29, 2012, Pettigrew Family Blog, Internet.

104. John W. Finley, "Bloody Angle, " *Buffalo Evening News,* May 28, 1894.

105. Hess, *Pickett's Charge,* pp. 15–21; Cowell, *Tactics at Gettysburg,* pp. 78–79; Wert, *A Glorious Army,* pp. 269, 274–275.

106. Moseley, ed., *The Stilwell Letters,* p. 5.

107. Gragg, *Covered with Glory,* p. 179; CVSR, NA; Tucker, *Lee and Longstreet at Gettysburg,* p. 119.

108. CVSR, NA; Rollins, ed., *Pickett's Charge,* pp. 69–70; Hess, *Pickett's Charge,* pp. 141–142.

109. Haskell, *The Battle of Gettysburg,* p. 96; Stewart, *Pickett's Charge,* p. 148; Gragg, *Covered in Glory,* pp. 178–181; Moseley, ed., *The Stilwell Letters,* p. 54.

110. Boritt, ed., *The Gettysburg Nobody Knows,* p. 130.

111. William J. Burns Diary, Save the Flags Collection, United States Military History Institute, Carlisle Barracks, Pennsylvania.

112. Gragg, *Covered in Glory,* pp. 179–181.

113. Moseley, ed., *The Stilwell Letters,* p. 203.

114. Ibid., p. 179; Haskell, *The Battle of Gettysburg,* pp. 97–98; Hess, *Pickett's Charge,* pp. 119–120; Foote, *The Civil War,* vol. 2, p. 550; Shultz, *"Double Canister at Ten Yards, "* p. 19; Boritt, ed., *The Gettysburg Nobody Knows,* p. 134; Time-Life Editors, *Echoes of Glory,* p. 34; Reardon, *Pickett's Charge,* p. 23.

115. Hirst letter to Sarah, n.d., ASC.

116. Haskell, *The Battle of Gettysburg,* p. 97; Gragg, *Covered in Glory,* p. 178.

117. Hirst letter to Sarah, n.d., ASC; Longacre, *Pickett*, p. 120; Boritt, *The Gettysburg Nobody Knows*, pp. 126, 134; John W. Finley, "Bloody Angle, " *Buffalo Evening News*, May 28, 1894; Hess, *Pickett's Charge*, pp. 22–23.

118. Reardon, *Pickett's Charge*, p. 19.

119. Robertson, *General A. P. Hill*, pp. 193, 195, 209, 217, 219, 222–223; *Annals of the War*, p. 313; Rollins, ed., *Pickett's Charge*, p. 360; Trudeau, *Gettysburg*, p. 453; Hess, *Pickett's Charge*, pp. 15–21; Dowdey, *Death of a Nation*, pp. 276, 280–281; Wert, *A Glorious Army*, p. 369; Carl Coppolino, "Lee's Illness Lost Gettysburg, " *Gettysburg Magazine*, no. 46 (January 2012), pp. 95–101.

120. Wert, *A Glorious Army*, pp. 269, 274–275; Hess, *Pickett's Charge*, pp. 15–21; Robertson, *General A. P. Hill*, pp. 218, 222–223.

121. Miers and Brown, *Gettysburg*, p. 174; Hess, *Pickett's Charge*, pp. 15–18.

122. Chandler, *The Campaigns of Napoleon*, pp. 375, 1087.

123. Hirst letter to Sarah, n.d., ASC.

124. Gragg, *Covered with Glory*, p. 47.

125. Moseley, ed., *The Stilwell Letters*, p. 40.

126. Gregory, *53rd Virginia Infantry and 5th Battalion Virginia Infantry*, p. 54; Robertson, *General A. P. Hill*, pp. 218–222.

127. Harrison, *Pickett's Men*, pp. 23, 44; Gragg, *Covered with Glory*, p. 178.

128. Durkin, ed., *John Dooley, Confederate Soldier*, p. 105.

129. CVSR, NA.

130. Armistead Biographical Information, Elizabeth Moore Papers, Collection No. 332, East Carolina Manuscript Collection, J. Y. Joyner Library, East Carolina University, Greenville, North Carolina; CVSR, NA; Pittsylvania Historical Society (PHC), *Pickett's Charge at Gettysburg* (Indian Rock Printing Company, 2006), pp. 5, 7; Hess, *Pickett's Charge*, p. 40; Motts, *"Trust in God and Fear Nothing, "* pp. 4, 10, 26, 28, 33, 48–49; Harrison, *Pickett's Men*, p. 36; Michael Halleran, "'The Widow's Son' Lewis Armistead at Gettysburg, " *Gettysburg Magazine*, no. 43 (July 2010), pp. 93–95; John W. Finley, "Bloody Angle, " *Buffalo Evenings News*, May 28, 1894.

131. John W. Finley, "Bloody Angle, " *Buffalo Evening News*, May 28, 1894.

132. PHS, *Pickett's Charge at Gettysburg*, p. 10.

133. Colonel Joseph Mayo, July 25, 1863, DU; CVSR, NA.

134. John W. Finley, "Bloody Angle, " *Buffalo Evening News*, May 28, 1894.

135. *Annals of the War*, p. 314.

136. Gragg, *Covered with Glory*, p. 50.

137. Moseley, ed., *The Stilwell Letters*, p. 104.

138. Lewis, Recollections from *1861 to 1865*, p. 82; Harrison and Busey, *Nothing but Glory*, p. 3; CVSR, NA.

139. CVSR, NA; Lewis, Recollections from *1861 to 1865*, p. 82; *Buffalo Evening News*, May 28, 1894.

140. The Weider History Group, Gettysburg, p. 72; CVSR, NA.

141. Ibid.

142. Hess, *Pickett's Charge*, p. 170.

143. Gregory, *53rd Virginia Infantry and 5th Battalion Virginia Infantry*, p. 54.

144. John A. Herndon to brother, July 11, 1863, CS; Coddington, *The Gettysburg Campaign*, p. 503.

145. William Weldon Bently to Mother, June 13, 1862, Alumni Civil War Letters, Diaries and Manuscripts, Virginia Military Institute Archives, Virginia Military Institute, Lexington, Virginia.

146. Cowell, *Tactics at Gettysburg*, p. 69.

147. Hess, *Pickett's Charge*, p. 182; Woodward, ed., *Mary Chesnut's Civil War*, p. 142.

148. Hess, *Pickett's Charge*, pp. 15, 187–188; Gragg, *Covered with Glory*, p. 182; Hess, *Pickett's Charge*, pp. 62–63; Coddington, *The Gettysburg Campaign*, pp. 490–491, 506; Davis, *Boy Colonel of the Confederacy*, pp. 302–304, 306, 309, 321–322; Smith, *The Twenty-fourth Michigan*, p. 127.

149. Hess, *Pickett's Charge*, pp. 77, 172; Gragg, *Covered with Glory*, p. 182; Gregory, *53rd Virginia Infantry and 5th Battalion Virginia Infantry*, p. 54; PHS, *Pickett's Charge at Gettysburg*, pp. 2–3, 5, 9.

150. Rollins, ed., *Pickett's Charge*, p. 115.

151. William A.Young and Patricia C. Young, *History of the 56th Virginia Infantry Regiment*, (Fort Walton Beach: James K. Baughman Publisher, 2009), p. 104.

152. Rollins, ed., *Pickett's Charge*, p. 179; CVSR, NA.

153. Harrison and Busey, *Nothing but Glory*, p. 43.

154. Hess, *Pickett's Charge*, p. 172; Gragg, *Covered with Glory*, p. 182.

155. Durkin, ed., *John Dooley, Confederate Soldier*, p. 105; Guelzo, *Gettysburg*, pp. 105, 302; Trudeau, *Gettysburg*, p. 283; CVSR, NA; Harrison and Busey, *Nothing but Glory*, p. 43; Creighton, *The Color of Courage*, pp. xviii–xix, 50–55, 125; Captain Henry Thweatt Owen Account, National Park Service, History E-Library, Internet; Paradis, *African Americans and the Gettysburg Campaign*, pp. 9, 59–60; Hess, *Pickett's Charge*, pp. 120, 174; Paradis, *African Americans and the Gettysburg Campaign*, pp. 59–60; *Gettysburg Times*, Gettysburg, Pennsylvania, July 11, 1878; Stewart, *Pickett's Charge*, p. 166.

156. CVSR, NA; Rollins, ed., *Pickett's Charge*, p. 200.

157. Rollins, ed., *Pickett's Charge*, pp. 11, 179; Harrison and Busey, *Nothing but Glory*, p. 42; Reardon, *Pickett's Charge*, p. 13.

158. Hess, *Pickett's Charge*, p. 77; Gragg, *Covered with Glory*, pp. 182–183.

159. "Ancestor in a Little Blue and a Lot of Gray, " Pettigrew Family, November 29, 2012, Pettigrew Family Blog, Internet.

160. Chapter VI

161. Rosen, *The Jewish Confederates*, pp. 126–131; Piston, *Lee's Tarnished Lieutenant*, p. 35; Si Sheppard, *The Jewish Revolt AD 66–74* (Oxford: Osprey Publishing Ltd., 2013), pp. 14–16.

162. Reverend James E. Poindexter, "Address on the Life and Services of Gen. Lewis A. Armistead" (Richmond, Va.: January 29, 1909), p. 3.

163. Campbell, "Hell in the Peach Orchard, " *ACW*, p. 44.

164. Wert, *A Glorious Army*, p. 273; CVSR, NA.

165. Faust, *This Republic of Suffering*, pp. 58–59; Moseley, ed., *The Stilwell Letters*, p. 29; Stewart, *Pickett's Charge*, p. 148.

166. William W. Bentley to Mother, June 13, 1862, VMI Archives, VMI.

167. Ross Family Correspondence, 1861–1864, Accession No. 21089, Virginia State Library, Richmond, Virginia; CVSR, NA.

168. CVSR, NA; James H. Walker, "The Charge of Pickett's Division by a Participant, " Virginia State Library, Richmond, Virginia.

169. Ibid.; Rankin, *Francis Marion*, pp. 1–299.

170. CVSR, NA; Rollins, ed., *Pickett's Charge*, pp. 69, 72.

171. Gragg, *Covered with Glory*, pp. 184–185.

172. Ibid., pp. 183–185.

173. Durkin, ed., *John Dooley, Confederate Soldier*, p. 105; CVSR, NA; Harrison, *Pickett's Men*, pp. 53–54.

174. Anderson and Anderson, *The Generals*, p. 421.

175. CVSR, NA; Rollins, ed., *Pickett's Charge*, p. 108; Kenneth S. Greenberg, ed., *Nat Turner, A Slave Rebellion in History and Memory* (Oxford: Oxford University Press, 2003), pp. xi–147.

176. Hess, *Pickett's Charge*, p. 155; CVSR, NA.

177. Stewart, *Pickett's Charge*, p. 163; Haskell, *The Battle of Gettysburg*, p. 96; Katcher, *The Army of Robert E. Lee*, p. 122.

178. Haskell, *The Battle of Gettysburg*, p. 97.

179. Crewdson, *Love and War*, pp. 13, 21.

180. Reardon, *Pickett's Charge*, p. 19.

181. Haskell, *The Battle of Gettysburg*, p. 97; *Annals of War*, p. 191.

182. Hess, *Pickett's Charge*, pp. 15–19, 30–33; Harrison and Busey, *Nothing but Glory*, pp. 32–34; Rollins, ed., *Pickett's Charge*, pp. 45–46, 109–110; Stewart, *Pickett's Charge*, pp. 54–55; Uffindell, *Napoleon's Immortals*, pp. 53–56; Hess, *Pickett's Charge*, pp. 22–23; Longacre, *Pickett*, p. 122; Lachouque, *The Anatomy of Glory*, pp. 160–164.

183. Rollins, ed., *Pickett's Charge*, p. 110.

184. Coco, *On the Bloodstained Field*, pp. 65–66; Harrison and Busey, *Nothing but Glory*, pp. 33–34; Stewart, *Pickett's Charge*, pp. 143; Coddington, *The Gettysburg Campaign*, p. 499.

185. Bradley M. Gottfried, "To Fail Twice,: Brockenbrough's Brigade at Gettysburg, " *Gettysburg Magazine*, no. 23, pp. 66–72; Hess, *Pickett's Charge*, p. 187; Gragg, *Covered with Glory*, pp. 182–185.

186. Gragg, *Covered with Glory*, p. 185; CNCSR, NA.

187. Coddington, *The Gettysburg Campaign*, p. 506; Gottfried, "To Fail Twice, " *GM*, p. 72; Stewart, *Pickett's Charge*, p. 148; Hess, *Pickett's Charge*, pp. 141–143, 161, 163.

188. Gottfried, "To Fail Twice, " *GM*, p. 72.

189. Coddington, *The Gettysburg Campaign*, pp. 502, 594; Hess, *Pickett's Charge*, pp. 15, 32–33, 62–63; Longacre, *Pickett*, p. 122; Cockrell, ed., *Gunner with Stonewall*, pp. xiv–xv, 73–74; CVSR, NA.

190. Cockrell, ed., *Gunner with Stonewall*, p. 74.

191. Ibid.; Hess, *Pickett's Charge,* p. 15.

192. Longacre, *Pickett,* p. 122.

193. Hess, *Pickett's Charge,* pp. 160–162.

194. Stewart, *Pickett's Charge,* pp. 135–136; Tucker, *Lee and Longstreet at Gettysburg,* p. 95; Robertson, *General A. P. Hill,* pp. 217–223; John D. McKenzie, *Uncertain Glory, Lee's Generalship Re-Examined* (New York: Hippocrene Books, 1996), pp. 147–149, 160; Piston, *Lee's Tarnished Lieutenant,* pp. 36, 58–60; *Annals of the War,* p. 313; Rollins, ed., *Pickett's Charge,* p. 10; Hess, *Pickett's Charge,* pp. 15, 17–19, 32–33, 160–163; Coddington, *The Gettysburg Campaign,* pp. 489, 502; Carl Coppolino, "Lee's Illness Lost Gettysburg, " *The Gettysburg Magazine,* vol. 46 (January 2012), pp. 93–101; Cowell, *Tactics at Gettysburg,* pp. 78–79.

195. Robertson, *General A. P. Hill,* pp. 216–222; Coppolino, "Lee's Illness Lost Gettysburg, " *GM,* pp. 95–101; Wert, *A Glorious Army,* p. 275; McKenzie, *Uncertain Glory,* p. 148.

196. *Annals of the War,* p. 313.

197. Durkin, ed., *John Dooley, Confederate Soldier,* pp. 102–103; Waters and Edmonds, *A Small but Spartan Band,* p. 74.

198. Robertson, *General A. P. Hill,* p. 223.

199. Oeffinger, *A Soldier's General,* pp. 196–197; Coddington, *The Gettysburg Campaign,* pp. 443–444; Hess, *Pickett's Charge,* p. 15.

200. Oeffinger, *A Soldier's General,* pp. 196–197; Cowell, *Tactics at Gettysburg,* pp. 68–79; Thomas, *Robert E. Lee,* pp. 290, 301–302; Hess, *Pickett's Charge,* pp. 15, 22–23; Wright, *A Glorious Army,* pp 269, 274–275; Foote, *The Civil War,* vol. 2, pp. 521–522, 528–529; Robertson, *General A. P. Hill,* pp. 216–223; Coddington, *The Gettysburg Campaign,* pp. 443–444, 462; Rollins, ed., *Pickett's Charge,* p. 10.

201. Rollins, ed., *Pickett's Charge,* p. 10; McKenzie, *Uncertain Glory,* p. 147; *Annals of the War,* p. 313; Hess, *Pickett's Charge,* pp. 15–19; Tucker, *Lee and Longstreet at Gettysburg,* p. 95.

202. Tower, ed., *Lee's Adjutant,* p. 53; Hess, *Pickett's Charge,* pp. 19–20; Robertson, *General A. P. Hill,* pp. 206, 218, 222; McKenzie, *Uncertain Glory,* pp. 146–149.

203. Hess, *Pickett's Charge,* pp. 19–20; Piston, *Lee's Tarnished Lieutenant,* pp. 2–3, 40; Thomas, *Robert E. Lee,* p. 290.

204. Thomas, *Robert E. Lee,* p. 290; Hess, *Pickett's Charge,* pp. 18–20; Conrad, *The Young Lions,* pp. 13, 17, 170, note 24.

205. McKenzie, *Uncertain Glory,* p. 160; Cockrell, ed., *Gunner with Stonewall,* p. 74; Tucker, *Lee and Longstreet at Gettysburg,* p. 95; *Annals of the War,* p. 313; Hess, *Pickett's Charge,* pp. 15, 22–23; McWhiney and Jamieson, *Attack and Die,* p. 120–121.

206. Joseph Graham to Graham, July 30, 1863, SHC.

207. Haskell, *The Battle of Gettysburg,* p. 95.

208. McWhiney and Jamieson, *Attack and Die,* p. 120.

209. Lewis, Recollections from *1861 to 1865,* p. 82; Halleran, "The Widow's Son" Lewis Armistead at Gettysburg, " *GM,* p. 95; Motts, *"Trust in God and Fear Nothing, "* pp. 8, 21–28; Hess, *Pickett's Charge,* pp. 15–23; Cowell, *Tactics at Gettysburg,* pp. 78–79; Cockrell, ed., *Gunner with Stonewall,* p. 74; *Annals of the War,* p. 313; Robertson, *General A. P. Hill,* p. 223.

210. Lewis, Recollections from *1861 to 1865,* p. 82; CVSR, NA.

211. CVSR, NA; Gregory, *53rd Virginia Infantry and 5th Battalion Virginia Infantry,* p. 54; PHS, *Pickett's Charge at Gettysburg,* p. 10; Motts, *"Trust in God and Fear Nothing,"* p. 48; Rollins, ed., *Pickett's Charge,* pp. 86, 108; Milton Harding, "Where General Armistead Fell," *Confederate Veteran,* vol. 19, no. 8 (August 1911), p. 371.

212. Anderson and Anderson, *The Generals,* p. 421.

213. Joseph Graham to Graham, July 30, 1863, SHC; Cockrell, ed., *Gunner with Stonewall,* p. 68.

214. Rollins, ed., *Pickett's Charge,* pp. 126–128, 373–374; Carhart, *Lost Triumph,* pp. xi–260; Cowell, *Tactics at Gettysburg,* pp. 77–81.

215. Reardon, *Pickett's Charge,* p. 13; Carhart, *Lost Triumph,* pp. xi–260.

216. Joseph Graham to Graham, July 30, 1863, SHC; McWhiney and Jamieson, *Attack and Die,* pp. 3–13.

217. Joseph Graham to Graham, July 30, 1863, SHC; McWhiney and Jamieson, *Attack and Die,* pp. 3–4; Reardon, *Pickett's Charge,* p. 13; Hess, *Pickett's Charge,* p. 11.

218. Joseph Graham to Graham, July 30, 1863, SHC.

219. CVSR, NA; Hess, *Pickett's Charge,* p. 15.

220. Robertson, *General A. P. Hill,* p. 203; Davis, *Boy Colonel of the Confederacy,* pp. 321–322; Tucker, *Lee and Longstreet at Gettysburg,* pp. 120–121.

221. Harrison, *Pickett's Men,* pp. 88–89, 99–100; Smith, *The Twenty-fourth Michigan,* pp. 127–128; Rollins, ed., *Pickett's Charge,* p. 87.

222. Smith, *The Twenty-fourth Michigan,* pp. 127–128; Wert, *A Glorious Army,* pp. 169, 274–275; Cowell, *Tactics at Gettysburg,* pp. 77–79.

223. *Annals of the War,* p. 200; Gottfried, "To Fail Twice," *GM,* pp. 66–72.

224. Clint Johnson, *Civil War Blunders* (Winston-Salem, N.C.: John F. Blair Publishers, 1997), pp. 154–155; Gragg, *Covered with Glory,* p. 182; Foote, *The Civil War,* vol. 2, p. 552; Katcher, *The Army of Robert E. Lee,* p. 236; Woodward, ed., *Mary Chesnut's Civil War,* p. 357; Gragg, *Covered with Glory,* p. 217.

225. Jim W. Dean, "Gettysburg, Vicksburg and the 4th of July," *Veterans Today,* July 4, 2013, Internet; CNCSR, NA; Smith, *The Twenty-fourth Michigan,* p. 41.

226. Wert, *A Glorious Army,* p. 269; Chandler, *The Campaigns of Napoleon,* pp. 133–191.

227. McWhiney and Jamieson, *Attack and Die,* pp. 3–4; Gregory, *53rd Virginia Infantry and 5th Battalion Virginia Infantry,* p. 27; Benjamin H. Trask, *9th Virginia Infantry,* (Lynchburg: H. E. Howard Publisher, 1984), p. 15; Motts, *"Trust in God and Fear Nothing,"* pp. 14–41, 48.

228. Trask, *9th Virginia Infantry,* p. 15; Halleran, "The Widow's Son Lewis Armistead at Gettysburg," *GM,* p. 95.

229. CVSR, NA; Trask, *9th Virginia Infantry,* p. 24.

230. CNCSR, NA; Longacre, *Pickett,* pp. 119–120; Hess, *Pickett's Charge,* p. 51; Stewart, *Pickett's Charge,* p. 136; *Times-Dispatch,* February 7, 1904.

231. CVSR, NA; *Times-Dispatch,* February 7, 1904; O'Grady, *Clear the Confederate Way!,* pp. 47–202; Lonn, *Foreigners in the Confederacy,* p. 96.

232. *Times-Dispatch,* February 7, 1909; Harrison and Busey, *Nothing but Glory,* p. 2; Longacre, *Pickett,* pp. x, 122; Harrison, *Pickett's Charge,* p. 102; Hess, *Pickett's Charge,* p. 166; Burke Davis, *Gray Fox, Robert E. Lee and the Civil War* (New York: The Fairfax Press, 1981), p. 241; Gordon, *General George E. Pickett in Life and Legend,* pp. 114–116; Priest, *Into the Fight,* p. 102.

233. Harrison, *Pickett's Charge,* p. 102; Gordon, *General George E. Pickett in Life and Legend,* pp. 114–116.

234. Hess, *Pickett's Charge,* p. 41; Harrison, *Pickett's Men,* pp. 18–19; CVSR, NA; Berkeley, "Rode with Pickett, " *CV,* p. 175.

235. Harrison, *Pickett's Men,* p. 20.

236. Ibid.

237. Ibid., p. 20.

238. Ibid., p. 21.

239. Motts, *"Trust in God and Fear Nothing, "* pp. 48–49; CVSR, NA.

240. *Richmond Daily Dispatch,* May 13, 1863; Henry Kyd Douglas, *I Rode with Stonewall* (Greenwich, Conn.: Fawcett Publications, Inc., 1961), pp. 47, 222; Woodward, ed., *Mary Chesnut's Civil War,* p. 503.

241. Woodward, ed., *Mary Chesnut's Civil War,* p. 791.

242. CVSR, NA; Cockrell, ed., *Gunner with Stonewall,* p. 74.

243. CVSR, NA; Young and Young, *History of the 56th Virginia Infantry Regiment,* pp. 8–10, 115, 307–308; David Mould and Missy Loewe, *Remembering Georgetown, A History of the Lost Port City* (Charleston, S.C.: The History Press, 2009), pp. 18–31, 54; Motts, *"Trust in God and Fear Nothing, "* p. 8; Cockrell, ed., *Gunner with Stonewall,* p. 74.

244. CVSR, NA; Young and Young, *History of the 56th Virginia Infantry Regiment,* pp. 7–12, 83, 297, 307–308; "Mechlenburg County, Virginia, " Wikipedia; "Brunswick Stew, " Wikipedia.

245. Woodward, ed., *Mary Chesnut's Civil War,* p. 331.

246. CVSR, NA.

247. Ibid.; Hess, *Pickett's Charge,* pp. 45–46; Young and Young, *History of the 56th Virginia Infantry Regiment,* pp. 11, 203.

248. Young and Young, *History of the 56th Virginia Infantry Regiment,* pp. 12, 207; CVSR, NA.

249. CVSR, NA; Young and Young, *History of the 56th Virginia Infantry Regiment,* pp. 12, 247, 333; Alan Pell Crawford, *Twilight at Monticello, The Final Years of Thomas Jefferson* (New York: Random House, 2008), pp. xv–189; Thomas P. Lowry, *The Story the Soldiers Wouldn't Tell* (Mechanicsburg, Pa.: Stackpole Books, 1994), p. 71.

250. CVSR, NA; Woodward, ed., *Mary Chesnut's Civil War,* p. 346.

251. CVSR, NA; Young and Young, *History of the 56th Virginia Infantry Regiment,* pp. 260–261.

252. Young and Young, *History of the 56th Virginia Infantry Regiment,* p. 323; CVSR, NA; Cockrell, ed., *Gunner with Stonewall,* p. 74.

253. Haskell, *The Battle of Gettysburg,* pp. 97–98, note 27, 100; Reardon, *Pickett's Charge,* p. 19.

254. Hirst letter to Sarah, n.d., ASC.

255. Ibid.; *Western Sentinel,* Winston, North Carolina, July 30, 1863; Hess, *Pickett's Charge,* p. 133.

256. Lewis, Recollections from *1861 to 1865,* pp. 82–83; Motts, *"Trust in God and Fear Nothing, "* pp. 40, 49; Longacre, *Pickett,* pp. x, 122–123; Bowden and Ward, *Last Chance for Victory,* pp. 463–464; Gragg, *Covered with Glory,* p. 195.

257. Motts, *"Trust in God and Fear Nothing, "* pp. 4–33; Anderson and Anderson, *The Generals,* p. 395.

258. CVSR, NA; *Richmond Daily Dispatch,* July 13, 1863; Creighton, *The Colors of Courage,* pp. 13, 35; Harrison and Busey, *Nothing but Glory,* p. 44; *Carolina Watchman,* August 5, 1863.

259. CVSR, NA.

260. CVSR, NA; Trask, *9th Virginia Infantry,* pp. 3, 7, 11, 13, 15, 26.

261. CVSR, NA; Trask, *9th Virginia Infantry,* pp. 11, 70.

262. Haskell, *The Battle of Gettysburg,* p. 100; Barra, "One Mile of Open Ground, " *CWT,* pp. 34–35; Trudeau, *Gettysburg,* p. 499; Rollins, ed., *Pickett's Charge,* p. 62.

263. Boritt, ed., *The Gettysburg Nobody Knows,* pp. 125–126; Johnson, *Napoleon,* pp. 55–56; Chandler, *The Campaigns of Napoleon,* p. 179; Stewart, *Pickett's Charge,* pp. 153; Coddington, *The Gettysburg Campaign,* p. 508; Rogers, *Napoleon's Army,* pp. 74–75.

264. Gragg, *Covered with Glory,* p. 185.

265. Reardon, *Pickett's Charge,* p. 19.

266. CVSR, NA.

267. Rollins, ed., *Pickett's Charge,* p. 303.

268. CVSR, NA.

269. Hess, *Pickett's Charge,* pp. 15–19, 32–33; Harrison and Busey, *Nothing but Glory,* p. 37; Wert, *A Glorious Army,* pp. 269, 274–275; Cowell, *Tactics at Gettysburg,* pp. 78–79.

270. CVSR, NA; Joseph T. Durkin, S.J., ed., *Confederate Chaplain, A War Journal,* (Milwaukee, Wis.: The Bruce Publishing Company, 1960), pp. 5, 54, 58; John C. Granberry to John W. Daniel, March 25, LV; Hess, *Pickett's Charge,* pp. 15–19, 32–33; Wert, *A Glorious Army,* pp. 269, 275.

271. John W. Finley, "Bloody Angle, " *Buffalo Evening News,* May 28, 1894.

272. Crewdson, *Love and War,* p. 88.

Chapter V

1. Hess, *Pickett's Charge,* pp. 117, 113.

2. Harrison and Busey, *Nothing but Glory,* p. 80; Persico, *My Enemy, My Brother,* p. 238; Stewart, *Pickett's Charge,* p. 265.

3. Shultz, *"Double Canister at Ten Yards, "* pp. 1–25; Rollins, ed., *Pickett's Charge,* pp. 257, 320–322; Hess, *Pickett's Charge,* pp. 113–114; Stewart, *Pickett's Charge,* pp. 125, 130, 142; Rod Gragg, *The Illustrated Gettysburg Reader, An Eyewitness History of the Civil War's Greatest Battle* (Washington, DC, Regnery, 2013), pp. 312–313; Hess, *Pickett's Charge,* pp. 113–117, 141.

4. Cowell, *Tactics at Gettysburg*, pp. 75–79; Shultz, *"Double Canister at Ten Yards,"* pp. 29–30.

5. Shultz, *"Double Canister at Ten Yards,"* p. 37.

6. Norborne Berkeley to family, no date, Gettysburg National Military Battlefield Park Gettysburg, Pennsylvania; Hess, *Pickett's Charge*, p. 79.

7. Lewis, *Recollections from 1860 to 1865*, p. 84; Durkin, ed., *John Dooley, Confederate Soldier*, p. 97; Rollins, ed., *Pickett's Charge*, pp. 179, 199; Harrison and Busey, *Nothing but Glory*, p. 20.

8. CVSR, NA; Harrison and Busey, *Nothing but Glory*, p. 79.

9. *Baltimore-Sun*, Baltimore, Maryland, December 4, 1905; CVSR, NA; Harrison and Busey, *Nothing but Glory*, p. 43; Hess, *Pickett's Charge*, p. 172.

10. Rollins, ed., *Pickett's Charge*, p. 200.

11. Boritt, ed., *The Gettysburg Nobody Knows*, p. 129; Rollins, ed., *Pickett's Charge*, p. 306; Harrison and Busey, *Nothing but Glory*, pp. 43, 50.

12. *Richmond Daily Dispatch*, Richmond, Virginia, July 13, 1863; CVSR, NA; Harrison and Busey, *Nothing but Glory*, p. 44.

13. CVSR, NA; Harrison and Busey, *Nothing but Glory*, p. 44.

14. CVSR, NA; Priest, *Into the Fight*, p. 101; Ralph Berrier, Jr., "Craig County Gave its All at the Battle of Gettysburg," July 3, 2013, *The Roanoke Times*, Roanoke, Virginia; Rollins, ed., *Pickett's Charge*, pp. 179, 181; Hess, *Pickett's Charge*, p. 47; Harrison and Busey, *Nothing but Glory*, pp. 50–51.

15. Berrier, Jr., "Craig County Gave its All at the Battle of Gettysburg," July 3, 2013, *The Roanoke Times*; CVSR, NA; Bradley M. Gottfried, *Stopping Pickett, The History of the Philadelphia Brigade* (Shippensburg, Pa.: White Mane Books, 1999), p. 170.

16. Rollins, ed., *Pickett's Charge*, p. 184; CVSR, NA; Harrison and Busey, *Nothing but Glory*, p. 50–51.

17. Boritt, ed., *The Gettysburg Nobody Knows*, p. 129; Harrison and Busey, *Nothing but Glory*, p. 51.

18. CVSR, NA; Trask, *9th Virginia Infantry*, p. 25.

19. CVSR, NA.

20. Rollins, ed., *Pickett's Charge*, p. 11; Bishop, *The Tennessee Brigade*, p. 207; Hess, *Pickett's Charge*, pp. 173–174, 220; Cowell, *Tactics at Gettysburg*, p. 76; Gragg, *Covered with Glory*, p. 186; Reardon, *Pickett's Charge*, pp. 20–21; Coddington, *The Gettysburg Campaign*, pp. 489, 503.

21. R. L. Murray, "Brig. Gen. Alexander Hays' Division at Gettysburg," *Gettysburg Magazine*, no. 42 (January 2010), p. 89.

22. Hess, *Pickett's Charge*, pp. 182–187.

23. Rollins, ed., *Pickett's Charge*, pp. 234, 321.

24. Coddington, *The Gettysburg Campaign*, pp. 482–483.

25. Stewart, *Pickett's Charge*, p. 171.

26. CVSR, NA; Hess, *Pickett's Charge*, pp. 172, 219–220.

27. McWhiney and Jamieson, *Attack and Die*, pp. 115, 121; Haskell, *The Battle of Gettysburg*, pp. 95–96, note 25; Rollins, ed., *Pickett's Charge*, p. 321; Schulz, *"Double Canister at Ten*

Yards, "p. 37; Stewart, *Pickett's Charge,* pp. 125–126, 130; Gragg, *Covered with Glory,* pp. 186–187; Coddington, *The Gettysburg Campaign,* pp. 482–483, 485; Reardon, *Pickett's Charge,* pp. 20–21.

28. Rollins, ed., *Pickett's Charge,* p. 180.

29. Hess, *Pickett's Charge,* p. 181.

30. John W. Finley, "Bloody Angle," *Buffalo Evening News,* May 28, 1894.

31. Ibid.; CVSR, NA.

32. CVSR, NA; Hess, *Pickett's Charge,* p. 172; John A. Herndon to brother, July 11, 1863, CS.

33. Murray, "Brig. Gen. Alexander Hays' Division at Gettysburg," *GM,* p. 89.

34. Rollins, ed., *Pickett's Charge,* p. 200; CVSR, NA.

35. CVSR, NA.

36. Ibid.; Harrison and Busey, *Nothing but Glory,* p. 51.

37. John W. Finley, "Bloody Angle," *Buffalo Evening News,* May 28, 1894.

38. CVSR, NA; Harrison and Busey, *Nothing but Glory,* p. 90.

39. Lewis, *Recollections from 1860 to 1865,* p. 84; PHS, *Pickett's Charge at Gettysburg,* p. 11; Rollins, ed., *Pickett's Charge,* p. 321.

40. John W. Finley, "Bloody Angle," *Buffalo Evening News,* May 28, 1894; CVSR, NA.

41. Wert, *A Glorious Army,* p. 273.

42. Crewdson, *Love and War,* p. 20; CVSR, NA.

43. Stewart, *Pickett's Charge,* p. 167.

44. Crewdson, *Love and War,* pp. 67–68.

45. Ibid., pp. 78, 87.

46. Ibid., pp. 95–97.

47. Murray, "Brig. Gen. Alexander Hays' Division at Gettysburg," *GM,* p. 89.

48. Katcher, *American Civil War Armies* (1), p. 46; Young and Young, *History of the 56th Virginia Infantry Regiment,* p. 340; CVSR, NA; Rollins, ed., *Pickett's Charge,* pp. 127–128, 321; Gragg, *Covered with Glory,* pp. 186–187; Shultz, *"Double Canister at Ten Yards,"* pp. 29–31, 37.

49. Hess, *Pickett's Charge,* p. 172.

50. CVSR, NA; Gottfried, *The Artillery of Gettysburg,* p. 97; Rollins, ed., *Pickett's Charge,* p. 234; Stewart, *Pickett's Charge,* pp. 170, 268; Shultz, *"Double Canister at Ten Yards,"* p. 28.

51. Coddington, *The Gettysburg Campaign,* p. 508.

52. Durkin, ed., *John Dooley, Confederate Soldier,* p. 105–106.

53. John W. Finley, "Bloody Angle," *Buffalo Evening News,* May 28, 1894; Stewart, *Pickett's Charge,* p. 170.

54. The Weider History Group, Gettysburg, p. 72; CVSR, NA.

55. Rollins, ed., *Pickett's Charge,* p. 244; Coddington, *The Gettysburg Campaign,* p. 756, note 41; *The Salem Gazette,* Salem, Massachusetts, April 4, 1876.

56. CVSR, NA; Harrison and Busey, *Nothing but Glory,* p. 49; Stewart, *Pickett's Charge,* p. 170.

57. Coddington, *The Gettysburg Campaign,* p. 513.

58. PHS, *Pickett's Charge at Gettysburg,* p. 11.

59. Durkin, ed., *John Dooley, Confederate Soldier,* p. 105; Rollins, ed., *Pickett's Charge,* p. 234; Coddington, *The Gettysburg Campaign,* p. 482.

60. CVSR, NA; William B. Robertson to Mattie, July 28, 1863, John W. Daniel Papers, 1874–1914, Library of Virginia, Richmond, Virginia.

61. Schultz, *"Double Canister at Ten Yards, "*pp. 31, 40; Gragg, *Covered with Glory,* p. 187.

62. *National Tribune,* Washington, DC, August 5, 1882.

63. Schultz, *"Double Canister at Ten Yards, "*p. 40.

64. Gottfried, *"To Fail Twice, " GM,* pp. 72, 74–75; Coddington, *The Gettysburg Campaign,* pp. 506–508; Stewart, *Pickett's Charge,* pp. 125–126; Hess, *Pickett's Charge,* pp. 190–191; Schultz, *"Double Canister at Close Range, "* p. 40; Murray, "Brig. Gen. Alexander Hays' Division at Gettysburg, " *GM,* p. 90; "Gen. Franklin Sawyer (1825–1892)" Find a Grave, Internet.

65. Gragg, *Covered with Glory,* p. 187; Stewart, *Pickett's Charge,* pp. 170, 172.

66. *The News and Observer,* March 24, 1887.

67. Coddington, *The Gettysburg Campaign,* pp. 506–507.

68. Joseph Graham to Graham, July 30, 1863, SHC; Rollins, ed., *Pickett's Charge,* pp. 109–110; Coddington, *The Gettysburg Campaign,* pp. 500–502; Hess, *Pickett's Charge,* pp. 15, 22–23.

69. Haskell, *The Battle of Gettysburg,* p. 94.

70. Joseph Graham to Graham, July 30, 1863, SHC.

71. Priest, *Into the Fight,* pp. 97–98, 100; CVSR, NA; Reardon, *Pickett's Charge,* p. 19; "James Keith Marshall (1839–1863), " Find a Grave, Internet; Murray, "Brig. Gen. Alexander Hays' Division at Gettysburg, " *GM,* p. 94.

72. Rollins, ed., *Pickett's Charge,* p. 299; "Major Frederick M. Edgell (1829–1877), " Find a Grave, Internet.

73. CVSR, NA; Priest, *Into the Fight,* pp. 97–98; Rollins, ed., *Pickett's Charge,* p. 299; Murray, "Brig. General Alexander Hays' Division at Gettysburg, " *GM,* p. 94.

74. Thomas J. Cureton to Colonel J. R. Lane, June 22, 1890, John R. Lane Papers, Southern Historical Collection, University of North Carolina, Chapel Hill, North Carolina.

75. Priest, *Into the Fight,* p. 98.

76. CVSR, NA; Rollins, ed., *Pickett's Charge,* p. 234; Hess, *Pickett's Charge,* p. 53; Harrison and Busey, *Nothing but Glory,* pp. 43–44; Priest, *Into the Fight,* pp. 98–99.

77. Hess, *Pickett's Charge,* pp. 191–192; Terry Cooks, "Rochester's Forgotten Regiment: The 108th New York at Gettysburg, " *Gettysburg Magazine,* No. 42 (January 2010), p. 106.

78. Gregory, *53rd Virginia Infantry and 5th Battalion Virginia Infantry,* p. 49.

79. Durkin, ed., *John Dooley, Confederate Soldier,* pp. 105–106.

80. CVSR, NA; Coco, *On the Bloodstained Field, I and II, 262 Human Interest Stories of the Campaign and the Battle of Gettysburg,* p. 68.

81. CVSR, NA.

82. Conrad, *The Young Lions,* p. 152; Davis, *The Battle of New Market,* p. 46; Mann, *They Were Heard From, VMI Alumni,* pp. 26–27.

83. *Times-Dispatch,* February 7, 1904; Coco, *Wasted Valor,* p. 127; CVSR, NA; Tucker, *Lee and Longstreet at Gettysburg,* pp. 197, 132.

84. CVSR, NA; Freeman Cleaves, *Meade of Gettysburg* (Norman: University of Oklahoma Press, 1960), pp. 353–354; Bradley M. Gottfried, *Stopping Pickett, The History of the Philadelphia Brigade* (Shippensburg, Pa.: White Mane Publishing Company, 1999), pp. 13–16.

85. Reardon, *Pickett's Charge,* p. 155; Stewart, *Pickett's Charge,* p. 255.

86. Durkin, ed., *John Dooley, Confederate Soldier,* pp. 105–106; Coddington, *The Gettysburg Campaign,* pp. 503–504; Stewart, *Pickett's Charge,* pp. 160, 177–178; Gregory, *53rd Virginia Infantry and 5th Battalion Virginia Infantry,* p. 54.

87. Murray, "Brig. Gen. Alexander Hays' Division at Gettysburg, " *GM,* p. 89.

88. Coddington, *The Gettysburg Campaign,* p. 504; Stewart, *Pickett's Charge,* pp. 177–178.

89. Stewart, *Pickett's Charge,* p. 154.

90. Harrison and Busey, *Nothing but Glory,* p. 29; Phillip Thomas Tucker, *Storming Little Round Top, The 15th Alabama and Their Fight for the High Ground, July 2, 1863* (New York: Da Capo Press, 2002), pp. 197–312; Glenn W. LaFantasie, *Twilight at Little Round Top, July 2, 1863–The Tide Turns at Gettysburg* (New York: Vintage Books, 2005), pp. 30–32; Stewart, *Pickett's Charge,* pp. 167, 170.

91. Thomas J. Cureton letter to Colonel J. R. Lane, June 22, 1890, John Lane Papers, Southern Historical Collection, Chapel Hill, North Carolina; CNCSR, NA.

92. Cureton to Lane, June 22, 1890, SHC.

93. Philip Katcher, *The Army of Robert E. Lee,* p. 122; Stewart, *Pickett's Charge,* p. 163.

94. CVSR, NA; Rollins, ed., *Pickett's Charge,* p. 211.

95. CVSR, NA; Harrison and Busey, *Nothing but Glory,* p. 44.

96. Faust, *This Republic of Suffering,* p. 6; Stewart, *Pickett's Charge,* p. 156.

97. William J. Burns Diary, Save the Flags Collection, United States Army Military History Institute, Carlisle Barracks, Pennsylvania.

98. Murray, "Brig. General Alexander Hays' Division at Gettysburg, " *GM,* p. 89.

99. Gregory, *53rd Virginia Infantry and 5th Battalion Virginia Infantry,* p. 55; Lewis, *Recollections from 1860 to 1865,* p. 84.

100. John E. Dooley, SJ, Papers, GU; Durkin, ed., *John Dooley, Confederate Soldier,* p. 106.

101. CVSR, NA.

102. *Times-Dispatch,* February 7, 1904; Harrison and Busey, *Nothing but Glory,* p. 21; Katcher, *The Army of Robert E. Lee,* p. 263; CVSR, NA; Tucker, *Lee and Longstreet at Gettysburg,* p. 122.

103. Durkin, ed., *John Dooley, Confederate Soldier,* p. 177.

104. CVSR, NA.

105. Boritt, ed., *The Gettysburg Nobody Knows,* p. 131; Murray, "Brig. Gen. Alexander Hays' Division at Gettysburg, " *GM,* p. 89.

106. CVSR, NA; Rollins, ed., *Pickett's Charge,* p. 171.

107. Stewart, *Pickett's Charge,* p. 178.

108. CVSR, NA; Harrison and Busey, *Nothing but Glory,* pp. 74–75.

109. Shultz, "*Double Canister at Ten Yards,* " pp. 24, 29–31, 33; Stewart, *Pickett's Charge,* pp. 170–171; CVSR, NA.

110. Gragg, *Covered with Glory,* pp. 188–189.

111. Lewis, *Recollections from 1860 to 1865*, p. 84; CVSR, NA.

112. Durkin, ed., *John Dooley, Confederate Soldier*, p. 106; John E. Dooley, SJ, Papers, Special Collections, Georgetown University, Georgetown, Virginia.

113. Murray, "Brig. Gen. Alexander Hays' Division at Gettysburg, " *GM*, p. 89.

114. Harrison and Busy, *Nothing but Glory*, p. 83.

115. CVSR, NA; Berkeley, "Rode with Pickett, " *CV*, p. 175; Evergreen Country Club Archives, Haymarket, Virginia.

116. Boritt, ed., *The Gettysburg Nobody Knows*, p. 129; Murray, "Brig. Gen. Alexander Hays' Division at Gettysburg, " *GM*, p. 90; Gragg, *Covered with Glory*, p. 189.

117. Gragg, *Covered with Glory*, p. 191; Christopher Mead to wife, July 6, 1863, Box 7, Robert L. Brake Collection, United States Army Military History Institute, Carlisle Barracks, Pennsylvania; Stewart, *Pickett's Charge*, pp. 172–176.

118. Hess, *Pickett's Charge*, p. 83.

119. Lewis, *Recollections from 1860 to 1865*, p. 55; McWhiney and Jamieson, *Attack and Die*, p. 49; Francis Lord, *Civil War Collector's Encyclopedia* (New York: Castle Books, 1965), pp. 243–245; Harrison and Busey, *Nothing but Glory*, p. 44; Murray, "Brig. Gen. Alexander Hays' Division at Gettysburg, " *GM*, p. 91; Hess, *Pickett's Charge*, p. 189; Gragg, *Covered with Glory*, p. 181.

120. Durkin, ed., *John Dooley, Confederate Soldier*, p. 106.

121. Berkeley, "Rode with Pickett, " *CV*, p. 175; Tucker, *Lee and Longstreet at Gettysburg*, pp. 126, 132.

122. CVSR, NA.

123. *Times-Dispatch*, February 7, 1904; Coco, *Wasted Valor*, pp. 127–128; Berkeley, "Rode with Pickett, " *CV*, p. 175; CVSR, NA; Hess, *Pickett's Charge*, p. 189; Harrison and Busey, *Nothing but Glory*, pp. 26, 44, 47; Tucker, *Lee and Longstreet at Gettysburg*, p. 132.

124. Durkin, ed., *John Dooley, Confederate Soldier*, pp. 108–109; Hess, *Pickett's Charge*, p. 173.

125. CVSR, NA.

126. *Times-Dispatch*, February 7, 1904.

127. CVSR, NA; Harrison and Busey, *Nothing but Glory*, p. 46.

128. Gregory, *53rd Virginia Infantry and 5th Battalion Virginia Infantry*, p. 55.

129. Murray, "Brig. Gen. Alexander Hays' Division at Gettysburg, " *GM*, pp. 87–91.

130. Ibid., p. 85.

131. Hess, *Pickett's Charge*, p. 210; Murray, "Gen. Brig. Alexander Hays' Division at Gettysburg, " *GM*, pp. 83–84; Persico, *My Enemy, My Brother*, p. 208.

132. *Charlotte Observer*, August 16, 1894; CNCSR, NA.

133. Hatch, *Glorious War*, pp. 146–147; Cowell, *Tactics at Gettysburg*, p. 81.

134. Stewart, *Pickett's Charge*, p. 267.

135. Hess, *Pickett's Charge*, pp. 143–144; Harrison and Busey, *Nothing but Glory*, pp. 102, 116; Stewart, *Pickett's Charge*, p. 179; Murray, "Brig. Gen. Alexander Hays' Division at Gettysburg, " *GM*, p. 90.

136. Rollins, ed., *Pickett's Charge*, p. 328; Hess, *Pickett's Charge*, pp. 114–115, 141, 143; Gragg, *Covered with Glory*, pp. 189–191; Murray, "Brig. Gen. Alexander Hays' Division at Gettysburg, " *GM*, pp. 89–90.

137. CVSR, NA; Hess, *Pickett's Charge*, pp. 144; Stewart, *Pickett's Charge*, p. 179.

138. John W. Finley, "Bloody Angle, " *Buffalo Evening News,* May 28, 1894; Stewart, *Pickett's Charge,* p. 179.

139. Stewart, *Pickett's Charge,* p. 179; CVSR, NA.

140. *Annals of the War,* p. 315; Hess, *Pickett's Charge,* pp. 15, 189; Stewart, *Pickett's Charge,* p. 180; Longacre, *Pickett,* pp. x, 122–125.

141. Longacre, *Pickett,* pp. x, 27.

142. Haskell, *The Battle of Gettysburg,* pp. 71–72; Longacre, *Pickett,* p. 122–123.

143. Reardon, *Pickett's Charge,* p. 13; Hess, *Pickett's Charge,* p. 105.

144. CVSR, NA.

145. Bishop, *The Tennessee Brigade,* p. 210; Stewart, *Pickett's Charge,* p. 180.

146. Anthony McDermott to John Bachelder, n.d., NHHS; Gottfried, *Stopping Pickett,* pp. 1–39, 124, 167–170, 178, 229; Hess, *Pickett's Charge,* pp. 141–142; Katharine Gilbert, "Col. O'Kane and His Men—Irish Heroes at Gettysburg, " *Irish Edition,* July 5, 2013, Internet; CVSR, NA; Rollins, ed., *Pickett's Charge,* pp. 323–324; Stewart, *Pickett's Charge,* pp. 145–146, 167; Harrison and Busey, *Nothing but Glory,* p. 116; McMurray, "Brig. Gen. Alexander Hays' Division at Gettysburg, " *GM,* p. 89; "The Dennis O'Kane Project, The 69th Pennsylvania Irish Volunteers, " Internet, Fleming, *Liberty!,* p. 140.

147. The Weider History Group, Gettysburg, p. 76.

148. Ibid., p. 326; Hess, *Pickett's Charge,* p. 86; Rollins, ed., *Pickett's Charge,* p. 325.

149. Hess, *Pickett's Charge,* pp. 85–86.

150. CVSR, NA; Stewart, *Pickett's Charge,* pp. 148–149, 170, 181; Harrison and Busey, *Nothing but Glory,* pp. 56, 58.

151. Harrison and Busey, *Nothing but Glory,* p. 65; Stewart, *Pickett's Charge,* pp. 177–178.

152. Murray, "Brig. Gen. Alexander Hays' Division at Gettysburg, " *GM,* p. 89; Hess, *Pickett's Charge,* p. 189; Stewart, *Pickett's Charge,* pp. 179–180; Harrison and Busey, *Nothing but Glory,* p. 83.

153. *Gettysburg Compiler,* Gettysburg, Pennsylvania, July 19, 1858; *Gettysburg Times,* July 11, 1878; Hess, *Pickett's Charge,* p. 189; Stewart, *Pickett's Charge,* p. 265; "Cordi Family Home Page, " Nicholas J. Cordi, Internet.

154. The Weider History Group, Gettysburg, p. 72.

155. John A. Herndon to brother, July 11, 1863, CS.

156. CVSR, NA; Persico, *My Enemy, My Brother,* p. 239; Stewart, *Pickett's Charge,* p. 184.

157. Hess, *Pickett's Charge,* pp. 15, 27–33; Wert, *A Glorious Army,* 269, 273–274.

158. Hess, *Pickett's Charge,* p. 120.

159. Ibid., pp. 76–80, 201, 219–222, 231; Cowell, *Tactics at Gettysburg,* p. 76.

Chapter VI

1. John W. Finley, "Bloody Angle, " *Buffalo Evening News,* May 28, 1894; Reynolds, *Andrew Pickens,* p. 16.

2. *Carolina Watchman,* August 5, 1863; Coddington, *The Gettysburg Campaign,* p. 503.

3. Lewis, *Recollections from 1860 to 1865*, p. 84; Bishop, *The Tennessee Brigade*, p. 212; Gragg, *Covered with Glory*, pp. 185, 191; John W. Finley, "Bloody Angle, " *Buffalo Evening News*, May 28, 1894; Rollins, ed., *Pickett's Charge*, p. 327; CVSR, NA; Hess, *Pickett's Charge*, pp. 33, 121, 172–173, 231; Harrison and Busey, *Nothing but Glory*, pp. 45, 87; Coco, *On the Bloodstained Field*, p. 205; Deborah Fitts, "New Gettysburg Look Has Fewer Cows and Crops, Lots More Grass, " *Civil War News* (October 2004), Internet; Rufus R. Dawes, *A Full Blown Yankee of the Iron Brigade, Service with the Sixth Wisconsin Volunteers* (Lincoln: University of Nebraska Press, 1999), p. 43.

4. Reardon, *Pickett's Charge*, p. 28.

5. Murray, "Brig. Gen. Alexander Hays' Division at Gettysburg, " *GM*, p. 91; Stewart, *Pickett's Charge*, pp. 167, 181–183; Coco, *On the Bloodstained Field I and II*, p. 31.

6. John W. Finley, "Bloody Angle, " *Buffalo Evening News*, May 28, 1894.

7. Wert, *A Glorious Army*, p. 274.

8. Gregory, *53rd Virginia Infantry and 5th Battalion Virginia Infantry*, p. 55; Gragg, *Covered with Glory*, p. 191; McWhiney, *Cracker Culture*, pp. xiii–271.

9. John W. Finley, "Bloody Angle, " *Buffalo Evening News*, May 28, 1894; Rollins, ed., *Pickett's Charge*, p. 327.

10. Bishop, *The Tennessee Brigade*, p. 212; Hess, *Pickett's Charge*, pp. 80–81, 210, 1104; Stewart, *Pickett's Charge*, p. 183.

11. Hess, *Pickett's Charge*, p. 210.

12. Bishop, *The Tennessee Brigade*, p. 212; Gragg, *Covered with Glory*, pp. 195–196; Smith, comp. , *Farms at Gettysburg*, p. 16; Longacre, *Pickett*, pp. 122–125.

13. Hess, *Pickett's Charge*, p. 302; Gragg, *Covered with Glory*, pp. 191–196; Bishop, *The Tennessee Brigade*, p. 212.

14. Gragg, *Covered with Glory*, pp. 191, 195–196.

15. CVSR, NA; Timberlake Papers, Virginia Historical Society, Richmond, Virginia; Stewart, *Pickett's Charge*, p. 183; Hess, *Pickett's Charge*, pp. 80–81, 223–224, 232–233; Gragg, *Covered with Glory*, p. 191.

16. Timberlake Papers, VHS; CVSR, NA.

17. Ibid.; Gregory, *53rd Virginia Infantry and 5th Battalion Virginia Infantry*, p. 55; Harrison and Busey, *Nothing but Glory*, p. 90; Hess, *Pickett's Charge*, pp. 80–81, 231; Stewart, *Pickett's Charge*, p. 183.

18. CVSR, NA.

19. Hess, *Pickett's Charge*, p. 224.

20. CVSR, NA.

21. Ibid.

22. *Richmond Times Dispatch*, September 28, 1936; CVSR, NA; Harrison and Busey, *Nothing but Glory*, p. 57; Hess, *Pickett's Charge*, pp. 80–81, 219–222, 231, 236–237, 248; Hess, *Pickett's Charge*, pp. 80, 141–146, 151, 182, 190; Cowell, *Tactics at Gettysburg*, p. 76; Gragg, *Covered with Glory*, pp. 191–196; John W. Finley, "Bloody Angle, " *Buffalo Evening News*, May 28, 1894; Rollins, ed., *Pickett's Charge*, p. 234; Stewart, *Pickett's Charge*, pp. 184–185; Shultz, *"Double Canister at Ten Yards, "* pp. 43–44, 51; Reardon, *Pickett's Charge*, pp. 21–23.

23. William B. Robertson to Mattie, LV.

24. Stewart, *Pickett's Charge*, p. 183.

25. Murray, "Brig. Gen. Alexander Hays' Division at Gettysburg, " *GM*, p. 90.

26. The Weider History Group, Gettysburg, p. 72.

27. Reardon, *Pickett's Charge*, p. 29.

28. Murray, "Brig. Gen. Alexander Hays' Division at Gettysburg, " *GM*, p. 90; Stewart, *Pickett's Charge*, p. 183.

29. Gregory, *53rd Virginia Infantry and 5th Battalion Virginia Infantry*, p. 55; Cowell, *Tactics at Gettysburg*, p. 76; Gragg, *Covered with Glory*, pp. 191–196.

30. Hess, *Pickett's Charge*, p. 202; Cowell, *Tactics at Gettysburg*, p. 76; Gragg, *Covered with Glory*, p. 191.

31. Murray, "Brig. Gen. Alexander Hays' Division at Gettysburg, " *GM*, p. 90; Hess, *Pickett's Charge*, p. 210; Longacre, *Pickett*, pp. 122–125; Gragg, *Covered with Glory*, pp. 192, 195–196; Stewart, *Pickett's Charge*, p. 183.

32. John W. Finley, "Bloody Angle, " *Buffalo Evening News*, May 28, 1894; Hess, *Pickett's Charge*, p. 231.

33. John W. Finley, "Bloody Angle, " *Buffalo Evening News*, May 28, 1894.

34. Ibid.; CVSR, NA.

35. Stewart, *Pickett's Charge*, p. 185.

36. CVSR, NA; Coco, *On the Bloodstained Field, I and II*, p. 68.

37. Rollins, ed., *Pickett's Charge*, pp. 75–76, 94, 106; CVSR, NA.

38. CVSR, NA; Harrison and Busey, *Nothing but Glory*, p. 74.

39. *Irish-American*, New York, New York, August 29, 1863; Tucker, *Irish Confederates*, pp. 90–94; Durkin, ed., *John Dooley, Confederate Soldier*, p. 144; O'Grady, *Clear the Confederate Way!*, pp. 35–46, 164; CVSR, NA; Charles T. Loehr, "The 'Old First' Virginia at Gettysburg, " *Southern Historical Society Papers*, vol. 32, (1904), p. 40; Harrison and Busey, *Nothing but Glory*, p. 47; Persico, *My Enemy, My Brother*, p. 231.

40. Coco, *On the Bloodstained Field, I and II*, p. 65.

41. Durkin, ed., *John Dooley, Confederate Soldier*, p. 115.

42. John A. Herndon to brother, July 11, 1863, CS.

43. CVSR, NA; Hess, *Pickett's Charge*, p. 170.

44. CVSR, NA.

45. McWhiney and Jamieson, *Attack and Die*, p. 115.

46. CNCSR, NA; Damian Shiels, *The Irish in the American Revolution* (Dublin: The History Press, 2013), pp. 107–108; Hess, *Pickett's Charge*, p. 210; Murray, "Brig. Gen. Alexander Hays' Division at Gettysburg, " *GM*, pp. 92–93; Gragg, *Covered with Glory*, p. 192.

47. Gottfried, *Stopping Pickett*, pp. 170, 172; Hess, *Pickett's Charge*, p. 201.

48. Harrison and Busey, *Nothing but Glory*, p. 116; Stewart, *Pickett's Charge*, p. 167; CVSR, NA.

49. *Annals of the War*, pp. 202–203.

50. CVSR, NA.

51. Ibid.

52. *Richmond Times Dispatch*, September 28, 1936; CVSR, NA; Hess, *Pickett's Charge*, p. 169.

53. Paul Clark Cooksey, "They Died as if on Dress Parade: The Annihilation of Iverson's Brigade at Gettysburg and the Battle of Oak Ridge, " *Gettysburg Magazine*, no. 20, pp. 89–112; Tucker, *Lee and Longstreet at Gettysburg*, pp. 131–132; Berkeley, "Rode with Pickett, " *CV*, p. 175.

54. CVSR, NA.

55. CVSR, NA.

56. Ibid.

57. Ibid.

58. "James Keith Marshall (1839–1863), " Find a Grave, Internet; Gragg, *Covered with Glory*, pp. 188–189, 192, 195; CNCSR, NA; Murray, "Brig. Gen. Alexander Hays' Division at Gettysburg, " *GM*, p. 90.

59. Lewis, *Recollections from 1860 to 1865*, p. 84; Gordon, *General George E. Pickett in Life and Legend*, p. 87; Hess, *Pickett's Charge*, pp. 80–81; Murray, "Brig. Gen. Alexander Hays' Division at Gettysburg, " *GM*, p. 90; Gragg, *Covered with Glory*, p. 191.

60. CVSR, NA; John W. Finley, "Bloody Angle, " *Buffalo Evening News*, May 28, 1894.

61. Durkin, ed., *John Dooley, Confederate Soldier*, p. 106; O'Grady, *Clear the Confederate Way!*, p. 161.

62. John A. Herndon to brother, July 11, 1863, CS.

63. CVSR, NA; Rollins, ed., *Pickett's Charge*, pp. 108; Hess, *Pickett's Charge*, p. 114.

64. CVSR, NA; Hess, *Pickett's Charge*, pp. 172, 221; Blackford, *Letters from Lee's Army*, p. 188.

65. Lewis, *Recollections from 1860 to 1865*, pp. 84–85.

66. Durkin, ed., *John Dooley, Confederate Soldier*, pp. 6, note 10, 106–107.

67. John W. Finley, *"Bloody Angle, " Buffalo Evening News*, May 28, 1894; CVSR, NA.

68. Gramm, *Gettysburg*, pp. 187–188; Tower, ed., *Lee's Adjutant*, p. 61; Cowell, *Tactics at Gettysburg*, p. 76; Barra, "One Mile of Open Ground, " *CWT*, pp. 34–35; Murray, "Brig. Gen. Alexander Hays' Division at Gettysburg, " *GM*, p. 89.

69. Cowell, *Tactics at Gettysburg*, p. 76; Gramm, *Gettysburg*, pp. 187–188; Barra, "One Mile of Open Ground, " *CWT*, pp. 34–35; Haskell, *The Battle of Gettysburg*, p. 100.

70. Durkin, ed., *John Dooley, Confederate Soldier*, p. 106.

71. Tower, ed., *Lee's Adjutant*, p. 61; Gramm, *Gettysburg*, pp. 187–188; Hess, *Pickett's Charge*, pp. 388, 398; Murray, "Brig. Gen. Alexander Hays' Division at Gettysburg, " *GM*, p. 89; Stewart, *Pickett's Charge*, p. 188; Barra, "One Mile of Open Ground, " *CWT*, pp. 34–35.

72. John W. Finley, "Bloody Angle, " *Buffalo Evening News*, May 28, 1894.

73. Ibid.

74. Hirst letter to Sarah, n.d., ASC.

75. Ibid.

76. CVSR, NA; *Times-Dispatch*, February 7, 1904; Coco, *Wasted Valor*, pp. 127–128; Harrison and Busey, *Nothing but Glory*, p. 137.

77. Coco, *Wasted Valor*, p. 124; CVSR, NA.

78. Coco, *Wasted Valor*, p. 124.

79. CVSR, NA.

80. The Weider History Group, Gettysburg, p. 77.

81. CVSR, NA; Erasmus Williams to John Daniels, n. d., John Daniels Papers, University of Virginia, Charlottesville, Virginia; Murray, "Brig. Gen. Alexander Hays' Division at Gettysburg, " *GM*, p. 89.

82. Wert, *A Glorious Army*, p. 274; Hess, *Pickett's Charge*, pp. 184–185.

83. Stewart, *Pickett's Charge*, pp. 174–184; Cowell, *Tactics at Gettysburg*, p. 76.

84. Joseph Graham to Graham, July 30, 1863, SHC; Murray, "Brig. Gen. Alexander Hays' Division at Gettysburg, " *GM*, p. 90; Harrison, *Pickett's Men*, pp. 99–100.

85. Joseph Graham to Graham, July 30, 1863, SHC; ; William S. Christian to John W. Daniels, October 24, 1904, John Warwick Daniels Papers, 1874–1914, Special Collections Department, University of Virginia, Charlottesville, Virginia; Wilson, *The Most Promising Man of the South*, pp. 50–73; *Carolina Watchman*, September 6, 1883; McWhiney and Jamieson, *Attack and Die*, pp. 60–61; Harrison, *Pickett's Men*, pp. 99–100; Crackel, *West Point*, pp. 103–105, 116, Hess, *Pickett's Charge*, pp. 15, 101; Hess, *Pickett's Charge*, pp. 210–211; Murray, "Brig. General Alexander Hays' Division at Gettysburg, " *GM*, p. 90; Kenneth Callahan, "Remembering Gettysburg: 8th Ohio Volunteer Infantry Was Critical to Blunting Pickett's Charge 150 Years Ago, " *The Plain Dealer*, Cleveland, Ohio, June 30, 2013; Gragg, *Covered with Glory*, pp. 182, 185, 192–198; Rollins, ed., *Pickett's Charge*, pp. 299–301, 306–307; Harrison and Busey, *Nothing but Glory*, pp. 60–61.

86. Cureton to Lane, June 22, 1890, SHC; Katcher, *The Army of Robert E. Lee*, p. 233.

87. Wilson, *The Most Promising Man of the South*, pp. 64–71; Harrison and Busey, *Nothing but Glory*, p. 37; Hess, *Pickett's Charge*, pp. 15, 248–250.

88. Joseph Graham to Graham, July 30, 1863, SHC.

89. *Annals of the War*, p. 196; Hess, *Pickett's Charge*, p. 252.

90. Cockrell, ed., *Gunner with Stonewall*, pp. 73–74; John A. Herndon to brother, July 11, 1863, CS.

91. Hess, *Pickett's Charge*, p. 224; Cowell, *Tactics at Gettysburg*, pp. 76, 141–143.

92. CVSR, NA; William A. Young, Jr., and Patricia C. Young, *History of the 56th Virginia Infantry Regiment* (Fort Walton Beach, Fla.: James K. Baughman, 2009), p. 203.

93. CVSR, NA; Young and Young, *History of the 56th Virginia Infantry Regiment*, pp. 214–215.

94. CVSR, NA; Young and Young, *History of the 56th Virginia Infantry Regiment*, pp. 220, 297, 326.

95. Hess, *Pickett's Charge*, pp. 15, 202; Wert, *A Glorious Army*, pp. 269, 274–275; *Annals of the War*, p. 315; CVSR, NA; Murray, "Brig. Gen. Alexander Hays' Division at Gettysburg, " *GM*, p. 90; Gragg, *Covered with Glory*, p. 196.

96. *Raleigh Observer*, November 30, 1877; Hess, *Pickett's Charge*, pp. 248–249.

97. *Fayetteville Observer*, August 24, 1863; Hess, *Pickett's Charge*, pp. 249–250.

98. *Charlotte Observer*, Charlotte, North Carolina, August 16, 1894.

99. Howard Coffin, *Nine Months to Gettysburg, Stannard's Vermonters and the Repulse of Pickett's Charge* (Woodstock, Vt.: The Countryman Press, 2011), pp. xiv, xvii–xix, 20–22, 57, 85, 201–211, 214, 219, 222–228; Rollins, ed., *Pickett's Charge*, pp. 219–220, 224;

Hess, *Pickett's Charge,* pp. 15, 32–33, 114, 130, 231; Harrison and Busey, *Nothing but Glory,* p. 67; Stewart, *Pickett's Charge,* pp. 149, 170, 181; Cowell, *Tactics at Gettysburg,* pp. 77–78.

100. Crewdson, *Love and War,* pp. 40–42, 81.
101. Ibid., pp. 64–65.
102. Longacre, *Pickett,* p. 120; CVSR, NA; Hess, *Pickett's Charge,* pp. 38, 156–157, 170; Harrison and Busey, *Nothing but Glory,* pp. 128–129; Coffin, *Nine Months to Gettysburg,* pp. 222–228; Gragg, *The Illustrated Gettysburg Reader,* pp. 322, 324; Wert, *A Glorious Army,* p. 270.
103. Bishop, *The Tennessee Brigade,* p. 229.
104. Reardon, *Pickett's Charge,* pp. 155–161; Champ Clark, *Gettysburg, The High Tide* (Alexandria: Time-Life Books, Inc., 1985) p. 126; Longacre, *Pickett,* pp. x, 2–3, 26–27; Sandburg, *Abraham Lincoln,* vol. 2, p. 355; Cockrell, ed., *Gunner with Stonewall,* p. 75; Gordon, *General George E. Pickett in Life and Legend,* pp. 77, 98–105; Longacre, *Pickett,* pp. ix–x, 3–5.
105. Gordon, *General George E. Pickett in Life and Legend,* p. 113.
106. Longacre, *Pickett,* p. x.
107. Reardon, *Pickett's Charge,* pp. 86, 155–158; CVSR, NA; Wilson, *The Most Promising Young Man of the South,* pp. 67, 69; Coddington, *The Gettysburg Campaign,* pp. 12; Longacre, *Pickett,* pp. ix–x, 2–5, 55–56, 122–123, 125, 166–167; Hess, *Pickett's Charge,* p. 15; Cockrell, ed., *Gunner with Stonewall,* p. 75; Harrison, *Pickett's Men,* pp. 29–31, 40–41, 64–65, 69; Piston, *Lee's Tarnished Lieutenant,* pp. 39–40, 45, 154; Clark, *Gettysburg,* p. 126; Gordon, *General George E. Pickett in Life and Legend,* pp. 75–116; Dugard, *The Training Ground,* p. 361; Mitchell, *Military Leaders in the Civil War,* pp. 146–148; Harrison and Busey, *Nothing but Glory,* p. 128; Longacre, *Pickett,* pp. 120, 122–123.
108. Kirkwood Otley, "Some War History, " *Times,* Richmond, Virginia, November 7, 1894; CVSR, NA.
109. Harrison and Busey, *Nothing but Glory,* p. 130.
110. Stewart, *Pickett's Charge,* p. 230.
111. Gordon, *General George E. Pickett in Life and Legend,* pp. 114–115; Longacre, *Pickett,* pp. 120, 121–122.
112. Reardon, *Pickett's Charge,* p. 158; Harrison, *Pickett's Men,* p. 31; Gordon, *General George E. Pickett in Life and Legend,* pp. 114–116; Longacre, *Pickett,* pp. 120, 121–122.
113. Reardon, *Pickett's Charge,* pp. 158–159; Wilson, *The Most Promising Young Man of the South,* p. 69.
114. Cockrell, ed., *Gunner with Stonewall,* p. 75.
115. Gordon, *General George E. Pickett in Life and Legend,* p. 114.
116. Stevens, ed., *As if it Were Glory,* p. 107.
117. Cockrell, ed., *Gunner with Stonewall,* p. 75; Longacre, *Pickett,* pp. 120, 122–123; Wilson, *The Most Promising Young Man in the South,* p. 69; Gordon, *General George E. Pickett in Life and Legend,* pp. 114–116, 147.
118. *Times-Dispatch,* February 7, 1904; Piston, *Lee's Tarnished Lieutenant,* pp. 1–172; Gordon, *General George E. Pickett in Life and Legend,* pp. 77, 91–116; Trudeau, *Gettysburg,*

pp. 351–352; Longacre, *Pickett*, pp. 116–123; Tucker, *Storming Little Round Top*, pp. 197–312; Harrison and Busey, *Nothing but Glory*, pp. 60–61; Hess, *Pickett's Charge*, pp. 15, 22–23; Mark Perry, *Conceived in Liberty, Joshua Chamberlain, William Oates, and the American Civil War* (New York: Viking, 1997), pp. 218–225; Cowell, *Tactics at Gettysburg*, pp. 78–79.

119. *Annals of the War*, pp. 313–314; Hess, *Pickett's Charge*, pp. 15, 32–33.

120. Gordon, *General George E. Pickett in Life and Legend*, pp. 114–115; Longacre, *Pickett*, pp. 120–123; Hess, *Pickett's Charge*, p. 15; Stewart, *Pickett's Charge*, p. 206.

121. Longacre, *Pickett*, pp. 125–126.

122. CVSR, NA; Hess, *Pickett's Charge*, p. 170; Tucker, *Lee and Longstreet at Gettysburg*, pp. 107, 130–132.

123. Hess, *Pickett's Charge*, p. 185.

124. "Ancestor in a Little Blue and a Lot of Gray, " The Pettigrew Family, November 29, 2012, Pettigrew Family Blog, Internet; Longacre, *Pickett*, pp. 120, 122–123, 125; Bishop, *The Tennessee Brigade*, p. 229.

125. Lewis, *Recollections from 1860 to 1865*, p. 83.

126. Harrison and Busey, *Nothing but Glory*, pp. 60–61; *Augusta Daily Constitutionalist*, July 23, 1863; Hess, *Pickett's Charge*, pp. 15, 32–33.

127. Cowell, *Tactics at Gettysburg*, pp. 78–79; Hess, *Pickett's Charge*, pp. 15, 32–33; Harrison and Busey, *Nothing but Glory*, pp. 60–61, 120.

128. James Marshall-Cornwall, *Napoleon as Military Commander* (New York: Barnes and Noble, Inc., 1967), p. 25; Hess, *Pickett's Charge*, pp. 15, 32–33.

129. Coddington, *The Gettysburg Campaign*, p. 489; Wert, *A Glorious Army*, pp. 269, 274.

130. CVSR, NA, p. 115; George Clark, "Wilcox's Alabama Brigade at Gettysburg, " *Confederate Veteran*, vol. 17, pp. 230–231; Harrison and Busey, *Nothing but Glory*, pp. 2, 60–61, 68–69, 133; Rollins, ed., *Pickett's Charge*, pp. 161, 165, 168; Waters and Edmonds, *A Small but Spartan Band*, p. 74; ; Hess, *Pickett's Charge*, pp. 15, 32–33, 226–227; Cowell, *Tactics at Gettysburg*, p. 76; Tucker, *Lee and Longstreet at Gettysburg*, pp. 114–115; Boritt, ed., *The Gettysburg Nobody Knows*, p. 23; Longacre, *Pickett*, pp. 122–126.

131. Hess, *Pickett's Charge*, pp. 15–19, 32–33, 306; Wert, *A Glorious Army*, pp. 269, 274–275; Coddington, *The Gettysburg Campaign*, p. 519; Cowell, *Tactics at Gettysburg*, pp. 78–79.

132. Coddington, *The Gettysburg Campaign*– p. 519.

133. Rollins, ed., *Pickett's Charge*, pp. 112, 166–167; Hess, *Pickett's Charge*, pp. 15, 22–23.

134. Carhart, *Lost Triumph*, pp. 2–6, 153–269; Cowell, *Tactics at Gettysburg*, p. 81; Hatch, *Glorious War*, pp. 1–3, 139–159.

135. Jeffrey D. Wert, *Custer, The Controversial Life of George Armstrong Custer* (New York: Simon and Schuster Publishers, 1997), pp. 83–85, 92–95; Carhart, *Lost Triumph*, pp. 188–240; Thomas, *Bold Dragoon*, pp. 241–249; Cowell, *Tactics at Gettysburg*, p. 81; Clark, *Gettysburg*, p. 132; *Annals of the War*, p. 215; Douglas, *I Rode with Stonewall*, p. 238; Wheeler, *The Last Cavaliers*, pp. 169–172; Thomas, *Robert E. Lee*, p. 291; Crewdson, *Love and War*, p. 90; Hatch, *Glorious War*, pp. 1–3, 139–159; Ernest L. Reedstrom, *Bugles, Banners and War Bonnets, A Study of George Armstrong Custer's Seventh Cavalry from Fort Riley to the Little Big Horn* (New York: Bonanza Books, 1986), pp. 248–249.

136. Carhart, *Lost Triumph*, pp. 188–240; Hatch, *Glorious War*, pp. 1–3, 139–159; Crewdson, *Love and War*, p. 90; Cowell, *Tactics at Gettysburg*, p. 81.

137. Thomas, *Bold Dragon*, p. 249; Cowell, *Tactics at Gettysburg*, p. 81; Hatch, *Glorious War*, pp. 1–3, 139–159.

138. *Annals of the War*, p. 215.

139. Meade, *The Life and Letters of General George Gordon Meade*, p. 109.

140. Carhart, *Lost Triumph*, pp. 188–240; Cowell, *Tactics at Gettysburg*, p. 81; Hatch, *Glorious War*, pp. 1–3, 139–159.

141. Cockrell, ed., *Gunner with Stonewall*, p. 74; Hess, *Pickett's Charge*, p. 15; Rollins, ed., *Pickett's Charge*, pp. 50–51.

142. Longacre, *Pickett*, pp. 122, 126.

143. Coffin, *Nine Months to Gettysburg*, p. xix; *Annals of the War*, pp. 313–216; Hatch, *Glorious War*, pp. 1–3, 139–159; Carhart, *Lost Triumph*, pp. 188–240; Cowell, *Tactics at Gettysburg*, pp. 78–79, 81.

144. Annals of the War, p. 313; Wert, *A Glorious Army*, pp. 269, 274–275; Tucker, *Lee and Longstreet at Gettysburg*, p. 95; Reardon, *Pickett's Charge*, pp. 21, 23–24.

145. Harrison and Busey, *Nothing but Glory*, p. 69; Wert, *A Glorious Army*, pp. 269, 274–275.

146. Hess, *Pickett's Charge*, p. 195.

147. Murray, "Brig. General Alexander Hays' Division at Gettysburg, " *GM*, p. 89.

148. CVSR, NA; Trask, *9th Virginia Infantry*, pp. 2–5, 10–11, 13, 26; Bevin Alexander, *Sun Tzu at Gettysburg, Ancient Military Wisdom in the Modern World* (New York: W. W. Norton and Company, 2011), p. 112; Cowell, *Tactics at Gettysburg*, p. 76; Hess, *Pickett's Charge*, pp. 141–143; Parramore, *Norfolk*, pp. 197, 209; Gleeson, *The Irish in the South*, p. 48; Hess, *Pickett's Charge*, pp. 224–225.

149. Lewis, *Recollections from 1860 to 1865*, p. 39.

150. CVSR, NA.

151. Ibid.; Gettysburg College Alumni Record, 1832–1932, Special Collections, Musselman Library, Gettysburg College, Gettysburg, Pennsylvania; Karen D. Drickamer to author, August 17, 2012.

152. CVSR, NA; Trask, *9th Virginia Infantry*, pp. 24, 60; Gettysburg College website, Internet; Drickamer to author, August 17, 2012; Gettysburg College Alumni Record, 1832–1932, Special Collections, ML; Sixteenth Commencement Program 1850, September 19, 1850, Special Collections, Musselman Library, Gettysburg College, Gettysburg, Pennsylvania; Natalie Sherif, "James Crocker: A Pennsylvania College Graduate Returns to Gettysburg, " 901 Stories from Gettysburg, Stories of the Gettysburg Battlefield, Civil War Institute, Gettysburg College, Gettysburg, Pennsylvania; Guelzo, Gettysburg, p. 104.

153. CVSR, NA; Serif, "James Crocker, " *CWI*.

154. Haskell, *The Battle of Gettysburg*, p. 101; CVSR, NA.

155. Rollins, ed., *Pickett's Charge*, pp. 292, 311; Murray, "Brig. Gen. Alexander Hays' Division at Gettysburg, " *GM*, p. 90; Hess, *Pickett's Charge*, pp. 101–102.

156. Gregory, *The 53rd Virginia Infantry and the 5th Battalion Virginia Infantry*, p. 56.

157. McWhiney and Jamieson, *Attack and Die*, p. 115.

158. CVSR, NA; Harrison and Busey, *Nothing but Glory*, p. 52.

159. CNCSR, NA; Charles D. Walker, *Memorial, Virginia Military Institute, Biographical Sketches of the Graduates and Eleves of the Virginia Military Institute Who Fell During the War Between the States* (Philadelphia, Pa.: J. B. Lippincott and Company, 1875), p. 369.

160. Colonel Joseph Mayo, July 25, 1863, DU; Lewis, *Recollections from 1860 to 1865*, p. 85.

161. CVSR, NA; Harrison and Busey, *Nothing but Glory*, p. 73.

162. CVSR, NA; Lord, *Civil War Collector's Encyclopedia*, p. 14; McWhiney and Jamieson, *Attack and Die*, pp. 48–58; Hess, *Pickett's Charge*, pp. 210–212; Rollins, ed., *Pickett's Charge*, pp. 293–294; Bowden and Ward, *Last Chance for Victory*, pp. 424–425; Hess, *Pickett's Charge*, p. 225; Murray, "Brig. Gen. Alexander Hays' Division at Gettysburg, " *GM*, pp. 83, 93; Gragg, *Covered with Glory*, pp. 163, 196.

163. CVSR, NA; Coco, *Killed in Action*, p. 110; Gottfried, *Stopping Pickett*, pp. 169–170, 172; Gragg, *Covered with Glory*, p. 196; John A. Herndon to brother, July 11, 1863, CS; Don Ernsberger, *At the Wall, The 69th Pennsylvania "Irish Volunteers" at Gettysburg* (Xlibris Corporation, 2006), pp. 107–108.

164. CVSR, NA; Gottfried, *Stopping Pickett*, pp. 169–170, 172; John A. Herndon to brother, July 11, 1863, CS.

165. Hess, *Pickett's Charge*, pp. Gragg, *Covered with Glory*, p. 196.

166. Reardon, *Pickett's Charge*, p. 23.

167. Hess, *Pickett's Charge*, pp. 207–211.

168. CNCSR, NA; Gragg, *Covered with Glory*, p. 197; Rollins, ed., *Pickett's Charge*, p. 311.

169. Hess, *Pickett's Charge*, pp. 211–213, 215; Murray, "Brig. Gen. Alexander Hays' Division at Gettysburg, " *GM*, p. 89.

170. CVSR, NA; Rollins, ed., *Pickett's Charge*, pp. 201–202; Gilles Bernard and Gerard Lachaux, *Waterloo Relics* (Paris: Histoire & Collections, 2006), p. 101; Gottfried, *Stopping Pickett*, pp. 170–172; Stewart, *Pickett's Charge*, p. 167.

171. Diary of Francis Moses Wafer, Queen's University Library, Kingston, Ontario, Canada; Hess, *Pickett's Charge*, p. 115.

172. CVSR, NA; Harrison and Busey, *Nothing but Glory*, pp. 83–84; John A. Herndon to brother, July 11, 1863, CS; O'Brien, *Irish Americans in the Confederate Army*, p. 97.

173. CVSR, NA.

174. CVSR, NA.

175. Harrison and Busey, *Nothing but Glory*, pp. 76, 83; Murray, "Brig. Gen. Alexander Hays' Division at Gettysburg, " *GM*, p. 89.

176. Haskell, *The Battle of Gettysburg*, p. 102; Hess, *Pickett's Charge*, pp. 141–144; Gottfried, *Stopping Pickett*, p. 170.

177. Rollins, ed., *Pickett's Charge*, pp. 328–329; Hess, *Pickett's Charge*, pp. 114–115, 141–144.

178. Myles Dungan, *Distant Drums, Irish Soldiers in Foreign Armies* (Belfast: Appletree Press, 1993), pp. 35–36; Hess, *Pickett's Charge*, pp. 141–144; Murray, "Brig. Gen. Alexander Hays' Division at Gettysburg, " *GM*, p. 90.

179. R. L. Murray, *"Hurrah for the Ould Flag!, " Captain Andrew Cowan and the First New York Independent Battery at Gettysburg* (Wolcott, N.Y.: Bendum Books, 1998), pp. 1–98, 121; Stewart, *Pickett's Charge*, p. 139; Gottfried, *Stopping Pickett*, pp. 169–170; McWhiney

and Jamieson, *Attack and Die,* p. 115; Hess, *Pickett's Charge,* pp. 120, 241; The Weider History Group, Gettysburg, p. 76; Murray, "Brig. Gen. Alexander Hays' Division at Gettysburg, " *GM,* p. 90; Harrison and Busey, *Nothing but Glory,* pp. 87–88.

180. Hess, *Pickett's Charge,* p. 120.
181. Harrison and Busey, *Nothing but Glory,* p. 116.
182. CVSR, NA; Harrison and Busey, *Nothing but Glory,* pp. 69–70.
183. Lewis, *Recollections from 1860 to 1865,* p. 85; John A. Herndon to brother, July 11, 1863, CS.
184. CVSR, NA; Harrison and Busey, *Nothing but Glory,* pp. 111, 116, 127.
185. John W. Finley, "Bloody Angle, " *Buffalo Evening News,* May 28, 1894; Cowell, *Tactics at Gettysburg,* p. 76; Murray, "Brig. Gen. Alexander Hays' Division at Gettysburg, " *GM,* p. 90; Hess, *Pickett's Charge,* pp. 141–145.
186. Catton, ed., *The Battle of Gettysburg,* p. 103.
187. CVSR, NA.
188. Murray, "Brig. General Alexander Hays' Division at Gettysburg, " *GM,* p. 92.
189. Crewdson, *Love and War,* p. 95; Carhart, *Lost Triumph,* pp. xi–260; Hatch, *Glorious War,* pp. 1–3, 139–159; Hess, *Pickett's Charge,* p. 164; Cowell, *Tactics at Gettysburg,* p. 81.

Chapter VII

1. Carhart, *Lost Triumph,* pp. xi–260; William Henry Cocke to Parents, Cocke Family Papers, 1794–1981, VHS; John A. Herndon to brother, July 11, 1863, CS; Cowell, *Tactics at Gettysburg,* p. 81.
2. John A. Herndon to brother, July 11, 1863, CS.
3. Reardon, *Pickett's Charge,* p. 24; Hess, *Pickett's Charge,* pp. 80, 118–119, 141–145, 196, 219, 261; Stewart, *Pickett's Charge,* pp. 185–188; Cowell, *Tactics at Gettysburg,* pp. 76–77; Murray, "Brig. Gen. Alexander Hays' Division at Gettysburg, " *GM,* p. 90.
4. Rollins, ed., *Pickett's Charge,* p. 344; Hess, *Pickett's Charge,* pp. 114, 141–143, 261; Cowell, *Tactics at Gettysburg,* pp. 76–77.
5. Stewart, *Pickett's Charge,* p. 187; Hess, *Pickett's Charge,* p. 245.
6. Hess, *Pickett's Charge,* pp. 196–197, 261; Rollins, ed., *Pickett's Charge,* pp. 324, 344; Anthony McDermott to John Bachelder, n.d., NHS.
7. Gottfried, *Stopping Pickett,* p. 170; Rollins, ed., *Pickett's Charge,* pp. 328–329, 344–345; Schultz, "Double Canister at Ten Yards, " p. 55; "Lt. Alonzo Cushing, Hero of Gettysburg, Awarded Medal of Honor, " National Public Radio, Washington, DC, Internet.
8. Anthony McDermott to John Backehder, n.d., NHHS; Rollins, ed., *Pickett's Charge,* p. 84; Schultz, "Double Canister at Ten Yards, " p. 55; Murray, "Brig. Gen. Alexander Hays' Division at Gettysburg, " *GM,* p. 89; Hess, *Pickett's Charge,* p. 261.
9. Rollins, ed., *Pickett's Charge,* p. 180; Hess, *Pickett's Charge,* p. 261.
10. Dungan, *Distant Drums,* pp. 4–5; CVSR, NA.
11. CVSR, NA.
12. Ibid.

13. John W. Finley, "Bloody Angle, " *Buffalo Evening News,* May 28, 1894.

14. CVSR, NA; Young and Young, *History of the 56th Virginia Infantry Regiment,* p. 307.

15. CVSR, NA; Harrison and Busey, *Nothing but Glory,* p. 101.

16. CVSR, NA; Harrison and Busey, *Nothing but Glory,* pp. 104–105.

17. Bishop, *The Tennessee Brigade,* pp. 210–211; Gottfried, *Stopping Pickett,* pp. 169–170, 172; Hess, *Pickett's Charge,* pp. 141–143, 192–193; Cowell, *Tactics at Gettysburg,* p. 76; Murray, "Brig. Gen. Alexander Hays' Division at Gettysburg, " *GM,* p. 90; Harrison and Busey, *Nothing but Glory,* p. 86.

18. Harrison and Busey, *Nothing but Glory,* p. 54.

19. Schultz, *"Double Canister at Ten Yards, "* p. 55.

20. CVSR, NA; Hess, *Pickett's Charge,* p. 221.

21. CVSR, NA; Coco, *On the Bloodstained Field,* p. 68.

22. CVSR, NA; Hess, *Pickett's Charge,* p. 267.

23. Ibid.

24. CVSR; Stewart, *Pickett's Charge,* p. 188; Cowell, *Tactics at Gettysburg,* p. 76; Gragg, *Covered with Glory,* pp. 186, 207.

25. Shiels, *The Irish in the American Civil War,* pp. 106–109; Hess, *Pickett's Charge,* pp. 193, 203; Stewart, *Pickett's Charge,* p. 52; Bishop, *The Tennessee Brigade,* pp. 210–211; Hess, *Pickett's Charge,* pp. 102, 204–205; Gragg, *Covered with Glory,* pp. 196, 207; Rollins, ed., *Pickett's Charge,* p. 79.

26. Bishop, *The Tennessee Brigade,* p. 211; CTSR, NA.

27. CNCSR, NA; Heth Family Papers, Special Collections Department, University of Virginia Library, Charlottesville, Virginia; F. Lewis Marshall letter to uncle, October 6, 1863 letter, Virginia Military Institute Archives, Manuscript, no. 0165, Lexington, Virginia; O'Grady, *Clear the Confederate Way!,* p. xii.

28. CNCSR, NA.

29. Durkin, ed., *John Dooley, Confederate Soldier,* p. 106; Dooley, SJ, Papers, GU; CVSR, NA; O'Grady, *Clear the Confederate Way!,* p. xii; Stewart, *Pickett's Charge,* p. 185.

30. John W. Finley, "Bloody Angle, " *Buffalo Evening News,* May 28, 1894; Hess, *Pickett's Charge,* p. 246.

31. Durkin, ed., *John Dooley, Confederate Soldier,* p. 107; CVSR, NA; O'Grady, *Clear the Confederate Way!,* p. 163; Hess, *Pickett's Charge,* pp. 229–230, 245, 261; John W. Finley, "Bloody Angle, " *Buffalo Evening News,* May 28, 1894.

32. CVSR, NA; O'Grady, *Clear the Confederate Way!,* pp. iv, 68, 256–257; Shiels, *The Irish in the American Civil War,* pp. 106–109.

33. CVSR, NA; Charles T. Loehr, "The 'Old First' Virginia at Gettysburg, " *Southern Historical Society Papers,* vol. 32 (1904), p. 40.

34. Rollins, ed., *Pickett's Charge,* p. 185; CVSR, NA.

35. CVSR, NA; O'Grady, *Clear the Confederate Way!,* pp. iv, 68; Rollins, ed., *Pickett's Charge,* p. 194; Gottfried, *Stopping Pickett,* pp. 14, 16, 169–170, 172.

36. CVSR, NA.

37. Colonel Joseph Mayo, July 25, 1863, DU; Rollins, ed., *Pickett's Charge,* pp. 172, 185.

38. Coffin, *Nine Months to Gettysburg*, pp. 20–22, 85, 225–228; Gottfried, *Stopping Pickett*, pp. 14, 16, 169-170-173.

39. John W. Finley, "Bloody Angle, " *Buffalo Evening News*, May 28, 1894; CVSR, NA; Hess, *Pickett's Charge*, p. 246; "Biography of Christopher Smith, Erie County, New York, Biographies, " Internet; Frederick Fuger Biography, Arlington National Military Cemetery, Arlington, Virginia.

40. Rollins, ed., *Pickett's Charge*, p. 202; Harrison and Busey, *Nothing but Glory*, p. 76.

41. *Carolina Watchman*, August 5, 1863.

42. CVSR, NA; Rollins, ed., *Pickett's Charge*, p. 185; Harrison and Busey, *Nothing but Glory*, pp. 71–72.

43. Blackford, ed., *Letters from Lee's Army*, pp. 188–189; CVSR, NA.

44. Hess, *Pickett's Charge*, pp. 228–229, 245.

45. Rollins, ed., *Pickett's Charge*, p. 202; CVSR, NA.

46. CVSR, NA.

47. Ibid.; Lonn, *Foreigners in the Confederacy*, pp. xi–xii, xiv, 1–32; O'Grady, *Clear the Way*, pp. ii, 158–165; Tucker, *Irish Confederates*, pp. 87–94; McWhiney, *Cracker Culture*, pp. xiii–271.

48. Hess, *Pickett's Charge*, p. 130; Stewart, *Pickett's Charge*, p. 189.

49. Wert, *A Glorious Army*, pp. 269, 274–275; Hess, *Pickett's Charge*, pp. 99–100; Harrison and Busey, *Nothing but Glory*, pp. 70, 80.

50. Coffin, *Nine Months to Gettysburg*, pp. 227–232; Rollins, ed., *Pickett's Charge*, pp. 219–220; Harrison and Busey, *Nothing but Glory*, p. 67. Thomas Herbert Davis Biography, Norwich University Museum, Norwich University, Norwich, Vermont

51. Rollins, *Pickett's Charge*, pp. 221, 224; Harrison and Busey, *Nothing but Glory*, p. 67.

52. Coffin, *Nine Months to Gettysburg*, p. 232; The Weider History Group, Gettysburg, p. 76; Harrison and Busey, *Nothing but Glory*, p. 87; Stewart, *Pickett's Charge*, pp. 185–186.

53. Coffin, *Nine Months to Gettysburg.*, pp. 10, 31; Rollins, ed., *Pickett's Charge*, p. 221.

54. Coffin, *Nine Months to Gettysburg*, pp. 232–233; John Gross, "A Grave Situation: Privately Purchased Identification Devices with Gettysburg Association, *Gettysburg Magazine* no. 42, (January 2010), p. 121.

55. Coffin, *Nine Months to Gettysburg*, pp. 232–233; Harrison and Busey, *Nothing but Glory*, pp. 60–61, 67; Hess, *Pickett's Charge*, p. 229.

56. John A. Herndon to brother, July 11, 1863, CS; Coffin, *Nine Months to Gettysburg*, p. 232; *National Tribune*, August 5, 1882; Hess, *Pickett's Charge*, pp. 15, 32–33, 217–218; Harrison and Busey, *Nothing but Glory*, pp. 60–61, 76, 80, 120; Cowell, *Tactics at Gettysburg*, pp. 76–79.

57. Kemper to Nannie L. Pollock, Museum Quality Americana Online; CVSR, NA; Tucker, *Longstreet and Lee at Gettysburg*, p. 132; Persico, *My Enemy, My Brother*, p. 205; Anthony McDermott to John Bachelder, n.d., NHHS; Harrison and Busey, *Nothing but Glory*, pp. 49, 65, 96; Reardon, *Pickett's Charge*, p. 24.

58. James L. Kemper to William H. Swallow, February 4, 1886, Gettysburg National Military Park, Gettysburg, Pennsylvania; James T. Carter, "Flag of the Fifty-Third Va. Regiment, " *Confederate Veteran*, vol. 10, (1902), p. 263; Maggie Maclean, Cremora

(Belle) Cave Kemper, February 28, 2009, Civil War Women, Women of the Civil War and Reconstruction Eras 1849–1877, Internet; Hess, *Pickett's Charge,* p. 43; Stewart, *Pickett's Charge,* p. 185; Harrison and Busey, *Nothing but Glory,* p. 96.

59. Stewart, *Pickett's Charge,* p. 185; CVSR, NA; Harrison and Busey, *Nothing but Glory,* p. 76.

60. John Finley, "Bloody Angle, " *Buffalo Evening News,* May 28, 1894; Harrison and Busey, *Nothing but Glory,* pp. 62, 68.

61. CVSR, NA; Coffin, *Nine Months to Gettysburg,* p. 233; Harrison and Busey, *Nothing but Glory,* pp. 96, 104; Hess, *Pickett's Charge,* p. 287; Tucker, *Lee and Longstreet at Gettysburg,* pp. 130–132.

62. CVSR, NA; Berkeley, "Rode with Pickett, " *CV,* p. 175; Harrison and Busey, *Nothing but Glory,* p. 49; Reardon, *Pickett's Charge,* p. 24; Hess, *Pickett's Charge,* p. 287; Tucker, *Lee and Longstreet at Gettysburg,* pp. 132–133.

63. Gottfried, *Stopping Pickett,* pp. 172–173, 229; Hess, *Pickett's Charge,* p. 224; Cowell, *Tactics at Gettysburg,* p. 76; Tucker, *Lee and Longstreet at Gettysburg,* pp. 131–132; CVSR, NA; Harrison and Busey, *Nothing but Glory,* p. 104.

64. CVSR, NA; *New York Times,* July 6, 1863; James Clay, "About the Death of General Garnett, " *Confederate Veteran,* vol. 33 (1905), p. 81; Berrier, "Craig County Gave its All at the Battle of Gettysburg, " *Roanoke Times,* July 3, 1863; *Baltimore-Sun,* December 3, 1905; Gottfried, *Stopping Pickett,* pp. 172–173; Hess, *Pickett's Charge,* pp. 224, 228, 265; Cowell, *Tactics at Gettysburg,* p. 76; Rollins, ed., *Pickett's Charge,* p. 181; Harrison and Busey, *Nothing but Glory,* pp. 78–79, 96.

65. Foote, *The Civil War,* vol. 2, pp. 559–560.

66. Walker, Memorial, Virginia Military Institute, p. 372.

67. CASR, NA.

68. John W. Finley, "Bloody Angle, " *Buffalo Evening News,* May 28, 1894.

69. Ibid.

70. CVSR, NA; *Richmond Times Dispatch,* September 28, 1936; Gottfried, *Stopping Pickett,* p. 173; Reardon, *Pickett's Charge,* p. 24; Hess, *Pickett's Charge,* pp. 265, 287; Harrison and Busey, *Nothing but Glory,* pp. 78, 96, 104.

71. CNCSR, NA; John W. Finley, "Bloody Angle, " *Buffalo Evening News,* May 28, 1894; Hess, *Pickett's Charge,* pp. 228, 265, 287.

72. John W. Finley, "Bloody Angle, " *Buffalo Evening News,* May 28, 1894; Hess, *Pickett's Charge,* p. 169; Harrison and Busy, *Nothing but Glory,* pp. 79–80.

73. John W. Finley, "Bloody Angle, " *Buffalo Evening News,* May 28, 1894; Hess, *Pickett's Charge,* pp. 169, 228.

74. Hess, *Pickett's Charge,* pp. 228, 265.

75. Bishop, *The Tennessee Brigade,* p. 212.

76. Armistead Biographical Information, Moore Papers, ECU; Motts, *"Trust in God and Fear Nothing, "* pp. 21–28; Harrison and Busey, *Nothing but Glory,* p. 54; John W. Finley, "Bloody Angle, " *Buffalo Evening News,* May 28, 1894; John A. Herndon to brother, July 11, 1863, CS; Hess, *Pickett's Charge,* p. 231; Dowdey, *Death of a Nation,* p. 271.

77. CVSR, NA; Hess, *Pickett's Charge,* p. 227; Harrison and Busey, *Nothing but Glory,* pp. 84, 89–90, 105.

78. CVSR, NA; Anthony McDermott to John Bachelder, n.d., NHHS; Gottfried, *Stopping Pickett*, p. 172; John W. Finley, "Bloody Angle, " *Buffalo Evening News*, May 28, 1894; Harrison and Busey, *Nothing but Glory*, p. 96; John A. Herndon to brother, July 11, 1863, 1863; Hess, *Pickett's Charge*, p. 228; Gregory, *53rd Virginia Infantry and 5th Battalion Virginia Infantry*, p. 58.

79. William Henry Cocke to parents, July 14, 1862, Cocke Family Papers, VHS.

80. Anthony McDermott to John Bacheldoer, n.d., NHHS; John W. Finley, "Bloody Angle, " *Buffalo Evening News*, May 28, 1894; Gottfried, *Stopping Pickett*, pp. 172–173, 229; Rollins, ed., *Pickett's Charge*, pp. 324–325; John A. Herndon to brother, July 11, 1863, CS; Hess, *Pickett's Charge*, pp. 222–232, 245; Foote, *The Civil War*, vol. 2, pp. 533–534; Motts, *"Trust Ii God and Fear Nothing, "* pp. 17, 19–20, 29–32.

81. Reardon, *Pickett's Charge*, p. 24; Hess, *Pickett's Charge*, pp. 228, 246.

82. CVSR NA; *Buffalo Evening News*, May 28, 1894; Hess, *Pickett's Charge*, pp. 155–156, 221; Harrison and Busey, *Nothing but Glory*, pp. 76–77, 102.

83. CVSR, NA; Anthony McDermott to John Bachelder, n.d., NHHS; Rollins, ed., *Pickett's Charge*, p. 185; Hess, *Pickett's Charge*, pp. 225–226, 229; Blackford, ed., *Letters from Lee's Army*, pp. 188–189. Hilary Valentine Harris to father, July 7, 1863, Pearce Museum, Navarro College, Corsicana, Texas.

84. CVSR, NA; Anthony McDermott to John Bachelder, n.d., NHHS; John W. Finley, "Bloody Angle, " *Buffalo Evening News*, May 28, 1894; Gottfried, *Stopping Pickett*, p. 172; The Weider History Group, Gettysburg, p. 76; Harrison and Busey, *Nothing but Glory*, pp. 76, 87–88, 98, 116; Stewart, *Pickett's Charge*, pp. 185–186.

85. Hess, *Pickett's Charge*, p. 242.

86. The Weider History Group, Gettysburg, p. 76.

87. Hess, *Pickett's Charge*, p. 242.

88. Anthony McDermott to John Bachelder, n.d., NHHS; Gottfried, *Stopping Pickett*, p. 172; Hess, *Pickett's Charge*, pp. 245–246.

89. Diary of William Burns, United States Army Military History Institute, Carlisle Barracks, Pennsylvania.

90. Rollins, ed., *Pickett's Charge*, p. 326.

91. Anthony McDermott to John Bachelder, n.d., NHHS.

92. CVSR, NA; Harrison and Busey, *Nothing but Glory*, pp. 84–85; Hess, *Pickett's Charge*, p. 227.

93. Berrier, "Craig County Gave its All at the Battle of Gettysburg, " *Roanoke Times*, July 3, 2013; CVSR, NA; Harrison and Busey, *Nothing but Glory*, p. 85.

94. CVSR, NA; John W. Finley, "Bloody Angle, " *Buffalo Evening News*, May 28, 1894; Harrison and Busey, *Nothing but Glory*, pp. 78, 84–85.

95. CVSR, NA; Harrison and Busey, *Nothing but Glory*, p. 105.

96. CVSR, NA; Stewart, *Pickett's Charge*, p. 186; John A. Herndon to brother, July 11, 1863, CS.

97. CVSR, NA; John A. Herndon to brother, July 11, 1863, CS.

98. Harrison, *Pickett's Men*, p. 98.

99. The Weider History Group, p. 76; Hess, *Pickett's Charge*, p. 242.

100. The Weider History Group, p. 76.

101. John W. Finley, "Bloody Angle, " *Buffalo Evening News*, May 28, 1894; Gottfried, *Stopping Pickett*, pp. 172–173; Motts, *"Trust In God And Fear Nothing, "* p. 45; Hess, *Pickett's Charge*, pp. 141–143, 204–205, 245–247, 261; Cowell, *Tactics at Gettysburg*, pp. 76–77; Stewart, *Pickett's Charge*, p. 188; Hess, *Pickett's Charge*, pp. 229–233, 245, 261; PHS, *Pickett's Charge at Gettysburg*, p. 11; Rollins, ed., *Pickett's Charge*, pp. 324–325; Bowden and Ward, *Last Chance for Victory*, pp. 463–464; John A. Herndon to brother, July 11, 1863, CS; William Henry Cocke to parents, Cocke Family Papers, 1794–1981, VHS; Harrison and Busey, *Nothing but Glory*, pp. 76, 86–87, 98, 102, 111–112, 127; CVSR, NA; Michael Halleran, "'The Widow's Son, ' Lewis Armistead at Gettysburg, " *Gettysburg Magazine*, no. 43 (July 2010), p. 93.

102. Hess, *Pickett's Charge*, p. 261.

103. Ibid.; CVSR, NA; Bowden and Ward, *Last Chance for Victory*, pp. 463–464; Harrison and Busey, *Nothing but Glory*, p. 113.

104. Rollins, ed., *Pickett's Charge*, p. 347.

105. Harrison and Busey, *Nothing but Glory*, p. 109; Hess, *Pickett's Charge*, pp. 246–247.

106. CVSR, NA.

107. John W. Finley, "Bloody Angle, " *Buffalo Evening News*, May 28, 1894.

108. Ibid.

109. Reardon, *Pickett's Charge*, p. 25.

110. CVSR, NA; Harrison and Busey, *Nothing but Glory*, pp. 112–113.

111. Clay, "About the Death of General Garnett, " *Confederate Veteran*, vol. 14 (February 1905), p. 81.

112. Lewis, *Recollections from 1860 to 1865*, p. 85.

113. Bishop, *The Tennessee Brigade*, pp. 211, 213, 217.

114. *Charlotte Daily Observer*, July 4, 1903; Hess, *Pickett's Charge*, p. 215.

115. CVSR, NA; Hess, *Pickett's Charge*, pp. 246–247, 268; Harrison and Busey, *Nothing but Glory*, p. 109.

116. Harrison and Busey, *Nothing but Glory*, pp. 101–102, 116; CVSR, NA.

117. CVSR, NA; Murray, "Brig. Gen. Alexander Hays' Division at Gettysburg, " *GM*, p. 89; Harrison and Busey, *Nothing but Glory*, pp. 73–74, 79–87, 116; Hess, *Pickett's Charge*, pp. 246–247.

118. CVSR, NA; Hess, *Pickett's Charge*, p. 267.

119. Bishop, *The Tennessee Brigade*, p. 213.

120. Anthony McDermott to John Bachelder, n.d., NHHS; John W. Finley, "Bloody Angle, " *Buffalo Evening News*, May 28, 1894; Gottfried, *Stopping Pickett*, p. 172; CVSR, NA; Rollins, ed., *Pickett's Charge*, p. 325; Ernberger, *At the Wall*, pp. 107–118; Hess, *Pickett's Charge*, p. 262.

121. John W. Finley, "Bloody Angle, " *Buffalo Evening News*, May 28, 1894; Ernberger, *At the Wall*, p. 111.

122. Ibid., pp. 91, 107–118.

123. Hess, *Pickett's Charge*, p. 262; Harrison and Busey, *Nothing but Glory*, pp. 109, 113; CVSR, NA.

124. John W. Finley, "Bloody Angle, " *Buffalo Evening News*; CVSR, NA; Hess, *Pickett's Charge,* p. 250; Cowell, *Tactics at Gettysburg,* p. 76.

125. PHS, *Pickett's Charge at Gettysburg,* pp. 4–6; CVSR, NA; Gottfried, *Stopping Pickett,* p. 173; Hess, *Pickett's Charge,* pp. 45, 250, 262; Harrison and Busey, *Nothing but Glory,* pp. 109, 113.

126. CVSR, NA; PHS, *Pickett's Charge at Gettysburg,* pp. 4–6; Harrison and Busey, *Nothing but Glory,* p. 90

127. CVSR, NA; PHS, *Pickett's Charge at Gettysburg,* p. 6; Gregory, *53rd Virginia Infantry and 5th Battalion Virginia Infantry,* pp. 59–60.

128. PHS, *Pickett's Charge at Gettysburg,* pp. 4–6; CVSR, NA; Gregory, *53rd Virginia Infantry and 5th Battalion Virginia Infantry,* p. 62; The Weider History Group, Gettysburg: Three Days of Courage and Sacrifice (Summer 2013), p. 72; Murray, "Hurrah for the Ould Flag!, " p. 29; Harrison and Busey, *Nothing but Glory,* p. 91; Shiels, *The Irish in the American Civil War,* p. 30.

129. Coco, *Wasted Valor,* pp. 127–129; CVSR, NA; Hess, *Pickett's Charge,* pp. 45–46; Harrison and Busey, *Nothing but Glory,* p. 91.

130. CVSR, NA; Harrison and Busey, *Nothing but Glory,* pp. 88–89, 101–102.

131. CVSR, NA; Harrison and Busey, *Nothing but Glory,* p. 89.

132. PHS, *Pickett's Charge at Gettysburg,* p. 6.

133. Ibid.; CVSR, NA; Gregory, *53rd Virginia Infantry and 5th Battalion Virginia Battalion,* pp. 61–62; Harrison and Busey, *Nothing but Glory,* pp. 113–114.

134. PHS, *Pickett's Charge at Gettysburg,* p. 6; Drewey B. Easley Papers, United States Military Institute, Carlisle Barracks, Pennsylvania; Rollins, ed., *Pickett's Charge,* pp. 203–204, 209; CVSR NA; Stewart, *Pickett's Charge,* pp. 192, 194–196; John A. Herndon to brother, July 11, 1863, CS; Harrison and Busey, *Nothing but Glory,* pp. 88, 101–102, 113; Halleran, "'The Widow's Son', " *GM,* p. 95; Hess, *Pickett's Charge,* pp. 11, 141–142, 204–205, 250, 273.

135. Lewis, *Recollections from 1860 to 1865,* p. 86; Easley Papers, CB.

136. CVSR, NA.

137. CVSR, NA.

138. Ibid; Harrison and Busey, *Nothing but Glory,* p. 104.

139. Diary of George Griggs, *Southern Historical Society Papers,* 6 (1878), p. 250; CVSR, NA; Harrison and Busey, *Nothing but Glory,* pp. 91–92.

140. CMSR, NA; Harrison and Busey, *Nothing but Glory,* pp. 91–92.

141. Hess, *Pickett's Charge,* pp. 204–205, 250; Gragg, *Covered with Glory,* p. 207.

142. Harrison and Busey, *Nothing but Glory,* pp. 102, 116; CVSR, NA; Durkin, ed., *John Dooley, Confederate Soldier,* pp. 72–73.

143. The Weider History Group, Gettysburg, p. 76; Hess, *Pickett's Charge,* p. 242.

144. Murray, *"Hurrah for the Ould Flag!, "* p. 92, note 32.

145. Ibid., p. 92; Hess, *Pickett's Charge,* p. 242.

146. Murray, *"Hurrah the Ould Flag!, "* p. 97.

147. Tower, ed., *Lee's Adjutant,* p. 61; CVSR, NA; Hess, *Pickett's Charge,* pp. 204–205, 248–261.

148. Reardon, *Pickett's Charge,* p. 25; Gottfried, *Stopping Pickett,* p. 173.

149. Rollins, ed., *Pickett's Charge,* p. 328.

150. Ibid., p. 327.

151. John A. Herndon to brother, July 11, 1863, CS; Reardon, *Pickett's Charge,* pp. 25, 30; Gottfried, *Stopping Pickett,* p. 173; Tom Huntington, "A Monumental Lie?, " *Civil War Times* (June 2014), p. 52; Ernsberger, *At the Wall,* p. 111; Hess, *Pickett's Charge,* p. 276; Stewart, *Pickett's Charge,* pp. 191–198.

152. CVSR, NA; Gottfried, *Stopping Pickett,* pp. 14, 16, 174–175; Gilbert, "Col. O'Kane and His Men—Irish Heroes at Gettysburg, " *IE*; Rollins, ed., *Pickett's Charge,* p. 348; Murray, *"Hurrah for the Ould Flag!, "* p. 97; Hess, *Pickett's Charge,* pp. 281–282; Stewart, *Pickett's Charge,* pp. 167, 198; Harrison and Busey, *Nothing but Glory,* p. 106.

153. Hess, *Pickett's Charge,* pp. 284–285.

154. Davis, *Gray Fox,* p. 243.

155. Gregory, *53rd Virginia Infantry and 5th Battalion Virginia Infantry,* p. 61; CVSR, NA.

156. The Weider History Group, *Gettysburg,* p. 76; CNYSR, NA; Hess, *Pickett's Charge,* p. 242; Harrison and Busey, *Nothing but Glory,* pp. 102, 105, 116; Murray, *"Hurrah for the Ould Flag!, "* pp. 98, 105, note 1, 119; Stewart, *Pickett's Charge,* p. 199–200.

157. Murray, *"Hurrah for the Ould Flag!, "* p. 98.

158. Ibid., p. 102.

159. Ibid., p. 105.

160. CVSR, NA; Gottfried, *Stopping Pickett,* p. 174; Hess, *Pickett's Charge,* p. 242; The Weider History Group, *Gettysburg,* p. 76; Harrison and Busey, *Nothing but Glory,* pp. 102, 105; Shultz, *"Double Canister at Ten Yards, "* pp. 57–58.

161. Harrison and Busey, *Nothing but Glory,* p. 116.

162. Murray, *"Hurrah for the Ould Flag!, "* p. 103.

163. Harrison and Busey, *Nothing but Glory,* pp. 102, 468; CVSR, NA.

164. Gottfried, *Stopping Pickett,* p. 175; Hess, *Pickett's Charge,* p. 243.

165. Gottfried, *Stopping Pickett,* pp. 174–175; Rollins, ed., *Pickett's Charge,* pp. 324–325.

166. CVSR, NA; Harrison and Busey, *Nothing but Glory,* pp. 102–103. John R. Morris to father July 10, 1863, Library of Virginia Archives, Richmond, Virginia.

167. Spessard Family Papers, CCHS; CVSR, NA; Rollins, ed., *Pickett's Charge,* p. 181; Harrison and Busey, *Nothing but Glory,* pp. 103, 105; Hess, *Pickett's Charge,* p. 228.

168. Spessard Family Papers, CCHS; Harrison and Busey, *Nothing but Glory,* p. 106.

169. CVSR, NA; J. R. McPherson, "A Private's Account of Gettysburg, " *Confederate Veteran,* vol. 6 (1898), p. 149.

170. Herndon to brother, July 11, 1863, CS.

171. Colonel Joseph Mayo Report, July 25, 1863, DU; Coffin, *Nine Months to Gettysburg,* pp. 231–233; Powell, "With Hood at Gettysburg, " *Weekly Times,* December 13, 1884; Ernsberger, *At the Wall,* p. 87; Hess, *Pickett's Charge,* p. 247.

172. Hess, *Pickett's Charge,* pp. 233, 245, 250.

173. *Fayetteville Observer,* March 27, 1864; Bishop, *The Tennessee Brigade,* p. 213; Rollins, ed., *Pickett's Charge,* p. 202; Hess, *Pickett's Charge,* pp. 80–81, 204–205, 245; Gragg, *Covered with Glory,* pp. 196–199, 207; Harrison and Busey, *Nothing but Glory,* pp. 85–86.

174. Reardon, *Pickett's Charge*, p. 23; Hess, *Pickett's Charge*, p. 252.

175. Hess, *Pickett's Charge*, pp. 215–216; Bob Bembridge, "Over the Wall and into History: New Jereyans at the Battle of Gettysburg, " *The New Jersey Monthly*, June 10, 2013, Internet.

176. Bishop, *The Tennessee Brigade*, p. 213; Hess, *Pickett's Charge*, pp. 250–251; Gragg, *Covered with Glory*, pp. 196, 201, 207.

177. CNCSR, NA; Rollins, ed., *Pickett's Charge*, p. 202; Hess, *Pickett's Charge*, pp. 204–205, 250–252; Gragg, *Covered with Glory*, pp. 196; Walker, Memorial, Virginia Military Institute, p. 372; Bishop, *The Tennessee Brigade*, pp. 213–214.

178. "Col. James Keith Marshall (1839–1863), " Find a Grave, Internet.

179. F. Lewis Marshall to Colonel Marshall, October 7, 1863, Alumni Civil War Letters, Diaries and Manuscripts, Virginia Military Institute Archives, Virginia Military Institute, Lexington, Virginia.

180. CNCSR, NA; Hess, *Pickett's Charge*, pp. 204–218, 250–253; Gragg, *Covered with Glory*, p. 198; Reardon, *Pickett's Charge*, pp. 23–24.

181. Hess, *Pickett's Charge*, p. 210; Gragg, *Covered with Glory*, pp. 179, 199–200; CNCSR, NA.

182. CNCSR, NA; Bembridge, "Over the Wall and into History, " *TNJM*, Internet; Gragg, *Covered with Glory*, pp. 164–165, 181, 200; Hess, *Pickett's Charge*, pp. 252–254.

183. *The News and Observer*, March 24, 1887; Hess, *Pickett's Charge*, pp. 253–254.

184. Reardon, *Pickett's Charge*, p. 23.

185. Bishop, *The Tennessee Brigade*, pp. 213–214; Reardon, *Pickett's Charge*, pp. 23–24; Hess, *Pickett's Charge*, pp. 204–205, 253–254; Cowell, *Tactics at Gettysburg*, p. 76.

186. Bishop, *The Tennessee Brigade*, pp. 213–215; Hess, *Pickett's Charge*, pp. 204–205.

187. Rollins, ed., *Pickett's Charge*, p. 202.

188. William J. Burns Diary, Save the Flags Collection, United States Army Military History Institute, Carlisle, Pennsylvania.

189. "In My Own Words": Commentary, webmousepublishing, Internet; Hess, *Pickett's Charge*, pp. 205–209, 252.

190. CVSR, NA; Rollins, ed., *Pickett's Charge*, p. 185.

191. Lewis, *Recollections from 1860 to 1865*, p. 86.

192. Joseph C. Mayo, "Pickett's Charge at Gettysburg, " *Southern Historical Society Papers*, vol. 34 (1906), p. 335; Carhart, *Lost Triumph*, pp. xi–260; Hatch, *Glorious War*, pp. 1–3, 139–159; Cowell, *Tactics at Gettysburg*, p. 81.

193. Hess, *Pickett's Charge*, p. 28.

194. Tower, ed., *Lee's Adjutant*, p. 61; Robertson, *General A. P. Hill*, pp. 222–224; Hess, *Pickett's Charge*, pp. 15–19, 32–33, 262, 301; Waters and Edmonds, *A Small but Spartan Band*, pp. 73–79; CVSR, NA; Bishop, *The Tennessee Brigade*, p. 213; McKenzie, *Uncertain Glory*, pp. 147, 160; Bowden and Ward, *Last Chance for Victory*, p. 466; *Annals of the War*, pp. 313–316; Cowell, *Tactics at Gettysburg*, pp. 78–79; Gragg, *Covered with Glory*, pp. 196, 200–201; Davis, *Gray Fox*, p. 244; Rollins, ed., *Pickett's Charge*, pp. 10, 265; Tucker, *Lee and Longstreet at Gettysburg*, p. 95; Hess, *Pickett's Charge*, pp. 15–19,

32–33, 70–73, 204–205, 306; Stewart, *Pickett's Charge,* pp. 205–206, 211; Wert, *A Glorious Army,* pp. 274–275, 282; Coffin, *Nine Months to Gettysburg,* pp. 227–239.

195. Waters and Edmonds, *A Small but Spartan Band,* p. 74; Hess, *Pickett's Charge,* p. 74.

196. Waters and Edmonds, *A Small but Spartan Band,* p. 73; Wert, *A Glorious Army,* pp. 274–275, 282; Stewart, *Pickett's Charge,* pp. 205–206.

197. *Annals of the War,* p. 313.

198. Wert, *A Glorious Army,* p. 275.

199. Rollins, ed., *Pickett's Charge,* p. 265.

200. Isaac R. Trimble, "Civil War Diary of I. R. Trimble, " *Maryland Historical Magazine,* vol. 17 (1922), p. 2; Hess, *Pickett's Charge,* pp. 256–257.

201. *Annals of the War,* p. 314.

202. Stevens, ed., *As if it Were Glory,* p. 105.

203. Harrison, *Pickett's Charge,* p. 98.

204. John A. Herndon to brother, July 11, 1863, CS; Hess, *Pickett's Charge,* p. 265; Stewart, *Pickett's Charge,* p. 192.

205. Harrison, *Pickett's Charge,* pp. 98–99.

206. Colonel Joseph Mayo, July 25, 1863, DU; Rollins, ed., *Pickett's Charge,* p. 271.

207. CVSR, NA; Rollins, ed., *Pickett's Charge,* pp. 185–187.

208. Lewis, *Recollections from 1860 to 1865,* p. 85.

209. Gregory, *53rd Virginia Infantry and 5th Battalion Virginia Infantry,* pp. 61, 64; CVSR, NA.

210. Tower, ed., *Lee's Adjutant,* p. 61; McKenzie, *Uncertain Glory,* p. 160; *Annals of the War,* pp. 313–316.

211. Thomas, *Robert E. Lee,* p. 301.

212. Wert, *A Glorious Army,* p. 275.

213. Ibid., p. 282.

214. Ibid., pp. 274–275, 282; Hess, *Pickett's Charge,* pp. 15, 32–33; Thomas, *Robert E. Lee,* p. 301; Robertson, *General A. P. Hill,* pp. 223–224; Cowell, *Tactics at Gettysburg,* pp. 78–79.

215. Gordon, *General George E. Pickett in Life and Legend,* p. 115; Hess, *Pickett's Charge,* pp. 14–15, 32–33; Robertson, *General A. P. Hill,* p. 223; Cowell, *Tactics at Gettysburg,* pp. 78–79.

216. Cockrell, ed., *Gunner with Stonewall,* pp. 74–75; McWhiney and Jamieson, *Attack and Die,* pp. 120–121; Gordon, *General George E. Pickett in Life and Legend,* p. 115; Hess, *Pickett's Charge,* pp. 15, 32–33; Cowell, *Tactics at Gettysburg,* pp. 78–79; Robertson, *General A. P. Hill,* p. 223; Wert, *A Glorious Army,* pp. 269, 274–275, 282; Rollins, ed., *Pickett's Charge,* pp. 46, 109–112; Hess, *Pickett's Charge,* pp. 266–227, 391; Stewart, *Pickett's Charge,* pp. 206–207; Harrison and Busey, *Nothing but Glory,* pp. 60–61.

217. Gordon, *General George E. Pickett in Life and Legend,* p. 115; Rollins, ed., *Pickett's Charge,* pp. 46, 109–110; Harrison and Busey, *Nothing but Glory,* pp. 60–61.

218. Cockrell, ed., *Gunner with Stonewall,* pp. 75–77.

219. Harrison and Busey, *Nothing but Glory,* p. 72. James L. Kemper Residence, Little Bits of History Along US Roadways, internet.

220. Cockrell, ed., *Gunner with Stonewall*, pp. 75–77; Rollins, ed., *Pickett's Charge*, pp. 21–22; CMSR, NA; Harrison and Busey, *Nothing but Glory*, pp. 60–61.

221. Harrison, *Pickett's Men*, p. 99.

222. Robertson, *General A. P. Hill*, p. 223; Hess, *Pickett's Charge*, pp. 15, 32–33; Thomas, *Robert E. Lee*, p. 302; Gordon, *General George E. Pickett in Life and Legend*, p. 115; Wert, *A Glorious Army*, pp. 274–275, 282; Cowell, *Tactics at Gettysburg*, pp. 78–79.

223. Thomas, *Robert E. Lee*, p. 302.

224. Robertson, *General A .P. Hill*, pp. 223–224; Dowdey, *Death of a Nation*, p. 253.

225. Hess, *Pickett's Charge*, pp. 15–19; Robertson, *General A. P. Hill*, p. 224; Wert, *A Glorious Army*, pp. 274–275, 282.

226. Stevens, ed., *As if it Were Glory*, pp. xiv, 110; Carhart, *Lost Triumph*, pp. xi–260; Hatch, *Glorious War*, pp. 1–3, 139–159; Cowell, *Tactics at Gettysburg*, p. 81.

227. Colonel Joseph Mayo, July 25, 1863, DU; Coffin, *Nine Months to Gettysburg*, pp. xvii–xx, 228–233; CVSR, NA; Hess, *Pickett's Charge*, pp. 130, 234–241; Harrison and Busey, *Nothing but Glory*, pp. 60–61; Longacre, *Pickett*, pp. 122, 126; Coddington, *The Gettysburg Campaign*, p. 519.

228. Colonel John Mayo, July 25, 1863, DU; CVSR, NA; Hess, *Pickett's Charge*, p. 241; Rollins, ed., *Pickett's Charge*, p. 173; Harrison and Busey, *Nothing but Glory*, p. 76.

229. Rollins, ed., *Pickett's Charge*, p. 173.

230. Ibid.; CVSR, NA; Thom Hatch, *Osceola and the Great Seminole War, A Struggle for Justice and Freedom* (New York: St. Martin's Press, 2012), pp. 1–256.

231. CVSR, NA; Rollins, ed., *Pickett's Charge*, pp. 173, 185.

232. June Kimble, "Tennesseans at Gettysburg—The Retreat, " *Confederate Veteran*, vol. 18 (1910), p. 461.

233. Coffin, *Nine Months to Gettysburg*, p. 233.

234. Rollins, ed., *Pickett's Charge*, p. 345.

235. Hess, *Pickett's Charge*, pp. 15, 32–33; Bowden and War, *Last Chance for Victory*, pp. 471–475; Harrison and Busey, *Nothing but Glory*, p. 97.

236. CVSR, NA.

Chapter VIII

1. Williams to Daniels, n.d., UV; Easley Papers, CB; Rollins, ed., *Pickett's Charge*, pp. 204, 234–235, 326; CVSR, NA; Hess, *Pickett's Charge*, pp. 204–205, 250; ; Gragg, *Covered with Glory*, pp. 199–200; *Observer*, November 6, 1877, Raleigh, North Carolina; Harrison and Busey, *Nothing but Glory*, pp. 55, 109–112; Bowden and Ward, *Last Chance for Victory*, pp. 463–464; Shultz, *"Double Shot Canister at Ten Yards, "* p. 55.

2. Rollins, ed., *Pickett's Charge*, p. 326.

3. CVSR, NA; Hess, *Pickett's Charge*, p. 262; Harrison and Busey, *Nothing but Glory*, p. 113.

4. CVSR, NA.

5. Williams to Daniels, n.d., UV; CVSR, NA.

6. CVSR, NA.

7. Williams to Daniel, n.d., UV; CVSR, NA.

8. Rollins, ed., *Pickett's Charge*, p. 326.

9. D. B. Easley, "With Armistead When He Was Killed, " *Confederate Veteran*, vol. 20 (1912), p. 379; CVSR, NA; Easley Papers, CB; Rollins, ed., *Pickett's Charge*, pp. 204, 346.

10. Williams to Daniels, n.d., UV; PHS, *Pickett's Charge at Gettysburg*, p. 6; Motts, *"Trust in God and Fear Nothing, "* p. 48; Rollins, ed., *Pickett's Charge*, pp. 204, 346; Halleran, "'The Widow's Son', " *GM,* p. 101; Easley, "With Armistead When He Was Killed, " *CV,* p. 379; CVSR, NA; Shultz, *"Double Canister at Ten Yards, "* p. 55; Ernsberger, *At the Wall,* pp. 70, 83, 86, 91, 93; Hess, *Pickett's Charge,* p. 262; Gottfried, *Stopping Pickett,* p. 175; Harrison and Busey, *Nothing but Glory,* pp. 110, 114.

11. The Weider History Group, Gettysburg, p. 72.

12. George W. Finley, "Bloody Angle, " *Buffalo Evening News,* Buffalo, New York, May 28, 1894; CVSR, NA.

13. Hess, *Pickett's Charge,* pp. 263–264.

14. Ibid., p. 268; CVSR, NA.

15. *Richmond Times Dispatch,* September 28, 1936; CVSR, NA.

16. Easley Papers, CB.

17. CVSR, NA.

18. Ibid.

19. Easley, "With Armistead When He Was Killed, " *CV,* p. p. 379; CVSR, NA; Harrison and Busey, *Nothing but Glory,* pp. 112–113, 115.

20. Finley, "Bloody Angle, " *Buffalo Evening News,* May 28, 1894.

21. Ibid.; CVSR, NA; Hess, *Pickett's Charge,* p. 264; Harrison and Busey, *Nothing but Glory,* p. 113.

22. Ibid.; Rollins, ed., *Pickett's Charge,* p. 347.

23. CVSR, NA; Hess, *Pickett's Charge,* pp. 15, 32–33.

24. Ibid.; Harrison and Busey, *Nothing but Glory,* p. 107; Stewart, *Pickett's Charge,* p. 206.

25. Coddington, *The Gettysburg Campaign,* p. 513.

26. Shultz, *"Double Canister at Ten Yards, "* pp. 56–57.

27. Homer Baldwin to father, July 7, 1863, Archives, Gettysburg National Military Battlefield Park, Gettysburg, Pennsylvania; Hess, *Pickett's Charge,* pp. 252–258.

28. Williams to Daniels, n.d., UV; PHS, *Pickett's Charge at Gettysburg,* p. 11; CVSR, NA.

29. Gottfried, *Stopping Pickett,* pp. 175–176; Rollins, ed., *Pickett's Charge,* p. 325.

30. PHS, *Pickett's Charge at Gettysburg,* pp. 11–12; CVSR, NA; Carter, "Flag of the Fifty-Third Va. Regiment, " *CV,* p. 263.

31. CVSR, NA; Carter, "Flag of the Fifty-Third Va. Regiment, " *CV,* p. 263; Steve Smith, "My Confederate Ancestors: Sergeant Thomas Booker Tredway and Capt. William Marshall Tredway, " *The Gilmore Blade,* Col. H. W. Gilmore Camp, Sons of Confederate Veterans, January 2011.

32. Williams to Daniels, n.d., UV; Motts, *"Trust in God and Fear Nothing, "* pp. 4–33, 45–48.

33. Durkin, ed., *John Dooley, Confederate Soldier*, p. 107.

34. Finley, "Bloody Angle, " *Buffalo Evening News*, May 28, 1894.

35. Lewis, *Recollections from 1860 to 1865*, p. 85.

36. Bishop, *The Tennessee Brigade*, pp. 214, 217; Hess, *Pickett's Charge*, p. 250.

37. Rollins, ed., *Pickett's Charge*, pp. 328–329, 333–335; Gragg, *Covered with Glory*, 199–200; CVSR, NA; CNCSR, NA; Shultz, *"Double Canister at Ten Yards, "* pp. 56–57.

38. Williams to Daniels, n.d., UV.

39. Finley, "Bloody Angle, " *Buffalo Evening News*, May 28, 1894; Carhart, *Lost Triumph*, pp. xi–260; Hatch, *Glorious War*, pp. 1–3, 139–159; Cowell, *Tactics at Gettysburg*, p. 81; Hess, *Pickett's Charge*, p. 262.

40. Diary of George Griggs, SHSP, p. 250; Harrison and Busey, *Nothing but Glory*, pp. 91–92.

41. CVSR, NA; Harrison and Busey, *Nothing but Glory*, p. 115; George K. Griggs, "Memorandum of Thirty-eighth Virginia Infantry, " *Southern Historical Society Papers*, vol. 24 (1886), p. 253.

42. Diary of Francis Moses Wafer, QUL; Hess, *Pickett's Charge*, p. 264; Shultz, *"Double Canister at Ten Yards, "* pp. 55–56.

43. Hatch, *Glorious War*, pp. 1–2, 139–154; Cowell, *Tactics at Gettysburg*, p. 81; Carhart, *Lost Triumph*, pp. xi–260.

44. CVSR, NA; Finley, "Bloody Angle, " *Buffalo Evening News*, May 28, 1894; Harrison and Busey, *Nothing but Glory*, pp. 102–103; Hess, *Pickett's Charge*, pp. 262, 269.

45. CVSR, NA; Harrison and Busey, *Nothing but Glory*, p. 103.

46. Norman F. Cantor, *Alexander the Great, Journey to the End of the Earth* (New York: HarperCollins Publishers, 2005), pp. 8–9; Finley, "Bloody Angle, " *Buffalo Evening News*, May 28, 1894.

47. Rollins, ed., *Pickett's Charge*, pp. 237–240, 252–253, 330, 345; Ernsberger, *At the Wall*, pp. 117–120; Gottfried, *Stopping Pickett*, pp. 175–178; Reardon, *Pickett's Charge*, p. 26; Harrison and Busey, *Nothing but Glory*, p. 98; Hess, *Pickett's Charge*, pp. 262, 280–286.

48. Bowden and Ward, *Last Chance for Victory*, p. 464.

49. Dungan, *Distant Drums*, p. 35.

50. Lewis, *Recollections from 1860 to 1865*, p. 85.

51. Rollins, ed., *Pickett's Charge*, pp. 246–247.

52. Daniel Bonds Recollections, Minnesota Historical Society, St. Paul, Minnesota; Harrison and Busey, *Nothing but Glory*, p. 106.

53. Daniel Bonds Recollections, MHS.

54. Finley, "Bloody Angle, " *Buffalo Evening News*, May 28, 1894.

55. CVSR, NA; Rollins, ed., *Pickett's Charge*, p. 253.

56. Rollins, ed., *Pickett's Charge*, p. 330; Hess, *Pickett's Charge*, p. 245.

57. Reardon, *Pickett's Charge*, p. 26.

58. Evault Boswell, *Texas Boys in Gray* (Plano: Republic of Texas Press, 2000), p. 78.

59. The Weider History Group, Gettysburg, p. 78.

60. Clay, "About the Death of General Garnett, " *CV*, p. 81.

61. Huntington, "A Monumental Lie?" *CWT*, p. 53.

62. Ibid.; Pennsylvania Civil War Battle Flags, Historical List of Pennsylvania Civil War Color-Bearers, Internet; Hess, *Pickett's Charge*, pp. 262, 289–291.

63. CVSR, NA.

64. *Buffalo Evening News*, May 28, 1894; Hess, *Pickett's Charge*, p. 269; CVSR, NA.

65. Lewis, *Recollections from 1860 to 1865*, p. 86.

66. Stewart, *Pickett's Charge*, p. 210.

67. Ibid., p. 236.

68. CVSR, NA; Diary of Walter A. Van Rensselaer, Gettysburg National Military Park, Gettysburg, Pennsylvania; Hess, *Pickett's Charge*, p. 287.

69. CVSR, NA.

70. CVSR, NA; Harrison and Busey, *Nothing but Glory*, pp. 99–100.

71. Harrison and Busey, *Nothing but Glory*, pp. 113–115; CVSR, NA.

72. Joseph H. De Castro Information, National Museum of the American Latino Commission, Washington, DC; Hess, *Pickett's Charge*, p. 287; Stewart, *Pickett's Charge*, p. 211.

73. Coffin, *Nine Months to Gettysburg*, pp. 235–237; Coddington, *The Gettysburg Campaign*, pp. 519–520.

74. Hess, *Pickett's Charge*, pp. 15, 32–33; Coffin, *Nine Months to Gettysburg*, p. 236; Coddington, *The Gettysburg Campaign*, pp. 519–520.

75. Rollins, ed., *Pickett's Charge*, pp. 246–247.

76. Coffin, *Nine Months to Gettysburg*, pp. 10, 22, 237, 296; Rollins, ed., *Pickett's Charge*, pp. 259–360.

77. Coffin, *Nine Months to Gettysburg*, p. 22.

78. *Carolina Watchman*, September 6, 1883; *Fayetteville Observer*, April 18, 1864.

79. W. B. Taylor to family, July 29, 1863, National Park Service Archives, Gettysburg National Military Park, Gettysburg, Pennsylvania.

80. *Richmond Enquirer*, March 18, 1864; Gragg, *Covered with Glory*, p. 238.

81. *Richmond Enquirer*, March 18, 1864; Gragg, *Covered with Glory*, pp. 52–53, 199–201, 203; CNCSR, NA; *Carolina Watchman*, September 15, 1887; *Fayetteville Observer*, April 18, 1864.

82. Gragg, *Covered with Glory*, pp. 209–210, 218–219.

83. Bishop, *The Tennessee Brigade*, pp. 216–217.

84. Hess, *Pickett's Charge*, pp. 333–334.

85. Rollins, ed., *Pickett's Charge*, p. 186; Coddington, *The Gettysburg Campaign*, pp. 519–520.

86. CVSR, NA; Harrison and Busey, *Nothing but Glory*, pp. 100–101.

87. CVSR, NA; Captain A. N. Jones Report, George Edward Pickett Papers, Perkins Library, Duke University, Durham, North Carolina.

88. CVSR, NA; Harrison and Busey, *Nothing but Glory*, p. 101.

89. Ibid.

90. Rollins, ed., *Pickett's Charge*, pp. 202–203.

91. CVSR, NA; Harrison and Busey, *Nothing but Glory*, p. 106.

92. Rollins, ed., *Pickett's Charge*, pp. 202–203; CVSR, NA.

93. Finley, "Bloody Angle, " *Buffalo Evening News,* May 28, 1894.

94. CVSR, NA; Harrison and Busey, *Nothing but Glory*, p. 113.

95. Gayle Diary, GNMP.

96. Boritt, ed., *The Gettysburg Nobody Knows,* p. 131.

97. Gragg, *Covered with Glory,* p. 211.

98. Harrison and Busey, *Nothing but Glory,* p. 92.

99. CVSR, NA; "Col. & Dr. R. W. Martin, " *Confederate Veteran,* vol. v (1897), p. 70.

100. Mary Lasswell, comp. and ed., *Rags and Hope, The Recollections of Val. C. Giles, Four Years with Hood's Brigade, Fourth Texas Infantry, 1861–1865,* (New York: Coward-McCann, 1961), p. 145.

101. Hirst letter to Sarah, n.d., ASC.

102. Durkin, ed., *John Dooley, Confederate Soldier,* p. 107.

103. Gragg, *Covered with Glory,* p. 205.

104. Reardon, *Pickett's Charge,* p. 26.

105. Cockrell, ed., *Gunner with Stonewall,* p. 75.

106. Ibid.

107. Haskell, *The Battle of Gettysburg,* p. 113.

108. *Carolina Watchman,* September 15, 1887.

109. Harrison and Busey, *Nothing but Glory,* p. 103.

110. Cockrell, ed., *Gunner with Stonewall,* p. 75.

111. Ibid.

112. Reardon, *Pickett's Charge,* p. 27.

113. Gragg, *Covered with Glory,* pp. 205–206, 231; CNCSR, NA.

114. Stewart, *Pickett's Charge,* pp. 222, 242.

115. Time-Life Editors, *Voices of the Civil War, Gettysburg,* p. 157; Stewart,, *Pickett's Charge,* pp. 15, 32–33; Hess, *Pickett's Charge,* pp. 15, 32–33; Dowdey, *Death of a Nation,* p. 253; Robertson, *General A. P. Hill,* pp. 223–224; Coddington, *The Gettysburg Campaign,* pp. 512–513.

116. Waters and Edmonds, *A Small but Spartan Band,* pp. 9, 78–79, 82, 184; Coddington, *The Gettysburg Campaign,* pp. 519–520; Rollins, ed., *Pickett's Charge,* p. 169; Coffin, *Three Months to Gettysburg,* p. 238; Hess, *Pickett's Charge,* pp. 15, 32–33, 296–305; Boritt, ed., *The Gettysburg Nobody Knows,* p. 23; Wert, *A Glorious Army,* pp. 269, 274–275; Reardon, *Pickett's Charge,* pp. 27, 29; Cowell, *Tactics at Gettysburg,* pp. 77–79.

117. Lasswell, comp. and ed., *Rags and Hope,* p. 191.

118. John A. Herndon to brother, July 11, 1863, CS.

119. Stewart, *Pickett's Charge,* p. 223.

120. Ibid., p. 227; CVSR, NA.

121. Anderson and Anderson, *The Generals,* p. 422.

122. Coco, *On the Bloodstained Field,* pp. 67–68.

123. Anderson and Anderson, *The Generals,* p. 424; Reardon, *Pickett's Charge,* p. 28; Durkin, ed., *John Dooley, Confederate Soldier,* p. 107.

124. Reardon, *Pickett's Charge,* p. 30.

125. Gabor Boritt, *The Gettysburg Gospel, The Lincoln Speech That Nobody Knows* (New York: Simon and Schuster, 2006), p. 4.

126. *Journal,* Boston, Massachusetts, July 6, 1863.

127. CVSR, NA; Trask, *9th Virginia Infantry,* p. 26.

128. Longacre, *Pickett,* pp. 3–4, 10.

129. Chandler, *The Campaigns of Napoleon,* pp. 1064–1094

130. Durkin, ed., *John Dooley, Confederate Soldier,* p. 107.

131. Coffin, *Nine Months to Gettysburg,* p. 10; Rollins, ed., *Pickett's Charge,* p. 257.

132. Harrison, *Pickett's Men,* pp. 40, 43.

133. Walker, "The Charge of Pickett's Division by a Participant, " *VSL*; CVSR, NA.

134. *Philadelphia Inquirer*, Philadelphia, Pennsylvania, July 6, 1863.

135. *The Times*, Philadelphia, Pennsylvania, March 26, 1882; CNCSR, NA;

136. Chandler, *The Campaigns of Napoleon,* pp. 338–339; Hess, *Pickett's Charge,* p. 36.

137. Chandler, *The Campaigns of Napoleon,* pp. 362–363, 425–438.

138. Ibid., p. 438.

139. Lewis, *Recollections from 1860 to 1865,* p. 86; Bara, "One Mile of Open Ground, " *CWT,* pp. 34–35; Chandler, *The Campaigns of Napoleon,* pp. 1064–1094; Gragg, *Covered with Glory,* p. 42; Boritt, ed., *The Gettysburg Nobody Knows,* p. 131.

140. Murray, "Brig. Gen. Alexander Hays' Division at Gettysburg, " *GM,* p. 95.

141. Ibid.

142. Cleaves, *Meade of Gettysburg,* pp. 157–169.

143. Joseph Graham to father, July 30, 1863, Papers of William A. Graham, SHSC, UNC.

144. Wert, *A Glorious Army,* pp. 269, 274–275; Coddington, *The Gettysburg Campaign,* pp. 519–520; Hess, *Pickett's Charge,* pp. 15, 32–33; Tucker, *Lee and Longstreet at Gettysburg,* pp. 95, 108; *Annals of the War,* pp. 313–316; McKenzie, *Uncertain Glory,* p. 160; Thomas, *Robert E. Lee,* p. 302; Cowell, *Tactics at Gettysburg,* pp. 77–78; Gordon, *General George E. Pickett in Life and Legend,* p. 115; Robertson, *General A. P. Hill,* pp. 223–224.

145. Lewis, *Recollections from 1860 to 1865,* p. 86.

146. Time-Life Editors, *Voices of the Civil War, Gettysburg,* p. 157.

147. Hess, *Pickett's Charge,* pp. 15, 32–33; Thomas, *Robert E. Lee,* p. 302; Mitchell, *Military Leaders in the Civil War,* pp. 146–148; Cowell, *Tactics at Gettysburg,* pp. 77–78.

148. Durkin, ed., *John Dooley Confederate Soldier,* p. 107.

149. Cahart, *Lee's Triumph,* pp. xi–260; Cowell, *Tactics at Gettysburg,* pp. 78–79, 81; Emory M. Thomas, *Bold Dragon, The Life of J.E.B. Stuart* (New York: Harper and Row, 1986), pp. 248–249; *Annals of the War,* p. 215; Chandler, *The Campaigns of Napoleon,* p. 363; Hess, *Pickett's Charge,* pp. 15, 32–33; Dowdey, *Death of a Nation,* pp. 253, 257; Thomas, *Robert E. Lee,* p. 302; Hatch, *Glorious War,* pp. 1–3, 139–159; Boritt, ed., *The Gettysburg Nobody Knows,* p. 114; Robertson, *General A. P. Hill,* pp. 223–224; Coddington, *The Gettysburg Campaign,* pp. 519–520.

150. Thomas, *Robert E. Lee,* p. 302; Robertson, *General A. P. Hill,* pp. 220, 222–224; McWhiney and Jamieson, *Attack and Die,* pp. 3–191; Hess, *Pickett's Charge,* pp. 15–19, 32–33.

151. Rollins, ed., *Pickett's Charge,* pp. 21–22; Hess, *Pickett's Charge,* pp. 15, 32–33.

152. Hess, *Pickett's Charge,* pp. 15, 32–33; Rollins, ed., *Pickett's Charge,* pp. 42–44; CVSR, NA.

153. Hess, *Pickett's Charge,* pp. 15, 32–33.

154. Cowell, *Tactics at Gettysburg,* pp. 78–79.

155. Murray, "Brig. Gen. Alexander Hays' Division at Gettysburg, " *GM,* p. 95.

156. CVSR, NA; Blackford, ed., *Letters from Lee's Army,* p. 188.

157. Boritt, ed., *The Gettysburg Nobody Knows,* p. 24.

158. Wert, *A Glorious Army,* p. 277.

159. Rollins, ed., *Pickett's Charge,* p. 1; CVSR, NA.

160. *Charlotte Observer,* Charlotte, North Carolina, November 16, 1892.

161. Reardon, *Pickett's Charge,* p. 28.

162. The Weider History Group, Gettysburg, p. 72; CVSR, NA.

163. Coco, *Wasted Valor,* p. 42.

164. Harrison and Busey, *Nothing but Glory,* pp. 138, 169; Priest, *Into the Fight,* p. 199.

165. Priest, *Into the Fight,* p. 199.

166. Hess, *Pickett's Charge,* pp. 333–334.

167. Ibid., p. 335.

168. Crewdsdon, *Love and War,* pp. 102–103.

169. Stewart, *Pickett's Charge,* pp. 237–238.

170. Faust, *The Republic of Suffering,* p. 69; Boritt, *The Gettysburg Gospel,* p. 6.

171. Elizabeth W. Farnham, July 7, 1863, Gettysburg National Military Park Library, Gettysburg, Pennsylvania; CVSR, NA.

172. Boritt, *The Gettysburg Gospel,* p. 5.

173. Diary of George Griggs, SHSP, p. 250.

174. Crewdson, *Love and War,* p. 103.

175. Boritt, *The Gettysburg Gospel,* p. 9.

176. Coco, *Wasted Valor,* pp. 27, 107.

177. Wert, *A Glorious Army,* p. 281.

178. Crewdson, *Love and War,* p. 105.

179. CVSR, NA; Harrison and Busey, *Nothing but Glory,* p. 139.

180. Diary of George Griggs, SHSP, p. 250; CVSR, NA.

181. R. F. White to his Ross cousins, August 2, 1863, Ross Family Correspondence, 1861–1864, Accession No. 21089, Virginia State Library, Richmond, Virginia; CVSR, NA; Biographical Information, Ross Family Correspondence, VSL.

182. Boritt, *The Gettysburg Gospel,* p. 11; Gragg, *Covered with Glory,* p. 213; Coco, *Wasted Valor,* pp.

183. Reid Mitchell, *Civil War Soldiers, Their Expectations and Experiences* (New York: Viking, 1988), p. 62.

184. Faust, *This Republic of Suffering,* p. 63.

185. Diary of George Griggs, SHSP, p. 250.

186. Durkin, ed., *John Dooley, Confederate Soldier,* p. 109; CVSR, NA; Boritt, *The Gettysburg Gospel,* pp. 19–20; Tucker, *Lee and Longstreet at Gettysburg,* p. 107

187. *Richmond Daily Dispatch,* July 13, 1863; CVSR, NA.

188. CVSR, NA; Boritt, *The Gettysburg Gospel*, pp. 20–21.
189. Coco, *Wasted Valor*, pp. 117–119.
190. Ibid., p. 119.
191. Ibid., p. 129.
192. Gage Family Collection, Special Collections, University of Mississippi Libraries, University of Mississippi, University, Mississippi; Stewart, *Pickett's Charge*, p. 203; Hess, *Pickett's Charge*, p. 334.
193. The Brave Tennesseans, Flickr, Internet.
194. CVSR, NA; Lewis, *Recollections from 1860 to 1865*, p. 87; Motts, *"Trust in God and Fear Nothing, "* p. 8; Hess, *Pickett's Charge*, p. 317; A. J. A. J. Langguth, *Union 1812, The Americans Who Fought in the Second War of Independence,* (London: Simon and Schuster, 2006), pp. 318–321.
195. Durkin, ed., *John Dooley, Confederate Soldier,* p. 121.
196. Halleran, *"'The Widow's Son', " GM*, p. 105; Motts, *"Trust in God and Fear Nothing, "* pp. 46, 48; The Weider History Group, Gettysburg, p. 7.
197. CVSR, NA.
198. Motts, *"Trust in God and Fear Nothing, "* pp. 4, 8, 48; Tucker, *Lee and Longstreet at Gettysburg,* p. 144.
199. CVSR, NA.
200. Gayle Diary, CVSR, NA.
201. CVSR, NA; CNCSR, NA.
202. Crewdson, *Love and War,* p. 107.
203. Blackford, ed., *Letters from Lee's Army,* p. 190.
204. Cowell, *Tactics at Gettysburg,* p. 78.

Chapter IX

1. Hatch, *Glorious War,* p. 152.
2. Shuffler, ed., *The Adventures of a Prisoner of War,* pp. 5–7, 53–54; Lasswell, comp. and ed., *Rags and Hope,* p. 103.
3. Lasswell, comp. and ed., *Rags and Hope,* p. 103; Hatch, *Glorious War,* pp. 1–3, 139–159; Carhart, *Lost Triumph,* pp. xi–260; Cowell, *Tactics at Gettysburg,* p. 81.
4. Reardon, *Pickett's Charge,* p. 30.
5. Time-Life Editors, *Voices of the Civil War, Gettysburg,* p. 157; Thomas, *Robert E. Lee,* pp. 301–302; Wert, *A Glorious Army,* pp. 274–275, 282.
6. John A. Herndon to brother, July 11, 1863, CS.
7. Cowell, *Tactics at Gettysburg,* p. 79.
8. Hess, *Pickett's Charge,* pp. 11–19, 32–33; Stewart, *Pickett's Charge,* pp. 205–206; Carhart, *Lost Triumph,* pp. xi–260; Hatch, *Glorious War,* pp. 1–3, 139–140.
9. Hess, *Pickett's Charge,* p. 19.
10. Gottfried, *"To Fail Twice, " GM*, p. 74.

11. George Wilson Booth, *Personal Reminiscences of a Maryland Soldier in the War Between the States, 1861–1865* (Gaithersburg, Md.: Butternut Press, 1986), p. 92; Wert, *A Glorious Army*, pp. 269, 274–274; Cowell, *Tactics at Gettysburg*, pp. 78–79.

12. Cowell, *Tactics at Gettysburg*, p. 77.

13. Foote, *The Civil War*, vol. 2, p. 523.

14. Terry L. Jones, ed., *The Civil War Memoirs of Captain William J. Seymour: Reminiscences of a Louisiana Tiger* (Baton Rouge: Louisiana State University Press, 1991), p. 79; Wert, *A Glorious Army*, pp. 274–275, 282; Creighton, *The Colors of Courage*, p. xix; Harrison and Busey, *Nothing but Glory*, pp. 60–61, 117; Cowell, *Tactics at Gettysburg*, pp. 78–79; Hess, *Pickett's Charge*, pp. 15, 32–33.

15. Gordon, *General George E. Pickett in Life and Legend*, p. 115; Longacre, *Pickett*, pp. 122, 126; Harrison and Busey, *Nothing but Glory*, pp. 60–61; Coddington, *The Gettysburg Campaign*, pp. 519–530; Wright, *A Glorious Army*, pp. 269, 275; Stewart, *Pickett's Charge*, pp. 206–207; Cowell, *Tactics at Gettysburg*, pp. 78–79; Dowdy, *Death of a Nation*, p. 285.

16. McWhiney and Jamieson, *Attack and Die*, pp. 120–121; Harrison and Busey, *Nothing but Glory*, pp. 60–62; Longacre, *Pickett*, pp. 122, 126; Stewart, *Pickett's Charge*, pp. 206–207.

17. Shultz, *"Double Canister at Ten Yards,"* pp. 1–67; Dowdey, *Death of a Nation*, p. 284.

18. Dowdey, *Death of a Nation*, p. 287.

19. Gordon, *General George E. Pickett in Life and Legend*, p. 116.

20. Longacre, *Pickett*, p. 126.

21. Harrison and Busey, *Nothing but Glory*, p. 61.

22. Ibid.

23. Coddington, *The Gettysburg Campaign*, p. 502.

24. Gordon, *General George E. Pickett in Life and Legend*, p. 115; Coddington, *The Gettysburg Campaign*, pp. 501, 519–520; Cowell, *Tactics at Gettysburg*, pp. 78–79; Robertson, *General A. P. Hill*, pp. 222–224; Harrison and Busey, *Nothing but Glory*, p. 61; Hess, *Pickett's Charge*, pp. 15, 32–33; Wert, *A Glorious Army*, pp. 269, 275.

25. Stackpole, *They Met at Gettysburg*, p. 248.

26. Durkin, ed., *John Dooley, Confederate Soldier*, p. 107.

27. Wert, *A Glorious Army*, pp. 281–282.

28. William Calder to mother, July 8, 1863, Box 8, Robert L. Brake Collection, United States Army Military History Institute, Carlisle Barracks, Carlisle, Pennsylvania.

29. Douglas, *riding With Stonewall*, p. 242.

30. Anderson and Anderson, *The Generals*, p. 384; Mitchell, *Military Leaders in the Civil War*, pp. 146–148; Coddington, *The Gettysburg Campaign*, pp. 519–520.

31. Lee, *Recollections and Letters of General Lee*, p. 415.

32. *Southern Illustrated News*, Richmond, Virginia, August 1, 1863.

33. Thomas, *Robert E. Lee*, pp. 301–302; Wert, *A Glorious Army*, pp. 274–275, 282.

34. George E. Pickett to LaSalle Corbell, July 23, 1863, Arthur Crew Inman Papers, 1856–1963, John Hay Library, Brown University, Providence, Rhode Island.

35. *Augusta Daily Constitutionalist,* Augusta, Georgia, July 7, 1863; Rollins, ed., *Pickett's Charge,* p. 265.

36. Hess, *Pickett's Charge,* p. 327.

37. Durkin, ed., *John Dooley, Confederate Soldier,* pp. 102–103; Hess, *Pickett's Charge,* pp. 15, 32–33, 306; Robertson, *General A. P. Hill,* pp. 222–224; Wert, *A Glorious Army,* pp. 274–275; Waters and Edmonds, *A Small but Spartan Band,* pp. 74–79; Coddington, *The Gettysburg Campaign,* pp. 519–520; Cowell, *Tactics at Gettysburg,* pp. 77–79; Tucker, *Lee and Longstreet at Gettysburg,* pp. 114–115; Coffin, *Three Months to Gettysburg,* pp. xviii–238.

38. Reardon, *Pickett's Charge,* p. 32.

39. Ibid., p. 32; Hess, *Pickett's Charge,* pp. 80–81, 182, 248.

40. William H. Cocke to William Cocke, July 11, 1863, Cocke Family Papers, 1794–1981, Virginia Historical Society, Richmond, Virginia.

41. *Raleigh Observer,* October 10, 1877, Raleigh, North Carolina; Coddington, *The Gettysburg Campaign,* pp. 506–507.

42. Louis G. Young to Major William J. Baker, February 10, 1864, Francis Donnell Winston Papers, 1787, 1828–1943, Southern Historical Collection, University of North Carolina, Chapel Hill, North Carolina; Louis G. Young Obituary, *Confederate Veteran Magazine,* vol. 30 (August 1922), p. 306.

43. *Fayetteville Observer,* April 18, 1864.

44. Louis G. Young to Major William J. Baker, February 10, 1864, Francis Donnell Winston Papers, 1787, 1828–1943, SHC; Young Obituary, *CV,* p. 306; Louis G. Young to William Pettigrew, July 2, 1862, Louis Round Wilson Special Collections Library, University of North Carolina, Chapel Hill, North Carolina.

45. *Annals of the War,* p. 315.

46. Ibid., p. 313.

47. Wert, *A Glorious Army,* pp. 274–275, 281–282.

48. Johnson, *Napoleon,* pp. 49–72; Alexander, *Sun Tzu and Gettysburg,* p. 45.

49. Rollins, ed., *Pickett's Charge,* p. 10.

50. Ibid.

51. Bowden and Ward, *Last Chance for Victory,* p. 439.

52. Alexander, *Sun Tzu at Gettysburg,* p. 124.

53. Tower, ed., *Lee's Adjutant,* pp. 1–2; *Annals of the War,* pp. 313–316.

54. William Calder to mother, July 8, 1863, Box 8, Robert L. Brake Collection, United States Army Military History Institute, Carlisle Barracks, Pennsylvania; Calder Family Papers, 1817–1886, Collection No. 00125, Southern Historical Collection, University of North Carolina, Chapel Hill, North Carolina..

55. Harrison and Busey, *Nothing but Glory,* p. 120; Cowell, *Tactics at Gettysburg,* pp. 78–79.

56. Thomas, *Robert E. Lee,* p. 301.

57. Ibid., pp. 301–302; Cowell, *Tactics at Gettysburg,* pp. 78–79; Hess, *Pickett's Charge,* pp. 15–20, 32–33; Time-Life Editors, *Voices of the Civil War, Gettysburg,* p. 148; Wert, *A Glorious Army,* pp. 274–275, 281–282; Coddington, *The Gettysburg Campaign,* pp. 519–520.

58. Time-Life Editors, *Voices of the Civil War, Gettysburg,* p. 157; CVSR, NA.

59. John A. Herndon to brother, July 11, 1863, CS.

60. Hess, *Pickett's Charge,* p. 326.

61. Durkin, ed., *John Dooley, Confederate Soldier,* p. 104.

62. Foote, *The Civil War,* vol. 2, 568.

63. John A. Herndon to brother, July 11, 1863, CS.

64. Charles Edward Lippitt Diary, Charles Edward Lippitt Diary and Medical Record Book, 1862–1853, Louis Round Wilson Special Collections Library, University of North Carolina Library, Chapel Hill, North Carolina.

65. CVSR, NA; Trask, *9th Virginia Infantry,* p. 29; Harrison and Busey, *Nothing but Glory,* p. 468.

66. CVSR, NA.

67. Ibid.

68. Ibid.

69. CVSR, NA; Benjamin Lyons Farinholt letter to Lelia May Farinholt, August 11, 1863, Benjamin Lyons Farinholt Papers, G. Selden Richardson, Richmond, Virginia; John Selby, *The Road to Yorktown* (New York: St. Martin's Press, 1976), pp. 179–198.

70. James T. Morehead Diary, James T. Morehead Papers, 1753–1919, Collection No. 00523, Southern Historical Collection, University of North Carolina, Chapel Hill, North Carolina.

71. CVSR, NA; O'Grady, *Clear the Confederate Ways!,* p. 164; Durkin, ed., *John Dooley, Confederate Soldier,* pp. 107–110.

72. CVSR, NA.

73. Ibid.; Spessard Family Papers, CCHS; Rollins, ed., *Pickett's Charge,* p. 181.

74. CSRV, NA; Spessard Family Papers, CCHS; Berrier, "Craig County Gave its All at the Battle of Gettysburg, " *Roanoke Times,* Roanoke, Virginia, July 3, 2013.

75. Spessard Family Papers, CCHS.

76. CNCSR, NA; C. M. Avery to Father, July 18; 1863, Tod Robinson Caldwell Papers, 1801–1890, UNC; *The News and Observer,* September 24, 1887.

77. Kemper to Nannie L. Pollock, September 7, 1863, Museum Quality Americana Online; CVSR, NA.

78. CVSR, NA; Barron, Barrow, and Rosenburg, *Forgotten Confederates, JCH,* pp. 33–34; Branch, "The Yale Men Who Died at Gettysburg, " *Yale Alumni Magazine,* July 3, 2013, Online; A. D. Pollock Papers, 1794–1944, SHC, UNC.

79. CNCSR, NA; Cowell, *Tactics at Gettysburg,* p. 81; Gragg, *Covered with Glory,* pp. 31–33, 211, 215–217.

80. Gragg, *Covered with Glory,* p. 236.

81. Longacre, *Pickett,* pp. 165–167; Charles Bracelen Flood, *Lee, The Last Years* (Boston, Mass.: Houghton Mifflin Company, 1981), p. 231.

82. George E. Pickett to LaSalle Corbell, July 23, 1863, Inman Papers, JHL; Longacre, *Pickett,* p. x.

83. Tower, ed., *Lee's Adjutant,* p. 101; Davis, *The Rise and Fall of the Confederate Government,* p. 428; Gramm, *Gettysburg,* p. 8; Alexander, *Sun Tzu at Gettysburg,* pp. 123–125; Nolan, *Lee Considered,* pp. 99–100; Thomas, *Robert E. Lee,* pp. 301–302.

84. Durkin, ed., *John Dooley, Confederate Soldier*, p. 107.

85. Waters and Edmonds, *A Small but Spartan Band*, p. 86; Reardon, *Pickett's Charge*, pp. 154–213.

86. Carhart, *Lost Triumph*, pp. xi–260; Cowell, *Tactics at Gettysburg*, p. 81.

87. Hess, *Pickett's Charge*, p. 397.

88. Carhart, *Lost Triumph*, pp. 1–269; Hatch, *Glorious War*, pp. 1–3, 139–159; Chandler, *The Campaigns of Napoleon*, p. 363; Cowell, *Tactics at Gettysburg*, pp. 77–78, 81.

89. Durkin, ed., *John Dooley, Confederate Soldier*, p. 107; Carhart, *Lost Triumph*, pp. 1–269; Thomas, *Robert E. Lee*, pp. 301–302; Hess, *Pickett's Charge*, pp. 15–19, 32–33; Robertson, *General A. P. Hill*, pp. 222–224; Wert, *A Glorious Army*, pp. 274–275, 281–282; Hatch, *Glorious War*, pp. 1–3, 139–159; Cowell, *Tactics at Gettysburg*, pp. 77–78, 81.

90. Alexander, *Sun Tzu at Gettysburg,*, p. 125.

91. *Richmond Sentinel*, Richmond, Virginia, July 16, 1863; Faust, *The Republic of Suffering*, p. xi; Connelly and Bellows, *God and General Longstreet*, p. 50; Mitchell, *Military Leaders in the Civil War*, p. 148; Gramm, *Gettysburg*, p. 8; Nolan, *Lee Considered*, pp. 99–100; Alexander, *Sun Tzu at Gettysburg*, p. 123; *Mercury*, Charleston, South Carolina, July 16 and 30, 1863; Stevens, ed., *As if it Were Glory*, p. 133.

92. *Richmond Dispatch*, June 12, 1861; Connelly and Bellows, *God and General Longstreet*, pp. 1–107; Curry, *God's Rebels*, pp. 1–6; Reardon, *Pickett's Charge*, pp. 154–213; Thomas, *Robert E. Lee*, pp. 301–302, 307.

93. *Richmond Dispatch*, June 12, 1861; Nolan, *Lee Considered*, p. 3; Curry, *God's Rebels*, pp. 1–6; Reardon, *Pickett's Charge*, pp. 154–213; CVSR, NA; CNCSR, NA.

94. CVSR, NA; *Final Report on the Battlefield of Gettysburg, New York Monuments Commission for the Battlefields of Gettysburg and Chattanooga* (2 vols) (Albany, N.Y.: J. B. Lyon Printer, 1900), vol. 2, pp. 1308–1309; Young and Young, *Into the Jaws of Hell*, p. 181; Christian S. Prillaman 1862 letter, Dr. James I. Roberton Collection, Blacksburg, Virginia; CVSR, NA.

95. Hess, *Pickett's Charge*, pp. 15–19, 32–33; Time-Life Editors, *Voices of the Civil War, Gettysburg*, p. 148; Cowell, *Tactics at Gettysburg*, pp. 78–79.

96. Wert, *A Glorious Army*, p. 281.

97. Mayo, "Pickett's Charge at Gettysburg," *SHSP*, p. 335.

98. Ibid.; Paul D. Escott, *After Secession, Jefferson Davis and the Failure of Confederate Nationalism* (Baton Rouge: Louisiana State University Press, 1978), pp. ix–xii, 19–255; Watkins, Sam, *"Co. Aytch," A Side Show of the Big Show* (New York: Collier Books, 1962), pp. 46–47.

99. Fawcett, ed., *How to Lose a War*, p. 290.

100. C. Van Woodward and Elisabeth Muhlenfeld, *The Private Mary Chesnut, The Unpublished Civil War Diaries* (New York: Oxford University Press, 1984), p. 258.

101. Henry T. Owen to wife, December 21, 1863, Henry T. Owen Papers, Virginia State Library, Richmond, Virginia; Harrison and Busey, *Nothing but Glory*, p. 275.

102. Woodward, ed., *Mary Chesnut's Civil War*, p. 591.

103. Ibid., p. 412.

104. *Richmond Daily Dispatch,* July 13, 1863.

105. Jane Mitchel to James Mitchel, June 10 (no year), Gettysburg National Military Park Library, Gettysburg, Pennsylvania; Tucker, *Irish Confederates,* pp. 90–91; *Irish-American,* August 29, 1863; Durkin, ed., *John Dooley, Confederate Soldier,* p. xv; CVSR, NA.

106. *Irish-American,* August 29, 1863.

107. Jane Mitchel to James Mitchel, June 10, GNMPL.

108. Time-Life Editors, *Voices of Gettysburg, Gettysburg,* p. 163.

109. F. Lewis Marshall to uncle, October 6, 1863, VMI; CNCSR, NA.

110. J. Roderick Heller and Carolyn A. Heller, eds., *The Confederacy Is on Her Way Up the Spout, Letters to South Carolina 1861–1865* (Columbia: University of South Carolina Press, 1998), p. 119.

111. Coco, *Wasted Valor,* p. 163.

112. *Lutheran Observer,* Baltimore, Maryland, August 21, 1863.

113. Coco, *Wasted Valor,* p. 174, note 44.

114. Ibid., p. 164.

115. Marc Charisse, "Yes, There Are Still Bodies on the Battlefield of Gettysburg, " *The Evening Sun,* Hanover, Pennsylvania.

116. *Hispanics and the Civil War: From Battlefield to Homefront* (Washington, DC: National Park Service, n.d.), pp. 1–10, 17; ; Phillip Thomas Tucker, ed., *Cubans in the Confederacy, Jose Agustin Quintero, Ambrosio Jose Gonzales, and Loreta Janeta Velazquez* (Jefferson, N.C.: McFarland and Company, Inc., Publishers, 2002), pp. 94, 98; CVSR, NA; CNCSR, NA; Waters and Edmonds, *A Small but Spartan Band,* p. 10; Ernsberger, *At the Wall,* pp. 11–137.

117. Waters and Edmonds, *A Small but Spartan Band,* p. 79; Compiled Service Records of Confederate Soldiers Who Served in Organizations from Florida, Record Group 109, National Archives, Washington, DC

118. CVSR, NA.

119. B. A. Botkin, ed., *Civil War Treasury of Tales, Legends and Folklore* (New York: Random House, 1960), p. 480.

120. CVSR, NA; William Henry Cocke to William Cocke, July 11, 1863, Cocke Family Papers, VHS.

121. Ibid.

122. Reardon, *Pickett's Charge,* pp. 4, 108–213; John A. Herndon to brother, July 11, 1863, CS; William Henry Cocke to Parents, July 14, 1862, Cocke Family Papers, 1794–1981, VHS.

123. Reardon, *Pickett's Charge,* pp. 3–4, 32, 34; Bishop, *The Tennessee Brigade,* p. 230.

Epilogue

1. Rollins, ed., *Pickett's Charge,* p. 74.

2. Cowell, *Tactics at Gettysburg,* pp. 78–79; Thomas, *Robert E. Lee,* pp. 301–302, 307; Longacre, *Pickett,* p. 117.

3. Thomas, *Robert E. Lee,* pp. 301–302.

4. Hess, *Pickett's Charge,* pp. 15–19, 32–33; Robertson, *General A. P. Hill,* pp. 217–224; Coddington, *The Gettysburg Campaign,* pp. 442–460; Carhart, *Lost Triumph,* pp. xi–260; Hatch, *Glorious War,* pp. 1–3, 139–159; McKenzie, *Uncertain Glory,* pp. 146–148, 158–160; Tower, ed., *Lee's Adjutant,* p. 61; Thomas, *Robert E. Lee,* pp. 296–302; Mitchell, *Military Leaders of the Civil War,* pp. 146–148; Cowell, *Tactics at Gettysburg,* pp. 78–79, 81; Piston, *Lee's Tarnished Lieutenant,* p. 49.

5. Bowden and Ward, *Last Chance for Victory,* p. 439; Cowell, *Tactics at Gettysburg,* pp. 78–79, 81.

6. Tower, ed., *Lee's Adjutant,* p. 61.

7. *Richmond Times Dispatch,* Richmond, Virginia, September 28, 1936; CVSR, NA.

8. Thomas, *Robert E. Lee,* pp. 296–302; Piston, *Lee's Tarnished Lieutenant,* p. 36.

9. Piston, *Lee's Tarnished Lieutenant,* p. 60.

10. Hess, *Pickett's Charge,* pp. 15, 32–33; Wert, *A Glorious Army,* pp. 269, 274–275; Coddington, *The Gettysburg Campaign,* pp. 519–520; Cowell, *Tactics at Gettysburg,* pp. 78–79.

11. Piston, *Lee's Tarnished Lieutenant,* p. 61.

12. Carhart, *Lost Triumph,* pp. 2–6, 163–269; Cowell, *Tactics at Gettysburg,* p. 81; Piston, *Lee's Tarnished Lieutenant,* pp. x–xi, 53–61; Stevens, *As if it Were Glory,* p. 110; Hatch, *Glorious War,* pp. 1–2, 139–157.

13. Boritt, ed., *The Gettysburg Nobody Knows,* p. 114; Hatch, *Glorious War,* pp. 1–2, 139–157; Cowell, *Tactics at Gettysburg,* p. 81.

14. Chandler, *The Campaigns of Napoleon,* p. 363; Hatch, *Glorious War,* pp. 1–2, 139–157; Thomas, *Robert E. Lee,* pp. 301–302; Carhart, *Lost Triumph,* pp. xi–206; Cowell, *Tactics at Gettysburg,* p. 81.

15. Tower, ed., *Lee's Adjutant,* p. 61; McKenzie, *Uncertain Glory,* p. 160; Longacre, *Pickett,* p. 117; Hess, *Pickett's Charge,* pp. 11, 306; Cowell, *Tactics at Gettysburg,* pp. 78–79.

16. Harrison, *Pickett's Men,* pp. xxv, 78–79, 98; Hess, *Pickett's Charge,* pp. 15–19, 32–33; Bowden and Ward, *Last Chance for Victory,* pp. 439, 471–472; Cowell, *Tactics at Gettysburg,* pp. 78–79, 81.

17. Harrison, *Pickett's Men,* pp. xxv, 79.

18. Ibid., pp. xxv, 88–89, 98.

19. Ibid., p. 88.

20. Ibid., pp. xxv, 98.

21. *Augusta Daily Constitutionalist,* Augusta, Georgia, July 23, 1863.

22. Thomas, *Robert E. Lee,* pp. 301–302.

23. Gordon, *General George E. Pickett in Life and Legend,* p. 115; Rollins, ed., *Pickett's Charge,* p. 22.

24. Rollins, ed., *Pickett's Charge,* p. 44; CVSR, NA

25. McKenzie, *Uncertain Glory,* pp. 158–159.

26. Tower, ed., *Lee's Adjutant,* p. 67; Hess, *Pickett's Charge,* pp. 15–19, 32–33.

27. Tower, ed., *Lee's Adjutant,* p. 101.

28. Joseph Graham to Graham, July 30, 1863, SHC.

29. Harrison, *Pickett's Men,* p. 186.

30. Ibid., p. 187.

31. Rollins, ed., *Pickett's Charge,* pp. 178–179.

32. Ibid., p. 362.

33. Dinkins, ed., *John Dooley, Confederate Soldier,* pp. 142, 217–218; Coddington, *The Gettysburg Campaign,* pp. 519–520; Hess, *Pickett's Charge,* pp. 15–19, 32–33; Thomas, *Robert E. Lee,* pp. 296–302; Harrison and Busey, *Nothing but Glory,* p. 125; Mitchell, *Military Leaders of the Civil War,* p. 148.

34. Boswell, *Texas Boys in Gray,* p. 78.

35. CVSR, NA; William A. Miler to sister, August 28, 1863, volume 168, Fredericksburg National Military Park, Fredericksburg, Virginia.

36. Flood, *Lee, The Last Years,* p. 261.

37. Ibid.; LaFantasie, *Twilight at Little Round Top,* p. 250; Hess, *Pickett's Charge,* pp. 15–19, 32–33.

38. Hess, *Pickett's Charge,* p. 386.

39. Polley, *Hood's Texas Brigade,* p. 172; LaFantasie, *Twilight at Little Round Top,* p. 72; Cantor, *Alexander the Great, Journey to the End of the Earth,* pp. 15–17; Wert, *A Glorious Army,* pp. 194–195.

40. Moseley, ed., *The Stilwell Letters,* p. 190.

41. *New York Times,* July 6, 1863; Stackpole, *They Met at Gettysburg,* p. 322.

42. Rosengarten, ed., *The Granite Farm Letters,* p. xii.

43. Stevens, ed., *As if it Were Glory,* pp. xiv, 104.

44. Boritt, ed., *The Gettysburg Nobody Knows,* p. 137.

45. Pickett to Corbell, July 23, 1863, JHL; Wert, *A Glorious Army,* pp. 269, 274–275; Coddington, *The Gettysburg Campaign,* pp. 519–520; Bowden and Ward, *Last Chance for Victory,* p. 439; Hess, *Pickett's Charge,* pp. 15–19, 32–33; Cowell, *Tactics at Gettysburg,* pp. 78–79.

46. Gregory, 53rd Virginia Infantry and 5th Battalion Virginia Infantry, p. 60; Wert, A Glorious Army, pp. 275, 281–282; Rollins, ed., Pickett's Charge, p. 373; CVSR, NA.

47. Sell, "Who Were Those Other Heroes with Armistead at the Guns," pp. 28, 32

48. Coco, On the Bloodstained Field, I and II, pp. 67–68.

Index